11 Years

CBSE

Class 12

Physics

Previous Year-wise Solved Papers

(2013 - 2023) Powered with Concept Notes

DISHA™

Publication Inc

DISHA Publication Inc.

45, 2nd Floor, Maharishi Dayanand Marg,
Corner Market, Malviya Nagar, new Delhi -110017
Tel: 49842349/ 49842350

By:

Sanjeev Kumar Jha

Typeset By
DISHA DTP Team

Buying books from DISHA

Just Got A Lot More Rewarding!!!

We at DISHA Publication, value your feedback immensely and to show our apperciation of our reviewers, we have launched a review contest.

To participate in this reward scheme, just follow these quick and simple steps:
- Write a review of the product you purchase on Amazon/Flipkart.
- Take a screenshot/photo of your review.
- Mail it to *disha-rewards@aiets.co.in*, along with all your details.

Each month, selected reviewers will win exciting gifts from DISHA Publication. Note that the rewards for each month will be declared in the first week of next month on our website.

https://bit.ly/review-reward-disha.

**Write To
Us At**

feedback_disha@aiets.co.in

CONTENTS

Chapterwise Division of Questions

The table below presents the chapter-wise division of the questions of the 19 papers. So this book can be put to dual usage-yearwise as well as chapter-wise. To find questions of a chapter just follow the question numbers in its row against the 19 papers. This table also depicts the Trend Analysis of 2023-2013 papers.

CH. No.	Chapter Name	Year of Examination								
		2023		2022		2021	2020		2019	
		All India	Delhi	Term-I	Term-II		All India	Delhi	All India	Delhi
1.	Electric Charges and Fields	5, 32	1, 22	1, 2, 3, 15, 23, 26, 27, 37, 45		Exam not held in 2021 due to Covid-19 pandemic	1, 35	7, 13, 21	17 & OR	1, 27 (OR)
2.	Electrostatic Potential and Capacitance	16, 30 & OR, (32 OR)	12, 34 & OR	14, 16, 28, 42, 50, 51			2, 22, 35 (OR)	11, 33, 21(OR), 37 & OR	1, 20,	13, 27
3.	Current Electricity	7, 9, 11, 29	17, 24, 33 & OR	4, 5, 6, 17, 22, 29, 33, 38, 40, 52, 53, 54, 55			3, 4, 21, 28	12, 28	24, 27 & OR	2, 6, 14 & OR
4.	Moving Charges and Magnetism	13, 15, 23, (35 OR)	2, 18, 23 & OR, 29	7, 8, 9, 10, 20, 30, 34, 47, 48			5, 25, 29 & OR, 36	6, 16, 20	2, 15 & OR	8, 18, 17(b)
5.	Magnetism and Matter	18	3	24, 39, 41, 46			11		3 & OR	20 & OR
6.	Electromagnetic Induction	(33 OR), 35	4, 25	11, 25, 31, 35			13	19, 34, 36(OR)	25 & OR	17(a)
7.	Alternating Current	26, 33	13, 27, 28	12, 13, 18, 19, 21, 32, 36, 43, 44, 49			12, 30, 36 (OR)	3, 9, 19(OR), 36	13 & OR	25& OR
8.	Electromagnetic Waves	1, 22	5, 21		7		16, 32	17, 22	5 & OR, 6	15
9.	Ray Optics and Optical Instruments	3, 14, 25, 27, (31 OR)	32 & OR, 35 & OR		4 & OR, 12		6, 7, 8, 15, 24 (OR), 37 & OR	10, 32, 35	9 & OR, 11, 12, 22	7, 19, 26 (OR)
10.	Wave Optics	17, 19, 31	6, 14, 26 & OR		7(OR), 6, 8		24, 31	1, 18, 23 & OR, 27	26 & OR,	4, 16 & OR, 26
11.	Dual Nature of Radiation and Matter	8, 12, 34 & OR	7, 11, 20 & OR, (30 OR)		1(OR), 5		10, 18(OR), 19	4, 8, 25	7	3 & OR, 11, 12
12.	Atoms	2, 24	10, 15, 30		11		9, 14, 26 & OR	26, 29	8 & OR, 16, 19	9 & OR
13.	Nuclei	6, (24 OR), 28	8, 19		1, 10		14(OR), 18, 23, 33	24, 30	21 & OR	21
14.	Semiconductor Electronics : Material Devices and Simple Circuits	4, 10, 20, 21	9, 16, 31		2, 3, 9		17, 20, 27, 34	2, 5, 14, 15, 31 & OR	4, 14, 23	22, 23
15.	Communication Systems								10, 18	5 & OR, 10, 24
	Total	**35**	**35**	**55**	**12**		**37**	**37**	**27**	**27**

Chapterwise Division of Questions

Chapter Number	Chapter Name	Year of Examination		
		2018	2017	
		All India	All India	Delhi
1.	Electric Charges and Fields	24 & OR	24 & OR	1, 18
2.	Electrostatic Potential and Capacitance	11 & OR	22	17
3.	Current Electricity	6, 7, 12,	1, 11, 17,	15, 26 & OR
4.	Moving Charges and Magnetism	1, 14 (a)	8, 21	13, 22
5.	Magnetism and Matter	13, 14 (b)	10	3
6.	Electromagnetic Induction	25	5, 16 & OR, 25 (OR)	2, 22(OR), 24
7.	Alternating Current	23, 25(OR)	25	11, 24(OR)
8.	Electromagnetic Waves	2, 8	2, 7	5, 6
9.	Ray Optics and Optical Instruments	15 (b), 17, 26	3, 15, 20, 26(OR)	9, 20, 23
10.	Wave Optics	15 (a), 16, 26 (OR)	6 & OR, 26	25& OR
11.	Dual Nature of Radiation and Matter	3, 9,	4, 14	14
12.	Atoms	18	9	7 & OR, 8
13.	Nuclei	4, 19	23	19
14.	Semiconductor Electronics : Material Devices and Simple Circuits	20, 21	13, 19	4, 12, 21
15.	Communication Systems	5, 10, 22	12, 18	10, 16
	Total	**26**	**26**	**26**

Chapterwise Division of Questions

Chapter Number	Chapter Name	Year of Examination			
		2016		2015	
		All India	Delhi	All India	Delhi
1.	Electric Charges and Fields	4	2, 11	4, 24 (OR)	2, 26
2.	Electrostatic Potential and Capacitance	15, 25 & OR	1, 15	20	17
3.	Current Electricity	2, 7, 11,	9, 26 & OR	5, 7, 21, 23, 24	5, 10, 16
4.	Moving Charges and Magnetism	16	3, 13, 16	26	18, 24
5.	Magnetism and Matter	1		17(OR)	
6.	Electromagnetic Induction	23, 26(OR)	14	17	24 (OR)
7.	Alternating Current	22, 26	5, 24 & OR	1, 15, 26(OR)	1, 22, 23
8.	Electromagnetic Waves	19	4, 17 & OR	18	11
9.	Ray Optics and Optical Instruments	3, 10, 14, 24 & OR	20, 22, 25(OR)	3, 10 & OR, 16, 25(OR)	3, 9, 12, 25(OR)
10.	Wave Optics	17 & OR	10, 25	14, 25	9(OR), 21, 25
11.	Dual Nature of Radiation and Matter	13	7, 12	9, 22	6, 13
12.	Atoms	6, 8 & OR	21	6	7, 14
13.	Nuclei	12	8	19	14(OR),
14.	Semiconductor Electronics : Material Devices and Simple Circuits	18, 21	19, 23	11, 12	8, 19, 20
15.	Communication Systems	5, 9, 20	6, 18	2, 8, 13	4, 15
	Total	**26**	**26**	**26**	**26**

Chapterwise Division of Questions

Chapter Number	Chapter Name	Year of Examination			
		2014		2013	
		All India	Delhi	All India	Delhi
1.	Electric Charges and Fields	3, 28(OR)	10, 16	1, 28(OR)	18(OR), 26
2.	Electrostatic Potential and Capacitance	10	3, 14, 24 & OR	11, 28	2, 18
3.	Current Electricity	12, 14, 21 & OR	1, 5, 13, 21	3, 4, 13 & OR, 19	7, 8, 28 & OR
4.	Moving Charges and Magnetism	1, 30 & OR	7, 15, 25	20, 27 & OR	12, 29
5.	Magnetism and Matter	17	9		1, 29(OR)
6.	Electromagnetic Induction	5, 20	4, 29 & OR	2, 5, 18 & OR	10, 21
7.	Alternating Current	7, 23		17	25
8.	Electromagnetic Waves	2, 11	26	7, 12	4, 14
9.	Ray Optics and Optical Instruments	8, 15, 22	6, 22, 23	14, 22, 26	5, 9, 11, 27
10.	Wave Optics	19, 29 & OR	11, 28 & OR	10, 25	3, 24, 27(OR)
11.	Dual Nature of Radiation and Matter	4, 27	17, 18	8, 23	6, 20
12.	Atoms	9 & OR	19	29	23
13.	Nuclei	6, 25	27	6, 29(OR)	19
14.	Semiconductor Electronics : Material Devices and Simple Circuits	13, 18, 24	12, 30 & OR	9, 16, 21	13, 16 & OR, 22
15.	Communication Systems	16, 26	2, 8, 20	15, 24	15, 17
	Total	**30**	**30**	**29**	**29**

CBSE Board Solved Paper

Time Allowed : 3 Hours   *Maximum Marks : 70*

General Instructions:

Read the following instructions very carefully and follow them :

(i) *This question paper contains **35** questions. **All** questions are compulsory.*

(ii) *Question paper is divided into **FIVE** sections – Section **A, B, C, D** and **E**.*

(iii) ***In section – A :** question number **1** to **18** are Multiple Choice (MCQ) type questions carrying **1** mark each.*

(iv) ***In section – B :** question number **19** to **25** are Short Answer-1 (SA-1) type questions carrying **2** marks each.*

(v) ***In section – C :** question number **26** to **30** are Short Answer-2 (SA-2) type questions carrying **3** marks each.*

(vi) ***In section – D :** question number **31** to **33** are Long Answer (LA) type questions carrying **5** marks each.*

(vii) ***In section – E :** question number **34** and **35** are case-based questions carrying **4** marks each.*

(viii) *There is no overall choice. However, an internal choice has been provided in 2 questions in Section – **B**, 2 questions in Section – **C**, 3 questions in Section – **D** and 2 questions in Section – **E**.*

(ix) *Use of calculators is NOT allowed.*

$c = 3 \times 10^8\,\text{m/s}$

$h = 6.63 \times 10^{-34}\,\text{Js}$

$e = 1.6 \times 10^{-19}\,\text{C}$

$\mu_0 = 4\pi \times 10^{-7}\,\text{T m A}^{-1}$

$\varepsilon_0 = 8.854 \times 10^{-12}\,\text{C}^2\,\text{N}^{-1}\,\text{m}^{-2}$

$$\frac{1}{4\pi\varepsilon_0} = 9 \times 10^9\,\text{Nm}^2\,\text{C}^{-2}$$

Mass of electron $(m_e) = 9.1 \times 10^{-31}\,\text{kg}$

Mass of neutron $= 1.675 \times 10^{-27}\,\text{kg}$

Mass of proton $= 1.673 \times 10^{-27}\,\text{kg}$

Avogadro's number $= 6.023 \times 10^{23}$ per gram mole

Boltzmann constant $= 1.38 \times 10^{-23}\,\text{JK}^{-1}$

SECTION - A

1. The ratio of the magnitudes of the electric field and magnetic field of a plane electromagnetic wave is

(a) 1   (b) $\dfrac{1}{c}$ (c) c   (d) $\dfrac{1}{c^2}$

2. Specify the transition of electron in the wavelength of the line in the Bohr model of hydrogen atom which gives rise to the spectral line of highest wavelength.

(a) $n = 3$ to $n = 1$ (b) $n = 3$ to $n = 2$

(c) $n = 4$ to $n = 1$ (d) $n = 4$ to $n = 2$

3. A ray of monochromatic light propagating in air, is incident on the surface of water. Which of the following will be the same for the reflected and refracted rays ?

(a) Energy carried   (b) Speed

(c) Frequency   (d) Wavelength

4. The formation of depletion region in a p-n junction diode is due to

(a) movement of dopant atoms

(b) diffusion of both electrons and holes

(c) drift of electrons only

(d) drift of holes only

5. An isolated point charge particle produces an electric field $\vec{E}$ at a point 3 m away from it. The distance of the point at which the field is $\dfrac{\vec{E}}{4}$ will be

(a) 2m   (b) 3m   (c) 4m   (d) 6m

6. The curve of binding energy per nucleon as a function of atomic mass number has a sharp peak for helium nucleus. This implies that helium nucleus is

(a) radioactive

(b) unstable

(c) easily fissionable

(d) more stable nucleus than its neighbours

7. A steady current of 8 mA flows through a wire. The number of electrons passing through a cross-section of the wire in 10 s is

(a) 4.0×10^{16} (b) 5.0×10^{17}

(c) 1.6×10^{16} (d) 1.0×10^{17}

8. Which one of the following elements will require the highest energy to take out an electron from them ?

Pb, Ge, C and Si

(a) Ge   (b) C   (c) Si   (d) Pb

9. A conductor of $10\ \Omega$ is connected across a 6 V ideal source. The power supplied by the source to the conductor is

(a) 1.8 W   (b) 2.4 W   (c) 3.6 W   (d) 7.2 W

10. In an extrinsic semiconductor, the number density of holes is 4×10^{20} m^{-3}. If the number density of intrinsic carriers is 1.2×10^{15} m^{-3}, the number density of electrons in it is

(a) $1.8 \times 10^{9}\,m^{-3}$ (b) $2.4 \times 10^{10}\,m^{-3}$

(c) $3.6 \times 10^{9}\,m^{-3}$ (d) $3.2 \times 10^{10}\,m^{-3}$

11. A cell of emf E is connected across an external resistance R. When current 'I' is drawn from the cell, the potential difference across the electrodes of the cell drops to V. The internal resistance 'r' of the cell is

(a) $\left(\dfrac{E - V}{E}\right)R$ (b) $\left(\dfrac{E - V}{R}\right)$

(c) $\dfrac{(E - V)R}{I}$ (d) $\left(\dfrac{E - V}{V}\right)R$

12. A photon of wavelength 663 nm is incident on a metal surface. The work function of the metal is 1.50 eV. The maximum kinetic energy of the emitted photo electrons is

(a) $3.0 \times 10^{-20}\,J$ (b) $6.0 \times 10^{-20}\,J$

(c) $4.5 \times 10^{-20}\,J$ (d) $9.0 \times 10^{-20}\,J$

13. Beams of electrons and protons move parallel to each other in the same direction. They

(a) attract each other

(b) repel each other

(c) neither attract nor repel

(d) force of attraction or repulsion depends upon speed of beams

14. A ray of light of wavelength 600 nm propagates from air into a medium. If its wavelength in the medium becomes 400 nm, the refractive index of the medium is

(a) 1.4   (b) 1.5   (c) 1.6   (d) 1.8

15. A long straight wire of radius 'a' carries a steady current 'I'. The current is uniformly distributed across its area of cross-section. The ratio of magnitude of magnetic field $\vec{B}_1$ at $\dfrac{a}{2}$ and $\vec{B}_2$ at distance 2a is

(a) $\dfrac{1}{2}$ (b) 1   (c) 2   (d) 4

Note: In question number **16** to **18** two statements are given – one labelled **Assertion (A)** and the other labelled **Reason (R)**. Select the correct answer to these questions from the codes **(a)**, **(b)**, **(c)** and **(d)** as given below :

(a) Both Assertion (A) and Reason (R) are true and Reason (R) is the correct explanation of Assertion (A).

(b) Both Assertion (A) and Reason (R) are true and Reason (R) is NOT the correct explanation of Assertion (A).

(c) Assertion (A) is true and Reason (R) is false.

(d) Assertion (A) is false and Reason (R) is also false.

16. **Assertion (A) :** Work done in moving a charge around a closed path, in an electric field is always zero.

Reason (R) : Electrostatic force is a conservative force.

17. **Assertion (A) :** In Young's double slit experiment all fringes are of equal width.

Reason (R) : The fringe width depends upon wavelength of light (λ) used, distance of screen from plane of slits (D) and slits separation (d).

18. **Assertion (A) :** Diamagnetic substances exhibit magnetism.

Reason (R) : Diamagnetic materials do not have permanent magnetic dipole moment.

SECTION - B

19. In a Young's double slit experiment, the separation between the two slits is d and distance of the screen from the slits is 1000 d. If the first minima falls at a distance d from the central maximum, obtain the relation between d and λ.

20. Draw energy band diagram for an n-type and p-type semiconductor at $T > 0$ K.

21. Answer the following giving reasons :

(i) A p-n junction diode is damaged by a strong current.

(ii) Impurities are added in intrinsic semiconductors.

22. (a) How are infrared waves produced ? Why are these waves referred to as heat waves ? Give any two uses of infrared waves.

OR

(b) How are X-rays produced ? Give any two uses of these.

23. Briefly explain why and how a galvanometer is converted into an ammeter.

24. (a) What is meant by ionisation energy ? Write its value for hydrogen atom ?

OR

(b) Define the term, mass defect. How is it related to stability of the nucleus ?

25. A point object in air is placed symmetrically at a distance of 60 cm in front of a concave spherical surface of refractive index 1.5. If the radius of curvature of the surface is 20 cm, find the position of the image formed.

SECTION - C

26. A series RL circuit with R = 10 Ω and L = $\left(\dfrac{100}{\pi}\right)$ mH is connected to an ac source of voltage V = 141 sin (100 πt), where V is in volts and t is in seconds. Calculate

(a) impedence of the circuit

(b) phase angle, and

(c) voltage drop across the inductor

27. A ray of light is incident on a glass prism of refractive index μ and refracting angle A. If it just suffers total internal reflection at the other face, obtain a relation between the angle of incidence, angle of prism and critical angle.

28. (a) (i) Distinguish between nuclear fission and fusion giving an example of each.

    (ii) Explain the release of energy in nuclear fission and fusion on the basis of binding energy per nucleon curve.

OR

(b) (i) How is the size of a nucleus found experimentally ? Write the relation between the radius and mass number of a nucleus.

    (ii) Prove that the density of a nucleus is independent of its mass number.

29. Two cells of emf E_1 and E_2 and internal resistances r_1 and r_2 are connected in parallel, with their terminals of the same polarity connected together. Obtain an expression for the equivalent emf of the combination.

30. (a) Two charged conducting spheres of radii a and b are connected to each other by a wire. Find the ratio of the electric fields at their surfaces.

OR

(b) A parallel plate capacitor (A) of capacitance C is charged by a battery to voltage V. The battery is disconnected and an uncharged capacitor (B) of capacitance 2C is connected across A. Find the ratio of

(i) final charges on A and B.

(ii) total electrostatic energy stored in A and B finally and that stored in A initially.

SECTION - D

31. (a) (i) State Huygen's principle. With the help of a diagram, show how a plane wave is reflected from a surface. Hence verify the law of reflection.

    (ii) A concave mirror of focal length 12 cm forms a three times magnified virtual image of an object. Find the distance of the object from the mirror.

OR

(b) (i) Draw a labelled ray diagram showing the image formation by a refracting telescope. Define its magnifying power. Write two limitations of a refracting telescope over a reflecting telescope.

    (ii) The focal lengths of the objective and the eyepiece of a compound microscope are 1.0 cm and 2.5 cm respectively. Find the tube length of the microscope for obtaining a magnification of 300.

32. (a) (i) Use Gauss' law to obtain an expression for the electric field due to an infinitely long thin straight wire with uniform linear charge density λ.

    (ii) An infinitely long positively charge straight wire has a linear charge density λ. An electron is revolving in a circle with a constant speed v such that the wire passes through the centre, and is perpendicular to the plane, of the circle. Find the kinetic energy of the electron in terms of magnitudes of its charge and linear charge density λ on the wire.

    (iii) Draw a graph of kinetic energy as a function of linear charge density λ.

OR

(b) (i) Consider two identical point charges located at points (0, 0) and (a, 0).

    (1) Is there a point on the line joining them at which the electric field is zero ?

    (2) Is there a point on the line joining them at which the electric potential is zero ?

Justify your answers for each case.

    (ii) State the significance of negative value of electrostatic potential energy of a system of charges.

Three charges are placed at the corners of an equilateral triangle ABC of side 2.0 m as shown in figure. Calculate the electric potential energy of the system of three charges.

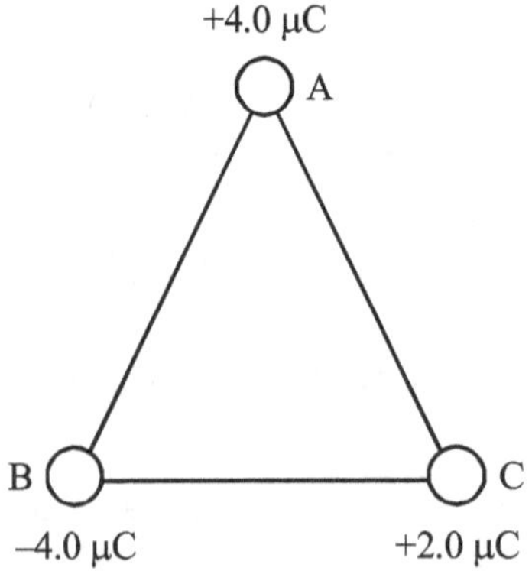

33. **(a)** **(i)** Define coefficient of self-induction. Obtain an expression for self-inductance of a long solenoid of length l, area of cross-section A having N turns.

   (ii) Calculate the self-inductance of a coil using the following data obtained when an AC source of frequency $\left(\dfrac{200}{\pi}\right)$ Hz and a DC source is applied across the coil.

AC Source			DC Source		
S.No.	V (Volts)	I (A)	S.No.	V (Volts)	I (A)
1	3.0	0.5	1	4.0	1.0
2	6.0	1.0	2	6.0	1.5
3	9.0	1.5	3	8.0	2.0

OR

(b) **(i)** With the help of a labelled diagram, describe the principle and working of an ac generator. Hence, obtain an expression for the instantaneous value of the emf generated.

   (ii) The coil of an ac generator consists of 100 turns of wire, each of area $0.5\ m^2$. The resistance of the wire is $100\ \Omega$. The coil is rotating in a magnetic field of 0.8 T perpendicular to its axis of rotation, at a constant angular speed of 60 radian per second. Calculate the maximum emf generated and power dissipated in the coil.

SECTION-E

Note : Questions number **34** and **35** are case study based questions. Read the following paragraph and answer the questions.

34. **(a)** Figure shows the variation of photoelectric current measured in a photo cell circuit as a function of the potential difference between the plates of the photo cell when light beams A, B, C and D of different wavelengths are incident on the photo cell. Examine the given figure and answer the following questions :

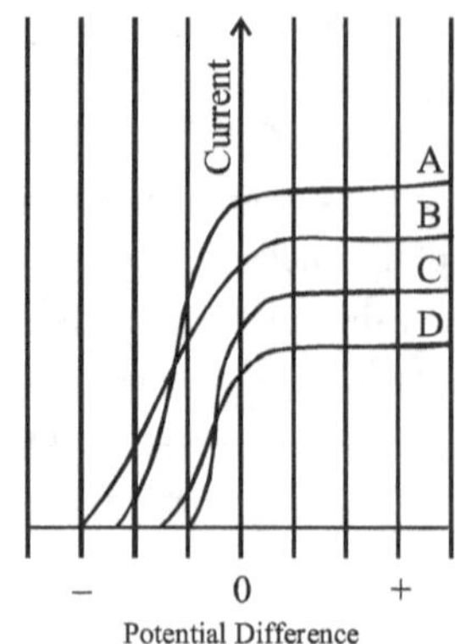

   (i) Which light beam has the highest frequency and why ?

   (ii) Which light beam has the longest wavelength and why ?

   (iii) Which light beam ejects photoelectrons with maximum momentum and why ?

OR

(b) What is the effect on threshold frequency and stopping potential on increasing the frequency of incident beam of light ? Justify your answer.

35. **(a)** Consider the experimental set up shown in the figure. This jumping ring experiment is an outstanding demonstration of some simple laws of Physics. A conducting non-magnetic ring is placed over the vertical core of a solenoid. When current is passed through the solenoid, the ring is thrown off.

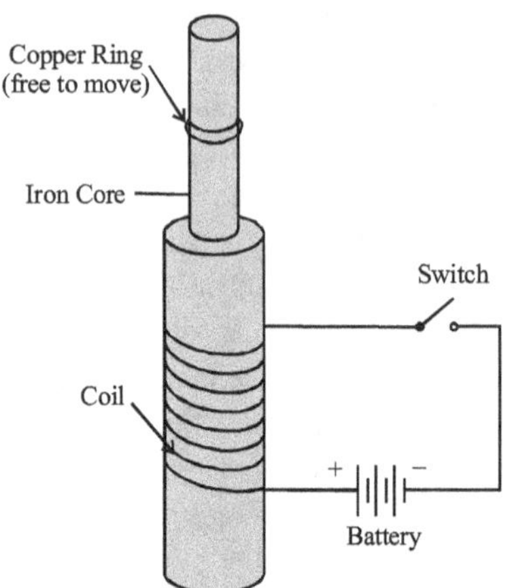

Answer the following questions:

   (i) Explain the reason of jumping of the ring when the switch is closed in the circuit.

   (ii) What will happen if the terminals of the battery are reversed and the switch is closed ? Explain.

   (iii) Explain the two laws that help us understand this phenomenon.

OR

(b) Briefly explain various ways to increase the strength of magnetic field produced by a given solenoid.

Solutions

1. **(c)** In free space, $E = cB$ **(1 Mark)**

2. **(b)** For minimum energy, we have longest wavelength
So, $n = 3$ to $n = 2$ will be most suitable answer.   **(1 Mark)**

3. **(c)** Frequency of light waves do not change with change in medium.   **(1 Mark)**

4. **(b)** The formation of depletion region in p-n junction diode is due to diffusion of both electron and holes.   **(1 Mark)**

5. **(d)** We have
$$E_{3m} = E \Rightarrow \frac{Kq}{3^2} = E \Rightarrow Kq = 9E$$
Let $\dfrac{E}{4}$ be the magnitude at of field at 'd' m away from it. So, $\dfrac{Kq}{d^2} = \dfrac{E}{4}$
$$\Rightarrow \frac{9E}{d^2} = \frac{E}{4} \Rightarrow d^2 = 36 \Rightarrow d = 6\,m$$
     (1 Mark)

6. **(d)** More binding energy per nucleon means more stability of nucleus.   **(1 Mark)**

7. **(b)** We have
$q = It \Rightarrow q = 8 \times 10^{-3} \times 10 = 0.08\,C = 8 \times 10^{-2}\,C$
So, no. of electrons $= 6.25 \times 10^{18} \times 8 \times 10^{-2}$
$$= 50.00 \times 10^{16} = 5 \times 10^{17}$$
     (1 Mark)

> **Note**
>
> *1 Coulomb charge means charge on 6.25×10^{18} electrons.*

8. **(b)** On moving down the group 14, size of atom increases. So, ionisation energy decreases. Therefore, carbon has highest ionisation energy.   **(1 Mark)**

9. **(c)** We have
$$P = \frac{V^2}{R} \quad \Rightarrow \quad P = \frac{6^2}{10} = 3.6\,Watt.$$
     (1 Mark)

10. **(c)** In semiconductors,
$n_e\, n_h = n_i^2$
$$n_e = \frac{n_i^2}{n_h} = \frac{(1.2 \times 10^{15})^2}{4 \times 10^{20}} = \frac{1.44 \times 10^{30}}{4 \times 10^{20}}$$
$$= 0.36 \times 10^{10} = 3.6 \times 10^9\,m^{-3}$$
     (1 Mark)

11. **(d)** We have $E = V + ir \Rightarrow ir = E - V \Rightarrow r = \dfrac{E - V}{i}$
$$\Rightarrow r = \left(\frac{E - V}{V}\right)R \Rightarrow r = \left(\frac{E}{V} - 1\right)R$$
     (1 Mark)

12. **(b)** Energy of photon, $E = \dfrac{1240}{663}\,eV = 1.87\,eV$
Work function, $\phi = 1.50\,eV$
So, $(K.E)_{max} = (1.87 - 1.50)\,eV$
$$= 0.37\,eV$$
$$= 0.592 \times 10^{-19}\,J = 5.92 \times 10^{-20}\,J$$
$$\approx 6 \times 10^{-20}\,J$$
     (1 Mark)

13. **(b)** The flow of positive charge is taken as the direction of current. So, here the currents are in opposite direction therefore they will repel each other.   **(1 Mark)**

14. **(b)** We have
$$\frac{\lambda_2}{\lambda_1} = \frac{\mu_1}{\mu_2} \quad \Rightarrow \quad \frac{400}{600} = \frac{1}{\mu} \Rightarrow \mu = \frac{3}{2}$$
     (1 Mark)

15. **(b)** We have
$$B = \frac{\mu_0\, ir}{2\pi a^2} \text{ for } r < a$$
$$= \frac{\mu_0\, i}{2\pi r} \text{ for } r \geq a$$
So, $B_1 = \dfrac{\mu_0\, i a}{2 \times 2\pi a^2} = \dfrac{\mu_0\, i}{4\pi a}$
$$B_2 = \frac{\mu_0\, i}{2\pi \times 2a} = \frac{\mu_0\, i}{4\pi a}$$
Thus, $\dfrac{B_1}{B_2} = 1$ **(1 Mark)**

16. **(a)** In conservative field, work done is independent of path chosen and work done in moving a charge around closed path is zero.   **(1 Mark)**

17. **(a)** Fringe width in YDSE is given as
$$\beta = \frac{\lambda D}{d} \cdot \text{ So, } \beta \propto \lambda$$
$$\propto D$$
$$\propto \frac{1}{d}$$
     (1 Mark)

18. **(b)** Dimagnetic material exhibits magnetism in reverse direction. And due to absence of unpaired electron in dimagnetic material it does not exhibit permanent dipole moment.   **(1 Mark)**

19. We have
$\dfrac{\beta}{2} = d$ [$\because$ Distance between maxima and minima is $\beta/2$]
$$\Rightarrow \quad \beta = 2d$$ **(1 Mark)**
$$\Rightarrow \quad \frac{\lambda \times 1000\,d}{d} = 2d \Rightarrow \lambda = \frac{1}{500}d$$
     (1 Mark)

20. Energy band diagram of both semiconductor at $T > 0$ K

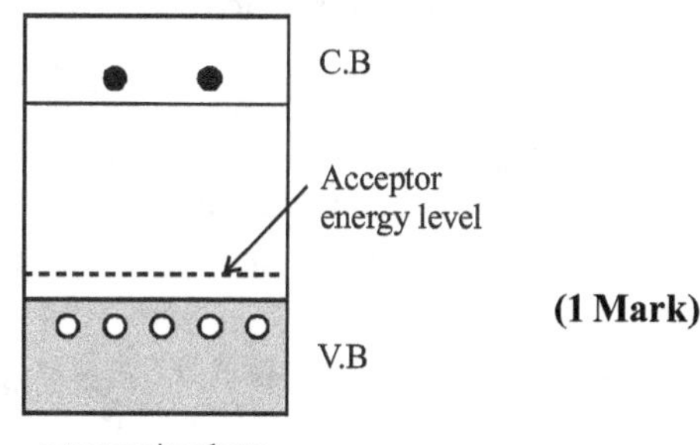

     (1 Mark)

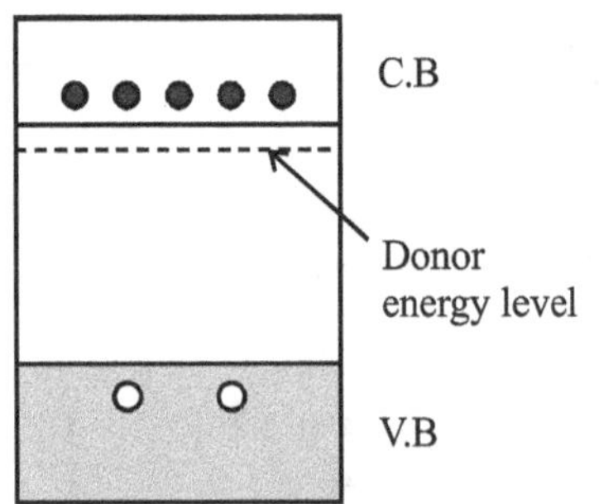

n-type semiconductor

(1 Mark)

21. (i) When a strong current passes through the semiconductor it heats up the crystal and covalent bond are broken. Hence because of excess number of free electrons it behaves like a conductor. **(1 Mark)**

(ii) The addition of impurities contributes free electrons or holes which increases the conductivity of the intrinsic semiconductor. **(1 Mark)**

22. (a) Infra-red waves are produced by hot bodies and molecules. **(½ Mark)**
They are also called heat waves because water molecules present in most of the materials readily absorb infra-red rays and their thermal motion increases, due to which material yet heated.
(½ Mark)
Two uses of infra-red waves are
(i) In remote switches of house-hold electric system.
(ii) Physical therapy to treat muscular strain.
(½ × 2 = 1 Mark)

OR

(b) X-rays are produced by Coolidge X-ray tube by bombarding a metal target by high energy electrons
Two uses of X-rays are **(1 Mark)**
(i) Medical application like detection of fractures, formation of stones etc.
(ii) To study crystal structure of solid.
(½ × 2 = 1 Mark)

23. An ammeter is made by connecting low resistance (shunt) in parallel to the galvanometer. When a low resistance is connected parallel to galvanometer, then most of the current passes through this resistance and thereby increasing its range. **(2 Marks)**

24. (a) Ionization energy is the minimum energy required to remove the most loosely bound electron of an isolated gaseous atom, positive ion, or molecule. **(1 Mark)**
For hydrogen atom, ionisation energy is 13.6 eV.
(1 Mark)

OR

(b) Mass defect is difference in the total mass of all the nucleons and mass of nucleus. **(1 Mark)**
i.e. Mass defect = mass of all nucleons
$$- \text{ mass of nucleus}$$
$$= [Zm_p + (A-Z)m_n] - m_{nucleus}$$
Higher is the mass defect, higher is the BEPN. So, higher is the stability. **(1 Mark)**

25. For spherical surface, we have
$$\frac{\mu_2}{V} - \frac{\mu_1}{u} = \frac{\mu_2 - \mu_1}{R} \qquad \textbf{(½ Mark)}$$
$$\Rightarrow \frac{1.5}{V} - \frac{1}{-60} = \frac{1.5-1}{-20} \quad \text{[For convex surface, R is } -ve\text{]}$$
(½ Mark)
$$\Rightarrow \frac{1.5}{V} = -\frac{0.5}{20} - \frac{1}{60} \Rightarrow \frac{1.5}{V} = -\frac{1}{40} - \frac{1}{60}$$
$$\Rightarrow \frac{1.5}{V} = \frac{-3-2}{120} \Rightarrow \frac{1.5}{V} = \frac{-5}{120} \qquad \textbf{(½ Mark)}$$
$$\Rightarrow V = -36\,cm \qquad \textbf{(½ Mark)}$$

26. (a) We have
$$Z = \sqrt{R^2 + X_L^2} = \sqrt{R^2 + \omega^2 L^2} \qquad \textbf{(½ Mark)}$$
$$= \sqrt{10^2 + 100^2 \pi^2 \times \frac{100^2}{\pi^2} \times 10^{-6}}$$
$$= \sqrt{10^2 + (100)^4 \times 10^{-6}}$$
$$= \sqrt{10^2 + 10^2}$$
$$= 10\sqrt{2}\ \Omega \qquad \textbf{(½ Mark)}$$

(b) The phase angle is given as
$$\cos\phi = \frac{R}{Z} = \frac{10}{10\sqrt{2}} = \frac{1}{\sqrt{2}} \Rightarrow \phi = 45° \qquad \textbf{(1 Mark)}$$

(c) $$I_0 = \frac{V_0}{Z} = \frac{141}{10\sqrt{2}} = \frac{141}{14.1} = 10\ A$$
$$I_{rms} = \frac{I_0}{\sqrt{2}} = \frac{10}{\sqrt{2}} \qquad \textbf{(½ Mark)}$$
So, voltage across inductor $= I_{rms} X_L$
$$= \frac{10}{\sqrt{2}} \times 100\pi \times \frac{100}{\pi} \times 10^{-3}$$
$$= 5\sqrt{2} \times 10^4 \times 10^{-3}$$
$$= 50\sqrt{2}\ \text{volt.} \qquad \textbf{(½ Mark)}$$

27. **At surface AC**
$$\mu_g \sin C = 1 \sin 90°$$
$$\Rightarrow \sin C = \frac{1}{\mu_g} = \frac{1}{\mu} \qquad \textbf{(1 Mark)}$$
We know that in prism $r_1 + r_2 = A$
So, $r_1 + C = A$
$$r_1 = A - C \qquad \textbf{(1 Mark)}$$
At surface AB
$$\sin i = \mu \sin r_1$$
$$\Rightarrow \sin i = \mu \sin (A - C)$$
$$\Rightarrow \sin i = \frac{1}{\sin C} \sin (A - C) \Rightarrow \sin i = \frac{\sin(A-C)}{\sin C}$$
(1 Mark)

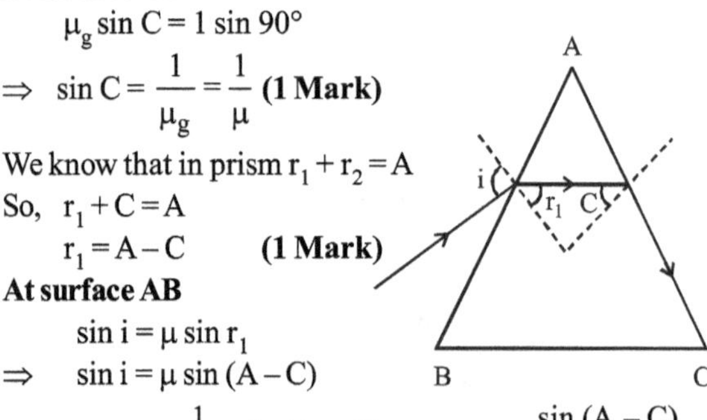

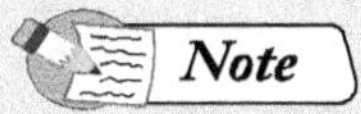

Note

* *If a light ray is incident normally on first surface i.e., $\angle i = 0°$ so refraction of first surface $\angle r_1 = 0°$.*
* *When angle of prism $A > C$ (critical angle) then no ray emerges from second surface of the prism.*

28. (a) (i)

Nuclear fission	Nuclear fusion
→ When the nucleus of an atom split into lighter nuclei through a nuclear reaction, the process is termed nuclear fission.	Nuclear fusion is a reaction through which two or more lighter nuclei collide with each other to form a heavier nucleus.
→ $^{235}_{92}U + ^{1}_{0}n \rightarrow$ $^{144}_{56}Ba + ^{89}_{36}Kr +$ $3^{1}_{0}n + 210$ MeV	$\rightarrow ^{1}_{1}H + ^{1}_{1}H \rightarrow ^{2}_{1}H +$ $e^+ + v +$ 0.42 MeV

(½ × 2 = 1 Mark)

(ii) We have BEPN curve as follows :

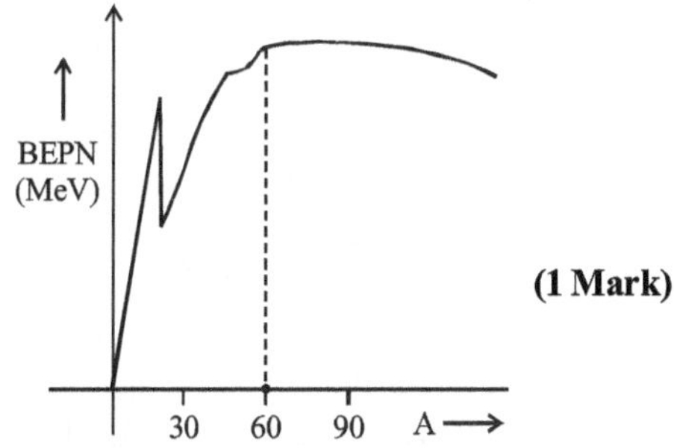

(1 Mark)

Fission Reactions

From the curve of binding energy, the heaviest nuclei are less stable than the nuclei near $A = 60$. This suggests that energy can be released if heavy nuclei split apart into smaller nuclei having masses nearer $A = 60$. This process is called fission. It is the process that powers atomic bombs and nuclear power reactors. **(½ Mark)**

Fusion Reactions

The curve of binding energy suggests a second way in which energy could be released in nuclear reactions. The lightest elements (like hydrogen and helium) have nuclei that are less stable than heavier elements up to $A \sim 60$. Thus, sticking two light nuclei together to form a heavier nucleus can release energy. This process is called fusion, and is the process that powers hydrogen (thermonuclear) bombs and (perhaps eventually) fusion energy reactors. **(½ Mark)**

OR

(b) (i) Size of a nucleus is experimentally estimated from Rutherford's α-particle scattering experiment.

(½ Mark)

If 'R' is radius of a nucleus of mass number 'A'. Then, $R = R_0 A^{1/3}$, where $R_0 = 1.2$ fm. **(1 Mark)**

(ii) The radius (size) R of nucleus is related to its mass number (A) as

$R = R_0 A^{1/3}$ where $R_0 = 1.1 \times 10^{-15}$ m **(½ Mark)**

If m is the average mass of a nucleon, then mass of nucleus = mA, where A is mass number

Volume of nucleus $= \dfrac{4}{3}\pi R^3$

$$= \dfrac{4}{3}\pi(R_0 A^{1/3})^3 = \dfrac{4}{3}\pi R_0^3 A \qquad \textbf{(½ Mark)}$$

∴ Density of nucleus,

$$\rho_N = \dfrac{mass}{volume} = \dfrac{mA}{\dfrac{4}{3}\pi R_0^3} \qquad \textbf{(½ Mark)}$$

Clearly nuclear density ρ_N is independent of mass number A.

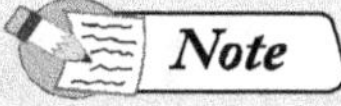

Note

Nuclear density, $\rho = \dfrac{3m}{4\pi R_0^3}$

Here, $R_0 = 1.2 \times 10^{-15}$m, m = Average of mass of a nucleon (mass of proton + mass of neutron) = 1.66×10^{-27} kg

This formula suggest that density of nuclear matter is same for all nuclei.

29. We have two cell E_1 and E_2 having resistance r_1 and r_2 respectively. They are connected in parallel as shown in figure.

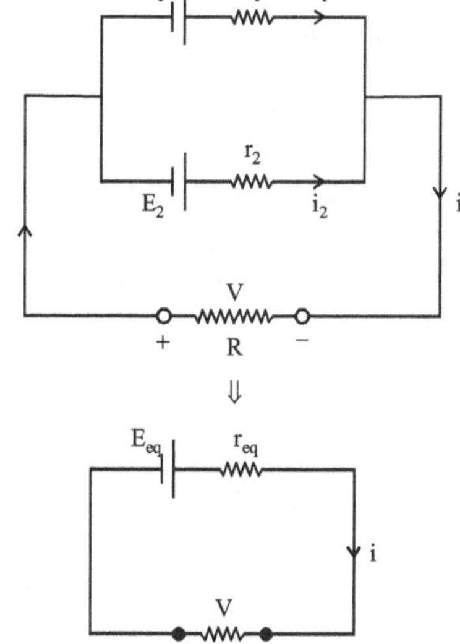

We have

$$V = E_1 - i_1 r_1 \Rightarrow i_1 = \dfrac{E_1 - V}{r_1}$$

$$V = E_2 - i_2 r_2 \Rightarrow i_2 = \dfrac{E_2 - V}{r_2}$$

Also, $V = E_{eq} - i r_{eq} \Rightarrow i = \dfrac{E_{eq} - V}{r_{eq}}$ **(1 Mark)**

As $i = i_1 + i_2$

$$\frac{E_{eq} - V}{r_{eq}} = \frac{E_1 - V}{r_1} + \frac{E_2 - V}{r_2}$$

$$\Rightarrow \quad \frac{E_{eq}}{r_{eq}} - \frac{V}{r_{eq}} = \left(\frac{E_1}{r_1} + \frac{E_2}{r_2}\right) - V\left(\frac{1}{r_1} + \frac{1}{r_2}\right) \quad \textbf{(1 Mark)}$$

Equating coefficient on both sides, we get

$$\frac{E_{eq}}{r_{eq}} = \left(\frac{E_1}{r_1} + \frac{E_2}{r_2}\right) \text{ and } \frac{1}{r_{eq}} = \frac{1}{r_1} + \frac{1}{r_2}$$

$$\Rightarrow \quad E_{eq} = r_{eq}\left(\frac{E_1}{r_1} + \frac{E_2}{r_2}\right) \text{ and } \frac{1}{r_{eq}} = \frac{1}{r_1} + \frac{1}{r_2}$$

$$\Rightarrow \quad E_{eq} = \frac{\dfrac{E_1}{r_1} + \dfrac{E_2}{r_2}}{\dfrac{1}{r_1} + \dfrac{1}{r_2}} \text{ and } \frac{1}{r_{eq}} = \frac{1}{r_1} + \frac{1}{r_2} \quad \textbf{(1 Mark)}$$

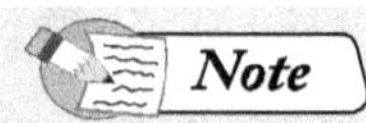

> **Note**
>
> *Parallel grouping of cells is used when r >> nR.*
> *Here, n = number of identical cells*

30. (a)

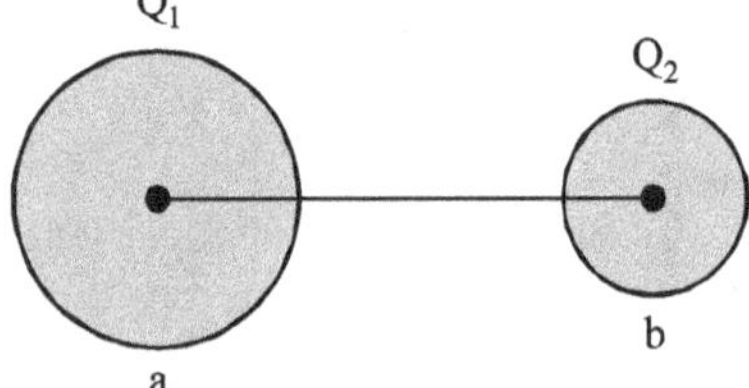

Let Q_1 and Q_2 be the charge on two sphere when they are connected by the wire.

As two sphere are connected by wire, they will have same potential.

So, $\dfrac{KQ_1}{a} = \dfrac{KQ_2}{b} \Rightarrow \dfrac{Q_1}{Q_2} = \dfrac{a}{b}$ **(1 Mark)**

Let E_1 and E_2 be the electric field at surface of 'a' and 'b'.

Then, $E_1 = \dfrac{KQ_1}{a^2}$ and $E_2 = \dfrac{KQ_2}{b^2}$ **(1 Mark)**

So, $\dfrac{E_1}{E_2} = \dfrac{Q_1}{Q_2} \cdot \dfrac{b^2}{a^2} = \dfrac{a}{b} \cdot \dfrac{b^2}{a^2} = \dfrac{b}{a}$ **(1 Mark)**

OR

(b) (i) We have

$$Q_i = Q_f$$

$$\Rightarrow \quad (Q_A)_i + (Q_B)_i = (Q_A)_f + (Q_B)_f$$

$$\Rightarrow \quad CV + 0 = (C + 2C)V_f$$

$$\Rightarrow \quad V_f = \frac{CV}{3C} \Rightarrow V_f = \frac{V}{3} \quad \textbf{(½ Mark)}$$

So, $(Q_A)_f = C \times \dfrac{V}{3} = \dfrac{CV}{3}$ **(½ Mark)**

$(Q_B)_f = 2C \times \dfrac{V}{3} = \dfrac{2CV}{3}$ **(½ Mark)**

(ii) $(U_A)_i = \dfrac{1}{2}CV^2$

$(U_B)_i = 0$ **(½ Mark)**

$(U_A)_f = \dfrac{1}{2}C\left(\dfrac{V}{3}\right)^2 = \dfrac{1}{18}CV^2$ **(½ Mark)**

$(U_B)_f = \dfrac{1}{2}2C\left(\dfrac{V}{3}\right)^2 = \dfrac{CV^2}{9}$ **(½ Mark)**

31. (a) (i) Huygen's principle states that every point on a given wavefront act as a source of secondary wavelets which travel in all direction with the velocity of light in the medium. The position of the new wavefront at any instant is a surface touching these secondary wavelets tangentially in the forward direction at that instant. **(1 Mark)**

Laws of reflection by Huygens' principle

Let us consider a plane wavefront AB incident on the plane reflection surface xy. Incident rays are normal to the wavefront AB.

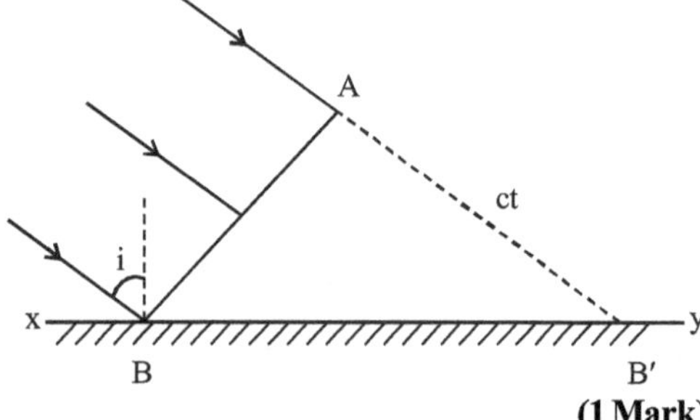

(1 Mark)

Let in time 't' the secondary wavelets reaches B' covering a distance ct. Similarly from each point on primary wavefront AB. Secondary wavelets start growing with the speed 'c'. To find reflected wavefront after time 't', let us draw a sphere of radius 'ct' taking 'B' as center and now a tangent is drawn from B' on the sphere the tangent $B'A'$ represents reflected wavefront after time t.

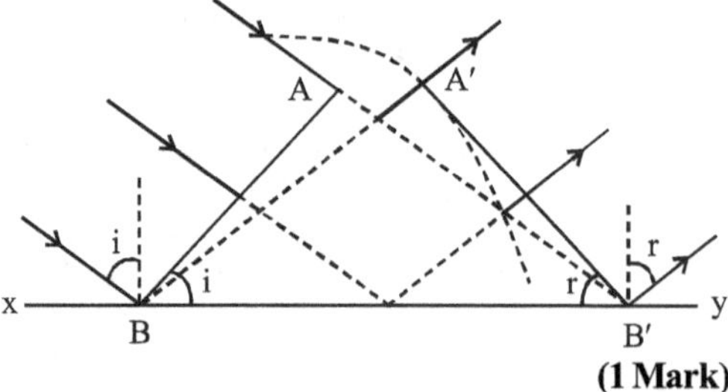

(1 Mark)

For every point on wavefront AB a corresponding point lie on the reflected wavefront $A'B'$.

So, comparing two triangle $\Delta BAB'$ and $\Delta B'A'B$

We get $AB' = A'B = ct$

$BB' = $ common

$\angle A = \angle A' = 90°$ **(½ Mark)**

Hence, two triangles are congruent, hence $\angle i = \angle r$. This proves law of reflection. Also incident ray, normal to point of incidence and reflected ray lie in same plane. This prove second law of reflection.   **(½ Mark)**

(ii) We have m = +3

So, $-\dfrac{v}{u} = +3$

$\Rightarrow$ v = –3u   **(½ Mark)**

By mirror formula $\dfrac{1}{v} + \dfrac{1}{u} = \dfrac{1}{f}$

$\Rightarrow \dfrac{1}{-3u} + \dfrac{1}{-u} = \dfrac{1}{f} \Rightarrow -\dfrac{4}{3u} = \dfrac{1}{12} \Rightarrow u = -16\,cm$

                                    (½ Mark)

OR

(b) (i) Refracting type telescope

A refracting type astronomical telescope, used to see the distant objects at large distances, consists of objective, i.e., a converging lens, or lens combination of larger focal length f_0 and larger aperture, and an eyepiece, i.e., also a converging lens, or lens combination, but of smaller focal length f_e and smaller aperture, placed coaxially.

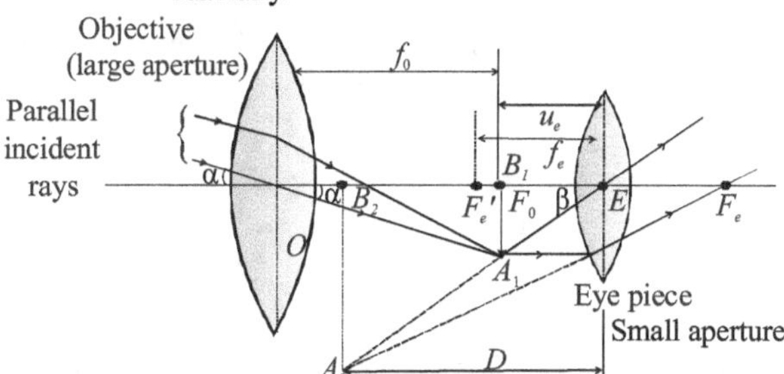

                                    (½ Mark)

Magnifying power (M) : Magnifying power (M), also called angular magnification of a telescope is defined as *the ratio of the visual angle subtended by the final image at the eye and the visual angle subtended by the object when the object lies in the actual position.* (In contrast to the definition of magnifying power of a microscope, the object is not placed at the near point in case of telescope)   **(½ Mark)**

$M = \dfrac{\beta}{\alpha} = \dfrac{\tan\beta}{\tan\alpha}$ $(\because \alpha, \beta$ are small)

$M = \dfrac{A_1B_1 / EB_1}{A_1B_1 / OB_1}$ (in ΔAB_1O and $\Delta\ AB_1E$)

$\Rightarrow M = \dfrac{OB_1}{EB_1}$ **(½ Mark)**

Using sign convention and taking u_e as object distance for eyepiece, we get

$M = \dfrac{+f_0}{-u_e} = -\dfrac{f_0}{u_e}$ ... (1)   **(½ Mark)**

This is the general formula for magnifying power of a telescope.

Magnifying power M, if eye is focussed at near point

For the eyepiece, $v = -D, v = -u_e, f = +f_e$, where , D = minimum distance of distinct vision

Using lens formula, we get $\dfrac{1}{v} - \dfrac{1}{u} = \dfrac{1}{f}$

or, $\dfrac{1}{-D} - \dfrac{1}{-u_e} = \dfrac{1}{f_e}$

$\therefore\ \ \dfrac{1}{u_e} = \dfrac{1}{f_e} + \dfrac{1}{D} = \dfrac{1}{f_e}\left(1 + \dfrac{f_e}{D}\right)$ ... (2)

                                    (½ Mark)

Put eq. (2) in (1), we get $M = -\dfrac{f_0}{f_e}\left(1 + \dfrac{f_e}{D}\right)$ ... (3)

In this case, the length of the telescope L $= f_0 + u_e$.

> **Note**
>
> *Negative sign in magnifying power of astronomical telescope shows that image is inverted.*

Magnifying power M when eye is focussed at ∞ (normal adjustment)

In this case, as already explained, we have $u_e = -f_e$
                                    ... (4)

Put eq. (4) in (1) to get $M = \dfrac{f_0}{f_e}$ ... (5)

                                    (½ Mark)

In this case, the length of the telescope L $= f_0 + f_e$.

This is the reason why the focal length of objective is taken large and of eyepiece small in case of a telescope. This also increases the resolving power of the telescope.

Further, linear or lateral magnification does not convey much meaning in case of a telescope because the size of final images too is negligible compared to actual size of the objects which are generally planets or stars.

Limitations of a refracting telescope over a reflecting telescope

(1) Image is fainter because of its large light gathering power.

(2) The resolving power (the ability to observe two object distinctly) is low, due to the large diameter of objective.   **(½ × 2 = 1 Mark)**

(ii) We have

$M = \dfrac{v_0}{u_0}\left(1 + \dfrac{D}{f_e}\right)$

As focal length of objective is small. So, $u_0 \approx f_0$
Also as focal length of eye is small. So, $v_0 \approx L$

$$\therefore M = \frac{L}{f_0}\left(1 + \frac{D}{f_e}\right) \qquad \text{(½ Mark)}$$

$$\Rightarrow 300 = \frac{L}{1}\left(1 + \frac{25}{2.5}\right) \Rightarrow 300 = L \times 11$$

$$\therefore \quad L = \frac{300}{11}\,cm \qquad \text{(½ Mark)}$$

32. (a) (i) Let us take an infinitely long positively charged straight wire having linear charge density 'λ' as shown in figure below.

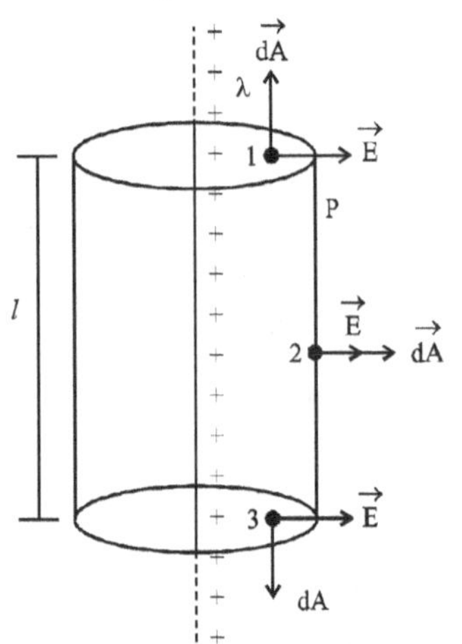

(1 Mark)

Suppose we have to determine electric field at 'P'. For this we will draw a gaussian surface as shown in fig.

Net flux through gaussian surface is

$$\phi = \oint \vec{E} \cdot \vec{dA}$$

$$\Rightarrow \quad \phi = \int_1 \vec{E}\cdot\vec{dA}^{\,0} + \int_2 \vec{E}\cdot\vec{dA} + \int_3 \vec{E}\cdot\vec{dA}^{\,0}$$

(½ Mark)

$$[\because \text{For surface 1 and 3, } \vec{E} \perp \vec{A}]$$

$$\Rightarrow \quad \phi = \int_2 \vec{E}\cdot\vec{dA} \Rightarrow \phi = \int E.dA$$

$$\Rightarrow \quad \phi = E \times \int dA$$

$$\Rightarrow \quad \phi = E \times 2\pi r l \qquad \text{(½ Mark)}$$

By Gauss law, $\phi = \dfrac{q_{in}}{\epsilon_0}$ (½ Mark)

$$\Rightarrow \quad E \times 2\pi r l = \frac{\lambda l}{\epsilon_0}$$

$$\Rightarrow E = \frac{\lambda}{2\pi \epsilon_0\, r} \text{ and direction is away from wire}$$

(½ Mark)

(ii) Here, the necessary centripetal force is provided by electrostatic attraction

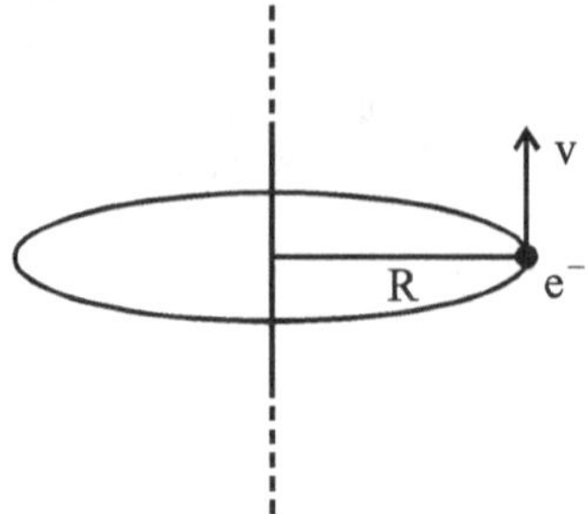

So, $\dfrac{mv^2}{R} = qE$ (½ Mark)

$$\Rightarrow \quad \frac{mv^2}{R} = \frac{e\lambda}{2\pi \epsilon_0\, R}$$

$$\Rightarrow \quad mv^2 = \frac{e\lambda}{2\pi \epsilon_0} \Rightarrow \frac{1}{2}mv^2 = \frac{e\lambda}{4\pi \epsilon_0}$$

$$\Rightarrow \quad K.E = \frac{e\lambda}{4\pi \epsilon_0} \qquad \text{(½ Mark)}$$

(iii) As $K.E = \dfrac{e\lambda}{4\pi \epsilon_0}$

$$\Rightarrow \quad K.E \propto \lambda$$

So, graph will be straight line passing through origin as shown below

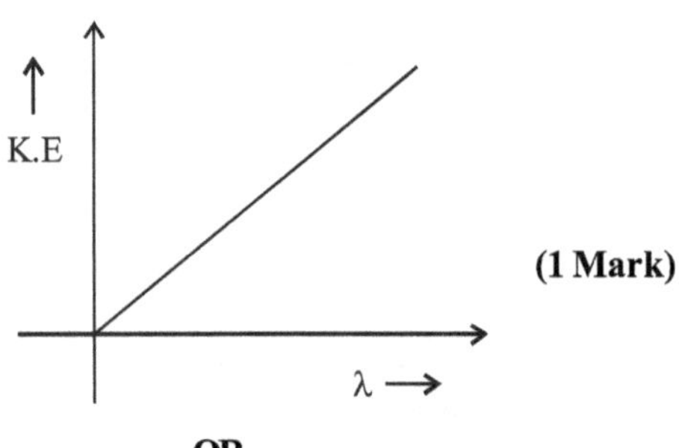

(1 Mark)

OR

(b) (i)

(1) At $x = a/2$, electric field due to both charge will cancel each other.

So at $x = a/2$, electric field will be zero.

(1 Mark)

(2) As potential is additive. So, net potential at any point can never be zero if both the charges are positive. (1 Mark)

(ii) Negative value of potential energy of a system of charges means positive amount of work is required against the electrostatic force to take the charges from the given location to infinity.

(1 Mark)

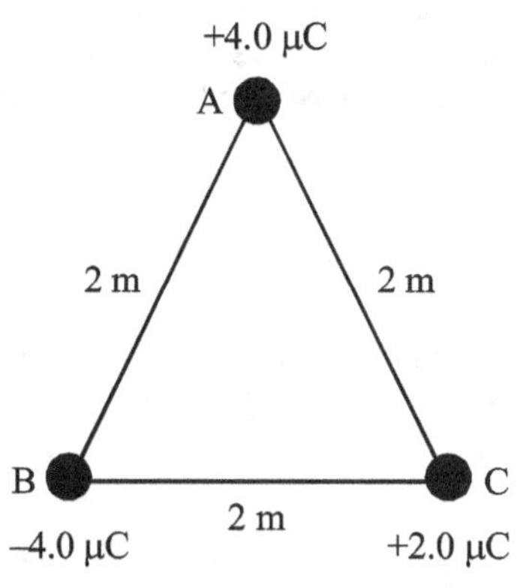

$$U = \frac{1}{4\pi \epsilon_0 \, r} \left[(4 \times -4) + (-4 \times 2) + (2 \times 4) \right] \times 10^{-12}$$

(½ Mark)

$$\Rightarrow \quad U = \frac{9 \times 10^9}{2} [-16 - 8 + 8] \times 10^{-12}$$

(½ Mark)

$$\Rightarrow \quad U = \frac{9 \times 10^9}{2} \times -16 \times 10^{-12} \qquad \textbf{(½ Mark)}$$

$$\Rightarrow \quad U = -72 \times 10^{-3} \, J = -72 \, mJ \qquad \textbf{(½ Mark)}$$

33. **(a)** **(i)** As induced emf, $|e| = \left| L \dfrac{di}{dt} \right|$

So, $|L| = \dfrac{|e|}{\left| \dfrac{di}{dt} \right|}$. If $\left| \dfrac{di}{dt} \right| = 1$ A/sec

Then, $|L| = |e|$

So, coefficient of self induction is equal to emf induced in inductor when current through it change at a rate of 1 |A| sec. **(1 Mark)**
Let the radius and length of air cored solenoid be 'r' and '*l*' respectively such that r << *l* and having n turns per unit length.

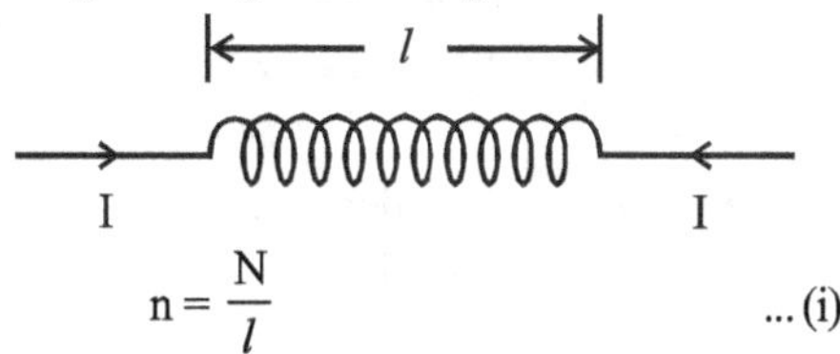

$$n = \frac{N}{l} \qquad \qquad \dots (i)$$

where, N = total number of turns.
If 'I' current flows through the coil, then magnetic field is given by

$$B = \mu_0 n I$$

where, n = number of turns per unit length
∴ Magnetic flux linked with each turn,

$$\phi = BA = \mu_0 n I A \qquad \textbf{(½ Mark)}$$

∴ Total magnetic flux linked with solenoid,

$$N\phi = (\mu_0 n I A)N \qquad \textbf{(½ Mark)}$$

But $\quad N\phi = LI \qquad \textbf{(½ Mark)}$

where, L is coefficient of self-induction,
$(\mu_0 n I A) = LI$

$$\Rightarrow \quad L = \mu_0 n A N = \mu_0 \left(\frac{N}{l} \right) AN = \frac{\mu_0 \, A N^2}{l}$$

This is required expression. **(½ Mark)**

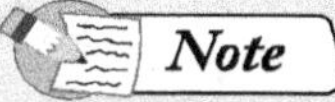 **Note**

The self-inductance of the solenoid depends on its number of turns, geometry and permeability of the medium.

(ii) From DC source, we can calculate resistance

$$R_1 = \frac{4}{1} = 4 \, \Omega, \quad R_2 = \frac{6}{1.5} = 4 \, \Omega$$

and $R_3 = \dfrac{8}{2} = 4 \, \Omega$

So, $R_{mean} = \dfrac{4 + 4 + 4}{3} = 4 \, \Omega$ **(½ Mark)**

From AC source, we can calculate impedance

$$Z_1 = \frac{3}{0.5} = 6 \, \Omega, \ Z_2 = \frac{6}{1} = 6 \, \Omega$$

and $Z_3 = \dfrac{9}{1.5} = 6 \, \Omega$

So, $Z_{mean} = \dfrac{6 + 6 + 6}{3} = 6 \, \Omega$ **(½ Mark)**

Now, $Z^2 = R^2 + \omega^2 L^2$

$$L^2 = \frac{Z^2 - R^2}{\omega^2}$$

$$L^2 = \frac{Z^2 - R^2}{4\pi^2 f^2} = \frac{(6^2 - 4^2) \times \pi^2}{4 \times \pi^2 \times 200^2} \textbf{ (½ Mark)}$$

$$= \frac{20}{4 \times 10 \times 4 \times 10^4} = \frac{1}{8} \times 10^{-4}$$

So, $L = \dfrac{1}{2\sqrt{2}} \times 10^{-2} = 0.36 \times 10^{-2} \, H$ **(½ Mark)**

$$= 3.6 \, mH$$

OR

(i) **AC generator or Dynamo**
It is used to convert mechanical energy into electrical energy. **(½ Mark)**
Principle and working : It works on the principle of electromagnetic induction. **(½ Mark)**
The main components of ac generator are :

(i) Armature coil : It consist of large number of turns of insulated copper wire wound over iron core.

(ii) Magnet : Strong permanent magnet (for small generator) or an electromagnet (for large generator) with cylindrical poles in shape.

(iii) Slip rings : The two ends of the armature coil are connected to two brass rings R_1 and R_2. These rings rotate along with the armature coil.

(iv) **Brushes :** Two carbon brushes (B_1 and B_2), are pressed against the slip rings. These brushes are connected to the load through which the output is obtained. **(1 Mark)**

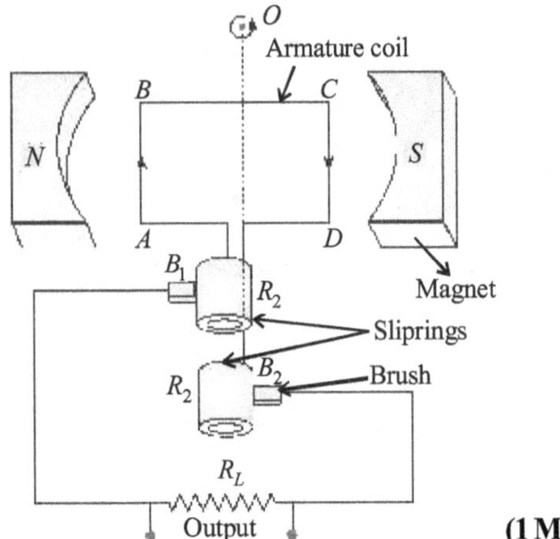

(1 Mark)

Working: When a coil is rotated in magnetic field, an emf is induced in the coil. The coil may be rotated by water energy, steam energy or oil energy. Let at any instant magnetic flux through armature coil,

$$N\phi_B = NBA\cos\theta = NBA\cos\omega t$$

The induced emf $e = -\dfrac{d\phi_B}{dt} = NBA\omega \sin\omega t$

or $e = e_0 \sin\omega t$, where $e_0 = NBA\omega$.
(½ Mark)

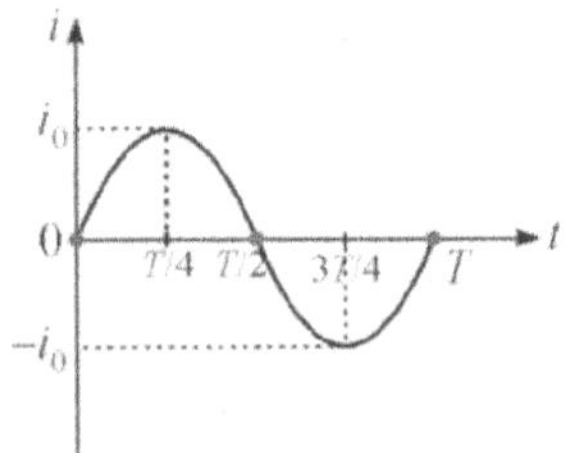

And induced current $i = \dfrac{e}{R} = \dfrac{e_0}{R}\sin\omega t = i_0 \sin\omega t$

The direction of current changes periodically and therefore the current is called alternating current. **(½ Mark)**

(ii) We have
$$e_{max} = NBA\omega$$
$$= 100 \times 0.8 \times 0.5 \times 60$$
$$= 2400\,V \qquad \text{(½ Mark)}$$

$$P_{av} = \dfrac{e_{rms}^2}{R} = \dfrac{e_{max}^2}{2R} = \dfrac{2400^2}{2 \times 100} = 28.8\,kW$$
(½ Mark)

34. (a) (i) 'B' has highest frequency because of its highest stopping potential. **(1 Mark)**

(ii) 'C' has longest wavelength because of its lowest stopping potential. **(1 Mark)**

(iii) 'B' ejects photoelectrons with maximum momentum because high momentum means high kinetic energy and therefore high stopping potential. **(2 Marks)**

OR

(b) **Effect on threshold frequency**

When frequency is increased there is no effect on threshold frequency because threshold frequency is property of metal. It does not depends on frequency of photon radiation. **(1 Mark)**

Effect on stopping potential

When frequency is increased, stopping potential get increased.

As $h\nu = h\nu_0 + eV_S \Rightarrow V_S = \dfrac{h}{e}\nu - \dfrac{h}{e}\nu_0$

We can see from equation that increasing frequency increases stopping potential. **(1 Mark)**

 *Note*

Slope of graph between stopping potential and frequency of the incident light gives the ratio of Planck's constant to electronic charge.

35. (a) (i) As the switch is closed in circuit, flux will change through the ring. Due to which current will be induced in it. The induced current opposes this change, and sets up its own magnetic field. This opposition is in effect as a repulsion (two like pole facing one another) and this cause rings to jump 20 cm to 50 cm in air. **(1 Mark)**

(ii) There will no change in repulsive forces, the only change that will occur is in the direction of induced current in the ring. **(1 Mark)**

(iii) Two laws that helps us in understanding this phenomenon are:

(i) Lenz law

(ii) Faraday's law **(2 × 1 = 2 Marks)**

OR

(b) Magnetic field inside the solenoid is given as
$$B = \mu_0\,\mu_r\,nI \qquad \text{(½ Mark)}$$
i.e. $B \propto \mu_r$

$\propto n$

$\propto I$

So, if permeability of core material is increased, magnetic field is increased. **(½ Mark)**

If number of turns per unit length is increased, again magnetic field is increased. **(½ Mark)**

If current is increased, then also magnetic field is increased. **(½ Mark)**

Delhi 2023

CBSE Board Solved Paper

Time Allowed : 3 Hours   *Maximum Marks : 70*

General Instructions:

Read the following instructions very carefully and follow them :

(i) *This question paper contains 35 questions. All questions are compulsory.*

(ii) *Question paper is divided into FIVE sections – Section A, B, C, D and E.*

(iii) *In section – A : question number 1 to 18 are Multiple Choice (MCQ) type questions carrying 1 mark each.*

(iv) *In section – B : question number 19 to 25 are Short Answer-1 (SA-1) type questions carrying 2 marks each.*

(v) *In section – C : question number 26 to 30 are Short Answer-2 (SA-2) type questions carrying 3 marks each.*

(vi) *In section – D : question number 31 to 33 are Long Answer (LA) type questions carrying 5 marks each.*

(vii) *In section – E : question number 34 and 35 are case-based questions carrying 4 marks each.*

(viii) *There is no overall choice. However, an internal choice has been provided in 2 questions in Section – B, 2 questions in Section – C, 3 questions in Section – D and 2 questions in Section – E.*

(ix) *Use of calculators is NOT allowed.*

$c = 3 \times 10^8 \, \text{m/s}$

$h = 6.63 \times 10^{-34} \, \text{Js}$

$e = 1.6 \times 10^{-19} \, \text{C}$

$\mu_0 = 4\pi \times 10^{-7} \, \text{T m A}^{-1}$

$\varepsilon_0 = 8.854 \times 10^{-12} \, \text{C}^2 \, \text{N}^{-1} \, \text{m}^{-2}$

$\dfrac{1}{4\pi\varepsilon_0} = 9 \times 10^9 \, \text{Nm}^2 \, \text{C}^{-2}$

Mass of electron $(m_e) = 9.1 \times 10^{-31} \, \text{kg}$

Mass of neutron $= 1.675 \times 10^{-27} \, \text{kg}$

Mass of proton $= 1.673 \times 10^{-27} \, \text{kg}$

Avogadro's number $= 6.023 \times 10^{23}$ per gram mole

Boltzmann constant $= 1.38 \times 10^{-23} \, \text{JK}^{-1}$

SECTION - A

1. A charge Q is placed at the centre of a cube. The electric flux through one if its face is

(a) $\dfrac{Q}{\varepsilon_0}$ (b) $\dfrac{Q}{6\varepsilon_0}$ (c) $\dfrac{Q}{8\varepsilon_0}$ (d) $\dfrac{Q}{3\varepsilon_0}$

2. Two long parallel wires kept 2 m apart carry 3A current each, in the same direction. The force per unit length on one wire due to the other is

(a) $4.5 \times 10^{-5} \, \text{Nm}^{-1}$, attractive

(b) $4.5 \times 10^{-7} \, \text{N/m}$, repulsive

(c) $9 \times 10^{-7} \, \text{N/m}$, repulsive

(d) $9 \times 10^{-5} \, \text{N/m}$, attractive

3. Which of the following has its permeability less than that of free space?

(a) Copper   (b) Aluminium

(c) Copper chloride   (d) Nickel

4. A square shaped coil of side 10 cm, having 100 turns is placed perpendicular to a magnetic field which is increasing at 1 T/s. The induced emf in the coil is

(a) 0.1 V   (b) 0.5 V   (c) 0.75 V   (d) 1.0 V

5. Choose the correct option related to wavelengths (λ) of different parts of electromagnetic spectrum.

(a) $\lambda_{x\text{-rays}} < \lambda_{\text{micro waves}} < \lambda_{\text{radio waves}} < \lambda_{\text{visible}}$

(b) $\lambda_{\text{visible}} > \lambda_{x\text{-rays}} > \lambda_{\text{radio waves}} > \lambda_{\text{micro waves}}$

(c) $\lambda_{\text{radio wave}} > \lambda_{\text{micro waves}} > \lambda_{\text{visible}} > \lambda_{x\text{-rays}}$

(d) $\lambda_{\text{visible}} < \lambda_{\text{micro waves}} < \lambda_{\text{radio waves}} < \lambda_{x\text{-rays}}$

6. In a Young's double-slit experiment, the screen is moved away from the plane of the slits. What will be its effect on the following?

(i) Angular separation of the fringes

(ii) Fringe-width

(a) Both (i) and (ii) remain constant

(b) (i) remains constant, but (ii) decreases

(c) (i) remains constant, but (ii) increases

(d) Both (i) and (ii) increase

7. The energy of a photon of wavelength λ is
   (a) $hc\lambda$　(b) hc/λ　(c) λ/hc　(d) $\lambda h/c$

8. The ratio of the nuclear densities of two nuclei having mass numbers 64 and 125 is
   (a) $\dfrac{64}{125}$　(b) $\dfrac{4}{5}$　(c) $\dfrac{5}{4}$　(d) 1

9. During the formation of a p-n junction
   (a) diffusion current keeps increasing
   (b) drift current remains constant
   (c) both the diffusion current and drift current remain constant
   (d) diffusion current remains almost constant but drift current increases till both currents become equal

10. The diagram shows four energy level of an electron in Bohr model of hydrogen atom. Identify the transition in which the emitted photon will have the highest energy.
    (a) I
    (b) II
    (c) III
    (d) IV

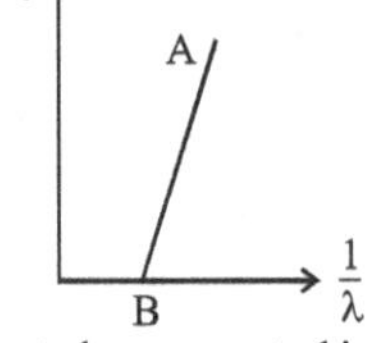

11. Figure shows a plot of stopping potential (V_0) versus $\dfrac{1}{\lambda}$, where λ is the wavelength of the radiation causing photoelectric emission from a surface. The slope of the line is equal to
    (a) ϕ_0　(b) $\dfrac{h}{e}$
    (c) $\dfrac{hc}{e}$　(d) $\dfrac{h^2 c}{e^2}$

12. The capacitors, each of 4 μF are to be connected in such a way that the effective capacitance of the combination is 6 μF. This can be achieved by connecting
    (a) All three in parallel
    (b) All three in series
    (c) Two of them connected in series and the combination in parallel to the third
    (d) Two of them connected in parallel and the combination in series to the third

13. An ideal inductor is connected across an AC source of voltage. The current in the circuit
    (a) is ahead of the voltage in phase by π.
    (b) lags voltage in phase by π.
    (c) is ahead of voltage in phase by $\pi/2$.
    (d) lags voltage in phase by $\pi/2$.

14. According to Huygens principle, the amplitude of secondary wavelets is
    (a) equal in both the forward and the backward directions.
    (b) maximum in the forward direction and zero in the backward direction.
    (c) large in the forward direction and small in the backward direction
    (d) small in the forward direction and large in the backward direction

15. The radius of the nth orbit in Bohr model of hydrogen atom is proportional to
    (a) n^2　(b) $\dfrac{1}{n^2}$　(c) n　(d) $\dfrac{1}{n}$

Note : In question number **16** to **18** two statements are given – one labelled **Assertion (A)** and the other labelled **Reason (R)**. Select the correct answer to these questions from the codes **(a)**, **(b)**, **(c)** and **(d)** as given below :
(a) Both Assertion (A) and Reason (R) are true and (R) is the correct explanation of (A).
(b) Both Assertion (A) and Reason (R) are true and (R) is NOT the correct exlanation of (A).
(c) Assertion (A) is true and Reason (R) is false.
(d) Assertion (A) is false and Reason (R) is also false.

16. **Assertion (A)** : In insulators, the forbidden gap is very large.
    Reason (R) : The valence electrons in an atom of an insulator are very tightly bound to the nucleus.

17. **Assertion (A)** : The equivalent resistance between points A and B in the given network is 2R.
    Reason (R) : All the resistors are connected in parallel

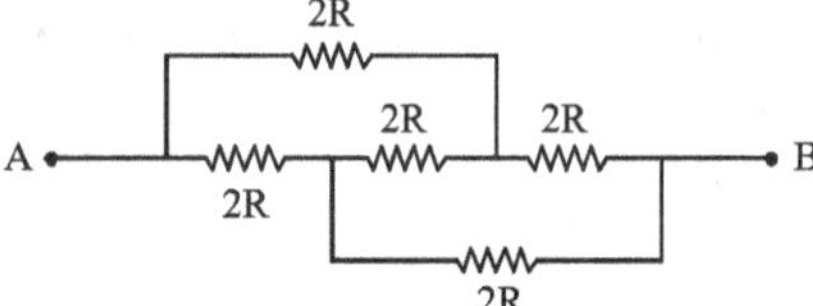

18. **Assertion (A)** : The deflecting torque acting on a current carrying loop is zero when its plane is perpendicular to the direction of magnetic field.
    Reason (R) : The deflecting torque acting on a loop of magnetic moment $\vec{m}$ in a magnetic field $\vec{B}$ is given by the dot product of $\vec{m}$ and $\vec{B}$.

SECTION - B

19. Draw a graph showing the variation of potential energy of a pair of nucleons as a function of their separation. Indicate the region in which the nuclear force is (a) attractive and (b) repulsive.

20. (a) How will the De Broglie wavelength associated with an electron be affected when the (i) velocity of the electron decreases ? and (ii) accelerating potential is increased ? Justify your answer.

    OR

    (b) How would the stopping potential for a given photosensitive surface change if (i) the frequency of the incident radiation were increased ? and (ii) the intensity of incident radiation were decreased ? Justify your answer.

21. Identify the electromagnetic radiation and write its wavelength range, which is used to kill germs in water purifier. Name the two sources of these radiations.

22. An electric dipole of dipole moment $(\vec{p})$ is kept in a uniform electric field $\vec{E}$. Show graphically the variation of torque acting on the dipole (τ) with its orientation (θ) in the field. Find the orientation in which torque is (i) zero and (ii) maximum.

23. (a) Write the expression for the Lorentz force on a particle of charge q moving with a velocity $\vec{v}$ in a magnetic field $\vec{B}$. When is the magnitude of this force maximum? Show that no work is done by this force on the particle during its motion from a point $\vec{r}_1$ to point $\vec{r}_2$.

OR

(b) A long straight wire AB carries a current I. A particle (mass m and charge q) moves with a velocity $\vec{v}$, parallel to the wire, at a distance d from it as shown in the figure. Obtain the expression for the force experienced by the particle and mention its directions.

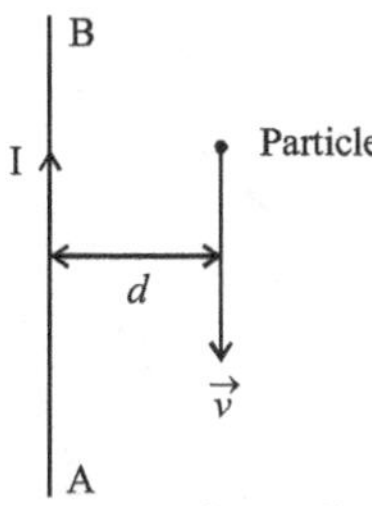

24. A potential difference (V) is applied across a conductor of length 'L' and cross-sectional area 'A'.

How will the drift velocity of electrons and the current density be affected if another identical conductor of the same material were connected in series with the first conductor ? Justify your answers.

25. Two coils C_1 and C_2 are placed close to each other. The magnetic flux ϕ_2 linked with the coil C_2 varies with the current I_1 flowing in coil C_1, as shown in the figure. Find

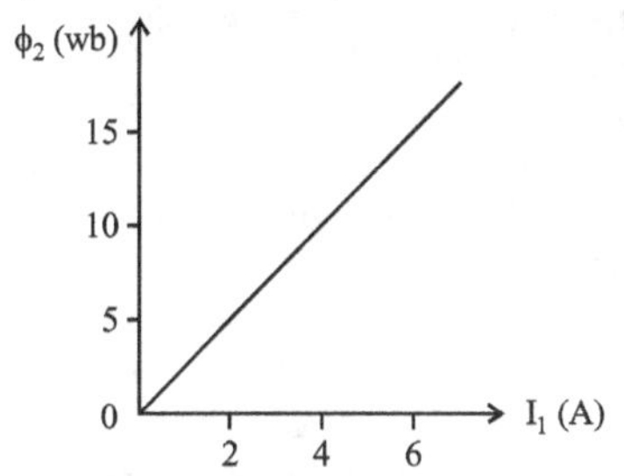

(i) the mutual inductance of the arrangement, and

(ii) the rate of change of current $\left(\dfrac{dI_1}{dt}\right)$ that will induce an emf of 100 V in coil C_2.

26. (a) A plane wave-front propagating in a medium of refractive index 'μ_1' is incident on a plane surface making an angle of incidence (i). It enters into a medium of refractive index $\mu_2 (\mu_2 > \mu_1)$.
Use Huygen's construction of secondary wavelets to trace the retracted wave-front. Hence verify Snell's law of refraction.

OR

(b) Using Huygen's construction, show how a plane wave is reflected from a surface. Hence verify the law of reflection.

27. A current of 1A flows through a coil when it is connected across a DC battery of 100 V. If DC battery is replaced by an AC source of 100 V and angular frequency 100 rad s^{-1}, the current reduces to 0.5 A. Find
(i) impedance of the circuit (ii) self-inductance of coil
(iii) phase difference between the voltage and the current.

28. The primary coil having N_p turns of an ideal transformer is supplied with an alternating voltage V_p. Obtain an expression for the voltage V_s induced in its secondary coil having N_s turns. Mention two main sources of power loss in real transformers.

29. (a) Briefly describe how the current sensitivity of a moving coil galvanometer can be increased.

(b) A galvanometer shows full scale deflection for current I_g. A resistance R_1 is required to convert it into a voltmeter of range $(0 - V)$ and a resistance R_2 to convert it into a voltmeter of range $(0 - 2V)$. Find the resistance of the galvanometer.

30. (a) (i) Write the limitations of Rutherford's model of atom.
(ii) The wavelength of the second line of the Balmer series in the hydrogen spectrum is 4861 Å. Calculate the wavelength of the first line of the same series.

OR

(b) (i) Increase in the intensity of the radiation causing photo-electric emission from a surface, does not affect the maximum K.E. of the photo electrons. Explain.
(ii) The photon emitted during the de-excitation from the first excited level to the ground state of hydrogen atom is used to irradiate a photo cathode in which stopping potential is 5 V. Calculate the work function of the cathode used.

31. (a) Draw the circuit arrangement for studying V-I characteristics of a p-n junction diode in (i) forward biasing and (ii) reverse biasing. Draw a typical V-I characteristics of a silicon diode. Describe briefly the following terms : (i) minority carriers injection in forward biasing and (ii) breakdown voltage in reverse biasing.

(b) Name two important processes involved in the formation of a p-n junction diode. With the help of a circuit diagram, explain the working of junction diode as a full wave rectifier. Draw its input and output waveforms. State the characteristic property of a junction diode that makes it suitable for rectification.

32. (a) (i) Draw a ray diagram to show the working of a compound microscope. Obtain the expression for the total magnification for the final image to be formed at the near point.

(ii) In a compound microscope an object is placed at a distance of 1.5 cm from the objective of focal length 1.25 cm. If the eye-piece has a focal length of 5 cm and the final image is formed at the near point, find the magnifying power of the microscope.

OR

(b) (i) Draw a ray diagram for the formation of image of an object by an astronomical telescope, in normal adjustment. Obtain the expression for its magnifying power.

(ii) The magnifying power of an astronomical telescope in normal adjustment is 2.9 and the objective and the eyepiece are separated by a distance of 150 cm. Find the focal lengths of the two lenses.

33. (a) (i) Explain how free electrons in a metal at constant temperature attain an average velocity under the action of an electric field. Hence obtain an expression for it.

(ii) Consider two conducting wires A and B of the same diameter but made of different materials joined in series across a battery. The number density of electrons in A is 1.5 times that in B. Find the ratio of drift velocity of electrons in wire A to that in wire B.

OR

(b) (i) A cell emf of (E) and internal resistance (r) is connected across a variable load resistance (R). Draw plots showing the variation of terminal voltage V with (i) R and (ii) the current (I) in the load.

(ii) Three cells, each of emf E but internal resistances $2r$, $3r$ and $6r$ are connected in parallel across a resistor R.

Obtain expressions for (i) current flowing in the circuit, and (ii) the terminal potential difference across the equivalent cell.

SECTION-E

Note: Questions number **34** and **35** are Case Study based questions. Read the following paragraph and answer the questions.

34. A capacitor is a system of two conductors separated by an insulator. The two conductors have equal and opposite charges with a potential difference between them. The capacitance of a capacitor depends on the geometrical configuration (shape, size and separation) of the system and also on the nature of the insulator separating the two conductors. They are used to store charges. Like resistors, capacitors can be arranged in series or parallel or a combination of both to obtain desired value of capacitance.

(i) Find the equivalent capacitances between points A and B in the given diagram.

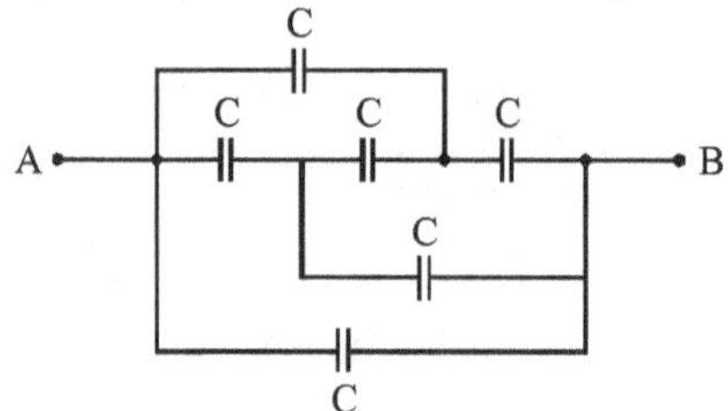

(ii) A dielectric slab is inserted between the plates of a parallel plate capacitor. The electric field between the plates decreases. Explain.

(iii) A capacitor A of capacitance C, having charge Q is connected across another uncharged capacitor B of capacitance 2C. Find an expression for (a) the potential difference across the combination and (b) the charge lost by capacitor A.

OR

(iii) Two slabs of dielectric constants 2K and K fill the space between the plates of a parallel plate capacitor of plate area A and plate separation d as shown in figure. Find an expression for capacitance of the system.

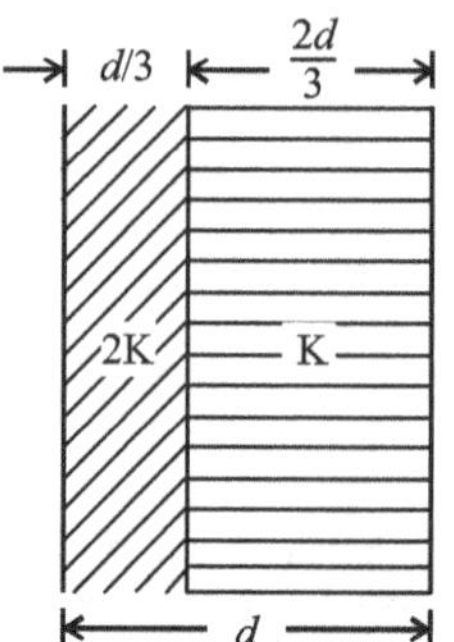

35. A lens is a transparent optical medium bounded by two surfaces; at least one of which should be spherical. Considering image formation by a single spherical surface successively at the two surfaces of a lens, lens maker's formula is obtained. It is useful to design lenses of desired focal length using surfaces of suitable radii of curvature. This formula helps us obtain a relation between u, v and f for a lens. Lenses form images of objects and they are used in a number of optical devices, for example microscopes and telescopes.

(i) An object AB is kept in front of a composite convex lens, as shown in figure. Will the lens produce one image? If not, explain.

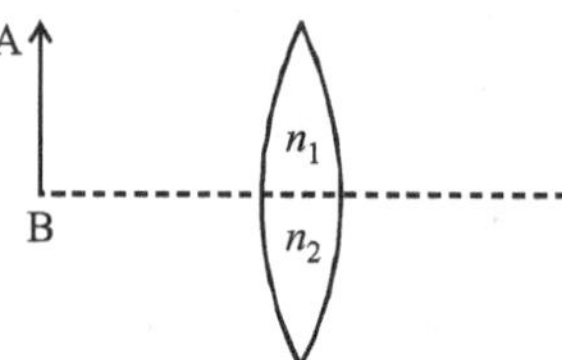

(ii) A real image of an object formed by a convex lens is observed on a screen. If the screen is removed, will the image still be formed? Explain.

(iii) A double convex lens is made of glass of refractive index 1.55 with both faces of the same radius of curvature. Find the radius of curvature required if focal length is 20 cm.

OR

(iii) Two convex lenses A and B of focal lengths 15 cm and 10 cm respectively are placed coaxially 'd' distance apart. A point object is kept at a distance of 30 cm in front of lens A. Find the value of 'd' so that the rays emerging from lens B are parallel to its principal axis.

Solutions

1. **(b)** Total flux through cube is $\dfrac{Q}{\varepsilon_0}$

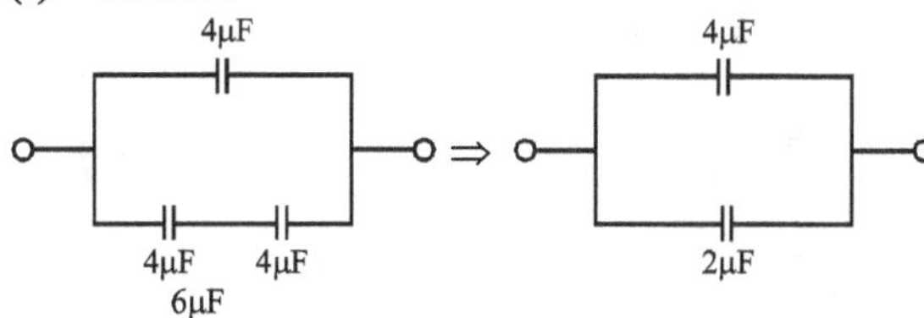

So, flux through one face is $\dfrac{\frac{Q}{\varepsilon_0}}{6}$ i.e. $\dfrac{Q}{6\varepsilon_0}$

(1 Mark)

2. **(c)** The force per unit length is given as

$$\dfrac{F}{l} = \dfrac{\mu_0}{2\pi}\dfrac{I_1 I_2}{d} = 2 \times 10^{-7} \times \dfrac{3 \times 3}{2}$$

$$= 9 \times 10^{-7}\,\text{N/m} \qquad \textbf{(½ Mark)}$$

As current in both wire is in same direction.

So, the two wire will repel each other.

(½ Mark)

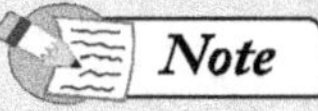

3. **(a)** Copper due its diamagnetic nature has permeability less than free space. **(½ Mark)**

4. **(d)** We have

$$e = \left|\dfrac{d\phi}{dt}\right| = NA\cos\theta\dfrac{dB}{dt} = 100 \times 0.1^2 \times \cos 0° \times 1 = 1\,\text{V}$$

(1 Mark)

5. **(c)** The correct order is

$$\lambda_{\text{radiowave}} > \lambda_{\text{microwaves}} > \lambda_{\text{visible}} > \lambda_{x\text{-rays}} \qquad \textbf{(1 Mark)}$$

6. **(c)** The angular width is given as

$$\theta = \dfrac{\lambda}{d} \Rightarrow \text{'θ' is independent of distance between screen}$$

and plane of slits **(½ Mark)**

and, the fringe width is given as $\beta = \dfrac{\lambda D}{d} \Rightarrow \beta \propto D$ i.e. if distance between screen and slit increases, fringe width also increases. **(½ Mark)**

7. **(b)** The energy of a photon of wavelength λ is given as

$$\dfrac{hc}{\lambda}$$

(1 Mark)

8. **(d)** The nuclear density is independent of the mass number. So, required ratio is 1. **(1 Mark)**

9. **(b)** During the formation of p-n junction, diffusion current keep on decreasing due to formation of barrier potential but as drift current is largely dependent on temperature it will remain constant. **(1 Mark)**

10. **(a)** In Ist transition, energy gap is highest. So emitted photon will have highest energy. **(1 Mark)**

11. **(c)** We have

$$eV_0 = \dfrac{hc}{\lambda} - \dfrac{hc}{\lambda_0}$$

$$V_0 = \left(\dfrac{hc}{e}\right)\dfrac{1}{\lambda} - \dfrac{hc}{\lambda_0 e}$$

Comparing it with straight line equation $y = mx + c$, we get

slope i.e. $m = \dfrac{hc}{e}$ **(1 Mark)**

12. **(c)** We have

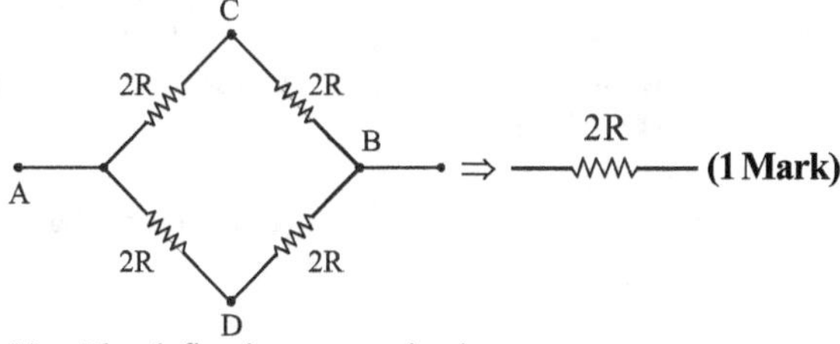

So, if two $4\mu F$ capacitors are connected in series and the combination in parallel to the third, we will have $6\mu F$ capacitance. **(1 Mark)**

13. **(d)** In purely inductive circuit, current lag the voltage in phase by $\pi/2$. **(1 Mark)**

14. **(b)** As energy cannot flow in backward directions, so amplitude of secondary wavelets is maximum in forward direction and zero in the backward direction. **(1 Mark)**

> **Note**
>
> *A wave front is always perpendicular to the direction of propogation of light.*

15. **(a)** As $R_n = 0.529 \times n^2\,\text{Å}$

So, $R_n \propto n^2$ **(1 Mark)**

16. **(a)** In insulators, the valence electrons in an atom are very tightly bound to the nucleus. So insulators forbidden gap is very large. **(1 Mark)**

17. **(c)**

The above is a wheatstone bridge having bridge resistance between C & D. So, our modified circuit is

(1 Mark)

18. **(a)** The deflecting torque is given as

$$\tau = BINA \sin\theta,$$

where θ is angle between area vector of loop and magnetic field.

Here $\theta = 0°$ So, $\tau = 0$

Also, $\vec{\tau} = \vec{M} \times \vec{B} \Rightarrow |\tau| = MB \sin\theta$

$\Rightarrow |\tau| = NIAB \sin\theta \qquad [\because M = NIA]$

$\Rightarrow |\tau| = BINA \sin\theta$ **(1 Mark)**

Torque is zero when the magnetic field is perpendicular to the plane of the loop. Torque is maximum when the magnetic field is perpendicular to the plane of the loop.

19.

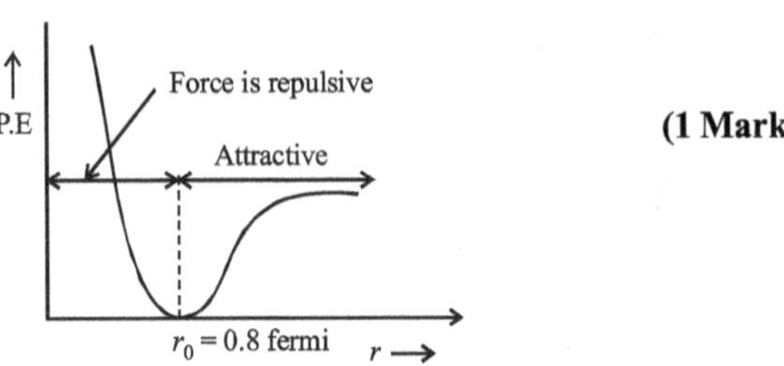

(1 Mark)

In the graph,

$\rightarrow$ For separation on greater than r_0, the force is attractive

$\rightarrow$ For separation less than r_0, the force is strongly repulsive **($\frac{1}{2} \times 2 = 1$ Mark)**

20. (a) We have, $\lambda = \dfrac{h}{mv} = \dfrac{h}{\sqrt{2mq\Delta V}}$

So, $\lambda \propto \dfrac{1}{v}$ and $\lambda \propto \dfrac{1}{\sqrt{\Delta V}}$ **(1 Mark)**

So decreasing velocity, increase de-Broglie wavelength and, increasing accelerating potential decreases de-Broglie wavelength. **(1 Mark)**

OR

(b) (i) As $h\nu = h\nu_0 = eV_s$

So, increasing frequency increases stopping potential. **(1 Mark)**

(ii) We can clearly see from above expression that stopping potential depends only on threshold frequency and work function, it is independent of intensity. **(1 Mark)**

21. UV rays is used to kill germs in water purifier. The UV region covers the wavelength range $1000 - 4000$Å. **(1 Mark)** The two main sources of UV radiation are :

(i) Sunlight is the main source of UV radiation.

(ii) UV radiation is produced either by heating a body to incandescent temperature. **($\frac{1}{2} \times 2 = 1$ Mark)**

22. We know that torque acting on a dipole placed in uniform electric field is given as

$$\tau = PE \sin \theta$$

So, graph between 'τ' and 'E' will look like as shown below

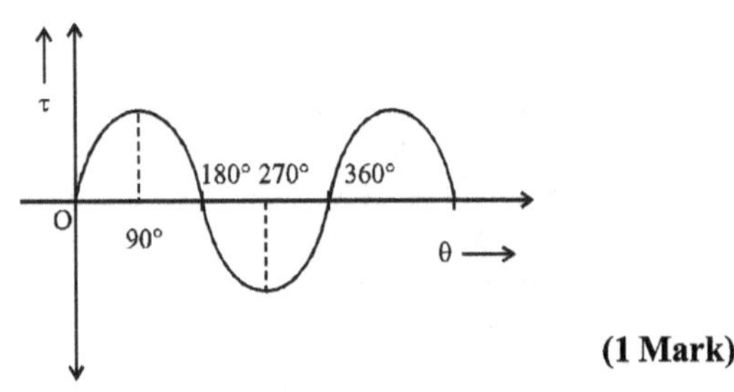

(1 Mark)

(i) For $\tau = 0 \Rightarrow PE \sin \theta = 0 \Rightarrow \sin \theta = 0 \Rightarrow \theta = 0°$ or $180°$
So, when dipole moment is parallel or anti-parallel to electric field, net torque on it is zero. **($\frac{1}{2}$ Mark)**

(ii) For maximum torque

$$\dfrac{d\tau}{d\theta} = 0 \ \Rightarrow \ \dfrac{d}{d\theta}(PE \sin \theta) = 0 \Rightarrow \cos \theta = 0$$
$$\Rightarrow \theta = 90° \text{ or } 270°$$ **($\frac{1}{2}$ Mark)**

23. (a) We know that Lorenz force is given as

$$\vec{F}_L = q\left[\vec{E} + (\vec{V} \times \vec{B}) \right]$$ **($\frac{1}{2}$ Mark)**

Here, $\vec{E} = 0$

So, $\vec{F}_L = q(\vec{V} \times \vec{B}) \Rightarrow F_L = q VB \sin \theta$

Clearly, F_L will be maximum when θ is $90°$ i.e. $\vec{V} \perp \vec{B}$. **($\frac{1}{2}$ Mark)**

As $\vec{F}$ is always perpendicular to $\vec{V}$, so body will undergo circular motion and therefore no work is done in moving from a point $\vec{r_1}$ to $\vec{r_2}$. **(1 Mark)**

OR

(b) Force on a charge particle placed in magnetic field is given as

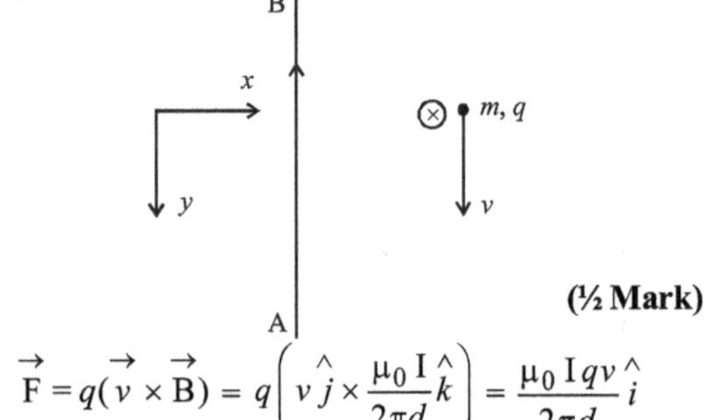

($\frac{1}{2}$ Mark)

$$\vec{F} = q(\vec{v} \times \vec{B}) = q\left(v\,\hat{j} \times \dfrac{\mu_0 I}{2\pi d}\hat{k} \right) = \dfrac{\mu_0 I q v}{2\pi d}\hat{i}$$ **($1\frac{1}{2}$ Marks)**

24. Drift velocity of an electron in conductor is given as

$$V_d = \dfrac{eE\tau}{2m} = \dfrac{eV\tau}{2ml}$$ **(1 Mark)**

As e, V, τ and m are constant

So, $V_d \propto \dfrac{1}{l}$. So, increasing 'l' decrease 'V_d'.

Now, current density is given as

$$J = \sigma E \Rightarrow J = \dfrac{\sigma V}{l} \ \Rightarrow J \propto \dfrac{1}{l}.$$

So, increasing 'l', decreases 'J'. **(1 Mark)**

25. (i) We have

$$N_2 \phi_2 = MI_1 \Rightarrow \phi_2 = \dfrac{M}{N_2}I_1$$

As $N_2 = 1$. So,

$$\phi_2 = MI_1$$

Comparing it with straight line equation

$$y = mx + c$$

We have, M = m = slope of ϕ_2 and I_1 curve

$$= \dfrac{10 - 5}{4 - 2} = \dfrac{5}{2}$$ **($\frac{1}{2}$ Mark)**

So, $M = \dfrac{5}{2}H$ **(½ Mark)**

(ii) As $e_2 = M\dfrac{d\mathrm{I}_1}{dt} \Rightarrow 100 = \dfrac{5}{2} \times \dfrac{d\mathrm{I}_1}{dt} \Rightarrow \dfrac{d\mathrm{I}_1}{dt} = 40$ A/sec **(1 Mark)**

26. **(a)** Let us consider a plane wavefront AB incident on the plane refracting surface xy. Incident rays are normal to the wavefront AB. Let first medium be air and second medium be glass.

Then, $\mu_1 = 1$ and $v_1 = c$
and, $\mu_2 = \mu_g$ and $v_2 = v$

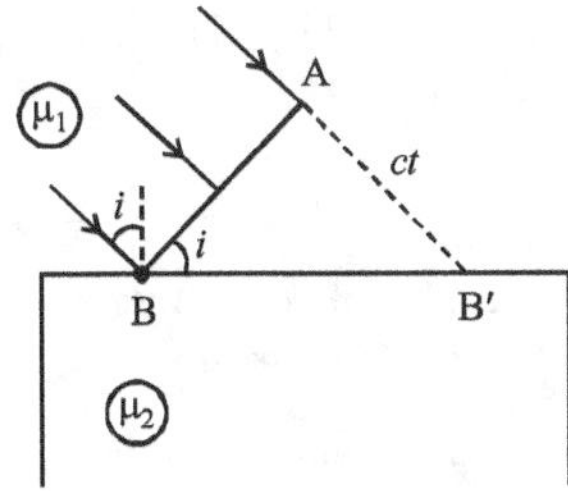

(½ Mark)

Let in time 't' the secondary wavelets from A reaches B′ covering a distance ct. Similarly from every point on primary wavefront AB, secondary wavelets start growing which travel with speed c in air and with speed 'v' in denser medium. **(½ Mark)**

To find refracted wavefront after time 't' let us draw a sphere of radius 'vt' in the denser medium taking B as center and now a tangent is drawn from B′ on the sphere. The tangent B′A′ represents refracted wavefront after time 't'. For every point on primary wavefront AB a corresponding point lies on the refracted wavefront A′B′. **(½ Mark)**

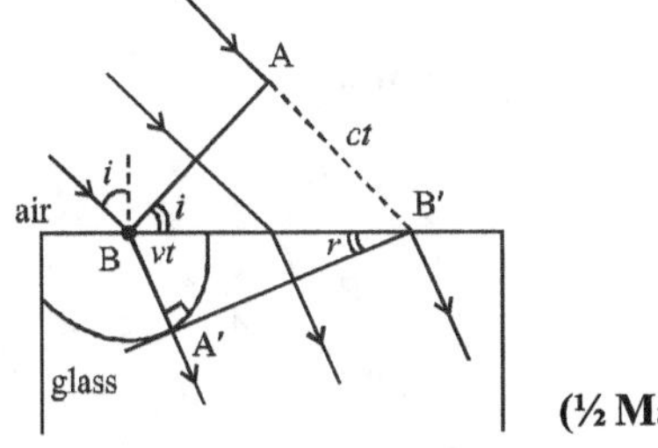

(½ Mark)

In ΔABB′ and ΔA′B′B

Snell's law can be proved

$\dfrac{\sin i}{\sin r} = \dfrac{ct/\mathrm{BB}'}{vt/\mathrm{BB}'} = \dfrac{c}{v} = {}^1\mu_2$ **(½ Mark)**

So, first law of refraction can be proved.

Also, the incident ray, refracted rays and normal to the rays, all lie in the same plane. This gives the second law of refraction.

OR

(b) Suppose we have a plane wavefront AB incident on the plane reflecting surface xy. Incident rays are normal to the wavefront AB.

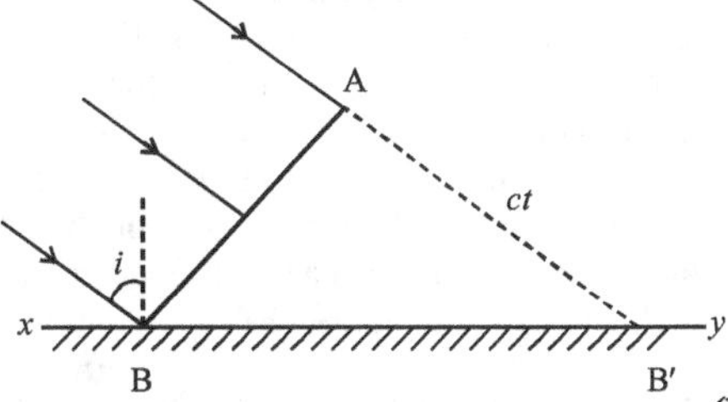

(½ Mark)

Let in time 't' the secondary wavelets reaches B′ covering a distance ct. Similarly from each point on primary wavefront AB. Secondary wavelets start growing with the speed 'c'. To find reflected wavefront after time 't', let us draw a sphere of radius 'ct' taking 'B' as center and now a tangent is drawn from B′ on the sphere the tangent B′A′ represents reflected wavefront after time t. **(½ Mark)**

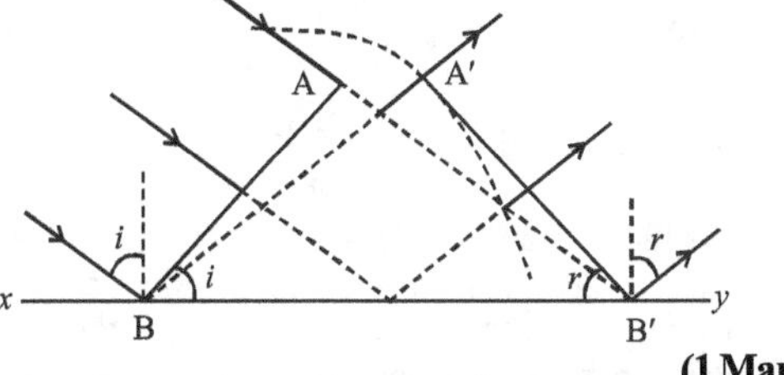

(1 Mark)

For every point on wavefront AB a corresponding point lie on the reflected wavefront A′B′.

So, comparing two triangle ΔBAB′ and ΔB′A′B

We have $\mathrm{AB}' = \mathrm{A}'\mathrm{B} = ct$

$\mathrm{BB}' = $ common

$\angle A = \angle A' = 90°$ **(½ Mark)**

Thus, two triangle are congruent, hence $\angle i = \angle r$. This proves first law of reflection. Also incident rays, normal to the point of incidence and reflected ray all lie in same plane. This gives second law of refraction. **(½ Mark)**

27. **(i)** When DC source is connected

$R = \dfrac{V}{I} = \dfrac{100}{1} = 100\,\Omega$ **(½ Mark)**

When AC source is connected

$Z = \dfrac{V_{\mathrm{rms}}}{I_{\mathrm{rms}}} = \dfrac{100}{0.5} = 200\,\Omega$ **(½ Mark)**

(ii) As, $Z^2 = X_L{}^2 + R^2$

$\Rightarrow X_L{}^2 = Z^2 - R^2 \Rightarrow X_L = \sqrt{200^2 - 100^2}$ **(1 Mark)**

$\Rightarrow 100 \times L = 173.2 \Rightarrow L = 1.732$H

(iii) We know that

$\cos\phi = \dfrac{R}{Z} = \dfrac{100}{200} = \dfrac{1}{2} \Rightarrow \phi = 60°$ **(1 Mark)**

 *Note*

For a DC source, $\omega = 0$. $\therefore$ Inductive reactance, $X_L = \omega L = 0$.

28. **Theory and working :** An alternating e.m.f. E_p is applied across the primary which produces current I_p in the primary circuit and a current I_s in the secondary circuit. The currents in the coils produce a magnetization in the soft-iron core and there is a corresponding magnetic field B inside the core. The field due to magnetization of the core is large as compared to the field due to the current in the coils. We assume that the field is constant in magnitude everywhere in the core and hence, its flux (BA) through each turn is same for the primary as well as for the secondary coil. Let the flux through each turn be Φ.

The emf induced in the primary, $E_p = -N_p \dfrac{d\Phi}{dt}$ and induced emf in the secondary, $E_S = -N_s \times \dfrac{d\Phi}{dt}$ **(½ Mark)**

If we neglect the resistance in the primary circuit, Kirchhoff's loop law applied to the primary circuit which gives,

$$E_p = N_p \frac{d\Phi}{dt} \qquad \text{......(i)} \quad \textbf{(½ Mark)}$$

Also, $$E_s = -N_s \frac{d\Phi}{dt} \qquad \text{......(ii)} \quad \textbf{(½ Mark)}$$

From (i) and (ii), $E_s = -\dfrac{N_s}{N_p} E_p$ **(½ Mark)**

The minus sign shows that E_s is 180° out of phase with E_p. Equⁿs. (i) and (ii) are valid for all values of currents in the primary and the secondary circuits. If there is no loss of power in output and input circuit then, **input power = output power**

i.e., $E_p \times I_p = E_s \times I_s$ or, $\dfrac{I_p}{I_s} = \dfrac{E_s}{E_p} = \dfrac{N_s}{N_p}$

But in practice there is always energy loss so, input power > output power.

Hence, $E_p \times I_p > E_s \times I_s$

Two main source of power losses in transformer are

(i) Hysteresis in the core

(ii) Coil resistance and eddy current. **(½ × 2 = 1 Mark)**

29. (a) We have

Current sensitivity, $\phi = \dfrac{NBA}{k}$

Clearly, $\phi \propto N$

$\propto B$

$\propto A$

$\propto \dfrac{1}{k}$

So, current sensitivity is increased by increasing

(i) Number of turns　　(ii) Magnetic field

(iii) Area of loop　　　　　　**(1½ Marks)**

and by decreasing spring constant

(b) Let R_g be resistance of galvanometer.

Then, at full scale deflection

Voltage across voltmeter, $V = I_g(R_g + R)$

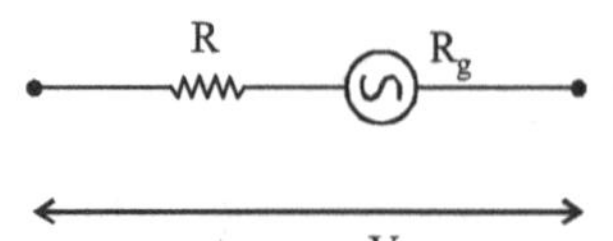

When $R = R_1$

$$1 = I_g(R_g + R_1) \qquad \text{... (i)} \quad \textbf{(½ Mark)}$$

When $R = R_2$

$$2 = I_g(R_g + R_2) \qquad \text{... (ii)} \quad \textbf{(½ Mark)}$$

Dividing (ii) from (i), we get

$$\frac{1}{2} = \frac{I_g(R_g + R_1)}{I_g(R_g + R_2)}$$

$\Rightarrow R_g + R_2 = 2R_g + 2R_1 \Rightarrow R_2 - 2R_1 = R_g$

$\Rightarrow R_g = R_2 - 2R_1$ **(½ Mark)**

Note

In order to increase the range of voltmeter n times the value of resistance to be connected in series with galvanometer is
$R = (n-1)R_g$
Here, R_g = resistance of galvanometer.

30. (a) (i) It cannot explain the stability of atom. As per the model, the orbital revolution of electrons is not stable as the revolving electrons in orbits will undergo acceleration and emit energy and ultimately collapse to nucleus. **(1 Mark)**

(ii) We have $\dfrac{1}{\lambda} = R_H\left(\dfrac{1}{n_1^2} - \dfrac{1}{n_2^2}\right)$ **(½ Mark)**

For Ist line

$$\frac{1}{\lambda_1} = R_H\left(\frac{1}{2^2} - \frac{1}{3^2}\right)$$

$$\frac{1}{\lambda_1} = R_H\left(\frac{5}{36}\right) \qquad \text{... (i)} \quad \textbf{(½ Mark)}$$

For IInd line

$$\frac{1}{\lambda_2} = R_H\left(\frac{1}{2^2} - \frac{1}{4^2}\right)$$

$$\frac{1}{\lambda_2} = R_H\left(\frac{12}{64}\right) \qquad \text{... (ii)} \quad \textbf{(½ Mark)}$$

Dividing (ii) by (i), we get

$$\frac{\lambda_2}{\lambda_1} = \frac{5}{36} \times \frac{64}{12} = 0.74$$

$\Rightarrow \lambda_2 = 0.74 \times \lambda_1 = 0.74 \times 4861 = 3600\,\text{Å}$ **(½ Mark)**

OR

(b) (i) Increase in intensity just increase number of photon falling per second. There is no increase in energy of photon. As kinetic energy of electron coming out of any metal depends only on energy of photon, so there will be no change in kinetic energy of photon. **(1 Mark)**

(ii) Energy of photon, $E = +13.6\left(\dfrac{1}{1^2} - \dfrac{1}{2^2}\right)e\,\text{V}$

$$= +13.6 \times \frac{3}{4} = 10.2\,\text{eV} \quad \textbf{(1 Mark)}$$

So, work function $= E(eV) - V_s$

$$\left[\phi = h\nu - eV_s \quad \phi = \frac{h\nu}{e} - V_s \quad \phi = E(eV) - V_s\right]$$

$$= 10.2 - 5 = 5.2 \, eV \qquad \textbf{(1 Mark)}$$

31. (a) (i)

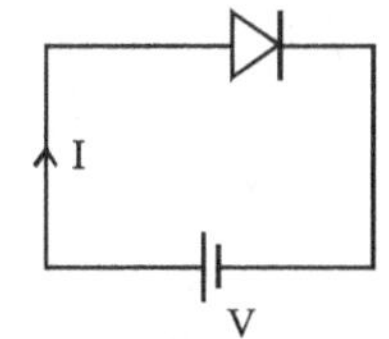

p-n junction in forward bias **(½ Mark)**

(ii)

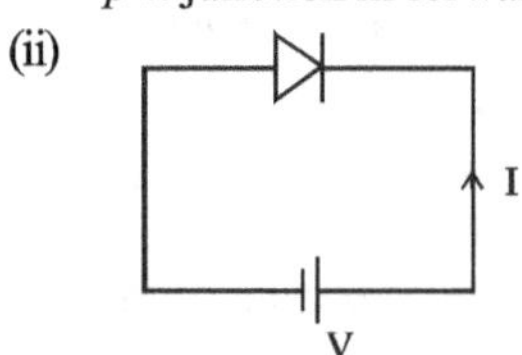

p-n junction in reverse bias **(½ Mark)**

V-I characteristic of a silicon diode

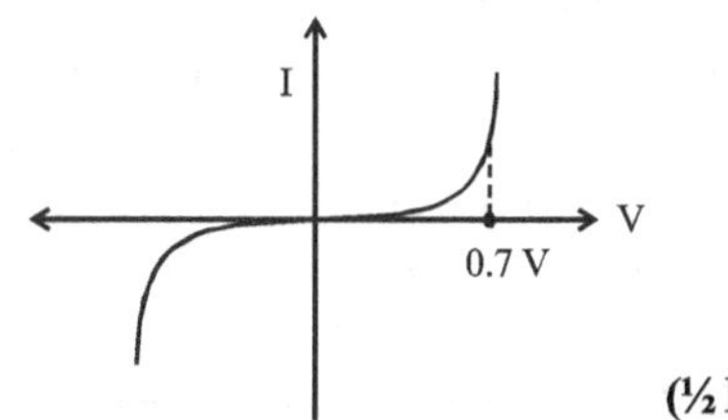

(½ Mark)

(i) **Minority carrier injection in forward biasing**
Due to the applied voltage, electron from n-side cross the depletion region and reach p-side (where they are minority carriers). Similarly, holes from p-side also cross the depletion region and reach n-side (where they are minority carriers). This process under forward bias is known as minority carrier injection. **(½ Mark)**

(ii) **Breakdown voltage in reverse biasing**
Breakdown voltage of a diode is the reverse bias voltage at which current increases suddenly across it. **(½ Mark)**

(b) Two important processes involved in formation of a p-n junction diode
(i) Diffusion of e^- and holes due to concentration difference
(ii) Formation of depletion layer **(½ × 2 = 1 Mark)**

p-n Junction Diode as a Full Wave Rectifier
The circuit uses two diodes connected to the ends of a centre tapped transformer. The voltage rectified by the two diodes is half of the secondary voltage i.e., each diode conducts for half cycle of input but alternately so that net output across load comes as half sinusoids with positive values only. For positive cycle diode D_1 conducts (FB) but D_2 is being out of phase is reverse biased and does not conduct. Thus output across R_L is due to D_1 only. In negative cycle of input D_1 is R.B. but D_2 is F.B. and conducts as with respect to centretap point A is negative but B is positive. Hence output across R_L is due to D_2.

(½ Mark)

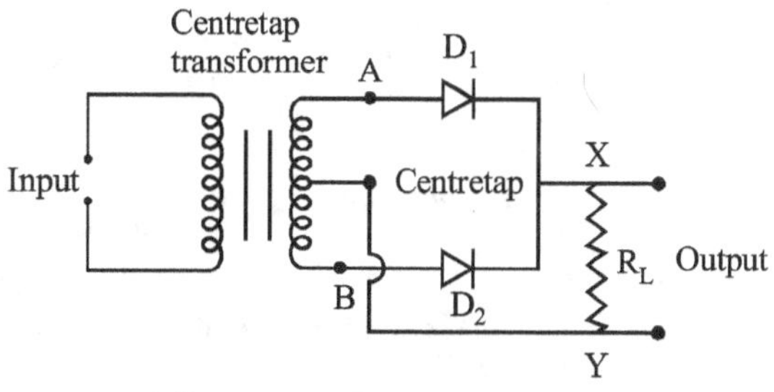

Full wave rectification circuit **(½ Mark)**

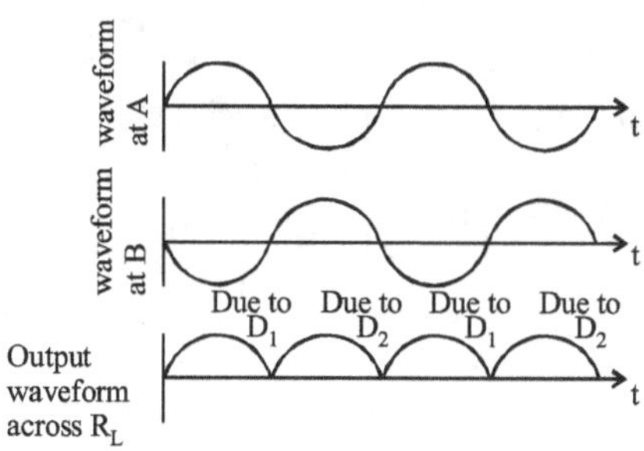

Output voltage waveform **(½ Mark)**

A p-n junction diode offers low resistance when forward biased and allow electricity to flow through it. In the reverse biased condition, it offers high resistance and does not allow electricity to flow through it. This property of junction diode makes it suitable for rectification.

32. (a) (i) **Compound Microscope**
It consists of two convergent lenses of short focal lengths and apertures, arranged co-axially. Lens (of focal length f_o) facing the object is called objective or field lens while the lens (of focal length fe) facing the eye, called eye-piece or ocular. The objective has a smaller aperture and smaller focal length than eye-piece. The separation between objective and eye-piece can be varied.

Magnifying power (MP) of compound microscope

$$MP = \frac{\text{Visual angle with instrument}}{\text{Max. visual angle for unaided eye}} = \frac{\theta}{\theta_0}$$

(½ Mark)

If the size of object is h and least distance of distinct vision is D, then

$$\theta_0 = \frac{h}{D} \quad \text{and} \quad \theta = \frac{h'}{u_e}$$

$$MP = \frac{\theta}{\theta_0} = \left[\frac{h'}{u_e}\right] \times \left[\frac{D}{h}\right] = \left[\frac{h'}{h}\right]\left[\frac{D}{u_e}\right] \qquad \textbf{(½ Mark)}$$

(1 Mark)

But for objective,

$$m = \frac{I}{O} = \frac{v}{u} \quad \text{i.e.,} \quad \frac{h'}{h} = -\frac{v}{u} \quad [\text{as } u \text{ is } -ve]$$

so, MP of compound microscope $= -\dfrac{v}{u}\left[\dfrac{D}{u_e}\right]$ .... (1)

Length of tube $L = v + u_e$ **(½ Mark)**

If the final image is at D (near point) : In this situation, as for eye - piece $v = D$

$$\frac{1}{-D} - \frac{1}{-u_e} = \frac{1}{f_e} \quad \text{i.e.,} \quad \frac{1}{u_e} = \frac{1}{D}\left[1 + \frac{D}{f_e}\right] \quad \textbf{(½ Mark)}$$

Substituting this value of u_e in eqⁿ. (1), we have

$$MP = -\frac{v}{u}\left[1 + \frac{D}{f_e}\right] \quad \text{with} \quad L = v + \frac{f_e D}{f_e + D} \quad \text{.... (2)}$$

                                                    (½ Mark)

(ii) We have

$u_0 = 1.5\,\text{cm}$

$f_0 = 1.25\,\text{cm}$

$f_e = 5\,\text{cm}$

So, magnifying power $= -\dfrac{v_0}{u_0}\left(1 + \dfrac{D}{f_e}\right)$ **(½ Mark)**

$$= \frac{-(-7.5)}{1.5}\left(1 + \frac{25}{5}\right)$$

$$= 5(1 + 5) = 30 \quad \textbf{(½ Mark)}$$

$$\left[\because \; \frac{1}{v_0} = \frac{1}{f_0} + \frac{1}{u_0} = \frac{1}{1.25} + \frac{1}{-1.5} = \frac{-0.25}{1.25 \times 1.5} = \frac{-1}{7.5}\right.$$

$$\left. V_0 = -7.5\,\text{cm}\right] \quad \textbf{(½ Mark)}$$

OR

(b) (i) **Astronomical Telescope (Refracting Type)**

A refracting type astronomical telescope, used to see the distant objects at large distances, consists of objective, i.e., a converging lens, or lens combination of larger focal length f_0 and larger aperture, and an eyepiece, i.e., also a converging lens, or lens combination, but of smaller focal length f_e and smaller aperture, placed coaxially.

Magnifying power (M) : Magnifying power (M), also called angular magnification of a telescope is defined as *the ratio of the visual angle subtended by the final image at the eye and the visual angle subtended by the object when the object lies in the actual position.* (In contrast to the definition of magnifying power of a microscope, the object is not placed at the near point in case of telescope)   **(1 Mark)**

$$M = \frac{\beta}{\alpha} = \frac{\tan\beta}{\tan\alpha} \quad (\because \alpha, \beta \text{ are small})$$

$$M = \frac{A_1 B_1 / EB_1}{A_1 B_1 / OB_1} \quad (\text{in } \Delta AB_1 O \text{ and } \Delta AB_1 E)$$

$$\Rightarrow M = \frac{OB_1}{EB_1} \quad \textbf{(½ Mark)}$$

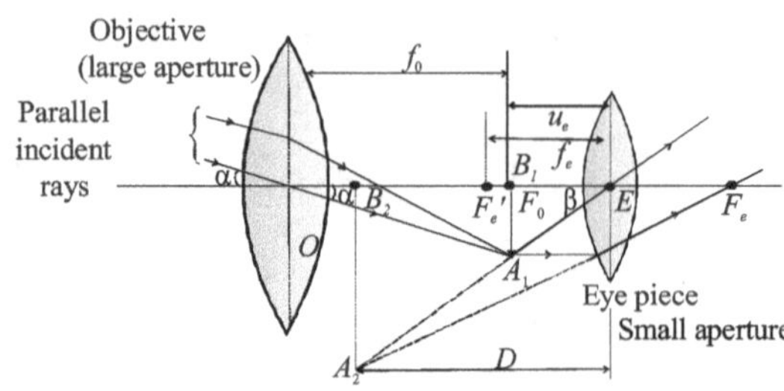

                                                    (1 Mark)

Using sign convention and taking u_e as object distance for eyepiece, we get

$$M = \frac{+f_0}{-u_e} = -\frac{f_0}{u_e} \quad \text{...(1)} \quad \textbf{(½ Mark)}$$

This is the general formula for magnifying power of a telescope.

Magnifying power M when eye is focussed at ∞ (normal adjustment)

In this case, as already explained, we have $u_e = -f_e$
                                                    ...(2)

Put eq. (2) in (1) to get $M = \dfrac{f_0}{f_e}$ ...(3)   **(½ Mark)**

In this case, the length of the telescope $L = f_0 + f_e$. This is the reason why the focal length of objective is taken large and of eyepiece small in case of a telescope. This also increases the resolving power of the telescope.

Further, linear or lateral magnification does not convey much meaning in case of a telescope because the size of final images too is negligible compared to actual size of the objects which are generally planets or stars.

(ii) We have

$$M = \frac{f_0}{f_e} = \frac{L - f_e}{f_e} = \frac{L}{f_e} - 1 \quad \textbf{(½ Mark)}$$

$$\Rightarrow \; 2.9 = \frac{150}{f_e} - 1 \Rightarrow 1.9 = \frac{150}{f_e}$$

$$f_e = \frac{150}{1.9} \approx 79\,\text{cm} \quad \textbf{(½ Mark)}$$

So, $f_0 = l - f_e = (150 - 79)\,\text{cm} = 71\,\text{cm}$ **(½ Mark)**

   **Note**

In a telescope, if abjective and eyepiece are interchanged magnification will change from $\left(\dfrac{f_o}{f_e}\right)$ *to* $\left(\dfrac{f_e}{f_o}\right)$ *i.e., it will change from m to* $\dfrac{1}{m}$ *i.e., will become* $\left(\dfrac{1}{m^2}\right)$ *times of its initial value.*

33. **(a)** **(i)** Drift velocity is defined as the velocity with which the free electrons get drifted towards the positive terminal under the effect of the applied external electric field. In addition to its thermal velocity, due to acceleration given by applied electric field, the electron acquires a velocity component in a direction opposite to the direction of the electric field. The gain in velocity due to the applied field is very small and is lost in the next collision. **(1 Mark)**

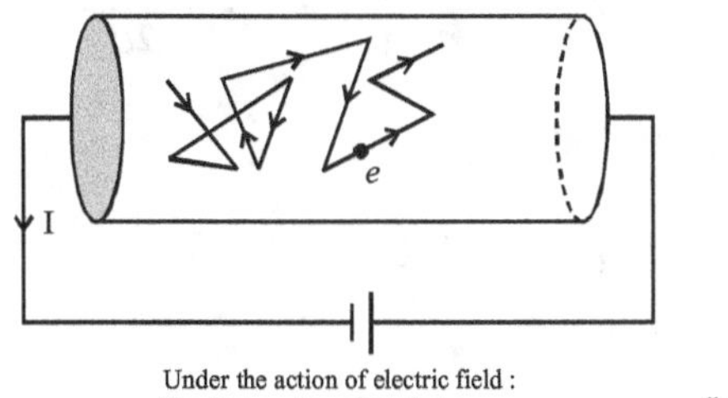

Under the action of electric field : Random motion of an electron with drift superimposed on it. **(½ Mark)**

At any given time, an electron has a velocity $\vec{v}_1$

$= \vec{u}_1 + \vec{a}\,\tau_1$, where $\vec{u}_1$ = the thermal velocity and $\vec{a}\,\tau_1$ = the velocity acquired by the electron under the influence of the applied electric field. τ_1 = the time that has elapsed since the last collision. Similarly, the velocities of the other electrons are **(½ Mark)**

$$\vec{v}_2 = \vec{u}_2 + \vec{a}\,\tau_2,$$
$$\vec{v}_3 = \vec{u}_3 + \vec{a}\,\tau_3, \dots \vec{v}_N = \vec{u}_N + \vec{a}\,\tau_N.$$
(½ Mark)

The average velocity of all the free electrons in the conductor is equal to the drift velocity $\vec{v}_d$ of the free electrons

$$\vec{v}_d = \frac{\vec{v}_1 + \vec{v}_2 + \vec{v}_3 + \dots + \vec{v}_N}{N}$$ **(½ Mark)**

$$= \frac{(\vec{u}_1 + \vec{a}\,\tau_1) + (\vec{u}_2 + \vec{a}\,\tau_2) + \dots + (\vec{u}_N + \vec{a}\,\tau_N)}{N}$$

$$= \frac{(\vec{u}_1 + \vec{u}_2 + \dots + \vec{u}_N)}{N} + \vec{a}\left(\frac{\tau_1 + \tau_2 + \dots + \tau_N}{N}\right)$$

$$\because \quad \frac{\vec{u}_1 + \vec{u}_2 + \dots + \vec{u}_N}{N} = \vec{0}$$ **(½ Mark)**

$$\therefore \quad \vec{v}_d = \vec{a}\left(\frac{\tau_1 + \tau_2 + \dots + \tau_N}{N}\right)$$

$$\Rightarrow \quad \vec{v}_d = \vec{a}\,\tau = -\frac{e\vec{E}}{m}\tau$$ **(½ Mark)**

 **Note**

Value of drift velocity is very small. Order of drift velocity is 10^{-4} m/s.

(ii) We have $V_d = \dfrac{I}{neA}$ **(½ Mark)**

$$\Rightarrow V_d \propto \frac{1}{n} \ [\because \text{ In series, I = constant}]$$

$$\Rightarrow \frac{(V_d)_A}{(V_d)_B} = \frac{n_B}{n_A} = \frac{n_B}{1.5 n_B} = \frac{1}{1.5} = \frac{2}{3} \ \textbf{(½ Mark)}$$

OR

(b) **(i)** We have

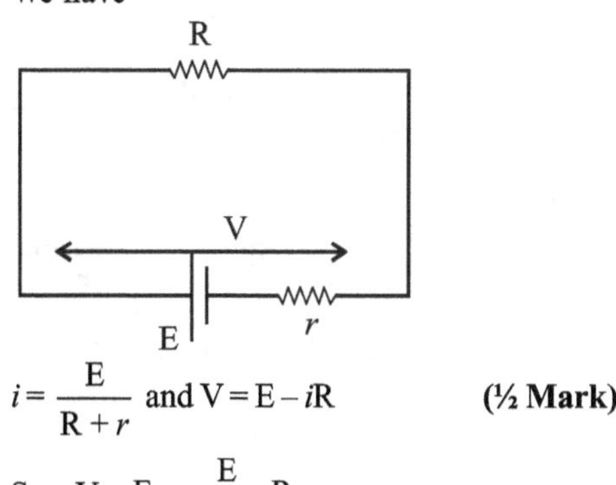

$$i = \frac{E}{R + r} \text{ and } V = E - iR$$ **(½ Mark)**

$$\text{So,} \quad V = E - \frac{E}{R + r}R$$

$$V = E\left(\frac{R + r - R}{R + r}\right) \Rightarrow V = E\left(\frac{r}{R + r}\right) \textbf{(½ Mark)}$$

when $R = 0 \Rightarrow V = E$
when $R \to \infty \Rightarrow V \to 0$

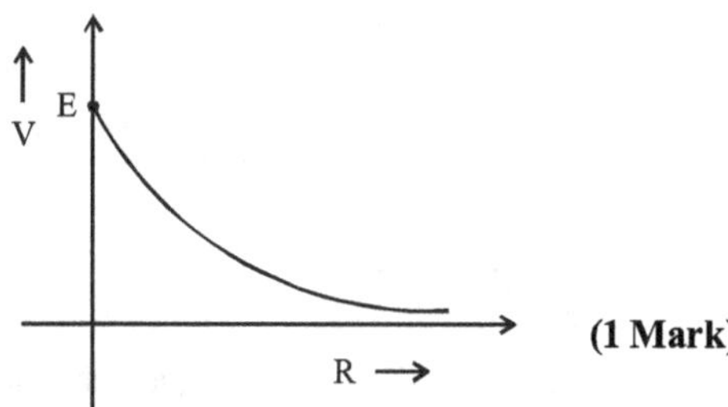

(1 Mark)

Also, when $i = 0$, $V = E$
i is very large $\Rightarrow$ V is very small

(1 Mark)

(ii)

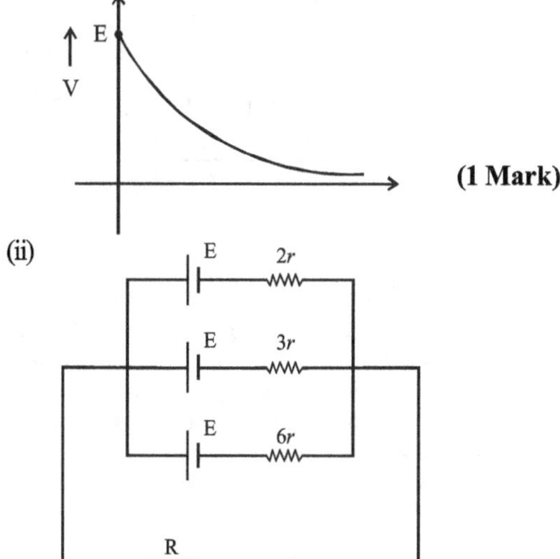

We have $E_{net} = E$ and $\dfrac{1}{r_{net}} = \dfrac{1}{2r} + \dfrac{1}{3r} + \dfrac{1}{6r}$

$\Rightarrow \quad \dfrac{1}{r_{net}} = \dfrac{3+2+1}{6r} \Rightarrow \dfrac{1}{r_{net}} = \dfrac{1}{r}$

$\Rightarrow \quad r_{net} = r$ (½ Mark)

So, $i = \dfrac{E_{net}}{R_{net}} = \dfrac{E}{R+r}$ (½ Mark)

As $V_{eq} = E_{eq} - i \cdot r_{eq} \Rightarrow V_{eq} = E - \dfrac{Er}{R+r}$ (½ Mark)

$\Rightarrow \quad V_{eq} = E\left(\dfrac{R+r-r}{R+r}\right) \Rightarrow V_{eq} = \dfrac{ER}{R+r}$ (½ Mark)

34. (i)

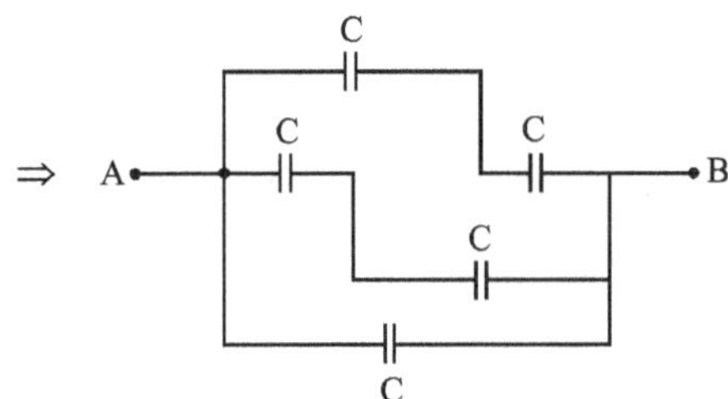

$\Rightarrow \quad \dfrac{C/2}{\text{---}||\text{---}}$ (1 Mark)

(ii) Due to insertion of dielectric slap, capacitance becomes 'K' times. As capacitor is not connected to battery, so charge will remain same.

As $Q_i = Q_f$

$\Rightarrow CV_i = KCV_f$

$\Rightarrow V_f = \dfrac{V_i}{K} \Rightarrow E_f d = \dfrac{E_i d}{K} \Rightarrow E_f = \dfrac{E_i}{K}$ (1 Mark)

(iii) (a) The common potential is given as

$V_0 = \dfrac{C_1 V_1 + C_2 V_2}{C_1 + C_2} = \dfrac{Q_1 + Q_2}{C_1 + C_2} = \dfrac{Q + 0}{3C} = \dfrac{Q}{3C}$

    (1 Mark)

Note

A capacitor of capacity C_1 charged to potential V_1 is connected to another capacitor of capacity C_2 and potential V_2. Now if batteries are connected to each other with reverse polarity i.e., positive plate of a capacitor connected to negative plate of other. Then common potential is given by
For numerical calculation we may assume as

$$V = \dfrac{Q_1 + Q_2}{C_1 + C_2} = \dfrac{C_1 V_1 - C_2 V_2}{C_1 + C_2}$$

(b) Charge lost by capacitor 'A'

$= Q - CV_0 \quad [\because Q_i = Q \text{ and } Q_f = CV_0]$

$= Q - \dfrac{C \cdot Q}{3C} = \dfrac{2Q}{3}$ (1 Mark)

OR

(iii) We have

$C_1 = \dfrac{2KA\in_0}{d/3}$ and $C_2 = \dfrac{KA\in_0}{2d/3}$ (½ Mark)

i.e. $C_1 = \dfrac{6KA\in_0}{d}$ and $C_2 = \dfrac{3KA\in_0}{2d}$ (½ Mark)

Let $C_0 = \dfrac{KA\in_0}{d}$

So, $C_{eq} = \dfrac{C_1 C_2}{C_1 + C_2} = \dfrac{6C_0 \cdot \frac{3}{2}C_0}{6C_0 + \frac{3}{2}C_0}$ (½ Mark)

$= \dfrac{\frac{18}{2}C_0}{\frac{15}{2}C_0} = \dfrac{6}{5}C_0 = \dfrac{6}{5}\dfrac{KA\in_0}{d}$ (½ Mark)

35. (i) The upper half will form image different than that of lower half, because due to different refractive index the lower and upper half will bend the ray by different amount.   (1 Mark)

(ii) Images are perception of any light reflected from a source. So, in short, No, you can't see an image without a screen. Screen here acts as a source from which the light creating the image reflect and our eye and brain percieve it.   (1 Mark)

(iii) By len's maker formula, for convex lens

$\dfrac{1}{f} = (u-1)\left(\dfrac{2}{R}\right) \Rightarrow \dfrac{1}{20} = (1.55-1)\left(\dfrac{2}{R}\right)$ (1 Mark)

$\Rightarrow \dfrac{1}{20} = 0.55 \times \dfrac{2}{R} \Rightarrow R = 0.55 \times 2 \times 20$

$\Rightarrow R = 22\,cm$ (1 Mark)

OR

(iii)

    (1 Mark)

We can see from diagram, the ray emerging from lens B are parallel to its principal axis.

Only if centre of curvature of A coincide with focus of B.

So, $d = 30\,cm + 15\,cm$

$\Rightarrow d = 45\,cm$ (1 Mark)

CBSE Board Solved Paper Term-II

Time Allowed : 2 Hours   *Maximum Marks : 35*

General Instructions:

(i) There are **12** questions in all. All questions are compulsory.

(ii) This question paper has three sections : Section A, Section B and Section C.

(iii) Section A contains three questions of two marks each, Section B contains eight questions of three marks each, Section C contains one case study-based question of five marks.

(iv) There is no overall choice. However, an internal choice has been provided in one question of two marks and two questions of three marks. You have to attempt only one of the choices in such questions.

(v) You may use log tables if necessary but use of calculator is not allowed.

SECTION - A

1. (a) (i) Distinguish between isotopes and isobars. **2**

    (ii) Two nuclei have different mass numbers A_1 and A_2. Are these nuclei necessarily the isotopes of the same element? Explain.

OR

  (b) (i) Name the factors on which photoelectric emission from a surface depends.

    (ii) Define the term 'threshold frequency' for a photosensitive material.

2. Explain the formation of the barrier potential in a p-n junction. **2**

3. Name the extrinsic semiconductors formed when a pure germanium is doped with (i) a trivalent and (ii) pentavalent impurity. Draw the energy band diagrams of extrinsic semiconductors so formed. **2**

SECTION - B

4. (a) Write two necessary conditions for total internal reflection.

  (b) Two prisms ABC and DBC are arranged as shown in figure.

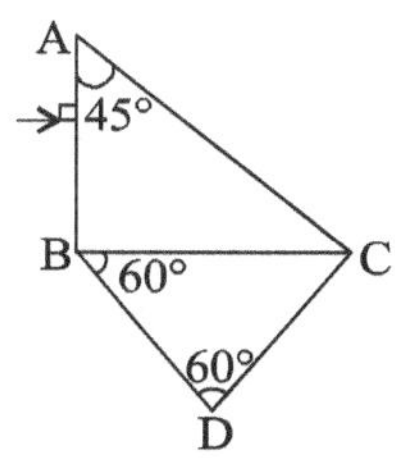

The critical angles for the two prisms with respect to air are 41.1° and 45° respectively. Trace the path of the ray through the combination. **3**

OR

(a) An object is placed in front of a converging lens. Obtain the conditions under which the magnification produced by the lens is (i) negative and (ii) positive.

(b) A point object is placed at O in front of a glass sphere as shown in figure.

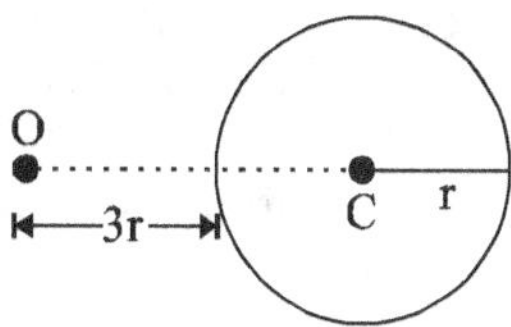

Show the formation of image by the sphere.

5. The work function of a metal is 2.31 eV. Photoelectric emission occurs when light of frequency 6.4×10^{14} Hz is incident on the metal surface. Calculate:

(i) the energy of the incident radiation, (ii) the maximum kinetic energy of the emitted electron and (iii) the stopping potential of the surface. **3**

6. A beam of light consisting of two wavelengths 600 nm and 500 nm is used in a Young's double slit experiment. The slit separation is 1.0 mm and the screen is kept 0.60 m away from the plane of the slits. Calculate:

(i) the distance of the second bright fringe from the central maximum for wavelength 500 nm, and

(ii) the least distance from the central maximum where the bright fringes due to both the wavelengths coincide. **3**

7. Electromagnetic waves of wavelengths λ_1, λ_2 and λ_3 are used in radar systems, in water purifiers and in remote switches of TV, respectively.
   (i) Identify the electromagnetic waves, and
   (ii) Write one source of each of them. **3**

   OR

   (i) State two conditions for two light sources to be coherent.
   (ii) Give two points of difference between an interference pattern due to a double – slit and a diffraction pattern due to a single slit.

8. In a diffraction pattern due to a single slit, how will the angular width of central maximum change, if
   (i) Orange light is used in place of green light,
   (ii) the screen is moved closer to the slit,
   (iii) the slit width is decreased?
   Justify your answer in each case. **3**

9. Briefly explain how emf is generated in a solar cell. Draw its I-V characteristics. **3**

10. (a) James Chadwick, in 1932, studied the emission of neutral radiations when Beryllium nuclei were bombarded with alpha particles. He concluded that emitted radiations were neutrons and not photons. Explain.
    (b) Two nuclei may have the same radius, even though they contain different number of protons and neutrons. Explain. **3**

11. (a) The energy of hydrogen atom in an orbit is -1.51 eV. What are kinetic and potential energies of the electron in this orbit?
    (b) The electron in a hydrogen atom is typically found at a distance of about 5.3×10^{-11} m from the nucleus which has a diameter of about 1.0×10^{-15} m. Assuming the hydrogen atom to be a sphere of radius 5.3×10^{-11} m, what fraction of its volume is occupied by the nucleus? **3**

SECTION - C

CASE STUDY

12. A compound microscope consists of two converging lenses. One of them, of smaller aperture and smaller focal length is called objective and the other of slightly larger aperture and slightly larger focal length is called eye-piece. Both the lenses are fitted in a tube with an arrangement to vary the distance between them. A tiny object is placed in front of the objective at a distance slightly greater than its focal length. The objective produces the image of the object which acts as an object for the eye-piece. The eye piece, in turn produces the final magnified image.

   $1 \times 5 = 5$

I. In a compound microscope the images formed by the objective and the eye-piece are respectively
   (a) virtual, real   (b) real, virtual
   (c) virtual, virtual   (d) real, real

II. The magnification due to a compound microscope *does not* depend upon
   (a) the aperture of the objective and the eye-piece
   (b) the focal length of the objective and the eye-piece
   (c) the length of the tube
   (d) the colour of the light used

III. Which of the following is *not correct* in the context of a compound microscope?
   (a) Both the lenses are of short focal lengths.
   (b) The magnifying power increases by decreasing the focal lengths of the two lenses.
   (c) The distance between the two lenses is more than $(f_0 + f_e)$.
   (d) The microscope can be used as a telescope by interchanging the two lenses.

IV. A compound microscope consists of an objective of 10X and an eye-piece of 20X. The magnification due to the microscope would be
   (a) 2   (b) 10
   (c) 30   (d) 200

V. The focal lengths of objective and eye-piece of a compound microscope are 1.2 cm and 3.0 cm respectively. The object is placed at a distance of 1.25 cm from the objective. If the final image is formed at infinity, the magnifying power of the microscope would be
   (a) 100   (b) 150
   (c) 200   (d) 250

Solutions

1. (a) (i) Isotopes are the atomic species of same element differing in mass number(A) but same in atomic number(Z).

Isobars are the atomic species of same element with same mass number(A) but different atomic number(Z). **[1 Mark]**

> **Note**
>
> *Nuclei having different atomic number (Z) and mass number (A) but same number of neutrons N = (A − Z) is called isotones. For examples $_4Be^9$ and $_5B^{10}$; $_6C^{13}$ and $_7N^{14}$, etc.*

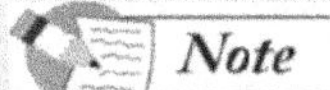

(ii) No, because different mass number may be due to different number of protons or neutrons. To be the isotopes of same element, protons number should be same. **[1 Mark]**

OR

(b) (i) The photoelectric emission from a surface depends on the frequency of incident light and nature of surface.

(ii) The minimum cut off frequency below which photoelectric effect doesn't take place is called threshold frequency. **[1 + 1 Mark]**

2. Formation of barrier potential in a P-n junction :

Electrons diffuse from n → p and holes diffuse from p → n side leaving a positively charged donor atom on n–side and negatively charged acceptor atom on p–side. This space charge region on either side is called depletion region. The n-material has lost electrons and p-material has acquired electrons. The n-material is thus positive relative to p-material. Due to which a potential difference is developed between n-type and p-type material which prevent the further diffusion of holes and electrons. This potential difference between junction is only called barrier potential.

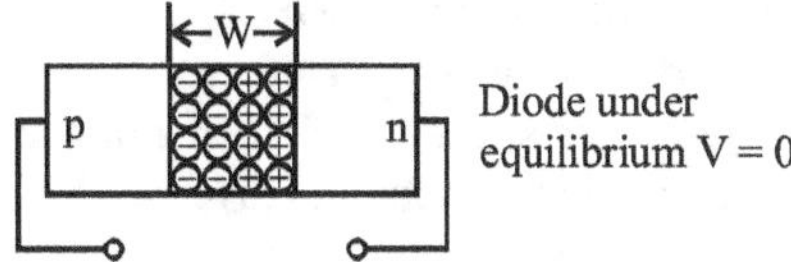

Diode under equilibrium V = 0

[2 Marks]

3. When pure germanium is doped with a trivalent impurity, p-type semiconductor is formed. When pure germanium is doped with a pentavalent impurity, n-type semicoductor is formed. **[1 Mark]**

Energy band diagram

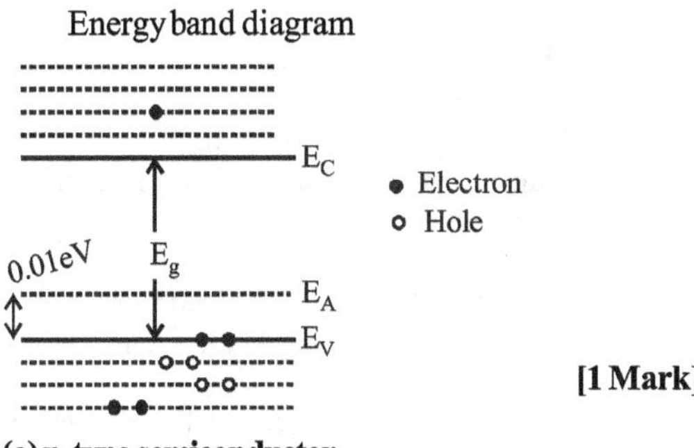

• Electron
○ Hole

[1 Mark]

(a) p-type semiconductor

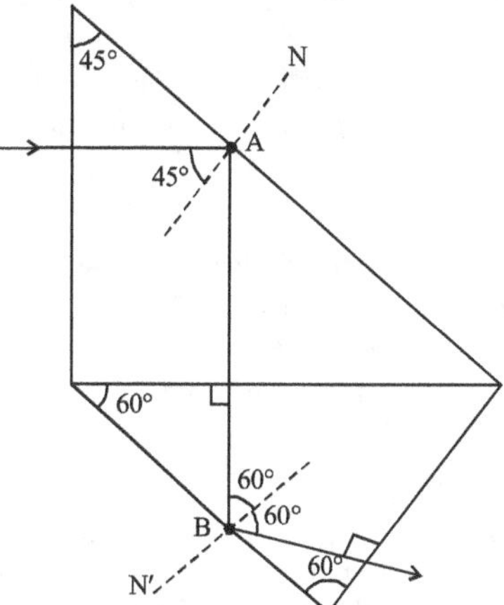

(b) n-type semiconductor

4. (a) Conditions for Total Internal Reflection
(i) The ray of light must travel from denser to rarer medium.
(ii) The angle of incidence must be greater than critical angle **[1 Mark]**

(b) Total internal reflection will take place at points A and B as angle of incidence at both points are greater than critical angle. When ray strikes surface finally at 90° to surface it will emerge out undeviated. **[2 Marks]**

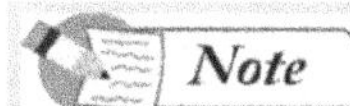

> **Note**
>
> *Brilliance of diamond is due to total internal reflection of light inside them. The critical angle for diamond – air interface $\cong$ 24.4° is very small. By cutting the diamond suitably, multiple total internal reflections can be made to occur.*

OR

(a) When an object is placed between focus (F) and pole (P) of converging lens, the magnification produced by lens is positive. In all other positions of object the magnification produce by converging lens is negative. **[1½ Marks]**

(b) Image formation by the sphere

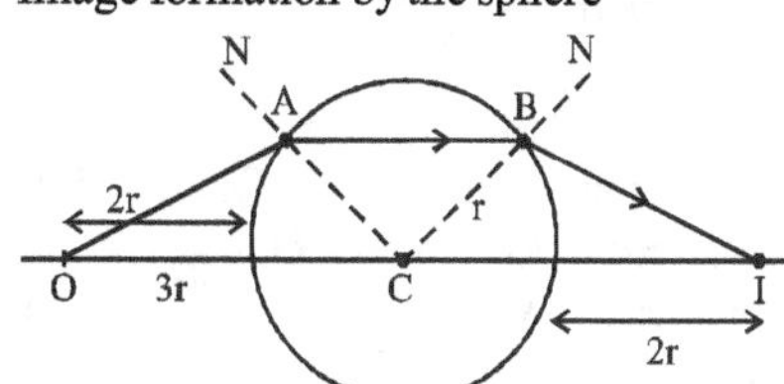

N and N′ are normals at the point of incidences. Rays will obey laws of refraction at point A refracted ray moves towards N and at point B refracted rays move away from N′.   **[1½ Marks]**

5. Given,

Work function of metal, $\phi = 2.31\,eV$

Frequency of incident light, $\nu = 6.4 \times 10^{14}\,Hz$

(a) Energy of incident radiation, $E = h\nu$

$= 6.63 \times 10^{-34} \times 6.4 \times 10^{14}$

$= 42.43 \times 10^{-20}\,J$ **[1 Mark]**

(b) Using Einstein's photoelectric equation

$E = \phi_0 + K.E$

$\Rightarrow K.E = E - \phi_0 = \dfrac{42.43 \times 10^{-20}}{1.6 \times 10^{-19}} - 2.31\,eV$

$\Rightarrow K.E = 2.652\,eV - 2.31\,eV$

$= 0.34\,eV$ **[1 Mark]**

(c) $K.E = eV_0$

where, $V_0 = $ stopping potential

$\therefore\quad V_0 = \dfrac{K.E}{e} = \dfrac{0.34\,eV}{e}$

$= 0.34\,V$ **[1 Mark]**

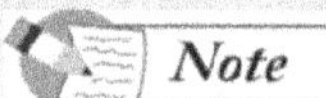

Note

Work function or threshold energy is the minimum energy of incident radiation, required to eject the electrons from metallic surface.

6. Given,

Slit separation, $d = 1\,mm = 1 \times 10^{-3}\,m$

Distance of screen from slits, $D = 0.60\,m$

(a) For wavelength, $\lambda_1 = 500\,nm$

Fringe width, $\beta = \dfrac{\lambda D}{d} = \dfrac{500 \times 10^{-9} \times 0.60}{1 \times 10^{-3}}$

$= 300 \times 10^{-6} = 0.3\,nm$

Distance of second bright fringe from central maximum $=$ $2\beta = 2 \times 0.3\,nm = 0.6\,nm$ **[1½ Marks]**

(b) We know that for n^{th} bright fringe

$x = \dfrac{n\lambda D}{d}$

Here, $x = $ common distance from bright fringes by both wavelength

$x = \dfrac{n_1 \lambda_1 D}{d} = \dfrac{n_2 \lambda_2 D}{d}\quad \left[\because\ x_n = \dfrac{n\lambda D}{d}\right]$

$\Rightarrow n_1 \lambda_1 = n_2 \lambda_2$

$\Rightarrow n_1 \times 600 \times 10^{-9} = n_2 \times 500 \times 10^{-9}$

$\Rightarrow 6n_1 = 5n_2 \Rightarrow \dfrac{n_1}{n_2} = \dfrac{5}{6}$

$\therefore$ 5th bright fringe due to wavelength 600 nm coincides with 6 bright fringe due to wavelength 500 nm.

$\therefore\quad x = \dfrac{5 \times 600 \times 10^{-9} \times 0.60}{1 \times 10^{-3}}$

$= 0.18 \times 10^{-2}\,m = 0.18\,cm$ **[1½ Marks]**

7. (i) Electromagnetic wave of wavelength λ_1 is Radio wave. Electromagnetic wave of wavelength λ_2 is ultraviolet rays. Electromagnetic wave of wavelength λ_3 is Infrared waves.   **[1½ Marks]**

(ii)

	Wave	Source of Production
λ_1	Radio wave	Produced by rapid acceleration and decelerations of electrons.
λ_2	Ultraviolet rays	Produced by movement of inner shell electrons from one energy level to a lower energy level.
λ_3	Infrared waves	Produced by vibration of atoms and molecules.

                                                                     [1½ Marks]

OR

(i) Conditions for two light sources to be coherent

(a) Both the sources should have same frequency.

(b) At any point, both source should maintain a constant phase difference.   **[1 Mark]**

(ii)

	Diffraction		Interference
1	The diffraction pattern has a central bright maximum which is twice as wide as other maxima.	1	The interference has a number of equally spaced bright and dark bands
2	The diffraction pattern is a superposition of waves originating from each point on a single slit.	2	The interference pattern is due to the superposition of waves emanating from the two narrow slits.

                                                                     [2 Marks]

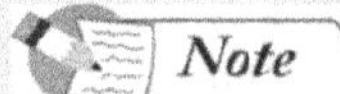

Note

Thin layer of oil on water surface and soap bubbles show various colours in white light due to interference of waves reflected from the two surfaces of the film.

In thin films interference takes place between the waves reflected from it's two surfaces and waves refracted through it.

8. We know that angular width of central maximum in diffraction pattern due to single slit is given by

Angular width, $\alpha = \dfrac{2\lambda}{a}$

Here, $\lambda = $ wavelength of light

$a = $ width of slit

(i) Wavelength of orange light is greater than the wavelength of green light. Therefore, if orange light is used, the angular width will increase because angular width $\propto \lambda$.

                                                                     [1 Mark]

(ii) Decrease of distance between the slit and the screen does not affect the angular width of central maximum.

                                                                     [1 Mark]

(iii) If slit width (a) is decreased, the angular width will increase as angular width $\propto \dfrac{1}{a}$ **[1 Mark]**

9. The following 3 basic processes occur in generation of emf by a solar cell.

(i) **Generation** of electron hole pair due to light ($h\nu > E_g$) close to junction. **[½ Mark]**

(ii) **Separation** of electrons and holes due to electric field of depletion region (Electrons reach n–side, holes p–side). **[½ Mark]**

(iii) **Collection** electrons are collected by front contact and holes by back contact (p–side: positive, n–side: negative) giving rise to photovoltage. **[½ Mark]**

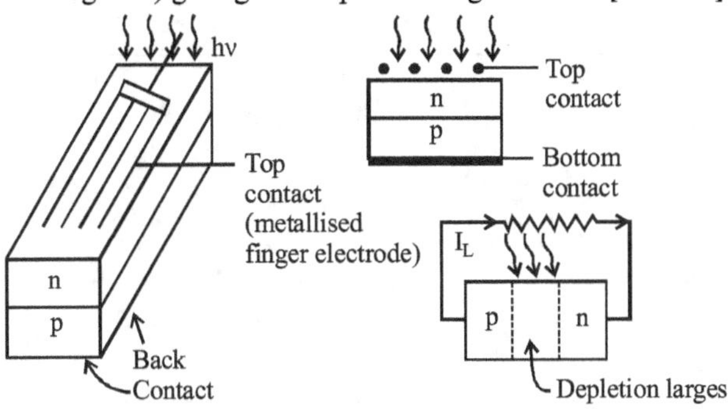

Solar cell (emf generation)

[½ Mark]

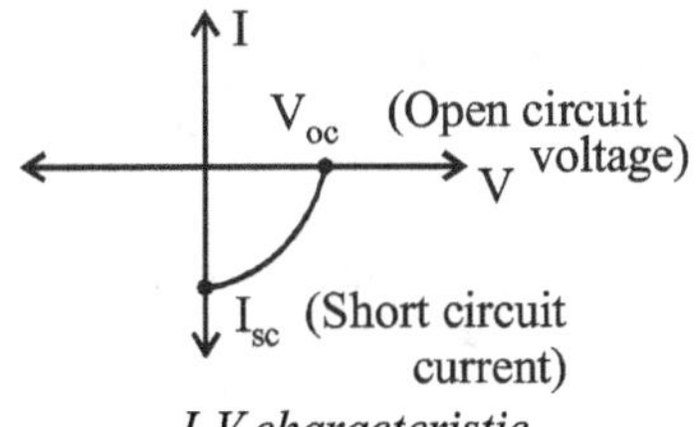

I-V characteristic

[1 Mark]

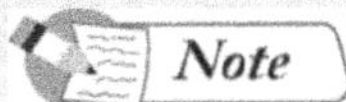

> **Note**
>
> *Solar cell is based on the photovoltic effect. One of the semiconductor region is made so thin that the light incident on it reaches the P-N junction and gets absorbed. It converts solar energy into electrical energy.*

10. (a) James Chadwick observed emission of neutral radiation when beryllium nuclei were bombarded with alpha particles. He found neutral radiation could knock out protons from light nuclei such as those of helium, carbon and nitrogen. At that time, only neutral radiation was photons. Using principles of conservation of energy and momentum, he showed that if neutral radiation consisted of photons, the energy of photons would be much higher than the energy from bombardment of beryllium nuclei with α particles. It makes him assume that neutral radiation consists of new type of neutral particles called neutrons. Using conservation of energy and momentum, he was able to determine the mass of new particle (neutron) as very nearly the same as mass of proton. **[2 Marks]**

(b) If two nuclei have same sum of number of protons and neutrons, then they will have same mass number (A). Radius of nucleus $\propto A^{1/3}$. **[1 Mark]**

So, they can have the same radii.

11. (a) The energy of hydrogen atom in an orbit, $E = -1.51\,eV$

Kinetic energy of electron $= -E = -(-1.51) = +1.51$ eV

Potential energy of electron $= -2 \times$ (Kinetic energy of electron)

$= -2 \times 1.51 = -3.02$ eV **[½ + ½ Mark]**

> **Note**
>
> *Potential energy of electron in n^{th} orbit of radius r_n*
>
> $$u = \frac{-KZe^2}{r_n} \text{ and kinetic energy } K = \frac{KZe^2}{2r_n} = \frac{|u|}{2} \text{ and}$$
>
> $$\text{total energy } E = K + u = \frac{-KZe^2}{2r_n}$$

(b) Given,

Radius of nucleus, $r = \dfrac{1.0 \times 10^{-15}\,m}{2}$

$= 0.5 \times 10^{-15}\,m$

Volume of nucleus, $V_1 = \dfrac{4}{3}\pi\,(0.5 \times 10^{-15})^3$

Volume of Hydrogen atom, $V_2 = \dfrac{4}{3}\pi\,(5.3 \times 10^{-11})^3$

Fraction of volume occupied by nucleus

$$= \frac{\frac{4}{3}\pi\,(0.5 \times 10^{-15})^3}{\frac{4}{3}\pi\,(5.3 \times 10^{-11})^3} = \frac{0.125 \times 10^{-45}}{148.87 \times 10^{-33}} = 0.839 \times 10^{-15}$$

$= 0.839 \times 10^{-15}$ **[2 Marks]**

12. **(I)** (b) In compound microscope, the image formed by objective is real and the image formed by eye-piece is virtual. **[1 Mark]**

(II) (a) Magnification due to compound microscope does not depend upon aperture of objective and eye piece. **[1 Mark]**

(III) (c) In compound microscope, two convergent lens are of short focal lengths. The magnifying power increases by decreasing the focal lengths of two lenses.

The distance between objective and eye piece of compound microscope is equal to sum of focal lengths of objective and eye piece i.e., $L = f_o + f_e$. **[1 Mark]**

(IV) (d) Magnifying power of compound microscope (M) = magnifying power of objective × magnifying power of eyepiece

$\Rightarrow M = 10 \times 20 = 200$ **[1 Mark]**

(V) (c) Given,

Focal length of objective lens, $f_o = 1.2$ cm

Focal length of eye-piece, $f_e = 3$ cm

Distance of object from objective, $u_o = 1.25$ cm

Using lens formula for objective

$$\frac{1}{v_o} - \frac{1}{u_o} = \frac{1}{f_o} \Rightarrow \frac{1}{v_o} = \frac{1}{1.2} - \frac{1}{1.25} \Rightarrow v_o = 30\,cm$$

Magnifying power of microscope, $M = \dfrac{v_0}{u_0}\left(\dfrac{D}{f_e}\right)$

$\therefore\quad M = \dfrac{30}{1.25}\left(\dfrac{25}{3}\right) = 200$ **[1 Mark]**

CBSE Board Solved Paper Term-I

Time Allowed : 1½ Hours   *Maximum Marks : 35*

General Instructions:
  (i)   This question paper contains three sections.
  (ii) Section A has **25** questions. Attempt any **20** questions.
  (iii) Section B has **24** questions. Attempt any **20** questions.
  (iv) Section C has **6** questions. Attempt any **5** questions.
  (v)   All questions carry equal marks.
  (vi) There is no negative marking.

SECTION - A

This section consists of 25 multiple choice questions with overall choice to attempt any 20 questions. In case more than desirable number of questions are attempted, ONLY first 20 will be considered for evaluation.

1. A negatively charged object X is repelled by another charged object Y. However an object Z is attracted to object Y. Which of the following is the most possible for the object Z ?
   (a) positively charged only
   (b) negatively charged only
   (c) neutral or positively charged
   (d) neutral or negatively charged

2. In an experiment three microscopic latex spheres are sprayed into a chamber and became charged with charges $+3e$, $+5e$ and $-3e$ respectively. All the three spheres came in contact simultaneously for a moment and got separated. Which one of the following are possible values for the final charge on the spheres ?
   (a) $+5e, -4e, +5e$ (b) $+6e, +6e, -7e$
   (c) $-4e, +3.5e, +5.5e$ (d) $+5e, -8e, +7e$

3. An object has charge of 1 C and gains 5.0×10^{18} electrons. The net charge on the object becomes –
   (a) $-0.80\,C$ (b) $+0.80\,C$ (c) $+1.80\,C$ (d) $+0.20\,C$

4. Kirchhoff's first rule $\Sigma I = 0$ and second rule $\Sigma IR = \Sigma E$ (where the symbols have their usual meanings) are respectively based on
   (a) conservation of momentum and conservation of charge
   (b) conservation of energy and conservation of charge
   (c) conservation of charge, conservation of momentum
   (d) conservation of charge, conservation of energy

5. The electric power consumed by a 220 V–100 W bulb when operated at 110 V is
   (a) 25 W   (b) 30 W
   (c) 35 W   (d) 45 W

6. Which of the following has negative temperature coefficient of resistance ?
   (a) metal
   (b) metal and semiconductor
   (c) semiconductor
   (d) metal and alloy

7. Two wires carrying currents I_1 and I_2 lie, one slightly above the other, in a horizontal plane as shown in figure. The region of vertically upward strongest magnetic field is

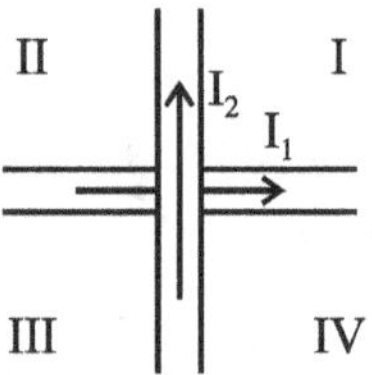

   (a) I   (b) II   (c) III   (d) IV

8. Two parallel conductors carrying current of 4.0 A and 10.0 A are placed 2.5 cm apart in vacuum. The force per unit length between them is –
   (a) $6.4 \times 10^{-5}\,N/m$ (b) $6.4 \times 10^{-2}\,N/m$
   (c) $4.6 \times 10^{-4}\,N/m$ (d) $3.2 \times 10^{-4}\,N/m$

9. If an ammeter is to be used in place of a voltmeter, then we must connect with the ammeter a –
   (a) low resistance in parallel
   (b) low resistance in series
   (c) high resistance in parallel
   (d) high resistance in series

10. The magnetic field at the centre of a current carrying circular loop of radius R, is B_1. The magnetic field at a point on its axis at a distance R from the center of the loop is B_2. Then the ratio (B_1/B_2) is

(a) $2\sqrt{2}$ (b) $\dfrac{1}{2\sqrt{2}}$ (c) $\sqrt{2}$ (d) 2

11. The self-inductance of a solenoid of 600 turns is 108 mH. The self-inductance of a coil having 500 turns with the same length, the same radius and the same medium will be

(a) 95 mH   (b) 90 mH   (c) 85 mH   (d) 75 mH

12. The rms current in a circuit connected to a 50 Hz ac source is 15 A. The value of the current in the circuit $\left(\dfrac{1}{600}\right)$ s after the instant the current is zero, is

(a) $\dfrac{15}{\sqrt{2}}$ A   (b) $15\sqrt{2}$ A   (c) $\dfrac{\sqrt{2}}{15}$ A   (d) 8 A

13. In a circuit the phase difference between the alternating current and the source voltage is $\dfrac{\pi}{2}$. Which of the following cannot be the element(s) of the circuit ?

(a) only C   (b) only L   (c) L and R   (d) L or C

14. The electric potential V at any point (x, y, z) is given by $V = 3x^2$ where x is in metres and V in volts. The electric field at the point (1 m, 0, 2m) is –

(a) 6 V/m along $-x$-axis   (b) 6 V/m along $+x$-axis

(c) 1.5 V/m along $-x$-axis   (d) 1.5 V/m along $+x$-axis

15. Which of the diagrams correctly represents the electric field between two charged plates if a neutral conductor is placed in between the plates ?

(a) 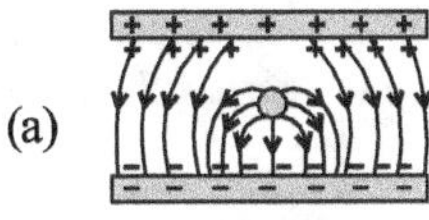   (b) 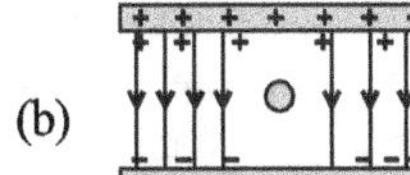

(c) 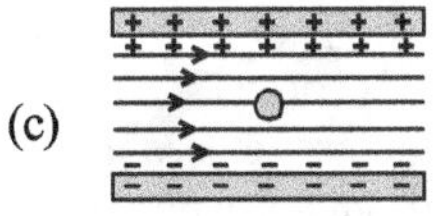   (d) 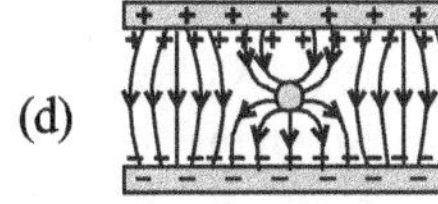

16. A variable capacitor is connected to a 200 V battery. If its capacitance is changed from 2 μF to X μF, the decrease in energy of the capacitor is 2×10^{-2} J. The value of X is

(a) 1 μF   (b) 2 μF

(c) 3 μF   (d) 4 μF

17. A potential difference of 200 V is maintained across a conductor of resistance 100 Ω. The number of electrons passing through it in 1s is

(a) 1.25×10^{19} (b) 2.5×10^{18}

(c) 1.25×10^{18} (d) 2.5×10^{16}

18. The impedance of a series LCR circuit is –

(a) $R + X_L + X_C$ (b) $\sqrt{\dfrac{1}{X_C^2} + \dfrac{1}{X_L^2} + R^2}$

(c) $\sqrt{X_L^2 - R_C^2 + R^2}$ (d) $\sqrt{R^2 + (X_L - X_C)^2}$

19. When an alternating voltage $E = E_0 \sin \omega t$ is applied to a circuit, a current $I = I_0 \sin\left(\omega t + \dfrac{\pi}{2}\right)$ flows through it. The average power dissipated in the circuit is

(a) $E_{rms} \cdot I_{rms}$ (b) $E_0 I_0$

(c) $\dfrac{E_0 I_0}{\sqrt{2}}$ (d) Zero

20. A current carrying wire kept in a uniform magnetic field, will experience a maximum force when it is

(a) perpendicular to the magnetic field

(b) parallel to the magnetic field

(c) at and angle of 45° to the magnetic field

(d) at and angle of 60° to the magnetic field

21. The voltage across a resistor, an inductor, and a capacitor connected in series to an ac source are 20 V, 15 V and 30 V respectively. The resultant voltage in the circuit is

(a) 5 V   (b) 20 V   (c) 25 V   (d) 65 V

22. In a dc circuit the direction of current inside the battery and outside the battery respectively are

(a) positive to negative terminal and negative to positive terminal

(b) positive to negative terminal and negative to positive terminal

(c) negative to positive terminal and positive to negative terminal

(d) negative to positive terminal and negative to positive terminal

23. The magnitude of electric field due to a point charge 2q, at distance r is E. Then the magnitude of electric field due to a uniformly charged thin spherical shell of radius R with total charge q at a distance $\dfrac{r}{2}$ ($r \gg R$) will be

(a) $\dfrac{E}{4}$ (b) 0   (c) 2E   (d) 4E

24. The horizontal component of earth's magnetic field at a place is 0.2 G whereas it's total magnetic field is 0.4 G. The angle of dip at the place is

(a) 30°   (b) 45°   (c) 60°   (d) 90°

25. The current in the primary coil of a pair of coils changes from 7 A to 3 A in 0.04 s. The mutual inductance between the two coils is 0.5 H. The induced emf in the secondary coil is –

(a) 50 V   (b) 75 V   (c) 100 V   (d) 220 V

SECTION - B

This section consists of 24 multiple choice questions with overall choice to attempt any 20 questions. In case more than desirable number of questions are attempted, ONLY first 20 will be considered for evaluation.

26. A square sheet of side 'a' is lying parallel to XY plane at $z = a$. The electric field in the region is $\vec{E} = cz^2\hat{k}$. The electric flux through the sheet is

(a) a^4c (b) $\frac{1}{3}a^3c$ (c) $\frac{1}{3}a^4c$ (d) 0

27. Three charges q, –q and q_0 are placed as shown in figure. The magnitude of the net force on the charge q_0 at point O is $\left[k = \dfrac{1}{(4\pi\varepsilon_0)} \right]$

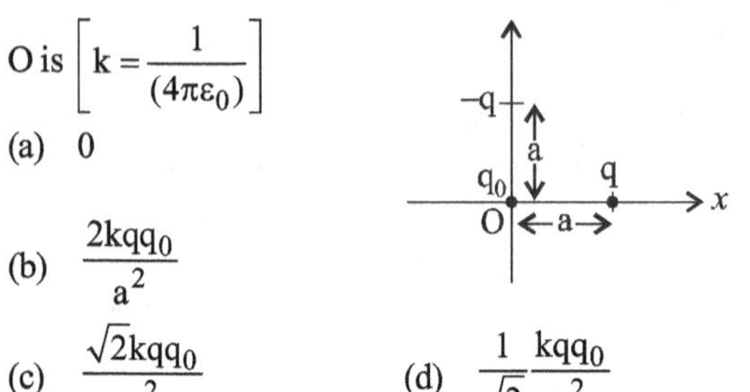

(a) 0

(b) $\dfrac{2kqq_0}{a^2}$

(c) $\dfrac{\sqrt{2}kqq_0}{a^2}$

(d) $\dfrac{1}{\sqrt{2}}\dfrac{kqq_0}{a^2}$

28. A + 3.0 nC charge Q is initially at rest at a distance of $r_1 = 10$ cm from a + 5.0 nC charge q fixed at the origin. The charge Q is moved away from q to a new position at $r_2 = 15$ cm. In this process work done by the field is

(a) 1.29×10^{-5} J (b) 3.6×10^5 J
(c) -4.5×10^{-7} J (d) 4.5×10^{-7} J

29. A car battery is charged by a 12 V supply, and energy stored in it is 7.20×10^5 J. The charge passed through the battery is–

(a) 6.0×10^4 C (b) 5.8×10^3 C
(c) 8.64×10^6 C (d) 1.6×10^5 C

30. A straight conducting rod of length l and mass m is suspended in a horizontal plane by a pair of flexible strings in a magnetic field of magnitude B. To remove the tension in the supporting string, the magnitude of the current in the wire is

(a) $\dfrac{mgB}{l}$ (b) $\dfrac{mgl}{B}$ (c) $\dfrac{mg}{lB}$ (d) $\dfrac{lB}{mg}$

31. A constant current is flowing through a solenoid. An iron rod is inserted in the solenoid along its axis. Which of the following quantities will not increase?

(a) The magnetic field at the centre
(b) The magnetic flux linked with the solenoid
(c) The rate of heating
(d) The self-inductance of the solenoid

32. A circuit is connected to an ac source of variable frequency. As the frequency of the source is increased, the current first increases and then decreases. Which of the following combinations of elements is likely to comprise the circuit?

(a) L, C and R (b) L and C
(c) L and R (d) R and C

33. If n, e, τ and m have their usual meanings, then the resistance of a wire of length l and cross-sectional area A is given by-

(a) $\dfrac{ne^2A}{2m\tau l}$ (b) $\dfrac{ml}{ne^2\tau A}$ (c) $\dfrac{m\tau A}{ne^2 l}$ (d) $\dfrac{ne^2\tau A}{2ml}$

34. A proton and an alpha particle move in circular orbits in a uniform magnetic field. Their speeds are in the ratio of 9 : 4. The ratio of radii of their circular orbits $\left(\dfrac{r_p}{r_{alpha}} \right)$ is

(a) $\dfrac{3}{4}$ (b) $\dfrac{4}{3}$ (c) $\dfrac{8}{9}$ (d) $\dfrac{9}{8}$

35. A coil of area 100 cm^2 is kept at an angle of 30° with a magnetic field of 10^{-1} T. The magnetic field is reduced to zero in 10^{-4} s. the unduced emf in the coil is

(a) $5\sqrt{3}$V (b) $50\sqrt{3}$V (c) 5.0V (d) 50.0V

36. A 15 Ω resister an 80 mH inductor and a capacitor of capacitance C are connected in series with a 50 Hz ac source. If the source voltage and current in the circuit are in phase, then the value of capacitance is

(a) 100 μF (b) 127 μF (c) 142 μF (d) 160 μF

37. Four objects W, X, Y and Z each with charge +q are hold fixed at four points of a square of side d as shown in the figure. Objects X and Z are on the midpoints of the sides of the square. The electrostatic force exerted by object W on object X is F. Then the magnitude of the force exerted by object W on Z is.

(a) $\dfrac{F}{7}$ (b) $\dfrac{F}{5}$

(c) $\dfrac{F}{3}$ (d) $\dfrac{F}{2}$

38. Two sources of equal emf are connected in series. This combination is in turn connected to an external resistance R. The internal resistance of two sources are r_1 and r_2 $(r_2 > r_1)$. If the potential difference across the source of internal resistance r_2 is zero then R equals to–

(a) $\dfrac{r_1 + r_2}{r_2 - r_1}$ (b) $r_2 - r_1$ (c) $\dfrac{r_1 r_2}{r_2 - r_1}$ (d) $\dfrac{r_1 - r_2}{r_1 r_2}$

39. Which of following statements is correct?
(a) Magnetic field lines do not form closed loops.
(b) Magnetic field lines start from north pole and end at south pole of a magnet.
(c) The tangent at a point on a magnetic field line represents the direction of the magnetic field at that point.
(d) Two magnetic field lines may intersect each other.

40. The equivalent resistance between A and B of the network shown in figure is

(a) 3R Ω (b) $\left(\dfrac{3}{2}\right)$R Ω

(c) 2R Ω (d) $\left(\dfrac{2}{3}\right)$R Ω

41. A bar magnet has magnetic dipole moment $\overline{M}$. Its initial position is parallel to the direction of uniform magnetic field $\vec{B}$. In this position, the magnitudes of torque and force acting on it respectively are–

  (a) 0 and MB   (b) MB and MB

  (c) 0 and 0   (d) $|\overline{M} \times \vec{B}|$ and 0

42. Two charges 14 μC and –4 μC are placed at (–12 cm, 0, 0) and (12 cm, 0, 0) in an external electric field $E = \left(\dfrac{B}{r^2}\right)$, where $B = 1.2 \times 10^6 \, N/(cm^2)$ and r is in metres.

The electrostatic potential energy of the configuration is

  (a) 97.9 J   (b) 102.1 J   (c) 2.1 J   (d) –97.9 J

43. A 300 Ω resistor and a capacitor of $\left(\dfrac{25}{\pi}\right)$ μF are connected in series to a 200 V – 50 Hz ac source. The current in the circuit is

  (a) 0.1 A   (b) 0.4 A   (c) 0.6 A   (d) 0.8 A

44. The core of a transformer is laminated to reduce the effect of

  (a) flux leakage   (b) copper loss

  (c) hysteresis loss   (d) eddy current

Question No. 45 to 49 are Assertion (A) and Reason (R) type questions. Given below are the two statements labelled as Assertion (A) and Reason (R). Select the most appropriate answer from the options given below :

(a) Both (A) & (R) are true and (R) is the correct explanation of (A)

(b) Both (A) & (R) are true and (R) is not the correct explanation of (A)

(c) (A) is true but (R) is false

(d) (A) is false and (R) is also false

45. **Assertion (A) :** A negative charge in an electric field moves along the direction of the electric field.

  Reason (R) : On a negative charge a force acts in the direction of the electric field.

46. **Assertion (A) :** The poles of a bar magnet cannot be separated.

  Reason (R) : Magnetic monopoles do not exist.

47. **Assertion (A) :** When radius of a current carrying loop is doubled, its magnetic moment becomes four times.

  Reason (R) : The magnetic moment of a current carrying loop is directly proportional to the area of the loop.

48. **Assertion (A) :** Higher the range, lower is the resistance of an ammeter

  Reason (R) : To increase the range of an ammeter additional shunt is added in series to it.

49. **Assertion (A) :** A step-up transformer cannot be used as a step-down transformer.

  Reason (R) : A transformer works only in one direction.

This section consists of 6 multiple choice questions with an overall choice to attempt any 5. In case more than desirable number of questions are attempted, ONLY first 5 will be considered for evaluation.

50. Equipotentials at a large distance from a collection of charges whose total sum is not zero are–

  (a) spheres   (b) planes

  (c) ellipsoids   (d) paraboloids

51. Four charges –q, –q, +q and +q are placed at the corners of a square of side 2 L is shown in figure. The electric potential at point A midway between the two charges + q and +q is–

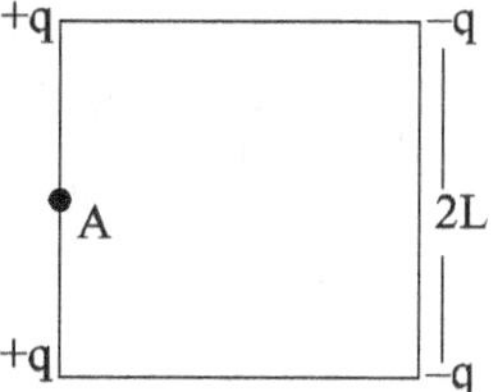

  (a) $\dfrac{1}{4\pi\varepsilon_0}\dfrac{2q}{L}\left(1-\dfrac{1}{\sqrt{5}}\right)$ (b) $\dfrac{1}{4\pi\varepsilon_0}\dfrac{2q}{L}\left(1+\dfrac{1}{\sqrt{5}}\right)$

  (c) $\dfrac{1}{4\pi\varepsilon_0}\dfrac{q}{2L}\left(1-\dfrac{1}{\sqrt{5}}\right)$ (d) zero

Case Study: (Qs. 52-55)

An experiment was set up with the circuit diagram shown in figure. Given that $R_1 = 10\,\Omega$, $R_2 = R_3 = 5\,\Omega$, $r = 0\,\Omega$ and E = 5V

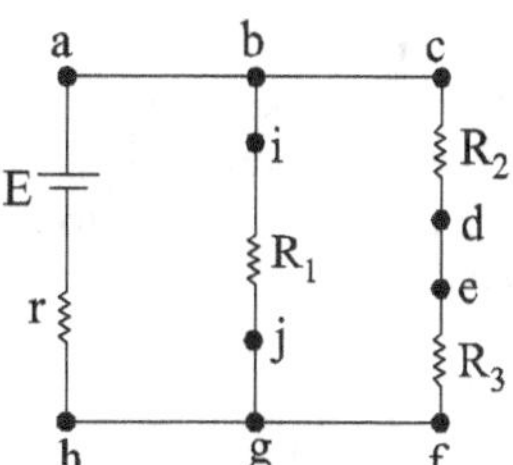

52. The points with the same potential are–

  (a) b, c, d   (b) f, h, j   (c) d, e, f   (d) a, b, j

53. The current through branch bg is–

  (a) 1 A   (b) $\dfrac{1}{3}$A   (c) $\dfrac{1}{2}$A   (d) $\dfrac{2}{3}$A

54. The power dissipated in R_1 is–

  (a) 2 W   (b) 2.5 W   (c) 3 W   (d) 4.5 W

55. The potential difference across R_3 is–

  (a) 1.5 V   (b) 2 V   (c) 2.5 V   (d) 3 V

Solutions

1. **(c)** As charged object Y repels negatively charged X so Y must be negatively charged object. And Z is attracted to Y so Z is neutral or positively charged.

2. **(b)** Net charge of three spheres with charges +3e, +5e, –3e = +5e.
   Also net charge of +6e, +6e, –7e = +5e
   So possible values for the final charge on the spheres are +6e, +6e, –7e

3. **(d)** The net charge on the object = $1C - ne$ [$\because Q = ne$]
   $= 1C - 5 \times 10^{18} \times 1.6 \times 10^{-19} C = +0.20\,C$

4. **(d)** Kirchhoff's first rule
   $\Sigma I = 0$ and second rule
   $\Sigma IR = V = IR$ are respectively based on conservation of charge and conservation of energy.

5. **(a)** For 220 V – 100W bulb
   $$P = \frac{V^2}{R} \Rightarrow R = \frac{V^2}{P} = \frac{(220)^2}{100} = 484\Omega$$
   So, electric power consumed when operated at 110V
   $$P = \frac{V^2}{R} = \frac{(110)^2}{484} = 25\,W$$

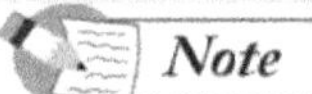

Note

If $V_{applied} < V_{rated}$ then % drop in output power of electrical

$device = \dfrac{P_R - P_{consumed}}{P_R} \times 100$ *(P_R = rated power)*.

6. **(c)** Temperature coefficient of resistivity, α $(°C)^{-1}$ of semiconductor is negative.

7. **(b)** In region II magnetic field due to both wires are vertically upwards and add.

8. **(d)** Force per unit length, $\dfrac{F}{l} = \dfrac{\mu_0}{2\pi} \dfrac{i_1 i_2}{r}$
   $$= \frac{4\pi \times 10^{-7} \times 4 \times 10\,N}{2\pi \times 2.5 \times 10^{-2}\,m} = 3.2 \times 10^{-4}\,N/m$$

9. **(d)** Ammeter has low resistance. Large current would flow when used directly across high voltage as voltmeter. High resistance is added in series to reduce current.

10. **(a)** B – magnetic field
    $$B_1 = B \text{ (center)} = \frac{\mu_0 i}{2R}$$
    $$B_2 \,(= B \text{ at } x = R) = \frac{\mu_0 i R^2}{2(R^2 + x^2)^{3/2}} \quad (\text{Put } x = R)$$
    $$= \frac{\mu_0 i R^2}{2(2R^2)^{3/2}}$$
    $$= \frac{\mu_0 i}{2 \times 2^{3/2} R} = \frac{\mu_0 i}{2 \times 2\sqrt{2}R} \qquad \therefore \frac{B_1}{B_2} = 2\sqrt{2}$$

11. **(d)** Self inductance $L = \dfrac{\mu_0 N^2 A}{l} \Rightarrow L \propto N^2$
    $108\,mH \propto (600)^2$
    new inductance $(L') \propto (500)^2$
    $$\Rightarrow \frac{L'}{108} = \frac{(500)^2}{(600)^2} \Rightarrow L' = \frac{(500)^2}{(600)^2} \times 108$$
    $$\therefore \quad L' = 75\,mH$$

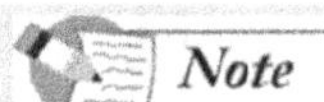

Note

Self inductance 'L' does not play any role till there is a constant current flowing in the circuit. It comes in to the picture only when there is a change in current.

12. **(a)** $i = i_0 \sin\omega t$
    $$i = 15\sqrt{2}\sin 2\pi \times 50 \times \frac{1}{600}$$
    $$= 15\sqrt{2}\sin\frac{\pi}{6} = \frac{15\sqrt{2}}{2} = \frac{15}{\sqrt{2}}\,A$$

13. **(c)** In L-R circuit phase difference between current and voltage is different from $90°$. It can be found by impedance triangle.

14. **(a)** Electric field is given by
    $$\bar{E} = \frac{-\partial V}{\partial x}\hat{i} - \frac{\partial V}{\partial y}\hat{j} - \frac{\partial V}{\partial z}\hat{k} = \frac{-\partial 3x^2}{\partial x}\hat{i} = -6x\hat{i}$$
    $$= -6 \times 1\hat{i} = -6\,V/m\hat{i}$$

15. **(d)** Negative charge will appear on the surface of neutral conductor near positive plate and positive charge on surface of conductor near negative plate. Field lines start from positive plate end at –ve charge of ball and start from +ve charge on conductor to –ve plate.

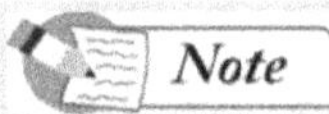

Note

Electric lines of force never intersect the conductor. They are perpendicular and slightly curved near the surface of conductor.

16. **(a)** Energy stored in a capacitor, $E = \dfrac{1}{2}CV^2$
    $\therefore$ Decrease in energy of the capacitor
    $$= \frac{1}{2} \times 2 \times 10^{-6} \times (200)^2 - \frac{1}{2} \times (x \times 10^{-6}) \times (200)^2$$
    $$\Rightarrow \frac{1}{2}(2 - x) \times 10^{-6} \times (200)^2 = 2 \times 10^{-2}$$
    $$\Rightarrow x = 10^{-6}\,F$$
    $$\Rightarrow x = 1\,\mu F$$

17. **(a)** From Ohm's law, current $i = \dfrac{V}{R} = \dfrac{200}{100}\,A$
    Also, $i = \dfrac{q}{t} = \dfrac{ne}{1s} = 2$
    or, $n \times 1.6 \times 10^{-19} = 2 \qquad \therefore n = \dfrac{2 \times 10^{19}}{1.6} = 1.25 \times 10^{19}$

18. **(d)** Impedance of the series LCR circuit
    $$= \sqrt{R^2 + (X_L - X_C)^2}$$

19. **(d)** Average power $= E_{rms}\,I_{rms}\cos\phi$
    $$= \frac{E_0}{\sqrt{2}}\frac{I_0}{\sqrt{2}}\cos 90° = 0$$

20. **(a)** Magnetic force $= i\vec{l} \times \vec{B} = i\,lB\sin\theta$
    When $\theta = 90°$ i.e., wire is $\perp$ to $\vec{B}$
    $F_{max} = ilB$

21. (c) $V_{resultant} = \sqrt{V_R^2 + (V_L - V_C)^2}$

$= \sqrt{20^2 + (15-30)^2} = 25V$

22. (c) In a dc circuit, the direction of current inside the battery is from −ve to +ve terminal and outside the battery it flows from +ve to −ve terminal.

23. (c) Electric field due to point charge $\dfrac{K2q}{r^2} = E$

So electric field due to shell outside $\dfrac{Kq}{\left(\dfrac{r}{2}\right)^2} = 2\left(\dfrac{K2q}{r^2}\right) = 2E$

24. (c) $B_H = B\cos\delta$

$0.2 = 0.4\cos\delta$

$\Rightarrow \quad \cos\delta = \dfrac{1}{2}$

$\therefore \quad$ Angle of dip $\delta = 60°$

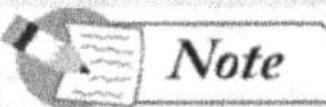 **Note**

Angle of dip is the angle between the direction of intensity of total magnetic field of earth and a horizontal line in the magnetic meridian.

25. (a) Induced $\text{emf} = \dfrac{Mdi}{dt}$

$= \dfrac{.5 \times (7-3)}{.04} = 50V$

26. (a) Electric flux = Electric field × area

$= EA = cz^2\hat{k}.a^2\hat{k}$

$= ca^2\hat{k}.a^2\hat{k} = ca^4$

27. (c) Forces due to q is F_q and that due to $-q$ F_{-q} are as shown.

Net force $= \sqrt{F_q^2 + F_{-q}^2}$

$= \sqrt{F^2 + F^2} \qquad$ (As $F_{-q} = F_q$)

$= \sqrt{2}F = \dfrac{\sqrt{2}Kqq_0}{a^2} \qquad \left(\because F = \dfrac{Kqq_0}{r^2}\right)$

28. (d) Work done by electric field $= \Delta U$

$= \left[\dfrac{Kq_1q_2}{r_1} - \dfrac{Kq_1q_2}{r_2}\right]$

$= K \times 3 \times 10^{-9} \times 5 \times 10^{-9}\left[\dfrac{1}{.01} - \dfrac{1}{.15}\right]$

$= 9 \times 10^9 \times 3 \times 10^{-9} \times 5 \times 10^{-9} [10 - 6.66] = 4.5 \times 10^{-7}J$

29. (a) Work done = qV

$\Rightarrow q = \dfrac{\text{Work done}}{V} = \dfrac{W}{V} = \dfrac{7.2 \times 10^5}{12} = 6 \times 10^4 C$

30. (c) Magnetic force = weight

$Bil = mg \qquad \therefore$ current $i = \dfrac{mg}{lB}$

Note

Magnetic force does no work when the charged particle is displaced while electric force does work in displacing the charged particle.

31. (c) Magnetic field at the centre of solenoid = μni

μ will change due to insertion of iron rod.

Rate of heat will not change as current is constant.

32. (a) In LCR circuit current first increases then decreases with increase in frequency.

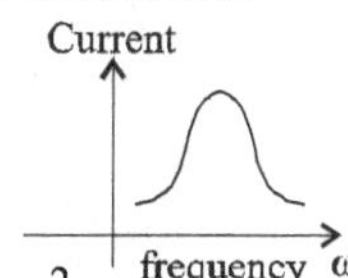

33. (b) Current density $J = \sigma E = \dfrac{1}{\rho}E = \dfrac{ne^2\tau}{m}E$

$\therefore \quad \sigma = \dfrac{ne^2\tau}{m}$

Resistance $(R) = \rho\dfrac{l}{A} = \dfrac{1}{\sigma}\dfrac{l}{A}$

Putting value of σ

$R = \dfrac{m}{ne^2\tau}\dfrac{l}{A}$

34. (d) Radius of circular path $r = \dfrac{mv}{qB}$

for proton $r_p = \dfrac{m_p v_p}{q_p B}$

for α-particle $r_\alpha = \dfrac{m_\alpha v_\alpha}{q_\alpha B}$

$\dfrac{r_p}{r_\alpha} = \left(\dfrac{m_p}{m_\alpha}\right) \times \left(\dfrac{q_\alpha}{q_p}\right) \times \left(\dfrac{V_p}{V_\alpha}\right) = \dfrac{1}{4} \times \dfrac{2}{1} \times \dfrac{9}{4} = \dfrac{9}{8}$

Note

If a particle enters a magnetic field normally to the magnetic field, then it starts moving in a circular orbit. The point at which, it enters the magnetic field lies on the circumference of the circular path.

35. (c) Induced emf, $e = -\dfrac{\Delta\phi}{\Delta t} = \dfrac{\phi_1 - \phi_2}{\Delta t}$

$= \dfrac{B_1 A\cos\theta - B_2 A\cos\theta}{\Delta t}$

$= \dfrac{10^{-1} \times 100 \times 10^{-4} \times \cos 60° - 0 \times 100 \times 10^{-4} \times \cos 60°}{10^{-4}}$

$= 5V$

Note: Area vector makes angle $90° - 30°$ with $\bar{B}$.

36. (b) As voltage and current are in phase so circuit is in resonance.

$\therefore \quad \omega^2 = \dfrac{1}{LC} \Rightarrow C = \dfrac{1}{\omega^2 L} = \dfrac{1}{(2\pi \times 50)^2 \times 80 \times 10^{-3}}$

$\Rightarrow \quad C = 1.27 \times 10^{-4} F = 127 \ \mu F$

37. (b) $F = \dfrac{Kq^2}{(d/2)^2} = \dfrac{4Kq^2}{d^2}$

Let W exerts F' force on Z

$\therefore \quad F' = \dfrac{Kq^2}{\left(\dfrac{\sqrt{5}d}{2}\right)^2} = \left(\dfrac{4}{5}\right)\dfrac{Kq^2}{d^2} = \dfrac{F}{5}$

38. (b) From circuit, current $i = \dfrac{2E}{R + r_1 + r_2}$

potential difference across source 2
$= E - ir_2$

$= E - \dfrac{2E}{R + r_1 + r_2} \times r_2 = 0$

$= \dfrac{E(R + r_1 + r_2 - 2r_2)}{R + r_1 + r_2} = 0$

$\therefore \quad R = r_2 - r_1$

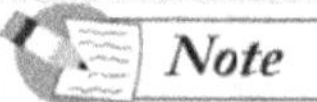 *Note*

Emf of cell is the potential difference across the terminals of a cell when it is not supplying any current. And potential difference is the voltage across the terminals of a cell when it is supplying current to external resistance.

39. **(c)** Tangent at a point on magnetic field lines give direction of field. Also it forms closed loop. And two magnetic field lines cannot intersect each other.

40. **(c)** Resistance which is shorted can be removed from the circuit.

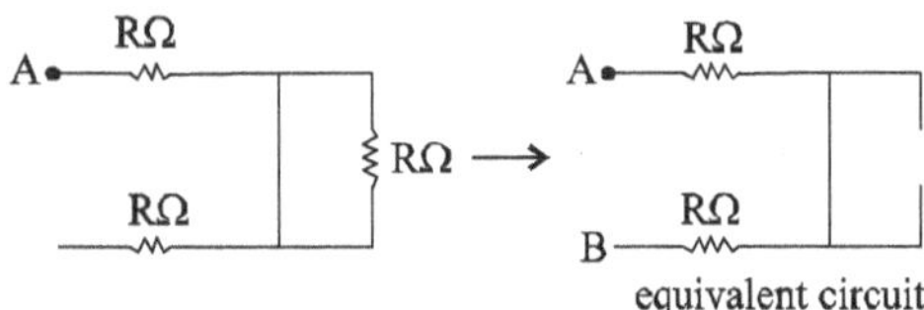

equivalent circuit

Therefore equivalent resistance $R_{AB} = R + R = 2R\Omega$

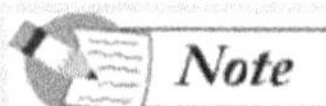 *Note*

Decoration of lights in festivals is an example of series grouping whereas all household appliances are connected in parallel grouping.

41. **(c)** Torque on magnetic dipole $\vec{M}$
$= \vec{M} \times \vec{B} = MB \sin\theta = MB \sin 0 = 0$
Force due to field is also zero as forces on both poles are in opposite direction so cancel each other.

42. **(a)** Electric potential (V)

$$V = -\int_r^\infty \vec{E}.d\vec{r} = -\int_r^\infty \dfrac{B}{r^2}dr = \dfrac{B}{r} = \dfrac{1.2 \times 10^6}{.12m} = 10^7 V$$

Potential energy of $14\mu C$
$u_1 = 14 \times 10^{-6} \times 10^7 J = 140 J$
Potential energy of $-4\mu C$
$u_2 = -4 \times 10^{-6} \times 10^7 = -40 J$

$$u_3 = \dfrac{Kq_1q_2}{r} = \dfrac{9 \times 10^9 \times 14 \times 10^{-6} \times (-4 \times 10^{-6})}{.24m}$$

$$[r = 12 - (-12)\, cm]$$

U (of configuration) $= -2.1$ J
$= u_1 + u_2 + u_3 = 140 + (-40) + (-2.1) = 97.9$ J

43. **(b)** Impedance $Z = \sqrt{R^2 + X_c^2}$

$$X_c = \dfrac{1}{\omega C} = \dfrac{1}{2\pi \times 50 \times \dfrac{25}{\pi} \times 10^{-6}} = 400\Omega$$

$$\therefore \quad Z = \sqrt{300^2 + 400^2} = 500\Omega$$

Current $i = \dfrac{V}{Z} = \dfrac{200}{500} = 0.4A$

44. **(d)** Core of a transformer is laminated mainly to reduce eddy current. It reduces the flux through which eddy current can flow.

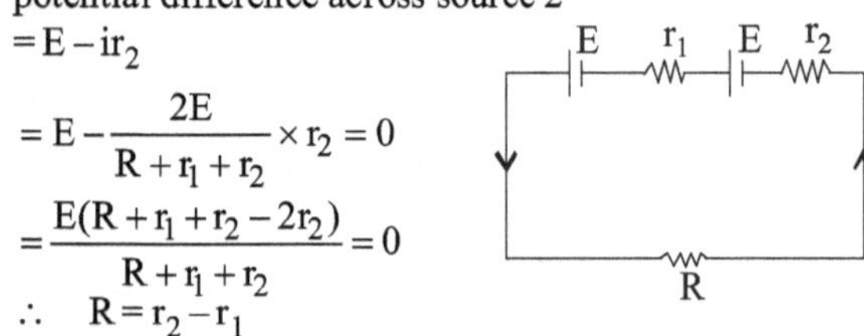 *Note*

Transformer is a device which raises or lowers the voltage in a.c. circuits through mutual induction. It works on a.c. only and never on d.c. It can increase or decrease either voltage or current but not both simultaneously.

45. **(d)** $-$ve charge moves in the opposite direction to the electric field, as it experiences force in the direction opposite to electric field.

46. **(a)** Magnetic poles always exist in pair, so poles of bar magnet cannot be separated.

47. **(a)** Magnetic moment is given by $\vec{M} = i\vec{A}$
As radius r gets double area $A = \pi r^2$ becomes 4 times and so does $\vec{M}$. Reason is correct as M is directly proportional to area of loop.

48. **(c)** Lower shunt resistance will draw more current through it and range of galvanometer and hence ammeter range will increase.
To increase range of ammeter smaller resistance should be added in parallel.

49. **(d)** Any step-up transformer can technically be used as a step down transformer by "reverse feeding" the transformer.

50. **(a)** At large distance collection of charge will act as point charge so, equipotential surface will be a sphere.

51. **(a)** Potential at point P due to charges at 1, 2, 3, 4 respectively are

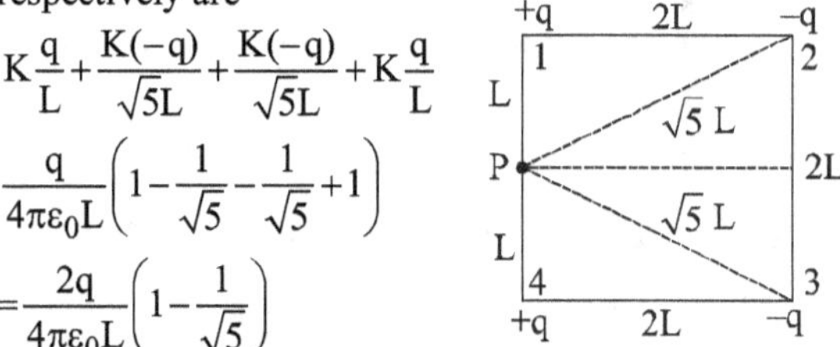

$$K\dfrac{q}{L} + \dfrac{K(-q)}{\sqrt{5}L} + \dfrac{K(-q)}{\sqrt{5}L} + K\dfrac{q}{L}$$

$$\dfrac{q}{4\pi\varepsilon_0 L}\left(1 - \dfrac{1}{\sqrt{5}} - \dfrac{1}{\sqrt{5}} + 1\right)$$

$$= \dfrac{2q}{4\pi\varepsilon_0 L}\left(1 - \dfrac{1}{\sqrt{5}}\right)$$

Note

Potential of a system of point charges at any point P,

$$V = \dfrac{KQ_1}{r_1} + \dfrac{KQ_2}{r_2} + \dfrac{K(-Q_3)}{r_3} + \dfrac{KQ_4}{r_4}$$

In general, $V = \sum\limits_{i=1}^{x} \dfrac{KQ_i}{r_i}$

52. **(b)** f, h, j are at same potential as there is no resistors between them.

53. **(c)** Current through branch bg

$$i_{bg} = \dfrac{V_{bg}}{R_{bg}} = \dfrac{5V}{R_1} = \dfrac{5}{10} = \dfrac{1}{2}A$$

54. **(b)** Power in $R_1 = V_{bg} \times i_{bg} = 5V \times \dfrac{1}{2}A = 2.5$ W

55. **(c)** From given circuit $i_{R_3} = \dfrac{V_{cf}}{R_2 + R_3} = \dfrac{5V}{5 + 5\Omega} = \dfrac{1}{2}A$

$$V_{R_3} = i_{R_3} \times R_3 = \dfrac{1}{2}A \times 5\Omega = \dfrac{5}{2}V = 2.5V$$

CBSE Board Sample Paper Term-II

Time Allowed : 2 Hours   *Maximum Marks : 35*

General Instructions:

(i) There are **12** questions in all. All questions are compulsory.

(ii) This question paper has three sections : Section A, Section B and Section C.

(iii) Section A contains three questions of two marks each, Section B contains eight questions of three marks each, Section C contains one case study-based question of five marks.

(iv) There is no overall choice. However, an internal choice has been provided in one question of two marks and two questions of three marks. You have to attempt only one of the choices in such questions.

(v) You may use log tables if necessary but use of calculator is not allowed.

SECTION - A

1. In a pure semiconductor crystal of Si, if antimony is added then what type of extrinsic semiconductor is obtained. Draw the energy band diagram of this extrinsic semiconductor so formed.

2. Consider two different hydrogen atoms. The electron in each atom is in an excited state. Is it possible for the electrons to have different energies but same orbital angular momentum according to the Bohr model? Justify your answer.

OR

Explain how does (i) photoelectric current and (ii) kinetic energy of the photoelectrons emitted in a photocell vary if the frequency of incident radiation is doubled, but keeping the intensity same?

Show the graphical variation in the above two cases.

3. Name the device which converts the change in intensity of illumination to change in electric current flowing through it. Plot I-V characteristics of this device for different intensities. State any two applications of this device.

SECTION - B

4. Derive an expression for the frequency of radiation emitted when a hydrogen atom de-excites from level n to level $(n-1)$. Also show that for large values of n, this frequency equals to classical frequency of revolution of an electron.

5. Explain with a proper diagram how an ac signal can be converted into dc (pulsating) signal with output frequency as double than the input frequency using pn junction diode. Give its input and output waveforms.

6. How long can an electric lamp of 100 W be kept glowing by fusion of 2 kg of deuterium?

Take the fusion reaction as

$$_1^2H + {}_1^2H \rightarrow {}_2^3He + n + 3.27 \text{ MeV}$$

7. Define wavefront. Draw the shape of refracted wavefront when the plane incident wave undergoes refraction from optically denser medium to rarer medium. Hence prove Snell's law of refraction.

8. (a) Draw a ray diagram of compound microscope for the final image formed at least distance of distinct vision?

(b) An angular magnification of 30X is desired using an objective of focal length 1.25 cm and an eye piece of focal length 5 cm. How will you set up the compound microscope for the final image formed at least distance of distinct vision?

OR

(a) Draw a ray diagram of Astronomical Telescope for the final image formed at infinity.

(b) A small telescope has an objective lens of focal length 140 cm and an eyepiece of focal length 5.0 cm. Find the magnifying power of the telescope for viewing distant objects when

(i) the telescope is in normal adjustment,

(ii) the final image is formed at the least distance of distinct vision.

9. Light of wavelength 2000 Å falls on a metal surface of work function 4.2 eV.
   (a) What is the kinetic energy (in eV) of the fastest electrons emitted from the surface?
   (b) What will be the change in the energy of the emitted electrons if the intensity of light with same wavelength is doubled?
   (c) If the same light falls on another surface of work function 6.5 eV, what will be the energy of emitted electrons?

10. The focal length of a convex lens made of glass of refractive index (1.5) is 20 cm.
   What will be its new focal length when placed in a medium of refractive index 1.25 ?
   Is focal length positive or negative? What does it signify?

11. (a) Name the e.m. waves which are suitable for radar systems used in aircraft navigation. Write the range of frequency of these waves.
   (b) If the Earth did not have atmosphere, would its average surface temperature be higher or lower than what it is now? Explain.
   (c) An e.m. wave exerts pressure on the surface on which it is incident. Justify.

OR

(a) "If the slits in Young's double slit experiment are identical, then intensity at any point on the screen may vary between zero and four times to the intensity due to single slit".
   Justify the above statement through a relevant mathematical expression.
(b) Draw the intensity distribution as function of phase angle when diffraction of light takes place through coherently illuminated single slit.

SECTION - C

CASE STUDY: MIRAGE IN DESERTS

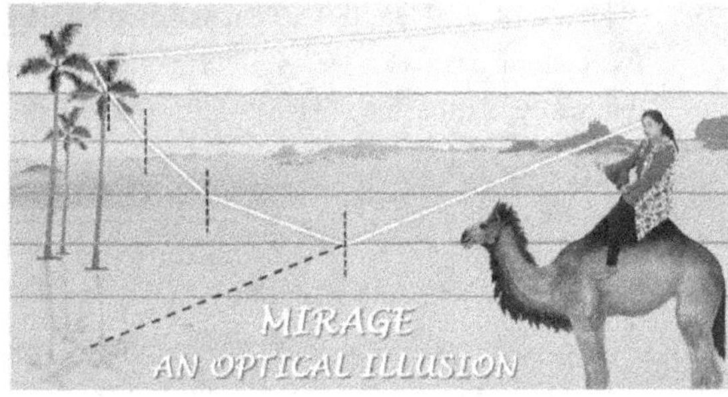

12. To a distant observer, the light appears to be coming from somewhere below the ground. The observer naturally assumes that light is being reflected from the ground, say, by a pool of water near the tall object.

Such inverted images of distant tall objects cause an optical illusion to the observer. This phenomenon is called mirage. This type of mirage is especially common in hot deserts.

Based on the above facts, answer the following questions:

(a) Which of the following phenomena is prominently involved in the formation of mirage in deserts?　　　1
   (i) Refraction, Total internal Reflection
   (ii) Dispersion and Refraction
   (iii) Dispersion and scattering of light
   (iv) Total internal Reflection and diffraction.

(b) A diver at a depth 12 m inside water $\left(a_{\mu_\omega} = \dfrac{4}{3}\right)$ sees the sky in a cone of semi-vertical angle　　　1

   (i) $\sin^{-1}\dfrac{4}{3}$ 　　　　　　(ii) $\tan^{-1}\dfrac{4}{3}$

   (iii) $\sin^{-1}\dfrac{3}{4}$ 　　　　　　(iv) $90°$

(c) In an optical fibre, if n_1 and n_2 are the refractive indices of the core and cladding, then which among the following, would be a correct equation?　　　1
   (i) $n_1 < n_2$ 　　　　　　(ii) $n_1 = n_2$
   (iii) $n_1 \ll n_2$ 　　　　　　(iv) $n_1 > n_2$

(d) A diamond is immersed in such a liquid which has its refractive index with respect to air as greater than the refractive index of water with respect to air. Then the critical angle of diamond-liquid interface as compared to critical angle of diamond-water interface will　　　1
   (i) depend on the nature of the liquid only
   (ii) decrease
   (iii) remain the same
   (iv) increase.

(e) The following figure shows a cross-section of a 'light pipe' made of a glass fiber of refractive index 1.68. The outer covering of the pipe is made of a material of refractive index 1.44. What is the range of the angles of the incident rays with the axis of the pipe for the following phenomena to occur.　　　1

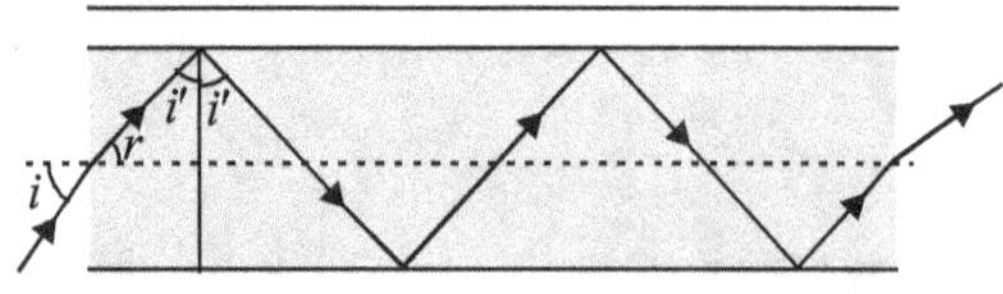

   (i) $0 < i < 90°$ 　　　　　　(ii) $0 < i < 60°$
   (iii) $0 < i < 45°$ 　　　　　　(iv) $0 < i < 30°$

Solutions

1. As given in the statement antimony is added to pure Si crystal, then a n-type extrinsic semiconductor would be so obtained, Since antimony(Sb) is a pentavalent impurity. Energy level diagram of n-type semiconductor **[1 Mark]**

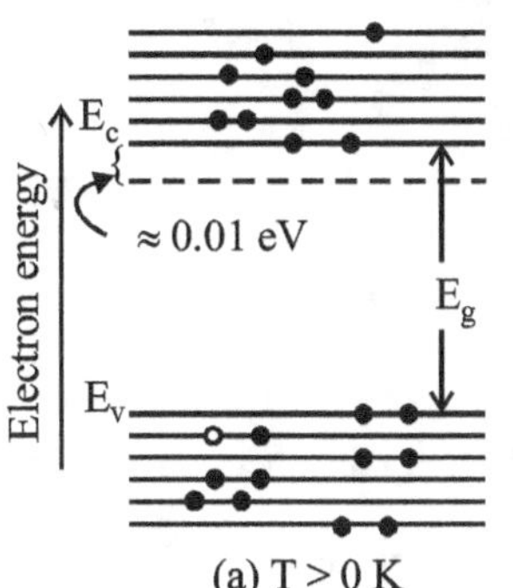

(a) T > 0 K   **[1 Mark]**

2. No   **[½ Mark]**

Because according to Bohr's model, $E_n = -\dfrac{13.6}{n^2}$ and electrons having different energies belong to different levels having different values of n.   **[½ Mark]**

So, their angular momenta will be different, as

$$L = mvr = \frac{nh}{2\pi}$$ **[1 Mark]**

OR

(i) The increase in the frequency of incident radiation has no effect on photoelectric current. This is because of incident photon of increased energy cannot eject more than one electron from the metal surface.   **[½ Mark]**

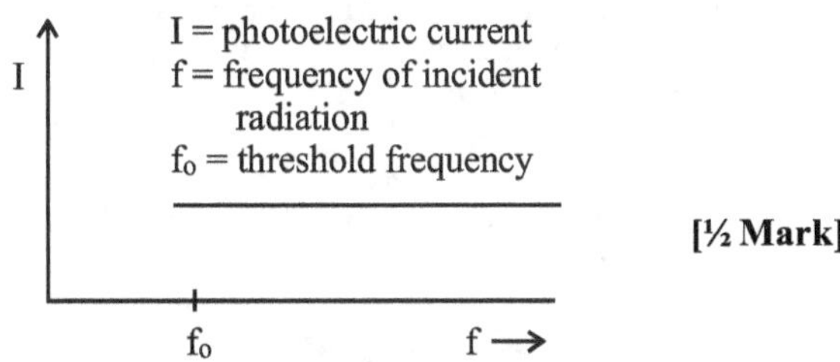

[½ Mark]

(ii) The kinetic energy of the photoelectron becomes more than the double of its original energy. As the work function of the metal is fixed, so incident photon of higher frequency and hence higher energy will impart more energy to the photoelectrons.   **[½ Mark]**

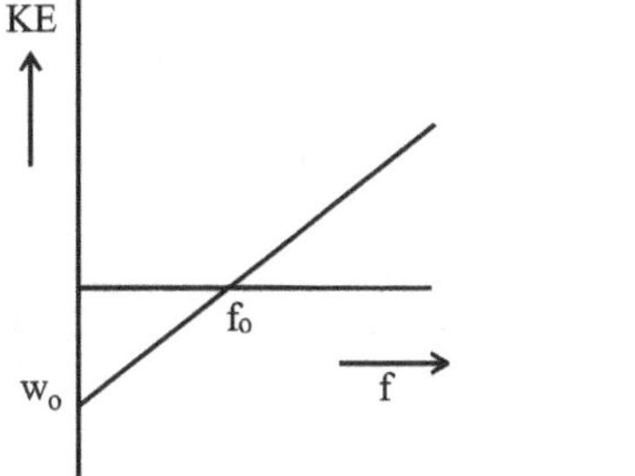

[½ Mark]

3. Photodiodes are used to detect optical signals of different intensities by changing current flowing through them.
[½ Mark]

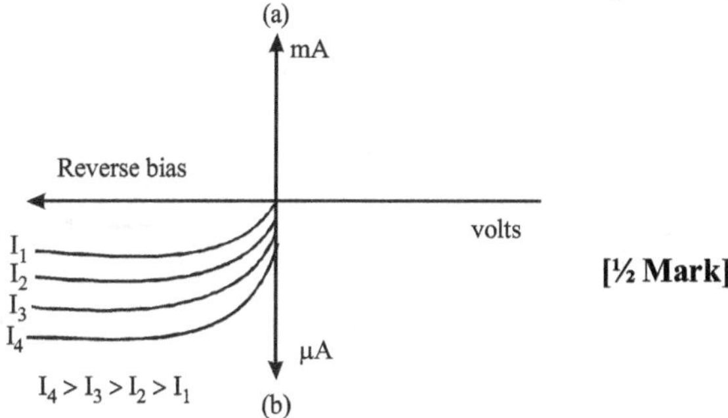

[½ Mark]

I-V Characteristics of a photodiode
Applications of photodiodes:
1. In detection of optical signals.
2. In demodulation of optical signals.
3. In light operated switches.
4. In speed reading of computer punched cards.
5. In electronic counters
(any two out of these or any other relevant application)
[½ × 2 = 1 Mark]

4. From Bohr's theory, the frequency f of the radiation emitted when an electron de – excites from level n_2 to level n_1 is given as

$$f = \frac{2\pi^2 mk^2 z^2 e^4}{h^3}\left[\frac{1}{n_1^2} - \frac{1}{n_2^2}\right]$$

Given $n_1 = n - 1$, $n_2 = n$, derivation of it

$$f = \frac{2\pi^2 mk^2 z^2 e^4}{h^3}\frac{(2n-1)}{(n-1)^2 n^2}$$ **[2 Marks]**

For large n, $2n - 1 = 2n$, $n - 1 = n$ and $z = 1$

Thus, $f = \dfrac{4\pi^2 mk^2 e^4}{n^3 h^3}$

which is same as orbital frequency of electron in n^{th} orbit.

$$f = \frac{v}{2\pi r} = \frac{4\pi^2 mk^2 e^4}{n^3 h^3}$$ **[1 Mark]**

5. A junction diode allows current to pass only when it is forward biased. So, if an alternating voltage is applied across a diode the current flows only in that part of the cycle when the diode is forward biased. This property is used to rectify alternating voltages and the circuit used for this purpose is called a rectifier.   **[1 Mark]**

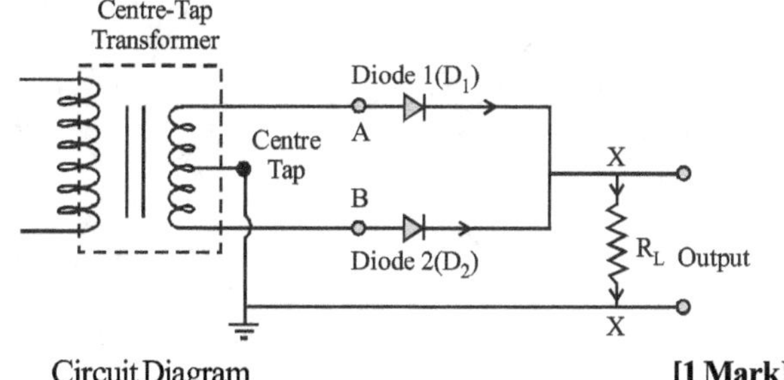

Circuit Diagram   **[1 Mark]**

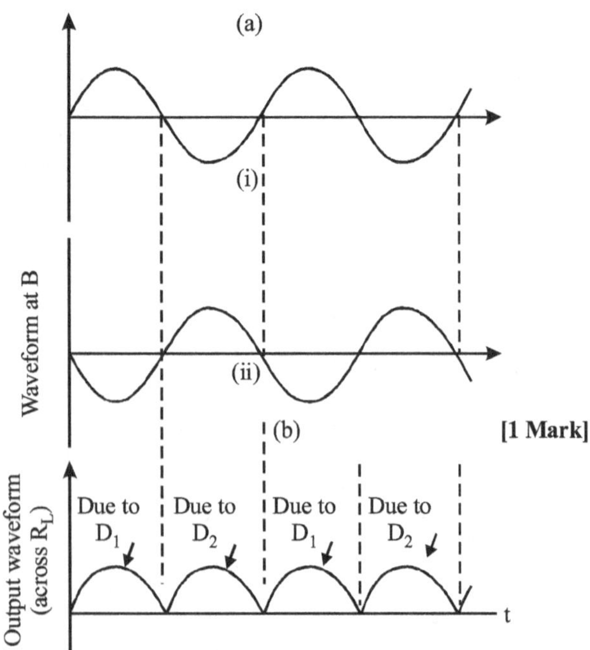

Working with input and output waveforms

6. Number of atoms present in 2 g of deuterium $= 6 \times 10^{23}$
   Number of atoms present in 2.0 Kg of deuterium $= 6 \times 10^{26}$
   [1 Mark]

   Energy released in fusion of 2 deuterium atoms
   $= 3.27$ MeV
   Energy released in fusion of 2.0 Kg of deuterium atoms

   $= \dfrac{3.27}{2} \times 6 \times 10^{26}$ MeV $= 9.81 \times 10^{26}$ MeV   **[1 Mark]**

   $= 15.696 \times 10^{13}$ J
   Energy consumed by bulb per sec $= 100$ J
   Time for which bulb will glow

   $= \dfrac{15.696 \times 10^{13}}{100}$ s $= 4.97 \times 10^{4}$ year **[1 Mark]**

7. A locus of points, which oscillate in phase is called a wavefront.

   OR

   A wavefront is defined as a surface of constant phase.
   [1 Mark]

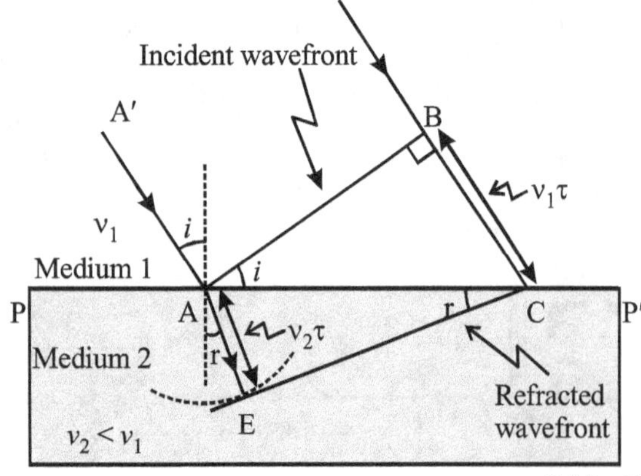

[1 Mark]

Diagram

Proof $n_1 \sin i = n_2 \sin r$ (Derivation)   **[1 Mark]**
This is the Snell's law of refraction.

8. (a) Diagram of Compound Microscope for the final image formed at D:

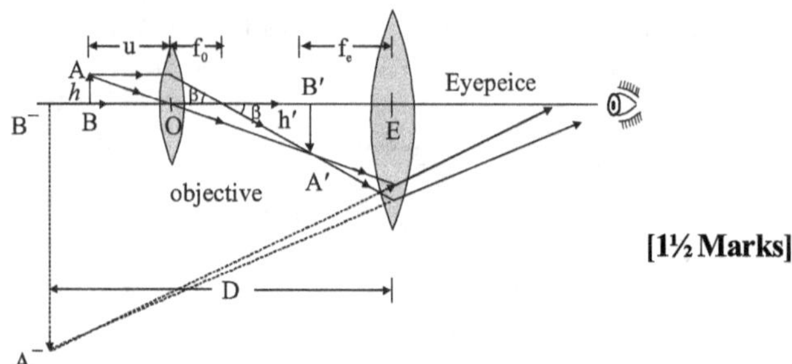

[1½ Marks]

(b) $m_0 = 30$, $f_0 = 1.25$ cm, $f_e = 5$ cm
when image is formed at least distance of distinct vision,
$D = 25$ cm
Angular magnification of eyepiece

$m_e = \left(1 + \dfrac{D}{f_e}\right) = 1 + \dfrac{25}{5} = 6$ **[½ Mark]**

Total Angular magnification, $m = m_0 m_e$

$\Rightarrow m_0 = \dfrac{m}{m_e} = \dfrac{30}{6} = 5$

As the objective lens forms the real image,

$m_0 = \dfrac{v_0}{u_0} = -5 \Rightarrow v_0 = -5u_0$

using lens equation, $u_0 = -1.5$ cm, $v_0 = -5 \times (-1.5)$ cm $= +7.5$ cm
[½ Mark]

Given $v_e = -D = -25$ cm, $f_e = +5$ cm, $u_e = ?$

using again lens equation $u_e = \dfrac{25}{6}$

Thus, object is to be placed at 1.5 cm from the objective and separation between the two lenses should be
$L = v_0 + |u_e| = 11.67$ cm

[½ Mark]

OR

8. (a) Ray diagram of astronomical telescope when image is formed at infinity.   **[1½ Marks]**

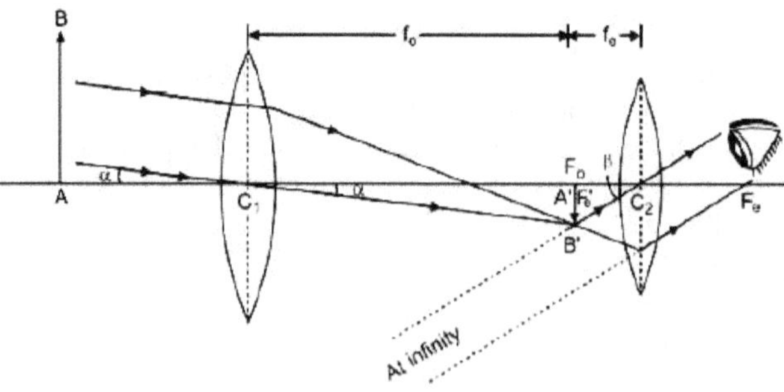

(b) (i) In normal adjustment : Magnifying power.
       $m = f_0/f_e = (140/5) = 28$ **[½ Mark]**
   (ii) When the final image is formed at the least distance of distinct vision (25 cm) :   **[1 Mark]**

$$m = \frac{f_o}{f_e}\left(1+\frac{f_e}{D}\right) = (28 \times 1.2) = \mathbf{33.6}$$

9. $\lambda = 2000\,\text{Å} = (2000 \times 10^{-10})\,\text{m}$
$W_o = 4.2\,\text{eV}$
$h = 6.63 \times 10^{-34}\,\text{JS}$
(a) Using Einstein's photoelectric equation
K.E. $= (6.2 - 4.2)\,\text{eV} = 2.0\,\text{eV}$ **[1 Mark]**
(b) The energy of the emitted electrons does not depend upon intensity of incident light; hence the energy remains unchanged. **[1 Mark]**
(c) For this surface, electrons will not be emitted as the energy of incident light (6.2 eV) is less than the work function (6.5 eV) of the surface. **[1 Mark]**

10. Given $a\mu_g = 1.5$
Focal length of the given convex lens when it is placed in air is
$f = +20\,\text{cm}$
Refractive index of the given medium with respect to air is
$a\mu_m = 1.25$
New focal length of the given convex lens when placed in a medium is f′

$$\frac{1}{f} = \left(a_{\mu_g}-1\right)\left[\left(\frac{1}{R_1}\right)+\left(\frac{1}{R_2}\right)\right] \quad \ldots(A) \qquad \textbf{[½ Mark]}$$

$$\frac{1}{f'} = \left(m_{\mu_g}-1\right)\left[\left(\frac{1}{R_1}\right)+\left(\frac{1}{R_2}\right)\right] \quad \ldots(B) \qquad \textbf{[½ Mark]}$$

Dividing (A) by (B), we get

$$\frac{f'}{f} = \frac{\left(a_{\mu_g}-1\right)}{\left(m_{\mu_g}-1\right)} = \frac{(1.5-1)}{(1.2-1)} = \frac{0.5}{0.2} = \frac{5}{2} = 2.5$$

$$f' = 2.5\,f = (2.5 \times 20)\,\text{cm} = +50\,\text{cm as } m_{\mu_g} = \frac{\mu_g}{\mu_m} = \frac{1.5}{1.25} = 1.2$$

[1 Mark]
New focal length is positive. **[½ Mark]**
The significance of the positive sign of the focal length is that given convex lens is still converging in the given medium. **[½ Mark]**

11. (a) Microwaves are suitable for the radar system used in aircraft navigation.
Range of frequency of microwaves is 108 Hz to 1011 Hz. **[1 Mark]**
(b) If the Earth did not have atmosphere, then there would be absence of greenhouse effect of the atmosphere. Due to this reason, the temperature of the earth would be lower than what it is now **[1 Mark]**
(c) An e.m. wave carries momentum with itself and given by P = Energy of wave(U)/ Speed of the wave(c) = U/c when it is incident upon a surface it exerts pressure on it. **[1 Mark]**

OR

11. (a) The total intensity at a point where the phase difference is ϕ, is

given by $I = I_1 + I_2 + 2\sqrt{I_1 I_2}\,\cos\phi$

intensities of two individual sources which are equal.
When ϕ is 0, $I = 4I_1$.
When ϕ is 90°, $I = 0$
Thus intensity on the screen varies between $4I_1$ and 0.
[2 Marks]

11. (b) Intensity distribution as function of phase angle, when diffraction of light takes place through coherently illuminated single slit
The intensity pattern on the screen is shown in the given figure

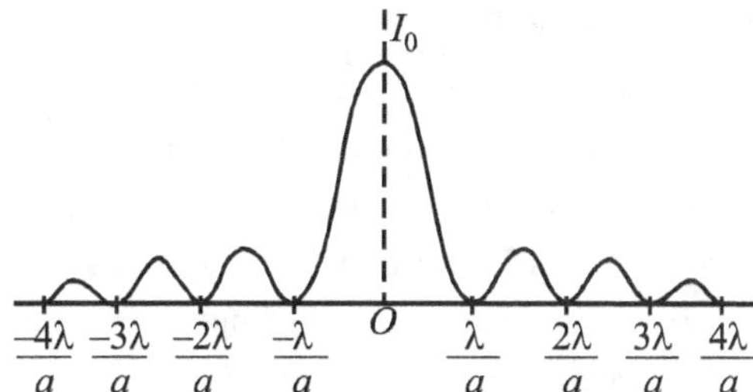

Width of central maximum **[1 Mark]**

12. (a) (i) Refraction, Total internal reflection **[1 Mark]**

(b) (iii) $\sin^{-1}\left(\dfrac{3}{4}\right)$

$$a_{\mu_\omega} = \frac{1}{\sin C} \qquad \textbf{[1 Mark]}$$

$$\Rightarrow \sin C = \frac{1}{a_{\mu_\omega}} \quad \Rightarrow \quad C = \sin^{-1}\left(\frac{1}{a_{\mu_\omega}}\right)$$

(c) (iv) $n_1 > n_2$ **[1 Mark]**
The refractive index of the core should be greater than the refractive index of the cladding.
(d) increases **[1 Mark]**

$$I_{\mu_d} = \frac{1}{\sin C} = \frac{\mu_d}{\mu_1}, \; \omega_{\mu_d} = \frac{1}{\sin C'} = \frac{\mu_d}{\mu_\omega}$$

$\mu_1 > \mu_\omega$
(e) Thus $C > C'$

(ii) $0 < i < 60°,\; 1_{\mu_2} = \dfrac{1}{\sin C'}$ **[1 Mark]**

$$\sin C' = \frac{1.44}{1.68} = 0.8571$$

Total internal reflection will occur if the angle i′ > i′c, i.e., if i′ > 59° or when $r < r_{max}$ where $r_{max} = 90° - 59° = 31°$.
Using Snell's law,

$$\frac{\sin i_{max}}{\sin r_{max}} = 1.68$$

or $\sin i_{max} = 1.68 \times \sin r_{max}$
$= 1.68 \times \sin 31° = 1.68 \times 0.5150 = 0.8662$
$= i_{max} = 60°$
Thus all incident rays which make angles in the range 0 < i < 60° with the axis of the pipe will suffer total internal reflections in the pipe.

CBSE Board Sample Paper Term-I

Time Allowed : 1½ Hours   *Maximum Marks : 35*

General Instructions:
   (i)   The Question Paper contains three sections.
   (ii) Section A has **25** questions. Attempt any **20** questions.
   (iii) Section B has **24** questions. Attempt any **20** questions.
   (iv) Section C has **6** questions. Attempt any **5** questions.
   (v)   All questions carry equal marks.
   (vi) There is no negative marking.

SECTION - A

*This section consists of **25** multiple choice questions with overall choice to attempt any **20** questions. In case more than desirable number of questions are attempted, ONLY first **20** will be considered for evaluation.*

1. Which of the following is NOT the property of equipotential surface?
    (a) They do not cross each other.
    (b) The rate of change of potential with distance on them is zero.
    (c) For a uniform electric field they are concentric spheres.
    (d) They can be imaginary spheres.

2. Two point charges $+8q$ and $-2q$ are located at $x = 0$ and $x = L$ respectively. The point on x axis at which net electric field is zero due to these charges is-
    (a) 8L   (b) 4L   (c) 2L   (d) L

3. An electric dipole of moment p is placed parallel to the uniform electric field. The amount of work done in rotating the dipole by 90° is-
    (a) 2pE   (b) pE   (c) pE/2   (d) Zero

4. Three capacitors $2\mu F$, $3\mu F$ and $6\mu F$ are joined in series with each other. The equivalent capacitance is-
    (a) $1/2\mu F$ (b) $1\mu F$ (c) $2\mu F$ (d) $11\mu F$

5. Two point charges placed in a medium of dielectric constant 5 are at a distance r between them, experience an electrostatic force 'F'. The electrostatic force between them in vacuum at the same distance r will be-
    (a) 5F   (b) F   (c) F/2   (d) F/5

6. Which statement is true for Gauss law-
    (a) All the charges whether inside or outside the gaussian surface contribute to the electric flux.
    (b) Electric flux depends upon the geometry of the gaussian surface.
    (c) Gauss theorem can be applied to non-uniform electric field.
    (d) The electric field over the gaussian surface remains continuous and uniform at every point.

7. A capacitor plates are charged by a battery with 'V' volts. After charging battery is disconnected and a dielectric slab with dielectric constant 'K' is inserted between its plates, the potential across the plates of a capacitor will become
    (a) Zero   (b) V/2   (c) V/K   (d) KV

8. The best instrument for accurate measurement of EMF of a cell is-
    (a) Potentiometer   (b) metre bridge
    (c) Voltmeter   (d) ammeter and voltmeter

9. An electric current is passed through a circuit containing two wires of same material, connected in parallel. If the lengths and radii of the wires are in the ratio of 3:2 and 2:3, then the ratio of the current passing through the wire will be
    (a) 2:3   (b) 3:2   (c) 8:27   (d) 27:8

10. By increasing the temperature, the specific resistance of a conductor and a semiconductor-
    (a) increases for both.
    (b) decreases for both.
    (c) increases for a conductor and decreases for a semiconductor.
    (d) decreases for a conductor and increases for a semiconductor.

11. We use alloys for making standard resistors because they have
    (a) low temperature coefficient of resistivity and high specific resistance
    (b) high temperature coefficient of resistivity and low specific resistance
    (c) low temperature coefficient of resistivity and low specific resistance
    (d) high temperature coefficient of resistivity and high specific resistance

12. A constant voltage is applied between the two ends of a uniform metallic wire, heat 'H' is developed in it. If another wire of the same material, double the radius and twice the length as compared to original wire is used then the heat developed in it will be-
    (a) H/2   (b) H   (c) 2H   (d) 4H

13. If the potential difference V applied across a conductor is increased to 2V with its temperature kept constant, the drift velocity of the free electrons in a conductor will–
    (a) remain the same.
    (b) become half of its previous value.
    (c) be double of its initial value.
    (d) become zero.

14. The equivalent resistance

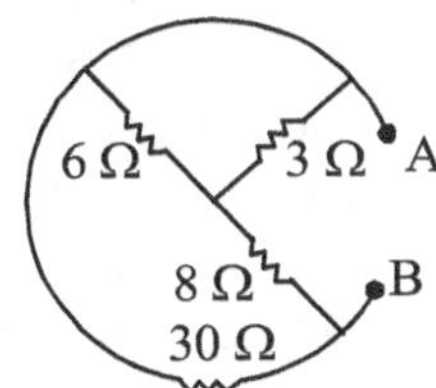

    (a) 3 ohms   (b) 5.5 ohms
    (c) 7.5 ohms   (d) 9.5 ohms

15. The SI unit of magnetic field intensity is
    (a) AmN^{-1} (b) $NA^{-1}m^{-1}$
    (c) $NA^{-2}m^{-2}$ (d) $NA^{-1}m^{-2}$

16. The coil of a moving coil galvanometer is wound over a metal frame in order to
    (a) reduce hysteresis
    (b) increase sensitivity
    (c) increase moment of inertia
    (d) provide electromagnetic damping

17. Two wires of the same length are shaped into a square of side 'a' and a circle with radius 'r'. If they carry same current, the ratio of their magnetic moment is
    (a) $2:\pi$ (b) $\pi:2$ (c) $\pi:4$ (d) $4:\pi$

18. The horizontal component of earth's magnetic field at a place is $\sqrt{3}$ times the vertical component. The angle of dip at that place is
    (a) $\pi/6$ (b) $\pi/3$ (c) $\pi/4$ (d) 0

19. The small angle between magnetic axis and geographic axis at a place is-
    (a) Magnetic meridian   (b) Geographic meridian
    (c) Magnetic inclination   (d) Magnetic Declination

20. Two coils are placed close to each other. The mutual inductance of the pair of coils depends upon the
    (a) rate at which current change in the two coils
    (b) relative position and orientation of the coils
    (c) rate at which voltage induced across two coils
    (d) currents in the two coils

21. A conducting square loop of side 'L' and resistance 'R' moves in its plane with the uniform velocity 'v' perpendicular to one of its sides. A magnetic induction 'B' constant in time and space pointing perpendicular and into the plane of the loop exists everywhere as shown in the figure. The current induced in the loop is

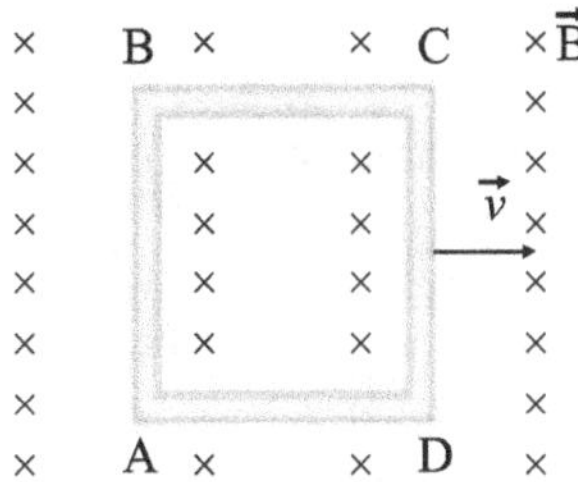

    (a) BLv/R Clockwise   (b) BLv/R Anticlockwise
    (c) 2BLv/R Anticlockwise (d) Zero

22. The magnetic flux linked with the coil (in Weber) is given by the equation –
    $$\phi = 5t^2 + 3t + 16$$
    The induced EMF in the coil at time, t = 4 will be-
    (a) –27 V   (b) –43 V   (c) –108 V   (d) 210 V

23. Which of the following graphs represent the variation of current (A) with frequency (f) in an AC circuit containing a pure capacitor?

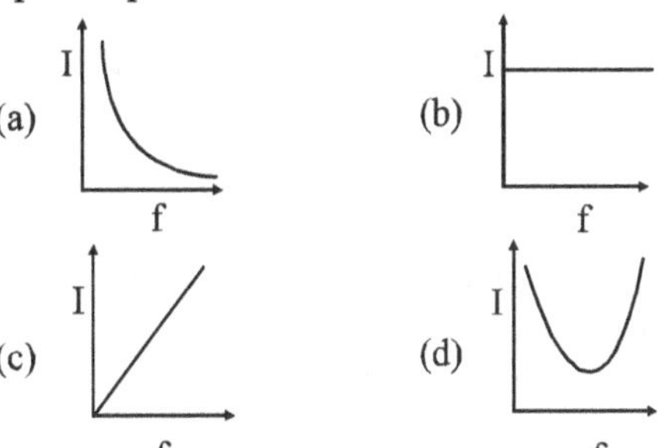

24. A 20 volt AC is applied to a circuit consisting of a resistance and a coil with negligible resistance. If the voltage across the resistance is 12 volt, the voltage across the coil is-
    (a) 16 V   (b) 10 V   (c) 8 V   (d) 6 V

25. The instantaneous values of emf and the current in a series ac circuit are-
    $E = E_0 \sin \omega t$ and $I = I_0 \sin (\omega t + \pi/3)$ respectively, then it is
    (a) Necessarily a RL circuit
    (b) Necessarily a RC circuit
    (c) Necessarily a LCR circuit
    (d) Can be RC or LCR circuit

SECTION - B

*This section consists of **24** multiple choice questions with overall choice to attempt any **20** questions. In case more than desirable number of questions are attempted, ONLY first **20** will be considered for evaluation.*

26. A cylinder of radius r and length l is placed in an uniform electric field parallel to the axis of the cylinder. The total flux for the surface of the cylinder is given by-

(a) zero   (b) πr^2 (c) $E\pi r^2$ (d) $2E\pi r^2$

27. Two parallel large thin metal sheets have equal surface densities 26.4×10^{-12} C/m^2 of opposite signs. The electric field between these sheets is-

(a) 1.5 N/C   (b) 1.5×10^{-16} N/C
(c) 3×10^{-10} N/C   (d) 3 N/C

28. Consider an uncharged conducting sphere. A positive point charge is placed outside the sphere. The net charge on the sphere is then,

(a) negative and uniformly distributed over the surface of sphere
(b) positive and uniformly distributed over the surface of sphere
(c) negative and appears at a point the surface of sphere closest to point charge.
(d) Zero

29. Three Charges 2q, –q and –q lie at vertices of a triangle. The value of E and V at centroid of triangle will be-

(a) E≠0 and V≠0   (b) E = 0 and V = 0
(c) E ≠ 0 and V = 0   (d) E = 0 and V ≠ 0

30. Two parallel plate capacitors X and Y, have the same area of plates and same separation between plates. X has air and Y with dielectric of constant 2. between its plates. They are connected in series to a battery of 12 V. The ratio of electrostatic energy stored in X and Y is-

(a) 4:1   (b) 1:4   (c) 2:1   (d) 1:2

31. Which among the following, is not a cause for power loss in a transformer-

(a) Eddy currents are produced in the soft iron core of a transformer.
(b) Electric Flux sharing is not properly done in primary and secondary coils.
(c) Humming sound produed in the tranformers due to magnetostriction.
(d) Primary coil is made up of a very thick copper wire.

32. An alternating voltage source of variable angular frequency 'w' and fixed amplitude 'V' is connected in series with a capacitance C and electric bulb of resistance R (inductance zero). When 'w' is increased-

(a) The bulb glows dimmer.
(b) The bulb glows brighter.

(c) Net impedance of the circuit remains unchanged.
(d) Total impedance of the circuit increases.

33. A solid spherical conductor has charge +Q and radius R. It is surrounded by a solid spherical shell with charge –Q, innerradius 2R, and outer radius 3R. Which of the following statements is true?

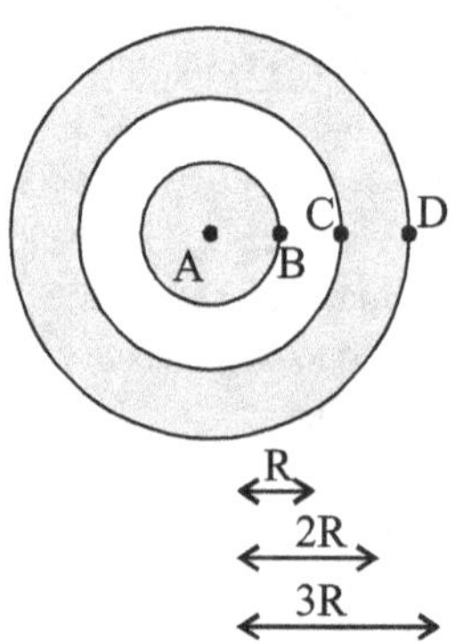

(a) The electric potential has a maximum magnitude at C and the electric field has a maximum magnitude at A.
(b) The electric potential has a maximum magnitude at D and the electric field has a maximum magnitude at B.
(c) The electric potential at A is zero and the electric field has a maximum magnitude at D.
(d) Both the electric potential and electric field achieve a maximum magnitude at B.

34. A battery is connected to the conductor of non-uniform cross section area. The quantities or quantity which remains constant is-

(a) electric field only
(b) drift speed and electric field
(c) electric field and current
(d) current only

35. Three resistors having values R_1, R_2 and R_3 are connected in series to a battery. Suppose R_1 carries a current of 2.0 A, R_2 has a resistance of 3.0 ohms, and R_3 dissipates 6.0 watts of power. Then the voltage across R_3 is-

(a) 1V   (b) 2V   (c) 3V   (d) 4V

36. A straight line plot showing the terminal potential difference (V) of a cell as a function of current (A) drawn from it, is shown in the figure. The internal resistance of the cell would be then-

(a) 2.8 ohms
(b) 1.4 ohms
(c) 1.2 ohms
(d) zero

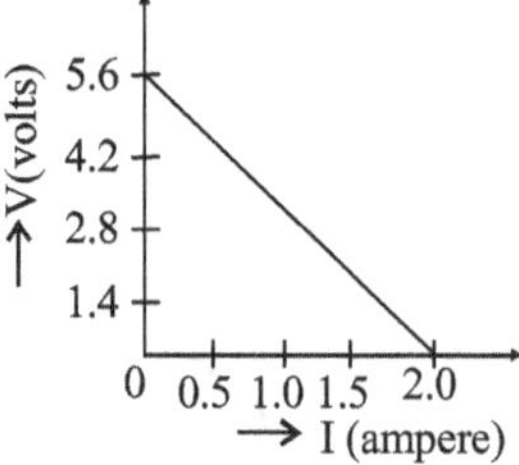

37. A 10 m long wire of uniform cross-section and 20 Ω resistance is used in a potentiometer. The wire is connected in series with a battery of 5 V along with an external resistance of 480 Ω. If an unknown emf E is balanced at 6.0 m length of the wire, then the value of unknown emf is-

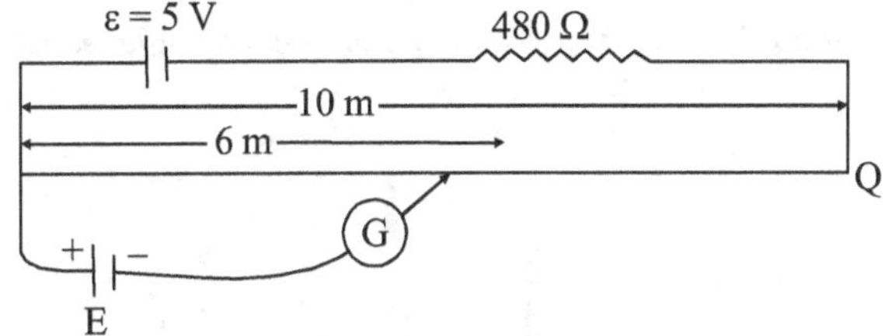

(a) 1.2 V   (b) 1.02 V   (c) 0.2 V   (d) 0.12 V

38. The current sensitivity of a galvanometer increases by 20%. If its resistance also increases by 25%, the voltage sensitivity will

(a) decrease by 1%   (b) increased by 5%

(c) increased by 10%   (d) decrease by 4%

39. Three infinitely long parallel straight current carrying wires A, B and C are kept at equal distance from each other as shown in the figure. The wire C experiences net force F. The net force on wire C, when the current in wire A is reversed will be

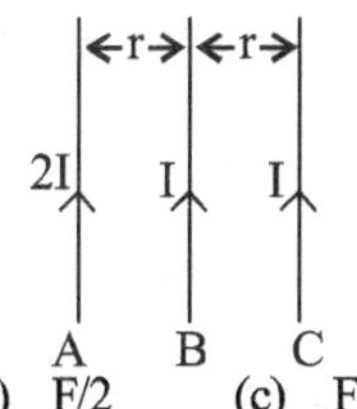

(a) Zero   (b) F/2   (c) F   (d) 2F

40. In a hydrogen atom the electron moves in an orbit of radius 0.5 Å making 10 revolutions per second, the magnetic moment associated with the orbital motion of the electron will be

(a) 2.512×10^{-38} Am^2 (b) 1.256×10^{-38} Am^2

(c) 0.628×10^{-38} Am^2 (d) zero

41. An air-cored solenoid with length 30 cm, area of cross-section 25 cm^2 and number of turns 800, carries a current of 2.5 A. The current is suddenly switched off in a brief time of 10^{-3}s. Ignoring the variation in magnetic field near the ends of the solenoid, the average back emf induced across the ends of the open switch in the circuit would be

(a) zero   (b) 3.125 volts

(c) 6.54 volts   (d) 16.74 volts

42. A sinusoidal voltage of peak value 283 V and frequency 50 Hz is applied to a series LCR circuit in which R = 3 Ω, L = 25.48 mH, and C = 796 μF, then the power dissipated at the resonant condition will be-

(a) 39.70 kW   (b) 26.70 kW

(c) 13.35 kW   (d) Zero

43. A circular loop of radius 0.3cm lies parallel to much bigger circular of radius 20 cm. The centre of the small loop is on the axis of the bigger loop. The distance between their centres is 15 cm. If a current of 2.0 A flows through the smaller loop, then the flux linked with the bigger loop is

(a) 3.3×10^{-11} weber   (b) 6×10^{-11} weber

(c) 6.6×10^{-9} weber   (d) 9.1×10^{-11} weber

44. If both the number of turns and core length of an inductor is doubled keeping other factors constant, then its self-inductance will be-

(a) Unaffected   (b) doubled

(c) halved   (d) quadrupled

45. Given below are two statements labelled as Assertion (A) and Reason (R)

Assertion (A): To increase the range of an ammeter, we must connect a suitable high resistance in series to it.

Reason (R): The ammeter with increased range should have high resistance.

Select the most appropriate answer from the options given below:

(a) Both A and R are true and R is the correct explanation of A

(b) Both A and R are true but R is not the correct explanation of A.

(c) A is true but R is false.

(d) A is false and R is also false.

46. Given below are two statements labelled as Assertion (A) and Reason (R)

Assertion (A): An electron has a high potential energy when it is at a location associated with a more negative value of potential, and a low potential energy when at a location associated with a more positive potential.

Reason (R): Electrons move from a region of higher potential to region of lower potential.

Select the most appropriate answer from the options given below:

(a) Both A and R are true and R is the correct explanation of A

(b) Both A and R are true but R is not the correct explanation of A.

(c) A is true but R is false.

(d) A is false and R is also false.

47. Given below are two statements labelled as Assertion (A) and Reason (R)

Assertion (A): A magnetic needle free to rotate in a vertical plane, orients itself (with its axis) vertical at the poles of the earth.

Reason (R): At the poles of the earth the horizontal component of earth's magnetic field will be zero.

Select the most appropriate answer from the options given below:

(a) Both A and R are true and R is the correct explanation of A

(b) Both A and R are true but R is not the correct explanation of A.

(c) A is true but R is false.

(d) A is false and R is also false.

48. Given below are two statements labelled as Assertion (A) and Reason (R)

Assertion (A): A proton and an electron, with same momenta, enter in a magnetic field in a direction at right angles to the lines of the force. The radius of the paths followed by them will be same.

Reason (R): Electron has less mass than the proton.

Select the most appropriate answer from the options given below:

(a) Both A and R are true and R is the correct explanation of A

(b) Both A and R are true but R is not the correct explanation of A.

(c) A is true but R is false.

(d) A is false and R is also false.

49. Given below are two statements labelled as Assertion (A) and Reason (R)

Assertion (A): On increasing the current sensitivity of a galvanometer by increasing the number of turns, may not necessarily increase its voltage sensitivity.

Reason (R): The resistance of the coil of the galvanometer increases on increasing the number of turns.

Select the most appropriate answer from the options given below:

(a) Both A and R are true and R is the correct explanation of A

(b) Both A and R are true but R is not the correct explanation of A.

(c) A is true but R is false.

(d) A is false and R is also false.

<h2 align="center">SECTION - C</h2>

*This section consists of **6** multiple choice questions with an overall choice to attempt any **5**. In case more than desirable number of questions are attempted, ONLY first 5 will be considered for evaluation.*

50. A small object with charge q and weight mg is attached to one end of a string of length 'L' attached to a stationary support. The system is placed in a uniform horizontal electric field 'E', as shown in the accompanying figure. In the presence of the field, the string makes a constant angle θ with the vertical. The sign and magnitude of q-

(a) positive with magnitude mg/E

(b) positive with magnitude (mg/E) tanθ

(c) negative with magnitude mg/E tanθ

(d) positive with magnitude E tanθ/mg

51. A free electron and a free proton are placed between two oppositely charged parallel plates. Both are closer to the positive plate than the negative plate.

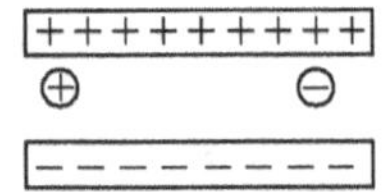

Which of the following statements is true?

I. The force on the proton is greater than the force on the electron.

II. The potential energy of the proton is greater than that of the electron.

III. The potential energy of the proton and the electron is the same.

(a) I only   (b) II only

(c) III and I only   (d) II and I only

<h2 align="center">Case Study</h2>

Read the following paragraph and answers the questions:

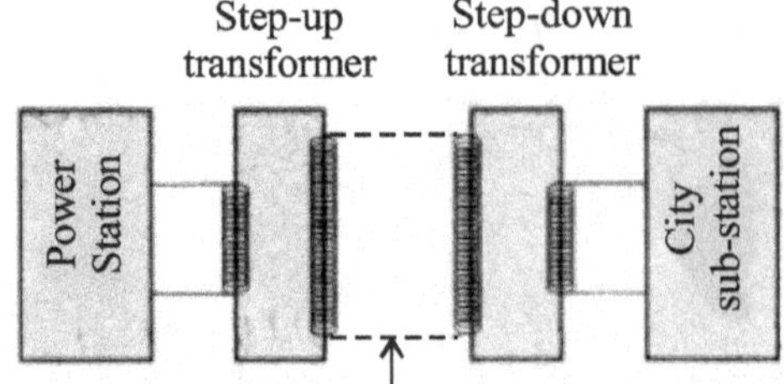

Long distance power transmissions

The large-scale transmission and distribution of electrical energy over long distances is done with the use of transformers. The voltage output of the generator is stepped-up. It is then transmitted over long distances to an area sub-station near the consumers. There the voltage is stepped down. It is further stepped down at distributing sub-stations and utility poles before a power supply of 240 V reaches our homes.

52. Which of the following statement is true?

(a) Energy is created when a transformer steps up the voltage

(b) A transformer is designed to convert an AC voltage to DC voltage

(c) Step–up transformer increases the power for transmission

(d) Step–down transformer decreases the AC voltage

53. If the secondary coil has a greater number of turns than the primary,

(a) the voltage is stepped-up (Vs > Vp) and arrangement is called a step-up transformer

(b) the voltage is stepped-down (Vs < Vp) and arrangement is called a step-down transformer

(c) the current is stepped-up (Is > Ip) and arrangement is called a step-up transformer

(d) the current is stepped-down (Is < Ip) and arrangement is called a step-down transformer

54. We need to step-up the voltage for power transmission, so that

(a) the current is reduced and consequently, the I^2R loss is cut down

(b) the voltage is increased, the power losses are also increased

(c) the power is increased before transmission is done

(d) the voltage is decreased so V^2/R losses are reduced

55. A power transmission line feeds input power at 2300 V to a step down transformer with its primary windings having 4000 turns. The number of turns in the secondary in order to get output power at 230 V are

(a) 4   (b) 40   (c) 400   (d) 4000

Solutions

1 **(c)** As all other statements are correct. In uniform electric field equipotential surfaces are never concentric spheres but are planes $\perp$ to Electric field lines.

2. **(c)** Let P is the observation point at a distance r from $-2q$ and at $(L+r)$ from $+8q$.

Given now, net EFI at $P = 0$

$\therefore \vec{E}_1$ = EFI (Electric Field Intensity) at P due to $+8q$

$\vec{E}_2$ = EFI (Electric Field Intensity) at P due to $-2q$

$\left|\vec{E_1}\right| = \left|\vec{E_2}\right|$

$\therefore \dfrac{k(8q)}{(L+r)^2} = \dfrac{k(2q)}{r^2}$

$\therefore \dfrac{4}{(L+r)^2} = \dfrac{1}{(r)^2}$

$4r^2 = (L+r)^2 \Rightarrow 2r = L+r$

$r = L$

$\therefore$ P is at $x = L + L = 2L$ from origin

3. **(b)** $W = pE(\cos\theta_1 - \cos\theta_2)$

$\theta_1 = 0°$

$\theta_2 = 90°$

$W = pE(\cos 0° - \cos 90°)$

$= pE(1-0) = pE$

4. **(b)** $\dfrac{1}{C_{series}} = \dfrac{1}{C_1} + \dfrac{1}{C_2} + \dfrac{1}{C_3}$

$= \dfrac{1}{2} + \dfrac{1}{3} + \dfrac{1}{6}$

$\dfrac{3+2+1}{6} = \dfrac{6}{6}$

$C_{series} = 1\ \mu F$

5. **(a)**

$Q_1 \underline{\hspace{2cm}} Q_2$ $K = 5$

      r

$F = \dfrac{1}{4\pi\varepsilon_0 k} \dfrac{Q_1 Q_2}{r^2}$

$Q_1 \underline{\hspace{2cm}} Q_2$ force in the charges in the air is

$F' = \dfrac{1}{4\pi\varepsilon_0} \dfrac{Q_1 Q_2}{r^2}$

$= K F = 5 F$

6. **(d)** All other statements except (d) are in correct. The electric field over the Gaussian surface remains continuous and uniform at every point.

7. **(c)**

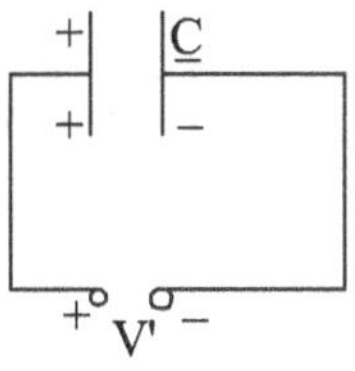

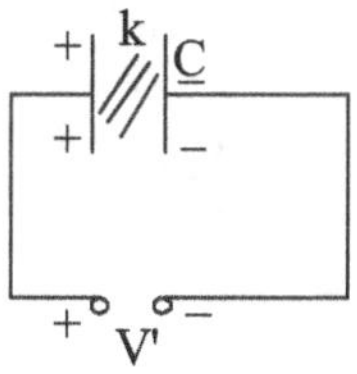

Battery is disconnected.

Q = Charge remains context

$C' = KC$

$Q' = C'V'$

$Q = C'V'$

$Q = KCV'$

$V' = \dfrac{Q}{KC} = \dfrac{V}{K}$

8. **(a)** Potentiometer

9. **(c)** $8 : 27$

$l_1 : l_2 = 3 : 2$

$r_1 : r_2 = 2 : 3$

$I_1 : I_2 = ?$

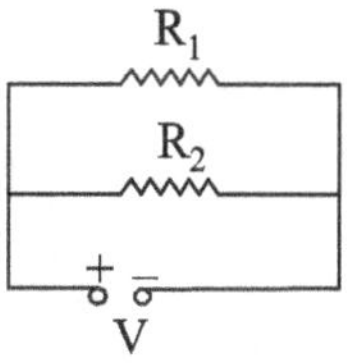

$R_1 = \rho \dfrac{l_1}{\pi r_1^2}$

$R_2 = \rho \dfrac{l_2}{\pi r_2^2}$

$\dfrac{R_1}{R_2} = \dfrac{l_1}{l_2} \dfrac{\pi r_2^2}{\pi r_1^2} = \dfrac{l_1}{l_2} \times \dfrac{r_2^2}{r_1^2}$

$= \dfrac{3}{2} \times \left(\dfrac{3}{2}\right)^2 = \dfrac{(3)^3}{(2)^3} = \dfrac{27}{8}$

$\therefore \dfrac{I_1}{I_2} = \dfrac{V/R_1}{V/R_2} = \dfrac{R_2}{R_1} = 8/27$

10. **(c)** Specific resistance of a conductor increases and for a semiconductor decreases with increase in temperature because for a conductor, a temperature.

coefficient of resistivity $\alpha = +ve$ and for a semiconductor, $\alpha = -ve$

11. **(a)** Alloys have low temperature coefficient of resistivity and high specific resistance. If α = low, the value of 'R' with temperature will not change much and specific resistance is high then required length of the wire will be less.

12. **(c)**

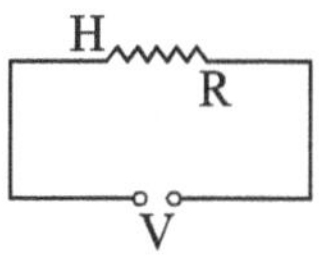

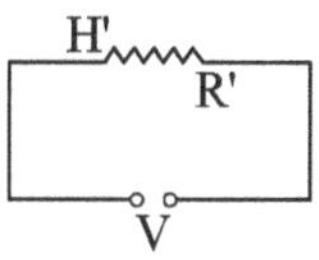

$R = \rho \dfrac{l}{A}$ $R' = \rho \dfrac{2l}{\pi(2r)^2}$

$R = \rho \dfrac{l}{\pi r^2}$ $R' = \rho \dfrac{2l}{\pi 4r^2}$

$H = \dfrac{V^2}{R} t \ \& \ H' = \dfrac{V^2}{R^1} t$ $\because V = $ constant

$$\frac{H'}{H} = \frac{V^2}{R'}\frac{R}{V^2}\frac{t}{t}$$

$$= \frac{R}{R'} = \rho \frac{1}{\pi r^2}\frac{2\pi r^2}{\rho l}$$

$$\frac{H'}{H} = \frac{2}{1} \quad \therefore H' = 2H$$

13. (b) We know

$$V_d = \frac{eE}{ml}\overline{\tau} = e\frac{V}{ml}\overline{\tau}$$

If temperature is kept constant, relaxation time $\overline{\tau}$ - will remain constant, and e, m are also constants.

$$V_d \propto V$$
$$V_d \propto 2V$$

14. (c) Redrawing the circuit, we get

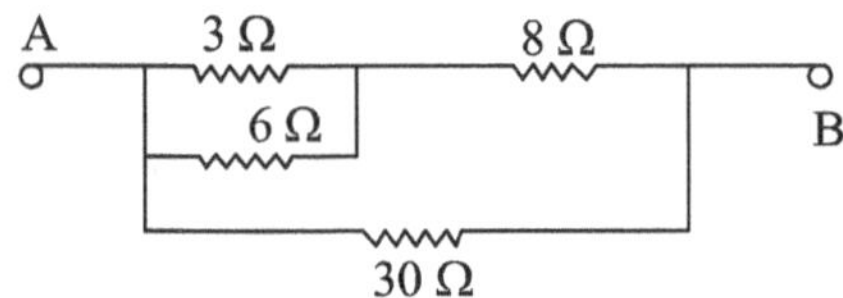

$$30\,\Omega$$

17. (c) l = length of wire

Area of a Square	**Area of a Circle**

$$= a^2 \qquad\qquad = \pi r^2$$

Also here $l = 4a$ Also here, $2\pi r = l$

$$a = \frac{l}{4} \qquad\qquad r = \frac{l}{2\pi}$$

$$\therefore \text{Area} = \frac{l^2}{16} \qquad \text{Now Area} = \pi\left(\frac{l}{2\pi}\right)^2$$

$$A_1 = \frac{l^2}{16} \qquad\qquad A_2 = \frac{l^2}{4\pi}$$

Now Magnetic moment = I A

$$\therefore M_1 = IA, \ \& \ M_2 = I A_2$$

Since I (current) is same in both

$$\therefore \frac{M_1}{M_2} = \frac{A_1}{A_2} = \frac{l^2}{16} \cdot \frac{4\pi}{l^2} = \frac{\pi}{4}$$

$$M_1 M_2 = \pi : 4$$

3Ω & 6Ω are in parallel.

$$\therefore R_1 = \frac{3\times 6}{3+6} = \frac{18}{9} = 2\Omega$$

Now R_1 and 8Ω in series
$$\therefore R_2 = R_1 + 8 = 2 + 8 = 10\Omega$$

Now R_2 and 30Ω in parallel

$$R_{eq} = \frac{R_2 \times 30}{R_2 + 30} = \frac{10\times 30}{10+30}$$

$$= \frac{300}{40} = \frac{30}{4} = \frac{15}{2}$$

$$= 7.5\Omega$$

15. (b) We know

$$B = \frac{F}{Il\sin\theta}$$

SI Unit of $B = \dfrac{N}{Am} = NA^{-1}m^{-1}$

16. (d) The coil of a moving coil galvanometer is wound over metallic frame to provide electromagnetic damping so it becomes dead beat galvanometer.

18. (a) Target law $B_v = B_H \tan\delta$

$$\tan\delta = \frac{B_v}{B_H}$$

Given $B_H = \sqrt{3}\,B_v$

$$\tan\delta = \frac{Bv}{\sqrt{3}\,Bv} = \frac{1}{\sqrt{3}}$$

$$\delta = 30° \text{ or } \frac{\pi}{6} \text{ radians.}$$

19. (d) Correct option is Magnetic declination or Angle of declination. It is the small angle between geographic axis & magnetic axis.

20. (b) Mutual inductance of a pair of two coils depends on the relative position and orientation of two coils, other statements are incorrect.

21. (d) Current induced is $I = \dfrac{|e|}{R}$

Now $|e| = \dfrac{d\phi}{dt}$

But there is no change of flux with time, as $\vec{B}, \vec{A}$ & θ all remain constant with time.

$\therefore$ No current is induced.

22. (b) $\phi = 5t^2 + 3t + 16$

$|e| = \dfrac{d\phi}{dt}$

$= \dfrac{d}{dt}[5t^2 + 3t + 16]$

$= 10t + 3$

$|e|_{t=4} = 10(4) + 3 = 43V$

$e = -43\,\text{Volts}$

23. (c) $I = \dfrac{V}{X_c}$ in Pure Capacitor

$= \dfrac{V}{\dfrac{1}{2\pi fc}} = V\,2\pi fc$

$\Rightarrow I \alpha f$

other parameters kept constant

24. (a)

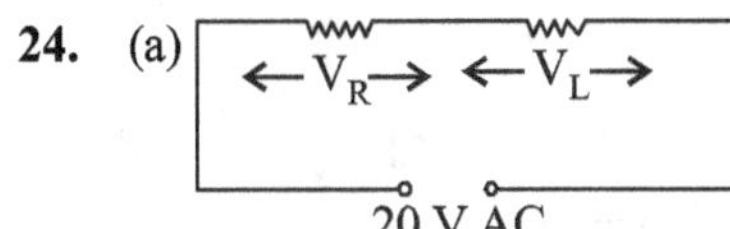

V_R = Effective Voltage across R

$\therefore V_R = I_{eff} R$

V_L = Effective Voltage across L

$V_L = I_{eff} \times L$

Net $V = \sqrt{V_R^2 + V_L^2}$

$= \sqrt{I_{eff}^2 R^2 + I_{eff}^2 \times L^2}$

$20 = \sqrt{(12)^2 + V_L^2} \Rightarrow (20)^2 = (12)^2 + V_L^2 \Rightarrow 400 = 144 + V_L^2$

$V_L = \sqrt{400 - 144} = \sqrt{256} = 16\,\text{Volts}$

25. (d) $E = E_0 \sin \omega t$

$I = I_0 \sin\left(\omega t + \dfrac{\pi}{3}\right)$

As i can lead the voltage in RC and LCR circuit, so it can be RC or LCR circuit.

26. (a) Since −ve electric flux

= + ve flux electric flux enclosed

with a cylinder here

$\therefore$ Total Electric

Flux = 0.

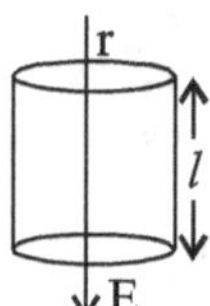

27. (d) Surface Charge density, $\sigma = 26.4 \times 10^{-12}\,\dfrac{C}{m^2}$

$E = \dfrac{\sigma}{2\varepsilon_0} + \dfrac{\sigma}{2\varepsilon_0}$

$= \dfrac{2\sigma}{2\varepsilon_0} + \dfrac{\sigma}{\varepsilon_0}$

$= \dfrac{26.4 \times 10^{-12}}{8.85 \times 10^{-12}}\,\dfrac{N}{C} = 3\dfrac{N}{C}$

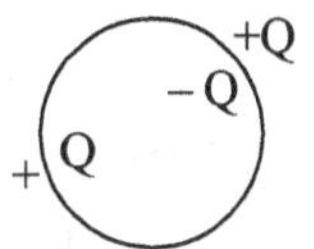

28. (d) Equal and opposite charges appear on the nearby conductor due to induction, but still net charge on the conductor is zero.

29. (c) Net E F I at G $\neq$ O

Net Potential at G,

$V = \dfrac{K2Q}{r} - \dfrac{KQ}{r} - \dfrac{KQ}{r} = 0$

30. (c)

$C_x = \dfrac{\varepsilon_0 A}{d}$ $C_y = \dfrac{2\varepsilon_0 A}{d}$

$$U_x = \frac{Q^2}{2C_x} \quad U_y = \frac{Q^2}{2C_y}$$

$$\therefore \frac{U_x}{U_y} = \frac{C_y}{C_x} = \frac{2C_x}{C_x} = \frac{2}{1}$$

31. (d) As primary coil made of thick copper wire has very less R. Therefore negligible power loss. Rest all options are reasons for power losses in a transformer.

32. (b)

$$X_c = \frac{1}{2\pi fc} = \frac{1}{\omega c} \downarrow \text{ i.e. } X_c \downarrow$$

$I \uparrow \therefore$ Brightness of the bulb will $\uparrow$.

33. (d) As all other statements seem incorrect in context with the given figure.

34. (d) Rest all quantities change with area of cross-section of a conductor.

35. (c) Given,

$I = 2\,A, R_2 = 3\,\Omega, P_3 = 6\,W$

Power across $R_3 = V_3 I$

$6\,W = I^2 R_3$

$$\frac{6}{4} = R_3 = \frac{3}{2} = 1.5\,\Omega$$

$V_3 = I R_3 = 2\,(1.5) = 3\,V$

36. (a) $I = O, V = E, \therefore E = 5.6\,V$

$$r = \frac{E}{I} = \frac{5.6}{2.0} = 2.8\,\Omega$$

37. (d) Let PQ is a potentiometer wore of length 10m,

$$I = \frac{E}{R + R'} = \frac{5}{480 + 20} = \frac{5}{500}$$

$$= \frac{1}{100} = 0.01\,A$$

$V_{PQ} = I R_{PQ} = 0.01 \times 20 = 0.2\,V$

If 10 m potentiometer wire balances $= 0.2\,V$

Then 1 m potentiometer wire balances $= \dfrac{0.2}{10}\,V$

Then 6 m potentiometer wire balances $= \dfrac{0.2}{10} \times 6\,V$

$$= \frac{1.2}{10} = 0.12\,V$$

38. (d) Given, $\quad I'_g = I_g + \dfrac{20}{100} I_g$

$$= \frac{120}{100} I_g = 1.2 I_g$$

$$R' = R + \frac{25}{100} R = \frac{125}{100} R$$

$$= 1.25\,R$$

$V'_g = ?$

$$V'_g = \frac{I'_g}{R'} = \frac{1.2 I_g}{1.25 R}$$

$$= \frac{120}{125} V_g = \frac{25}{25} V_g$$

% change $= \dfrac{V'_g - V_g}{V_g} \times 100$

$$= \frac{\left(\dfrac{24}{25} V_g - V_g\right)}{V_g} \times 100$$

$$= \frac{(24 - 25)}{25} \times 100$$

$$= \frac{-1}{25} \times 100 = 4\%$$

Decrease by 4%.

39. (a) Let F_1 is force per unit, length between A & C

$$\therefore \text{ i.e. } F_1 = \frac{\mu_0}{4\pi} \frac{2I \times I}{2r}$$

And F_2 is force per unit, length between B & C

$$\therefore \quad F_2 = \frac{\mu_0}{4\pi} \frac{I \times I}{r}$$

Now net force on 'C' is per unit length

$$F_1 + F_2 = \frac{\mu}{4\pi} \frac{I^2}{r} (1 + 1)$$

$$= \frac{2\mu_0}{4\pi} \frac{I^2}{r} = F \text{ (given)}$$

$F'_1 = $ Repulsive force between A & C

$$= \frac{\mu_0}{4\pi} \frac{2I^2}{2r}$$

$F'_2 = F_2 = $ A reactive force between B & C

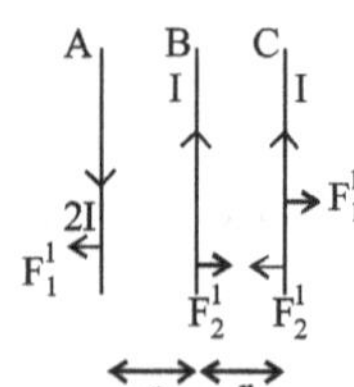

$\therefore$ Net force on 'C' $F_1' - F_2' = 0$

$\because$ $\qquad F_1' = F_2' = \dfrac{\mu}{4\pi} \dfrac{2I^2}{2r}$

$\therefore$ Net Force on 'C' is zero.

40. (b) $R = 0.5$ Å

$\omega = 10$ rps $= 10 \times 2\pi$ rad/s

$\nu = 10$ Hz

$M = IA = e\nu\pi r^2$

$= 1.6 \times 10^{-19} \times 10 \times 3.14 \times 0.5 \times 0.5 \times 10^{-10} \times 10^{-10}$

$= 1.256 \times 10^{-38}$ Am^2

41. (b) Magnetic field inside a solenoid

$$B = \mu_0 \dfrac{N}{l} I'$$

Flux linked with 'N' turns

Initial flux $\phi_1 = NBA = N\mu_0 \dfrac{N}{l} IA$

$$= \mu_0 \dfrac{N^2}{l} IA$$

$$= \dfrac{4\pi \times 10^{-7} \times 800 \times 800 \times 2.5 \times 2.5 \times 10^{-4}}{0.30}$$

$= 16.74 \times 10^{-3}$ Wb

Final flux $\phi_2 = 0$

Average back emf $|e| = \dfrac{d\phi}{dt} = \dfrac{16.74 \times 10^{-3} - 0}{10^{-3}}$

$= 16.74$ V

42. (c) $V_0 = 283$ V, $f = 50$ Hz

$R = 3\,\Omega$, $L = 25.48$ mH

$C = 796\,\mu$F

$P|_{\text{at resonance}} = ?$

Power dissipated $P = I^2 R$

$$I = \dfrac{I_0}{\sqrt{2}} = \dfrac{1}{\sqrt{2}}\left(\dfrac{283}{3}\right)$$

$= 66.7$ A

$P = I^2 R$

$= (66.7)^2 3$

$= 13.35$ kW

43. (d) Let flux linked with smaller loop is ϕ_1 and with bigger loop is ϕ_2.

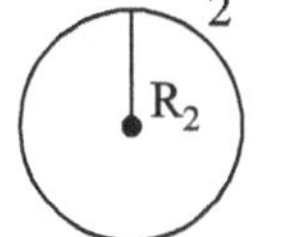

Given $R_2 = 0.2$ m

$R_1 = 0.003$ m

$x = 15$ cm $= 0.15$ m

Now $\phi_1 = B_2 A_1$

$$= \dfrac{\mu_0}{4\pi}\left[\dfrac{2\pi R_2^2 I_2}{(R_2^2 + x^2)^{3/2}}\right] \pi R_1^2$$

$$M = \dfrac{\phi_1}{I_2} = \dfrac{\mu_0}{4\pi} \dfrac{2\pi R_2^2 \pi R_1^2}{(R_2^2 + x^2)^{3/2}}$$

Now $\phi_2 = MI_1$

$$= \dfrac{\mu_0}{4\pi} \dfrac{2\pi R_2^2 \pi R_1^2}{(R_2^2 + x^2)^{3/2}} \cdot I_1$$

$= 9.1 \times 10^{-11}$ Weber

44. (b) $L = \mu_0 \dfrac{N^2}{l} A$

$$L' = \mu_0 \dfrac{(2N)^2}{2l} A$$

$$= 2\mu_0 \dfrac{N^2}{l} A = 2L$$

45. (d) As both statements are false. To increase the range of an ammeter, suitable low R (or shunt) should be connected in parallel to it. The ammeter with increased range has low resistance.

46. (c) Statements correct but reason is wrong because electrons move from a region of low potential to high potential.

47. (a) The given statement is correct and reason is the correct explanation of the above statement. At poles, magnetic needle orients itself vertically because horizontal components of earth's field is zero there.

48. (b) We know $\dfrac{mv^2}{r} = Bqv \sin\theta = Bqv \sin\theta$

Centripetal force = magnetic lorentz force

$\sin\theta = \sin 90° = 1$ ($\angle$ between $\vec{V}\,\&\,\vec{B} = 90°$)

$$\dfrac{mv^2}{r} = Bqv$$

$$\dfrac{mv}{r} = Bq$$

$$r = \dfrac{mv}{Bq} = \dfrac{p}{Bq} = \dfrac{\text{linear momentum}}{Bq}$$

Since $r = \dfrac{p}{Bq}$

Given p, B are same

Also q for proton & electron is same except its sign

$\therefore$ Radius is same. So statement is correct but reason is not the correct explanation of the given assertion.

49. (a) When we increase current sensitivity by increasing no. of turns, then resistance of coil also increases. So increasing current sensitivity does not necessarily imply that voltage sensitivity will increase because $V_g = \dfrac{I_g}{R}$

$\therefore$ if $I_g \uparrow$ & $R \uparrow$ by different amounts, then V_g may increase or decrease.

50. (b) $F_e = mg \tan\theta$

$qE = mg \tan\theta$

$q = \left(\dfrac{mg}{E}\right) \tan\theta$

$\tan\theta = \dfrac{F_e}{mg}$

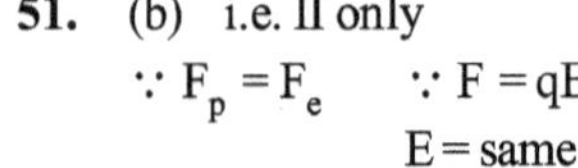

51. (b) i.e. II only

$\because F_p = F_e \qquad \because F = qE$

$E = $ same

$'q' = $ same

Now, $P\varepsilon = qV(r)$

$(P.\,\varepsilon)_p > (P.\,\varepsilon)_e$

52. (d) i.e. step down transformer decreases the ac voltage.

53. (a) i.e. $= \dfrac{N_s}{N_p} = \dfrac{E_s}{E_p}$

i.e. if no. of turns in secondary coil are more than no. of turns in primary, then voltage is increased or stepped up in secondary, so called step up transformer.

54. (a) i.e. current is reduced if voltage is stepped – up so corresponding I^2R losses are cut down.

55. (c) Given $E_i = 2300V$

$E_0 = 230\,V$

$N_p = 4000$

$N_s = ?$

$\dfrac{E_i}{E_0} = \dfrac{N_p}{N_s} \Rightarrow \dfrac{2300}{230} = \dfrac{4000}{x}$

$x = 400 = N_s = $ No. of turns in secondary coil

CBSE Board Solved Paper

Time Allowed : 3 Hours   *Maximum Marks : 70*

General Instructions:

(i) This question paper comprises four sections - A, B, C and D.

(ii) There are **37** questions in the question paper. All questions are compulsory.

(iii) Section A : Q. no. **1** to **20** are very short-answer questions and carry 1 mark each.

(iv) Section B : Q. no. **21** to **27** are short-answer questions and carry 2 marks each.

(v) Section C : Q. no. **28** to **34** are long-answer questions and carry 3 marks each.

(vi) Section D : Q. no. **35** to **37** are also long answer questions and carry 5 marks each.

(vii) There is no overall choice. However, an internal choice has been provided in two questions of one mark, two questions of two marks, one questions of three marks and all the three questions of five marks weightage. You have to attempt only one of the choices in such questions.

(viii) However, separate instructions are given with each section and question, wherever necessary.

(ix) Use of calculators and log tables is not permitted.

(x) You may use the following values of physical constants wherever necessary.

$c = 3 \times 10^8$ m/s

$h = 6.63 \times 10^{-34}$ Js

$e = 1.6 \times 10^{-19}$ C

$\mu_0 = 4\pi \times 10^{-7}$ T m A^{-1}

$\varepsilon_0 = 8.854 \times 10^{-12}$ C^2 N^{-1} m^{-2}

$\dfrac{1}{4\pi\varepsilon_0} = 9 \times 10^9$ N m^2 C^{-2}

Mass of electron (m$_e$) = 9.1×10^{-31} kg

Mass of neutron = 1.675×10^{-27} kg

Mass of proton = 1.673×10^{-27} kg

Avogadro's number = 6.023×10^{23} per gram mole

Boltzmann constant = 1.38×10^{-23} JK^{-1}

SECTION - A

Note: *Select the most appropriate option from those given below each question:*

1. If the net electric flux through a closed surface is zero, then we can infer
   (a) no net charge is enclosed by the surface.
   (b) uniform electric field exists within the surface.
   (c) electric potential varies from point to point inside the surface.
   (d) charge is present inside the surface.

2. An electric dipole consisting of charges $+q$ and $-q$ separated by a distance L is in stable equilibrium in a uniform electric field $\vec{E}$. The electrostatic potential energy of the dipole is
   (a) qLE
   (b) zero
   (c) $-qLE$
   (d) $-2\,qEL$

3. A potentiometer can measure emf of a cell because
   (a) the sensitivity of potentiometer is large.
   (b) no current is drawn from the cell at balance.
   (c) no current flows in the wire of potentiometer at balance.
   (d) internal resistance of cell is neglected.

4. Two resistors R_1 and R_2 of 4 Ω and 6 Ω are connected in parallel across a battery. The ratio of power dissipated in them, $P_1 : P_2$ will be
   (a) $4 : 9$
   (b) $3 : 2$
   (c) $9 : 4$
   (d) $2 : 3$

5. The magnetic dipole moment of a current carrying coil does **not** depend upon
   (a) number of turns of the coil.
   (b) cross-sectional area of the coil.
   (c) current flowing in the coil.
   (d) material of the turns of the coil.

6. Larger aperture of objective lens in an astronomical telescope
   (a) increases the resolving power of telescope.
   (b) decreases the brightness of the image.
   (c) increases the size of the image.
   (d) decreases the length of the telescope.

7. A biconvex lens of glass having refractive index 1.47 is immersed in a liquid. It becomes invisible and behaves as a plane glass plate. The refractive index of the liquid is
   (a) 1.47   (b) 1.62
   (c) 1.33   (d) 1.51

8. For a glass prism, the angle of minimum deviation will be smallest for the light of
   (a) red colour.   (b) blue colour.
   (c) yellow colour.   (d) green colour.

9. Which of the following statements is **not** correct according to Rutherford model ?
   (a) Most of the space inside an atom is empty.
   (b) The electrons revolve around the nucleus under the influence of coulomb force acting on them.
   (c) Most part of the mass of the atom and its positive charge are concentrated at its centre.
   (d) The stability of atom was established by the model.

10. Photons of energies 1 eV and 2 eV are successively incident on a metallic surface of work function 0.5 eV. The ratio of kinetic energy of most energetic photoelectrons in the two cases will be
    (a) 1 : 2   (b) 1 : 1
    (c) 1 : 3   (d) 1 : 4

Note: *Fill in the blanks with appropriate answer :*

11. The magnetic field and angle of dip at a place on the earth are 0.3 G and 30°, respectively. The value of vertical component of the earth's magnetic field at the place is __________.

12. Laminated iron sheets are used to minimize ________ currents in the core of a transformer.

13. The number of turns of a solenoid are doubled without changing its length and area of cross-section. The self-inductance of the solenoid will become __________ times.

14. According to Bohr's atomic model, the circumference of the electron orbit is always an ________ multiple of de Broglie wavelength.

OR

In β-decay, the parent and daughter nuclei have the same number of ______________.

15. A ray of light on passing through an equilateral glass prism, suffers a minimum deviation equal to the angle of the prism. The value of refractive index of the material of the prism is ________.

Note: *Answer the following :*

16. Write the mathematical form of Ampere-Maxwell circuital law.

17. How does an increase in doping concentration affect the width of depletion layer of a *p-n* junction diode?

18. The nuclear radius of $^{27}_{13}\text{Al}$ is 3.6 fermi. Find the nuclear radius of $^{64}_{29}\text{Cu}$.

OR

A proton and an electron have equal speeds. Find the ratio of de Broglie wavelengths associated with them.

19. The variation of the stopping potential (V_0) with the frequency (v) of the light incident on two different photosensitive surfaces M_1 and M_2 is shown in the figure. Identify the surface which has greater value of the work function.

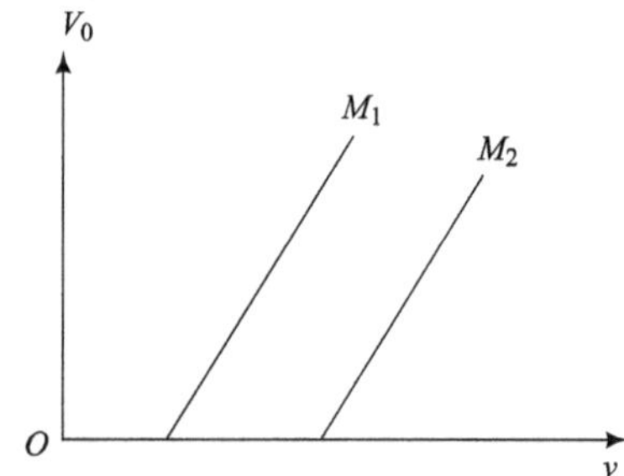

20. Why cannot we use Si and Ge in fabrication of visible LEDs?

21. Explain the principle of working of a meter bridge. Draw the circuit diagram for determination of an unknown resistance using it.

22. The space between the plates of a parallel plate capacitor is completely filled in two ways. In the first case, it is filled with a slab of dielectric constant K. In the second case, it is filled with two slabs of equal thickness and dielectric constants K_1 and K_2 respectively as shown in the figure. The capacitance of the capacitor is same in the two cases. Obtain the relationship between K, K_1 and K_2.

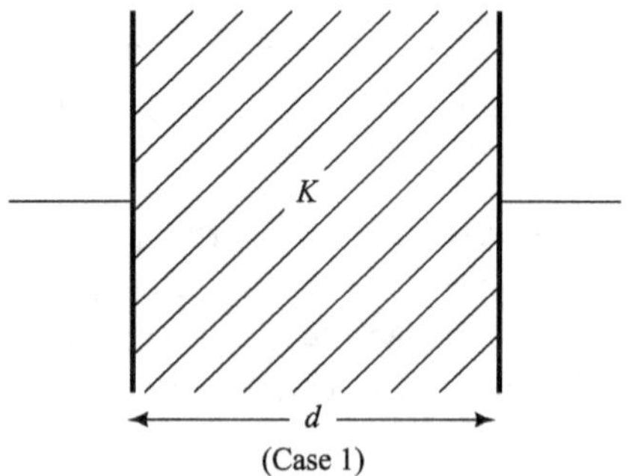

(Case 1)

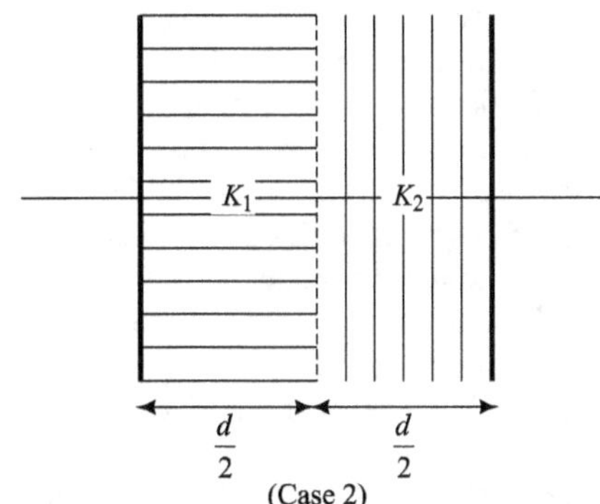

(Case 2)

23. Define the term 'Half-life' of a radioactive substance. Two different radioactive substances have half-lives T_1 and T_2 and number of undecayed atoms at an instant N_1 and N_2, respectively. Find the ratio of their activities at that instant.

24. Define wavefront of a travelling wave. Using Huygens principle, obtain the law of refraction at a plane interface when light passes from a denser to rarer medium.

OR

Using lens maker's formula, derive the thin lens formula $\dfrac{1}{f} = \dfrac{1}{v} - \dfrac{1}{u}$ for a biconvex lens.

25. Two long straight parallel wires A and B separated by a distance d, carry equal current I flowing in same direction as shown in the figure.

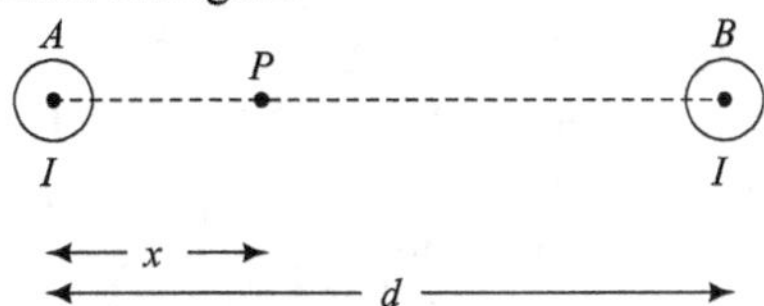

(a) Find the magnetic field at a point P situated between them at a distance x from one wire.

(b) Show graphically the variation of the magnetic field with distance x for $0 < x < d$.

26. Using Bohr's atomic model, derive the expression for the radius of nth orbit of the revolving electron in a hydrogen atom.

OR

(a) Write two main observations of photoelectric effect experiment which could only be explained by Einstein's photoelectric equation.

(b) Draw a graph showing variation of photocurrent with the anode potential of a photocell.

27. Explain the terms 'depletion layer' and 'potential barrier' in a p-n junction diode. How are the (a) width of depletion layer, and (b) value of potential barrier affected when the p-n junction is forward biased?

SECTION - C

28. (a) Two cells of emf E_1 and E_2 have their internal resistances r_1 and r_2 respectively. Deduce an expression for the equivalent emf and internal resistance of their parallel combination when connected across an external resistance R. Assume that the two cells are supporting each other.

(b) In case the two cells are identical, each of emf $E = 5$ V and internal resistance $r = 2\Omega$, calculate the voltage across the external resistance $R = 10\ \Omega$.

29. (a) Write an expression of magnetic moment associated with a current (I) carrying circular coil of radius r having N turns.

(b) Consider the above mentioned coil placed in YZ plane with its centre at the origin. Derive expression for the value of magnetic field due to it at point $(x, 0, 0)$.

OR

(a) Define current sensitivity of a galvanometer. Write its expression.

(b) A galvanometer has resistance G and shows full scale deflection for current I_g.

   (i) How can it be converted into an ammeter to measure current upto $I_0\ (I_0 > I_g)$?

   (ii) What is the effective resistance of this ammeter?

30. A resistance R and a capacitor C are connected in series to a source $V = V_0 \sin \omega t$.

Find :

(a) The peak value of the voltage across the (i) resistance and (ii) capacitor.

(b) The phase difference between the applied voltage and current. Which of them is ahead?

31. What is the effect on the interference fringes in Young's double slit experiment due to each of the following operations? Justify your answers.

(a) The screen is moved away from the plane of the slits.

(b) The separation between slits is increased.

(c) The source slit is moved closer to the plane of double slit.

32. (a) Write the expression for the speed of light in a material medium of relative permittivity ε_r and relative magnetic permeability μ_r.

(b) Write the wavelength range and name of the electromagnetic waves which are used in (i) radar systems for aircraft navigation, and (ii) Earth satellites to observe the growth of the crops.

33. The nucleus $^{235}_{92}Y$, initially at rest, decays into $^{231}_{90}X$ by emitting an α-particle

$$^{235}_{92}Y \longrightarrow\ ^{231}_{90}X + ^{4}_{2}He\ + \text{energy}.$$

The binding energies per nucleon of the parent nucleus, the daughter nucleus and α-particle are 7.8 MeV, 7.835 MeV and 7.07 MeV, respectively. Assuming the daughter nucleus to be formed in the unexcited state and neglecting its share in the energy of the reaction, find the speed of the emitted α-particle. (Mass of α-particle = 6.68×10^{-27} kg)

34. (a) Draw circuit diagram and explain the working of a zener diode as a dc voltage regulator with the help of its I-V characteristic.

(b) What is the purpose of heavy doping of p- and n-sides of a zener diode?

SECTION - D

35. (a) Using Gauss law, derive expression for electric field due to a spherical shell of uniform charge distribution σ and radius R at a point lying at a distance x from the centre of shell, such that

(i) $0 < x < R$, and

(ii) $x > R$.

(b) An electric field is uniform and acts along $+x$ direction in the region of positive x. It is also uniform with the same magnitude but act in $-x$ direction in the region of negative x. The value of the field is $E = 200$ N/C for $x > 0$ and $E = -200$ N/C for $x < 0$. A right circular cylinder of length 20 cm and radius 5 cm has its centre at the origin and its axis along the x-axis so that one flat face is at $x = +10$ cm and the other is at $x = -10$ cm.

Find:

(i) The net outward flux through the cylinder.

(ii) The net charge present inside the cylinder.

OR

(a) Find the expression for the potential energy of a system of two point charges q_1 and q_2 located at $\vec{r_1}$ and $\vec{r_2}$, respectively in an external electric field $\vec{E}$.

(b) Draw equipotential surfaces due to an isolated point charge $(-q)$ and depict the electric field lines.

(c) Three point charges $+1$ μC, -1 μC and $+2$ μC are initially infinite distance apart. Calculate the work done in assembling these charges at the vertices of an equilateral triangle of side 10 cm.

36. (a) Derive the expression for the torque acting on the rectangular current carrying coil of a galvanometer. Why is the magnetic field made radial ?

(b) An α-particle is accelerated through a potential difference of 10 kV and moves along x-axis. It enters in a region of uniform magnetic field $B = 2 \times 10^{-3}$ T acting along y-axis. Find the radius of its path. (Take mass of α-particle $= 6.4 \times 10^{-27}$ kg)

OR

(a) With the help of a labelled diagram, explain the working of a step-up transformer. Give reasons to explain the following :

(i) The core of the transformer is laminated.

(ii) Thick copper wire is used in windings.

(b) A conducting rod PQ of length 20 cm and resistance 0.1 Ω rests on two smooth parallel rails of negligible resistance AA' and CC'. It can slide on the rails and the arrangement is positioned between the poles of a permanent magnet producing uniform magnetic field $B = 0.4$ T. The rails, the rod and the magnetic field are in three mutually perpendicular directions as shown in the figure. If the ends A and C of the rails are short circuited, find the

(i) external force required to move the rod with uniform velocity $v = 10$ cm/s, and

(ii) power required to do so.

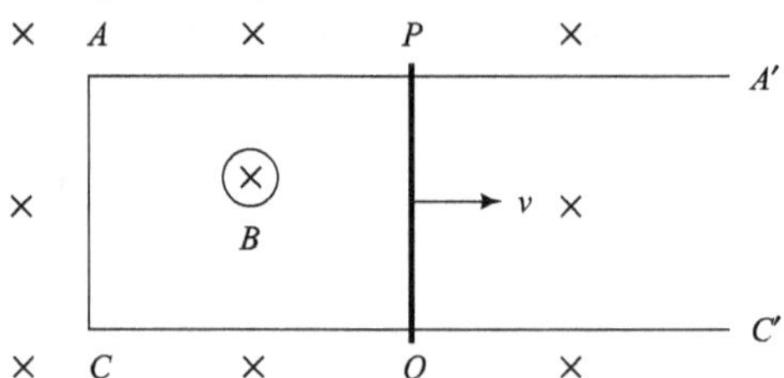

37. (a) Draw the ray diagram of an astronomical telescope when the final image is formed at infinity. Write the expression for the resolving power of the telescope.

(b) An astronomical telescope has an objective lens of focal length 20 m and eyepiece of focal length 1 cm.

(i) Find the angular magnification of the telescope.

(ii) If this telescope is used to view the Moon, find the diameter of the image formed by the objective lens. Given the diameter of the Moon is 3.5×10^6 m and radius of lunar orbit is 3.8×10^8 m.

OR

(a) An object is placed in front of a concave mirror. It is observed that a virtual image is formed. Draw the ray diagram to show the image formation and hence derive the mirror equation $\dfrac{1}{f} = \dfrac{1}{u} + \dfrac{1}{v}$.

(b) An object is placed 30 cm in front of a plano-convex lens with its spherical surface of radius of curvature 20 cm. If the refractive index of the material of the lens is 1.5, find the position and nature of the image formed.

Solutions

SECTION - A

1. Option (a) is correct.

According to Gauss's theorem

$$\phi = \frac{\Sigma q_{in}}{\varepsilon_0}$$

So, electric flux through a closed surface is zero if $\Sigma\, q_{in} = 0$ i.e. electric flux is zero if not net charge is enclosed by surface.

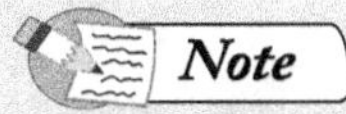

Note

Electric field in $\oint \vec{E}\cdot\vec{dA}$ is complete electric field. It may be partly due to charge within the surface and partly due to charge outside the surface. If there is no charge enclosed in the Gaussian surface, then $\oint \vec{E}\cdot\vec{dA} = 0$.

The electric field due to a charge outside the Gaussian surface contributes zero net flux through the surface because as many lines due to that charge enter the surface as leave it.

2. Option (c) is correct.

Potential energy of a dipole in external field U is given as

$$U = -\vec{P}\cdot\vec{E}$$

For stable equilibrium $\theta = 0°$

So, $U = -p\,E \cos 0° = -pE$

$\therefore \qquad U = -qLE$

3. Option (b) is correct.

At balance, no current flow through cell

So, EMF of cell = Potential difference between A and J

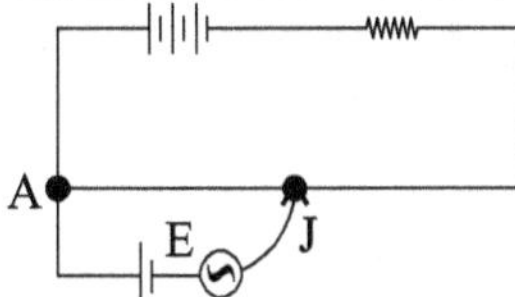

4. Option (b) is correct.

We have, $P_1 = \dfrac{V^2}{R_1}$ and $P_2 = \dfrac{V^2}{R_2}$

So, $\dfrac{P_1}{P_2} = \dfrac{R_2}{R_1} = \dfrac{6}{4} = \dfrac{3}{2}$

5. Option (d) is correct.

For a current carrying coil, magnetic moment is given as

$M = NiA$

i.e. $M \propto N$

$M \propto i$

and, $M \propto A$

So, 'M' is independent of material of turns.

6. Option (a) is correct.

Resolving power of telescope, R.P. $= \dfrac{a}{1.22\lambda}$ where a = aperture of objective lens.

7. Option (a) is correct.

If $\mu_{lens} = \mu_{liquid}$ then lens immersed in liquid becomes invisible.

8. Option (a) is correct.

Angle of minimum deviation δ is given as

$$\delta = (\mu - 1)A$$

Now $\qquad \lambda_{red} > \lambda_{violet}$

$\therefore \qquad \mu_{red} < \mu_{violet}$

So δ_{red} is smallest.

9. Option (d) is correct.

Rutherford suggested that the electrons revolve around the nucleus in a circular path. But any charged particle in circular motion undergoes acceleration and radiate energy. So, the electron would eventually lose energy and finally fall into the nucleus making the atom highly unstable. Thus, his model could not explain atom's stability.

10. Option (c) is correct.

We have,

$K.E.$ = Photon energy − Work function.

$\therefore \qquad \dfrac{K.E_1}{K.E_2} = \dfrac{1-0.5}{2-0.5} = \dfrac{0.5}{1.5} = \dfrac{1}{3}$

11. Vertical component of magnetic field B_V is given as

$\qquad B_V = B \sin \delta$, where δ = angle of dip

Given $\qquad B = 0.3$

$\qquad\qquad \delta = 30°$

$\therefore \qquad B_V = 0.3 \sin 30°$

or, $\qquad B_V = 0.15$ G

12. Laminations about the transformer's core give small gaps in between, which enhances the coil's resistance. This resistance will decrease the total current and thus hold the eddy current losses.

13. Self-inductance of a long solenoid is given as

$$L = \frac{\mu_0 N^2 A}{l}$$

$\therefore \qquad L \propto N^2$

So, the self inductance of the solenoid will become *4 times.*

14. According to Bohr's atomic model, magnitude of the electron's angular momentum is quantized.

i.e., $L = mvr = n\left(\dfrac{h}{2\pi}\right)$ where n is an integer (n = 1, 2, 3 .....)

$\Rightarrow 2\pi r(\text{circumference}) = n\left(\dfrac{h}{mv}\right) = n\left(\dfrac{h}{p}\right)$

$\Rightarrow 2\pi r = n\lambda$

So, circumference of electron orbit is integral multiple of de-Broglie wavelength.

OR

Nucleons (neutrons + protons)

15. Here $\qquad A = 60°\ \delta = 60°$

As, $\mu = \dfrac{\sin\left(\dfrac{A+\delta_{min}}{2}\right)}{\sin\dfrac{A}{2}} \Rightarrow \mu = \dfrac{\sin 60°}{\sin 30°}$

$\therefore\ \mu = \sqrt{3}.$

16. Mathematical form of ampere-Maxwell circuital law

$$\oint_l \vec{B}.\overrightarrow{dl} = \mu_0\left[I + \varepsilon_0\dfrac{d\phi_E}{dt}\right] \qquad \textbf{(1 Mark)}$$

17. An increase in doping concentration decrease the width of depletion layer of *a p-n* junction diode. **(1 Mark)**

18. Using, $R = R_0\,A^{1/3}$

$$\dfrac{R_2}{R_1} = \left(\dfrac{A_2}{A_1}\right)^{1/3} \qquad \textbf{(½ Mark)}$$

$$\Rightarrow R_2 = R_1\left(\dfrac{A_2}{A_1}\right)^{1/3}$$

$$R_2 = 3.6\left(\dfrac{64}{27}\right)^{1/3} = 3.6\left(\dfrac{4}{3}\right) \qquad \textbf{(½ Mark)}$$

$$\Rightarrow R_2 = 4.8 \text{ fermi}$$

OR

de Broglie wavelength $\lambda = \dfrac{h}{P} = \dfrac{h}{mv}$ **(½ Mark)**

$$\dfrac{\lambda_p}{\lambda_e} = \dfrac{h/m_p v_p}{h/m_e v_e}$$

Given $\qquad v_p = v_e$

$$\therefore \qquad \dfrac{\lambda_p}{\lambda_e} = \dfrac{m_e}{m_p} \qquad \textbf{(½ Mark)}$$

19. From the graph, we can conclude that M_2 will have greater value of work function due to higher value of threshold frequency. **(1 Mark)**

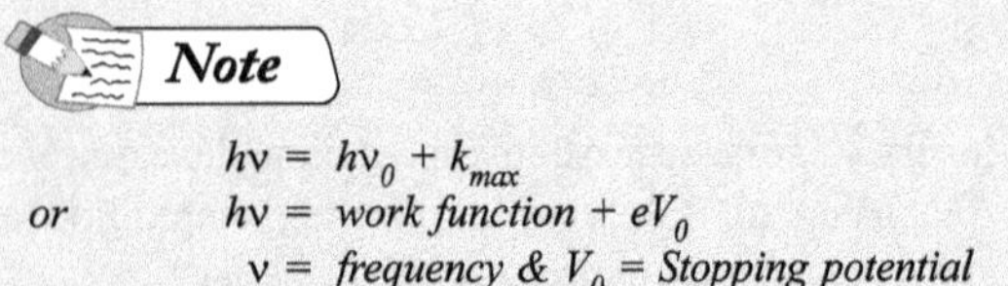

20. For visible LEDs, the band gap of semiconductor must be within 1.8 eV to 3 eV. But the band gap of Ge and Si is less than 1.8 eV. So, they cannot be used to fabricate visible LEDs. **(1 Mark)**

SECTION - B

21. Working principle of meter bridge:
The working principle of meter bridge is based on wheatstone bridge. It is an arrangement of four resistances

used to determine one of these resistances quickly in terms of the remaining three resistances. **(½ Mark)**
When the bridge is balanced,

$$\dfrac{R}{S} = \dfrac{l}{100-l}\ ;\ l = \text{balanced length.} \textbf{(½ Mark)}$$

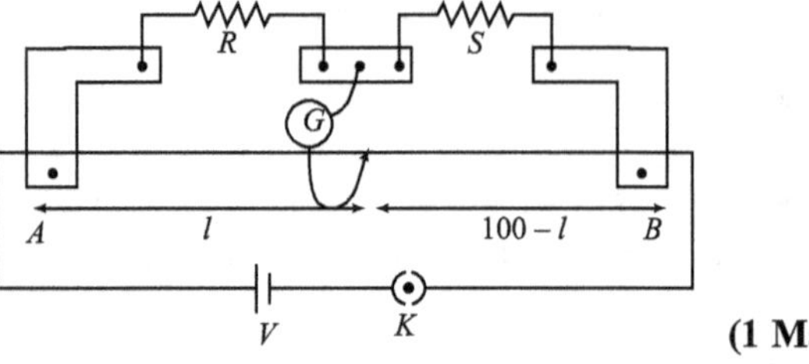

(1 Mark)

22. Capacitance of capacitor in case *I*

$$C_1 = \dfrac{K\varepsilon_0 A}{d.} \qquad \textbf{(½ Mark)}$$

For, case 2, the capacitor are connected in series. Therefore equivalent capacitance would be

$$\dfrac{1}{C_2} = \dfrac{1}{\dfrac{K_1\varepsilon_0 A}{d/2}} + \dfrac{1}{\dfrac{K_2\varepsilon_0 A}{d/2}} \qquad \textbf{(½ Mark)}$$

$$\Rightarrow \dfrac{1}{C_2} = \dfrac{d}{2\varepsilon_0 A}\left[\dfrac{1}{K_1} + \dfrac{1}{K_2}\right]$$

$$\Rightarrow C_2 = \dfrac{2\varepsilon_0 A}{d}\left[\dfrac{K_1 K_2}{K_1 + K_2}\right] \qquad \textbf{(½ Mark)}$$

Given that $C_1 = C_2$

$$\therefore \qquad \dfrac{k\varepsilon_0 A}{d} = \dfrac{2\varepsilon_0 A}{d}\left[\dfrac{K_1 K_2}{K_1 + K_2}\right]$$

$$\boxed{K = \left[\dfrac{2K_1 K_2}{K_1 + K_2}\right]} \qquad \textbf{(½ Mark)}$$

23. *Half-life:* The time-interval in which one half of the undecayed nuclei originally present in radioactive sample becomes radioactive is called half-life of the radioactive substance. **(1 Mark)**

Activity $\qquad R = \lambda N$

$$\therefore \qquad \dfrac{R_1}{R_2} = \dfrac{\lambda_1}{\lambda_2} \times \dfrac{N_1}{N_2}$$

We know that,

$$\lambda = \dfrac{0.693}{T_{1/2}} \qquad \textbf{(½ Mark)}$$

$$\therefore \qquad \dfrac{\lambda_1}{\lambda_2} = \dfrac{(T_{1/2})_2}{(T_{1/2})_1}$$

$$\Rightarrow \qquad \dfrac{R_1}{R_2} = \dfrac{(T_{1/2})_2}{(T_{1/2})_1} \times \dfrac{N_1}{N_2} = \left(\dfrac{T_2}{T_1}\right)\left(\dfrac{N_1}{N_2}\right) \textbf{(½Mark)}$$

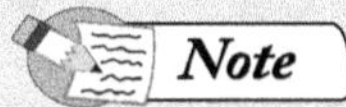

Note

The activity of a radioactive substance decreases as the number of undecayed nuclei decreases with time.

$$\text{Activity } (R) \propto \frac{1}{\text{Half-life } (T_{1/2})}$$

24. *Wavefront: A* locus of the points which oscillates in the same phase is called a wavefront. Thus, *a* wavefront is defined as *a* surface of constant phase. **(½ Mark)**

Law of refraction at rarer medium

Consider a plane wavefront *AB* incident on a plane surface, separating two media 1 and 2. Let v_1 and v_2 be the velocities of light in the two media with $v_2 > v_1$.

According to Huygen's principle, every point on the wavefront AB is a source of secondary wavelet. Let the secondary wavelets from B strike the surface AC at C in t seconds

$$\therefore BC = v_1 t \qquad \text{(½ Mark)}$$

In time 't', the secondary wavelet from A will travel a distance $v_2 t$ in the rarer medium bacause the valocity of light in rarer medium is v_2 with A as centre and $C_2 \times t$ as radius, draw an arc D.

$$\therefore AD = v_2 \times t \qquad \text{(½ Mark)}$$

From point C, draw a plane tangent to the secondary wavelet D. Then CD is the refracted wavefront.

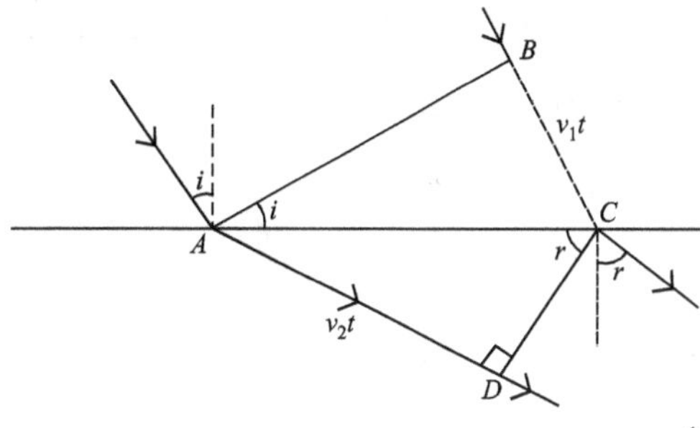

(1 Mark)

We have, $\sin i = \dfrac{BC}{AC} = \dfrac{v_1 t}{AC}$

$$\sin r = \dfrac{AD}{AC} = \dfrac{v_2 t}{AC}$$

$$\therefore \frac{\sin i}{\sin r} = \frac{v_1}{v_2} = \frac{\mu_2}{\mu_1} = {}^1\mu_2$$

This proves Snell's law of reflection. **(1 Mark)**

OR

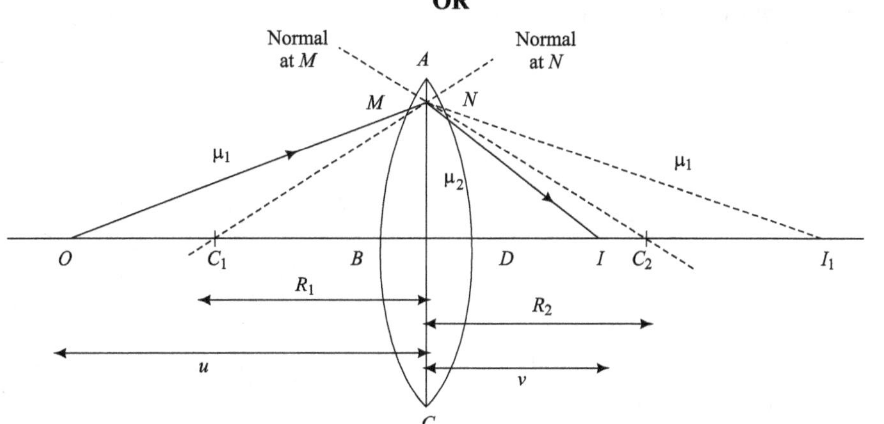

(½ Mark)

For refraction at surface *ABC*, we have

$$\frac{\mu_2}{v_1} - \frac{\mu_1}{u} = \frac{\mu_2 - \mu_1}{R_1} \qquad \text{...(1)}$$

For refraction at surface *ADC*, we have

$$\frac{\mu_1}{v} - \frac{\mu_2}{v_1} = \frac{\mu_1 - \mu_2}{R_2} \qquad \text{...(2)}$$

adding equation (1) and (2), we get

$$\frac{\mu_1}{v} - \frac{\mu_1}{u} = (\mu_2 - \mu_1)\left[\frac{1}{R_1} - \frac{1}{R_2}\right] \qquad \text{(½ Mark)}$$

$$\frac{1}{v} - \frac{1}{u} = \left[\frac{(\mu_2 - \mu_1)}{\mu_1}\right]\left[\frac{1}{R_1} - \frac{1}{R_2}\right] \qquad \text{...(3)}$$

If the object is placed at infinity ($u = \infty$), the image will be formed at the focus, *i.e.* $v = f$

Therefore

$$\frac{1}{f} - \frac{1}{\infty} = (\mu_{21} - 1)\left[\frac{1}{R_1} - \frac{1}{R_2}\right]$$

$$\frac{1}{f} = (\mu_{21} - 1)\left[\frac{1}{R_1} - \frac{1}{R_2}\right] \qquad \text{...(4)} \ \text{(½ Mark)}$$

From eq. (3) and (4), we have

$$\frac{1}{v} - \frac{1}{u} = \frac{1}{f} \rightarrow \text{Thin lens formula. (½ Mark)}$$

25. (a)

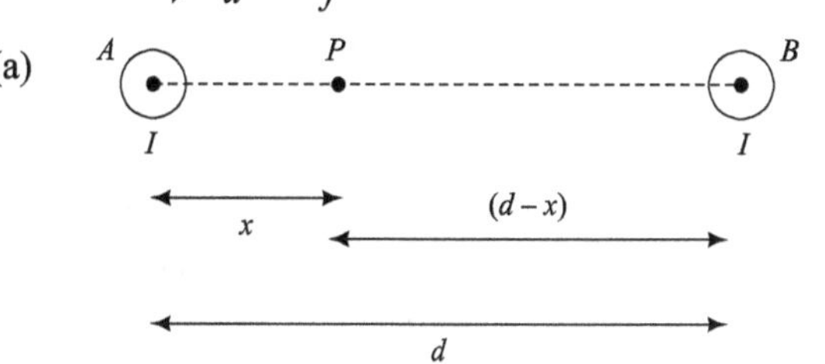

Field at P due to wire at A

$$\vec{B}_A = \frac{\mu_0 I}{2\pi x} \text{ (upward)}$$ **(½ Mark)**

Field at P due to wire at B

$$\vec{B}_B = \frac{\mu_0 I}{2\pi(d-x)} \text{ (downward)}$$ **(½ Mark)**

Therefore, total field at P

$$\vec{B} = \vec{B}_A + \vec{B}_B$$

$$\Rightarrow \quad \vec{B} = \frac{\mu_0 I}{2\pi x} - \frac{\mu_0 I}{2\pi(d-x)}$$

$$\Rightarrow \quad \vec{B} = \frac{\mu_0 I}{2\pi}\left[\frac{1}{x} - \frac{1}{d-x}\right]$$

$$\Rightarrow \quad \vec{B} = \frac{\mu_0 I}{2\pi}\left[\frac{d-x-x}{x(d-x)}\right]$$

$$\Rightarrow \quad \vec{B} = \frac{\mu_0 I(d-2x)}{2\pi x(d-x)} \text{ upward.}$$ **(½ Mark)**

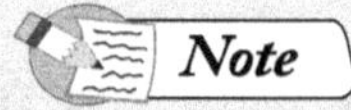

Note

The value of Magnetic field at a point on the centre of separation of two linear parallel conductors carrying equal currents in the same direction is zero.

(b)

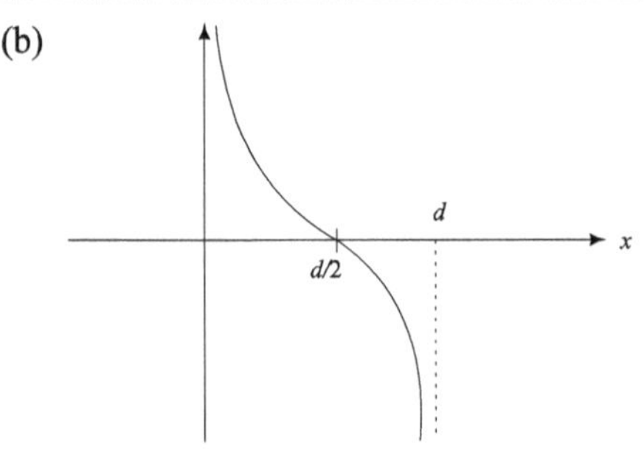

(½ Mark)

26. The electrostatic force of attraction between nucleus and the electron is

$$F = \frac{KZe.e}{r^2}$$

$$\Rightarrow \quad F = \frac{KZe^2}{r^2}$$ **(½ Mark)**

To keep the electron in its orbit, the centripetal force on the electron must be equal to the electrostatic attraction. Therefore,

$$\frac{mv^2}{r} = \frac{KZe^2}{r^2}$$

$$\Rightarrow \quad r = \frac{KZe^2}{mv^2} \quad \text{...(1)}$$ **(½ Mark)**

$m =$ mass of electron

$v =$ speed of electron

According to Bohr's quantisation condition for angular momentum,

$$L = mvr = \frac{nh}{2\pi}$$

$$\Rightarrow \quad r = \frac{nh}{2\pi mv} \quad \text{...(2)}$$ **(½ Mark)**

From (1) and (2)

$$v = \frac{2\pi KZe^2}{nh}$$

Putting the value of v in eqn (2), we get

$$\boxed{r = \frac{n^2 h^2}{4\pi^2 mKZe^2}}$$ **(½ Mark)**

OR

(a) The two main observation of photoelectric effect experiment which could only be explained by Einstein's photoelectric equations are:

(i) The photoelectric emission is an instantaneous process i.e. there is no time lag between emission of electron and falling of light.

(ii) For a given photosensitive material, there exist a certain minimum cut-off frequency below which no photoelectrons are emitted, howsoever high is the intensity of incident radiations. This frequency is called threshold frequency. **(½ × 2 = 1 Mark)**

(b)

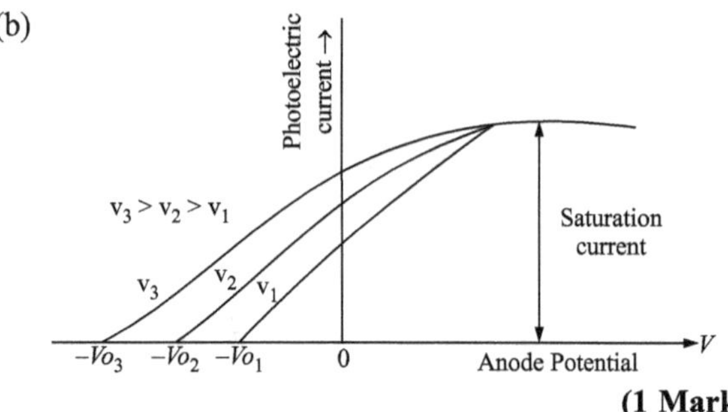

(1 Mark)

27. *Potential barrier:* The accumulation of negative charges in the *p*-region and positive charges in the *n*-region sets up a potential difference across the junction. This act as a barrier and is called barrier potential. **(½ Mark)**

Depletion layer: It is a layer of immobile ion formed near the p-n junction by diffusion of majority charge carriers and electron hole recombination. **(½ Mark)**

(a) Width of depletion layer decreases in forward bias. **(½ Mark)**

(b) The value of potential barrier reduces in forward bias. **(½ Mark)**

28. (a) From the circuit, we can write

$$V_1 = E_1 - I_1 r_1 \quad \text{...(1)}$$

$$V_2 = E_2 - I_2 r_2 \quad \text{...(2)}$$

Since E_1 and E_2 are parallel

$$V_1 = V_2 = V$$

and

$$I = I_1 + I_2$$

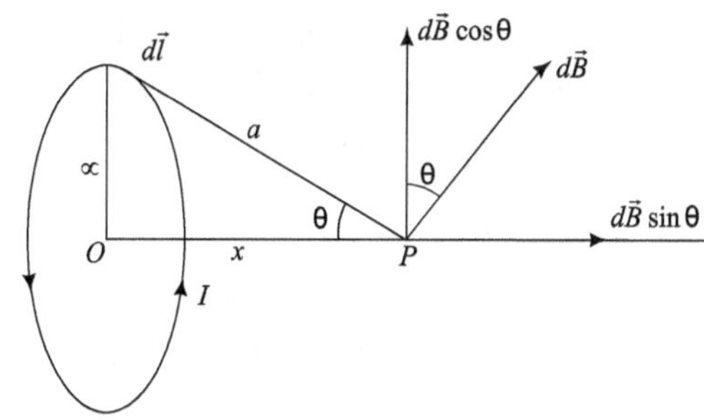

From (1),

$$I_1 = \frac{E_1 - V}{r_1} \qquad \textbf{(½ Mark)}$$

From (2)

$$I_2 = \frac{E_2 - V}{r_2} \qquad \textbf{(½ Mark)}$$

Similarly, for equivalent cell

$$I = \frac{E_{eq} - V}{r_{eq}}$$

$$\therefore \qquad I = I_1 + I_2$$

$$\frac{E_{eq} - V}{r_{eq}} = \left(\frac{E_1}{r_1} + \frac{E_2}{r_2}\right) - V\left[\frac{1}{r_1} + \frac{1}{r_2}\right] \quad \textbf{(½ Mark)}$$

$$\frac{E_{eq}}{r_{eq}} - V\left[\frac{1}{r_{eq}}\right] = \left[\frac{E_1 r_2 + E_2 r_1}{r_1 r_2}\right] - V\left[\frac{1}{r_1} + \frac{1}{r_2}\right]$$

$$\therefore \qquad \frac{1}{r_{eq}} = \frac{1}{r_1} + \frac{1}{r_2}$$

and

$$E_{eq} = r_{eq}\left[\frac{E_1 r_2 + E_2 r_1}{r_1 r_2}\right]$$

$$E_{eq} = \left[\frac{E_1 r_2 + E_2 r_1}{r_1 + r_2}\right] \qquad \textbf{(½ Mark)}$$

(b) Given $E_1 = E_2 = 5$ V

$$r_1 = r_2 = 2\ \Omega$$

$$\therefore \qquad E_{eq} = \frac{5 \times 2 + 5 \times 2}{2 + 2} = \frac{20}{4} = 5\ \text{V}$$

$$r_{eq} = \frac{r_1 r_2}{r_1 + r_2} = \frac{4}{4} = 1\ \Omega \qquad \textbf{(½ Mark)}$$

$$I = \frac{E_{eq}}{R + r_{eq}} = \frac{5}{10 + 1} = \frac{5}{11}\ \text{A}$$

Voltage across $R \Rightarrow V = IR$

$$V = \frac{5}{11} \times 10 = \frac{50}{11}\ \text{V} \qquad \textbf{(½ Mark)}$$

29. (a) Magnetic moment associated with a current carrying circular coil of radius r having N turns,

$$\vec{M} = NI(\pi r^2)\,\hat{n} \qquad \textbf{(1 Mark)}$$

(b)

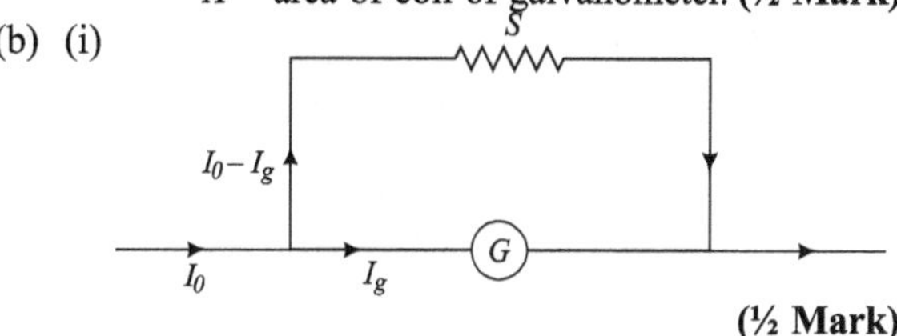

(½ Mark)

From Biot-savart law, the magnetic field at point $P(x, 0, 0)$ due to current element $\vec{dl}$,

$$\vec{dB} = \frac{\mu_0}{4\pi}\frac{I\,dl\sin 90°}{a^2} \qquad \textbf{(½ Mark)}$$

Now, the vertical component $\vec{dB}\cos\theta$ will cancel out by symmetrically opposite $\vec{dl}$ element.

So, $\vec{B}$ at $P \Rightarrow B = \int dB\sin\theta$

$$B = \frac{\mu_0 I}{4\pi a^2}\sin\theta\int dl$$

Now $\quad \int dl = 2\pi r$

$$\therefore \qquad B = \frac{\mu_0 I}{4\pi a^2} \times \frac{r}{a} \times 2\pi r \quad \left[\because \sin\theta = \frac{r}{a}\right] \textbf{(½ Mark)}$$

$$B = \frac{\mu_0 I r^2}{2a^3}$$

$$\vec{B} = \frac{\mu_0 I r^2}{2(r^2 + x^2)^{3/2}}\,\hat{i}.$$

For coil having N turns,

$$\vec{B} = \frac{\mu_0 I N r^2}{2(r^2 + x^2)^{3/2}}\,\hat{i}. \qquad \textbf{(½ Mark)}$$

OR

(a) Current sensitivity

It is defined as the deflection produced in the galvanometer when a unit current flows through it.

(½ Mark)

Current sensitivity $I_C = \dfrac{NBA}{K}$

Where　N = no. of turns in the coil

　　　　B = Magnetic field

　　　　A = area of coil of galvanometer. **(½ Mark)**

(b) (i)

(½ Mark)

Galvanometer can be converted into ammeter by connecting a shunt (small resistance) S with parallel to galvanometer.

Let I_0 be the maximum current that can be measured then at $I = I_0$, current through galvanometer is I_g, where I_g = maximum current that can be passed through galvanometer.

As galvanometer and shunt are connected in parallel, so,

Potential across G = Potential across the S

$$I_g\,G = (I_0 - I_g)S$$

$$\therefore \quad S = \frac{I_g}{I_0 - I_g}G. \qquad \textbf{(½ Mark)}$$

(ii) Effective resistance of this ammeter will be

$$\frac{1}{R_A} = \frac{1}{G} + \frac{1}{S}$$

$$R_A = \frac{GS}{G+S}. \qquad \textbf{(1 Mark)}$$

Note

Shunt can be used to convert any galvanometer into ammeter of desired range.

It protects the galvanometer coil from burning.

30. (a)

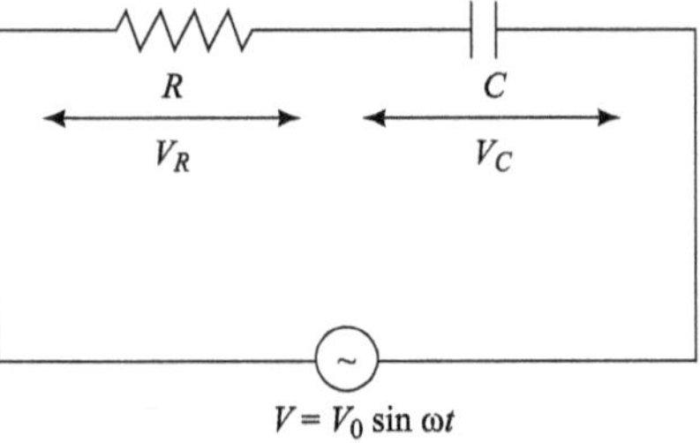

Total impedance of circuit

$$Z = \sqrt{R^2 + X_C^{\,2}} \qquad \textbf{(½ Mark)}$$

$\therefore$ Current in circuit

$$I = \frac{V_0}{\sqrt{R^2 + X_C^2}} \qquad \textbf{(½ Mark)}$$

Peak voltage across

(i) Resistance R

$$V_R = IR = \frac{V_0 R}{\sqrt{R^2 + X_C^2}} \qquad \textbf{(½ Mark)}$$

(ii) Capacitor C

$$V_C = I X_C$$
$$= \frac{V_0 X_C}{\sqrt{R^2 + X_C^2}} \qquad \textbf{(½ Mark)}$$

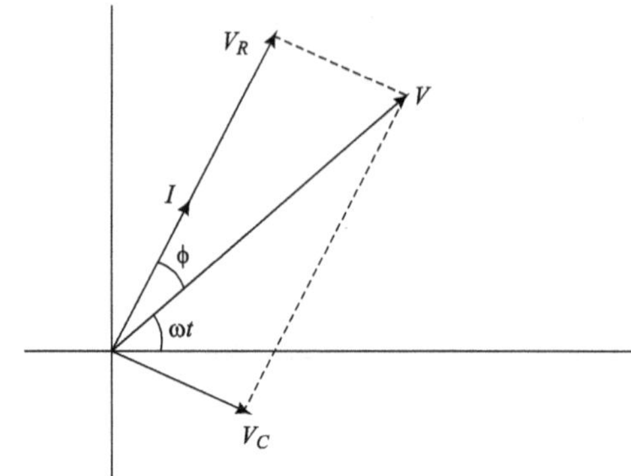

$\textbf{(½ Mark)}$

(b) $\tan \phi = \dfrac{V_C}{V_R} \Rightarrow \phi = \tan^{-1}\!\left(\dfrac{V_C}{V_R}\right) = \tan^{-1}\!\left(\dfrac{X_C}{R}\right)$

$\therefore$ Phase difference between V and I is $\tan^{-1}\!\left(\dfrac{X_C}{R}\right)$

$\textbf{(½ Mark)}$

31. (a) Fringe width $\beta = \dfrac{\lambda D}{d}$

Since $\beta \propto D$, the fringe width will increase, as screen is moved away. **(1 Mark)**

(b) $\beta \propto \dfrac{1}{d}$, therefore fringe width will decrease, as separation between slits is increased. **(1 Mark)**

(c) Let s be the width of the source slit and S its distance from plane of two slit. For interference fringes to be distinctly seen, the condition

$$\frac{s}{S} < \frac{\lambda}{d}$$

should be satisfied, otherwise, the interference patterns produced will overlap. **(1 Mark)**

Note

Fringe width is the separation between any two consecutive bright or dark fringes.

Angular fringe width $= \dfrac{\lambda}{d} = \dfrac{\beta}{D}$

32. (a) Velocity of light v will be

$$v = \frac{1}{\sqrt{\mu_0 \mu_r \varepsilon_0 \varepsilon_r}}$$

Now, since $c = \dfrac{1}{\sqrt{\mu_0 \varepsilon_0}}$

$$\therefore \quad v = \frac{c}{\sqrt{\mu_r \varepsilon_r}} \qquad \textbf{(1 Mark)}$$

(b) (i) Microwaves – 0.3 m to 10^{-3} m **(1 Mark)**

(ii) Infrared – 5×10^{-3} m to 10^{-6} m **(1 Mark)**

33. Total B.E of $^{235}_{92}Y = 7.8 \times 235 = 1833\ MeV$ (½ Mark)

Total B.E of $^{231}_{90}X = 7.835 \times 231 = 1809.9\ MeV$ (½ Mark)

Total B.E of $^4_2He = 7.07 \times 4 = 28.28\ MeV$ (½ Mark)

Energy released in the decay, Q

$$Q = B.E \text{ of } X + B.E \text{ of } He - B.E \text{ of } Y$$
$$= 1809.9 + 28.28 - 1833 = 5.18\ MeV \text{ (½ Mark)}$$

$K.E$ of a particle, $\dfrac{1}{2}mv^2 = Q$

$\therefore$ Speed, $v = \sqrt{\dfrac{2Q}{m}}$ (½ Mark)

$$v = \sqrt{\dfrac{2 \times 5.18 \times 1.6 \times 10^{-13}}{6.68 \times 10^{-27}}}$$

$$v = 1.58 \times 10^7\ ms^{-1} \quad \text{(½ Mark)}$$

34. (a)

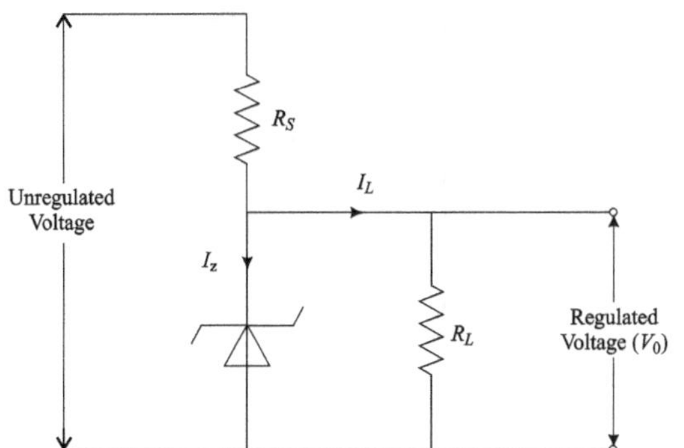

(1 Mark)

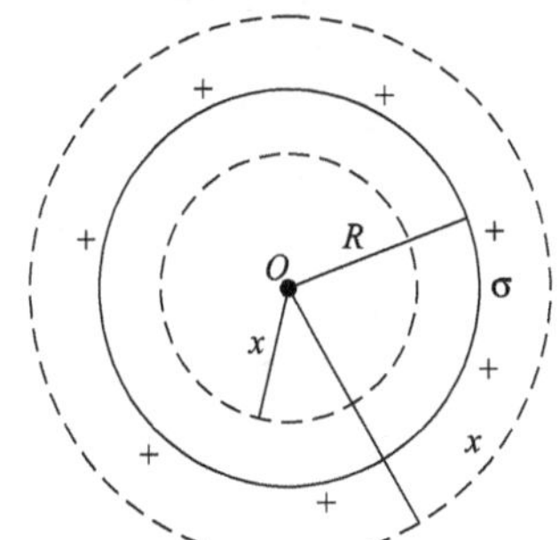

(½ Mark)

Working of a zener diode as voltage regulator: If the voltage across zener diode is greater that breakdown voltage if input voltage increases, the current through R_S and Zener diode also increases. This increases the voltage drop across R_S without any change in the voltage across the zener diode. This is because in the breakdown region, Zener voltage remains constant even though current through the Zener diode changes. Similarly, if the input voltage decreases, the voltage

across R_S decreases without any change in the voltage across the Zener diode. Thus any increase/decrease of the input voltage results in increase/decrease of the voltage drop across R_S without any change in voltage across Zener diode. Hence the Zener diode act as voltage regulator. **(1 Mark)**

(b) Due to heavy doping of P and n sides, the width of junction layer is small and the barrier field is high.

(½ Mark)

Diode can conduct current only in one direction whereas zener diode allows the conduction in both direction. It is a highly doped p-n junction which is not damaged by high reverse current. A normal diode will be permanently damaged for a large reverse current, but a zener diode will not.

35. (a)

(i) $0 < x < R$

As x lies inside the shell, the charge enclosed by the gaussian surface is zero

$$q = 0$$

Flux through the Gaussian surface

$$\phi = E \times 4\pi x^2 \quad \text{(½ Mark)}$$

Applying Gauss's theorem,

$$\phi = \dfrac{q}{\varepsilon_0}$$

$$E \times 4\pi x^2 = 0$$

$\therefore \qquad E = 0$ (½ Mark)

(ii) $x > R$

The total charge q inside the gaussian surface is the charge on the shell of radius R and area $4\pi R^2$.

$\therefore \qquad q = 4\pi R^2 \sigma$ (½ Mark)

Flux through gaussian surface

$$\phi = E \times 4\pi x^2$$

Applying gauss theorem,

$$\phi = \dfrac{q}{\varepsilon_0}$$

$$E \times 4\pi x^2 = \dfrac{4\pi R^2 \sigma}{\varepsilon_0}$$

$$E = \dfrac{\sigma R^2}{\varepsilon_0 x^2} \quad \text{(½ Mark)}$$

(b)

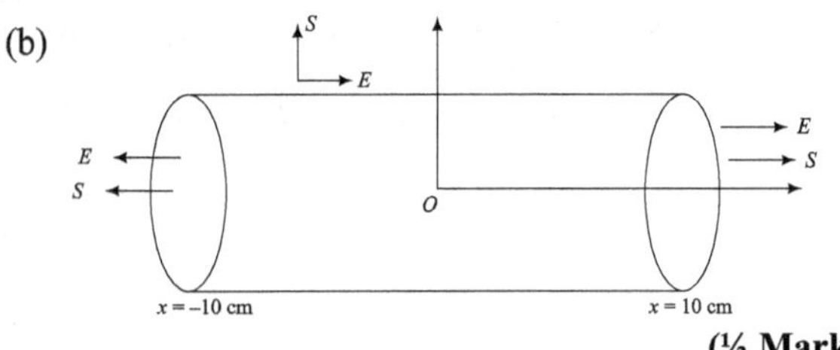

(½ Mark)

(i) Outward flux through left face is

$$\phi = \vec{E}.\Delta\vec{S}$$
$$= +200 \times \pi(0.05)^2\left(-\hat{i}\right).\left(-\hat{i}\right)$$
$$= +1.57 \ Nm^2C^{-1}. \qquad \text{(½ Mark)}$$

Outward flux through right face

$$\phi = \vec{E}.\Delta\vec{S}$$
$$= 200 \times \pi(0.05)^2 \ \hat{i}.\hat{i}$$
$$\phi = +1.57 \ Nm^2C^{-1} \qquad \text{(½ Mark)}$$

Flux through the curved surface of the cylinder

$$\phi = E\Delta S \cos 90° = 0 \qquad \text{(½ Mark)}$$

∴ Net outward flux through the cylinder

$$\phi = 1.57 + 1.57$$
$$= 3.14 \ Nm^2C^{-1} \qquad \text{(½ Mark)}$$

(ii) The net charge inside the cylinder

$$q = \varepsilon_0\phi_E$$
$$= 8.854 \times 10^{-12} \times 3.14$$
$$q = 2.78 \times 10^{-11} \ C \qquad \text{(½ Mark)}$$

OR

(a) Work done to bring q_1 from ∞ in external electric field $\vec{E}$

$$w_1 = q_1 \ V(\vec{r}_1) \qquad \text{(½ Mark)}$$

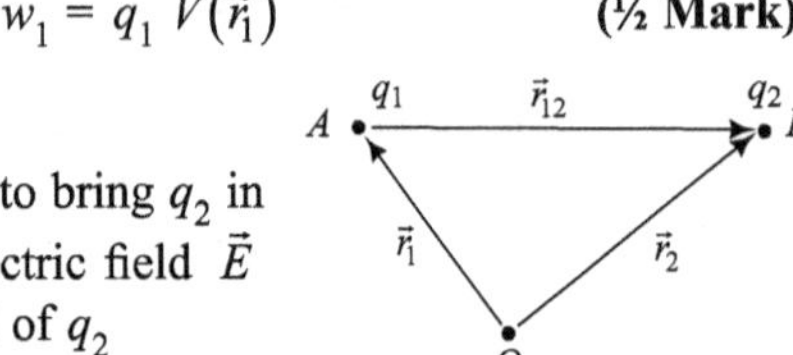

Work done to bring q_2 in external electric field $\vec{E}$ and of field of q_2

$$w_2 = q_2 V(\vec{r}_2) + \frac{Kq_1q_2}{r_{12}} \qquad \text{(1 Mark)}$$

Potential energy of system

$$U = w_1 + w_2$$
$$= q_1 V(\vec{r}_1) + q_2 V(\vec{r}_2) + \frac{Kq_1q_2}{r_{12}} \qquad \text{(½ Mark)}$$

(b)

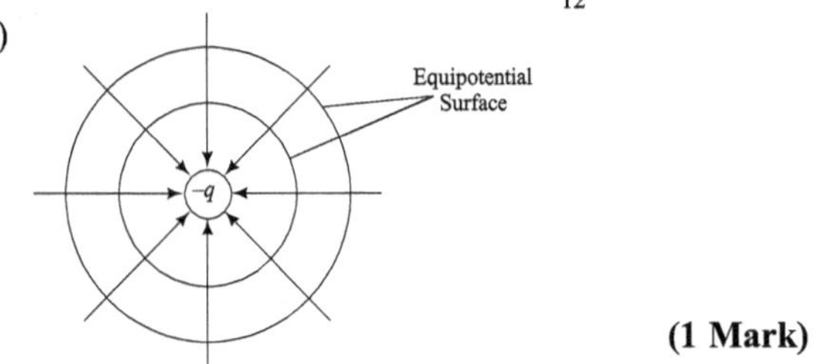

(1 Mark)

The direction of electric field is perpendicular to the equipotential surfaces or lines.
A metallic surface of any shape is an equipotential surface.

(c) Potential energy of the system

$$U = U_{12} + U_{23} + U_{13}$$
$$U = \frac{1}{4\pi\varepsilon_0 r}[q_1q_2 + q_2q_3 + q_1q_3] \qquad \text{(1 Mark)}$$
$$U = \frac{9\times10^9}{10\times10^{-12}}[+1 \times -1 + (+1) \times (+2) + (-1)(+2)] \times 10^{-12}$$
$$U = 9 \times 10^{-2} \ (-1 + 2 - 2)$$
$$U = -0.09 \ J \qquad \text{(1 Mark)}$$

36. (a)

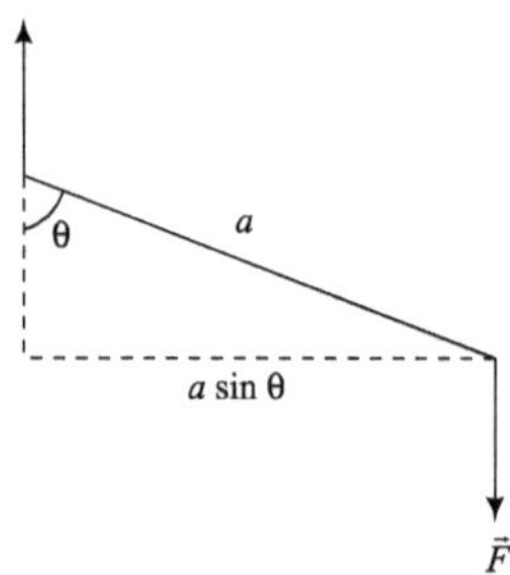

(1 Mark)

As we can see from figure,

   I = current flowing through coil *PQRS*
a, b = sides of rectangular coil *PQRS*
  $A = ab$ = area of the coil
  N = number of turns in the coil.

(½ Mark)

The magnetic forces on sides *PQ* and *SR* are equal, opposite and collinear, so their resultant is zero. According to Fleming's rule, the side *PS* experiences a normal inward force equal to *NIbB* while the side *QR* experiences an equal normal outward force. The two forces on sides *PS* and *QR* are equal and opposite. They form a couple and exert a torque given by

$$\tau = \text{Force} \times \text{Perpendicular distance}$$
$$= NIbB \times a \sin 90°$$
$$= NIB \ (ab)$$

$$\tau = NIBA \quad \textbf{(1½ Mark)}$$

Magnetic field is taken radial in galvanometer coil in order to create $\theta = 90°$ at every orientation of coil in the magnetic field so that current varies linearly with deflection. **(½ Mark)**

(b) Radius of circular path

$$r = \frac{1}{B}\sqrt{\frac{2mV}{q}} \quad \textbf{(1½ Mark)}$$

$$r = \frac{1}{2\times10^{-3}}\sqrt{\frac{2\times6.4\times10^{-27}\times10\times10^{3}}{2\times1.6\times10^{-19}}}$$

$$r = 10 \; m.$$

OR

Working of a step-up transformer:
As the alternating current flows through the primary, it generates an alternating magnetic flux in the core which also passes through the secondary. This changing flux sets up an induced emf in the secondary, also a self-induced emf in the primary. If there is no leakage of magnetic flux, then flux linked with each turn of the primary will be equal to that linked with each turn of the secondary. **(1 Mark)**

(i) Core is laminated to block or minimise the paths of eddy current to minimise heat loss against resistance of core. **(½ Mark)**

(ii) Thick copper wire is used in order to reduce the resistance of transformer coil to minimise heat loss. **(½ Mark)**

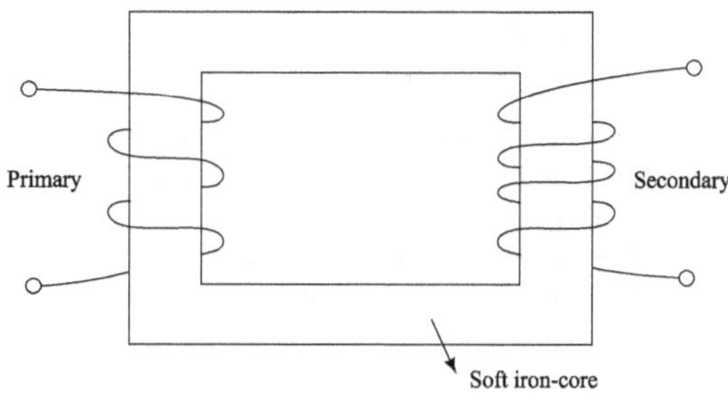

(1 Mark)

> **Note**
>
> *Transformer increases or decreases either a.c. voltage or current but not both simultaneously.*
> *Step-up transformer increases voltage and decreases current. Step-down transformer decreases voltage and increases current.*

(b) (i) Force $F = I\,l\,B$

$$F = \left(\frac{Blv}{R}\right)lB = \frac{B^{2}l^{2}v}{R} \quad \textbf{(½ Mark)}$$

$$= \frac{(0.4)^{2}\times(20\times10^{-2})^{2}\times(10\times10^{-2})}{0.1}$$

$$F = 6.4\times10^{-3}\,N \quad \textbf{(½ Mark)}$$

(ii) Power $P = Fv$ **(½ Mark)**

$$= 6.4\times10^{-3}\times10\times10^{-2}$$

$$= 6.4\times10^{-4}\;\text{watt} \quad \textbf{(½ Mark)}$$

37. (a)

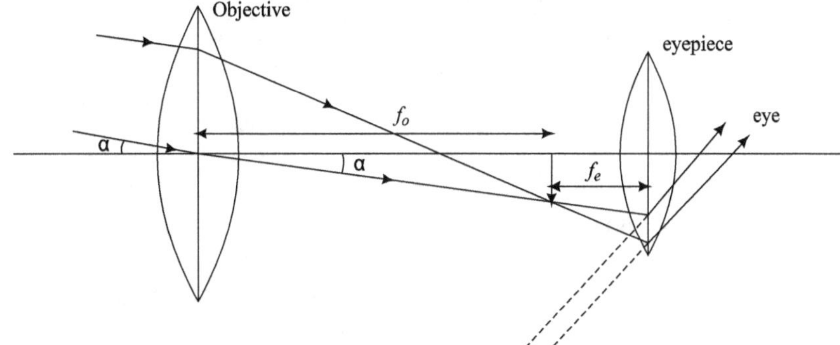

(2 Marks)

$$\text{Resolving power} = \frac{D}{1.22\lambda} \quad \textbf{(1 Mark)}$$

(b) (i) Angular magnification

$$m = \frac{f_0}{f_e} \quad \textbf{(½ Mark)}$$

$$m = \frac{20}{0.01} = 2000 \quad \textbf{(½ Mark)}$$

(ii) Let d be the diameter of the image in metres. Then angle subtended by the moon will be

$$\alpha = \frac{\text{Diameter at moon}}{\text{Radius of lunar orbit}}$$

$$= \frac{3.5\times10^{6}}{3.8\times10^{8}} \quad \textbf{(½ Mark)}$$

Angle subtended by the image formed by the objective will also be equal to α and is given by

$$\alpha = \frac{\text{Diameter of image of moon}}{f_o}$$

$$\alpha = \frac{d}{20}$$

$$\therefore \quad \frac{d}{20} = \frac{3.5\times10^{6}}{3.8\times10^{8}}$$

or $\quad d = 0.18 \; m$ **(½ Mark)**

In telescope, aperture of objective lens is greater than eye-piece and in compound microscope aperture of eye-piece is greater than objective lens.

If objective and eye-piece of a telescope are interchanged, it will not behave as a microscope but object appears very small.

OR

(a) Consider an object AB placed on the principle axis of a concave mirror between its pole P and focus F. A virtual and errect image $A'B'$ is formed behind mirror, after reflection from concave mirror.

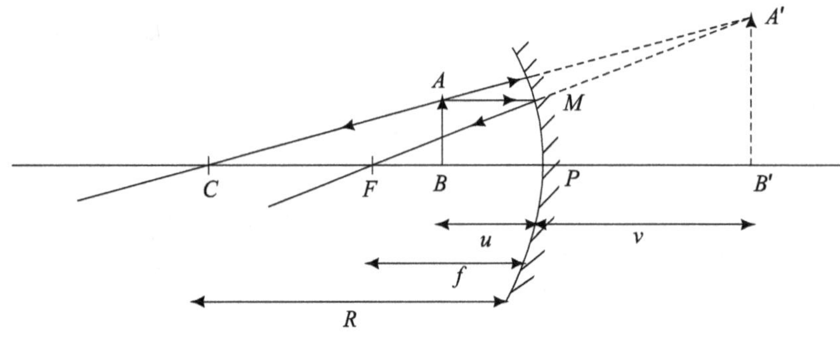

(1 Mark)

Here, $\triangle ABC \sim \triangle A'B'C'$,

$$\frac{AB}{A'B'} = \frac{CB}{CB'} = \frac{CP - BP}{CP + PB'} = \frac{-2f + u}{-2f + v} \quad ...(1) \text{ (½ Mark)}$$

Also, $\triangle MPF \sim \triangle A'B'F$, therefore,

$$\frac{MP}{A'B'} = \frac{FP}{FB'} = \frac{FP}{FP + PB'} \quad \text{(½ Mark)}$$

$$\therefore \quad \frac{AB}{A'B'} = \frac{-f}{-f + v} \qquad [\because MP = AB] \ ...(2)$$

From equation (1) and (2), we get

$$\frac{-2f + u}{-2f + v} = \frac{-f}{-f + v} \quad \text{(½ Mark)}$$

$$\Rightarrow \quad -fv - fu + uv = 0$$
$$uv = fv + fu$$

Dividing both sides by uvf, we get,

$$\frac{1}{f} = \frac{1}{u} + \frac{1}{v} \quad \text{(½ Mark)}$$

(b) Lens-maker formula,

$$\frac{1}{f} = (\mu - 1)\left[\frac{1}{R_1} - \frac{1}{R_2}\right] \quad \text{(½ Mark)}$$

$$\frac{1}{f} = (1.5 - 1)\left[\frac{1}{20} - \frac{1}{\infty}\right]$$

$$\frac{1}{f} = \frac{0.5}{20} = \frac{1}{40}$$

$$\Rightarrow \quad f = 40 \text{ cm}$$

Now, $\quad \dfrac{1}{f} = \dfrac{1}{v} - \dfrac{1}{u}$ **(½ Mark)**

$$\frac{1}{40} = \frac{1}{v} - \frac{1}{(-30)}$$

$$\frac{1}{v} = \frac{1}{40} - \frac{1}{30}$$

$$v = \frac{-40 \times 30}{10}$$

$$v = -120 \text{ cm} \quad \text{(½ Mark)}$$

Image is virtual, erect and enlarged in front of lens 120 cm away. **(½ Mark)**

Delhi *2020*

CBSE Board Solved Paper

Time Allowed : 3 Hours · *Maximum Marks : 70*

General Instructions:

(i)   This question paper comprises **four** sections - A, B, C and D.

(ii)   There are **37** questions in the question paper. All questions are compulsory.

(iii)   Section A : Q. no. **1** to **20** are very short-answer type questions carrying **1** mark each.

(iv)   Section B : Q. no. **21** to **27** are short-answer type questions carrying **2** marks each.

(v)   Section C : Q. no. **28** to **34** are long-answer type questions carrying **3** marks each.

(vi)   Section D : Q. no. **35** to **37** are also long answer type questions carrying **5** marks each.

(vii)   There is no overall choice in the questions paper. However, an internal choice has been provided in **two** questions of **one** mark, **two** questions of **two** marks, **one** question of **three** marks and all the **three** questions of **five** marks. You have to attempt **only one** of the choices in such questions.

(viii)   However, separate instructions are given with each section and question, wherever necessary.

(ix)   Use of calculators and log tables is not permitted.

(x)   You may use the following values of physical constants wherever necessary.

$c = 3 \times 10^8$ m/s

$h = 6.63 \times 10^{-34}$ Js

$e = 1.6 \times 10^{-19}$ C

$\mu_0 = 4\pi \times 10^{-7}$ T m A^{-1}

$\varepsilon_0 = 8.854 \times 10^{-12}$ C^2 N^{-1} m^{-2}

$\dfrac{1}{4\pi\varepsilon_0} = 9 \times 10^9$ N m^2 C^{-2}

Mass of electron $(m_e) = 9.1 \times 10^{-31}$ kg

Mass of neutron $= 1.675 \times 10^{-27}$ kg

Mass of proton $= 1.673 \times 10^{-27}$ kg

Avogadro's number $= 6.023 \times 10^{23}$ per gram mole

Boltzmann constant $= 1.38 \times 10^{-23}$ JK^{-1}

SECTION - A

Note: *Select the most appropriate option from those given below each question.*

1.   The relationship between Brewster angle 'θ' and the speed of light 'v' in the denser medium is ___
   (a) $v \tan \theta = c$
   (b) $c \tan \theta = v$
   (c) $v \sin \theta = c$
   (d) $c \sin \theta = v$

2.   Photo diodes are used to detect
   (a) radio waves
   (b) gamma rays
   (c) IR rays
   (d) optical signals

3.   The selectivity of a series LCR a.c. circuit is large, when
   (a) L is large and R is large
   (b) L is small and R is small
   (c) L is large and R is small
   (d) $L = R.$

4.   The graph showing the correct variation of linear momentum (p) of a charge particle with its de-Broglie wavelength (λ) is –

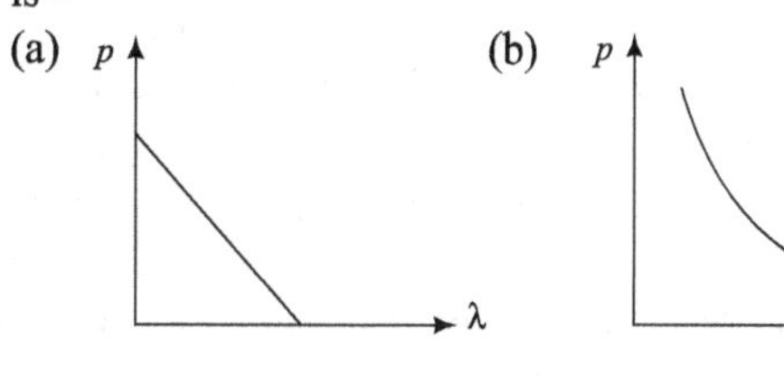

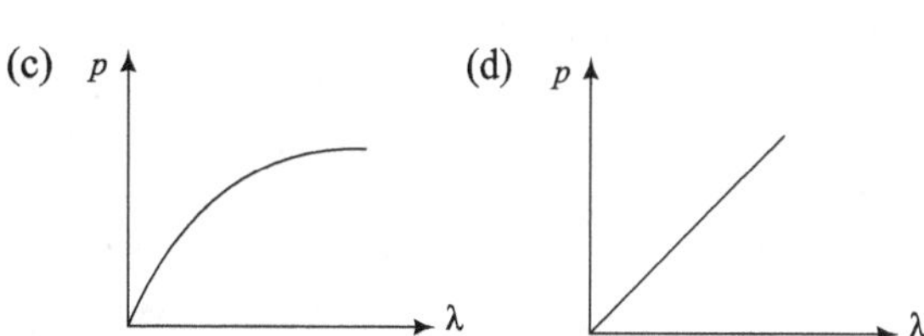

5. The wavelength and intensity of light emitted by a LED depend upon

    (a) forward bias and energy gap of the semiconductor

    (b) energy gap of the semiconductor and reverse bias

    (c) energy gap only

    (d) forward bias only

6. A charge particle after being' accelerated through a potential difference 'V' enters in a uniform magnetic field and moves in a circle of radius r. If V is doubled, the radius of the circle will become

    (a) $2r$ (b) $\sqrt{2r}$

    (c) $4r$ (d) $r\sqrt{2}$

7. The electric flux through a closed Gaussian surface depends upon

    (a) Net charge enclosed and permittivity of the medium

    (b) Net charge enclosed, permittivity of the medium and the size of the Gaussian surface

    (c) Net charge enclosed only

    (d) Permittivity of the medium only

8. If photons of frequency v are incident on the surfaces of metals A & B of threshold frequencies $v/2$ and $v/3$ respectively, the ratio of the maximum kinetic energy of electrons emitted from A to that from B is

    (a) $2:3$ (b) $3:4$

    (c) $1:3$ (d) $\sqrt{3}:\sqrt{2}$

9. The power factor of a series LCR circuit at resonance will be

    (a) 1 (b) 0

    (c) $1/2$ (d) $1/\sqrt{2}$

10. A biconcave lens of power P vertically splits into two identical plano concave parts. The power of each part will be

    (a) $2P$ (b) $P/2$

    (c) P (d) $P/\sqrt{2}$

Note: *Fill in the blanks with appropriate answer.*

11. The physical quantity having SI unit $NC^{-1}\,m$ is __________.

12. A copper wire of non-uniform area of cross-section is connected to *a d.c.* battery. The physical quantity which remains constant along the wire is __________.

13. A point charge is placed at the centre of a hollow conducting sphere of internal radius 'r' and outer radius '$2r$'. The ratio of the surface charge density of the inner surface to that of the outer surface will be __________.

14. The ______, a property of materials C, Si and Ge depends upon the energy gap between their conduction and valence bands.

15. The ability of a junction diode to __________ an alternating voltage, is based on the fact that it allows current to pass only when it is forward biased.

Note: *Answer the following :*

16. Define the term 'current sensitivity' of a moving coil galvanometer.

17. Depict the fields diagram of an electromagnetic wave propagating along positive X-axis with its electric field along Y-axis.

18. Write the conditions on path difference under which (i) constructive (ii) destructive interference occur in Young's double slit experiment.

19. Plot a graph showing variation of induced e.m.f. with the rate of change of current flowing through a coil.

OR

A series combination of an inductor (L), capacitor (C) and a resistor (R) is connected across an ac source of emf of peak value E_0 and angular frequency (ω). Plot a graph to show variation of impedance of the circuit with angular frequency (ω).

20. An electron moves along $+x$ direction. It enters into a region of uniform magnetic field $\vec{B}$ directed along $-z$ direction as shown in fig. Draw the shape of trajectory followed by the electron after entering the field.

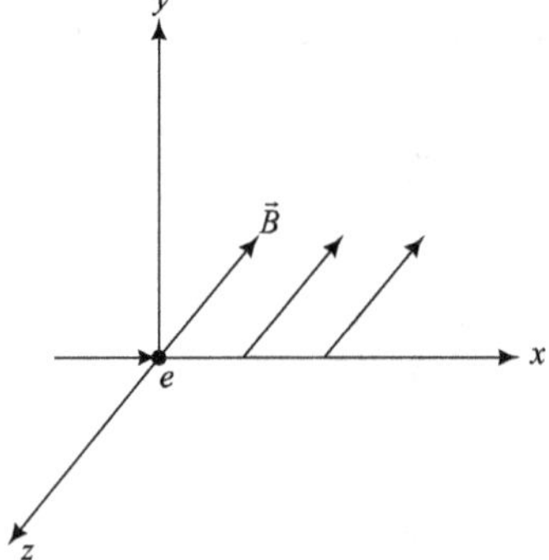

OR

A square shaped current carrying loop $MNOP$ is placed near a straight long current carrying wire AB as shown in the fig. The wire and the loop lie in the same plane. If the loop experiences a net force F towards the wire, find the magnitude of the force on the side 'NO' of the loop.

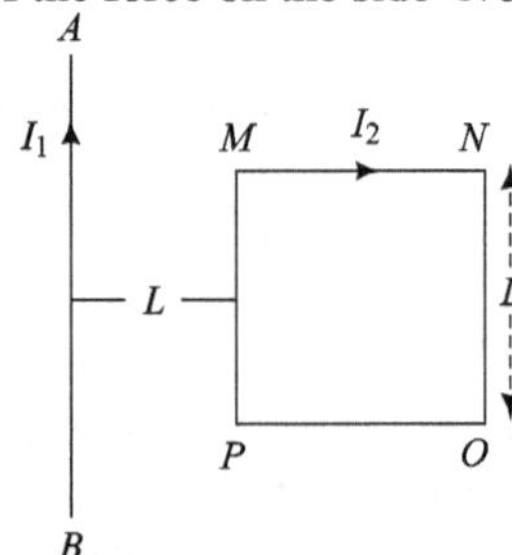

21. Derive the expression for the torque acting on an electric dipole, when it is held in a uniform electric field. Identify the orientation of the dipole in the electric field, in which it attains a stable equilibrium.

OR

Obtain the expression for the energy stored in a capacitor connected across a dc battery. Hence define energy density of the capacitor.

22. Gamma rays and radio waves travel with the same velocity in free space. Distinguish between them in terms of their origin and the main application.

23. Light from a sodium lamp (S) passes through two polaroid sheets P_1 and P_2 as shown in fig. What will be the effect on the intensity of the light transmitted (i) by P_1 and (ii) by P_2 on rotating polaroid P_1 about the direction of propagation of light ? Justify your answer in both cases.

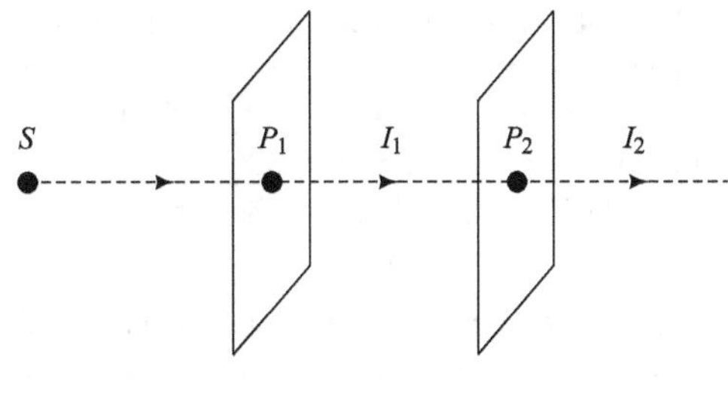

OR

Define the term 'wave front of light'. A plane wave front AB propagating from denser medium (1) into a rarer medium (2) is incident on the surface P_1P_2 separating the two media as shown in fig.

Using Huygen's principle, draw the secondary wavelets and' obtain the refracted wave front in the diagram.

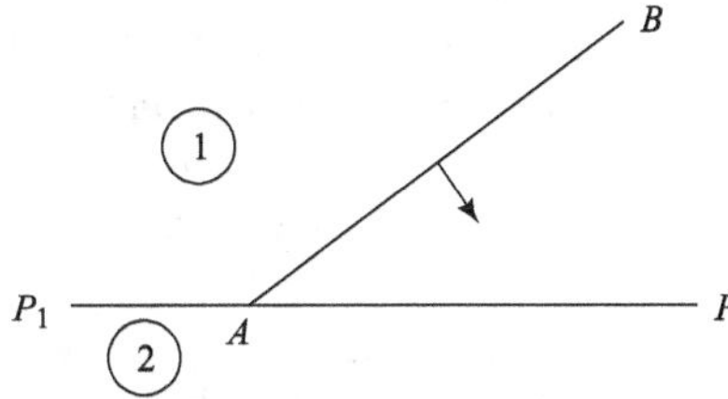

24. A heavy nucleus P of mass number 240 and binding energy 7.6 MeV per nucleon splits in to two nuclei Q and R of mass numbers 110, 130 and binding energy per nucleon 8.5 MeV and 8.4 MeV, respectively. Calculate the energy released in the fission.

25. Figure shows the stopping potential (V_0) for the photo electron versus ($1/\lambda$) graph, for two metals A and B, λ being the wavelength of incident light.

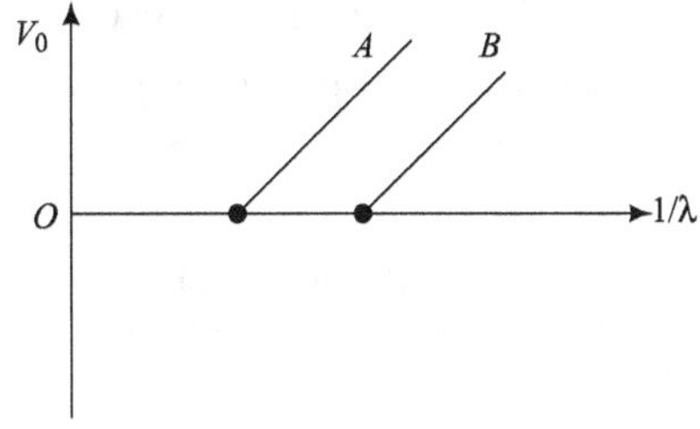

(a) How is the value of Planck's constant determined from the graph?

(b) If the distance between the light source and the surface of metal A is increased, how will the stopping potential for the electrons emitted from it be effected ? Justify your answer.

26. Use Bohr's model of hydrogen atom to obtain the relationship between the angular momentum and the magnetic moment of the revolving electron.

27. In a single slit diffraction experiment, the width of the slit is increased. How will the (i) size and (ii) intensity of central bright band be affected? Justify your answer.

SECTION -C

28. (a) Differentiate between electrical resistance and resistivity of a conductor.

(b) Two metallic rods, each of length L, area of cross A_1 and A_2, having, resistivities ρ_1 and ρ_2 are connected in parallel across a d.c. battery. Obtain the expression for the effective resistivity of this combination.

29. Calculate the de-Broglie wavelength associated with the electron revolving in the first excited state of hydrogen atom. The ground state energy of the hydrogen atom is $-13.6\ eV$.

30. (a) Define the term decay constant of a radioactive substance.

(b) The half life of $^{238}_{92}$U undergoing α decay is 4.5×10^9 years. Calculate the activity of 10 g sample of $^{238}_{92}$U.

31. What is a solar cell ? Draw its V-I characteristics. Explain the three processes involved in its working.

OR

Draw the circuit diagram of a full wave rectifier. Explain its working showing its input and output waveforms.

32. An optical instrument uses a lens of power 100 D for objective lens and 50 D for its eyepiece. When the tube length is kept at 25 cm, the final image is formed at infinity.

(a) Identify the optical instrument.

(b) Calculate the magnification produced by the instrument.

33. (a) Two point charges q_1 and q_2 are kept at a distance of r_{12} in air. Deduce the expression for the electrostatic potential energy of this system.

(b) If an external electric field (E) is applied on the system, write the expression for the total energy of this system.

34. When a conducting loop of resistance 10 Ω and area 10 cm^2 is removed from an external magnetic field acting normally, the variation of induced current in the loop with time is shown in the figure.

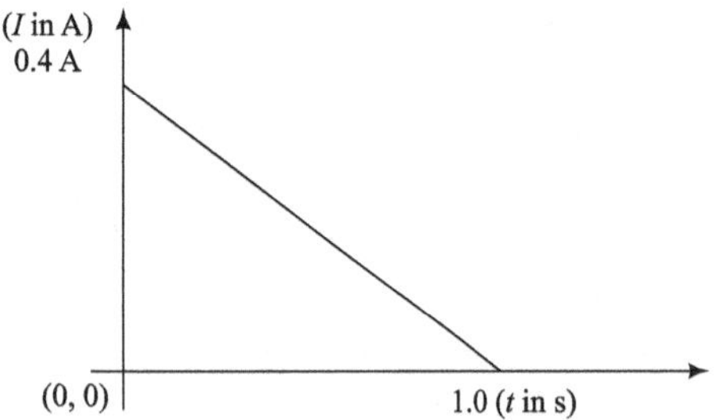

Find the

(i)   total charge passed through the loop.

(ii) change in magnetic flux through the loop.

(iii) magnitude of the magnetic field applied.

SECTION - D

35. (a) Define the term 'focal length of a mirror'. With the help of a ray diagram, obtain the relation between its focal length and radius of curvature.

(b) Calculate the angle of emergence (e) of the ray of light incident normally on the face AC of a glass prism ABC of refractive index $\sqrt{3}$. How will the angle of emergence change qualitatively, if the ray of light emerges from the prism into a liquid of refractive index 1.3 instead of air?

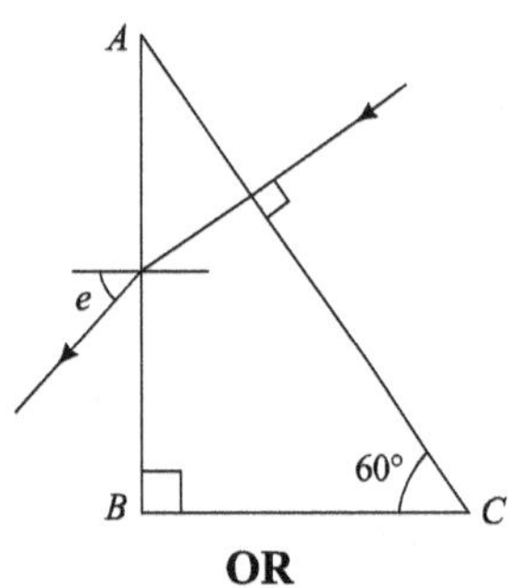

OR

(a) Define the term 'resolving power of a telescople'. How will the resolving power be effected with the increase in

(i) Wavelength of light used.

(ii) Diameter of the objective lens.

Justify your answers.

(b) A screen is placed 80 cm from an object. The image of the object on the screen is formed by a convex lens placed between them at two different locations separated by a distance 20cm. Determine the focal length of the lens.

36. (a) Show that an ideal inductor does not dissipate power in an ac circuit,

(b) The variation of inductive reactance (X_L) of an inductor with the frequency (f) of the ac source of 100 V and variable frequency is shown in the fig.

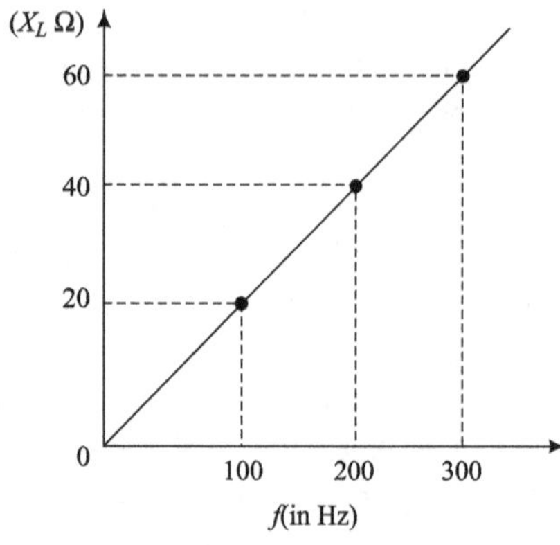

(i)   Calculate the self-inductance of the inductor.

(ii) When this inductor is used in series with a capacitor of unknown value and a resistor of 10 Ω at 300 s^{-1}, maximum power dissipation occurs in the circuit. Calculate the capacitance of the capacitor.

OR

(a) A conductor of length 'l' is rotated about one of its ends at a constant angular speed 'ω' in a plane perpendicular to a uniform magnetic field B. Plot graphs to show variations of the emf induced across the ends of the conductor with (i) angular speed ω and (ii) length of the conductor l.

(b) Two concentric circular loops of radius 1 cm and 20 cm are placed coaxially.

(i)   Find mutual inductance of the arrangement.

(ii) If the current passed through the outer loop is changed at a rate of 5 A/ms, find the emf induced in the inner loop. Assume the magnetic field on the inner loop to be uniform.

37. (a) Write two important characteristics of equipotential surfaces.

(b) A thin circular ring of radius r is charged uniformly so that its linear charge density becomes λ. Derive an expression for the electric field at a point P at a distance x from it along the axis of the ring. Hence, prove that at large distances ($x \gg r$), the ring behaves as a point charge.

OR

(a) State Gauss's law on electrostatics and derive an expression for the electric field due to a long straight thin uniformly charged wire (linear charge density λ) at a point lying at a distance r from the wire.

(b) The magnitude of electric field (in NC^{-1}) in a region varies with the distance r(in m) as

$E = 10r + 5$

By how much does the electric potential increase in moving from point at $r = 1$ m to a point at $r = 10$ m.

Solutions

SECTION - A

1. Option (a) is correct.

Brewster law, $\mu = \tan\theta$

$\Rightarrow \qquad \tan\theta = \dfrac{c}{v}$

$\therefore \qquad v\tan\theta = c$

> **Note**
>
> *Polarised sunglasses is one general example for the application of Brewster law. The polarised glasses reduce glare that is reflecting directly from the sun and also from horizontal surface like road and water.*

2. Option (d) is correct.

3. Option (c) is correct.

4. Option (b) is correct.

de-Broglie wavelength, $\lambda = \dfrac{h}{P} \Rightarrow \lambda \propto \dfrac{1}{P}$

5. Option (a) is correct.

6. Option (b) is correct.

$$\frac{1}{2}mv^2 = eV$$

$\therefore \qquad v = \sqrt{\dfrac{2eV}{m}}$ and $r = \dfrac{mu}{qB}$

So $\qquad r = \dfrac{m}{qB}\sqrt{\dfrac{2eV}{m}}$

$$r = \frac{1}{qB}\sqrt{2meV} \Rightarrow r \propto \sqrt{V}$$

7. Option (a) is correct.

8. Option (b) is correct.

$$K.E. = h\nu - h\nu_0$$

$$(K.E)_A = h\nu - \frac{h\nu}{2} = \frac{h\nu}{2}$$

$$(K.E)_B = h\nu - \frac{h\nu}{3} = \frac{2h\nu}{3}$$

$$\frac{(K.E)_A}{(K.E)_B} = \frac{h\nu/2}{2h\nu/3} = \frac{3}{4}$$

9. Option (a) is correct.

Power factor $\cos\phi = \dfrac{R}{Z}$

At resonance, $R = Z$ $\therefore$ $\cos\phi = 1$

10. Option (b) is correct.

For biconcave lens, $R_1 = -R$ $R_2 = +R$

$$\frac{1}{f} = (\mu-1)\left[\frac{-1}{R} - \frac{1}{R}\right] = \frac{-2(\mu-1)}{R}$$

For planoconcave lens, $R_1 = \infty$ $R_2 = +R$

$$\frac{1}{f'} = (\mu-1)\left[\frac{1}{\infty} - \frac{1}{R}\right] = \frac{-(\mu-1)}{R}$$

$\therefore \qquad \dfrac{1}{f} = \dfrac{2}{f'} \Rightarrow f' = 2f$

So, power will be halved.

11. Voltage/potential difference.

$$\boxed{NmC^{-1} \Rightarrow J/C \Rightarrow V}$$

12. Resistivity

> **Note**
>
> *Resistivity (ρ) is the intrinsic property of the substance. It is independent of shape and size of the body i.e., length of the wire (l) and area of cross-section (A) of the wire.*

13. Charge $-q$ will be induced on the inner surface and $+q$ on the outer surface.

$\therefore \qquad \sigma_1 = \dfrac{-q}{4\pi r^2}$ $\sigma_2 = \dfrac{q}{4\pi(2r)^2}$

$$\frac{\sigma_1}{\sigma_2} = \frac{4}{1}$$

14. Electrical conductivity/resistivity

15. Rectify.

16. *Current sensitivity:* It is defined as the deflection produced in the galvanometer when a unit current flows through it.

$$I_S = \frac{NBA}{K}$$

$N =$ no. of turns in coil

$B =$ Magnetic field

$A =$ area of coil of galvanometer.   **(1 Mark)**

$K =$ torsional constant

17.

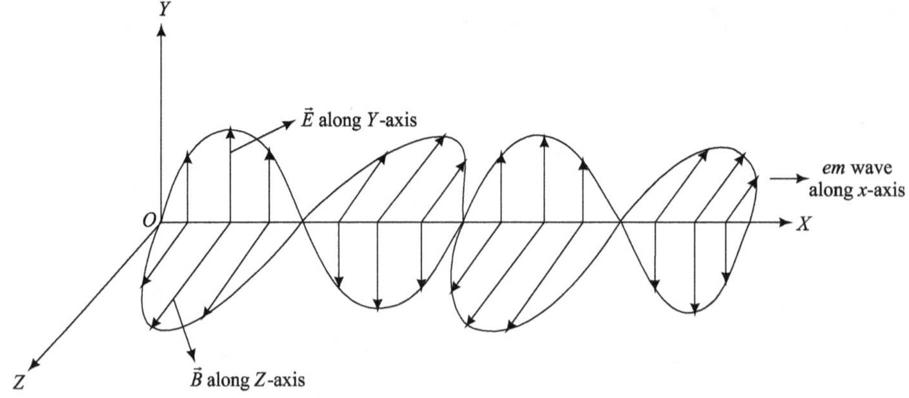

(1 Mark)

18. (i) Path difference in constructive interference

$P = n\lambda,\ n = 0, \pm1, ...$

(ii) Path difference in destructive interference

$P = (2n-1)\dfrac{\lambda}{2},\ n = \pm1, \pm2, ...$ **(½ + ½ = 1 Mark)**

19.

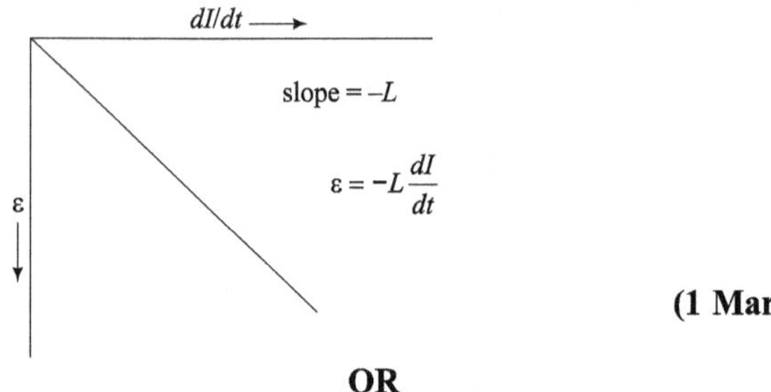

(1 Mark)

OR

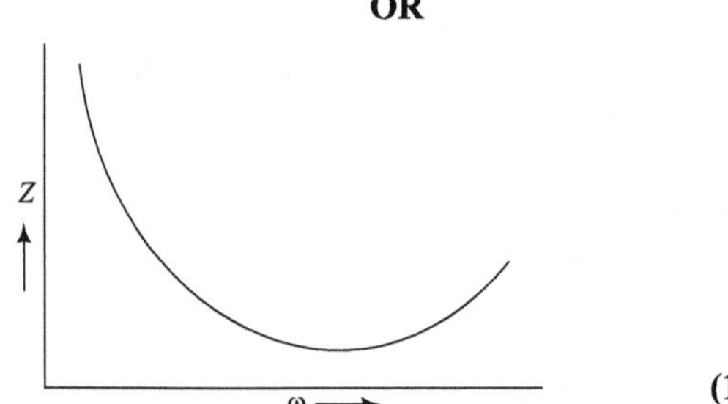

(1 Mark)

20.

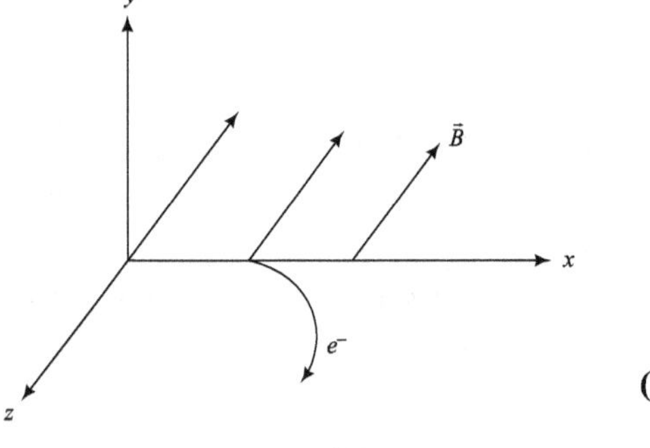

(1 Mark)

OR

Force on side 'NO' of loop   **(1 Mark)**

$$= \frac{\mu_0 I_1 I_2}{2\pi 2L} \times L$$

$$= \frac{\mu_0 I_1 I_2}{4\pi}$$

> **Note**
>
> *The force on length l of each of two long, straight, parallel wires carrying currents I_1 and I_2 and separated by a distance 'd'*
>
> $F = \dfrac{\mu_0}{4\pi} \cdot \dfrac{2I_1 I_2}{d} \times l$

SECTION - B

21. Torque on a dipole in a uniform electric field:

Consider an electric dipole consisting of charges $+q$ and $-q$ and of length $2a$ placed in a uniform electric field $\vec{E}$ making an angle θ with it. It has a dipole moment of magnitude $\vec{P} = q \times 2a$ **(½ Mark)**

Since force exerted on charge $+q$ and $-q$ by field is equal and opposite (qE), therefore the net translating force on a dipole in a uniform electric field is zero.

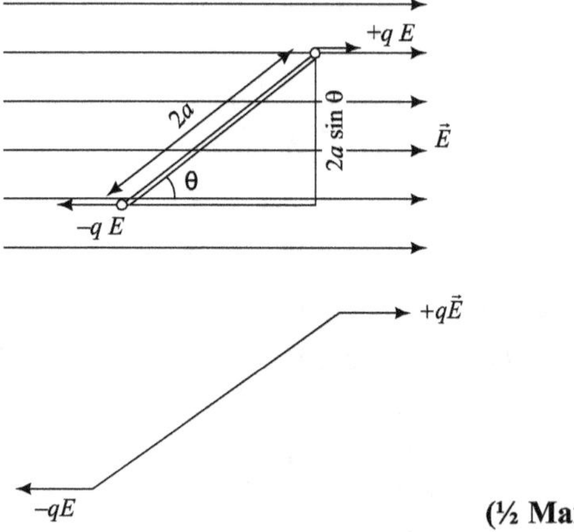

(½ Mark)

But two equal and opposite forces act at different points of the dipole. They form a couple which exerts a torque.

Torque τ = Force $\times \perp$ ar distance b/w two force

$$\tau = qE \times 2a \sin\theta$$

$$\tau = pE \sin\theta$$

$\therefore \quad \tau = \vec{P} \times \vec{E}$ **(½ Mark)**

Stable equilibrium $\rightarrow \theta = 0°$ *i.e.* dipole is parallel to external electric field. **(½ Mark)**

OR

Consider a capacitor of capacitance C. Suppose at any instant the plates 1 and 2 have charges Q' and $-Q'$ respectively. Then the potential difference between the two plates will be

$$V' = \frac{Q'}{C}$$ **(½ Mark)**

Now, let a small additional charge dQ' be transferred from plate 2 to plate 1. The work done will be

$$dw = V' \cdot dQ'$$

$$dw = \frac{Q'}{C} \cdot dQ'$$ **(½ Mark)**

The total work done in transferring a charge Q from plate 2 to plate 1 will be

$$w = \int dw = \int_0^Q \frac{Q'}{C} dQ'$$

$$w = \frac{1}{C}\left[\frac{Q'^2}{2}\right]_0^Q$$

$$w = \frac{1}{C}\frac{Q^2}{2}$$ **(½ Mark)**

This work done is stored as electric potential energy U of capacitor.

$$U = \frac{1}{2C}Q^2$$

Energy density: Energy stored per unit volume or the energy density of electric field

$$u = \frac{U}{Ad}$$

$$u = \frac{1}{2}\varepsilon_0 E^2$$ **(½ Mark)**

22.

Gamma Ray	Radio Wave
Origin: radioactive nuclei and nuclear reaction	Accelerated motion of charges in conducting wire
Application in radio therapy and to study nuclear reactions	In radio and television communication system and in radio astronomy.

(1 × 2 = 2 Marks)

23. (i) Intensity of light after passing through P_1 will be cut down to half of original.
Original intensity = I_0

Intensity after passing through $P_1 = \dfrac{I_0}{2}$ **(1 Mark)**

(ii) As P_1 is now rotated, the intensity of light will follow malus law.

Intensity after passing through $P_2 = \dfrac{I_0}{2}\cos^2\theta$ when P_2 is rotated

Where θ = angle between plane of P_1 and P_2 **(1 Mark)**

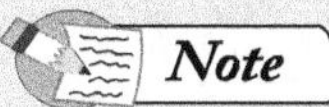

Note

Polaroid is used to produce the plane polarised light. It is based on the principle of selective absorption. It allow the light oscillations parallel to the transmission axis to pass through them.

OR

A locus of the points which oscillates in the same phase is called a wavefront. Thus, a wavefront is defined as a surface of constant phase. **(1 Mark)**

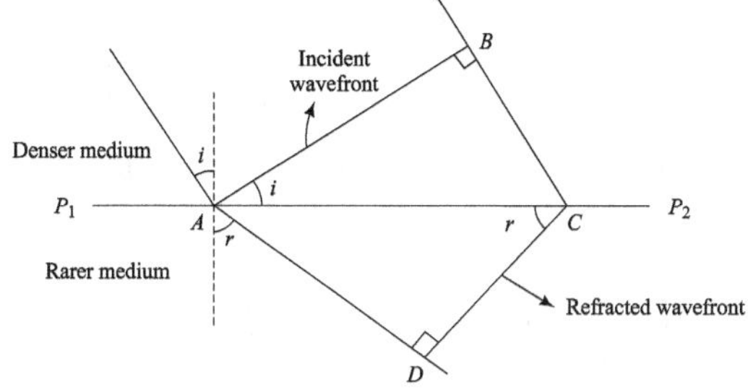

(1 Mark)

24. *B.E* of nucleus $P = 7.6 \times 240 = 1824$ MeV **(½ Mark)**
B.E of nucleus $Q = 8.5 \times 110 = 935$ MeV **(½ Mark)**
B.E of nucleus $R = 8.4 \times 130 = 1092$ MeV **(½ Mark)**
Energy released in fission = $1092 + 935 - 1824$
$$= 2027 - 1824$$
$$= 203 \text{ MeV}$$ **(½ Mark)**

25. (a) Einstein's photoelectron equation

$$eV_0 = h\nu - w_0$$

$$eV_0 = \frac{hc}{\lambda} - w_0$$

$$V_0 = \left(\frac{hc}{e}\right)\frac{1}{\lambda} - \frac{w_0}{e}$$

Comparing this equations with $y = mx + C$

Slope of graph V_0 *vs* $\dfrac{1}{\lambda}$ is $\dfrac{hc}{e}$.

$\therefore$ Planck's constant $h = \text{slope} \times \dfrac{e}{c}$ **(1 Mark)**

(b) The stopping potential V_0 remains same because it is independent of the intensity. **(½ Mark)**

Note

Intensity $\propto$ no. of incident photons $\propto$ no. of emitted photoelectrons per time $\propto$ photocurrent $\propto \dfrac{1}{(\text{distance})^2}$

If frequency of incident light increases keeping intensity is constant, stopping potential increases but there is no change in photoelectric current.

26. We know that circulating electron around a heavy nucleus constitutes a current given by $I = \dfrac{e}{T}$

where T = time period of revolution

$$T = \frac{2\pi R}{V}$$

R = radius of orbit
V = velocity of electron

$$\therefore \quad I = \frac{eV}{2\pi R} \qquad \textbf{(½ Mark)}$$

Now, magnetic moment associated with this circulating electron given by,

$$m_l = IA$$

$$m_l = \frac{eV}{2\pi R}.\pi R^2$$

$$m_l = \frac{eVR}{2} \qquad ...(1) \qquad \textbf{(½ Mark)}$$

Angular momentum of circulating electron L,

$$L = mVR$$

So, $\quad VR = \dfrac{L}{m} \qquad ...(2) \qquad$ **(½ Mark)**

m = mass of electron

From (1) and (2)

$$\boxed{m_l = \frac{eL}{2m}}$$

(½ Mark)

27. (i) Size of central maximum = $\dfrac{D2\lambda}{a}$

Size $\propto \dfrac{1}{a(\text{slit width})}$

$\therefore$ Size of central bright will decrease. **(1 Mark)**

(ii) Intensity of central maximum (bright band) will increase. **(1 Mark)**

SECTION - C

28.

(a)	Resistance	Resistivity
Definition	The resistance of a conductor is the property by virtue of which it opposes the flow of charges through it.	Resistivity of a material may be defined as the resistance of a conductor of that material, having unit length and unit area of cross-section.
Factors affecting	Resistance depends on length, area and nature of conductor.	Resistivity is independent of size and shape of conductor.

(2 × 1 = 2 Mark)

(b) $R_1 = \dfrac{\delta_1 l}{A_1} \quad R_2 = \dfrac{\delta_2 l}{A_2}$

$$\frac{1}{R_{eq}} = \frac{1}{R_1} + \frac{1}{R_2} = \frac{A_1}{\delta_1 l} + \frac{A_2}{\delta_2 l} = \frac{1}{l}\left[\frac{A_1\delta_2 + A_2\delta_1}{\delta_1\delta_2}\right] \quad \textbf{(½ Mark)}$$

$$R_{eq} = \frac{\delta l}{A} = \frac{(\delta_1\delta_2)l}{A_1\delta_2 + A_2\delta_1} \qquad \textbf{(½ Mark)}$$

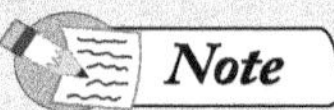 **Note**

If $A_1 \neq A_2$, then it is very complicated to solve this problem. Hence, this questions seems incorrect.

29. Energy of electron revolving in first excited state of hydrogen atom

$$E = \frac{13.6}{(2)^2} \left[\because E_n = \frac{-13.6}{n^2}, n = 2\right]$$

$$E = \frac{13.6}{4}\,\text{eV}$$

$$E = 3.4 \times 1.6 \times 10^{-19}\,J \qquad \textbf{(1½ Marks)}$$

de-Broglie wavelength associated with it will be then

$$\lambda = \frac{h}{\sqrt{2mE}}$$

$$\lambda = \frac{6.63\times10^{-34}}{\sqrt{2\times9.1\times10^{-31}\times3.4\times1.6\times10^{-19}}}$$

$$\lambda = 0.67\,nm \qquad \textbf{(1½ Marks)}$$

30. (a) *Decay constant:* The radioactive decay constant may be defined as the reciprocal of the time interval during which the number of active nuclei in a given radioactive sample reduces to $(1/e)$ times of its initial value. **(1 Mark)**

(b) Here $T_{1/2} = 4.5 \times 10^9$ years

$$= 4.5 \times 10^9 \times 3.156 \times 10^7 \text{ sec} \qquad \textbf{(½ Mark)}$$

given mass = 10 g Atomic mass = 238

Number of atoms in 10 g uranium

$$N = \frac{10}{238} \times 6.023 \times 10^{23} \text{ atoms.} \qquad \textbf{(½ Mark)}$$

Activity of the sample, $R = \lambda N$

$$= \frac{0.693}{T_{1/2}} N \qquad \textbf{(½ Mark)}$$

$$R = \frac{0.693\times10\times6.023\times10^{23}}{4.5\times3.156\times10^{16}\times238}$$

$$R = 1.235 \times 10^{45}\,Bq \qquad \textbf{(½ Mark)}$$

31. *Solar cell:* It is a junction diode which converts solar energy into electricity. **(½ Mark)**

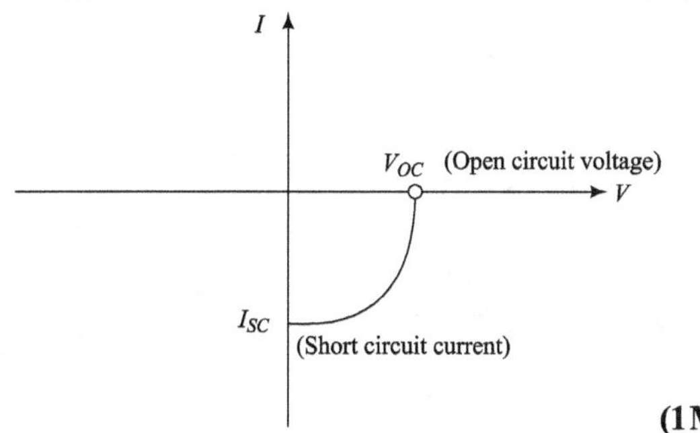

(1 Mark)

Working of solar cell

The generation of emf by a solar cell, when light falls on it, is due to the following three basic processes,

(i) generation   (ii) separation

(iii) collection

- Generation of electron hole pair due to light close to junction.
- Separation of electrons and holes due to electric field of the depletion region. Electron are swept to n-side and holes to p-side.
- The electrons reaching the n-side are collected by the front contact and holes reaching p-sides are collected by the back contact. Thus p-side becomes positive and n-side becomes negative giving rise to photo voltage. **(½ × 3 = 1½ Marks)**

OR

Working of a full wave rectifier:

(i) During the one half cycle (of input ac) diode D_1 alone gets forward biased and conducts. During the other half cycle, it is diode D_2 that conducts.

(ii) Because of the use of the centre tapped transformer the current through the loads flows in the same direction in both the half cycles. **(1 Mark)**

Circuit diagram of a full wave rectifier

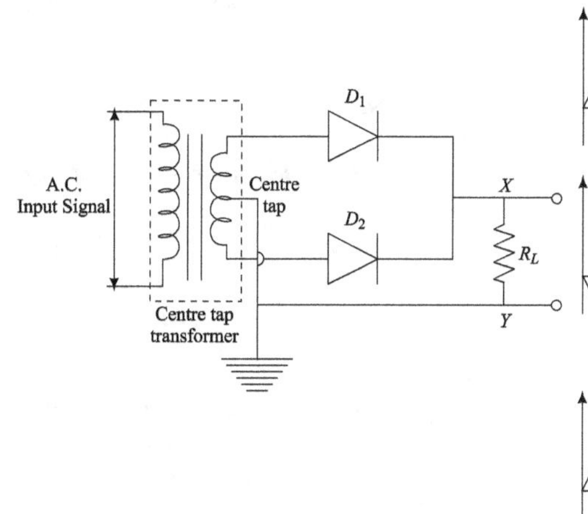

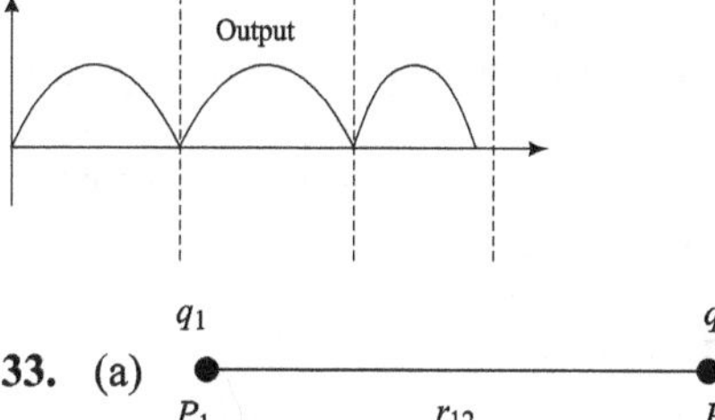

(1 + 1 = 2 Marks)

32. (a) The optical instrument is compound microscope. **(1 Mark)**

(b) $P_o = 100D \Rightarrow f_o = \dfrac{1}{100} = 0.01$ m = 1 cm **(½ Mark)**

$P_e = 50D \Rightarrow f_e = \dfrac{1}{50} = 0.02$ m = 2 cm **(½ Mark)**

Magnification, $m = \dfrac{L}{f_o}\dfrac{D}{f_e}$ **(½ Mark)**

$L = 25$ cm

$D = 25$ cm (near point)

$m = \dfrac{25}{1} \times \dfrac{25}{2} = 312.5$ **(½ Mark)**

33. (a)

q_1 q_2
P_1 r_{12} P_2

Suppose a point charge q_1 is at rest in space (air), as shown. It takes no work to bring the first charge q_1 because there is no field yet to work against.

Potential due to charge q_1 at a point P_2 at distance r_{12} from P_1 will be

$$V_1 = \frac{1}{4\pi\varepsilon_0}\frac{q_1}{r_{12}}$$ **(1 Mark)**

If charge q_2 is moved in from infinity to P_2, the work required is,

w_2 = potential × charge

$$w_2 = V_1 \times q_2 = \frac{q_1 q_2}{4\pi\varepsilon_0 r_{12}}$$ **(½ Mark)**

This work done is stored as the potential energy U of the system, so

$$u = \frac{1}{4\pi\varepsilon_0}\frac{q_1 q_2}{r_{12}}.$$ **(½ Mark)**

(b) Potential energy when external electric field (E) is applied on the system,

$$u = q_1 V(\vec{r_1}) + q_2 V(\vec{r_2}) + \frac{1}{4\pi\varepsilon_0}\frac{q_1 q_2}{r_{12}}$$

where $V(\vec{r_1})$ and $V(\vec{r_2})$ are electric potential of field $\vec{E}$ at the points having position vectors $\vec{r_1}$ and $\vec{r_2}$.   **(1 Mark)**

34. (i) Area under current time graph gives charge.

$\therefore$ Total charge passed through loop $= \dfrac{1}{2} \times 0.4 \times 1$
$= 0.2$ C   **(1 Mark)**

(ii) Charge $= \dfrac{\text{change in flux in loop}}{\text{Resistance of loop}}$

$0.2 = \dfrac{\text{change in magnetic flux}}{10}$

$\Delta\phi$, change in magnetic flux $= 0.2 \times 10$
$= 2$ Wb   **(1 Mark)**

(iii) $\phi = B\,A\cos\theta$

Here $\theta = 0 [\because$ field is acting normal to coil, so angle b/w area vector and field will be 0°]

$\therefore \qquad \phi = BA$

$B = \dfrac{\phi}{A}$

$B = \dfrac{2}{10 \times 10^{-4}} = 2 \times 10^{-5}\,T$ **(1 Mark)**

SECTION - D

35. (a) Focal length of mirror: It is the distance between pole and focus of the mirror.   **(1 Mark)**

Consider a ray AB parallel to the principle axis, incident at point B of a spherical mirror (here concave). After reflection from mirror, this ray converges to point F. According to law of reflection,

$$\angle i = \angle r$$

As AB is parallel to PC,

$$\angle\alpha = \angle i$$

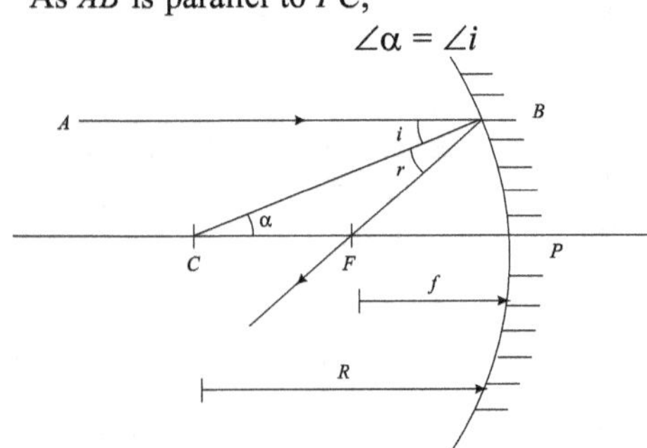

$\therefore$ In ΔBFC, $\qquad \angle r = \angle\alpha$
Hence $\qquad\qquad CF = FB.$
For a mirror of small aperture,
$FB \simeq FP \therefore CF \simeq FP$
Hence $\quad CP = CF + FP = FP + FP = 2FP$

or $\quad R = 2f$ or $f = \dfrac{R}{2}$.   **(2½ Marks)**

(b) Angle of refraction at face AB is 30° (from geometry).

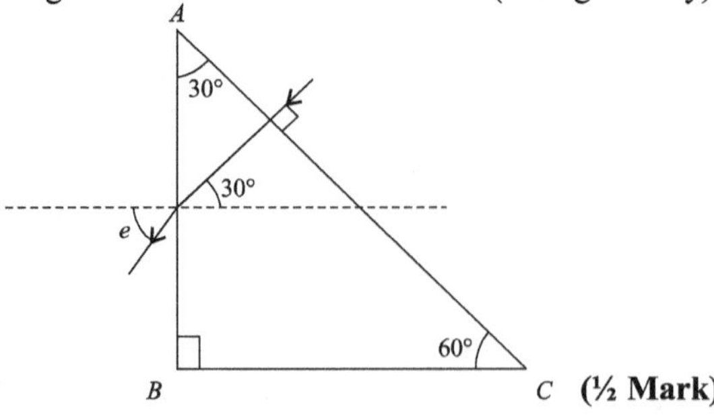

                    (½ Mark)

Therefore applying, Snell's law at face AB we get.

$$\frac{\sin 30°}{\sin e} = \frac{1}{\sqrt{3}}$$

$$\sin e = \sin 30° \times \sqrt{3}$$

$$\sin e = \frac{\sqrt{3}}{2}$$

$\therefore \qquad e = 60°$ **(½ Mark)**

Angle of emergence will decrease, if the ray of light emerges from prism into a liquid of refractive index 1.3 instead of air.   **(½ Mark)**

 *Note*

If light ray is incident normally on first surface i.e., $\angle i = 0$ it means $\angle r_1 = 0$.
If $\angle i = \angle e$ and $\angle r_1 = \angle r_2$ then deviation produced is minimum.

OR

(a) Resolving power of a telescope is defined as the reciprocal of the smallest angular separation ($d\theta$) between two distant objects, whose images are just seen in telescope as separate.   **(1 Mark)**

$$R.P. = \frac{D}{1.22\lambda}$$

$D =$ diameter of objective lens
$\lambda =$ wavelength of light.   **(½ Mark)**

(i) As $R.P. \propto \dfrac{1}{\lambda}$, resolving power will decrease as wavelength increases.

(ii) $R.P. \propto D$, therefore resolving power will increase as diameter of objective lens increases.
                    (½ + ½ = 1 Mark)

(b)

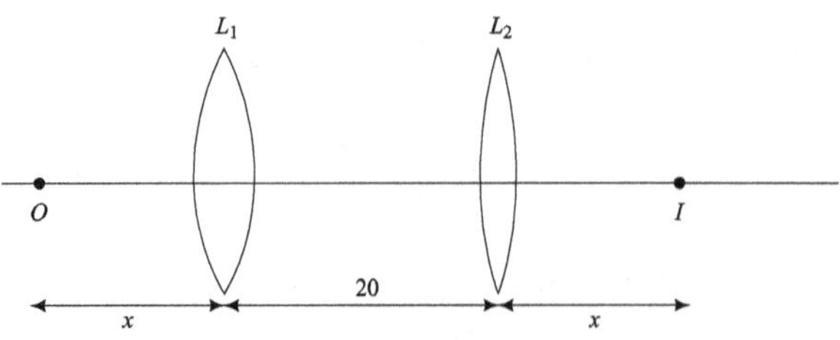

                    (½ Mark)

Let O and I be position of object and image respectively.

(½ Mark)

Now $x + 20 + x = 80$

$\therefore x = 30$ cm   **(½ Mark)**

When the lens is in position L_1, we have,

$u = -x = -30$ cm, $v = 20 + x = 50$ cm

$\therefore \dfrac{1}{f} = \dfrac{1}{v} - \dfrac{1}{u} = \dfrac{1}{50} + \dfrac{1}{30}$ **(½ Mark)**

$\dfrac{1}{f} = \dfrac{3+5}{150}$

$f = \dfrac{150}{8} = 18.75$ cm   **(½ Mark)**

36. (a) When a.c. is applied to an ideal inductor, current lags behind the voltage in phase by $\pi/2$ rad.

So, $V = V_o \sin \omega t$

$I = I_o \sin\left(\omega t - \dfrac{\pi}{2}\right)$ **(½ Mark)**

$= -I_o \cos \omega t$

$P_{av} = \dfrac{1}{T}\displaystyle\int_o^T VI\,dt$

$P_{av} = \dfrac{-1}{T}\displaystyle\int_o^T V_o I_o \sin \omega t \cos \omega t\,dt$ **(½ Mark)**

$P_{av} = \dfrac{-V_o I_o}{2T}\displaystyle\int_o^T \sin 2\omega t\,dt$

$P_{av} = +\dfrac{V_o I_o}{2T}\left[\dfrac{\cos 2\omega t}{2\omega}\right]_o^T$ **(½ Mark)**

$P_{av} = +\dfrac{V_o I_o}{2\pi\omega}[\cos 2\,\omega T - \cos 0]$

$P_{av} = \dfrac{+V_o I_o}{4T\omega}[1 - 1]$ ($\because$ even value of cosine is 1)

$P_{av} = 0$ **(½ Mark)**

Thus, the average power dissipated per cycle in an inductor is zero.

(b) (i) $L = \dfrac{X_L}{2\pi f}$

$L = \dfrac{1}{2\pi}$ slope of $X_L - f$ graph   **(½ Mark)**

$L = \dfrac{1}{2\pi} \times \dfrac{20-0}{100-0}$

$L = \dfrac{1}{100\pi} = 3.18 \times 10^{-3}$ H.   **(½ Mark)**

(ii) Since inductor is connected in series with capacitor and resistor, this becomes *a LCR* circuit. **(½ Mark)**

Given

$f = 300$ Hz

$X_L = 60\ \Omega$ (at 300 Hz)

$R = 10\ \Omega$

Now at resonance ($X_L = X_C$), maximum power dissipation occur.   **(½ Mark)**

Therefore $X_C = X_L = 60\ \Omega$

$X_C = \dfrac{1}{2\pi f C}$ **(½ Mark)**

$C = \dfrac{1}{2\pi f X_C}$

$C = \dfrac{1}{2 \times 3.14 \times 300 \times 60}$

$C = 8.84 \times 10^{-6}\ F$ **(½ Mark)**

OR

(a) Emf induced in rotating conductor is $\varepsilon = \dfrac{1}{2}\,\beta\,\omega l^2$

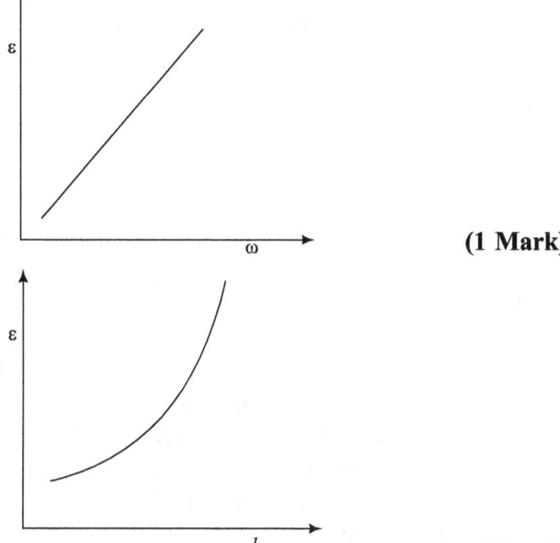

(1 Mark)

(1 Mark)

(b) (i) Let I be the current in outer coil.

So the magnetic field associated with inner coil will be

$B = \dfrac{\mu_o I}{2R}$; R = radius of outer coil.   **(½ Mark)**

$\therefore$ Magnetic flux linked with inner coil =

$\phi = \dfrac{\mu_o I}{2R} \times \pi r^2$ **(½ Mark)**

$r =$ radius of inner coil.

Mutual inductance $M = \dfrac{\phi}{I}$ **(½ Mark)**

$M = \dfrac{\mu_o I \pi r^2}{2RI}$

$M = \dfrac{\mu_o \pi r^2}{2R}$

$M = \dfrac{4\pi \times 10^{-7} \times \pi \times (10^{-2})^2}{2 \times 20 \times 10^{-2}}$

$M = 9.85 \times 10^{-10}$ M.   **(½ Mark)**

(ii) $\varepsilon = -M\dfrac{dI}{dt}$ **(½ Mark)**

$\dfrac{dI}{dt} = 5$ A/ms $= 5 \times 10^3$ A/S

$\therefore \quad \varepsilon = -9.85 \times 5 \times 10^{-10} \times 10^3\ V$

$\varepsilon = 49.25 \times 10^{-7}\ V.$ **(½ Mark)**

37. (a) Two important characteristics of equipotential surfaces are:

(i) No work is done in moving a test charge over an equipotential surface.

(ii) Electric field is always normal to the equipotential surface at every point. **(2 × 1 = 2 Marks)**

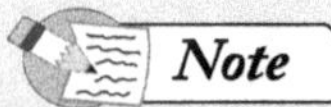

Note

Some other characteristics of equipotential surfaces

(i) For a uniform electric field, the equipotential surfaces are a family of plane perpendicular to the field lines.

(ii) Equipotential surfaces can never cross each other.

(b)

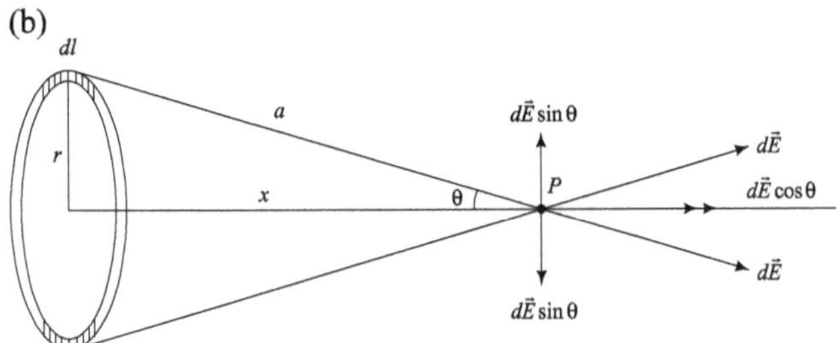

(1 Mark)

Suppose that the ring is placed with its plane perpendicular to the x-axis, as shown in figure. Consider a small element dl of the ring.

As the total charge q is uniformly distributed, the charge dq on the element dl is

$dq = \lambda \, dl.$

$\therefore$ The magnitude of the field $d\vec{E}$ produced by the element dl at the field point P is

$$d\vec{E} = K\frac{\lambda dl}{a^2}$$ **(½ Mark)**

Since the $\perp ar$ components of any two diametrically opposite elements are equal and opposite, they all cancel out in pairs. Only axial components will add up to produce the resultant field $\vec{E}$ at point P, which is given by

$$E = \int_{0}^{2\pi r} dE\cos\theta \Rightarrow E = \int_{0}^{2\pi r} \frac{K\lambda dl}{a^2}\cdot\frac{x}{a}$$ **(½ Mark)**

$$E = \int_{0}^{2\pi r} \frac{K\lambda x}{a^3}dl \Rightarrow E = \frac{K\lambda x}{a^3}\left[2\pi r\right]$$

$$E = \frac{K\lambda x}{(r^2 + x^2)^{3/2}}\cdot 2\pi r$$

$$\Rightarrow E = \frac{\lambda x 2\pi r K}{(r^2 + x^2)^{3/2}} \Rightarrow \lambda = \frac{q}{2\pi r}$$

$$\therefore \quad E = \frac{qxK}{(r^2 + x^2)^{3/2}}$$ **(½ Mark)**

For $x \gg r$, $E = \frac{qKx}{x^3} = \frac{qK}{x^2} = \frac{1}{4\pi\varepsilon_o}\frac{q}{x^2}.$ **(½ Mark)**

OR

(a) Gauss's law: Gauss's law states that the total flux through a closed surface is $\dfrac{1}{\varepsilon_o}$ times the net charge enclosed by the closed surface.

$$\phi_E = \oint_s \vec{E}.d\bar{s} = \frac{q}{\varepsilon_o}$$ **(1 Mark)**

Electric field due to long straight charged wire

Consider a thin long straight wire having a uniform linear charge density λ. By symmetry, the field $\vec{E}$ of the line charge is directed radially outward and its magnitude is same at all points equidistant from the line charge.

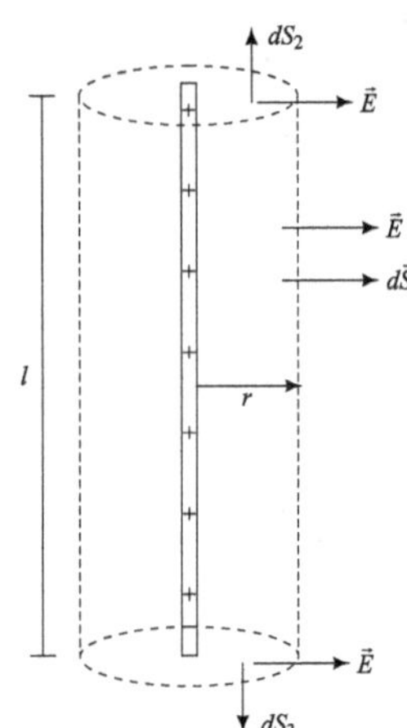

(1 Mark)

Flux $\phi_E = \int \vec{E}.d\vec{S}$

$$= \int \vec{E}\cdot d\vec{S}_1 + \int \vec{E}\cdot d\vec{S}_2 + \int \vec{E}\cdot d\vec{S}_3$$

$$\phi_E = \int Eds_1 \cos\theta° + \int Eds_2 \cos 90° + \int Eds_3 \cos 90°$$ **(½ Mark)**

$$\phi_E = \int Eds_1 + 0 + 0$$
$$= E \times \text{area of curved surface}$$
$$\phi_E = E \times 2\pi rl$$ **(½ Mark)**

Charge enclosed by gaussian surface, $q = \lambda l$

$$\phi_E = \frac{q}{\varepsilon_o}$$

$$\Rightarrow \frac{\lambda l}{\varepsilon_o} = E \times 2\pi rl$$

$$\boxed{E = \frac{\lambda}{2\pi\varepsilon_o r}}$$ **(1 Mark)**

(b) $E = 10r + 5$

$$E = \frac{-dV}{dr} \Rightarrow dV = -Edr$$ **(½ Mark)**

$$V = -\int_{1}^{10} Edr \Rightarrow V = -\int_{1}^{10}(10r+5)dr$$

$$V = -\left[\frac{10r^2}{2} + 5r\right]_1^{10}$$

$$V = -[540] \, V$$

Potential increases by -540 V **(½ Mark)**

CBSE Board Solved Paper

Time Allowed : 3 Hours   *Maximum Marks : 100*

General Instructions:
(i)   All questions are compulsory. There are **27** questions in all.
(ii) This question paper has four sections : Section **A**, Section **B**, Section **C** and Section **D**.
(iii) Section **A** contains **five** questions of **one** mark each, Section **B** contains **seven** questions of **two** marks each, Section **C** contains **twelve** questions of **three** marks each, and Section **D** contains **three** questions of **five** marks each.
(iv) There is no overall choice. However, an internal choice(s) has been provided in **two** questions of **one** mark, **two** questions of **two** marks, **four** questions of **three** marks and **three** questions of **five** marks weightage. You have to attempt only **one** of the choices in such questions.
(v)   You may use the following values of physical constants wherever necessary :
$c = 3 \times 10^8$ m/s
$h = 6.63 \times 10^{-34}$ Js
$e = 1.6\ 10^{-19}$ C
$\mu_0 = 4\pi \times 10^{-7}$Tm A^{-1}
$\varepsilon_0 = 8.854 \times 10^{-12}$ C^2 N^{-1} m^{-2}

$\dfrac{1}{4\pi\varepsilon_0} = 9 \times 10^9$N m^2 C^{-2}

Mass of electron $(m_e) = 9.1 \times 10^{-31}$ kg

Mass of neutron $= 1.675 \times 10^{-27}$ kg

Mass of proton $= 1.673 \times 10^{-27}$ kg

Avogadro's number $= 6.023 \times 10^{23}$ per gram mole

Boltzmann constant $= 1.38 \times 10^{-23}$ JK^{-1}

SECTION - A

1. Draw equipotential surfaces for an electric dipole.

2. A proton is accelerated through a potential difference V, subjected to a uniform magnetic field acting normal to the velocity of the proton. If the potential difference is doubled, how will the radius of circular path described by the proton in the magnetic field change?

3. The magnetic susceptibility of magnesium at 300 K is 1.2 $\times 10^5$. At what temperature will its magnetic susceptibility become 1.44×10^5?

OR

The magnetic susceptibility χ of given material is -0.5. Identify the magnetic material.

4. Identify the semiconductor diode whose *V-I* characteristics are as shown.

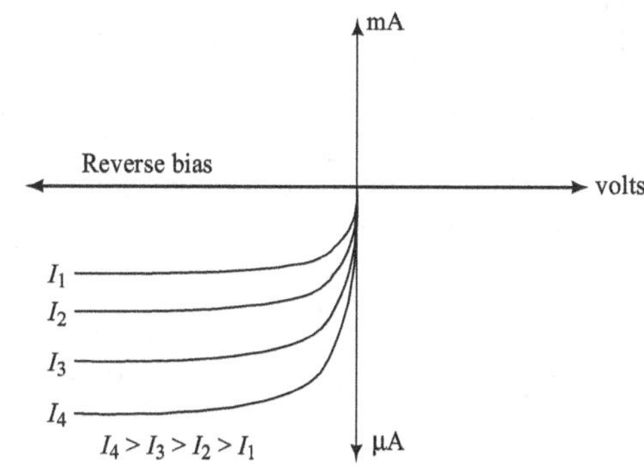

5. Which part of the electromagnetic specturm is used in RADAR? Give its frequency range.

OR

How are electromagnetic waves produced by accelerating charges?

SECTION - B

6. A capacitor made of two parallel plates, each of area 'A' and separation 'd' is charged by an external *dc* source. Show that during charging, the displacement current inside the capacitor is the same as the current charging the capacitor.

7. A photon and a proton have the same de-Broglie wavelength λ. Prove that the energy of photon is $(2m\lambda)c/h$ times the kinetic energy of the proton.

8. A photon emitted during the de-excitation of electron from a state n to the first excited state in hydrogen atom, irradiates a metallic cathode of work function 2eV, in a photo cell, with stopping potential of 0·55 V. Obtain the value of the quantum number of the state n.

OR

A hydrogen atom in the ground state is excited by an electron beam of 12.5 eV energy. Find the maximum number of lines emitted by the atom from its excited state.

9. Draw a ray diagram of an astronomical telescope showing image formation in normal adjustment position. Write the expression for its magnifying power.

OR

Draw a labelled ray diagram to show image formation by a compound microscope and write the expression for its resolving power.

10. Write the relation between the height of a TV antenna and maximum range up to which signals transmitted by antenna can be received. How is this expression modified in the case of line of sight communication by space waves ? In which range of frequencies, is this mode of communication used?

11. Under which conditions can a rainbow be observed ? Distinguish between a primary and secondary rainbow.

12. Explain the following
   (i) Sky appears blue.
   (ii) The Sun appears reddish at (a) sunset, and (b) sunrise.

SECTION - C

13. A capacitor C and resistor R are connected in series with an a.c. source of voltage of frequency 50 Hz. The potential difference across C and R are respectively $120V$, $90V$ and the current in the circuit is 3A. Calculate
   (i) the impedance of the circuit (ii) the value of the inductance, which when connected in series with C and R will make the power factor of circuit unity.

OR

The figure shows a series LCR circuit connected to a variable frequency 230 V source.

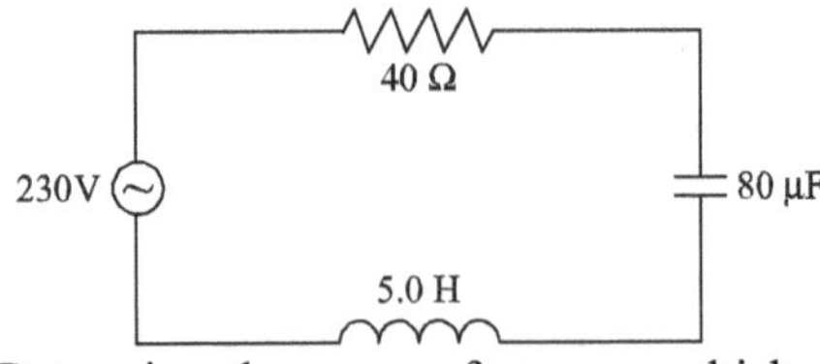

   (a) Determine the source frequency which drives the circuit in resonance.
   (b) Calculate the impedance of the circuit and amplitude of the current at resonance.
   (c) Show that the potential drop across LC combinations is zero at resonanting frequency.

14. Give the reason to explain why n and p regions of a Zener diode are heavily doped. Find the current through the Zener diode in the circuit given below : (Zener breakdown voltage is 15V)

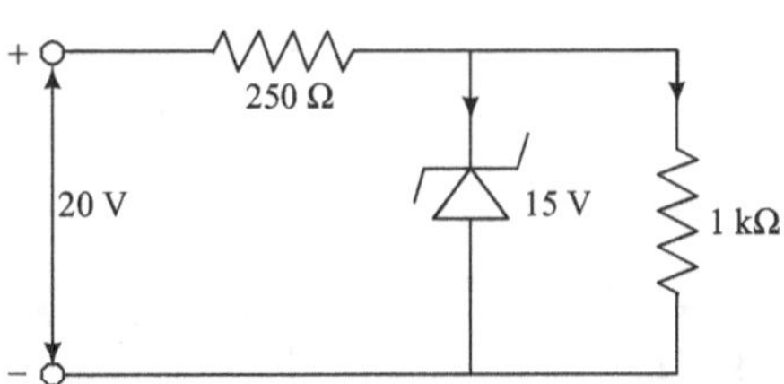

15. Draw a labelled diagram of cyclotron. Explain its working principle. Show that cyclotron frequency is independent of the speed and radius of the orbit.

OR

   (a) Derive, with the help of a diagram, the expression for magnetic field inside a very long solenoid having n turns per unit length carrying a current I.
   (b) How is a toroid different from a solenoid?

16. Prove that the magnetic moment of electron revolving around a nucleus in an orbit of radius 'r' with orbital speed v is equal to evr/2. Hence using Bohr's postulate of quantization of angular momentum, deduce the expression for magnetic moment of hydrogen atom in ground state.

17. Two long charged plane sheets of charge densities σ and -2σ C/m^2 are arranged vertically with a separation of d between them. Deduce the expressions for the electric field at points (i) to the left of first sheet, (ii) to the right of second sheet and (iii) between two sheets.

OR

A spherical conducting shell of inner radius r_1 and outer radius r_2 has charge Q.
   (a) A charge q is placed at the centre of the shell. Find out the surface charge density on the inner and outer surfaces of the shell.
   (b) Is the electric field inside a cavity (with no charge) zero; independent of fact whether the shell is spherical or not? Explain.

18. A signal of low frequency fm is to be transmitted using a carrier wave of frequency fc. Derive the expression for amplitude modulated wave and deduce the expressions for the lower and upper side bands produced. Hence, obtain the expression for modulation index.

19. Draw a plot of α-particle scattering by a thin fail of gold to show the variation of the number of scattered particles with scattering angle. Describe briefly how the large angle scattering explains the existence of the nucleus inside the atom. Explain with the help of impact parameter picture, how Rutherford scattering serves a powerful way to determine an upper limit on the size of the nucleus.

20. A 200 µF parallel plate capacitor having plate separation of 5 mm is charged by a 100 V dc source. It remains connected to the source. Using an insulated handle, the distance between the plates is doubled and a dielecteric slab of thickness 5mm and dielectric constant 10 is introduced between the plates. Explain with reason, how the (i) capacitance, (ii) electric field between plates, (iii) energy density of the capacitor will change?

21. Why it is difficult to detect the presence of an anti-neutrino, during β-decay? Define the term decay constant of a radioactive nucleus and derive the expression for its mean life in terms of decay constant.

OR

   (a) State two distinguish features of nuclear force.

(b) Draw a plot showing the variation of potential energy of a pair of nucleons as a function of their separation. Mark the regions on the graph where the force is (i) attractive and (ii) repulsive.

22. A triangular prism of refractive angle 60° is made of a transparent material of refractive index $2/\sqrt{3}$. A ray of light is incident normally on face KL as shown in figure. Trace the path of the ray as it passes through the prism and calculate the angle of emergence and angle of deviation.

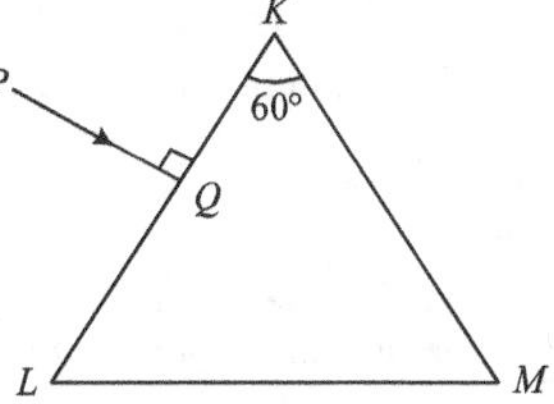

23. Prove that in a common-emitter amplifier, the output and input differ in phase by 180°.

In a transistor, the change of base current by 30 μA produces change of 0.02 V in the base-emitter voltage and a change of 4 mA in the collector current. Calculate the current amplification factor and the load resistance used, if the voltage gain of amplifier is 400.

24. Show, on a plot, variation of resistivity of (i) a conductor, and (ii) a typical semiconductor as a function of temperature.

Using the expression for the resistivity in terms of number density and relaxation time between the collisions, explain how resistivity in the case of a conductor increases while it decreases in a semiconductor, with the rise of temperature.

SECTION - D

25. (a) Derive an expression for the induced emf developed when a coil of N turns, and area of cross-section A, is rotated at a constant angular speed w in a uniform magnetic field B.

(b) A wheel with 100 metallic spokes each 0.5m long is rotated with speed of 120 rev/min in the plane normal to the horizontal component of the Earth's magnetic field. If the resultant magnetic field at that place is 4×10^{-4} T and the angle of dip at the place is 30°, find the emf induced between the axle and the rim of the wheel.

OR

(a) Derive the expression for magnetic energy stored in an inductor when a current I develops in it. Hence obtain the expression for the magnetic energy density.

(b) A square loop of sides 5 cm carrying a current of 0·2 A in the clockwise direction is placed at a distance of 10 cm from an infinitely long wire carrying current of 1 A as shown. Calculate (i) resultant magnetic force, and (ii) torque, if any, acting on the loop.

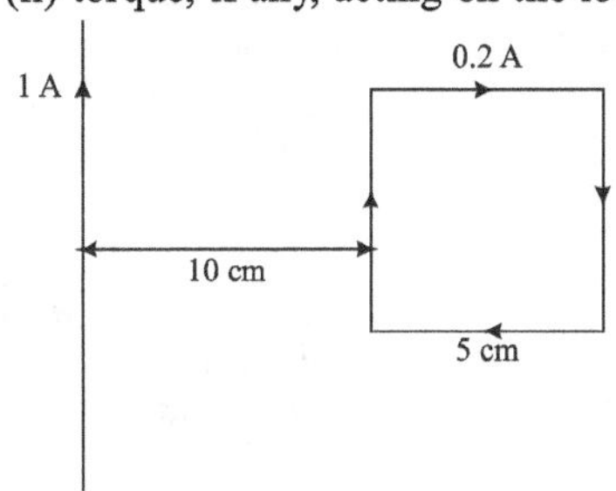

26. Explain with the help of diagram, how plane polarized light can be produced by scattering of light from the Sun.

Two polaroids P_1 and P_2 are placed with their pass axes perpendicular to each other. Unpolarised light of intensity I is incident on P_1. A third polaroid P_3 is kept between P_1 and P_2 such that its pass axis makes an angle 45° with that of P_1. Calculate the intensity of light transmitted through P_1, P_2 and P_3.

OR

(a) Why cannot the phenomenon of interference be observed by illuminating two pin holes with two sodium lamps ?

(b) Two monochromatic source waves having displacements $y_1 = a \cos \omega t$ and $y_2 = a \cos (\omega t + \phi)$ from two coherent sources interfere to produce an interference pattern. Derive the expression for the resultant intensity and obtain the conditions for constructive and destructive interference.

(c) Two wavelengths of sodium light of 590 nm and 596 nm, are used in turn to study the diffraction taking place at a single slit of aperture 2×10^{-6} m. If the distance between slit and the screen is 1·5m, calculate the separation between the positions of the second maxima of diffraction pattern obtained in the two cases.

27. (a) Describe briefly, with the help of a circuit diagram, the method of measuring the internal resistance of a cell.

(b) Give reason why a potentiometer is preferred over a voltmeter for the measurement of emf of a cell.

(c) In the potentiometer circuit below, calculate the balancing length l. Give reason, whether the circuit will work, if the driver cell of emf 5V is replaced with a cell of 2V, keeping all other factors constant.

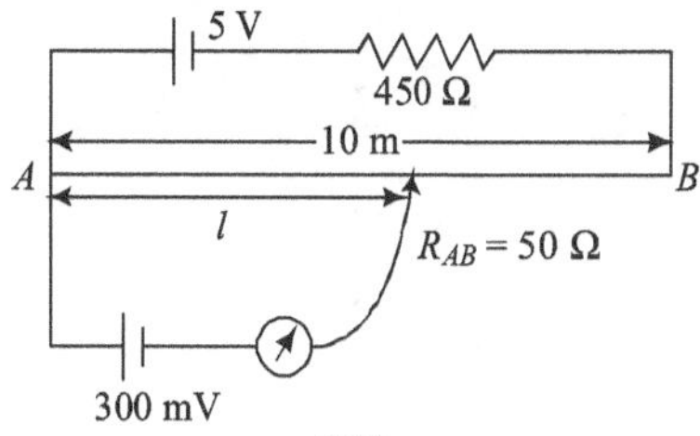

OR

(a) State the working principle of a meter bridge used to measure an unknown resistance.

(b) Give reason
(i) why the connection between the resistors in a metre bridge are made of thick copper strips,
(ii) why is it generally prefered to obtain the balance length near the mid-point of the bridge wire.

(c) Calculate the potential difference across the 4 Ω resistor in given electrical circuit, using Kirchhoff's law.

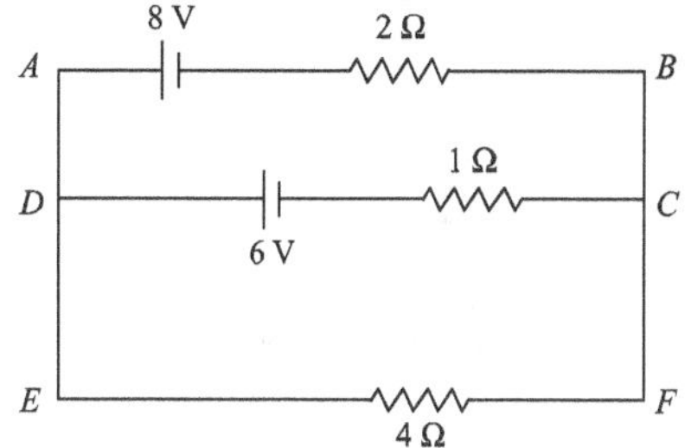

Solutions

SECTION - A

1. Equipotential surfaces for an electric dipole.

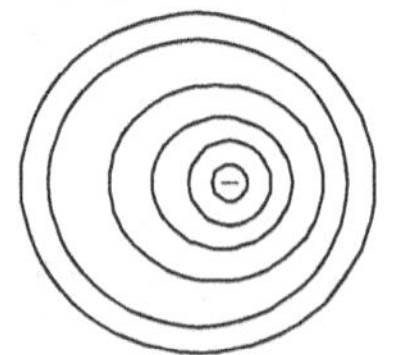 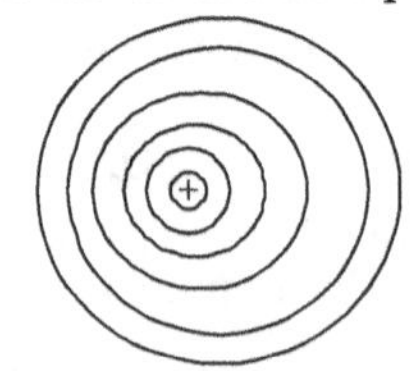

(1 Mark)

2. Radius of circular orbit for a charge particle moving in uniform magnetic field B with velocity v is

$$r = \frac{mu}{qB}$$ **(1 Mark)**

where m = mass of particle

The kinetic energy of proton when accelerated through potential V should be equal to qV.

$$\therefore \quad \frac{1}{2}mv^2 = qV$$

$$\Rightarrow \quad v = \sqrt{\frac{2qV}{m}}$$

$$\therefore \quad r = \frac{m}{qB}\left[\frac{2qV}{m}\right]^{1/2}$$

When potential is doubled, the radius

$$r' = \frac{1}{B}\sqrt{\frac{2m(2V)}{q}}$$

$$r' = \frac{1}{B}\sqrt{\frac{4mV}{q}}$$

$$\therefore \quad \frac{r'}{r} = \sqrt{\frac{4}{2}} = \sqrt{2}$$

3. Magnetic susceptibility χ is

$$\chi = \frac{C\mu_0}{T}$$ **(1 Mark)**

where c = curie constant

μ_0 = permeability of free space

T = temperature.

at $\quad T_1 = 300$ K

$$\chi_1 = \frac{C\mu_0}{T_1}$$

$$1.2 \times 10^5 = \frac{C\mu_0}{300} \qquad ...(1)$$

at $\quad T_2\chi_2 = \frac{C\mu_0}{T_2}$

$$1.44 \times 10^5 = \frac{C\mu_0}{T_2} \qquad ...(2)$$

Dividing eqⁿ (1) by (2)

$$\frac{1.2\times10^5}{1.44\times10^5} = \frac{T_2}{300}$$

$$\Rightarrow \quad T_2 = \frac{1.2\times10^5}{1.44\times10^5}\times300 \quad T_2 = 250 \text{ K}$$

OR

Material is diamagnetic because magnetic susceptibility of diamagnetic substance is $-1 \leq \chi < 0$. **(1 Mark)**

> **Note**
>
> *Magnetic susceptibility, c of diamagnetic = negative*
> *Paramagnetic = small and positive*
> *Ferromagnetic = large and positive*

4. The *V-I* characteristics shown in figure is of photodiode.

(1 Mark)

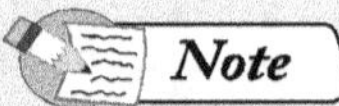

> **Note**
>
> *Photodiode is a reverse biased p-n junction in which current carriers are generated by photons through photo excitaition. Also, current in the photodiode changes with the change in light intensity.*

5. Microwaves are used in RADAR. **(½ + ½ = 1 Mark)**
Its frequency range is 10^{10} to 10^{12} Hz.

OR

An accelerating charge or an oscillating charge produces an oscillating electeric field in space, which produces an oscillating magnetic field, which in turn, is a source of oscillating electric field and soon. Thus, oscillating electric and magnetic field regenerate each other, as electromagnetic wave propagates through space. **(1 Mark)**

SECTION - B

6. The total current through capacitor, when charged by an external *dc* source is

$$i = i_c + i_d$$

where i_c = conduction current or current charging the capacitor **(2 Mark)**

i_d = displacement current due to changing electric field between the plates of capacitor.

Outside the capacitor plates, we have only conduction current $i = i_c$ and no displacement current, $i_d = 0$.

$\therefore$ Outside capacitor $i = i_c$ ...(1)

Inside the capacitor plates, we have only displacement current $i = i_d$ and no conduction current, $i_c = 0$.

$\therefore$ Inside capacitor $i = i_d$ ...(2)

From (1) and (2), $i = i_c = i_d$.

> **Note**
>
> *Ampere - Maxwell law which uses displacement current is given as,*
>
> $$\oint \vec{B}\cdot d\vec{l} = \mu_0 i_c + \mu_0\varepsilon_0\frac{d\phi_E}{dt}$$
>
> *where* $\quad i_d = \frac{\varepsilon_0 d\phi_E}{dt}$
>
> *This law establish the fact that an electric field changing with time give rise to a magnetic field and therefore displacement current is the source of magnetic field, even when there is no actual charge movement.*

7. Energy of photon is

$$E_{Pho} = h\nu_{Pho}$$
$$= \frac{hc}{\lambda_{Pho}} \qquad ...(1)$$

$$[\because \nu\lambda = C = \text{speed of light}]$$

where λ_{Pho} = de-Broglie wavelength of photon.

Kinetic energy of proton E_k is

$$E_k = \frac{1}{2}mv^2 \qquad ...(2)$$

De-Broglie wavelength of proton,

$$\lambda_p = \frac{h}{mv}$$

$$\Rightarrow \qquad mv = \frac{h}{\lambda_p} \qquad ...(3)$$

Using (3) and (2), we get

$$E_k = \frac{1}{2}m\left[\frac{h^2}{m^2\lambda_p^2}\right]$$

$$E_k = \frac{1\,h^2}{2\,m\lambda_p^2} \qquad ...(4)$$

Given that $\lambda_p = \lambda_{Pho} = \lambda$　　**(1 Mark)**

So, equation (1) is

$$E_{Pho} = \frac{hc}{\lambda}$$

Multiply and divide above equation by $\dfrac{h}{2m\lambda}$

$$E_{Pho} = \frac{hc}{\lambda} \times \frac{h}{2m\lambda} \times \frac{2m\lambda}{h}$$

$$E_{Pho} = \frac{2m\lambda c}{h}\left[\frac{h^2}{2m\lambda^2}\right]$$

From equation (4)

$$E_{Pho} = \left(\frac{2m\lambda c}{h}\right)E_k \qquad \textbf{(1 Mark)}$$

8. Given,

Work function of metal $\phi_0 = 2\ eV$　　**(2 Mark)**

Stopping potential, $eV_s = 0.55\ V$

From einstein's photoelectric equation, the energy of photon emitted is

$$h\nu = \phi_0 + eV_S$$
$$= 2 + 0.55$$
$$h\nu = 2.55\ eV$$

From Bohr's third postualate, the energy of photon emitted should be equal to the energy difference of stationary orbit.

$$\therefore \qquad h\nu = E_i - E_f$$

$$h\nu = \frac{-13.6}{n^2} - \left(\frac{-13.6}{(2)^2}\right)[\because \text{for Ist excited state } n = 2]$$

$$\Rightarrow \qquad 2.55 = \frac{-13.6}{n^2} + 3.4$$

$$-0.85 = \frac{-13.6}{n^2}$$
$$n^2 = 16$$
$$\Rightarrow \qquad n = 4$$

OR

Energy states of hydrogen atom is

$$E_n = \frac{-13.6}{n^2}$$

where n = principle quantum number.

Energy of ground state $i.e.$ for $n = 1$

$$E_1 = -13.6\,eV$$

When energy of value $12.5\,eV$ is supplied to atom, it will get excited and will make transition from ground state to excited state.

Energy of excited state $= -13.6 + 12.5 = -1.1\ eV$

For hydrogen atom, this should be equal to

$$E_n = \frac{-13.6}{n^2} = -1.1$$

$$n^2 = \frac{-13.6}{-1.1} = 12.3$$
$$n = 3.5$$
$$n \sim 3. \qquad \textbf{(2 Mark)}$$

So, the maximum number of lines emitted by atom are 3.

> **Note**
>
> *Another way to ask this question*
> **Q.** *A 12.5 eV electron beam is used to excite a gaseous hydrogen atom at room temperature. Determine the wave-lengths and the corresponding series of the lines emitted.*

9.

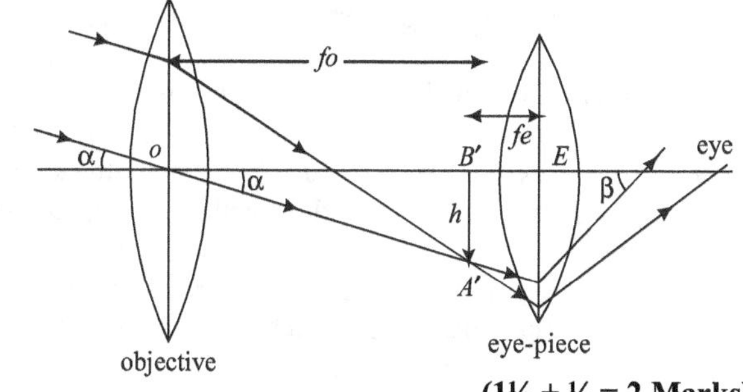

(1½ + ½ = 2 Marks)

Magnifying power of telescope is

$$m = \frac{fo}{fe}$$

where　fo = focal length of objective

　　　　fe = focal length of eye-piece.

> **Note**
>
> *Magnifying power of telescope, when final image is formed at least distance of distinct vision,*
>
> $$m = \frac{f_0}{f_e}\left(1 + \frac{f_0}{D}\right)$$

OR

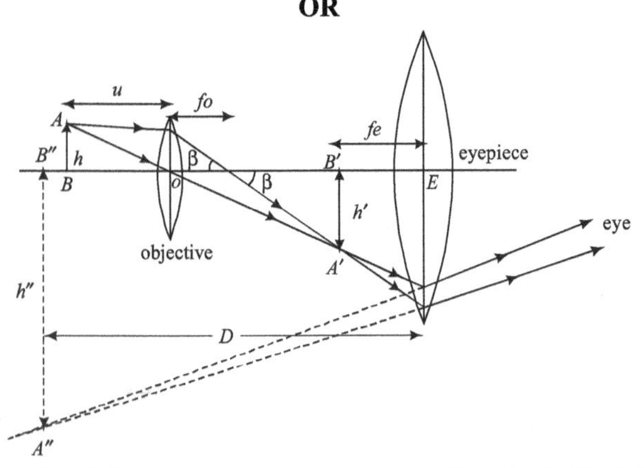

Resolving power of microscope,   **(1½ + ½ = 2 Marks)**

$$R.P. = \frac{2n\sin\beta}{1.22\lambda}$$

λ = wavelength incident light

n = refractive index of medium between object and objective lens.

10. The relation between height of a *TV* antenna 'h' and maximum range of signals 'd' is   **(1 + 1 + 1 Marks)**

$$d = \sqrt{2hR}$$

For space-wave communication, this relation is modified as,

$$d = \sqrt{2h_R R} + \sqrt{2h_T R}$$

where h_R = height of receiving antenna

h_T = height of transmitting antenna.

R = Radius of earth.

Frequency range of space-wave communication is above 40 *MHz*.

11. Conditions under which rainbow can be observed:-

(1 + 1 = 2 Marks)

(i) Rain/water droplets should be present in atmosphere.

(ii) Observer should be standing with his back towards observer

Primary rainbow: The primary rainbow is formed by rays which undergo one internal reflection. Intensity of primary rainbow is high.

Secondary rainbow: The secondary rainbow is formed by rays which undergo two internal reflection. The intensity of secondary rainbow is low.

12. (i) The blue colour of the sky is due to the scattering of sunlight by molecules of atmosphere. Since blue light have short wavelength, they are scattered the most and hence sky appear blue.   **(1 Mark)**

(ii) When sun is near the horizon at sunset or sunrise, the light rays have to travel a larger thickness of the atmosphere. The lower wavelengths in the blue region are almost completely scattered away by air molecules. The higher wavelengths in the red region are least scattered and reach our eye. Hence, sun appear reddish at sunset and sunrise.   **(1 Mark)**

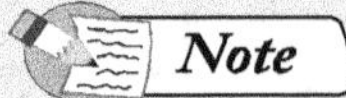

Scattering of the light takes place when the size of the scattering object is very small as compared to the wavelength of light. Intensity of light corresponding to a wavelength in the scattered light varies inversely as the fourth power of the wavelngth amount of scattering $\alpha \dfrac{1}{\lambda 4}$.

SECTION - C

13. (i) Current in circuit $I = 3A$

Potential difference across capacitor, $V_C = 120\ V$

Potential difference across resistor, $V_R = 90V$.

$\therefore \qquad R = \dfrac{V_R}{I} = \dfrac{90}{3} = 30\Omega$

$X_C = \dfrac{V_C}{I} = \dfrac{120}{3} = 40\ \Omega$

Total impedance of circuit Z

$$= \sqrt{R^2 + (X_C)^2}$$

$$Z = \sqrt{(30)^2 + (40)^2}$$

$$Z = \sqrt{2500}$$

$$Z = 50\ \Omega \qquad \textbf{(1½ Marks)}$$

(ii) When inductor of inductance 'L' is connected in series with C and R, power factor becomes 1.

When power factor of *LCR* circuit is 1, that means

$X_C = X_L$

$X_C = 40\ \Omega$

$X_L = WL$

Given $\nu = 50$ Hz

so $w = 2\pi\nu$

$= 2\pi \times 50$

$w = 100\ \pi$

So, $100\ \pi\ L = 40$

$$L = \frac{2}{5\pi}\ \text{Henry.} \qquad \textbf{(1½ Marks)}$$

OR

(a) Given, $C = 80\ \mu F = 80 \times 10^{-6}\ F$

$L = 5.0\ H$

$R = 40\ \Omega$

Resonance frequency $w = \dfrac{1}{\sqrt{LC}}$

$$\omega = \frac{1}{\sqrt{5 \times 80 \times 10^{-6}}}$$

$$\omega = \frac{1}{\sqrt{400 \times 10^{-6}}}$$

$$\omega = \frac{1000}{20} = 50\ \text{Hz} \qquad \textbf{(1 Mark)}$$

(b) Impedance Z of *LCR* circuit,

$$Z = \sqrt{R^2 + (X_C - X_L)^2}$$

At resonance, $X_C = X_L$ so
$$Z = R = 40\ \Omega$$
Value of voltage is given as $= 230$ V. This the ums value of voltage. So peak value of voltage V_m is

$$V_m = 230\sqrt{2} \qquad \left[\because V_{rms} = \frac{V_m}{\sqrt{2}}\right]$$

$\therefore$ Amplitude of current $= \dfrac{V_m}{Z} = \dfrac{V_m}{R}$

$$= \frac{230\sqrt{2}}{40} = 8.1\ \text{A} \qquad \textbf{(1 Mark)}$$

(c) At resonance, current is 8.1 A.

$\therefore$ Potential difference across capacitor $V_C = I\,X_C$

$$V_C = (8.1) \times \frac{1}{50 \times 80 \times 10^{-6}}$$

$$\left[\because X_C = \frac{1}{WC}\right]$$

$$V_C = 2033\ \text{V}$$

Similarly, potential difference across inductor $V_L = I\,X_L$.

$$V_L = (8.1) \times 50 \times 5$$
$$V_L = 2033\ \text{V}$$

So $\qquad V_C - V_L = 0.$ $\qquad\qquad$ **(1 Mark)**

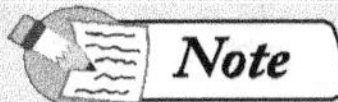

Note

The resonance phenomenon occur when $X_L = X_C$ in LCR circuit. For resonance to occur, the presence of both L and C elements in circuit is must, otherwise there will be no possibility of voltage cancellation.

14. The n and p region of a zener diode are heavily doped because when they are heavily doped, the electric field at the junction is extremly high to knock-off electrons from valance band and also the width of depletion region is very thin.

If voltage across zener is 15V, then voltage across 250 Ω resistor will be $20 - 15 = 5$V. $\qquad$ **(1½ + 1½ = 3 Marks)**

So current through 250 Ω resistor

$$I = \frac{5}{250} = 0.02\ \text{A}$$

1 KΩ resistor and zener diode are in parallel. So voltage across 1 KΩ resistor is also 15 V.

So, current through 1KΩ resistor $= \dfrac{15}{1000} = 0.015$ A.

From circuit diagram,

Current through 250 Ω = current through zener diode + current through 1 kΩ resistor

$\therefore\ 0.02$ = current through zener diode + 0.015

$\Rightarrow$ current through zener diode $= 0.02 - 0.015 = 0.005$ A.

15.

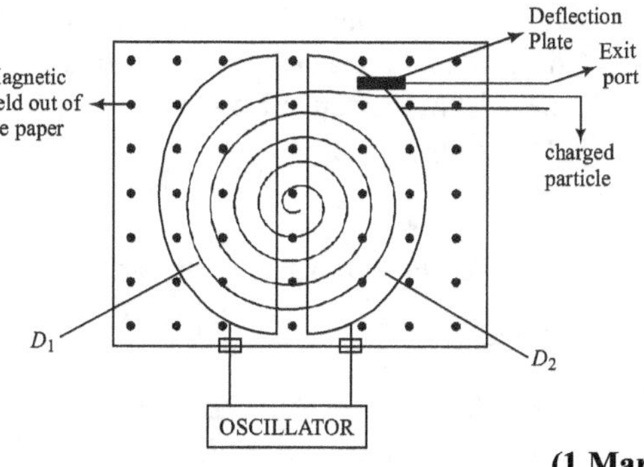

(1 Mark)

Working principle of cyctron:- A charged particle can be accelerated to gigh energies by making it pass through cross electric and magnetic field a number of times without changing its frequency of revolution.

Let a charged particle of charge q, enters the region of magnetic field $\vec{B}$ that is normal to its velocity $\vec{v}$.

Due to magnetic field, the particle will follow a circular path. The necessary centripetal force is provide by magnetic force.

So, Magnetic force = Centripetal force.

$$q\left[\vec{V} \times \vec{B}\right] = \frac{mv^2}{r}$$

$$q\,VB \sin 90° = \frac{mv^2}{r}$$

$$q\,VB = \frac{mv^2}{r} \qquad r = \frac{mv}{qB}$$

Period of revolution T, is

$$T = \frac{2\pi r}{v} = \frac{2\pi}{v} \times \frac{mv}{qB}$$

$$T = \frac{2\pi m}{qB}$$

Now frequency of revolution is

$$f = \frac{1}{T} \quad \Rightarrow \quad f = \frac{qB}{2\pi m} \qquad \textbf{(2 Marks)}$$

which is independent of velocity and radius of orbit.

Note

The key to the operation of the cyclotron is that the frequency at which the particle circulates in the magnetic field must be equal to the frequency of the electrical oscillator.

OR

(a)

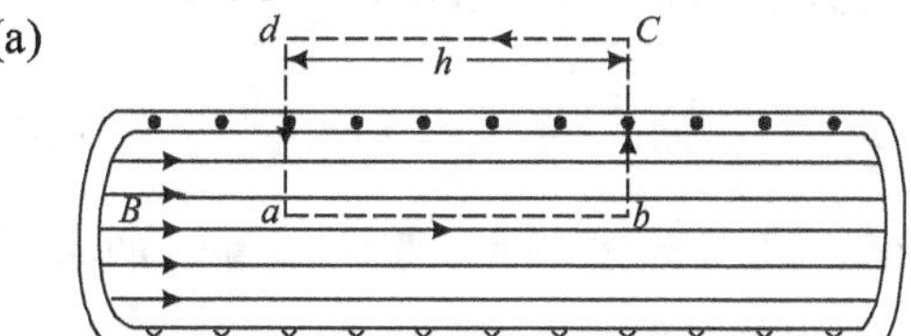

The magnetic field inside a closely wound long solenoid is uniform everywhere and zero outside it.

Let n be the number of turns per unit length. To determine the magnetic field $\vec{B}$ at any inside point, consider a rectangular loop abcd as the Amperian loop. According to ampere's law,

$$\oint \vec{B} \cdot d\vec{e} = \mu_0 \times I_e$$

For, 'dc' $\vec{B} = 0$ (outside solenoid)

Along 'ad' and 'bc', the angle between $\vec{B}$ and $d\vec{e}$ is 90°. So $B \, dl \cos 90° = 0$.

Therefore, 'ad', 'bc' and 'dc' make no contribution.

Along 'ab', total current $I_e = I \times (nh)$ where I is the current in solenoid.

$$\therefore \quad \oint \vec{B} \cdot d\vec{e} = \mu_0 \, I(nh)$$

$$BL = \mu_0 I \, (nh)$$

Relevant length of amperian loop $L = h$.

$$\therefore \quad Bh = \mu_0 \, Inh$$

$$\boxed{B = \mu_0 \, In}$$

(b) Difference between solenoid and toriod.

A solenoid is a long wire wound over a cylinder in the form of helix. Solenoid behaves as bar magnet.

A toroid is a circular ring on which a large number of turns of a wire are closely wound. Toroid does not behave as bar magnet.

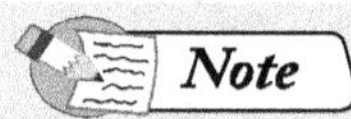

Note

If an iron core of magnetic permeability m_r is kept inside the solenoid, then magnetic field due to solenoid will be

$$B = \mu_r \, \mu_0 \, nL$$

16. Magnetic moment is

$$m = IA$$

where I is current and A = area

When electron of charge 'e', revolve around nucleus, with time period T, then current I is

$$I = \frac{e}{T}$$

If r = orbital radius

and v = orbital speed

Then $T = \dfrac{\text{Distance}}{\text{speed}} = \dfrac{2\pi r}{v}$

$$\therefore \quad I = \frac{ev}{2\pi r}$$

Area of orbit $A = \pi r^2$

So magnetic moment m will be $m = \dfrac{ev}{2\pi r} \times \pi r^2$

as $\boxed{m = \dfrac{evr}{2}}$ ...(1) **(1½ Marks)**

According to Bohr's quantization of angular momentum,

$$L = \frac{nh}{2\pi}$$

where n = principle quantum number

     h = planck's constant.

For circular orbit $L = m_e Vr$, where m_e = mass of electron.

$$\therefore \quad m_e vr = \frac{nh}{2\pi}$$

$$vr = \frac{nh}{2\pi m_e}$$

For ground state $n = 1$

$$\therefore \quad vr = \frac{h}{2\pi m_e}$$

Putting the value of vr in 'm' equation (1),

$$m = \frac{e}{2}\left[\frac{h}{2\pi m_e}\right]$$

$$m = \frac{eh}{4\pi m_e}$$ **(1½ Marks)**

Note

Bohr's quantization of angular momentum given as

$$L = \frac{nh}{2\pi}$$

is dimensionally correct because the dimension of angular momentum and planck's constants is same.

17. 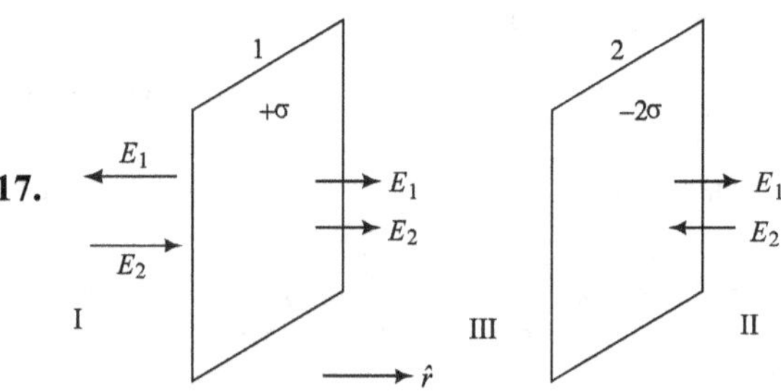

(1 + 1 + 1 = 3 Marks)

Electric field due to charge plane sheet is

$$\vec{E} = \frac{\sigma}{2\varepsilon_0}\hat{r}$$

(i) Electric field to the left of first sheet

$$\vec{E}_I = \vec{E}_1 + \vec{E}_2$$

$$= \frac{-\sigma}{2\varepsilon_0}\hat{r} + \frac{2\sigma}{2\varepsilon_0}\hat{r}$$

$$\vec{E}_I = \frac{\sigma}{2\varepsilon_0}\hat{r}$$

(ii) Electric field to the right of second sheet

$$\vec{E}_{II} = \vec{E}_1 + \vec{E}_2$$

$$\vec{E}_{II} = \frac{\sigma}{2\varepsilon_0}\hat{r} - \frac{(2\sigma)}{2\varepsilon_0}\hat{r}$$

$$\vec{E}_{II} = \frac{-\sigma}{2\varepsilon_0}\hat{r}$$

(iii) Electric field between the sheets

$$\vec{E}_{III} = \vec{E}_1 + \vec{E}_2$$

$$\vec{E}_{III} = \frac{\sigma}{2\varepsilon_0}\hat{r} + \frac{(2\sigma)}{2\varepsilon_0}\hat{r} = \frac{3\sigma}{2\varepsilon_0}\hat{r}$$

OR

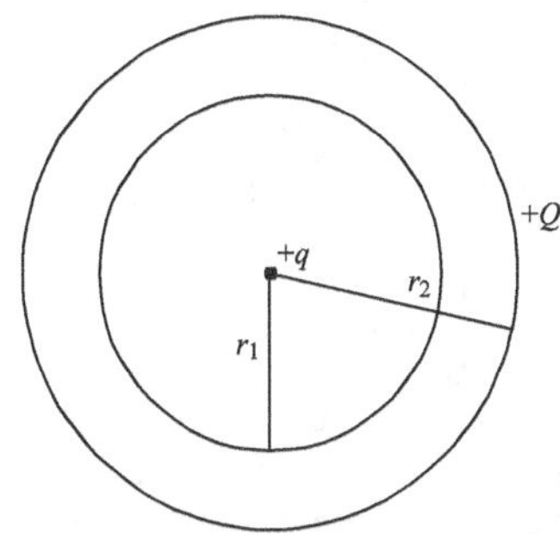

(a) Surface charge density σ is

$$\sigma = \frac{q}{A}$$

where q = total charge
A = surface area

Surface charge density on inner surface of shell σ, is

$$\sigma_1 = \frac{q}{4\pi\varepsilon_0 r_1^2} \qquad [\because A = 4\pi r^2 \text{ for sphere}]$$

Surface charge density on outer surface of shell σ_2 is
(1½ Marks)

$$\sigma_2 = \frac{Q+q}{4\pi r_2^2}$$

(b) Gauss law states that

$$\phi_E = \frac{q}{\varepsilon_0}$$

where ϕ_E = electric flux through gaussian surface
q = total charge enclosed in gaussian surface.
Consider a gaussian surface inside the cavity. It is given the cavity does not have any charge in it.
So, $q = 0$ inside gaussian surface.

$$\therefore \qquad \phi_E = 0$$

Since flux is zero, therefore electric field inside cavity with no charge is zero. This does not depend on shape and size of sheet as long as charge inside cavity is zero.

(1½ Marks)

18. Let $c(t) = A_C \sin(w_C t)$ represents carrier wave of angular frequency wc.

$m(t) = A_m \sin(w_m t)$ represents modulating signal of angular frequency w_m.

Then, the modulated signal $c_m(t)$ can be written as

$$C_m(t) = (A_C + A_m \sin w_m t) \sin wct$$

$$C_m(t) = A_C\left(1 + \frac{Am}{A_C}\sin w_C t\right)\sin wet \qquad \textbf{(1½ Marks)}$$

$$C_m(t) = A_C \sin w_c t + \frac{Am}{A_C} A_C \sin w_c t \sin wmt$$

Here we define modulation index μ as

$$\mu = \frac{A_m}{A_C} \qquad \textbf{(1½ Marks)}$$

$$\therefore \quad c_m(t) = A_C \sin w_C t + \mu A_C \sin w_C t \sin wmt$$

Using trigonometric identity

$$\sin A \sin B = \frac{1}{2}\left[\cos(A-B) - \cos(A+B)\right]$$

$$C_m(t) = A_C \sin w_c t + \frac{\mu A_C}{2}\cos(w_c - wm)t - \frac{\mu A_C}{2}$$
$$\cos/w_c + w_m t$$

Here $w_c - w_m$ = lower side band frequencies

$w_c + w_m$ = upper side band frequencies. **(1 Mark)**

> **Note**
>
> *Modulation index* $\mu = \dfrac{A_m}{A_c}$ *is always equal to or less than unity.*
>
> *When μ exceeds unity, the carrier wave is over modulated.*

19.   **(1 Mark)**

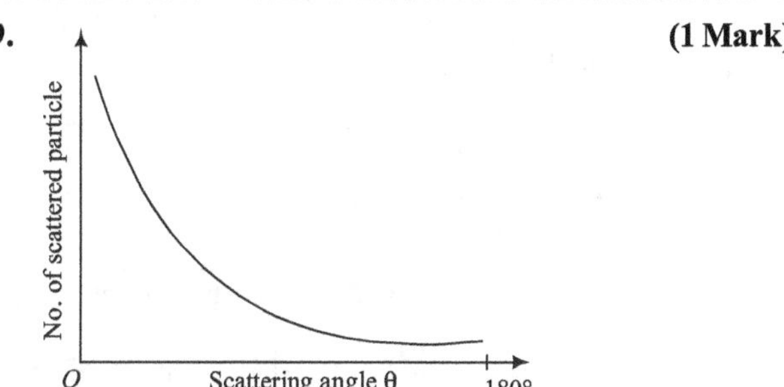

From the graph, it is conclude that only a small fraction of incident particles undergo head on collision having large scattering angle. This implies that the mass of the atom is concentrated in a small volume. Since α-particle rebound back, massive positively charged nucleus reside inside the atom occupying small region.

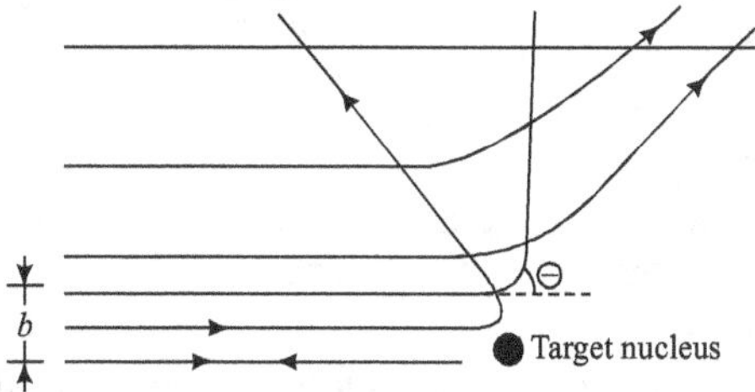

(2 Marks)

From above diagram, we can conclude that small impact parameter 'b' suffers large scattering angle that it show the upper limit to the size of nucleus.

> **Note**
>
> *Another way to ask this question:-*
> **Q.** *In study of Geiger - Mardon experiment on scattering of α-particles by a thin foil of gold, draw the trajectory of α-particle in coulomb field of target nucleus. Explain briefly how one gets the information on the size of nucleus from this study.*

20. Given, capacitor without dielectric

$$C_0 = \frac{\varepsilon_0 A}{d} = 200 \ \mu F \qquad \ldots(1)$$

where $d = 5$ mm

when dielectric of dielectric constant k is introduced (of thickness t), then $d \to 2d$.

$$\therefore \quad C' = \frac{\varepsilon_0 A}{2d - d + \dfrac{t}{k}} \qquad \ldots(2)$$

$\therefore$ The effective separation between plates is

$$2d - t + \frac{t}{k} = 2 \times 5 - 5 + \frac{5}{10} = 5.5 \ \text{mm} \quad \textbf{(½ Mark)}$$

(i) From (1) and (2)

$$\frac{C'}{C_0} = \frac{d}{2d - t + \dfrac{t}{k}}$$

$$C' = 200 \times \frac{5}{5.5} \approx 182 \ \mu F \qquad \textbf{(1 Mark)}$$

(ii) Electric field is given as

$$E = \frac{v}{d}$$

New electric field will be,

$$E' = \frac{V}{\text{effective distance between plates}}$$

$$E' = \frac{100}{5.5 \times 10^{-3}} = 18182 \ \text{V/m.} \quad \textbf{(1 Mark)}$$

(iii) Electrostatic energy without dielectric $E_1 = \dfrac{1}{2} C_0 V^2$

Electrostatic energy with dielectric $E_2 = \dfrac{1}{2} C' V^2$

$$\frac{E_2}{E_1} = \frac{C^1}{C_0} = \frac{2000}{11 \times 200} = \frac{10}{11}.$$

$$\therefore \qquad E_2 = \frac{10}{11} E_1. \qquad \textbf{(½ Mark)}$$

21. Anti-neutrino are difficult to detect in β-decay because they are charge less particle and interact very weakly with other matters. **(½ Mark)**

Decay constant:- Decay constant is defined as the reciprocal of the time duration in which undecayed radioactive nuclei reduce to $1/e$ times the nuclei present initially.

Mean life $\qquad \tau = \dfrac{\text{total life of all nuclei}}{\text{total number of nuclei}}$ **(1 Mark)**

$$\tau = \frac{\displaystyle\int_0^\infty t\,dN}{N_0}$$

From radioactive decay law

$$\frac{dN}{dt} = \lambda N = \lambda N_0 e^{-\lambda t}$$

where λ = decay constant.

$$\therefore \qquad \tau = -\int_0^\infty \frac{t(\lambda N_0 e^{-\lambda t}\,dt)}{N_0}$$

$$\tau = \lambda \int_0^\infty t e^{-\lambda t}\,dt$$

$$\tau = \lambda \left[t\frac{e^{-\lambda t}}{\lambda}\Big|_0^\infty - \int_0^\infty \frac{e^{-\lambda t}}{-\lambda}\cdot 1 \right]$$

$$\tau = \lambda \left[0 + \frac{1}{\lambda^2} \right] \Rightarrow \boxed{\tau = \frac{1}{\lambda}} \qquad \textbf{(1½ Marks)}$$

OR

(a) Two distinguish features of nuclear forces are:-
(i) It is attractive in nature
(ii) It is short range force which is independent of charge.
(1 + 1 = 2 Marks)

(b)

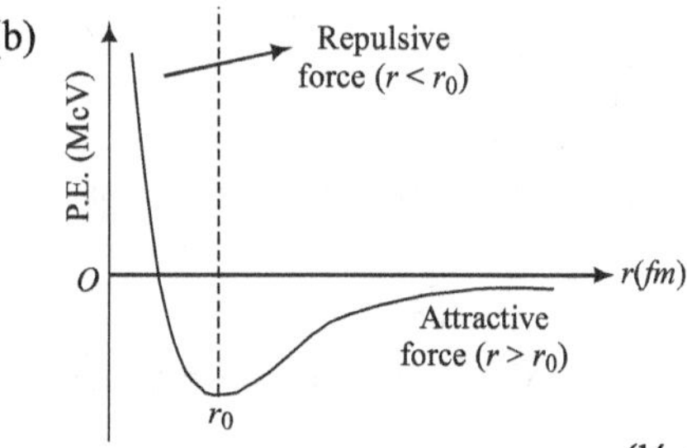

(½ + ½ = 1 Mark)

22. Since ray falls normally on face KL, the angle of incidence at face KM is 60°. ($\because A = 60°$)

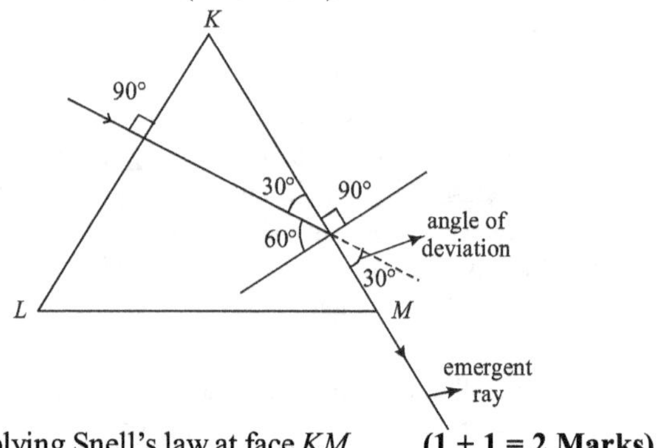

Applying Snell's law at face KM **(1 + 1 = 2 Marks)**

$$\frac{\sin i}{\sin r} = n_{ap}$$

where n_{ap} = refractive index of wrt prism

$$n_{ap} = \frac{1}{2/\sqrt{3}}$$

$$\therefore \qquad \frac{\sin 60°}{\sin r} = \frac{1}{2/\sqrt{3}}$$

$$\sin r = \frac{2}{\sqrt{3}} \sin 60°$$

$$\sin r = \frac{2}{\sqrt{3}} \times \frac{\sqrt{3}}{2} = 1$$

$$\therefore \qquad r = 90°$$

$\Rightarrow$ angle of emergence is 90°. **(1 Mark)**

Angle of deviation is equal to 30° as seen from ray diagram.

23. In common-emitter amplifier.

Input voltage signal $V_i = \Delta I_B \, ri$

where $I_B =$ base current

    $ri =$ input resistance

Output voltage $V_0 = -\Delta I_C R_L$

where $I_C =$ Collector current

    $R_L =$ Load resistance.

Voltage gain or voltage amplification A_V is

$$A_V = \frac{V_0}{V_i} = \frac{-\Delta I_C R_L}{\Delta I_B \, ri}$$

$$A_V = -\beta_{ac} \times \text{resistance gain}$$

The negative sign indicates that output is $180°$ out of phase wrt input signal.   **(1 Mark)**

Given $\Delta I_B = 30 \, \mu A = 30 \times 10^{-6} \, A$

    $\Delta I_C = 4 \, mA = 4 \times 10^{-3} \, A$

Current amplification $\beta ac = \dfrac{\Delta I_C}{\Delta I_B}$

$$= \frac{4 \times 10^{-3}}{30 \times 10^{-6}} = \frac{400}{3} \qquad \textbf{(1 Mark)}$$

Base emitter voltage $V_{BE} = ri \, \Delta I_B$

$\therefore$ $ri = \dfrac{0.02}{30 \times 10^{-6}}$ $[\because V_{BE} = 0.02 \, V \text{ (given)}]$

$$ri = \frac{2}{3} \times 10^3 \, \Omega$$

Voltage gain $A_V = -\beta \dfrac{R_L}{r_i}$

    $A_V = 100 \text{ (given)}$

$\therefore$ $R_L = \dfrac{A_V \, ri}{\beta}$ [neglecting the $-ve$ sign]

$$= \frac{100 \times 2 \times 10^3 \times 3}{400 \times 3}$$

$$R_L = 2 \times 10^3 \, \Omega. \qquad \textbf{(1 Mark)}$$

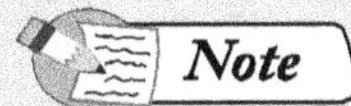

Note

The AC voltage gain in common-emitter amplifier is larger compared to that in common-base amplifier, but the resistance gain is smaller. In common-emitter amplifier, the output voltage signal is obtained across the collector and the emitter is 180° out of phase with input-signal applied across the base.

24.

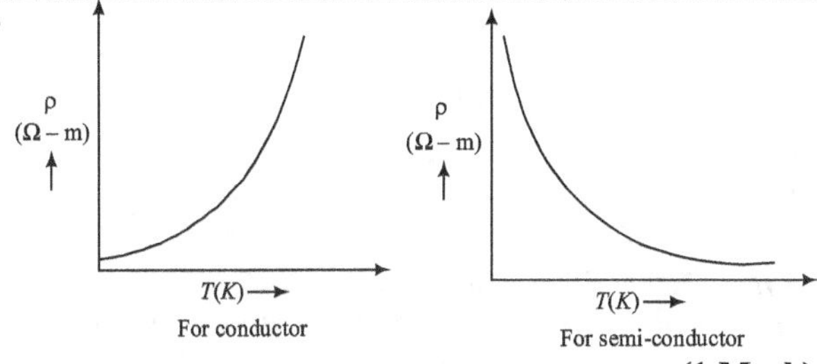

    (1 Mark)

Resistivity ρ is

$$\rho = \frac{m}{ne^2 \tau} \qquad \qquad \dots(1)$$

where $n =$ number density of free electron

    $\tau =$ relaxation time.

As we increase the temperature, τ decreases as average speed of electron increases.

For conductor, 'n' is not dependent on temperature. So, with increase in temperature, τ will decrease increasing resistivity of conductor (from eq^n (1)).

For semiconductor, 'n' increases with increase in temperature. This increase is dominant over decrease in τ. Therefore, from eq^n (1) with increase in temperature, resistivity will decrease as 'n' increases.   **(2 Marks)**

SECTION - D

25. **(a)** When the coil having N turns is rotated with a constant angular speed w, the angle θ between the magnetic field $\vec{B}$ and area vector $\vec{A}$ of coil at any instant t is $\theta = \omega t$.

Magnetic flux $\phi = \vec{B} \cdot \vec{A}$

$$\phi = BA \cos \theta$$

$$= BA \cos \omega t$$

From Faraday's law, the induced emf is

$$\varepsilon = -\frac{N d\phi}{dt}$$

$$\varepsilon = -N\left[\frac{d}{dt}(BA \cos \omega t)\right]$$

$$\varepsilon = +NBA \, \omega \sin \omega t$$

$$\varepsilon = \varepsilon_0 \sin \omega t$$

where $\varepsilon_0 = NBA \, \omega$ **(2½ Marks)**

(b) Given $l = 0.5 \, m$

frequency $\nu = 120 \, rpm$

$$= \frac{120}{60} = 2 \text{ rps.}$$

$\therefore$ $w = 2\pi\nu = 4\pi \, rad/S$

    $B = 4 \times 10^{-4} \, T$ and $\delta = 30°$

Horizontal component of B,

    $B_H = B \cos \delta$

$$= 4 \times 10^{-4} \times \cos 30°$$

$$= 4 \times 10^{-4} \times \frac{\sqrt{3}}{2}$$

$$= 2\sqrt{3} \times 10^{-4} \, T$$

emf induced $\varepsilon = \dfrac{1}{2} B_H \omega l^2$

$$\varepsilon = \frac{1}{2} \times 2\sqrt{3} \times 10^{-4} \times 4\pi \times (0.5)^2$$

$$\varepsilon = 5.4 \times 10^{-4} \text{ volts.} \qquad \textbf{(2½ Marks)}$$

OR

(a) When external voltage is applied across inductor, it induces emf in inductor called self induced emf. This opposes any change in current in a circuit. So, work is needed to be done against self-induced emf to establish current. This work done is stored as magnetic potential energy. For the current I at any instant, the rate of work done is

$$\frac{dw}{dt} = |\varepsilon|\, I \qquad \left(\because \text{Power} = \frac{w}{t} = VI\right)$$

$$\varepsilon = -L\frac{dI}{dt} \text{ is the self induced emf.}$$

$$\therefore \quad \frac{dw}{dt} = LI\frac{dI}{dt}$$

$$dw = LIdI$$

$$w = \int_0^I LIdI$$

$$w = L\left[\frac{I^2}{2}\right]_0^I$$

$$w = \frac{1}{2}LI^2 \qquad \textbf{(2 Marks)}$$

$$\therefore \quad \text{Magnetic potential energy } E = \frac{1}{2}LI^2$$

$$\text{Energy density} = \frac{E}{\text{volume}}$$

$$= \frac{\frac{1}{2}LI^2}{\text{volume}} \qquad \textbf{(1 Mark)}$$

(b)

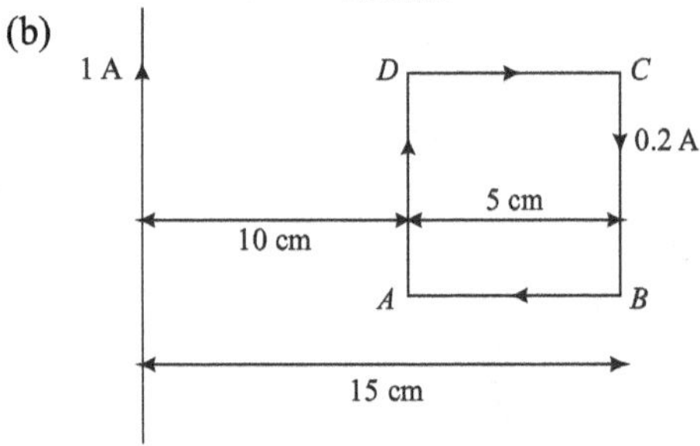

Force on arm DC and AB will be equal and opposite, cancelling out each other. Hence they do not contribute. Force per unit length between two parallel current carrying conductor

$$f = \frac{\mu_0 I_1 I_2}{2\pi d}$$

where d =distance between conductor.
Force per unit length on arm AD,

$$f_1 = \frac{\mu_0 1 \times 0.2}{2\times \pi \times 10 \times 10^{-2}}$$

$$f_1 = 4\times 10^{-7} \text{ N } m^{-1}$$

This force is attractive in nature as current are parallel. Force per unit length on arm BC

$$f_2 = \frac{\mu_0 \times 1 \times 0.2}{2\pi \times 15 \times 10^{-2}}$$

$$= 2.6\times 10^{-7} \text{ N } m^{-1}$$

This force is replusive in nature as current as are antiparallel.

Net force $\qquad\qquad F = (f_1 - f_2)\, l$

$$F = (4 - 2.6)\times 10^{-7} \times 5 \times 10^{-2}$$

$$F = 7\times 10^{-7} \text{ N attractive.} \qquad \textbf{(1½ Marks)}$$

Net torque will be zero as lines of action of forces coincide. **(1½ Marks)**

26. The incident sunlight is unpolarised. Under the influence of electric field of wave, the electrons in molecules of earth's atmosphere starts accelerating in direction according to wave oscillations. (Both $\bullet$ and $\updownarrow$ dirn).

Charges accelerating parallel to arrow do not radiate energy towards observer since their acceleration has no component in transverse direction. The radiation scattered by the molecules therefore is polarised (dot direction).

(1½ + 1½ Marks)

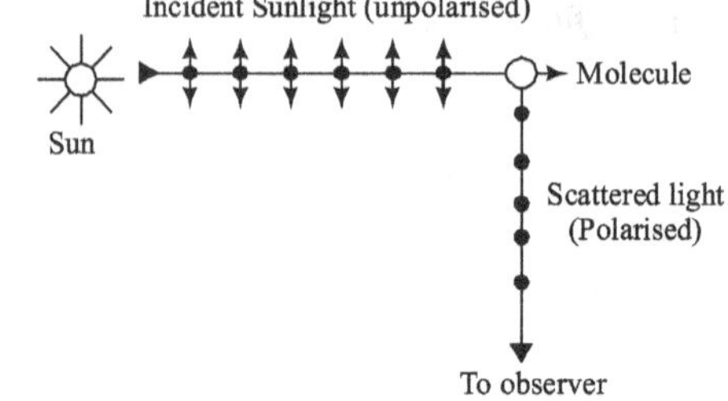

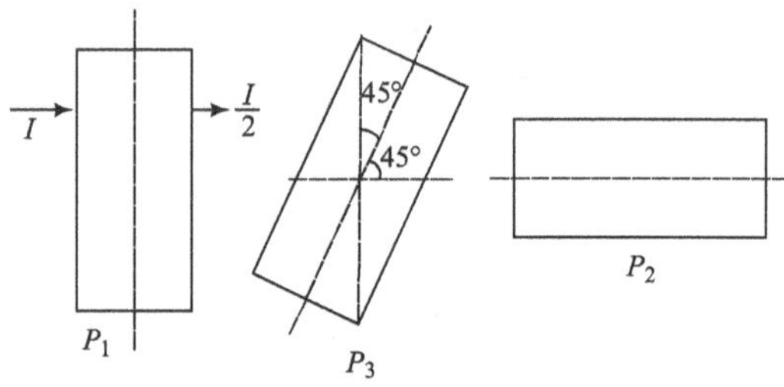

Intensity of transmitted light by $p_1 = \dfrac{I}{2} = I_1$ **(½ Mark)**

Intensity of transmitted light by P_2 by Malus' law is

$$I_2 = I_1 \cos^2 45°$$

$$I_2 = \frac{I}{2}\left(\frac{1}{\sqrt{2}}\right)^2 = \frac{I}{4} \qquad \textbf{(½ Mark)}$$

Intensity of light transmitted by P_3 using Malus' law

$$I_3 = I_2 \cos^2 45°$$

$$I_3 = \frac{I}{4}\left(\frac{1}{\sqrt{2}}\right)^2 = \frac{I}{8} \qquad \textbf{(½ Mark)}$$

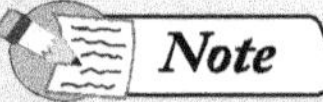 *Note*

Diffraction and interference effects is observed for both longitudinal and transverse wave. But polarization phenomena is special to transverse waves only.

OR

(a) Two different sodium lamps can never act as coherent sources because light wave emitted from an ordinary sources undergoes abrupt phase changes in times of order 10^{-10} seconds. So there phase difference will never be fixed, a necessary condition for coherent source. **(1 Mark)**

(b) Given, $y_1 = a \cos wt$

$y_2 = a \cos (wt + \phi)$

According to super position principle, resultant displacement y will be

$$y = y_1 + y_2$$
$$y = a \cos wt + a \cos (wt + \phi)$$

using trigometric identity,

$$\cos A + \cos B = 2\cos\left(\frac{A+B}{2}\right)\cos\left(\frac{A-B}{2}\right)$$

$$\therefore \quad y = 2a\left[\cos\left(\frac{wt - wt - \phi}{2}\right)\cos\left(\frac{wt + wt + \phi}{2}\right)\right]$$

$$y = 2a\cos\left(\frac{-\phi}{2}\right)\cos\left(\frac{2wt+\phi}{2}\right)$$

$\cos(-\theta) = \qquad\qquad \cos\theta \quad y = 2a \cos (\phi/2) \cos (wt + \phi/2)$

The amplitude of resultant displacement is

$$A = 2a \, \cos\left(\frac{\phi}{2}\right)$$

Intensity $I \propto A^2$

Intensity of $y_1/y_2 \; I_0 \propto a^2$

Intensity of $YI = 4a^2 \cos^2 \dfrac{\phi}{2}$

$$I = 4I_0 \cos^2 \frac{\phi}{2}$$

For $\phi = 0, \pm 2\pi, \pm 4\pi$

$I = 4I_0$ – condition for constructive interference

For $\phi = \pm\pi, 3\pi, \pm 5\pi$

$I = 0$ – condition for destructive interference.

(2 Marks)

(c) Condition for position of secondary maxima

$$y = \left(2n + \frac{1}{2}\right)\frac{\lambda D}{a}$$

where $a = 2 \times 10^{-6}$ m $D = 1.5$ m

For second maxima $n = 2$

$$y = \frac{5\lambda D}{2} \frac{1}{a}$$

$$y_1 = \frac{5\lambda_1 D}{2}\frac{1}{a} \text{ for } \lambda_1 = 590 \text{ nm}$$

$$y_2 = \frac{5\lambda_2 D}{2}\frac{1}{a} \text{ for } \lambda_2 = 596 \text{ nm}$$

$$\therefore \quad y_2 - y_1 = \frac{5D}{2a}(\lambda_2 - \lambda_1)$$

$$= \frac{5 \times 1.5 \times 6 \times 10^{-9}}{2 \times 2 \times 10^{-6}}$$

$$y_2 - y_1 = 11.25 \times 10^{-3} \text{ m.} \qquad \textbf{(2 Marks)}$$

27. (a)

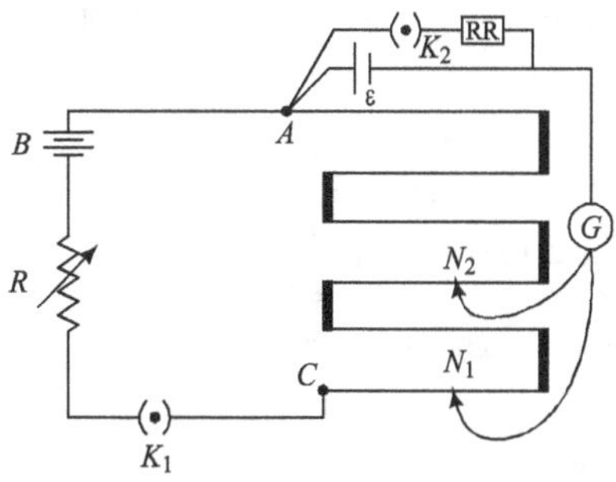

To find internal resistance of cell of *emf* ε, Ist plug K_1, keeping K_2 open. Then balance length l_1 (AN_1) is

$$\varepsilon = \phi l_1 \qquad\qquad ...(1)$$

where ϕ = potential gradient.

when K_2 is plugged in, keeping K_1 open, balance length l_2 (AN_2) is

$$V = \phi \, l_2 \qquad\qquad ...(2)$$

where V = potential drop across resistance box

We know, $V = \varepsilon - Ir$

and $V = IR$

$$\therefore \qquad V = \varepsilon - \frac{V}{R}r$$

$$V + \frac{Vr}{R} = \varepsilon$$

$$\Rightarrow \qquad \frac{\varepsilon}{V} = \left(\frac{r+R}{R}\right) \qquad\qquad ...(3)$$

From (1) and (2)

$$\frac{\varepsilon}{V} = \frac{l_1}{l_2} \qquad\qquad ...(4)$$

Equating equation (3) and (4)

$$\frac{l_1}{l_2} = \frac{R+r}{R}$$

$$\Rightarrow \qquad r = R\left[\frac{l_1}{l_2} - 1\right] \qquad\qquad \textbf{(2½ Marks)}$$

(b) The potentiometer is preferred over voltmeter for the measurement of emf of cell because it draws no current from voltage source being measured. **(1 Marks)**

(c) Given $R_{AB} = 50 \, \Omega$

$R = 450 \, \Omega$

$V = 5 \, V$

$$\therefore \qquad \text{Current} = \frac{V}{R + R_{AB}} = \frac{5}{50 + 450} = 0.01 \text{ A}$$

Voltage across AB, $V_{AB} = 0.01 \times 50 = 0.5$ V

Potential gradient $\phi = \dfrac{V_{AB}}{l} = \dfrac{0.5}{10} = 0.05 \; Vm^{-1}$

Balance length $l = \dfrac{V}{K} = \dfrac{300 \times 10^{-3}}{0.05}$

$$l = 6 \text{ m.}$$

when $V = 5\ V$ is replaced by $2\ V$ cell, then current in circuit will be

$$I = \frac{2}{500} = 0.004\ \text{A}$$

Voltage across AB, $V_{AB} = 0.004 \times 50$
$$= 200\ \text{mV}$$

Since $V_{AB} = 200$ mV is less than 300 mV, the circuit will not work. **(1½ Marks)**

OR

(a) Working principle of metre bridge is based on wheatstone bridge. When bridge is balanced,

$$\frac{R_1}{R_2} = \frac{l_1}{100 - l_1}$$

where l_1 = balanced length. **(1½ Marks)**

(b) (i) Thick copper strips offer minimum resistance and hence avoid error due to end resistances.

$$R \propto \frac{l}{A}$$ **(1 Mark)**

(ii) The metre bridge is most sensitive when the four resistances forming wheatstone bridge are equal. This is possible only if the balance point is near middle of the wire. **(1 Mark)**

(c) 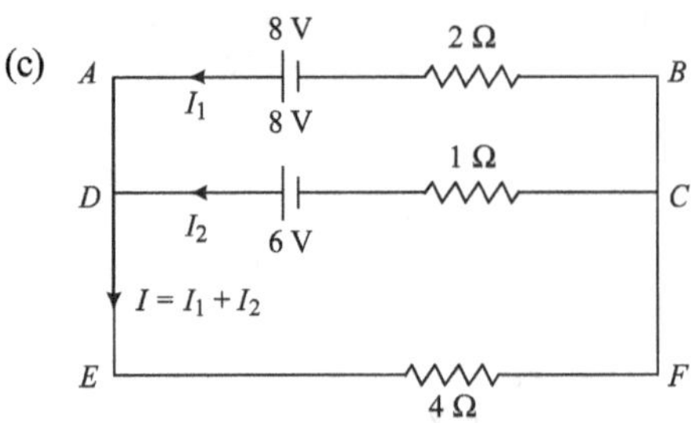

Applying kirchhoff's voltage rule in loop $ABCDA$,
$$-8 + 2I_1 - 1I_2 + 6 = 0$$
$$2I_1 - I_2 = 2 \quad ...(1)$$

Applying kirchhoff's voltage rule in loop $DEFCD$,
$$-4(I_1 + I_2) - I_2 + 6 = 0$$
$$4I_1 + 5I_2 = 6 \quad ...(2)$$

Solving equation (1) and (2) we get
$$I_1 = \frac{8}{7} A \text{ and } I_2 = \frac{2}{7} A$$

$$\therefore \qquad I = \frac{10}{7} A$$

So voltage across $4\ \Omega$ resistor $= 4 \times I$
$$= 4 \times \frac{10}{7} = \frac{40}{7} V.$$ **(1½ Marks)**

CBSE Board Solved Paper

Time Allowed : 3 Hours   *Maximum Marks : 70*

General Instructions:

(i) All questions are compulsory. There are **27** questions in all.

(ii) This question paper has four sections : Section **A**, Section **B**, Section **C** and Section **D**.

(iii) Section **A** contains **five** questions of **one** mark each, Section **B** contains **seven** questions of two marks each, Section **C** contains **twelve** questions of **three** marks each, and Section **D** contains **three** questions of **five** marks each.

(iv) There is no overall choice. However, an internal choice(s) has been provided in **two** questions of **one** mark, **two** questions of **two** marks, **four** questions of **three** marks and **three** questions of **five** marks weightage. You have to attempt only **one** of the choices in such questions.

(v) You may use the following values of physical constants wherever necessary :

$c = 3 \times 10^8$ m/s

$h = 6.63 \times 10^{-34}$ Js

$e = 1.6 \; 10^{-19}$ C

$\mu_0 = 4\pi \times 10^{-7}$ Tm A^{-1}

$\varepsilon_0 = 8.854 \times 10^{-12}$ C^2 N^{-1} m^{-2}

$\dfrac{1}{4\pi\varepsilon_0} = 9 \times 10^9$ Nm^{2}C^{-2}

Mass of electron $(m_e) = 9.1 \times 10^{-31}$ kg

Mass of neutron $= 1.675 \times 10^{-27}$ kg

Mass of proton $= 1.673 \times 10^{-27}$ kg

Avogadro's number $= 6.023 \times 10^{23}$ per gram mole

Boltzmann constant $= 1.38 \times 10^{-23}$ JK^{-1}

SECTION - A

1. Draw the pattern of electric field lines, when a point charge –Q is kept near an uncharged conducting plate.

2. How does the mobility of electrons in a conductor change, if the potential difference applied across the conductor is doubled, keeping the length and temperature of the conductor constant?

3. Define the term "threshold frequency", in the context of photoelectric emission.

OR

Define the term "Intensity" in photon picture of electromagnetic radiation.

4. What is the speed of light in a denser medium of polarising angle 30°?

5. In sky wave mode of propagation, why is the frequency range of transmitting signals restricted to less than 30 MHz?

OR

On what factors does the range of coverage in ground wave propagation depend?

SECTION - B

6. Two bulbs are rated (P_1, V) and (P_2, V). If they are connected (i) in series and (ii) in parallel across a supply V, find the power dissipated in the two combinations in terms of P_1 and P_2.

7. Calculate the radius of curvature of an equi-concave lens of refractive index 1.5, when it is kept in a medium of refractive index 1.4, to have a power of –5D ?

OR

An equilateral glass prism has a refractive index 1.6 in air. Calculate the angle of minimum deviation of the prism, when kept in a medium of refractive index $4\sqrt{\dfrac{2}{5}}$.

8. An α particle and a proton of the same kinetic energy are in turn allowed to pass through a magnetic field B, acting normal to the direction of motion of the particles. Calculate the ratio of radii of the circular paths described by them.

9. State Bohr's quantization condition of angular momentum. Calculate the shortest wavelength of the Bracket series and state to which part of the electromagnetic spectrum does it belong.

OR

Calculate the orbital period of the electron in the first excited state of hydrogen atom.

10. Why a signal transmitted from a TV tower cannot be received beyond a certain distance ? Write the expression for the optimum separation between the receiving and the transmitting antenna.

11. Why is wave theory of electromagnetic radiation not able to explain photo electric effect? How does photon picture resolve this problem ?

12. Plot a graph showing variation of de Broglie wavelength (λ) associated with a charged particle of mass m, versus $1/\sqrt{V}$, where V is the potential difference through which the particle is accelerated. How does this graph give us the information regarding the magnitude of the charge of the particle ?

SECTION - C

13. (a) Draw the equipotential surfaces corresponding to a uniform electric field in the z-direction.
    (b) Derive an expression for the electric potential at any point along the axial line of an electric dipole.

14. Using Kirchhoff's rules, calculate the current through the 40 Ω and 20 Ω resistors in the following circuit:

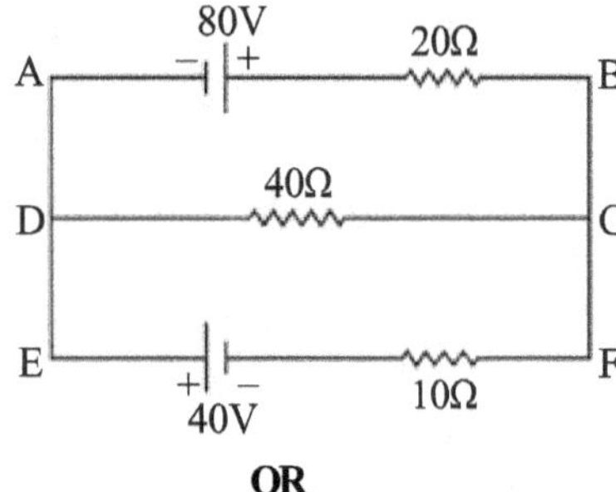

OR

What is end error in a metre bridge ? How is it overcome ? The resistances in the two arms of the metre bridge are R = 5Ω and S respectively.
When the resistance S is shunted with an equal resistance, the new balance length found to be 1.5 l_1, where l_1 is the initial balancing length. Calculate the value of S.

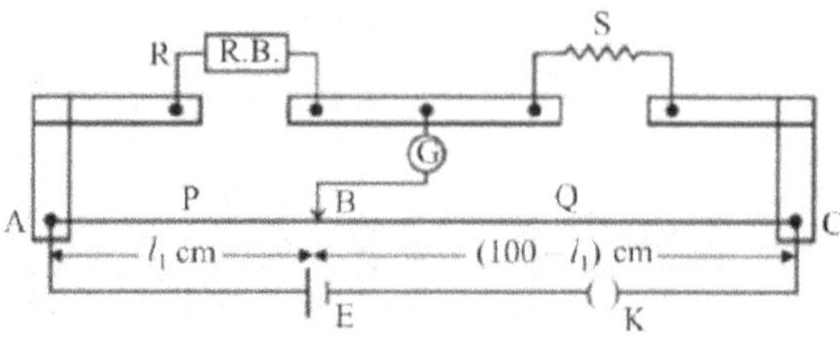

15. (a) Identify the part of the electromagnetic spectrum used in (i) radar and (ii) eye surgery. Write their frequency range.
    (b) Prove that the average energy density of the oscillating electric field is equal to that of the oscillating magnetic field.

16. Define the term wave front. Using Huygens's wave theory, verify the law of reflection.

OR

Define the term, "refractive index" of a medium. Verify Snell's law of refraction when a plane wavefront is propagating from a denser to a rarer medium.

17. (a) Define mutual inductance and write its S.I. unit.
    (b) A square loop of side 'a' carrying a current I2 is kept at distance x from an infinitely long straight wire carrying a current I1 as shown in the figure. Obtain the expression for the resultant force acting on the loop.

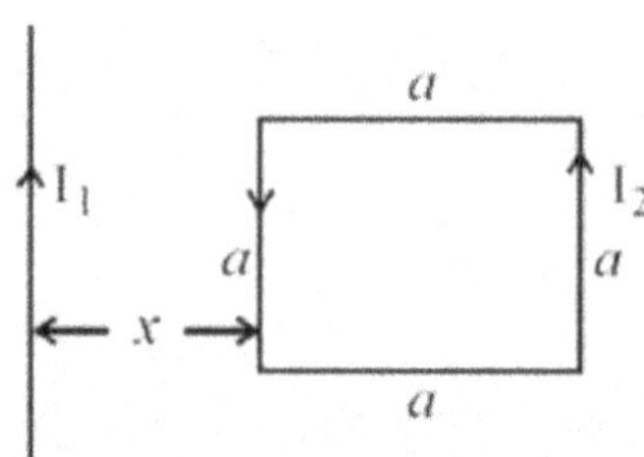

18. (a) Derive the expression for the torque acting on a current carrying loop placed in a magnetic field.
    (b) Explain the significance of a radial magnetic field when a current carrying coil is kept in it.

19. Draw a labelled ray diagram of an astronomical telescope in the near point adjustment position.

A giant refracting telescope at an observatory has an objective lens of focal length 15 m and an eyepiece of focal length 1.0 cm. If this telescope is used to view the Moon, find the diameter of the image of the Moon formed by the objective lens. The diameter of the Moon is 3.48×10^6 m, and the radius of lunar orbit is 3.8×10^8 m.

20. (a) State Gauss's law for magnetism. Explain its significance.
    (b) Write the four important properties of the magnetic field lines due to a bar magnet.

OR

Write three points of differences between para-, dia- and ferro- magnetic materials, giving one example for each.

21. Define the term 'decay constant' of a radioactive sample. The rate of disintegration of a given radioactive nucleus is 10000 disintegrations/s and 5,000 disintegrations/s after 20 hr. and 30 hr. respectively from start. Calculate the half-life and initial number of nuclei at t = 0.

22. (a) Three photo diodes D1, D2 and D3 are made of semiconductors having band gaps of 2.5 eV, 2 eV and 3 eV respectively. Which of them will not be able to detect light of wavelength 600 nm?

    (b) Why photodiodes are required to operate in reverse bias ? Explain.

23. (a) Describe briefly the functions of the three segments of n-p-n transistor.

    (b) Draw the circuit arrangement for studying the output characteristics of n-p-ntransistor in CE configuration. Explain how the output characteristics is obtained.

OR

Draw the circuit diagram of a full wave rectifier and explain its working. Also, give the input and output waveforms.

24. (a) If A and B represent the maximum and minimum amplitudes of an amplitude modulated wave, write the expression for the modulation index in terms of A & B.

    (b) A message signal of frequency 20 kHz and peak voltage 10 V is used tomodulate a carrier of frequency 2 MHz and peak voltage of 15 V. Calculate themodulation index. Why the modulation index is generally kept less than one ?

SECTION - D

25. (a) In a series LCR circuit connected across an ac source of variable frequency, obtain the expression for its impedance and draw a plot showing its variation with frequency of the ac source.

    (b) What is the phase difference between the voltages across inductor and thecapacitor at resonance in the LCR circuit ?

    (c) When an inductor is connected to a 200 V dc voltage, a current of 1A flowsthrough it. When the same inductor is connected to a 200 V, 50 Hz ac source,only 0.5 A current flows. Explain, why ? Also, calculate the self-inductance of the inductor.

OR

(a) Draw the diagram of a device which is used to decrease high ac voltage into a low ac voltage and state its working principle. Write four sources of energy loss in this device.

(b) A small town with a demand of 1200 kW of electric power at 220 V is situated20 km away from an electric plant generating power at 440 V. The resistance ofthe two-wire line carrying power is 0.5 &!per km. The town gets the power from the line through a 4000-220 V step-down transformer at a sub-station in thetown. Estimate the line power loss in the form of heat.

26. (a) Describe any two characteristic features which distinguish between interference and diffraction phenomena. Derive the expression for the intensity at a point of the interference pattern in Young's double slit experiment.

    (b) In the diffraction due to a single slit experiment, the aperture of the slit is 3 mm. If monochromatic light of wavelength 620 nm is incident normally on the slit,calculate the separation between the first order minima and the 3rd order maximaon one side of the screen. The distance between the slit and the screen is 1.5 m.

OR

(a) Under what conditions is the phenomenon of total internal reflection of lightobserved? Obtain the relation between the critical angle of incidence and therefractive index of the medium.

(b) Three lenses of focal lengths +10 cm, −10 cm and +30 cm are arranged coaxiallyas in the figure given below. Find the position of the final image formed by thecombination.

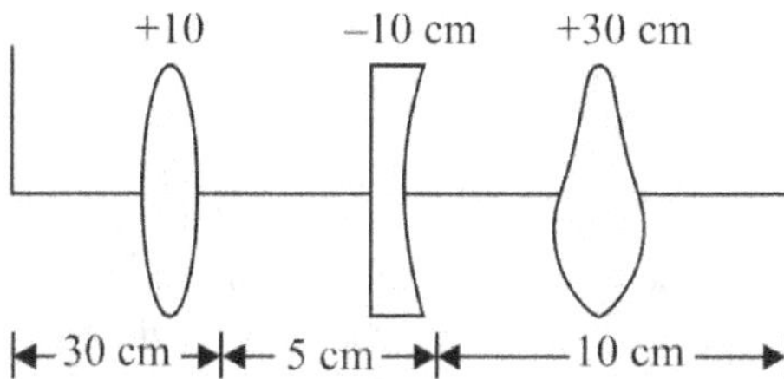

27. (a) Describe briefly the process of transferring the charge between the two plates of a parallel plate capacitor when connected to a battery. Derive an expression for the energy stored in a capacitor.

    (b) A parallel plate capacitor is charged by a battery to a potential difference V. It is disconnected from battery and then connected to another uncharged capacitor of the same capacitance. Calculate the ratio of the energy stored in the combination to the initial energy on the single capacitor.

OR

(a) Derive an expression for the electric field at any point on the equatorial line of an electric dipole.

(b) Two identical point charges, q each, are kept 2m apart in air. A third point charge Q of unknown magnitude and sign is placed on the line joining the charges such that the system remains in equilibrium. Find the position and nature of Q.

Solutions

SECTION - A

1. The pattern of electric field lines, when a point charge –Q is kept near an uncharged conducting plate is given below:

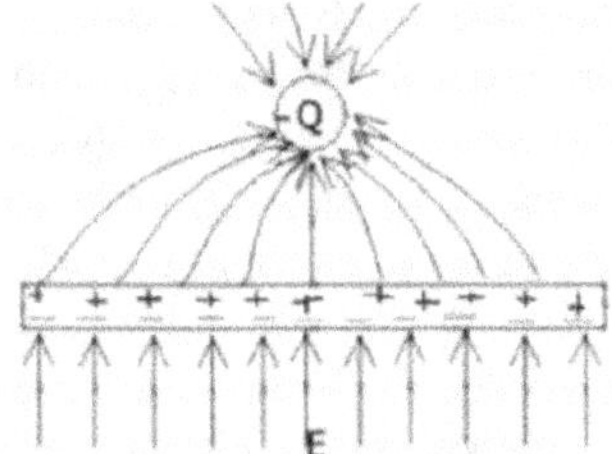

(1 Mark)

As we can see from figure, due to charge –Q, +q charge will be induced on the top surface of conducting plate and –q charge on the bottom surface of conducting plate. Therefore, Electric lines of forces should fall normally (90°) away from the conducting plate.

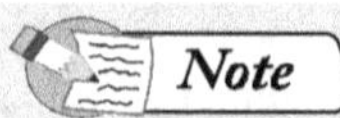
> ### Note
>
> *Electric lines of force do not pass through a conductor. Hence, the interior of the conductor is free from the influence of the electric field. Also, electric lines of force start from positive charges and end at negative charges.*

2. Mobility of electrons is defined as magnitude of drift velocity per unit electric field.

$$\text{Mobility} \quad \mu = \frac{v_d}{E} \qquad \text{...(i)}$$

Where v_d = drift velocity and E = electric field

From equation (i), it is clear that mobility is independent of applied voltage. Therefore, if the potential difference applied across the conductor is doubled, keeping the length and temperature of the conductor constant, mobility will remain unchanged. **(1 Mark)**

3. **Threshold frequency-** In photoelectric effect, for a given metal there exists a minimum frequency of incident radiation below which no emission of photoelectrons takes place. This frequency is called threshold frequency. **(1 Mark)**

OR

Intensity in photon picture of electromagnetic radiation is defined as the number of photons incident per unit area per unit time.

The SI unit of intensity is W/m^2. **(1 Mark)**

4. According to Brewster's law,

$$\mu = \tan i_p$$

Where μ = refractive index of denser medium

i_p = polarising angle

Given, $i_p = 30°$

Applying Brewster's law, we get

$$\mu = \tan 30° = \frac{1}{\sqrt{3}} \qquad \text{...(i)}$$

Refractive index of medium is defined as

$$\mu = \frac{\text{speed of light in vacuum}}{\text{speed of light in medium}}$$

Therefore, from equation (i), we can write

$$\frac{1}{\sqrt{3}} = \frac{3 \times 10^8}{\text{speed of light in denser medium}}$$

∴ Speed of light in denser medium is $3\sqrt{3} \times 10^8$ m/s.

(1 Mark)

5. Sky wave propagation is a equal mode of propagation in which communication of radio waves takes place due to reflection from the ionosphere because the ionosphere layer of atmosphere acts as a reflector for range frequencies below 30MHz. So, electromagnetic waves of frequencies higher than 30 MHz penetrate the ionosphere and do not reflect back. **(1 Mark)**

> ### Note
>
> *The sky wave propagation is a consequence of total internal reflection of radiowaves. Higher we go in the ionosphere, free electron density increases and refractive index decreases. Therefore, refractive index of ionosphere (μ) is less than of free electron (μ_0) i.e., $\mu < \mu_0$. So refractin occurs till it reaches critical angle and afterwards, it reflects electromagnetic waves back on earth's surface.*

OR

There are two factors on which range of coverage in ground wave propagation depends
(a) Transmitted power
(b) Frequency of signal **(1 Mark)**

SECTION - B

6. Power dissipated 'P' in any device is given as

$$P = \frac{V^2}{R}$$

For first bulb, let resistance be R_1. Then

$$P_1 = \frac{V^2}{R_1}$$

$$\therefore \quad R_1 = \frac{V^2}{P_1} \qquad \text{...(i)}$$

Similarly, for second bulb, let resistance be R_2. Then

$$P_2 = \frac{V^2}{R_2}$$

$$\therefore \quad R_2 = \frac{V^2}{P_2} \qquad \text{...(ii)}$$

(a) Equivalent resistance in series is given as

$$R_{series} = R_1 + R_2$$

From equation (i) and (ii),

$$R_{series} = \frac{V^2}{P_1} + \frac{V^2}{P_2} = V^2\left(\frac{P_1 + P_2}{P_1 P_2}\right)$$

Therefore, power in series will be

$$P_{series} = \frac{V^2}{R_{series}}$$

Substituting the value of R_{series}

$$P_{series} = \frac{V^2}{V^2\left(\dfrac{P_1 + P_2}{P_1 P_2}\right)} = \left(\frac{P_1 P_2}{P_1 + P_2}\right) \qquad \textbf{(1 Mark)}$$

(b) Equivalent resistance in parallel is given as

$$\frac{1}{R_{parallel}} = \frac{1}{R_1} + \frac{1}{R_2}$$

From equation (i) and (ii),

$$\frac{1}{R_{parallel}} = \frac{P_1}{V^2} + \frac{P_2}{V^2} = \frac{1}{V^2}(P_1 + P_2)$$

Therefore, power in parallel will be

$$P_{parallel} = \frac{V^2}{R_{parallel}}$$

Substituting the value of $R_{parallel}$

$$P_{parallel} = V^2 \times \frac{1}{V^2}(P_1 + P_2)$$

$$\therefore \qquad P_{parallel} = (P_1 + P_2) \qquad \textbf{(1 Mark)}$$

7. Lens maker formula is given as

$$\frac{1}{f} = \left(\frac{n_2}{n_1} - 1\right)\left(\frac{1}{R_1} - \frac{1}{R_2}\right)$$

R_1 and R_2 = radius of curvature of two refracting surfaces
For equi-concave lens $R_1 = -R$ and $R_2 = R$.

$$P = \frac{1}{f} \qquad \therefore \quad f = \frac{1}{P} = \frac{1}{-5} = -0.2m \qquad \textbf{(1 Mark)}$$

Substituting the values of f, n_1, n_2 in lens maker formula

$$\frac{1}{-0.2} = \left(\frac{1.5}{1.5} - 1\right)\left(\frac{1}{-R} - \frac{1}{R}\right)$$

$$\frac{1}{-0.2} = \left(\frac{0.1}{1.4}\right)\left(-\frac{2}{R}\right)$$

$$R = \left(\frac{1}{14}\right)(2 \times 0.2) = \frac{0.2}{7} = 0.0285m \ \textbf{(1 Mark)}$$

$\therefore$ Radius of curvature of an equi-concave lens 0.0285m or 2.85cm.

 **Note**

Refractive index of material of lens depends upon the medium in which it is kept. In the formula, $\dfrac{1}{f} = (\mu - 1)\left(\dfrac{1}{R_1} - \dfrac{1}{R_2}\right)$. *If lens is placed in a medium other than air, due to change in refractive index* (μ), *focal length of the lens changes. If lens is immersed in a liquid whose refractive index with respect to air is less than refractive index of material of lens, then focal length increases and vice versa.*

OR

Given,
Refractive index of prism 'n_2' = 1.6

Refractive index of medium 'n_1' = $4\sqrt{2/5}$

Because the prism is equilateral glass prism, angle of prism 'A' will be 60°.
Refractive index of prism w.r.t refractive of medium

$$\frac{n_{prism}}{n_{medium}} = \frac{n_2}{n_1} = \frac{\sin\left(\dfrac{A + D_m}{2}\right)}{\sin\left(\dfrac{A}{2}\right)} \qquad \textbf{(1 Mark)}$$

Where D_m = angle of minimum deviation
Substituting the values of n_2, n_1, A in above equation

$$\frac{1.6}{4\sqrt{2}\big/5} = \frac{\sin\left(\dfrac{60° + D_m}{2}\right)}{\sin\left(\dfrac{60°}{2}\right)}$$

$$\frac{1.6 \times 5}{4\sqrt{2}} = \frac{\sin\left(\dfrac{60° + D_m}{2}\right)}{\sin 30°}$$

$\sin 30° = 1/2$, so

$$\frac{8}{4\sqrt{2}} = \frac{\sin\left(\dfrac{60° + D_m}{2}\right)}{\dfrac{1}{2}}$$

$$\frac{1}{\sqrt{2}} = \sin\left(\dfrac{60° + D_m}{2}\right)$$

Solving the above equation, we get,

$$\sin^{-1}\frac{1}{\sqrt{2}} = \left(\frac{60° + D_m}{2}\right)$$

Now the value of $\sin^{-1}\dfrac{1}{\sqrt{2}} = 45°$.

So, $45° = \left(\dfrac{60° + D_m}{2}\right)$

$\Rightarrow \qquad 90° = 60° + D_m$

$\therefore$ Angle of minimum deviation $D_m = 30°$.   **(1 Mark)**

8. Let
Mass of α particle = m_α
Mass of proton = m_p
Radius α particle = r_α
Radius of proton = r_p
Velocity of á particle = v_α
Velocity of proton = v_p
Radius of circular path, when a charged particle enters in the magnetic field at right angle is given as

$$r = \frac{mv}{qB}$$

So, radius of α particle will be

$$r_\alpha = \frac{m_\alpha v_\alpha}{q_\alpha B} \qquad \text{...(i)}$$

And, radius of proton will be $r_p = \dfrac{m_p v_p}{q_p B}$ ...(ii)

It is given in question that kinetic energy of alpha particle and proton is same. Therefore

$$\frac{1}{2} m_\alpha v_\alpha^2 = \frac{1}{2} m_p v_p^2$$

$$\therefore \qquad \frac{m_p}{m_\alpha} = \frac{v_\alpha^2}{v_p^2} \qquad \text{...(iii)}$$

(½ Mark)

From equation (i) and (ii), the ratio of radii of alpha particle and proton will be

$$\frac{r_\alpha}{r_p} = \frac{\dfrac{m_\alpha v_\alpha}{q_\alpha B}}{\dfrac{m_p v_p}{q_p B}} \qquad \text{Now, } q_\alpha = 2q_p$$

$$\therefore \qquad \frac{r_\alpha}{r_p} = \frac{2 m_\alpha v_\alpha}{m_p v_p} \qquad \text{...(iv)}$$

(½ Mark)

Using equation (iii), we can write equation (iv) as

$$\frac{r_\alpha}{r_p} = \frac{2 m_\alpha}{m_p} \times \sqrt{\frac{m_p}{m_\alpha}} = 2\sqrt{\frac{m_\alpha}{m_p}} \qquad \textbf{(½ Mark)}$$

Mass of alpha particle $= 4 \times$ mass pf proton.

$$\therefore \qquad \frac{r_\alpha}{r_p} = 2\sqrt{\frac{4 m_p}{m_p}} = 2\sqrt{4} = 2 \times 2 = 4 = \frac{4}{1} \textbf{(½ Mark)}$$

Ratio of radii of circular paths of alpha particle to proton is 4:1.

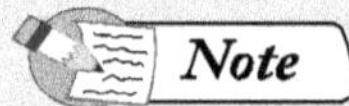

When a charged particle moves in magnetic field acting perpendicular to the velocity of the particle, then particle will describe a circular path. If charge particle has velocity not perpendicular to magnetic field, particle will describe a helical motion.

9. **Bohr's quantization condition of angular momentum:** Bohr's quantization condition of angular momentum states that the angular momentum of orbiting electron is integral multiple of **h/2π** where 'h' is the plank's constant. Thus, the angular momentum (L_n) of the orbiting electron is quantised.

$$L_n = n\frac{h}{2\pi} \qquad \textbf{(½ Mark)}$$

Where n = principle quantum number.

Wavelength of bracket series is

$$\frac{1}{\lambda} = R\left(\frac{1}{4^2} - \frac{1}{n^2}\right) \qquad \textbf{(½ Mark)}$$

Where R = Rydberg constant = 1.09×10^7 m^{-1}

For shortest wavelength of bracket series n $\to \infty$.

$$\frac{1}{\lambda_m} = R\left(\frac{1}{4^2} - \frac{1}{\infty^2}\right) = \frac{R}{16} \qquad \textbf{(½ Mark)}$$

$$\lambda_m = \frac{16}{R} = \frac{16}{1.09 \times 10^7} = 14.67 \times 10^{-7} \text{ m} \quad \textbf{(½ Mark)}$$

Shortest wavelength of bracket series $\lambda_m = 14.67 \times 10^{-7}$ m lies in infrared region.

OR

Orbital period T_n of hydrogen atom in nth orbit is

$$T_n = \frac{2\pi r_n}{v_n} \qquad \textbf{(½ Mark)}$$

Where r_n = radius of nth circular orbit

        v_n = velocity of hydrogen atom in nth orbit

Radius of nth circular orbit of hydrogen atom is

$$r_n = a_o n^2$$

Where a_o = Bohr's radius = 5.29×10^{-11} m.

Velocity of hydrogen atom in nth orbit is

$$v_n = \frac{2.19 \times 10^6}{n} \qquad \textbf{(½ Mark)}$$

So, Orbital period T_n of hydrogen atom in nth orbit becomes

$$T_n = \frac{2\pi a_o n^2}{\dfrac{2.19 \times 10^6}{n}} = \frac{2\pi \times 5.29 \times 10^{-11} \times n^2}{\dfrac{2.19 \times 10^6}{n}}$$

$$T_n = 1.5 \times 10^{-16} \times n^3 \qquad \textbf{(½ Mark)}$$

For first excited state $n = 2$.

Therefore, T_2 will be

$T_2 = 1.5 \times 10^{-16} \times 2^3 = 1.5 \times 10^{-16} \times 8 = 1.2 \times 10^{-15}$ seconds

$\therefore$ The orbital period of the electron in the first excited state of hydrogen atom is 1.2×10^{-15} seconds.   **(½ Mark)**

10. A signal transmitted from a TV tower cannot be received beyond a certain distance due to curvature of earth. For TV signals, communication is essentially limited to the path of line of sight. The direct waves get blocked at some point by the curvature of earth.   **(1 Mark)**

Optimum separation between the receiving and the transmitting antenna is

$$R = \sqrt{2R_e h_t} + \sqrt{2R_e h_r}$$

where R_e = radius of earth

      h_t = height of transmitting tower

      h_r = height of receiving tower.   **(1 Mark)**

11. There are two main aspects of experimental results which cannot be explained by wave theory.

(1) According to wave picture, no matter what the frequency of incident radiation is, a sufficiently intense beam of radiation should be able to eject electron out of metal surface. A threshold frequency, therefore, should not exist.

However, it is observed that there is a threshold frequency below which photoelectric effect is not observed.

(2) Secondly if electrons absorbs the energy of the wave, the emission of the electron must be delayed with respect to the instance light falls on the substance, but it is immediate. **(½ × 2 = 1 Mark)**

According to the photon picture if frequency of photon í is greater than ϕ/h (ϕ is work function and h is Planck's constant), the photoelectricemission will happen almost instantaneously even if intensity is low. **(1 Mark)**

12. De Broglie wavelength, λ associated with charged particle of mass m is given as

$$\lambda = \frac{h}{\sqrt{2mqV}}$$

Since for a charged particle, mass and its charge is constant,

$$\therefore \qquad \lambda \propto \frac{1}{\sqrt{V}}$$

So, the graph between τ and $1/\sqrt{V}$ is a straight line with slope equals to $h/\sqrt{(2mq)}$.

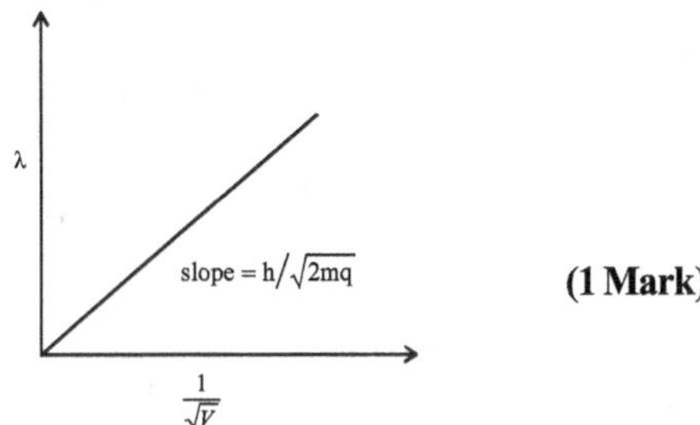

(1 Mark)

To calculate the charge of the particle from the graph, first find the slope of the graph. Then equate the value of slope

$$\text{slope} = \frac{h}{\sqrt{2mq}} \qquad \therefore \quad q = \frac{h^2}{2m \times (slope)^2} \text{ (1 Mark)}$$

SECTION - C

13. (a) The equipotential surfaces

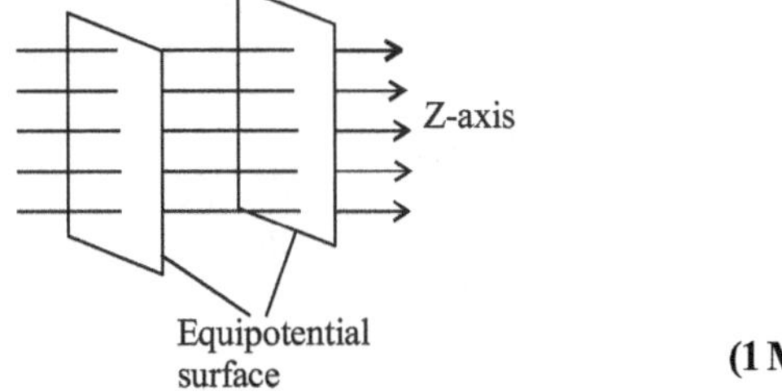

(1 Mark)

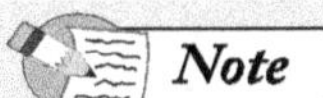 **Note**

Electric field is always perpendicular to an equipotential surface and as a result, work done in moving a charge between two points on an equipotential surface is zero.

(b) Electric potential at an axial point of a dipole:
Consider an electric dipole consisting of two-point charges $-q$ and $+q$, separated by distance 2a. Let R be the point on axis of dipole where we have to find electric potential.

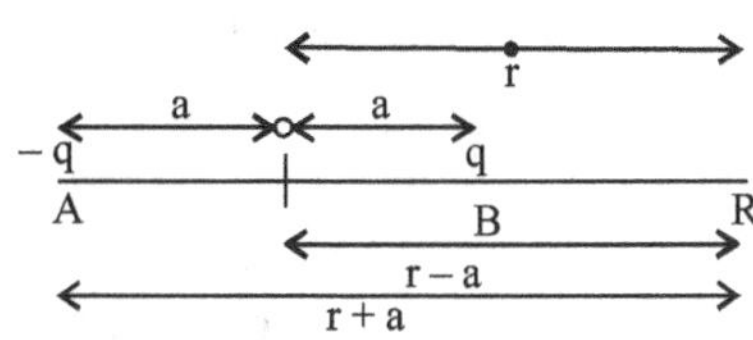

Electric potential V at any point due to a point charge is given as

$$V = \frac{q}{4\pi\epsilon_0 r}$$

Where r = distance between the point charge and point.
So, electric potential due to charge -q of dipole

$$V_{-q} = \frac{1}{4\pi\epsilon_0} \times -\frac{q}{AR} \qquad \text{(½ Mark)}$$

And electric potential due to q of dipole

$$V_q = \frac{1}{4\pi\epsilon_0} \times \frac{q}{BR} \qquad \text{(½ Mark)}$$

Total electric potential due to dipole at point R is
$$V = V_{-q} + V_q$$

$$V = \frac{1}{4\pi\epsilon_0} \times -\frac{q}{AR} + \frac{1}{4\pi\epsilon_0} \times \frac{q}{BR}$$

$$V = \frac{1}{4\pi\epsilon_0} \times \left[\frac{-q}{(r+a)} + \frac{q}{(r-a)}\right]$$

$$V = \frac{q}{4\pi\epsilon_0} \times \left[\frac{1}{r-a} - \frac{1}{r+a}\right]$$

$$V = \frac{q}{4\pi\epsilon_0} \times \left[\frac{r+a-r+a}{(r-a)(r+a)}\right]$$

$$V = \frac{q}{4\pi\epsilon_0} \times \left[\frac{2a}{r^2 - a^2}\right] \qquad ...(i) \quad \text{(½ Mark)}$$

Where we have used identity $(a - b)(a + b) = a^2 - b^2$.
Dipole moment $p = q \times 2a$. Using this in equation (i), we get

$$V = \frac{1}{4\pi\epsilon_0} \times \left[\frac{p}{r^2 - a^2}\right]$$

For short dipole, $a^2 \ll r^2$

$$\therefore \qquad V = \frac{1}{4\pi\epsilon_0} \times \frac{p}{r^2} \qquad \text{(½ Mark)}$$

14.

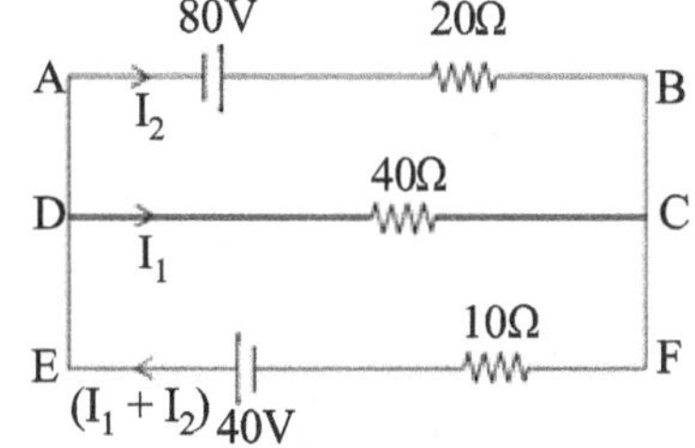

On applying Kirchhoff's voltage law in FEDCF,

$$-10(I_1 + I_2) + 40 - 40 I_1 = 0 \qquad \text{(½ Mark)}$$
$$-10 I_1 - 10 I_2 + 40 - 40 I_1 = 0$$
$$-50 I_1 - 10 I_2 = -40$$
$$5 I_1 + I_2 = 4 \qquad ...(i) \qquad \text{(1 Mark)}$$

Again, applying Kirchhoff's voltage law in CDAB,

$$40\,I_1 + 80 - 20\,I_2 = 0 \qquad \textbf{(½ Mark)}$$
$$40\,I_1 - 20\,I_2 = -80$$
$$I_2 - 2\,I_1 = 4 \qquad \text{...(ii)}$$

Solving equation (i) and (ii), we get

$$I_1 = 0\text{A} \quad \text{and} \quad I_2 = 4\text{A}. \qquad \textbf{(1 Mark)}$$

Note

The product of resistance and current in an arm of the loop is taken as positive if the direction of current in that arm is in the same sense as one moves, and is taken as negative if the direciotn of current in an arm is opposite to the sense as one moves. Also, while traversing a loop emf of a cell is taken negative if negative pole of the cell is encountered first otherwise positive.

OR

End error in metre bridge:

The end error in the meter bridge may arise when the zero mark of the scale provided along the bridge wire may not start from the position where the bridge wire leaves the copper strip and 100 cm mark of the scale may not be at position, where the bridge wire just touches the other copper strip.

The end error can be removed by repeating the experiment by interchanging the known and unknown resistances and taking the mean of the resistances determined.

Given resistance R = 5Ω.

Balanced length $l = l_1$

So, applying the metre bridge balanced condition,

$$\frac{R}{S} = \frac{l_1}{100 - l_1} \qquad \text{...(i)}$$

Shunting resistance S with equal resistance means applying equal resistance in parallel with S. Then equivalent resistance of S becomes

$$\frac{1}{S_{eq}} = \frac{1}{S} + \frac{1}{S} \Rightarrow S_{eq} = \frac{S}{2} \qquad \textbf{(½ Mark)}$$

The new balance length = $1.5l_1$.

$$\therefore \quad \frac{R}{S_{eq}} = \frac{1.5l_1}{100 - 1.5l_1}$$

$$\frac{R}{\dfrac{S}{2}} = \frac{1.5l_1}{100 - 1.5l_1} \Rightarrow \frac{2R}{S} = \frac{1.5l_1}{100 - 1.5l_1} \qquad \text{...(ii)}$$

(½ Mark)

Using equation (i) in equation (ii) we get,

$$2 \times \frac{l_1}{100 - l_1} = \frac{1.5l_1}{100 - 1.5l_1}$$
$$150 - 1.5\,l_1 = 200 - 3\,l_1$$
$$3\,l_1 - 1.5\,l_1 = 200 - 150$$
$$1.5l_1 = 50 \qquad \text{...(iii)} \qquad \textbf{(½ Mark)}$$

Using equation (ii) and (iii)

$$\frac{2R}{S} = \frac{50}{100 - 50} = 1 \qquad \textbf{(½ Mark)}$$

Putting the value of R= 5Ω

$$2 \times \frac{5}{S} = 1 \Rightarrow S = 10\ \Omega \qquad \textbf{(½ Mark)}$$

Note

When the bridge is balanced, then on interchanging the positions of the galvanometer and the cell, there is no effect on the balance condition of the bridge. Also, the sensitivity of the bridge depends upon the values of the resistance. The bridge is maximum sensitivity when all the four resistances are of the same order.

15. (a) The part of the electromagnetic spectrum used in

  (i) Radar- microwaves with frequency range from 1 GHz to 2 GHz.

  (ii) Eye surgery- UV rays with frequency range from 10^{15} Hz to 10^{17} Hz. **(1 Mark)**

(b) The average energy density of ocillating electric field is

$$U_E = \frac{1}{4}\,\epsilon_0 E_0^2 \qquad \textbf{(½ Mark)}$$

where E = amplitude of oscillating electric field.

The average energy density of oscillating magnetic field is

$$U_B = \frac{B_0^2}{4\mu_o} \qquad \textbf{(½ Mark)}$$

where B = amplitude of oscillating electric field.

Amplitude of electric field and magnetic field are related as

$$\frac{E_o}{B_o} = c \qquad \text{where } c = \text{speed of light} \qquad \text{...(i)}$$

(½ Mark)

Also,

$$c = \frac{1}{\sqrt{\mu_o\,\epsilon_o}} \qquad \text{...(ii)}$$

Substituting the value of E_o and ϵ_o from equation (i) and (ii) respectively in U_E,

$$U_E = \frac{1}{4} \times \frac{1}{c^2\mu_o} \times (cB_o)^2$$

$$U_E = \frac{1}{4} \times \frac{B_0^2}{\mu_o} = U_B \qquad \textbf{(½ Mark)}$$

16. Wavefront: A wavefront is defined as the continuous locus of all such particles of a medium which are vibrating in the same phase at any instant. **(1 Mark)**

Law of reflection:

As shown in the figure, consider a plane wavefront AB incident on the plane reflecting surface XY at an angle i.

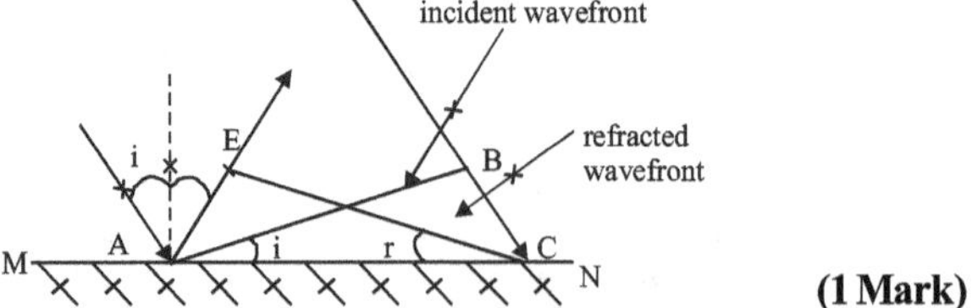

(1 Mark)

The reflected wave front CE can be constructed using Huygens' theory. Taking BC as radius , draw a sphere at point A. Then CE will be the tangent from this sphere to point C. Since, radius of this sphere AE is equal to BC *i.e.* AE = BC ,we can write,

In $\triangle$ EAC and $\triangle$ BAC

$$AC = \text{common}$$
$$\angle B = \angle E = 90°$$
$$AE = BC$$

$\therefore$ By SAS congruency, $\triangle EAC \cong \triangle BAC$.

Therefore, $\angle BAC (= i)$ becomes equal to $\angle ECA (= r)$. **(1 Mark)**

i.e., angle of incidence '*i*' is equal to angle of reflection '*r*'. this proves law of reflection.

OR

Refractive index: The refractive index of medium is defined as ratio of the speed of light in vacuum to its speed in that medium.

If μ = refractive index then,

$$\mu = \frac{\text{speed of light in vacuum}}{\text{speed of light in medium}} = \frac{c}{v} \qquad \textbf{(1 Mark)}$$

Snell's law:

To derive Snell's law from Huygens theory, consider a refracting surface XY separating medium 1 and 2.

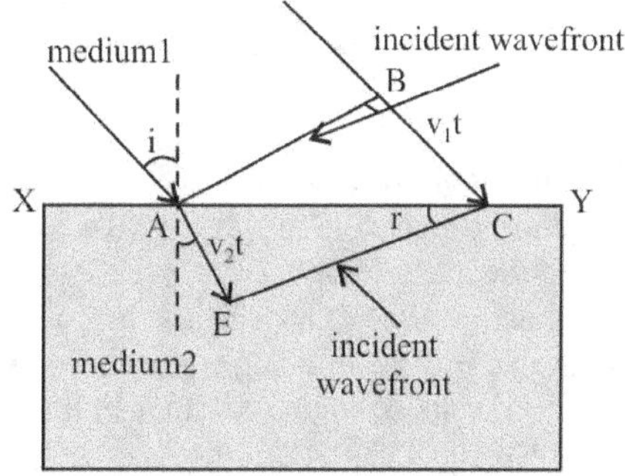

Let $\quad v_1$ = velocity of light in medium 1

$\qquad v_2$ = velocity of light in medium 2

Let a plane wave front AB incident at an angle i on refracting surface XY. If '*t*' is the time taken to travel by wave front from B to C then, distance BC will be

$$BC = v_1 t$$

To construct the refracted wave front, draw a sphere of radius $v_2 t$ from point A in medium 2. Let CE represent a tangent plane drawn from the point C on to the sphere.

Then, $AE = v_2 t$ = radius of the sphere in medium 2 and CE would represent the refracted wave front.

Now, in $\triangle$ ABC

$$\sin i = \frac{BC}{AC} = \frac{v_1 t}{AC} \qquad \text{...(i)}$$

And in $\triangle AEC$

$$\sin r = \frac{AE}{AC} = \frac{v_2 t}{AC} \qquad \text{...(ii)}$$

$$\therefore \quad \frac{\sin i}{\sin r} = \frac{\dfrac{v_1 t}{AC}}{\dfrac{v_2 t}{AC}} = \frac{v_1}{v_2} \qquad \text{...(iii)}$$

(1 Mark)

From the definition of refractive index given above we can write, refractive index of medium 1 μ_1 as

$$\mu_1 = \frac{c}{v_1}$$

Refractive index of medium 2

$$\mu_2 = \frac{c}{v_2}$$

Using refractive index of medium 1 and 2 in equation (iii),

$$\frac{\sin i}{\sin r} = \frac{\dfrac{c}{\mu_1}}{\dfrac{c}{\mu_2}} = \frac{\mu_2}{\mu_1} \qquad \textbf{(1 Mark)}$$

This proves Snell's law using Huygens theory.

17. (a) **Mutual inductance**: Mutual induction is the phenomenon of production of induced emf in one coil due to change of current in the neighbouring coil. Its S.I. unit is henry (H). **(1 Mark)**

(b) We know that the magnetic force between the two parallel current carrying conducting wire

$$F = \frac{\mu_o}{2\pi} \times \frac{I_1 I_2 L}{r}$$

where $\quad r$ = distance between current carrying conductors

$\qquad L$ = length of conductor

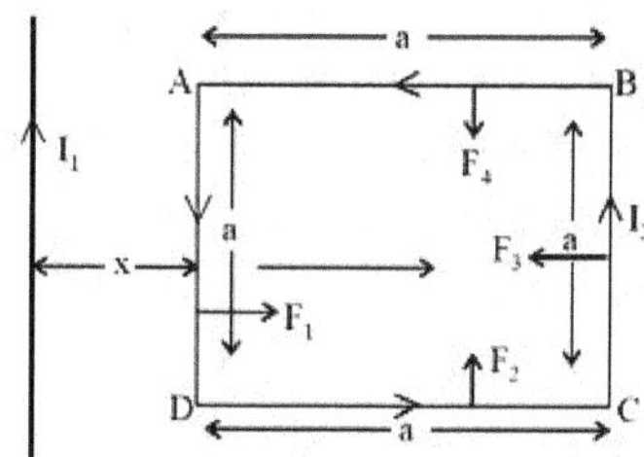

The square loop ABCD and infinitely long straight wire work as two parallel current carrying conducting wires AD and BC. Since current in BC is parallel with AB, force on BC due to AB will be attractive and current in AD is anti-parallel to AB, force on AD due to AB will be repulsive.

Force on AD due to AB

$$F_1 = \frac{\mu_o}{2\pi} \times \frac{I_1 I_2 a}{x} \qquad \textbf{(½ Mark)}$$

Force on BC due to AB

$$F_2 = \frac{\mu_o}{2\pi} \times \frac{I_1 I_2 a}{(x+a)} \qquad \textbf{(½ Mark)}$$

As we seen above diagram, the force on AB and CD will be equal in magnitude but opposite direction, so they will be cancelled to each other.

Since $F_1 > F_2$, therefore total force on loop ABCD will be

$$F = F_1 - F_2$$

$$F = \frac{\mu_o}{2\pi} \times \frac{I_1 I_2 a}{x} - \frac{\mu_o}{2\pi} \times \frac{I_1 I_2 a}{(x+a)} \qquad \textbf{(½ Mark)}$$

$$F = \frac{\mu_o I_1 I_2 a}{2\pi} \times \left[\frac{1}{x} - \frac{1}{x+a} \right]$$

$$F = \frac{\mu_o I_1 I_2 a^2}{2\pi x (x+a)} \qquad \textbf{(½ Mark)}$$

18. (a) Torque on a rectangular current loop in a magnetic field

Force on a current carrying conductor is given as

$F = I \, (l \times B) = IlB \sin\theta$

where I = current flowing in the loop.

θ = angle between length of conductor and magnetic field.

Consider a rectangular loop of length b and breadth a in a uniform magnetic field B.

The magnetic field B is directed in the plane of loop from north to south (left to right in diagram).

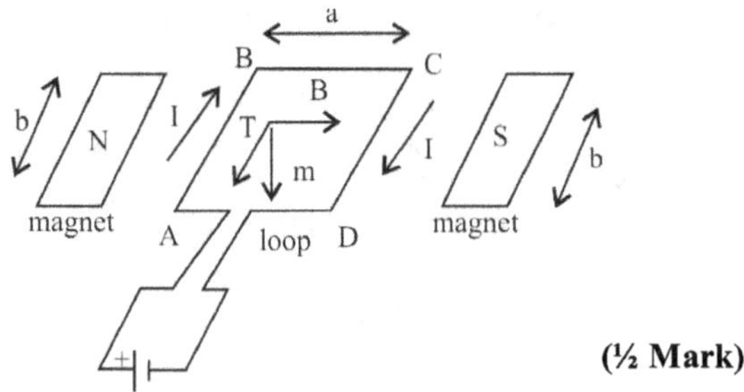

(½ Mark)

For arms AD and BC θ is 0°. So, field exerts no force on arm AD and BC of the loop.

Let F_1 = force on arm AB.

F_2 = force on arm CD.

Length of arm AB and DC is b

So, magnitude of force

$F_1 = I \, (b \times B) = IbB \quad (\because \theta \text{ is } 90°)$

Similarly, the magnitude of force $F_2 = I \, (b \times B) = IbB$ **(½ Mark)**

Using Fleming's left-hand rule, one can easily see that direction of F_1 is into the plane and direction of F_2 is out of the plane.

So, magnitude of F_1 and F_2 is same but in opposite direction. Therefore, net force on the loop is zero.

But there will be torque (couple) due to two same but opposite force F_1 and F_2.

Torque is given as

$$T = r \times F$$

where r is the length of torque arm

Length of the torque arm is a/2 for both AB and CD.

$\therefore \quad$ Total torque $\tau = \dfrac{a}{2} \times F_1 + \dfrac{a}{2} \times F_2$ **(½ Mark)**

θ between both F_1 and F_2 and a/2 is 90°.

$\therefore \qquad \tau = \dfrac{a}{2} F_1 + \dfrac{a}{2} F_2$

Substituting the value of F_1 and F_2, we get

$\tau = \dfrac{a}{2}(IbB + IbB) \Rightarrow \tau = \dfrac{a}{2} \times 2IbB = I(ab)B = IAB$ **(½ Mark)**

where $A = ab$ = area of rectangular loop.

(b) In radial magnetic field, torque on loop is maximum for all position of coils. This is because in radial magnetic field torque on a current carrying loop is $\tau = I$ (area of loop) = constant. **(1 Mark)**

> **Note**
>
> *When normal to the coil is along the direction of magnetic field, then current loop is in stable equilibrium. Any small rotation of the coil produces a torque which bring the coil back to its original position. When normal to the coil is antiparallel to magnetic field, then coil is in unstable equilibrium.*

19.

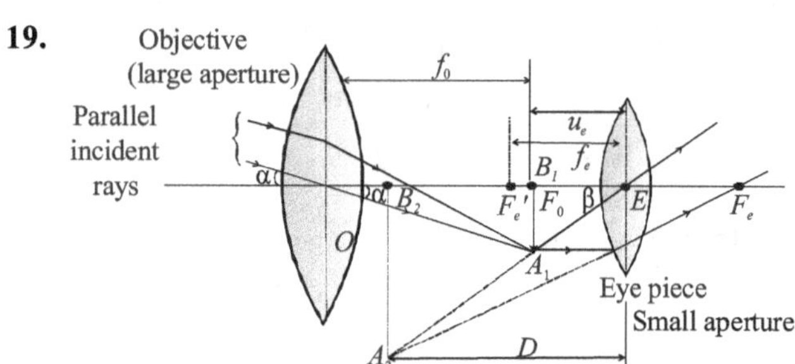

Given **(1½ Marks)**

Focal length of objective lens $f_o = 15$m.

Focal length of eyepiece $f_e = 1$cm $= 0.01$m.

Diameter of moon $d = 3.48 \times 10^6$m.

Radius of lunar orbit $r = 3.8 \times 10^8$ m.

From figure we can see that angle subtended by moon at objective lens is equal to angle subtended by image of moon formed by the objective.

Angle subtended by moon at objective lens, α, is

$\alpha = \dfrac{\text{diametre of moon}}{\text{radius of lunar orbit}} = \dfrac{3.48 \times 10^6}{3.8 \times 10^8}$ **(½ Mark)**

Angle subtended by image of moon formed by objective lens,

$\beta = \dfrac{\text{diametre of image of moon}}{f_o}$

$\beta = \dfrac{\text{diametre of image of moon}}{15}$ **(½ Mark)**

Since α and β are equal, therefore

$\dfrac{3.48 \times 10^6}{3.8 \times 10^8} = \dfrac{\text{diametre of image of moon}}{15}$

$\therefore$ Diametre of image of moon $= \dfrac{3.48 \times 10^6}{3.8 \times 10^8} \times 15 = 13.73 cm$

(½ Mark)

20. (a) Gauss's law of magnetism:

Gauss's law of magnetism states that the surface integral of a magnetic field over a closed surface is always zero. The surface integral of a magnetic field over a surface gives magnetic flux through that surface. So, Gauss's law of magnetism can also be stated as follows:

The net magnetic flux through a closed surface is zero.

(½ Mark)

Significance :

Gauss's law of magnetism indicates that there are no sources or sinks of magnetic field inside a closed surface. Hence isolated magnetic poles do not exist. **(½ Mark)**

(b) Properties of magnetic field lines are:

1. Magnetic field lines are closed curves which start in air from the N pole and end the S pole and then return to the N pole through the interior of the magnet.
2. The lines of forces never cross each other. If they do so, that would mean there are two directions of magnetic field at the point of intersection, which is impossible.
3. The relative closeness of the lines of force gives a measure of the strength of the magnetic field.
4. The tangent to the field line gives direction of the field at that point. **(½ × 4 = 2 Marks)**

Note

When a bar magnet is dropped into a pile of iron-fillings, the maximum amount of fillings get deposited near the ends of the magnet and almost nil in the middle. The pattern suggests that attraction is maximum at two ends of the bar magnet.

OR

Property	Diamagnetic	Paramagnetic	Ferromagnetic
Effect of magnets	They are feebly repelled by magnets	They are feebly attracted by magnets	They are strongly attracted by magnets
Susceptibility χ_m	Susceptibility is small and negative $-1 \leq \chi_m < 0$	Susceptibility is small and positive.	Susceptibility is very large and positive.
Relative permeability value (μ_r)	Slightly less than 1.0 $\mu_r < 1$	Slightly greater than 1.0 $\mu_r > 1$	Of the orders of thousands. $\mu_r > 1000$.
Examples	Bi, Cu, Pb, H_2O	Al, Na, Ca	Fe, Ni, Co

(3 Marks)

21. Decay constant: The radioactive decay constant may be defined as the reciprocal of the time interval during which the number of active nuclei in a given radioactive sample reduces to $1/e$ times of its initial value. **(1 Marks)**

The radioactive decay law states that
$$N = N_o e^{-\lambda t}$$
where N = number of undecayed nuclei at any instant t
N_o = number of nuclei at initial time $t = 0$.
λ = decay constant.

So, decay constant λ is **(½ Mark)**
$$\lambda = \frac{1}{t} ln\left(\frac{N_o}{N}\right)$$

Disintegration rate R is
$$R = R_o e^{-\lambda t} = \lambda N$$
where $R_o = \lambda N_o$ disintegration rate at t = 0.

Disintegration rate at t = 20hr, is R1 = 10,000/s

Disintegration rate at t = 30hr, is R2 = 5,000/s

$$10,000 = R_o e^{-\lambda 20} \qquad (i)$$

and $\quad 5000 = R_o e^{-\lambda 30}$ $\qquad\qquad (ii)$

Dividing equation (i) and (ii), we get

$$\frac{10,000}{5000} = \frac{R_o e^{-\lambda 20}}{R_o e^{-\lambda 30}} \Rightarrow 2 = e^{\lambda \times 10} \Rightarrow ln2 = 10\lambda \quad \textbf{(½ Mark)}$$

Multiplying the R.H.S of above equation by 3600 to convert hours into sec, we get

$$\lambda = \frac{ln2}{36000} = 1.92 \times 10^{-5} s^{-1}$$

Half-life and decay constant of a radioactive nucleus are related as

$$T_{\frac{1}{2}} = \frac{ln2}{\lambda} = 36000 \text{ seconds} = 10 \text{ hours}.$$

To find initial number of nuclei, we will first have to calculate number of nuclei at t = 10 hr or 20 hr. Using disintegration rate at t = 10 hr,
$$R = \lambda N \Rightarrow 10,000 = 1.92 \times 10^{-5} \times N$$

$$\therefore \quad N = \frac{10,000}{1.92 \times 10^{-5}} = 5.2 \times 10^8 \text{ nuclei} \quad \textbf{(½ Mark)}$$

Using radioactive decay law at t = 10 hr
$$N = N_o e^{-\lambda t}$$

$$\Rightarrow N_o = \frac{N}{e^{-\lambda t}} = \frac{5.2 \times 20^8}{e^{-1.92} \times 10^{-5} \times 10 \times 3600} \quad \textbf{(½ Mark)}$$
$$= 10.4 \times 10^8 \text{ nuclei}.$$

22. (a) Wavelength of incident light λ = 600 nm

Energy of the photon associated with this light is
$$E = hv$$
Where h = Planck's constant
v = frequency of light
$v\lambda = c$ = speed of light

$$\therefore E = \frac{hc}{\lambda} = \frac{1240}{600} = 2.1eV \qquad \textbf{(1 Mark)}$$

Given, Band gap of diode D1 = 2.5 eV
Band gap of diode D2 = 2 eV
Band gap of diode D3 = 3 eV
Diode will detect light only when band gap of diode is less than energy of incident light.
So, only diode D2 will detect the light as its band gap is less than energy of incident light, *i.e.,* 2 < 2.1eV. **(1 Mark)**

(b) The whole point of a photodiode is to detect light, and it does this by measuring the effect the light has on the current. When photodiode is illuminated with light, the fractional increase in majority carriers is much less than the fractional increase in minority carriers. Consequently, the increase in forward bias current is more readily measurable than increase in forward bias current. Therefore, photodiodes are preferable used in the reverse bias condition for measuring light intensity. **(1 Mark)**

23. (a) The three segments of n-p-n transistors are as follows:

(1) Emitter (E)- It is a section on one side of the transistor. It is forward biased in n-p-n transistor and supplies a large number of majority carriers for the flow of current.

(2) Base (B)- It is the middle section of transistor. It is very lightly doped and thin. It controls the flow of majority carriers from emitter to collector

(3) Collector (C)- It is a section on other side of transistor and larger in size than emitter. It is reversed bias in n-p-n transistor and collects the majority charge carries from base. **(½ × 3 = 1½ Marks)**

(b) The circuit arrangement for studying the output characteristics of n-p-n transistor in CE configuration is given below

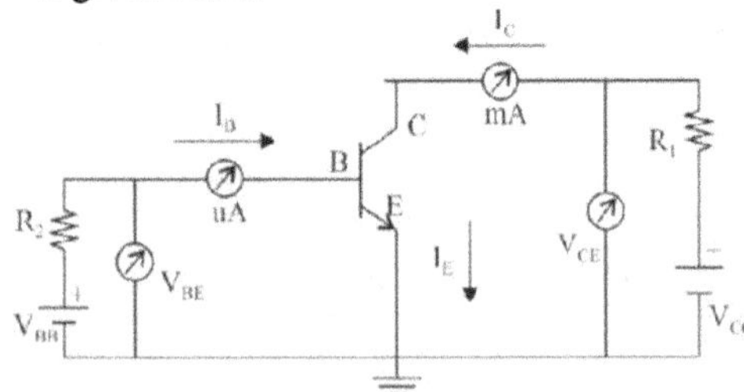

(1 Mark)

Output characteristics of n-p-n transistor in CE configuration

The graph showing the variation of collector current Ic with collector -emitter voltage V_{CE} at a constant base current IB is called output characteristics of n-p-n transistor in CE configuration.

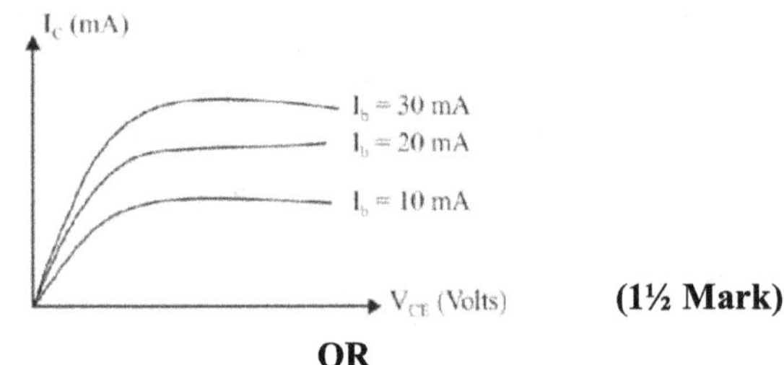

(1½ Mark)

OR

Circuit diagram of full wave rectifier is given below

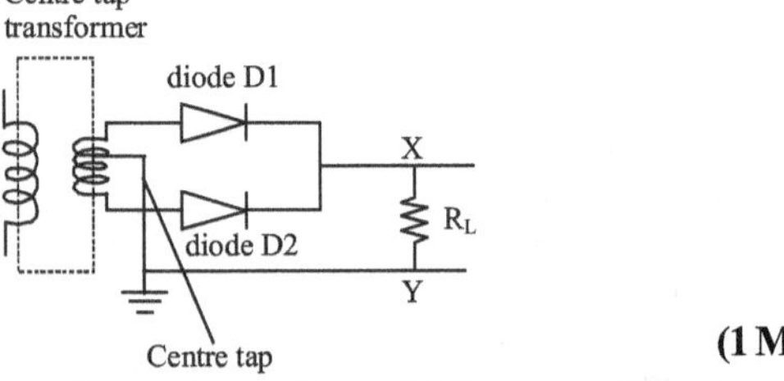

(1 Mark)

Input and output waveform of full wave rectifier:

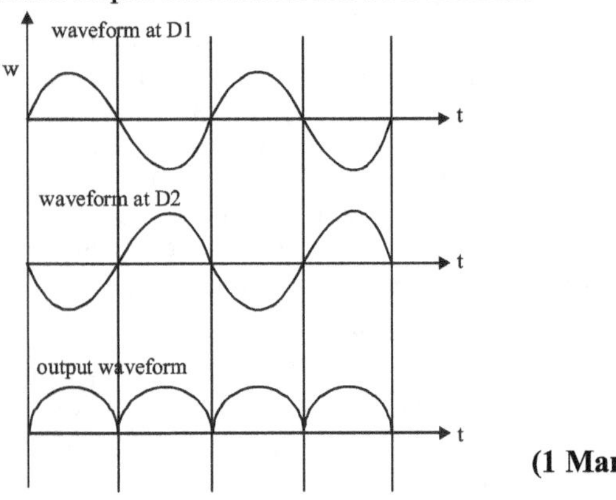

(1 Mark)

Working of full wave rectifiers

(1) The full wave rectifiers consists of a transformer, two junction diodes D1 and D2 and a load resistance R_L. The a.c. input signal is fed to the primary coil of the transformer.

(2) During positive half cycle of input a.c, end A of the secondary winding becomes positive and end B negative. Thus, diode D1 becomes forward biased, whereas diode D2 reverse biased.

(3) So, diode D1 allows the current to flow through it, while diode D2 does not, and current in the circuit flows from D1 and through load R_L form x to y.

(4) Again during negative half cycle of input a.c, end A of the secondary winding becomes negative and end B positive, thus diode D1 becomes reverse biased, whereas diode D2 forward biased.

(5) Because , in both the half cycle of input a.c. electric current through load R_L flows in the same direction, so. d.c is obtained across R_L. **(1 Mark)**

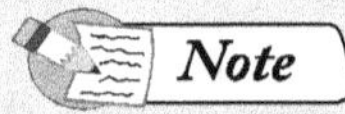 **Note**

Full wave rectifier is used to convert alternating voltage into direct voltage as current flows in the same direction during both half cycles of input alternating current.

24. (a) Maximum amplitude A_{max}=A
Minimum amplitude A_{min}=B
Modulation index is given as

$$\mu = \frac{A_{max} - A_{min}}{A_{max} + A_{min}} \quad \mu = \frac{A - B}{A + B}$$ **(1 Mark)**

(b) Modulation index

$$\mu = \frac{amplitude\ of\ modulated\ carrier\ wave}{amplitude\ of\ original\ carrier\ wave}$$ **(1 Mark)**

Amplitude of modulated wave=10V
Amplitude of original carrier wave=15V

$$\therefore \quad \mu = \frac{10}{15} = \frac{2}{3}$$ **(1 Mark)**

25. (a) **Impedance in series LCR circuit:** Consider a resistance R, an inductance L, and a capacitance C are connected in series to a source of alternating emf E of frequency ω, given by

$E = E_o \sin (\omega t)$

Let I = current in the circuit.

Voltage across resistance $V_R = IR$

Voltage across inductor, $V_L = IX_L$
Voltage across capacitor $V_C = IX_C$
Where X_C and X_L are capacitive resistance and inductive resistance respectively.

$$X_c = \frac{1}{\omega C} \text{ and } X_L = wL$$

(i) Voltage across resistance is in phase with current. So, they are in same direction in phasor diagram.
(ii) Voltage across inductor leads current by $\pi/2$. So, V_L lies $\pi/2$ anti-clockwise w.r.t V_R in phasor diagram.
(iii) Voltage across capacitor lags current by $\pi/2$. So, V_C lies $\pi/2$ clockwise w.r.t V_R in phasor diagram.

So, the phasor diagram is as follows:

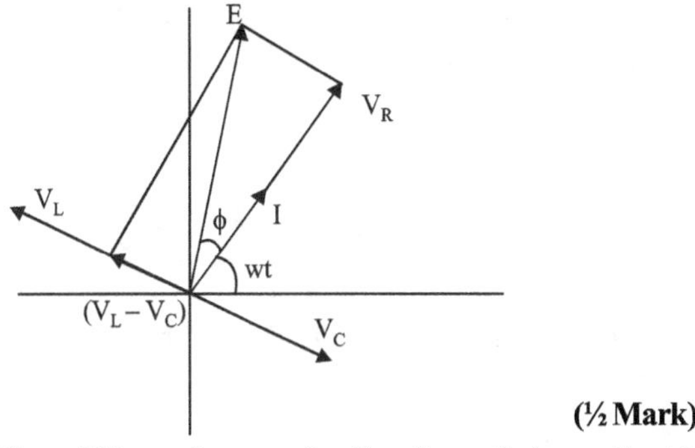

(½ Mark)

As V_L and V_C are in opposite directions, their resultant is $(V_L - V_C)$. By parallelogram law, the resultant of V_R and $(V_L - V_C)$ must be equal to the applied emf E.

Now, using Pythagoras theorem
$$E_0^2 = V_R^2 + (V_L - V_C)^2$$
$$= (IR)^2 + (X_L I - X_C I)^2$$
$$= I^2[R^2 + (X_L - X_C)^2]$$
$$I = \frac{E_o}{\sqrt{R^2 + (X_L - X_C)^2}}$$

(½ Mark)

If we compare the above equation with ohm's law which is

$$I = \frac{V}{R}$$

then $\sqrt{R^2 + (X_L - X_C)^2}$ becomes effective resistance of LCR circuit and it is called impedance of LCR circuit. It is denoted by Z.
Putting the value of X_C and X_L, we get

$$Z = \sqrt{R^2 + \left(\omega L - \frac{1}{\omega C}\right)^2}$$

(½ Mark)

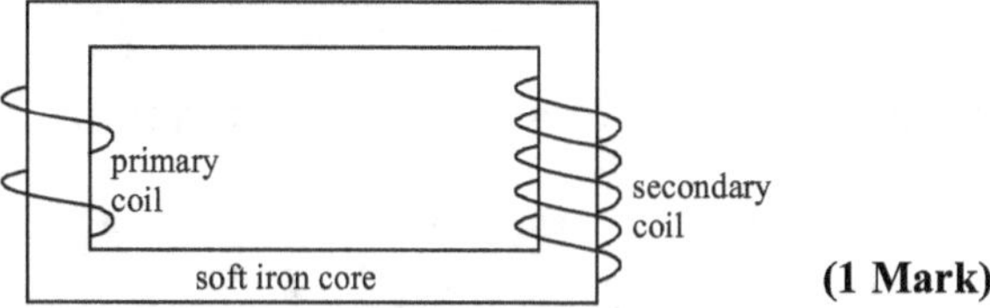

(½ Mark)

(b) The phase difference between voltage across inductor and the capacitor at resonance in the LCR circuit is π.
(1 Mark)

(c) When inductor is connected to dc source it offer no resistance as $\omega = 0$. So, $XL = \omega L = 0$.

So, current in the circuit will be totally due to resistance R

$$I = \frac{V}{R} = \frac{200}{1} = 200\Omega$$

(½ Mark)

But when inductor is connected to ac source it will offer extra resistance X_L in addition to resistance R.
Total impedance then will be

$$Z = \sqrt{X_L^2 + R^2}$$

$$Z = \frac{V}{1} \Rightarrow Z = \frac{200}{0.5} = 400\Omega$$

(½ Mark)

Since Z > R, current will be less when inductor is connected to a.c. source.

$$Z^2 = X_L{}^2 + R^2 \Rightarrow (400)^2 = X_L{}^2 + (200)^2$$
$$\therefore \qquad X_L = 200\sqrt{3}\,\Omega$$

(½ Mark)

Frequency of source $v = 50$Hz.
$X_L = \omega L = 2\pi v L$

$$\Rightarrow L = \frac{X_L}{2\pi v} \Rightarrow L = \frac{200\sqrt{3}}{2\pi \times 50} = \frac{2\sqrt{3}}{\pi} henry$$

(½ Mark)

OR

(a) The device which is used to decrease high ac voltage into a low ac voltage is transformer. **(½ Mark)**
Working principle of transformer:
It works on the principle of mutual inductance. When a changing current is passed through one of the two inductively coupled coils, an induced emf is set up in the other coil. **(½ Mark)**
The diagram of transformer is given below:

(1 Mark)

Four sources of energy loss in transformer are as follow:

(1) Copper Loss: some energy is lost due to heating of copper wires used in the primary and secondary coil.

(2) Eddy current loss: The alternating magnetic flux induces the eddy currents in the iron core which leads to some energy loss in the form of heat.

(3) Flux leakage : Total fluxes linked with the primary do not completely pass through the secondary which denotes the loss in the flux.

(4) Hysteresis loss : The energy loss takes place in magnetising and demagnetising the iron core over every cycle. **(½ × 4 = 2 Marks)**

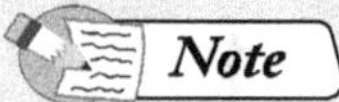

In transformer, the same flux links both the primary and the secondary as very little flux escapes from the core. The primary resistance and current are assumed to be small.

(b) Given

Power supplied to town $P = 1200\ kW = 1200 \times 10^3\ W$

Voltage at which the power is sent through $V = 4000\ V$.

Length of two wire line $= 2 \times 20\ km = 40\ km$

Resistance per unit length $= 0.5\ \Omega/km$

So, total line resistance = Length of two wire line × Resistance per unit length
$$= 2 \times 20 \times 0.5 = 20W$$

Rms value of current in the line

$$I = \frac{power}{voltage} = \frac{1200 \times 10^3}{4000} = 300A \qquad \textbf{(½ Mark)}$$

Line power loss in the form of heat $= I^2R$
$$= (300)^2 20 = 1800\ kW. \qquad \textbf{(½ Mark)}$$

26. (a) Difference between interference and diffraction

Interference	Diffraction
Interference is the result of superposition of secondary waves starting from two different wavefronts originating from two coherent sources.	Diffraction is the result of superposition of secondary waves starting from different parts of the same wave front.
All bright and dark fringes are of equal width and all bright fringes are of same intensity.	The width of central maxima is twice the width of any secondary maxima and they are not of same intensity.

$$\textbf{(2 × 1 = 2 Marks)}$$

Expression for intensity at any point in interference pattern:

Consider the displacement of two coherent source S_1 and S_2 at any point P on the screen at any time *t*.

Displacement of wave from S_1, $y_1 = a_1 \sin \omega t$

Displacement of wave from S_2, $y_2 = a_2 \sin (\omega t + \phi)$

Where ϕ = constant phase difference between them.

By superposition principle, the displacement of resultant wave at point P,

$$y = y_1 + y_2$$
$$y = a_1 \sin \omega t + a_2 \sin(\omega t + \phi)$$

If we take the amplitude of both the waves equal then
$$a_1 = a_2 = a$$

Resultant displacement would then become
$$y = a\,[\sin\omega t + \sin(\omega t + \phi)] \qquad \textbf{(½ Mark)}$$

Using the trigonometry identity

$$\sin A + \sin B = 2\sin\frac{A+B}{2}\cos\frac{A-B}{2}$$

Amplitude of resultant wave is

$$A = 2a\cos\frac{\phi}{2}$$

Now, intensity of a wave $\propto$ (amplitude)^2
So, intensity of resultant wave will be

$$I = \left(2a\cos\frac{\phi}{2}\right)^2 = 4a\cos^2\frac{\phi}{2} \qquad \textbf{(½ Mark)}$$

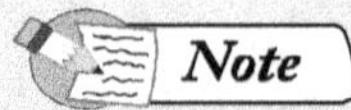

In interference, intensity of light is simply being redistributed, i.e., energy is being transferred from regions of destructive interference to the regions of constructive interference. Thus, the principle of energy conservation is being obeyed in the process of interference of light.

(b) Given

Wavelength of light $\lambda = 620\ nm = 620 \times 10^{-9} m$

Width of slit (a) $= 3\ mm = 3 \times 10^{-3} m$

Distance of screen from slit (D) $= 1.5\ m$

Distance of first order minima from central maxima x_1 is

$$x_1 = \frac{D\lambda}{2a} \qquad \textbf{(½ Mark)}$$

Distance of third order maxima from central maxima x_2 is

$$x_2 = \frac{3D\lambda}{a} \qquad \textbf{(½ Mark)}$$

Separation between the third order maxima and first order minima will be $x_2 - x_1$.

$$x_2 - x_1 = \frac{3D\lambda}{a} - \frac{D\lambda}{2a}$$

$$\Rightarrow x_2 - x_1 = \frac{5D\lambda}{2a} = \frac{5 \times 1.5 \times 620 \times 10^{-9}}{2 \times 10^{-3}} \qquad \textbf{(1 Mark)}$$

$$= 7.75 \times 10^{-4}\ m$$

Separation between the third order maxima and first order minima is 7.75×10^{-4} m.

OR

(a) Total internal reflection

The phenomenon in which a ray of light travelling at an angle of incidence greater than the critical angle from denser to rarer medium is totally reflected back into the medium is called total internal reflection.

Conditions for total internal reflection are:

(1) Light must travel from optically denser medium to rarer medium.

(2) Angle of incidence should be greater than the critical angle for the given two media. $\qquad \textbf{(2 × 1 = 2 Marks)}$

From snell's law we know that

$$\frac{\sin i}{\sin r} = \frac{\mu_2}{\mu_1}$$

where μ_1 = refractive index of denser medium

μ_2 = refractive index of rarer medium, at critical angle, angle of refraction becomes $90°$, *i.e.,* when $i = i_c$, $r = 90°$.

$$\Rightarrow \frac{\sin i_c}{\sin 90°} = \frac{\mu_2}{\mu_1} \Rightarrow \sin i_c = \frac{\mu_2}{\mu_1}$$

If rarer medium is air then we can take $\mu_2 = 1$ and $\mu_1 = \mu$.

$$\therefore \ \sin i_c = \frac{1}{\mu} \qquad \textbf{(1 Mark)}$$

(b) Given

Object distance $u = -30$ cm for first lens

For first lens $u_1 = -30$ cm

Image distance $= v_1$

Focal length $f_1 = 10$ cm

Applying lens formula for first lens

$$\frac{1}{v_1} - \frac{1}{u_1} = \frac{1}{f_1} \Rightarrow \frac{1}{v_1} - \frac{1}{-30} = \frac{1}{10} \qquad \textbf{(½ Mark)}$$

Image formed by first lens $v_1 = 15$ cm.

The image formed by first lens will act as object for second lens. For second lens $v_2 = (15 - 5)$ cm $= 10$cm to the right of second lens. Hence it will act as virtual object.

So, for second lens focal length $f_2 = -10$ cm.

$$\frac{1}{v_2} - \frac{1}{u_2} = \frac{1}{f_2} \Rightarrow \frac{1}{v_2} - \frac{1}{10} = \frac{1}{-10} \qquad \textbf{(½ Mark)}$$

The image formed by second lens $v_2 = \infty$.

The virtual image is formed at an infinite distance to the right of the second lens. This acts as an object for third lens.

For third lens, focal length $f_3 = 30$ cm. Applying lens formula

$$\frac{1}{v_3} - \frac{1}{u_3} = \frac{1}{f_3} \Rightarrow \frac{1}{v_3} - \frac{1}{\infty} = \frac{1}{30} \qquad \textbf{(½ Mark)}$$

The image formed by third lens $v_3 = 30$.   **(½ Mark)**

The final image is formed 30 cm to the right of the third lens.

27. **(a)** The process of transferring the charge between the two plates of a parallel plate capacitor when connected to a battery:

When plates A and B of a parallel plate capacitor are connected to the terminals of a battery, the battery sets up electric field in the connecting wires. The electric field drives charge Q from plate B, connected to the negative terminal of the battery to plate A connected to the positive terminal.

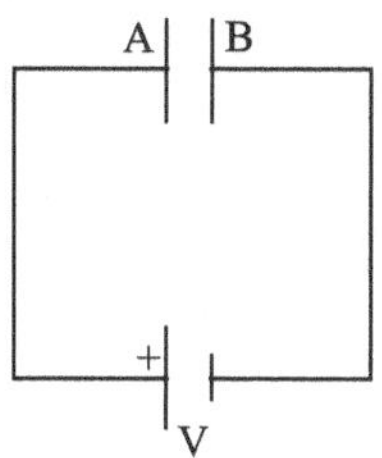

The charge transfer takes place till the potential difference across the capacitor plates equals the emf of battery.

(1 Mark)

Energy stored in capacitor

Let 'dw' amount of work done in transferring 'dq' charge from plate A to plate B.

dw = Vdq   **(½ Mark)**

where V = potential between plates of capacitor.

For capacitor of capacitance C and charge q, voltage across the plates of capacitor is given as

$$V = \frac{q}{C}$$

$$\therefore \quad dw = \frac{q}{C} dq \qquad \textbf{(½ Mark)}$$

The total work done in transferring the charge from 0 to Q is

$$\int dw = \int_0^Q \frac{q}{C} dq$$

$$W = \left[\frac{q^2}{2C}\right]_0^Q = \frac{Q^2}{2C} \ or \ W = \frac{1}{2}CV^2 \qquad \textbf{(1 Mark)}$$

This work done is stored as the energy in capacitor.

(b) Initial energy stored in capacitor U_i is

$$U_i = \frac{1}{2}CV^2$$

When the capacitor is connected to another uncharged capacitor with capacitance C, charge will flow between them until the voltage becomes V/2 across each capacitor.

Then final energy stored in combination of capacitor

$$U_f = \frac{1}{2}C\left(\frac{V}{2}\right)^2 + \frac{1}{2}C\left(\frac{V}{2}\right)^2 = \frac{1}{4}CV^2 \qquad \textbf{(1 Mark)}$$

Therefore, the ratio of the energy stored in the combination to the initial energy in the single capacitor

$$\frac{U_f}{U_i} = \frac{\frac{1}{4}CV^2}{\frac{1}{2}CV^2} = \frac{1}{2} \qquad \textbf{(1 Mark)}$$

The ratio of the energy stored in the combination to the initial energy in the single capacitor is 1 : 2.

OR

(a) The electric field at any point on the equatorial line of an electric dipole

Consider an electric dipole consisting of two charges -q and +q separated by a distance 2a. Let P be the equatorial point at a distance 'r' from the centre of dipole.

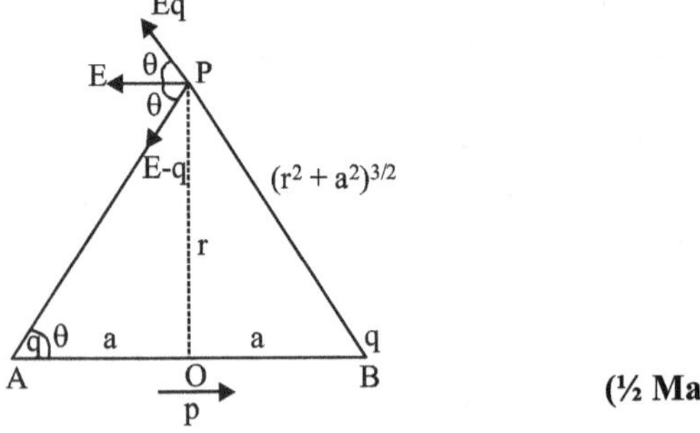

(½ Mark)

Electric field due to a point charge at distance r is given as

$$E = \frac{1}{4\pi\epsilon_o} \times \frac{q}{r^2}$$

So, electric field due to charge, q at point P

$$E_q = \frac{1}{4\pi\epsilon_o} \times \frac{q}{r^2 + a^2} , \textit{ directed along BP}$$ (½ Mark)

Similarly, electric field due to -q at point P

$$E_{-q} = \frac{1}{4\pi\epsilon_o} \times \frac{q}{r^2 + a^2} , \textit{ directed along AP}$$ (½ Mark)

Therefore, the magnitudes of E_q and E_{-q} are equal.

The component of E_q and E_{-q} normal to the axis of dipole will cancel out each other as they are equal and opposite.

But the components parallel to the dipole axis will add up. So, the total electric field which is opposite to dipole moment p

$$E = -(E_q \cos\theta + E_{-q} \cos\theta) = -2E_q \cos\theta$$ (½ Mark)

Negative sign is due to the fact that the total electric field is opposite to dipole moment p.

From figure $\cos\theta = \dfrac{a}{\sqrt{a^2 + r^2}}$

$$\therefore E = -2 \times \frac{1}{4\pi\epsilon_0} \times \frac{q}{r^2 + a^2} \times \frac{a}{\sqrt{a^2 + r^2}}$$ (½ Mark)

$$\Rightarrow E = \frac{1}{4\pi\epsilon_0} \times \frac{-p}{(r^2 + a^2)^{\frac{3}{2}}}$$

where p = dipole moment = $2qa$

If the point P is located far away from the dipole, then

$$E = \frac{1}{4\pi\epsilon_o} \times \frac{-p}{r^3}$$

Direction of electric field at any point on the equatorial line will be antiparallel to the dipole moment p.

> **Note**
>
> *The magnitude and direciton of dipole field depend not only on the distance r but also on the angle between the position vector $\vec{r}$ and dipole moment p. The electric field due to a dipole at large distance falls off at a much faster rate $\left(\alpha\, \dfrac{1}{r^3}\right)$ than electric field due to single charge $\left(\alpha\, \dfrac{1}{r^2}\right)$.*

(b) For the system to remain in equilibrium, force on Q due to q and q should be zero.

```
  q                 Q                 q
A ◄─────────────────────────────────► B
      ◄──────x──────►◄────2 − x────►
```

Let Q be at a distance x from q. Then, force on Q due to q kept at A

$$F_1 = \frac{Qq}{4\pi\epsilon_o x^2}$$ (½ Mark)

Similarly, force on Q due to q kept at B

$$F_2 = \frac{Qq}{4\pi\epsilon_o (2-x)^2}$$ (½ Mark)

Now, $F_1 = F_2$ for system to be in equilibrium.

$$\therefore \frac{Qq}{4\pi\epsilon_o\, x^2} = \frac{Qq}{4\pi\epsilon_o (2-x)^2}$$

$2 - x = x \Rightarrow x = 1$ m.   (1 Mark)

Hence, the charge Q should be at the mid-point of the line joining the two-charges and should be of opposite polarity.

All India *2018*

CBSE Board Solved Paper

Time Allowed : 3 Hours   *Maximum Marks : 70*

(i) There are **26** questions in all. All questions are compulsory.

(ii) This question paper has **five** sections: Section **A**, Section **B**, Section **C**, Section **D** and Section **E**.

(iii) Section **A** contains **five** questions of **one** mark each, Section **B** contains **five** questions of **two** marks each, Section **C** contains **twelve** questions of **three** marks each, Section **D** contains **one** value based question of **four** marks and Section **E** contains **three** questions of **five** marks each.

(iv) There is no overall choice. However, an internal choice has been provided in **one** question of **two** marks, **one** question of **three** marks and all the **three** questions of **five** marks weightage. You have to attempt only **one** of the choices in such questions

(v) You may use the following values of physical constants wherever necessary:

$c = 3 \times 10^8$ m/s

$h = 6.63 \times 10^{-34}$ Js

$e = 1.6 \ 10^{-19}$ C

$\mu_o = 4\pi \times 10^{-7}$ Tm A^{-1}

$\varepsilon_0 = 8.854 \times 10^{-12}$ C^2 N^{-1} m^{-2}

$$\frac{1}{4\pi\varepsilon_0} = 9 \times 10^9 \text{N m}^2 \text{ C}^{-2}$$

Mass of electron $(m_e) = 9.1 \times 10^{-31}$ kg

Mass of neutron $= 1.675 \times 10^{-27}$ kg

Mass of proton $= 1.673 \times 10^{-27}$ kg

Avogadro's number $= 6.023 \times 10^{23}$ per gram mole

Boltzmann constant $= 1.38 \times 10^{-23}$ JK^{-1}

SECTION - A

1. A proton and an electron travelling along parallel paths enter a region of uniform magnetic field, acting perpendicular to their paths. Which of them will move in a circular path with higher frequency?

2. Name the electromagnetic radiations used for (a) water purification, and (b) eye surgery.

3. Draw graphs showing variation of photoelectric current with applied voltage for two incident radiations of equal frequency and different voltage for two incident radiations of equal frequency and different intensities. Mark the graph for the radiation of higher intensity.

4. Four nuclei of an element undergo fusion to form a heavier nucleus, with release of energy. Which of the two - the parent or the daughter nucleus - would have higher binding energy per nucleon?

5. Which mode of propagation is used by short wave broadcast services?

SECTION - B

6. Two electric bulbs P and Q have their resistances in the ratio of 1 : 2. They are connected in series across a battery. Find the ratio of the power dissipation in these bulbs.

7. A 10 V cell of negligible internal resistance is connected in parallel across a battery of emf 200 V and internal resistance 38W as shown in the figure. Find the value of current in the circuit.

OR

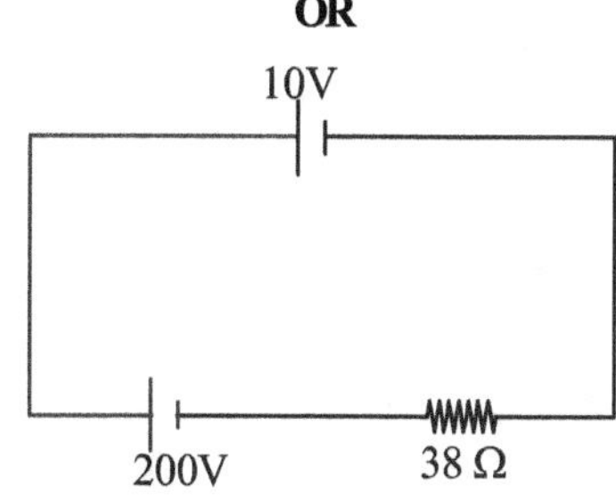

In a potentiometer arrangement for determining the emf of a cell, the balance point of the cell in open circuit is 350 cm. When a resistance of 9 Ω is used in the external circuit of the cell, the balance point shifts to 300 cm. Determine the internal resistance of the cell.

8. (a) Why are infra-red waves often called heat waves? Explain.

(b) What do you understand by the statement, "Electromagnetic waves transport momentum"?

9. If light of wavelength 412.5 nm is incident on each of the metals given below, which one will show photoelectric emission and why?

Metal	Work Function (eV)
Na	1.92
K	2.15
Ca	3.20
Mo	4.17

10. A carrier wave of peak voltage 15 V is used to transmit a message signal. Find the peak voltage of the modulating signal in order to have a modulation index of 60%.

SECTION - C

11. Four point charges Q, q, Q and q are placed at the corners of a square of side 'a' as shown in the figure.

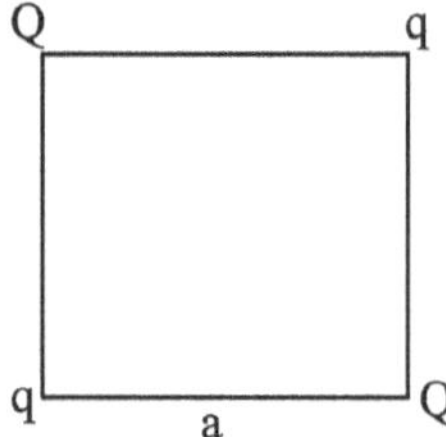

Find the

(a) resultant electric force on a charge Q, and

(b) potential energy of this system.

OR

(a) Three point charges q, –4q and 2q are placed at the vertices of an equilateral triangle ABC of side 'ℓ' as shown in the figure. Obtain the expression for the magnitude of the resultant electric force acting on the charge q.

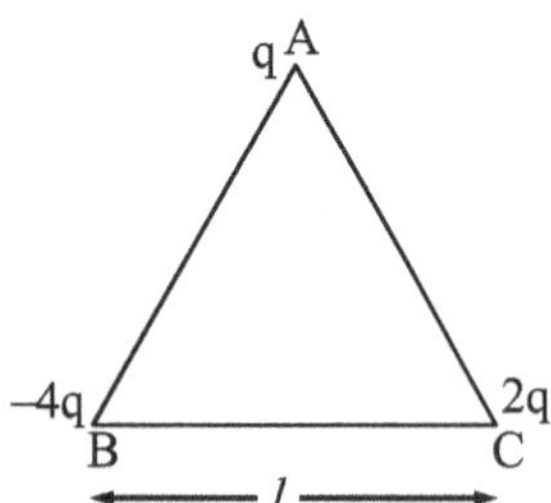

(b) Find out the amount of the work done to separate the charges at infinite distance.

12. (a) Define the term 'conductivity' of a metallic wire. Write its SI unit.

(b) Using the concept of free electrons in a conductor, derive the expression for the conductivity of a wire in terms of number density and relaxation time. Hence obtain the relation between current density and the applied electric field E.

13. A bar magnet of magnetic moment 6 J/T is aligned at 60° with a uniform external magnetic field of 0.44 T. Calculate (a) the work done turning the magnet to align its magnetic moment (i) normal to the magnetic field, (ii) opposite to the magnetic field, and (b) the torque on the magnet in the final orientation in case (ii).

14. (a) An iron ring of relative permeability μ_r has windings of insulated copper wire of n turns per meter. When the current in the winding is I, find the expression for the magnetic field in the ring.

(b) The susceptibility of a magnetic material is 0.9853. Identify the type of magnetic material. Draw the modification of the field pattern on keeping a piece of this material in a uniform magnetic field.

15. (a) Show using proper diagram how unpolarised light can be linearly polarised by reflection from a transparent glass surface.

(b) The figure shows a ray of light falling normally on the face AB of an equilateral glass prism having refractive index $\frac{3}{2}$, placed in water of refractive index $\frac{4}{3}$. Will this ray suffer total internal reflection on striking the face AC? Justify your answer.

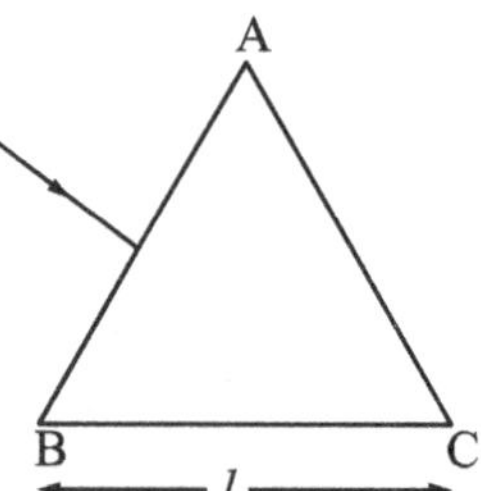

16. (a) If one of two identical slits producing interference in Young's experiment is covered with glass, so that the light intensity passing through it is reduced to 50%, find the ratio of the maximum and minimum intensity of the fringe in the interference pattern.

(b) What kind of fringes do you expect to observe if white light is used instead of monochromatic light?

17. A symmetric biconvex lens of radius of curvature R and made of glass of refractive index 1.5, is placed on a layer of liquid placed on top of a plane mirror as shown in the figure. An optical needle with its tip on the principal axis of the lens is moved along the axis until its real, inverted image coincides with the needle itself. The distance of the needle from the lens is measured to be x. On removing the liquid layer and repeating the experiment, the distance is found to be y. Obtain the expression for the refractive index of the liquid in terms of x and y.

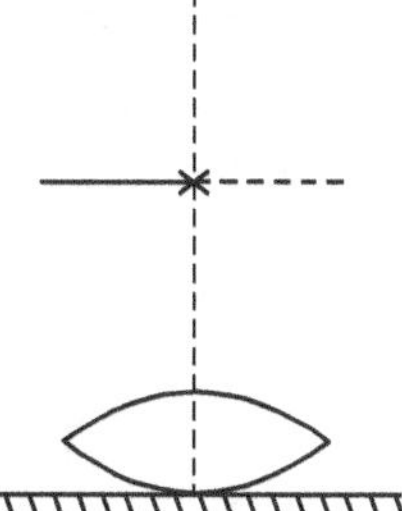

18. (a) State Bohr's postulate to define stable orbits in hydrogen atom. How does de-Broglie's hypothesis explain the stability of these orbits?
    (b) A hydrogen atom initially in ground state absorbs a photon which excites it to the $n = 4$ level. Estimate the frequency of the photon.
19. (a) Explain the processes of nuclear fission and nuclear fusion by using the plot of binding energy per nucleon (BE/A) versus the mass number A.
    (b) A radioactive isotope has a half-life of 10 years. How long will it take for the activity to reduce to 3.125%?
20. (a) A student wants to use two p-n junction diodes to convert alternating current into direct current. Draw the labelled circuit diagram she would use and explain how it works.
    (b) Give the truth table and circuit symbol for NAND gate.
21. Draw the typical input and output characteristics of an n-p-n transistor in CE configuration. Show how these characteristics can be used to determine (a) the input resistance (r_i) and (b) current amplification factor (β).
22. (a) Give three reasons why modulation of a message signal is necessary for long distance transmission.
    (b) Show graphically an audio signal, a carrier wave and an amplitude modulated wave.

SECTION - D

23. The teachers of Geeta's school took the students on a study trip to a power generating station, located nearly 200 km away from the city. The teacher explained that electrical energy is transmitted over such a long distance to their city, in the form of alternating current (ac) raised to a high voltage. At the receiving end in the city, the voltage is reduced to operate the devices. As a result, the power loss is reduced. Geeta listened to the teacher and asked questions about how the ac is converted to a higher or lower voltage.
    (a) Name the device used to change the alternating voltage to a higher or lower value. State one cause for power dissipation in this device.
    (b) Explain with an example, how power loss is reduced if the energy is transmitted over long distances as an alternating current rather than a direct current.
    (c) Write two values each shown by the teachers and Geeta.

SECTION - E

24. (a) Define electric flux. Is it a scalar or a vector quantity? A point charge q is at a distance of $d/2$ directly above the centre of a square of side d, as shown in the figure. Use Gauss's law to obtain the expression for the electric flux through the square.

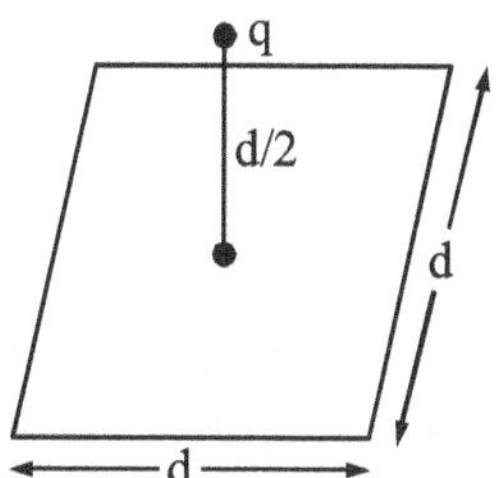

    (b) If the point charge is now moved to a distance 'd' from the centre of the square and the side of the square is doubled, explain how the electric flux will be affected.

OR

    (a) Use Gauss's law to derive the expression for the electric field (E) due to a straight uniformly charged infinite line of charge density ρ C/m.
    (b) Draw a graph to show the variation of E with perpendicular distance r from the line of charge.
    (c) Find the work done in bringing a charge q from perpendicular distance r_1 to r_2 $(r_2 > r_1)$.

25. (a) State the principle of an ac generator and explain its working with the help of a labelled diagram. Obtain the expression for the emf induced in a coil having N turns each of cross-sectional area A, rotating with a constant angular speed 'ω' in a magnetic field $\vec{B}$, directed perpendicular to the axis of rotation.
    (b) An aeroplane is flying horizontally from west to east with a velocity of 900 km/hour. Calculate the potential difference developed between the ends of its wings having a span of 20 m. The horizontal component of the Earth's magnetic field is 5×10^{-4} T and the angle of dip is 30°.

OR

A device X is connected across an ac source of voltage $V = V_0 \sin\omega t$. The current through X is given as
$$I = I_0 \sin\left(\omega t + \frac{\pi}{2}\right).$$

    (a) Identify the device X and write the expression for its reactance.
    (b) Draw graphs showing variation of voltage and current with time over one cycle of ac, for X.
    (c) How does the reactance of the device X vary with frequency of the ac? Show this variation graphically.
    (d) Draw the phasor diagram for the device X.

26. (a) Draw a ray diagram to show image formation when the concave mirror produces a real, inverted and magnified image of the object.
    (b) Obtain the mirror formula and write the expression for the linear magnification.
    (c) Explain two advantages of a reflecting telescope over a refracting telescope.

OR

    (a) Define a wavefront. Using Huygens' principle, verify the laws of reflection at a plane surface.
    (b) In a single slit diffraction experiment, the width of the slit is made double the original width. How does this affect the size and intensity of the central diffraction band? Explain.
    (c) When a tiny circular obstacle is placed in the path of light from a distant source, a bright spot is seen at the centre of the obstacle. Explain why?

Solutions

SECTION - A

1. Charges will trace a circular path as soon as they will enter a region of uniform magnetic field (acting perpendicular to their paths)

Frequency, $f = \dfrac{qB}{2\pi m}$

$\Rightarrow\ f \propto \dfrac{1}{m}$ or frequency $\propto \dfrac{1}{mass}$

As electron has less mass, so, it will move with higher frequency. **(1 Mark)**

2. Electromagnetic radiation used for
(a) Water purification– Ultraviolet rays
(b) Eye surgery– Infrared rays   **(½ + ½ = 1 Mark)**

3.

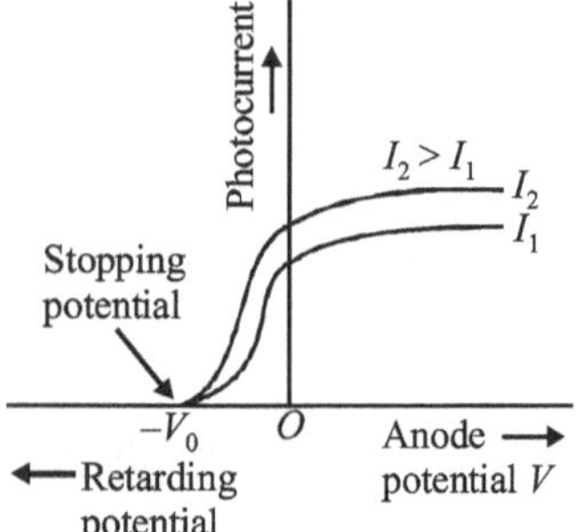

(1 Mark)

 **Note**

For a given material, the photoelectric current is directly proportional to the intensity of the incident light. The stopping potential is independent of Intensity of incident light.

4. Binding energy per nucleon

$= \dfrac{BE}{mass\ number(A)}$

The binding energy per nucleon of the fused heavier nuclei > binding energy per nucleon of the lighter nuclei. So, binding energy is more per nucleon in daughter nuclei. **(1 Mark)**

5. The sky wave mode of propagation is limited to 40 MHz. This is because the waves of this and higher frequencies are not reflected by the atmosphere but are transmitted. The critical frequency for sky wave mode of porpagation is 40 MHz. **(1 Mark)**

SECTION - B

6. For series combination, power dissipated (P) by a bulb is directly proportional to its resistance (R).
i.e., $P \propto R$ $[\because P = I^2 R]$ **(1 Mark)**
$P_1/P_2 = R_1/R_2 = 1 : 2.$ **(1 Mark)**

7. Let i be the current in the circuit and its direction is in anticlockwise direction.

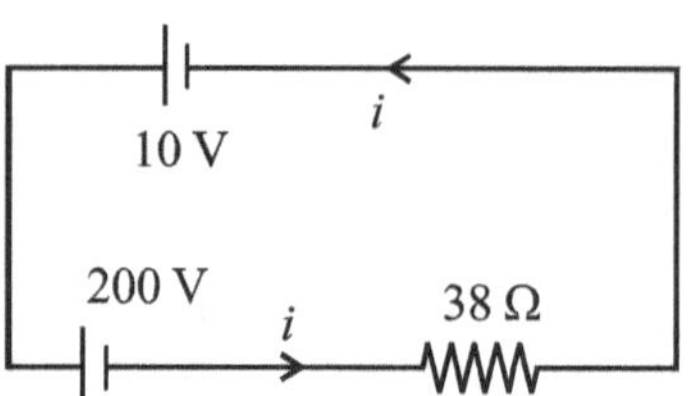

Applying kirchhoff's voltage law, $E - V + iR = 0$ **(1 Mark)**
$10 - 200 + 38i = 0$
$\Rightarrow\ 38\, i = 190 \Rightarrow i = 5A$ **(1 Mark)**

OR

Given : $R = 9W,\ l_1 = 350,\ l_2 = 300$
Internal resistance of a cell is given by,

$r = R\left(\dfrac{l_2}{l_1} - 1\right)$ **(1 Mark)**

Substituting values of $l_2,\ l_1$ and R, we get

$r = R\left(\dfrac{350}{300} - 1\right) = 9\left(\dfrac{7}{6} - 1\right) = 1.5\Omega.$ **(1 Mark)**

8. (a) The water molecules present in most materials readily absorb infrared waves (many other molecules, like, CO_2, NH_3, also absorb infrared waves). After absorption, their thermal motion increases, so, they heat up and heat their surroundings. hence infra–red waves often called heat waves. **(1 Mark)**
(b) It means when EM waves strike a surface, a pressure is exerted on the surface. **(1 Mark)**

 **Note**

The electromagnetic wave like other waves carries energy and momentum. Since it carries momentum, an electromagnetic wave also exert pressure called radition pressure.

Radiation pressure, $p = \dfrac{u}{c}$

9. To show photoelectric emission, work function of metal should be less than the energy incident on it.

Energy incident $E = \dfrac{hc}{\lambda}$

Given, $\lambda = 412.9 \times 10^{-9}\,m$

$\therefore\ E = \dfrac{6.67 \times 10^{-34} \times 3 \times 10^8}{412.5 \times 10^{-9}} = 0.048 \times 10^{-7}\,J$

$\Rightarrow E = \dfrac{0.048 \times 10^{-17}}{1.6 \times 10^{-19}}\,eV = 3\ eV.$ **(1 Mark)**

$$\because \quad 1 \text{ joule} = \frac{1}{1.6 \times 10^{-19}} \text{ eV}$$

Na and K will show photoelectric effect. **(1 Mark)**

10. Given : Modulation index, $\mu = 60\% = 0.60$

Amplitude of carrier wave, $Ac = 15$ V

Amplitude of modulating wave, $Am = ?$

$$\mu = \frac{A_m}{A_c} \Rightarrow 0.60 = \frac{A_m}{15} \Rightarrow A_m = 9V. \qquad \textbf{(2 Marks)}$$

 **Note**

If the modulation index (μ) is greater than 1 i.e., $\mu > 1$, the carrier wave will be over modulated and distortion will occur during reception as negative peak of modulating signal will be missing. Therefore, μ is kept less than one.

SECTION - C

11. (a) Force on charge, Q due to other charges is shown in the figure

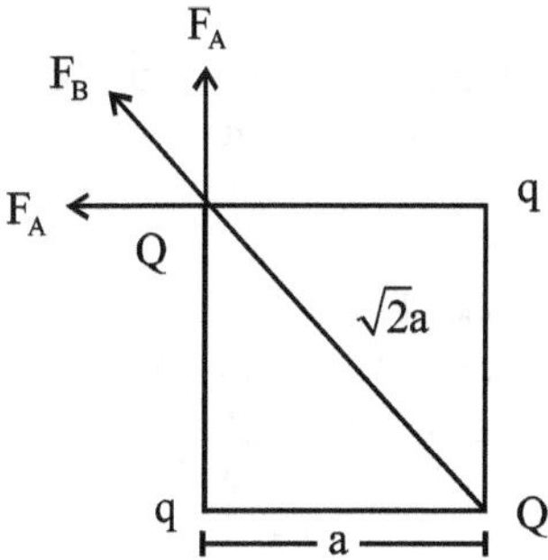

Here, F_A is force acting on Q due to q

F_B is force acting on Q due to Q

Using Coulomb's law

$$F_A = K\frac{Qq}{a^2} \text{ and } F_B = K\frac{Q^2}{a^2} \left[\text{here, } K = \frac{1}{4\pi \in_o} \right] \qquad \textbf{(½ Mark)}$$

Net force is equal to resultant of two perpendicular forces F_A (acting in different direction) + force F_B

$$F_{net} = \sqrt{2}\, F_A + F_B \Rightarrow F_{net} = k\left[\sqrt{2}\frac{Qq}{a^2} + \frac{Q^2}{2a^2} \right] \qquad \textbf{(1 Mark)}$$

(b) Potential energy of a system of two charges (q_1 and q_2) separated by a distance 'a' is given by

$$V = k\frac{q_1 q_2}{a} \qquad \textbf{(½ Mark)}$$

There are 6 pairs, as shown in the figures.

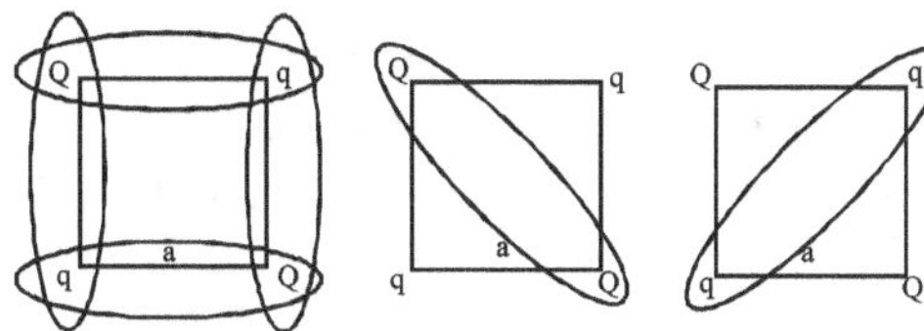

∴ Electrostatic potential energy of the system =

$$\frac{4kQq}{a} + \frac{kQ^2}{\sqrt{2}a} + \frac{kq^2}{\sqrt{2}a} \qquad \textbf{(1 Mark)}$$

 **Note**

Electrostatic potential energy of a system of N point charges equal to the total amount of work done in assembling all the charges at the given position from infinity.

OR

(a) The forces on the charge q due to other charges are shown in the figure

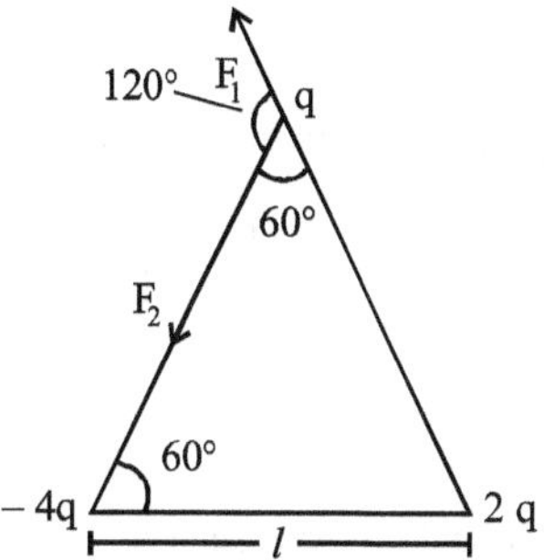

The resultant electric force acting on the charge q is the resultant of forces F_1 and F_2

Using Coulomb's law,

$$|F_1| = k\frac{2qq}{l^2} = k\frac{2q^2}{l^2} \text{ and}$$

$$|F_2| = k\frac{4qq}{l^2} = k\frac{4q^2}{l^2}$$

Now, resulant force

$$F = \sqrt{F_1^2 + F_2^2 + 2F_1 F_2 \cos\theta}$$

$$= \sqrt{F_1^2 + F_2^2 + 2F_1 F_2 \cos 120°} \qquad \textbf{(1 Mark)}$$

Resultant force

$$F = \sqrt{F_1^2 + F_2 - 2F_1 F_2} \qquad \left[\because \cos 120° = -\frac{1}{2} \right]$$

$$F = \sqrt{F_1^2 + F_2^2 - F_1 F_2}$$

Since $F_2 = 2F_1$

$$\therefore \qquad F = \sqrt{(F_1)^2 + (2F_1)^2 - 2F_1^2}$$

$$F = \sqrt{5F_1^2 - 2F_1^2}$$

$$F = F_1\sqrt{3}$$

$$F = \frac{K2q^2}{l^2} \times \sqrt{3} \qquad \textbf{(1 Mark)}$$

(b) The amount of the work done to separate the charges at infinite distance is difference in initial and final potential energy *i.e.*,

Work done = (final potential energy) – (initial potential energy)

Final potential energy (when charges are at infinite distance) = 0

Initial potential energy

$$= -k\frac{4q^2}{\ell} - k\frac{8q^2}{\ell} + k\frac{2q^2}{\ell}$$

$$= -k\frac{10q^2}{\ell} \qquad \textbf{(½ Mark)}$$

∴ Work done = (final potential energy) – (initial

potential energy) $= 0 - \left(-k\frac{10q^2}{\ell}\right)$

∴ Work done $= k\frac{10q^2}{\ell} \qquad \textbf{(½ Mark)}$

12. (a) The reciprocal of the resistivity (r) of a material is called its conductivity and is denoted by σ.

$$i.e., \ \sigma = \frac{1}{\rho} \qquad \textbf{(½ Mark)}$$

The SI unit of conductivity: siemen per meter (sm^{-1})

$$\textbf{(½ Mark)}$$

(b) The average time difference between two successive collisions of drifting electrons inside the conductor under the influence of electric field is known as relaxation time.

Drift speed and relaxation time are related as:

$$V_d = -\frac{eE\tau}{m}$$

As current $I = -ne\,Av_d$

$$I = -neA\left(-\frac{eE\tau}{m}\right)$$

$$I = \frac{ne^2 A\tau}{m}\left(\frac{V}{l}\right) \qquad \left(\because E = \frac{V}{l}\right)$$

$$\Rightarrow \frac{V}{I} = \frac{ml}{ne^2 A\tau} = \rho\frac{l}{A} = R$$

$$\rho = \frac{m}{ne^2\tau} \qquad \textbf{(1 Mark)}$$

Now, we know that conductivity of a conductor (σ) is mathematically defined as the reciprocal of resistivity of the conductor. Thus, $\rho = \dfrac{1}{\sigma}$

$$\therefore \text{Conductivity, } \sigma = \frac{ne^2\tau}{m}$$

Now, from above equations

$$\frac{I}{A} = \sigma E \text{ Current density is given as } J = \frac{I}{A}$$

Thus, $J = \sigma E$ **(1 Mark)**

13. (a) (i) Work done, $W = \vec{M}\vec{B}\,(\cos\theta_1 - \cos\theta_2)$

$$= 6 \times 0.44 \times (\cos 60° - \cos 90°)$$

$$= 6 \times 0.44 \times (0.5 - 0) = 1.32 \qquad \textbf{(1 Mark)}$$

(ii) $W = \vec{M}\vec{B}\,(\cos\theta_2 - \cos\theta_1)$

$$= 6 \times 0.44 \times (\cos 60° - \cos 180°)$$

$$= 6 \times 0.44 \times [0.5 - (-1)] = 3.96J \qquad \textbf{(1 Mark)}$$

(b) Torque, $t = \vec{M} \times \vec{B} = 6 \times 0.44 \times \sin 180° = 0.$ **(1 Mark)**

14. (a) Here, an iron ring of relative permeability mr having windings of insulated copper wire of *n* turns per meter. It means it is acting as toroid.

A toroid consists of hollow circular ring on which a large number of turns of a wire are closely wound as shown in figure. Let N be the number of turns and I be the current passed through the toroid. r be the average radius. If the coils are closely spaced, the field inside the toroidal coil is tangent to the dotted circular path and is same at all points.

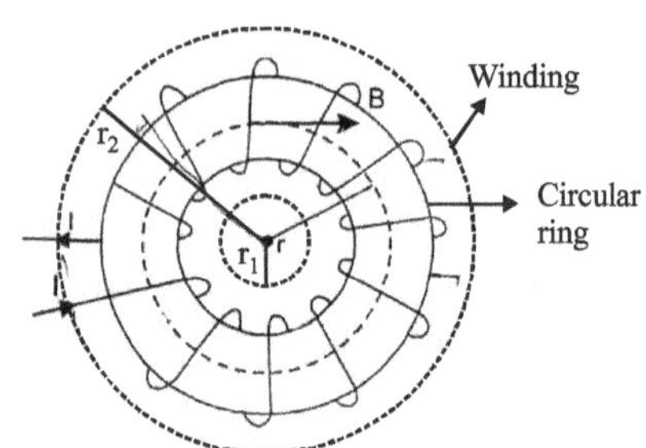

By Ampere's circuital law,

$$\oint \vec{B}\cdot\overrightarrow{dL} = B\oint dL = B\,(2\pi r) = \mu_0\mu_r NI \qquad \textbf{(1 Mark)}$$

or $B = \dfrac{\mu_0 u_r NI}{2\pi r} = \mu_0 nI$ **(½ Mark)**

$\because$ $n = \dfrac{N}{2\pi r}$ (number of turns per unit length)

This is the expression for magnetic field.

(b) Susceptibility of a paramagnetic substance is positive but small. Hence, the given magnetic material is paramagnetic in nature.   **(½ Mark)**

The field pattern on keeping a piece of this material in a uniform magnetic field is shown in figure:

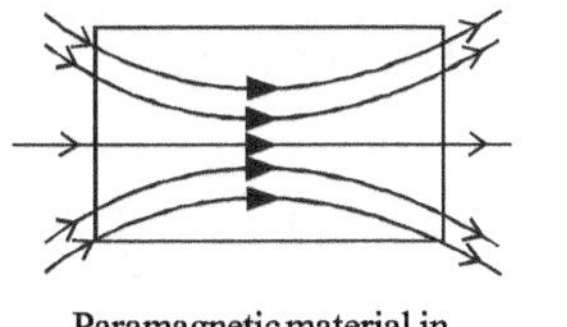

(1 Mark)

Paramagnetic material in external magneitc field

15. (a) **Unpolarized light :** When the vibrations of electric field vector are symmetricaly distributed in a direction perpendicular to the direction of propagation of light wave, is termed as unpolarized light

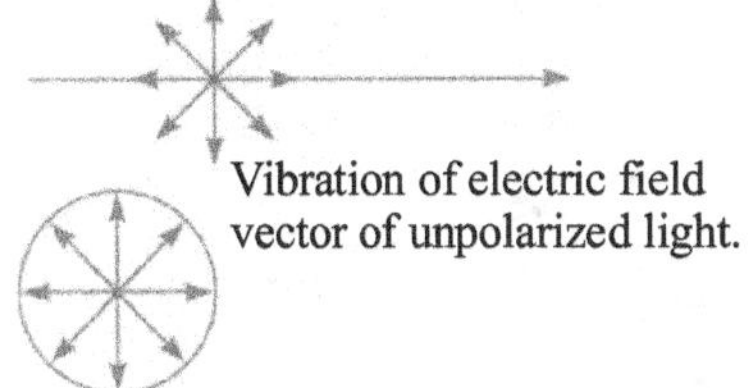

Vibration of electric field vector of unpolarized light.

(1 Mark)

Polarization by reflection from a transparent medium

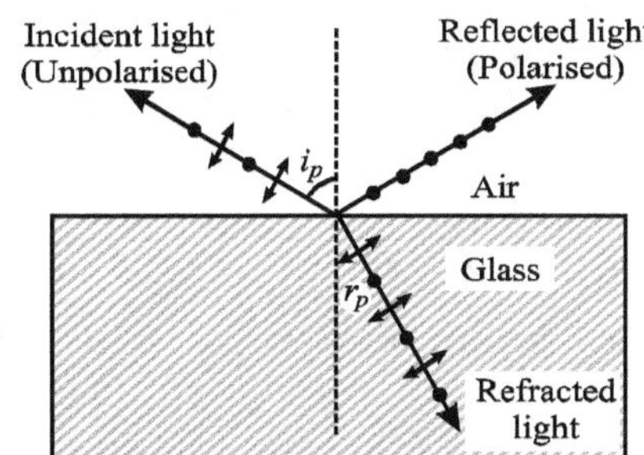

When an unpolarized light beam is incident on a refracting transparent medium at a particular angle of incidence, known as polarising angle i_p, the reflected light is plane polarized. Thus, plane polarized light is produced by reflection. **(1 Mark)**

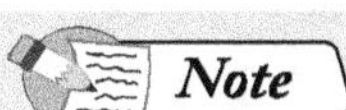
Note

When light is incident on a transparent surface at the polarising angle, the reflected and refracted rays are perpendicular to each other.

(b) Let the ray suffers total internal reflection, for limiting ray,

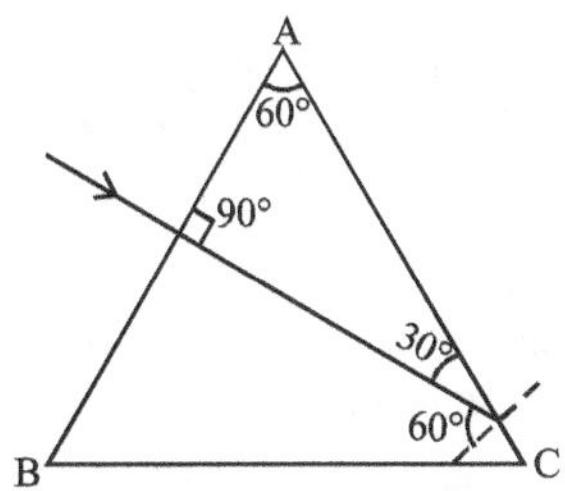

Angle of incidence $= i$, angle of emergence $= 90°$

Applying Snell's law,

$(n_g) \sin i = n_1 (\sin 90°)$

$\Rightarrow \sin i = (n_1)/(n_g) \Rightarrow \sin i = 8/9 = 0.88.$

In the given question, angle of incidence (inside prism) is 60°.

Now, $\sin 60° = \sqrt{3/2} = 0.816.$

Clearly angle of incidence is smaller so, total internal reflection in this case will not take place. **(1 Mark)**

16. (a) Let intensity in first case is I, therefore intensity in second case is $I/2$ according to question.

$i.e., I_1 = I$ and $I_2 = I/2$

Intensity ratio $\dfrac{I_{max}}{I_{min}} = \left(\dfrac{\sqrt{I_1} + \sqrt{I_2}}{\sqrt{I_1} - \sqrt{I_2}} \right)^2$ **(1 Mark)**

or, $\dfrac{I_{max}}{I_{min}} = \left(\dfrac{\sqrt{I} + \sqrt{I/2}}{\sqrt{I} - \sqrt{I/2}} \right)^2$

$= \left(\dfrac{\sqrt{I}(\sqrt{2}+1)}{\sqrt{I}(\sqrt{2}-1)} \right)^2 = \left(\dfrac{(\sqrt{2}+1)}{(\sqrt{2}-1)} \right)^2$ **(1 Mark)**

(b) The interference pattern due to different colour component of white light overlap. The central bright fringes for different colours are at the same position. Therefore, central fringes are white. And on the either side of the central white fringe (*i.e.*, central maxima) coloured bands will appear.

The fringe closed on either side of central white fringe is red and the farthest will be blue. After a few fringes, no clear fringe pattern is seen. **(1 Mark)**

17. Let us first consider the situation when no liquid between lens and plane mirror and the image is formed at y cm position of object.

As the image is formed on the object position itself, the object must be placed at focus of biconvex lens.

$f_O = y$ cm

Radius of curvature of convex lens can be calculated as,

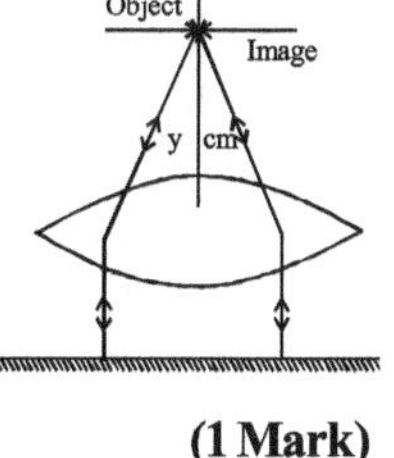

$\dfrac{1}{f} = \left({}^a\mu_g - 1 \right) \left(\dfrac{1}{R_1} - \dfrac{1}{R_2} \right)$

or $\dfrac{1}{y} = \left(\dfrac{3}{2} - 1 \right) \left(\dfrac{1}{R} - \dfrac{1}{-R} \right)$

or $\dfrac{1}{y} = \dfrac{1}{2} \left(\dfrac{2}{R} \right) \Rightarrow R = y$ cm **(1 Mark)**

Now a liquid is filled between lens and plane mirror and the image is formed at position of object at x cm.

The image is formed on the position of object itself, the object must be placed at focus of equivalent lens of Biconvex of glass and Plano convex lens of liquid.

$$\frac{1}{f_{eq}} = \frac{1}{f} + \frac{1}{f_2}$$

Equivalent focal length $f_{eq} = x$ cm   ...(i)

Focal length of Biconvex lens $f_1 = y$ cm

Focal length of plano convex lens

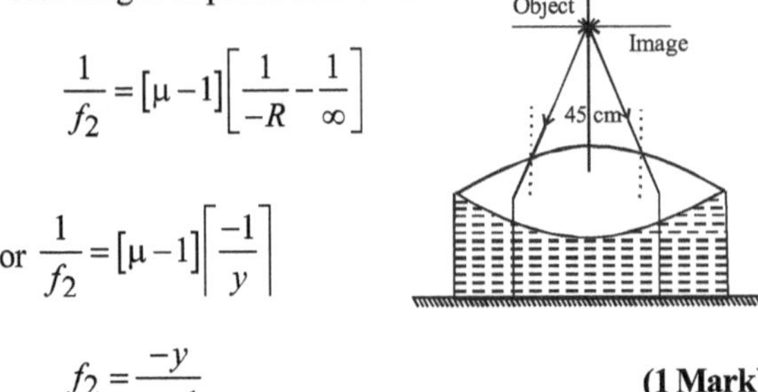

$$\frac{1}{f_2} = [\mu - 1]\left[\frac{1}{-R} - \frac{1}{\infty}\right]$$

or $$\frac{1}{f_2} = [\mu - 1]\left[\frac{-1}{y}\right]$$

$$f_2 = \frac{-y}{\mu - 1}$$ **(1 Mark)**

Now equation (i),

$$\frac{1}{f_{eq}} = \frac{1}{f_1} + \frac{1}{f_2}, \quad \frac{1}{x} = \frac{1}{y} - \left(\frac{\mu - 1}{y}\right)$$ **(1 Mark)**

Solving we get, $\mu = 2 - \dfrac{y}{x}$

18. (a) According to Bohr postulate, electrons revolve around the nucleus only in those discrete orbits which are non radiating and for which the angular momentum of the revolving electron is an integral multiple of $h/2\pi$. These discrete orbits are known as stationary or stable orbits.

According to de-Broglie, wavelength of matter waves is given by

$$\lambda = \frac{h}{mv_n}$$ **(½ Mark)**

where v_n = speed of electron in n^{th} orbit

For stable orbit, we must have perimeter of orbit = $n\lambda$

$$\therefore \quad 2\pi r_n = \frac{nh}{mv_n} \quad \Rightarrow \quad mv_n r_n = \frac{nh}{2\pi}$$ **(1 Mark)**

This is Bohr's second postulate of quantisation of orbital angular momentum

(b) Given $n_i = 1$, $n_f = 4$

For H-atom, $E_1 = -13.6$ eV and

$$E_4 = \frac{E_1}{n^2} = \frac{E_1}{4^2} = \frac{-13.6}{16} = -0.85 \text{ eV}$$

$$\therefore \quad E_f - E_i = -0.85 - (-13.6) = 12.75 \text{ eV}$$
$$= 12.75 \times 1.6 \times 10^{-19} \text{ J} = 20.4 \times 10^{-19} \text{ J. } \textbf{(1 Mark)}$$

Frequency of photon absorbed is,

$$\upsilon = \frac{E_f - E_i}{h} = \frac{20.4 \times 10^{-19}}{6.6 \times 10^{-34}} = 3.09 \times 10^{15} \text{ Hz.}$$

$$[\because h\upsilon = E_f - E_i]$$ **(½ Mark)**

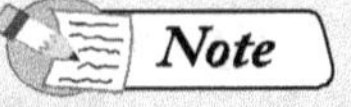

Note

The lowest state of the atom is called the ground state, this state has lowest energy. The energy of this state is -13.6 eV.

19. The binding energy curve per nucleon is shown below

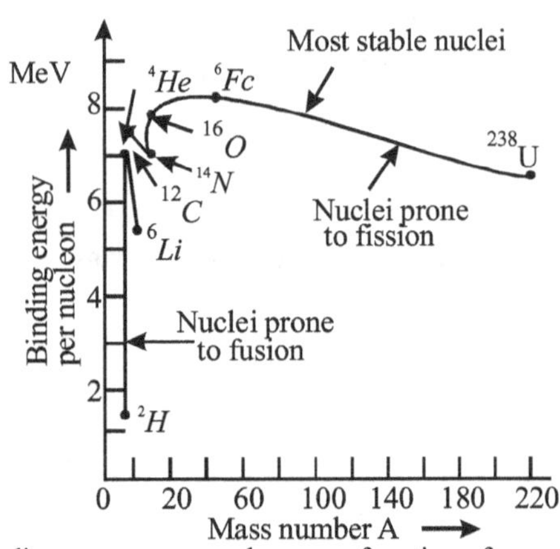

Binding energy per nucleon as a function of mass number A

    (1 Mark)

The binding energy per nucleon in range $30 < A < 170$ has a broad maximum to average binding energy per nucleon = 8.5 MeV. The higher value of binding energy per nucleon is due stability of these nucleon. Also neutron-proton ratio is higher in this range of mass number which leads to stability of the nuclei. Also, the nuclear force is strongly attractive, enough to overcome the Colombian repulsive force acting between positively charged protons.

The curve reveals that binding energy per nucleon is smaller for heavier nuclei than the middle level nuclei. This shows that heavier nuclei are less stable than middle level nuclei. In nuclear fission, binding energy per nucleon of reactants (heavier nuclei) changes from nearly 7.6 MeV to 8.4 MeV.

Higher value of the binding energy of the nuclear product results in the liberation of energy during the phenomena of nuclear fission.

In nuclear fusion, binding energy per nucleon of lighter nuclei into heavier one changes from low value of binding energy per nucleon to high value and release of energy takes place in fusion *e.g.*, two $_1H^2$ ($Be \approx 1.5$ MeV/nucleon) combine to form $_2He^4$ (Binding energy per nucleon $\simeq 7$ MeV/nuclei) and therefore the energy is liberated during nuclear fusion. **(1 Mark)**

(b) According to the question, $N = N_o 3.12\%$

$$\Rightarrow \quad \frac{N}{N_o} = 3.12\% \Rightarrow \frac{N}{N_o} = \frac{1}{32}$$

$$\Rightarrow \quad \frac{N}{N_o} = \left(\frac{1}{2}\right)^n = \left(\frac{1}{32}\right) = \left(\frac{1}{5}\right)^5$$

$$n = \frac{t}{T_{1/2}} = 5$$

$$\therefore t = 5 \times T_{1/2}$$

Number of years it will take for the activity to reduce to $3.12\% = 5 \times$ half life $= 5 \times 10 = 50$ years. **(1 Mark)**

20. (a) **P-N junction diode as a full wave rectifier:** The circuit uses two diodes connected to the ends of a centre tapped transformer. The voltage rectified by the two diodes is half of the secondary voltage *i.e.*, each diode conducts for half cycle of input but alternately so that net output across load comes as half sinusoids with positive values only.

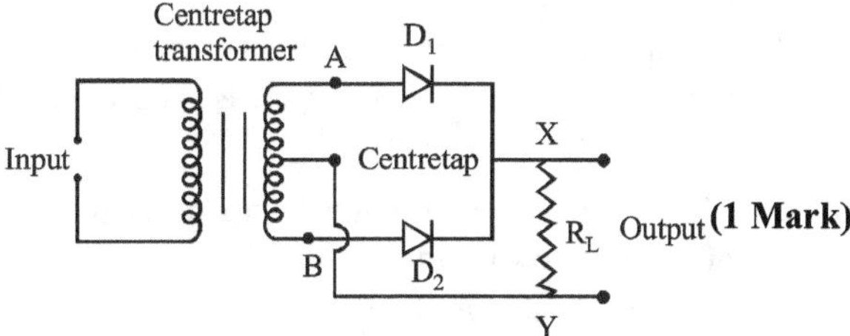

(1 Mark)

For positive cycle diode D_1 conducts (FB) but D_2 is being out of phase is reverse biased and does not conduct. Thus output across R_L is due to D_1 only. In negative cycle of input D_1 is R.B. but D_2 is F.B. and conducts as with respect to centretap point A is negative but B is positive. Hence output across R_L is due to D_2.

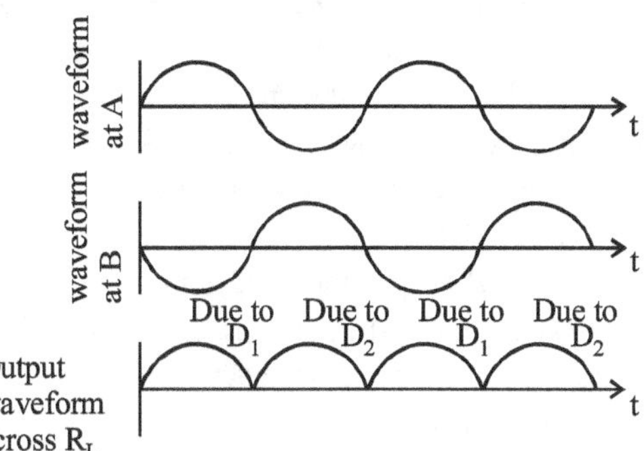

(1 Mark)

(b) Symbol of NAND logic gate :

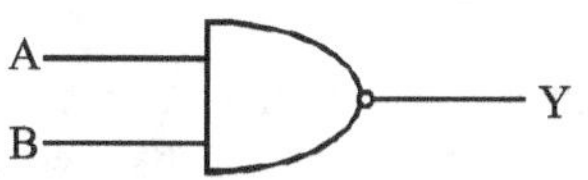

Truth table: NAND gate

A	B	Y
0	0	1
0	1	1
1	0	1
1	1	0

(1 Mark)

Note

NAND logic gate is also called universal gate because combinations of NAND gates can be used to produce an OR gate, AND gate and NOT gate.

21. **Input characteristics :** It is a graph between base voltage V_B and the base current I_B for a constant value of collector voltage V_C.

(½ Mark)

Output characteristics : It is a graph between collector voltage V_{CE} and collector current Ic for a constant value of base current I_B.

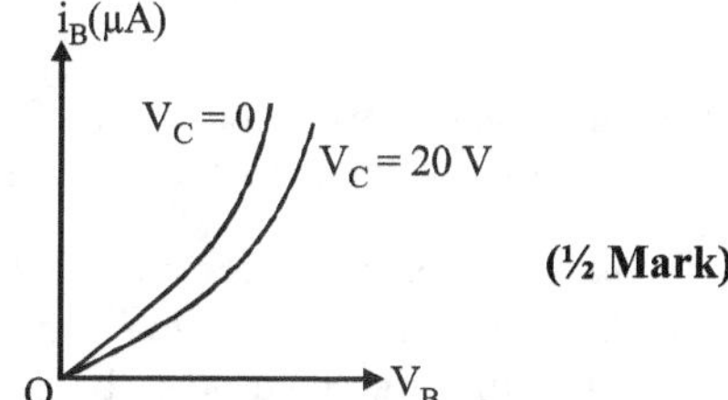
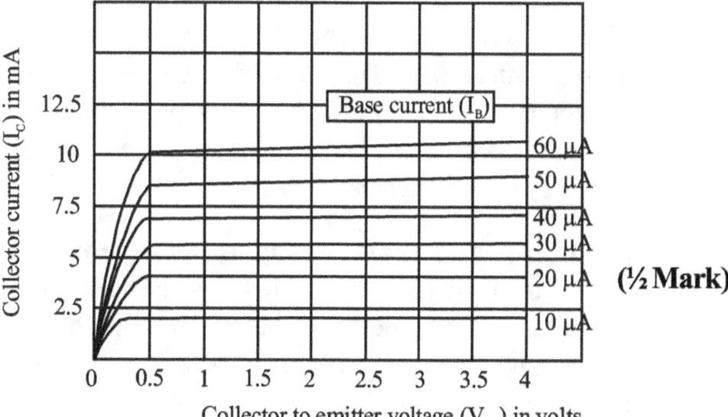

(½ Mark)

(a) **Input resistance** (r_i): It is the ratio of change in base emitter voltage (ΔV_{BE}) to the resulting change in base current (ΔI_B) at constant collector-emitter voltage (V_{CE}). This is dynamic (ac resistance) and as can be seen from the input characteristic, its value varies with the operating current in the transistor:

$$r_i = \left(\frac{\Delta V_{BE}}{\Delta I_B}\right)_{V_{CE}}$$

The value of r_i can be anything from a few hundreds to a few thousand ohms.   **(1 Mark)**

(b) Current gain is the ratio of the change in collector current to the change in base current at a constant collector-emitter voltage (V_{CE}) when the transistor is in active state. *i.e.,* Current gain $b = \dfrac{\Delta I_c}{\Delta I_b}$

This is also known as small signal current gain and its value is very large.

If we simply find the ratio of I_C and I_B we get what is called *dc* β of the transistor

Hence, $\beta_{dc} = \dfrac{I_c}{I_B}$

Since I_C increases with I_B almost linearly and $I_C = 0$ when $I_B = 0$, the values of both βdc and bac are nearly equal. So, for most calculations βdc can be used. Both bac and bdc vary with V_{CE} and I_B (or I_C) slightly.

(1 Mark)

22. (a) Three reasons why modulation of a message signal is necessary for long distance transmission are:

(i) **Size of antenna or aerial:** The size of the antenna should at least be equal to *l*/4 in dimension so as to detect time variation properly. For electro magnetic waves of frequency 20 kHz, wavelength = 15 km, such large antennas are not practically possible. So we translate low frequency signal into high frequency before transmission.

(ii) **Effective power radiation:** The power radiated by a linear antenna is $(l/l)^2$. This means that long wavelength base band signals would have less power during transmission but we need more power, hence high frequency (low *l*) signals are better.

(iii)**Mixing up of signals during transmission:** To prevent many signals transmitted at same time from mixing, it is important that a bandwidth be allotted to each signal separately which is possible for high frequency only (low frequency signal has limited range). The above limitations suggest that if low frequency message is translated into high frequency transmission then original signal can be sent in a more effective way. Hence modulation by means of message signal superimposed on a high frequency carrier wave is done, This reduces antenna size, increases power, gives a unique band width to each signal and prevents mixing of signals.   **(½ × 3 = 1½ Marks)**

(b) (i)

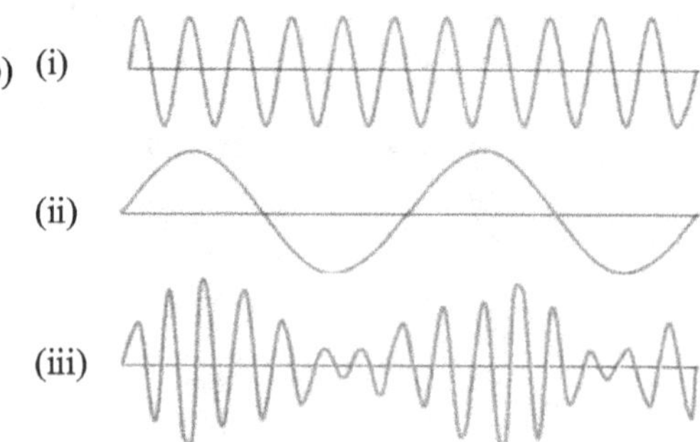

(ii)

(iii)

Here, (i) an audio signal; (ii) a carrier wave; (iii) amplitude modulated wave.   **(½ × 3 = 1½ Marks)**

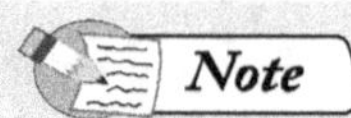

> *Note*

In amplitude modulation, the audio signal is super imposed on a carrier wave in such a manner that the frequency of the modulated wave is same as that of carrier wave but its amplitude varies in accordance with amplitude of audio signal.

SECTION - D

23. (a) Device – Transformer.   **(1 Mark)**

Reason for power loss: Heating and flux leakage

(b) In long distance transmission of energy through transmission lines, the power loss is mainly due to heat loss (due to resistance).

This resistive loss of power is proportional to square of current flowing through the lines *i.e.,* $H \propto I^2$. To minimise heat loss, we need to minimise the current flowing in the wire.

In case of dc, if the current flowing in the wire decrease then, the power losses will decrease but simultaneous power received at the receiving station will also decrease.

In order to achieve the required amount of power at the receiving station, we transmit the ac signal by stepping up the voltage with lower value of current as ac gives the flexibility of stepping up or down the voltage.

In this way the power losses are reduced while maintaining the required amount of power at the receiving station.   **(2 Marks)**

(c) Two values shown by the teacher are:

(i) Responsible (ii) Providing good education and undertaking the doubts of student.

Two values shown by Geeta are: (i) Curious (ii) Gaining knowledge.   **(1 Mark)**

SECTION - E

24. (a) Electric flux is defined as the number of electric filed lines crossing the per unit area. It is a scalar quantity.

(1 Mark)

When cube is of side d and point charge q is at the center of the cube then the total electric flux due to this charge will pass evenly through the six faces of the cube. So, the electric flux through one face will be equal to 1/6 of the total electric flux due to this charge.

Flux through 6 faces $= \dfrac{q}{\epsilon_0}$ **(1 Mark)**

$\therefore$ Flux through 1 face, $= \dfrac{q}{6\,\epsilon_0}$ **(1 Mark)**

(b) If we moved point charge d from centre and square side changes to $2d$, still the point charge can be imagined at the center of a cube of side $2d$. Again the flux through one face of the cube will be 1/6 of the total electric flux due to the charge q.

Hence, the electric flux through the square will not change and it will remain the same *i.e.*, $q/6\,\epsilon_0$.

(2 Marks)

OR

(a) Electric field due to an infinitely long straight wire : Consider an infinitely long line charge having linear charge density λ. To determine its electric field at distance r, consider a cylindrical Gaussian surface of radius r and length 1 coaxial with the charge. By symmetry, the electric field E has same magnitude at each point of the curved surface S_1 and is directed radially outward.

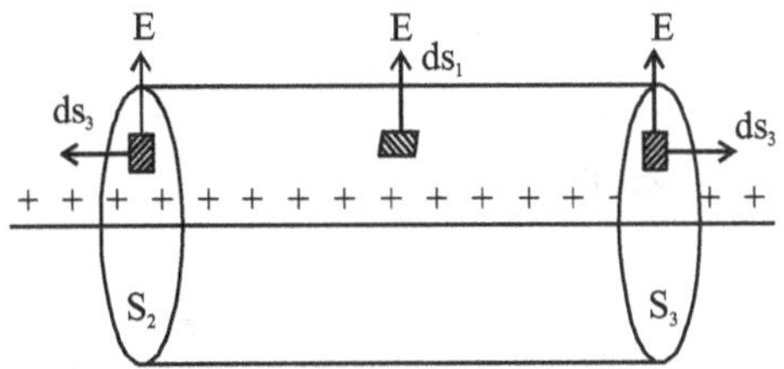

Total flux through the cylindrical surface,

$$\oint \vec{E}\cdot\vec{ds} = \oint_{S_1} \vec{E}\cdot\vec{ds_1} + \oint_{S_2} \vec{E}\cdot\vec{ds_2} + \oint_{S_3} \vec{E}\cdot\vec{ds_3}$$

$$= \oint_{S_1} E ds_1 \cdot \cos 0° + \oint_{S_2} E ds_2 \cdot \cos 90° + \oint_{S_3} E ds_3 \cdot \cos 90°$$

$$= E\int ds_1 = E \times 2\pi r l$$

(1 Mark)

As l is the charge per unit length and l is the length of the wire, so charge enclosed, $q = \lambda l$

By Gauss's theorem,

$$\oint_{S} \vec{E}\cdot\vec{ds} = \frac{q}{\varepsilon_0} \quad \text{or,} \quad E \times 2\,\pi\,rl = \frac{\lambda l}{\varepsilon_0}$$

$$E = \frac{\lambda}{2\pi\varepsilon_0 r}$$

This is the required expression.   **(1 Mark)**

 *Note*

Gauss's law is true for any closed surface, no matter what its shape or size be, Gauss's law is often useful when the system has same symmetry. This is facilitated by the choice of a suitable Gaussian surface.

(b) From above equation, we can observe, $E \propto \dfrac{1}{r}$

The graph showing the variation of E with perpendicular distance 'r' from the line of charge

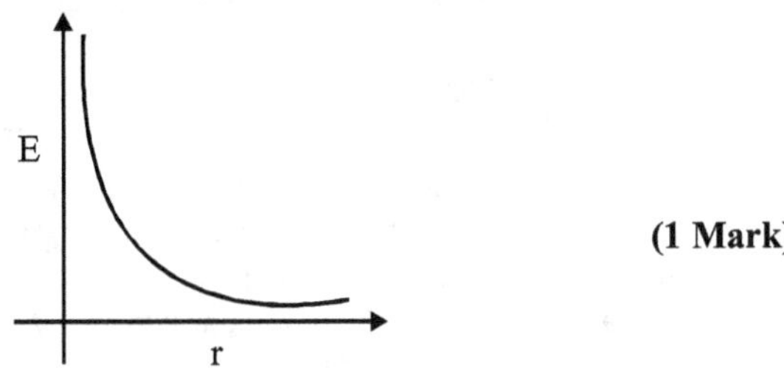

(1 Mark)

(c) Let the charge has move by an infinitely small distance dr.

$$V = \int \vec{E}\cdot d\vec{r}$$

$$\Rightarrow V = \int_{r_1}^{r_2} \frac{\lambda}{2\pi\,\epsilon_o r}\,dr = \frac{\lambda}{2\pi\,\epsilon_o} \int_{r_1}^{r_2} \frac{1}{r}$$ **(1 Mark)**

$$= \frac{\lambda}{2\pi\,\epsilon_o}\left[\log\frac{r_2}{r_1} \right]$$

Work done, $W = qV = \dfrac{q\lambda}{2\pi\,\epsilon_o}\left[\log\dfrac{r_2}{r_1} \right]$ **(1 Mark)**

25. (a) **AC Generator:** It is used to convert mechanical energy into electrical energy.

Principle: It works on the principle of electromagnetic induction.   **(1 Mark)**

Construction: The main components of ac generator are :

(i) **Armature coil:** It consist of large number of turns of insulated copper wire wound over iron core.

(ii) **Magnet:** Strong permanent magnet (for small generator) or an electromagnet (for large generator) with cylindrical poles in shape.

(iii) Slip rings: The two ends of the armature coil are connected to two brass rings R_1 and R_2. These rings rotate along with the armature coil.

(iv) Brushes: Two carbon brushes (B_1 and B_2), are pressed against the slip rings. These brushes are connected to the load through which the output is obtained.

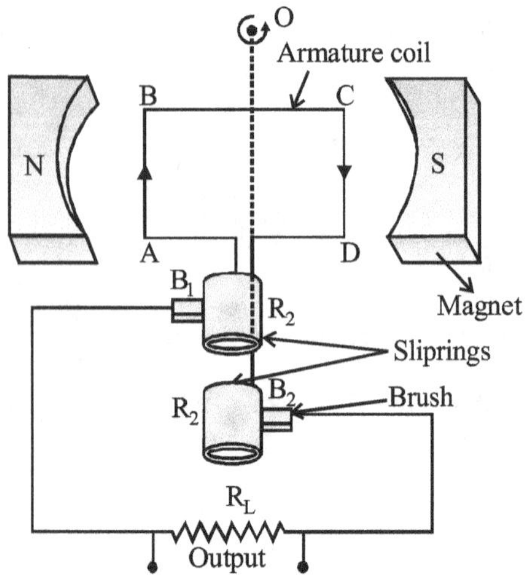

(1 Mark)

Expression for the emf induced:

When the coil is rotated with a constant angular speed ω, the angle θ between the magnetic field vector B and the area vector A of the coil at any instant t is $\theta = \omega t$ (assuming $\theta = 0°$ at $t = 0$)

As a result, the effective area of the coil exposed to the magnetic field lines changes with time, and the flux at any time t is $\phi_B = BA \cos \theta = BA \cos \omega t$

From Faraday's law, the induced EMF for the rotating coil of N turns

$$\varepsilon = -N\frac{d\phi}{dt} = -NBA\frac{d}{dt}(\cos \omega t) \qquad \text{(½ Mark)}$$

Thus, the instantaneous value of the EMF $\varepsilon = NBA\omega \sin \omega t$ where $NBA\omega$ is the maximum value of the EMF. If we denote $NBA\omega$ as ε_0, then EMF,

$$\varepsilon = \varepsilon_0 \sin \omega t \qquad \text{(½ Mark)}$$

> **Note**
>
> *The value of sine function varies between +1 and −1, the sign, or polarity of emf changes with time. The emf has its extreme value when $\theta = 90°$ or $\theta = 270°$ as the change of flux is greatest at these points. The direction of current changes periodically, so the current is AC.*

(b) Given : Horizontal component of earth's magnetic field, $B_H = 5 \times 10^{-4}$ T

Angle of dip, $\delta = 30°$

wings distance, $l = 20$ m

velocity of aeroplane,

$v = 900$ km/h $= 250$ m/s

Potential difference, e = ?

Magneic field,

$$B = \frac{B_H}{\cos \delta} = \frac{5 \times 10^{-4}}{\cos 30°} = \frac{5 \times 10^{-4}}{\sqrt{3}} \qquad \textbf{(1 Mark)}$$

Potential difference, e = B*l*V

$$= \frac{5 \times 10^{-4}}{\sqrt{3}} \times 20 \times 250 \cong 1.5\text{V} \qquad \textbf{(1 Mark)}$$

OR

(a) According to the question, the current is leading the voltage by 90°, so the device X is capacitor.

The expression for reactance is $X_C = 1/\omega C = 1/(2\pi v C)$

(2 Marks)

(b) Graph showing variation of voltage and current with time over one cycle of ac

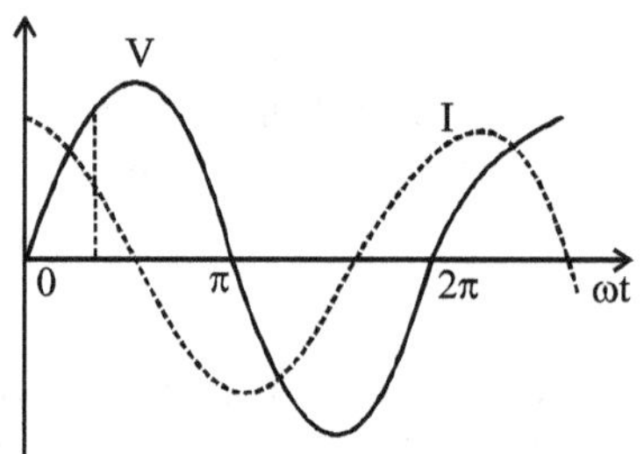

(1 Mark)

(c) The reactance varies inversely with frequency

(1 Mark)

(d) Phasor diagram for the device:

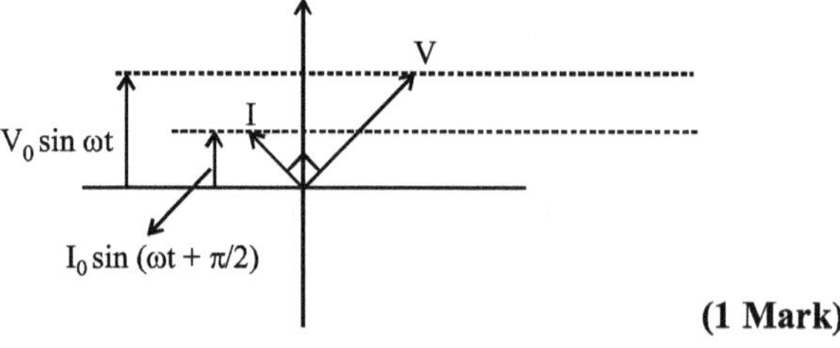

(1 Mark)

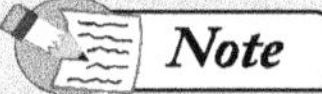

> **Note**
>
> *The capacitive reactance is inversely proportional to the capacitance and frequency of the current. As frequency of DC current is zero, so when capacitor is connected to DC source, the capacitor blocks DC and acts as open circuit.*

26. (a) Ray diagram

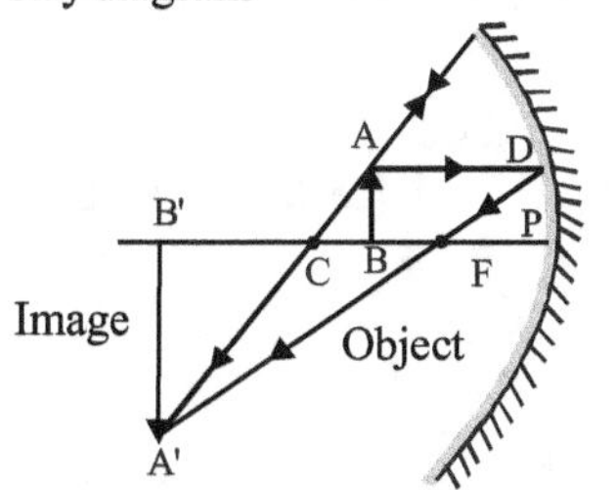

(1 Mark)

(b) A relationship among the object distance (u), the image distance (v) and the focal length (f) of a mirror is called the mirror formula.

The formula is given by $\dfrac{1}{f}=\dfrac{1}{u}+\dfrac{1}{v}$

Proof: Take an object AB beyond C of a concave mirror MM'. A ray AD parallel to principal axis passes through focus after reflection. Another ray AE which is passing through C comes back along the same path after reflection. These two reflected rays intersect at A'. From A' draw perpendicular $A'B'$ on the principal axis. So $A'B'$ is real and inverted image which is formed between C and F which is smaller than the object in size.

Draw DG perpendicular to the principal axis. So, applying sign convention, we get

$PB=-u;\ PB'=-v;\ PF=-f;\ PC=-2f$

In $\triangle ABC$ and $\triangle A'B'C$, $\angle ABC=\angle A'B'C=90°$

$\angle ACB=\angle A'CB'$ (Vertically opposite angles)

$\therefore\ \triangle ABC\sim\triangle A'B'C\ (AA\ \text{similarity})$

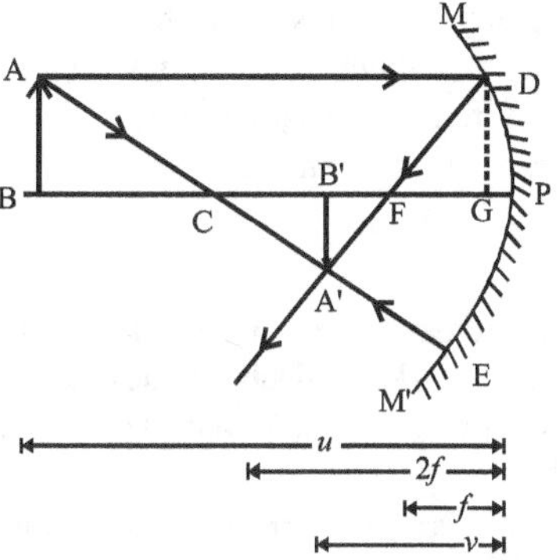

(1 Mark)

$\dfrac{AB}{A'B'}=\dfrac{BC}{B'C}$ (Corresponding sides of similar triangles are in proportion)   ....(1)

In $\triangle DGF$ and $\triangle A'B'F$, $\angle DGF=\angle A'B'F=90°$

$\qquad\angle DFG=\angle A'FB'$ (Vertically opposite angles)

$\triangle DGF\sim\triangle A'B'F\ (AA\ \text{similarity})$

$\dfrac{DG}{A'B'}=\dfrac{GF}{B'F}$ (Corresponding sides of similar triangles are in proportion)

But $AB=DG$ (the perpendicular distance between two parallel lines are equal)

$\therefore\ \dfrac{AB}{A'B'}=\dfrac{GF}{B'F}$ ...(2)

From eq. (1) and (2), we get,

$\dfrac{BC}{B'C}=\dfrac{GF}{B'F}$ ...(3)

Let us assume that mirror is very small,

$\therefore$ G and P are very close to each other so that GF = PF.

From (3), $\dfrac{BC}{B'C}=\dfrac{PF}{B'F}$

$\Rightarrow\dfrac{PB-PC}{PC-PB'}=\dfrac{PF}{PB'-PF}$

$\Rightarrow\dfrac{-u-(-2f)}{-2f-(-v)}=\dfrac{-f}{-v-(-f)}$

$\Rightarrow\dfrac{-u+2f}{-2f+v}=\dfrac{-f}{-v+f}$

$\Rightarrow(-v+f)(-u+2f)=-f(-2f+v)$

$\Rightarrow\ vu-2fv-fu+2f^2=2f^2-fv$

$\Rightarrow uv=-fv+2fv+fu$

$\therefore\ uv=vf+uf$

Dividing both sides by uvf,

$\dfrac{uv}{uvf}=\dfrac{vf}{uvf}+\dfrac{uf}{uvf}\ \Rightarrow\ \dfrac{1}{f}=\dfrac{1}{u}+\dfrac{1}{v}$ **(1 Mark)**

If the mirror is plane, the size of the image is always equal to the size of the object *i.e.*, **magnification is unity**. But the case is different for a curved mirror. The size of the image is different from the size of the object in such a 'mirror'. Image may be greater or smaller in size than the object depending upon the nature of the mirror or the location of the object.

Let I and O be the size of the image and the object respectively. The ratio $\dfrac{I}{O}$ is called **magnification**, and it is denoted by m.

Magnification, $m=\dfrac{I}{O}=-\dfrac{v}{u}$ **(1 Mark)**

This is called **linear magnification**.

(c) (i) Images are brighter (as compared to that in a refracting type telescope).

(ii) Chromatic aberration is absent in reflecting type telescope.   **(½ × 2 = 1 Mark)**

OR

(a) A **wavefront** is defined as the continuous locus of all the particles of a medium, which are vibrating in the same phase or it is a surface of constant phase.   **(1 Mark)**

Huygens' principle:

(1) Every points on the given wavefront (called primary wavefront) acts as a fresh source of new disturbance (secondary wavelets), which travel in all directions with the velocity of light in the medium.

(2) A surface touching these secondary wavelets, tangentially in the forward direction at any instant gives the new wavefront at that instant. This is called secondary wavefront.

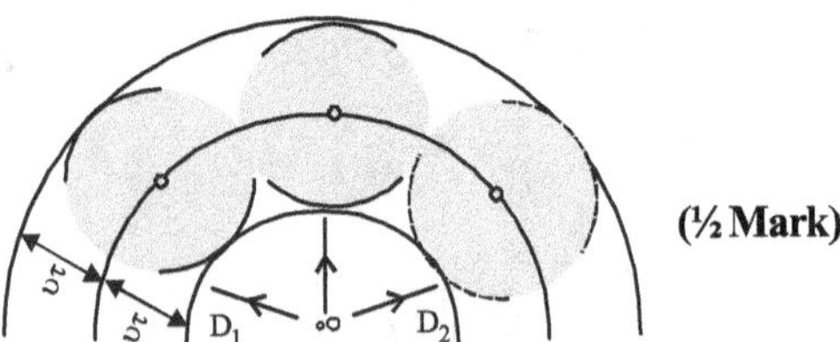

(½ Mark)

The above model has one shortcoming: we also have a backwave which is shown as D_1D_2 in figure. Huygens argued that the amplitude of the secondary wavelets is maximum in the forward direction and zero in the backward direction, by making this assumption, Huygens could explain the absence of the backwave.

Let a plane wavefront AB is incident on the plane mirror MM'. As per Huygen's wave theory, every point on wavefront again behaves like a light source and emits secondary wavelets. In the time taken by the wave to reach from A to C, the secondary wavelets from B gets spread over a hemisphere of radius.

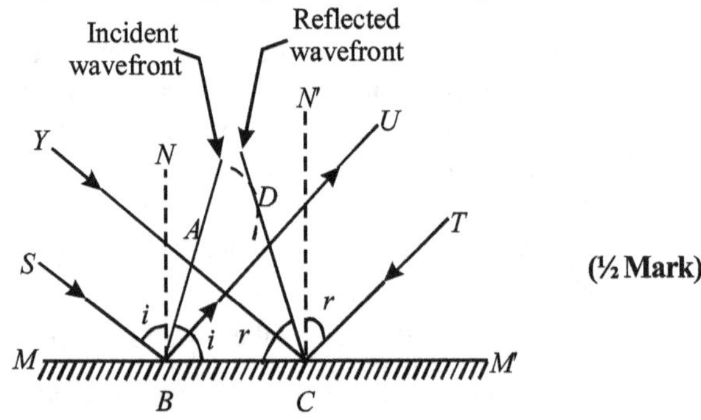

(½ Mark)

where, c is velocity of light and t is the time taken by wave in going from A to C. The tangent plane CD drawn from the point C over this hemisphere of radius ct gives new reflected wavefront CD corresponding to incident wavefront AB.

Let i and r be angles of incidence and reflection respectively.

Now, in $\triangle ABC$ and $\triangle DCB$

$\angle BAC = \angle CDB$ [each 90°, ray $\perp$ wavefront]

$BC = BC$ (common)

$AC = DB$ [From Eq. (i)]

$\Rightarrow \triangle ABC \cong \triangle DCB$

(RHS congruence)   (½ Mark)

$\Rightarrow \angle ABC = \angle DCB$

or $i = r$

$$\left[\because SB \perp AB \Rightarrow \angle NBA = 90° - i \text{ and } BN \perp BC \Rightarrow \angle ABC = i \right]$$

Similarly, $\angle N'CT = \angle DCB = r$

$\Rightarrow$ Angle of incidence = Angle of reflection

Also, incident ray, reflected ray and normal meet at one point on a plane.   (½ Mark)

Thus, laws of reflection are verified using Huygen's principle.

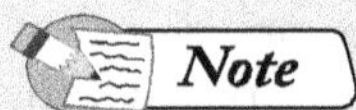 *Note*

Huygen's argued that the amplitude of the secondary wavelets is maximum in the forward direction and zero in the backward direction. Hence, the backward secondary wavefront is absent.

(b) As the number of point sources increases, their contribution towards intensity also increases. Intensity varies as square of the slit width. Thus, when the width of the slit is made double the original width, intensity will get four times of its original value.

Width of central maximum is given by,

$$\beta = \frac{2D\lambda}{b}$$

So, with the increase in size of slit, the width of central maxima decreases. Hence, double the size of the slit would results as half the width of the central maxima.

(1 Mark)

(c) The waves diffracted from the edge of the circular obstacle interfere constructively at the centre of the shadow producing a bright spot.   (1 Mark)

All India *2017*
CBSE Board Solved Paper

Time Allowed : 3 Hours   *Maximum Marks : 70*

General Instructions:

(i) There are **26** questions in **all. All** questions are compulsory.

(ii) This question paper has five sections: Section **A**, Section **B**, Section **C**, Section **D** and Section **E**.

(iii) Section **A** contains **five** questions of **one** mark each, Section **B** contains **five** questions of **two** marks each, Section **C** contains **twelve** questions of **three marks** each, Section **D** contains **one** value based question of **four** marks and Section **E** contains **three** questions of **five** marks each.

(iv) There is no overall choice. However, an internal choice has been provided in **one** question of **two** marks, **one** question of **three** marks and all the **three** questions of **five** marks weightage. You have to atempt only **one** of the choices in such questions.

(v) You may use the following values of physical constants wherever necessary:

$c = 3 \times 10^8$ m/s

$h = 6.63 \times 10^{-34}$ Js

$e = 1.6 \; 10^{-19}$ C

$\mu_o = 4\pi \times 10^{-7}$ Tm A^{-1}

$\varepsilon_0 = 8.854 \times 10^{-12}$ C^2 N^{-1} m^{-2}

$\dfrac{1}{4\pi\varepsilon_0} = 9 \times 10^9$ N m^2 C^{-2}

Mass of electron $(m_e) = 9.1 \times 10^{-31}$ kg

Mass of neutron $= 1.675 \times 10^{-27}$ kg

Mass of proton $= 1.673 \times 10^{-27}$ kg

Avogadro's number $= 6.023 \times 10^{23}$ per gram mole

Boltzmann constant $= 1.38 \times 10^{-23}$ JK^{-1}

SECTION - A

1. Nichrome and copper wires of same length and same radius are connected in series. Current I is passed through them. Which wire gets heated up more? Justify your answer.

2. Do electromagnetic waves carry energy and momentum?

3. How does the angle of minimum deviation of a glass prism vary, if the incident violet light is replaced by red light? Give reason.

4. Name the phenomenon which shows the quantum nature of electromagnetic radiation.

5. Predict the polarity of the capacitor in the situation described below:

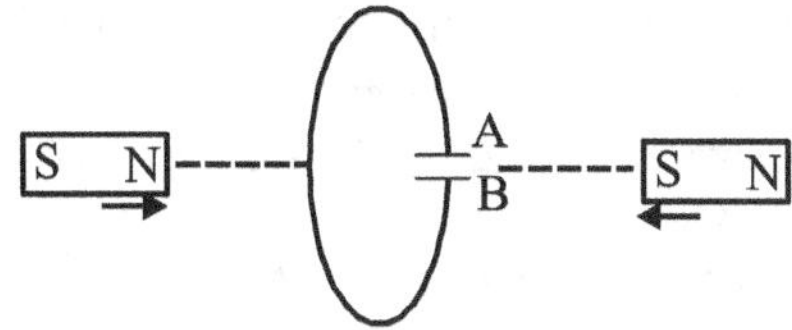

SECTION - B

6. Draw the intensity pattern for single slit diffraction and double slit interference. Hence, state two differences between interference and diffraction patterns.

OR

Unpolarised light is passed through a polaroid P_1. When this polarised beam passes through another polaroid P_2 and if the pass axis of P_2 makes angle θ with the pass axis of P_1, then write the expression for the polarised beam passing through P_2. Draw a plot showing the variation of intensity when θ varies from 0 to 2π.

7. Identify the electromagnetic waves whose wavelengths vary as

(a) 10^{-12} m $< \lambda < 10^{-8}$ m

(b) 10^{-3} m $< \lambda < 10^{-1}$ m

Write one use for each.

8. Find the condition under which the charged particles moving with different speeds in the presence of electric and magnetic field vectors can be used to select charged particles of a particular speed.

9. A 12.5 eV electron beam is used to excite a gaseous hydrogen atom at room temperature. Determine the wavelengths and the corresponding series of the lines emitted.

10. Write two properties of a material suitable for making (a) a permanent magnet, and (b) an electromagnet.

SECTION - C

11. (a) The potential difference applied across a given resistor is altered so that the heat produced per second increases by a factor of 9. By what factor does the applied potential difference change?

    (b) In the figure shown, an ammeter A and a resistor of 4 Ω are connected to the terminals of the source. The emf of the source is 12V having an internal resistance of 2Ω. Calculate the voltmeter and ammeter readings.

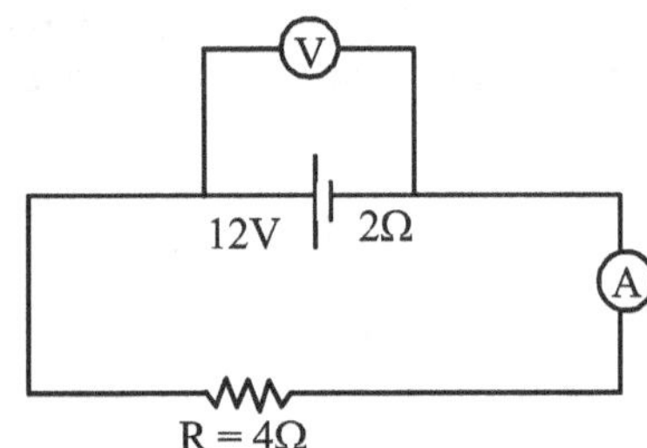

12. (a) How is amplitude modulation achieved?

    (b) The frequencies of two side bands in an AM wave are 640 kHz and 660 kHz respectively. Find the frequencies of carrier and modulating signal. What is the bandwidth required for amplitude modulation?

13. (a) In the following diagram, is the junction diode forward biased or reverse biased?

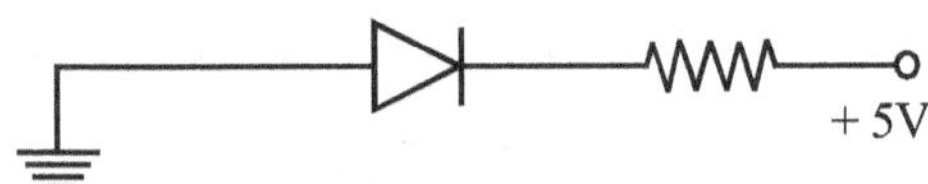

    (b) Draw the circuit diagram of a full wave rectifier and state how it works.

14. Using photon picture of light, show how Einstein's photoelectric equation can be established. Write two features of photoelectric effect which cannot be explained by wave theory.

15. (a) Monochromatic light of wavelength 589 nm is incident from air on a water surface. If μ for water is 1.33, find the wavelength, frequency and speed of the refracted light.

    (b) A double convex lens is made of a glass of refractive index 1.55 with both faces of the same radius of curvature. Find the radius of curvature required, if the focal length is 20 cm.

16. Define mutual inductance between a pair of coils. Derive an expression for the mutual inductance of two long coaxial solenoids of same length wound one over the other.

OR

Define self-inductance of a coil. Obtain the expression for the energy stored in an indicator L connected across a source of emf.

17. (a) Write the principle of working of a metre bridge.

    (b) In a metre bridge, the balance point is found at a distance l_1 with resistances R and S as shown in the figure.

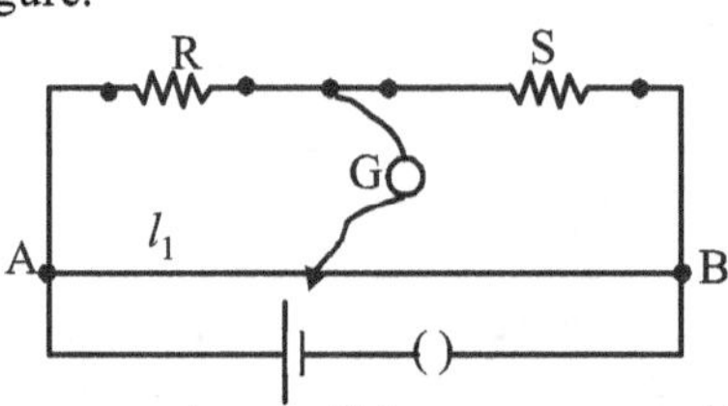

    An unknown resistance X is now connected in parallel to the resistance S and the balance point is found at a distance l_2. Obtain a formula for X in terms of l_1, l_2 and S.

18. Draw a block diagram of a generalized communication system. Write the functions of each of the following:

    (a) Transmitter   (b) Channel

    (c) Receiver

19. (a) Write the functions of the three segments of a transistor.

    (b) The figure shows the input waveforms A and B for 'AND' gate. Draw the output waveform and write the truth table for this logic gate.

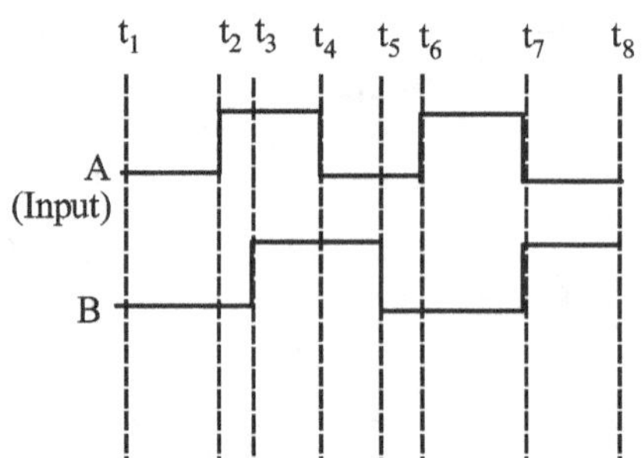

20. (a) Draw a ray diagram depicting the formation of the image by an astronomical telescope in normal adjustment.

    (b) You are given the following three lenses. Which two lenses will you use as an eyepiece and as an objective to construct an astronomical telescope? Give reason.

Lenses	Power (D)	Aperture (cm)
L_1	3	8
L_2	6	1
L_3	10	1

21. (a) State Biot - Savart law and express this law in the vector form.

    (b) Two identical circular coils, P and Q each of radius R, carrying currents 1 A and $\sqrt{3}$A respectively, are placed concentrically and perpendicular to each other lying in the XY and YZ planes. Find the magnitude and direction of the net magnetic field at the centre of the coils.

22. Two identical parallel plate capacitors A and B are connected to a battery of V volts with the switch S closed. The switch is now opened and the free space between the plates of the capacitors is filed with a dielectric of dielectric constant K. Find the ratio of the total electrostatic energy stored in both capacitors before and after the introduction of the dielectric.

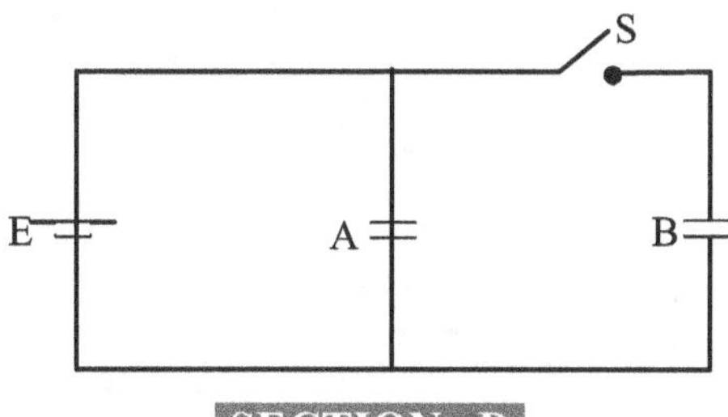

SECTION - D

23. Asha's mother read an article in the newspaper about a disaster that took place at Chernobyl. She could not understand much from the article and asked a few questions from Asha regarding the article. Asha tried to answer her mother's questions based on what she learnt in Class XII Physics.

(a) What was the installation at Chernobyl where the disaster took place? What, according to you, was the cause of the disaster?

(b) Explain the process of release of energy in the installation at Chernobyl.

(c) What, according to you, were the values displayed by Asha and her mother?

SECTION - E

24. (a) Derive an expression for the electric field E due to a dipole of length '2a' at a point distant r from the centre of the dipole on the axial line.

(b) Draw a graph of E versus r for $r \gg a$.

(c) If this dipole were kept in a uniform external electric field E_0, diagrammatically represent the position of the dipole in stable and unstable equilibrium and write the expressions for the torque acting on the dipole in both the cases.

OR

(a) Use Gauss's theorem to find the electric field due to a uniformly charged infinitely large plane thin sheet with surface charge density σ.

(b) An infinitely large thin plane sheet has a uniform surface charge density +σ. Obtain the expression for the amount of work done in bringing a point charge q from infinity to a point, distant r, in front of the charged plane sheet.

25. A device 'X' is connected to an ac source $V = V_0 \sin \omega t$ The variation of voltage, current and power in one cycle is shown in the following graph:

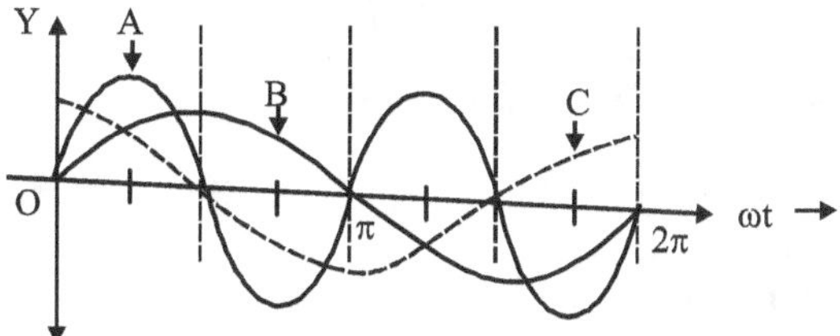

(a) Identify the device 'X'.

(b) Which of the curves A, B and C represent the voltage, current and the power consumed in the circuit? Justify your answer.

(c) How does its impedance vary with frequency of the ac source? Show graphically.

(d) Obtain an expression for the current in the circuit and its phase relation with ac voltage.

OR

(a) Draw a labelled diagram of an ac generator. Obtain the expression for the emf induced in the rotating coil of N turns each of cross-sectional area A in the presence of a magnetic field $\vec{B}$.

(b) A horizontal conducting rod 10 m long extending form east to west is falling with a speed 5.0 ms⁻¹ at right angles to the horizontal component of the Earth's magnetic field, 0.3×10^{-4} Wb m⁻². Find the instantaneous value of the emf induced in the rod.

26. (a) Define wavefront. Use Huygens' principle to verify the laws of refraction.

(b) How is linearly polarised light obtained by the process of scattering of light? Find the Brewster angle for air-glass interface, when the refractive index of glass = 1.5.

OR

(a) Draw a ray diagram to show the image formation by a combination of two thin convex lenses in contact. Obtain the expression for the power of this combination in terms of the focal lengths of the lenses.

(b) A ray of light passing from air through an equilateral glass prism undergoes minimum deviation when the angle of incidence is $\dfrac{3}{4}$th of the angle of prism. Calculate the speed of light in the prism.

Solutions

SECTION - A

1. Nichrome wire is heated more.

Heat dissipated in a wire is given by Joule's heating law

$$H = I^2Rt = I^2 \frac{\rho \ell}{A} t$$

$H \propto \rho$ ($\because$ I, ℓ and A remains same)

As $\rho_{nichrome} > \rho_{copper}$

$\therefore$ H $_{nichrome}$ > H $_{copper}$ **(½ + ½ = 1 Mark)**

2. Yes. As an electromagnetic wave is constituted by varying or oscillating electric and magnetic fields, it carries both energy and momentum. **(1 Mark)**

Energy, $E = \dfrac{hc}{\lambda}$ and momentum, p = E/C.

C = Speed of light

> **Note**
>
> *The electromagnetic wave energy is shared equally by electric and magnetic field.*

3. The angle of minimum deviation of a glass prism decreases, if the incident violet light is replaced with red light. **(½ + ½ = 1 Mark)**

As we know $\mu = \sin \dfrac{\left(\dfrac{A+\delta_m}{2}\right)}{\sin \dfrac{A}{2}}$ and from cauchy's

equation, $\mu = A + \dfrac{B}{\lambda^2} + \dfrac{C}{\lambda^4} + \dots$

$\lambda_{Red} > \lambda_{violet}$ so $\mu_{Red} < \mu_{violet}$ and therefore, angle of minimum deviation $\delta_{m\ Red} < \delta_{m\ violet}$.

4. Photoelectric effect shows the quantum nature of electromagnetic radiation. **(1 Mark)**

> **Note**
>
> *Photoelectric effect follow law of conservation of energy as it involves conversion of light energy into electrical energy.*

5. Polarity of capacitor Plate A will be positive with respect to Plate B. According to Lenz law, Plate A of the capacitor is at a higher potential than Plate B. **(1 Mark)**

SECTION - B

6.

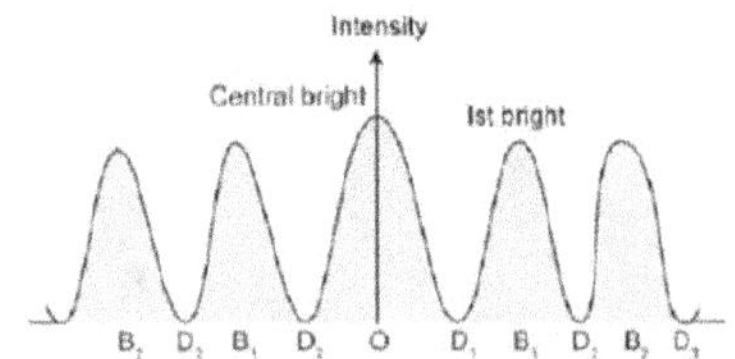

Intensity pattern for double slit diffraction

Intensity pattern for single slit diffraction **(½ Mak)**

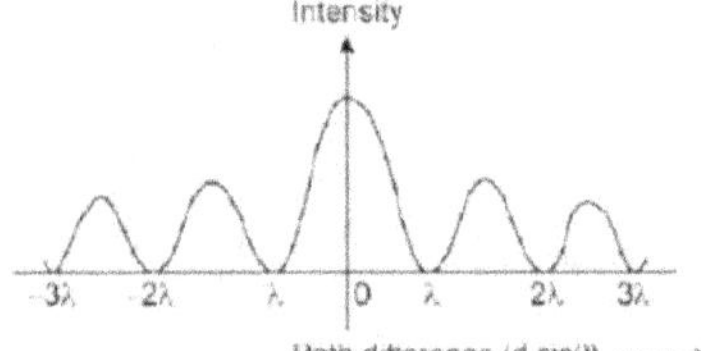

(½ Mark)

Difference between interference pattern and diffraction pattern.

Interference	Diffraction
It is due to the superposition of two waves coming from two coherent sources.	It is due to the superposition of secondary wavelets originating from different parts of the same wavefront.
Width of the interference bands is equal.	Width of diffraction bands is not the same.

(½ × 2 = 1 Mark)

OR

According to law of Malus, when a beam of completely plane polarised light is incident on an analyser at an angle, θ, resultant intensity of light (I) transmitted from the analyser

$$I \propto \cos^2\theta.$$

or, $I = I_0 \cos^2\theta$ ...(i) **(1 Mark)**

when $\theta = 0°$ or $\theta = 180°$ (polarizer and analyzer parallel)

$\cos \theta = \pm 1$

$\therefore$ $I = I_0$ ...(ii)

when $\theta = 90°$ $\cos \theta = \cos 90° = 0$

$\therefore$ $I = 0$ ...(iii)

Graph showing the variation of intensity when θ varies from 0 to 2π

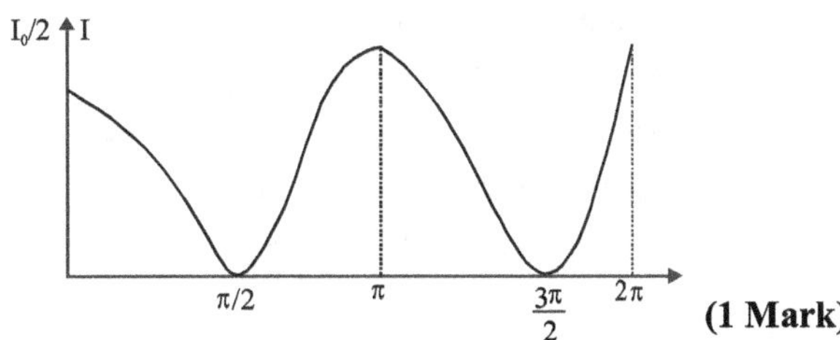

(1 Mark)

$$\therefore \quad [\cos^2\theta]av = \frac{1}{2\pi}\int_0^{2\pi}\cos^2\theta\,d\theta = \frac{1}{2\pi}\int_0^{2\pi}\frac{(1+\cos 2\theta)}{2}\,d\theta$$

$$= \frac{1}{2\pi\times 2}\left[0+\frac{\sin 2\theta}{2}\right]_0^{2\pi} = \frac{1}{2}$$

Therefore from malus law, expression

$$I = I_0\cos^2\theta = I_0\times\frac{1}{2} = \frac{I_0}{2}$$

$$\therefore \quad I = \frac{I_0}{2}$$

 **Note**

In unpolarised light, vibrations are probable in all the directions in a plane perpendicular to the direction of propagation.
$\therefore$ *θ can have any value from 0 and 2π*

7. (a) **X-rays:** Use-In medical diagnosis to detect fracture in bones, stones in kidney etc.
   (b) **Microwaves:** Use-In microwave oven.

   (1 + 1 = 2 Marks)

8. Let a charge q moving with velocity v in the presence of electric field E and magnetic field B.
   The force on an electric charge q due to both E and B
   $$F = q\,[E(r) + v \times B\,(r)]$$
   $$F = F_{electric} + F_{magnetic} \qquad \text{...(i)} \ \textbf{(1 Mark)}$$
   Let us consider a simple case in which electric field, E and magnetic field, B are perpendicular to each other and also perpendicular to the velocity of the particle.
   $$F_E = qE = qEj \ . \ F_B = q\,v\times B$$
   or, $\quad F_B = q(v\hat{i}\times B\hat{k}) = -qB\hat{j}$
   $$\therefore \quad F = q(E - vB)\hat{j}$$

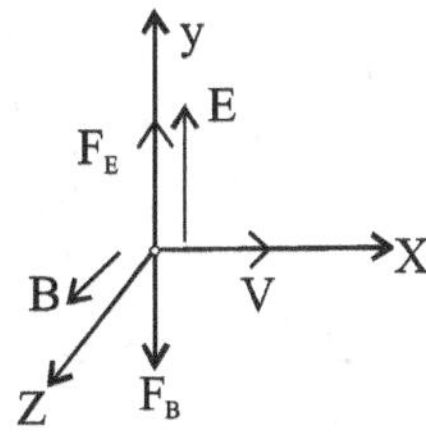

   i.e., Electric and magnetic forces are in opposite directions.
   Suppose we adjust the values of E and B such that magnitudes of the two forces are equal, then the total force on the charge is zero and the charge will move in the fields undeflected. This happens when

   $$qE = qvB \quad or, \quad v = \frac{E}{B} \qquad \textbf{(1 Mark)}$$

This condition can be used to select charged particles of a particular velocity out of a beam containing charges moving with different speeds. The crossed E and B fields serve as a velocity selector.

 **Note**

Another way to ask this question
Q. Find the condition when a charged particle is passed undeflected through a region of crossed magnetic and electric field.

9. When gaseous hydrogen is bombarded with an electron beam, the energy of the gaseous hydrogen
   $= -13.6 + 12.5 \text{ eV} = -1.1 \text{ eV}.$

   Orbital energy $E = \dfrac{-13.6}{(n)^2}\text{eV}$

   For n = 3, $\ E = \dfrac{-13.6}{(3)^2}\text{eV} = \dfrac{-13.6}{9}\text{eV} = -1.5\text{ eV}$ **(½ Mark)**

   This energy is approximately equal to the energy of gaseous hydrogen. This implies that the electron has jumped from n = 1 to n = 3 level.
   During its de-excitation, electrons can jump from n = 3 to n = 1 directly, which forms a line of the Lyman series of the hydrogen spectrum. For Lyman series,

   $$\frac{1}{\lambda} = R\left[\frac{1}{1^2} - \frac{1}{n^2}\right]$$

   For first member n = 3

   $$\therefore \quad \frac{1}{\lambda_1} = R\left[\frac{1}{1^2} - \frac{1}{(3)^2}\right] = R\left[\frac{1}{1} - \frac{1}{9}\right]$$

   $$\therefore \quad \frac{1}{\lambda_1} = 1.097\times 10^7\left[\frac{9-1}{9}\right]$$

   $(\because$ Rydberg constant R $= 1.097\times 10^7 \text{m}^{-1})$

   $$\therefore \quad \frac{1}{\lambda_1} = 1.097\times 10^7\times\frac{8}{9} \quad or, \ \lambda_1 = 1.025\times 10^{-7}\text{ m}$$

   (½ Mark)

   For $n = 3$

   $$\therefore \quad \frac{1}{\lambda_2} = R\left[\frac{1}{1^2} - \frac{1}{(2)^2}\right] = R\left[\frac{1}{1} - \frac{1}{4}\right]$$

   $$\therefore \quad \frac{1}{\lambda_2} = 1.097\times 10^7\left[\frac{4-1}{4}\right]$$

   $$\therefore \quad \frac{1}{\lambda_2} = 1.097\times 10^7\times\frac{3}{4} \quad or, \ \lambda_2 = 1.215\times 10^{-7}\text{ m}$$

   (½ Mark)

   For Balmer series $\dfrac{1}{\lambda} = R\left[\dfrac{1}{2^2} - \dfrac{1}{n^2}\right]$

   For first member $n = 3$

   $$\therefore \quad \frac{1}{\lambda_3} = R\left[\frac{1}{2^2} - \frac{1}{(3)^2}\right] = 1.097\text{m}\times 10^7\times\left[\frac{1}{4} - \frac{1}{9}\right]$$

   or, $\ \lambda_3 = 6.56\times 10^{-7}\text{m}$ **(½ Mark)**

Note

Another way to ask question:-
Q. A hydrogen atom in ground state is excited by an electron beam of 12.5 eV energy. Find the maximum number of lines emitted by atom and hence their wavelength from its excited state?

10. (a) Two properties of material suitable for making permanent magnets are
(i) high coercivity
(ii) high retentivity   **(½ × 2 = 1 Mark)**
(b) Two properties of material suitable for making electromagnets are
(i) low coercivity
(ii) low retentivity.   **(½ × 2 = 1 Mark)**

SECTION - C

11. (a) According to question, heat produced per second (H/t) increases 9 times by changing potential difference (V)

i.e., $H' = 9H$

$$\therefore \quad \frac{V'^2 t}{R} = 9 \times \frac{V^2 t}{R} \quad \text{(½ Mark)}$$

[from joule's heating law, $H = I^2 Rt = \dfrac{V^2 t}{R}$]

$\therefore \qquad V'^2 = 9 \times V^2$

or, $V' = 3V$

Hence applied potential difference increases by a factor of 3.   **(1 Mark)**

(b) Given : emf of cell /source E 12 V
Internal resistance $r = 2\Omega$
External resistance $R = 4\Omega$

$$\text{Current } I = \frac{E}{R+r} = \frac{12}{4+2} = \frac{12}{6} = 2\,A \quad \text{(½ Mark)}$$

Using $V = E - Ir$
$V = 12 - (2 \times 2) = 8\ V$
Thus, reading of the ammeter will be 2 A and of the voltmeter will be 8 V.   **(1 Mark)**

12. (a) In amplitude modulation, the amplitude of the carrier varies in accordance with the information signal. At the input of the transistor as CE, the low frequency modulating signals are superimposed on high frequency carrier wave. The output signal is carrier signal varying in amplitude in accordance with biasing modulation voltage. Thus, AM wave is produced.   **(1 Mark)**

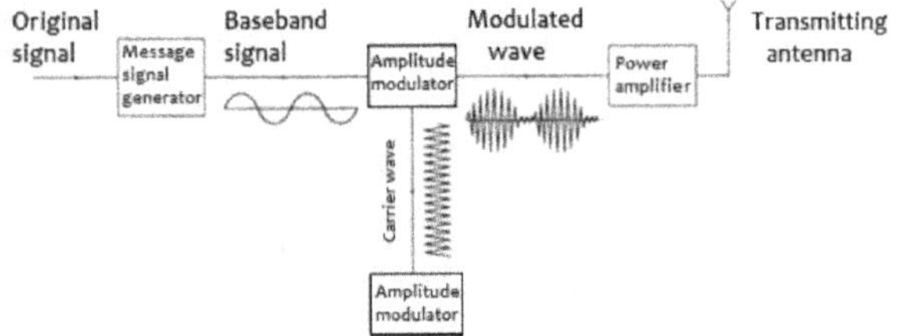

(b) According to question,
Upper side band frequency, $f_c + f_m = 660\,\text{kHz}$ ....(i)
Lower side band frequency, $f_c - f_m = 640\,\text{kHz}$ ...(ii)
Adding equation (i) and (ii), we get
$$2f_c = 660\ \text{kHz} + 640\ \text{kHz}$$
$\therefore \qquad f_c = 650\ \text{kHz}$ **(1 Mark)**
Now $f_c + f_m = 660\ \text{kHz}$
$\therefore \qquad f_m = 660\ \text{kHz} - 650\ \text{kHz}$
$\therefore \qquad f_m = 10\ \text{kHz}$

Band width for amplitude modulation
$$= \text{Upper side} - \text{lower side}$$
$$= (f_c + f_m) - (f_c - f_m) = 2f_m$$
$\therefore$ Band width for amplitude modulation
$$= 2 \times 10\ \text{kHz} = 20\ \text{kHz} \quad \textbf{(1 Mark)}$$

Note

The measure of amplitude modulation is given by modulation index $\mu = \dfrac{A_m}{A_c}$, where A_m is amplitude of message signal and A_c is amplitude of carrier wave.
It is kept below 1 to aviod any distortion.

13. (a) Reverse biased as P-crystal of the diode is earthed *i.e.,* at lower potential and N-crystal is at higher potential (5V)   **(1 Mark)**

(b) **P-N junction diode as a full wave rectifier :** The circuit uses two diodes connected to the ends of a centre tapped transformer. The voltage rectified by the two diodes is half of the secondary voltage i.e., each diode conducts for half cycle of input but alternately so that net output across load comes as half sinusoids with positive values only.

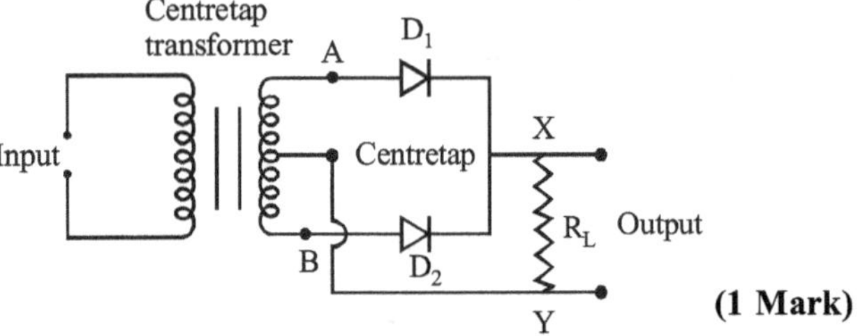

(1 Mark)

For positive cycle diode D_1 conducts (FB) but D_2 is being out of phase is reverse biased and does not conduct. Thus output across R_L is due to D_1 only. In negative cycle of input D_1 is R.B. but D_2 is F.B. and conducts as with respect to centretap point A is negative but B is positive. Hence output across R_L is due to D_2.

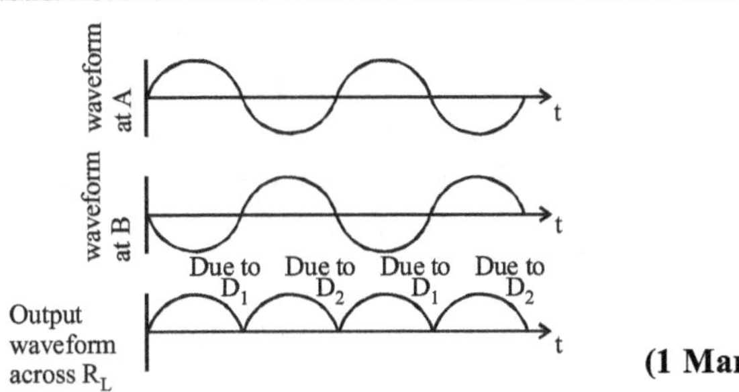

(1 Mark)

14. When a photon of energy 'hv' falls on a metal surface then,

   (i) a part of energy is used to overcome the surface barrier and come out of the metal surface *i.e.*, work function and is expressed as $\phi_o = hv_o$

   and (ii) the remaining part of energy is used in giving a velocity 'v' to the emitted photoelectron and is equal to the maximum kinetic energy of photo electrons

   i.e., $\qquad KE_{max} = \left(\dfrac{1}{2}mv_{max}^2\right)$

   According to the law of conservation of energy,

   $$hv = \phi_o + \dfrac{1}{2}mv_{max}^2 = hv_o + \dfrac{1}{2}mv_{max}^2$$

   $$\therefore \ \dfrac{1}{2}mv_{max}^2 = KE_{max} = hv - hv_o = h(v - v_o)$$

   or $KE_{max} = hv - \phi_o$ ....(i)

   This equation (i) is called Einstein's photoelectric equation. **(1 Mark)**

   Two features of photoelectric effect which cannot be explained by wave theory:

   (i) Maximum kinetic energy of emitted electrons is independent of the intensity of incident light.

   (ii) There exists a 'threshold frequency' for each photosensitive material. **(2 × 1 = 2 Marks)**

15. (a) Given: wavelength of incident light

   $\lambda_{air} = 589nm = 589 \times 10^{-9}\,m$

   Refractive index of water, $^a\mu_w = 1.33$

   Frequency of the refractive light

   $$f = \dfrac{C}{\lambda_{air}} = \dfrac{3 \times 10^8}{589 \times 10^{-9}}$$

   Speed of light in air, $C = 3 \times 10^8$ m/s

   or, $f = 5.09 \times 10^{14}$ Hz **(½ Mark)**

   Wavelength of refracted light $\lambda_{water} = \dfrac{\lambda_{air}}{^a\mu_w}$

   $$= \dfrac{589 \times 10^{-9}}{1.33} = 4.42 \times 10^{-7}\,m$$ **(½ Mark)**

   Speed of refracted light, $V_{water} = \dfrac{C}{^a\mu_w}$

   $$= \dfrac{3 \times 10^8}{1.33} = 2.2 \times 10^8\,ms^{-1}$$ **(½ Mark)**

(b) Given : focal length of lens, f = 20 cm and refractive index of lens, $\mu = 1.55$

   Let the radius of the curvature of each of the two surfaces of the lens be R.

   If $R_1 = R$ then $R_2 = -R$

   Using lens maker's formula ,

   $$\dfrac{1}{f} = (\mu - 1)\left[\dfrac{1}{R_1} - \dfrac{1}{R_2}\right]$$ **(½ Mark)**

   or, $\quad \dfrac{1}{20} = (1.55 - 1)\left[\dfrac{1}{R} + \dfrac{1}{R}\right] = \dfrac{1.1}{R}$

   $\therefore$ R = 20 × 1.1 = 22 cm **(1 Mark)**

> **Note**
>
> *For double concave lens*
> $R_1 = -R$ and $R_2 = +R$
> *For plano-convex lens*
> $R_1 = +R$ and $R_2 = \infty$
> *For plano-concave lens*
> $R_1 = \infty$ and $R_2 = +R$

---

16. Mutual inductance is the property of two coils by the virtue of which each opposes any change in the strength of current flowing through the other by developing an induced emf.

   (1 Mark)

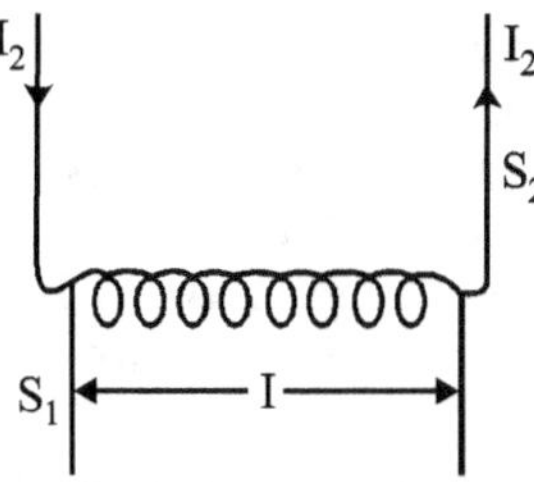

   Consider two coils (Primary and secondary) placed very near to each other. Let N_1 and N_2 be the number of turns in the coils and i_1 be the current flowing in the first coil.

   Let, due to this current, the magnetic flux linked with each turn of the secondary coil be ϕ_2. If N_2 be the number of turns in the secondary coil, then the number of flux-linkages in the coil will be $N_2\phi_2$. This number is proportional to the current i_1 flowing in the primary coil,

   i.e. $N_2\phi_2 \propto i_1 \qquad$ or $\qquad N_2\phi_2 = Mi_1$,

   where M is a constant called the **'coefficient of mutual induction'** or **'mutual inductance'** between the two coils. From the above equation, we have $M = N_2\phi_2/i_1$. In this equation, if $i_1 = 1$, then $M = N_2\phi_2$. Hence the coefficient of mutual induction between two coils is equal to the number of magnetic flux-linkage in one coil when a unit current flows in the other.

   From Faraday's Law $e = -\dfrac{\Delta\phi}{\Delta t} = -\dfrac{\Delta(N_2\phi_2)}{\Delta t}$ **(1 Mark)**

   But $N_2\phi_2 = Mi_1 \qquad \therefore e = -\dfrac{\Delta(Mi_1)}{\Delta t} = -\dfrac{M\Delta i_1}{\Delta t}$

If $\dfrac{\Delta i_1}{\Delta t} = 1$ ampere@second then $e = -M$

Hence, the coefficient of mutual induction between two coils is equal to the numerical value of the induced emf in one coil which is produced due to unit rate of change of current in the other.

The unit of the coefficient of mutual induction is 'henry'.

For a solenoid having a primary coil of N_1 turns and a secondary coil of N_2 turns, the coefficient of mutual inductance is given by

$M = \dfrac{\mu_r \mu_0 N_1 N_2 A}{\ell}$ where ℓ is the length of solenoid and A is the area of one turn of the secondary coil. **(1 Mark)**

OR

Self-inductance of a coil is a property of a coil by virtue of which it opposes any change in self-flux linked with the coil. **(1 Mark)**

When a current is passed through a coil, it produces a magnetic field. A flux is linked with the magnetic field produced by the coil. This flux is called self-flux.

Self-flux is directly proportional to the current flowing through the coil. If I is current flowing through a coil and 'ϕ' is the magnetic flux linked with its own magnetic field, then

$$\phi \propto I \qquad \text{or,} \qquad \phi = LI$$

where L is the proportionality constant and is known as self-inductance.

Expression for the energy stored in an inductor :
Consider a simple circuit having a coil, a battery and a key. The coil has a self-inductance L. On pressing the key K, current flows through the circuit. However, self-inductance gives rise to induced current which opposes the growth of current in the circuit.

Thus, to increase the current from zero to its maximum value I_o, some work has to be done.

This work done is stored as the magnetic field of the inductor. Similarly, when the key is opened, the induced emf tends to maintain current in the circuit.

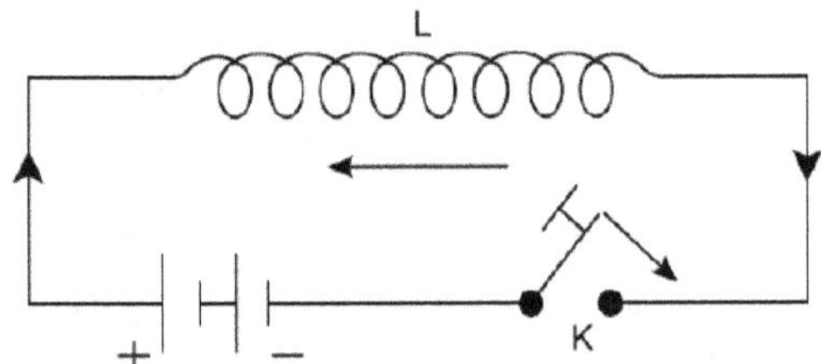

Let, I current flows through the coil of self-inductance L at any instant t when rate of change of current in coil is $\dfrac{dI}{dt}$.

$\therefore$ Induced emf, $E = -L\dfrac{dI}{dt}$ **(1 Mark)**

$\therefore$ Work done in establishing the current in small time interval dt is given by

$$dW = Pdt = -\varepsilon I dt = -\left(-L\dfrac{dI}{dt}\right)I dt$$

$$dW = LIdI$$

$\therefore$ Total work done in increasing the current from zero to I.

$$\therefore \qquad W = \int_0^I LIdI = L\int_0^I IdI$$

$$= L\left[\dfrac{I^2}{2}\right]_0^I = \dfrac{1}{2}L\left(I^2 - 0^2\right)$$

$$W = \dfrac{1}{2}LI^2 \qquad\qquad \textbf{(1 Mark)}$$

 **Note**

The self-induced emf is also called back emf as it opposes any change in the current in a circuit. The self-inductance plays the role of inertia analogue of mass in mechanics.

17. (a) **Principle of working of a meter bridge:** Meter bridge works on the principle of Wheatstone bridge. According to the principle, the balancing condition for balancing length l_1,

$$\dfrac{R}{S} = \dfrac{P}{Q} = \dfrac{\sigma l_1}{\sigma(100 - l_1)}$$

$$\Rightarrow \dfrac{R}{S} = \dfrac{l_1}{100 - l_1} \Rightarrow R = S\dfrac{l_1}{100 - l_1} \quad \textbf{(1 Mark)}$$

where σ is the resistance per unit length of the wire and l_1 is the length of the wire from one end where null point is obtained. The bridge is most sensitive when null point is somewhere near the middle point of the wire. This is due to end resistances.

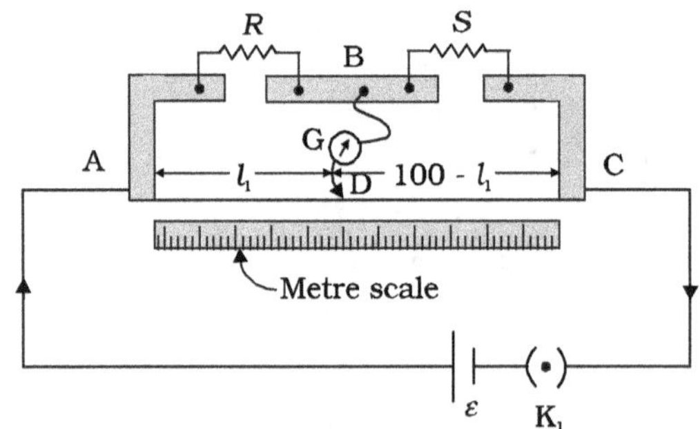

A meter bridge. Wire AC is 1 m long.

(b) For balancing length l_1, the condition is

$$\dfrac{R}{S} = \dfrac{l}{100 - l_1} \qquad\qquad ...(i)$$

When a resistance x is connected in parallel with S, the net resistance becomes

$$S_{new} = \dfrac{XS}{X + S}$$

For balancing length l_2, the condition is

$$\dfrac{R}{S_{new}} = \dfrac{l_2}{100 - l_2}$$

$$\therefore \quad \frac{R(X+S)}{XS} = \frac{l_2}{100-l_2} \qquad \ldots(ii)$$

From eqn. (i) and (ii)

$$\frac{l_1}{100-l_1} \times \frac{X+S}{X} = \frac{l_2}{100-l_2} \qquad \textbf{(1 Mark)}$$

$$\therefore \quad \frac{X+S}{X} = \frac{l_2}{100-l_2} \times \frac{100-l_1}{l_1}$$

$$\therefore \quad \frac{X+S}{X} = \frac{l_2(100-l_1)}{l_1(100-l_2)}$$

$$\Rightarrow \frac{S}{X}+1 = \frac{l_2(100-l_1)}{l_1(100-l_2)}$$

$$\therefore \quad \frac{S}{X} = \frac{l_2(100-l_1)}{l_1(100-l_2)} - 1$$

$$= \frac{l_2(100-l_1)-l_1(100-l_2)}{l_1(100-l_2)}$$

$$\therefore \quad \frac{X}{S} = \frac{l_1(100-l_2)}{l_2(100-l_1)-l_1(100-l_2)}$$

$$\text{or,} \quad X = S \times \frac{l_1(100-l_2)}{l_2(100-l_1)-l_1(100-l_2)} \qquad \textbf{(1 Mark)}$$

18. Block diagram of a generalised communication system:

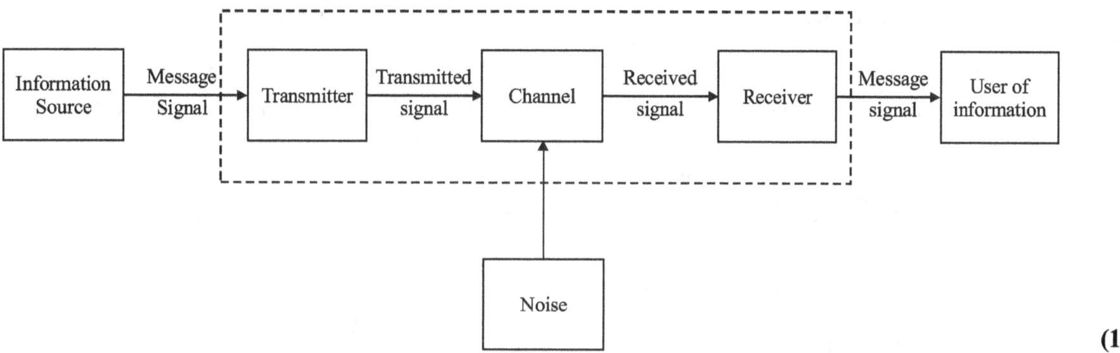

(1½ Marks)

Functions of

(a) Transmitter: A transmitter is an arrangement which processes the incoming message signal to a form suitable for transmission through a channel and subsequent reception.

(b) Channel: Channel is the medium through which the signal is transmitted from the transmitter to the receiver.

(c) Receiver: A receiver extracts the desired message signals from the received signals at the channel output.

(½ × 3 = 1½ Marks)

19. (a) Three segments of a transmitter are (i) Emitter (E), (ii) Base (B) and (iii) Collector.

   (i) **Emitter:** It is of moderate size and heavily doped. It supplies a large number of majority carriers for the current flow through the transistor.

   (ii) **Base:** It is the control segment and is very thin and lightly doped.

   (iii) **Collector:** It is the segment which collects a major portion of the majority carriers supplied by the emitter. It is moderately doped and large in size as compared to the emitter.

(½ × 3 = 1½ Marks)

(b) The corresponding output waveform of the input waveforms A and B for 'AND' gate.

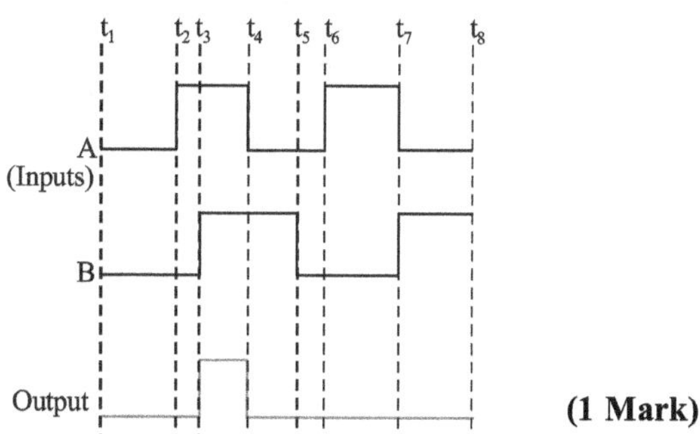

(1 Mark)

Truth table for AND gate

A	B	$Y = A \cdot B$
0	0	0
0	1	0
1	0	0
1	1	1

(½ Mark)

20. (a) Ray diagram depicting the formation of the image by an astronomical telescope in normal adjustment.

Ray diagram of astronomical telescope.

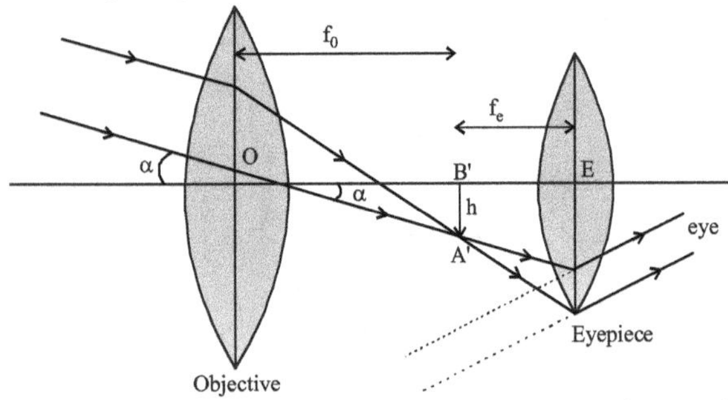

(2 Mark)

(b) Lens L_1 – Objective; Lens L_2 – Eye-piece

Lens L_1 has higher aperture of 8 cm. So, it can gather more light and will have high resolving power. Hence, L_1 should be used as the objective lens. Lens L_3 has high power of 10 D. So, it will give higher magnification. Hence, lens L_3 should be used as an eye-piece. **(1 Mark)**

21. (a) Biot–Savart law states that the magnetic field (dB) due to the current element dl at any point P is

   (i) directly proportional to the current, I *i.e.*, dB $\propto$ I

   (ii) directly proportional to the length dl of the element *i.e.*, dB $\propto$ dl

   (iii) directly proportional to sin θ, where θ is the angle between dl and r, *i.e.,* dB $\propto$ sin θ   **(1 Mark)**

   (iv) inversely proportional to the square of the distance r from the current element AB *i.e.*, dB $\propto \dfrac{1}{r^2}$

Therefore, we have   **(½ Mark)**

$$dB \propto \frac{Idl \sin \theta}{r^2}$$

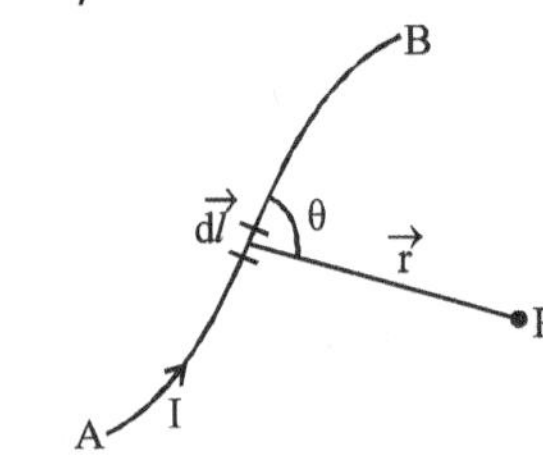

$$\therefore dB = \frac{\mu_0}{4\pi} \frac{Idl \sin \theta}{r^2}$$

In vector notation, $dB = \dfrac{\mu_0}{4\pi} \dfrac{Idl \times r}{r^3}$ **(1 Mark)**

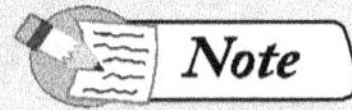
Note

From Biot-Savart law, we notice that magnetic field is linear in the source $Id\vec{l}$ *and is produced by a vector source. This law follow super position principle.*

(b) Two coils P and Q are placed as shown in the figure:

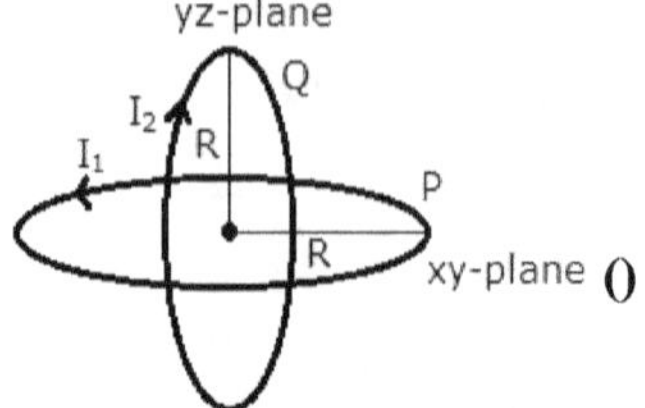

Given: Current through coil P, I_1 = 1 A

Current through coil Q, $I_2 = \sqrt{3}$ A

The magnetic field due to coil P at its centre

$$B_P = \frac{\mu_0 I_1}{2R} \text{ along z-axis}$$

The magnetic field due to coil Q at its centre

$$B_Q = \frac{\mu_0 I_2}{2R} \text{ along X-axis}$$

Hence, the field structure is as shown in figure

Therefore, the resultant field at the centre of the coils,

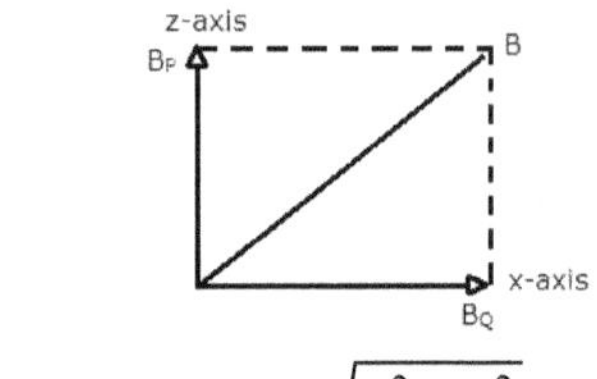

$\therefore \qquad B = \sqrt{B_P^2 + B_Q^2}$

$\therefore \qquad B = \sqrt{\left(\dfrac{\mu_0 I_1}{2R}\right)^2 + \left(\dfrac{\mu_0 I_2}{2R}\right)^2}$ **(1 Mark)**

$\qquad = \sqrt{\left(\dfrac{\mu_0}{2R}\right)^2 + 3\left(\dfrac{\mu_0^2}{2R}\right)^2}$

$\therefore \qquad B = 2\left(\dfrac{\mu_0}{2R}\right) = \dfrac{\mu_0}{R}$ **(1 Mark)**

Direction of this field is in the x–z plane.

22. As two capacitors are connected in parallel

So, the potential on each of them remains the same.

Charge on each, $Q_A = CV = Q_B$

Hence, the energy stored in the system

$$U_{initial} = \frac{1}{2}CV^2 + \frac{1}{2}CV^2 = CV^2 \quad ...(i) \textbf{ (1 Mark)}$$

When a dielectric slab of dielectric constant (k) is introduced, the capacitance changes to KC.

As the switch is open, only voltage across capacitor, A remains the same.

The voltage across capacitor, B changes to

V' = Q/C'

= Q/KC = V/K

Hence, new energy stored in the system

$$U_{final} = \frac{1}{2}KCV^2 + \frac{1}{2}KC\frac{V^2}{K^2}$$ **(1 Mark)**

$$\therefore \quad U_{final} = \frac{1}{2}KCV^2 + \frac{1}{2}\frac{CV^2}{K}$$

$$= \frac{1}{2}CV^2\left(k + \frac{1}{K}\right)$$

$$\therefore \quad \frac{U_{initial}}{U_{final}} = \frac{1}{K + \dfrac{1}{K}} = \frac{K}{K^2 + 1} \qquad \textbf{(1 Mark)}$$

SECTION - E

23. (a) Nuclear power plant.

The cause of disaster took place at chernobyl nuclear power plant was fire in the reactor and release of harmful radiations in the atmosphere. **(2 Marks)**

(b) Process of release of energy: Inside a reactor, nuclear energy is first converted to heat energy. This heat energy is then converted to mechanical energy of the turbine which is finally converted to electrical energy. **(1 Mark)**

(c) Values displayed by Asha: Awareness about real-life scenarios, helping nature towards her mother.

Values displayed by Asha's mother: Curiosity towards an worldwide incident. **(1 Mark)**

SECTION - E

24. (a) Consider an electric dipole consisting of two point charges +q and –q separated by a small distance 2a. Electric field intensity at point P due to charge –q

$$E_1 = \frac{1}{4\pi\varepsilon_0}\frac{q}{AP^2} = \frac{1}{4\pi\varepsilon_0}\frac{q}{(r+a)^2}$$

It is along PA. **(½ Mark)**

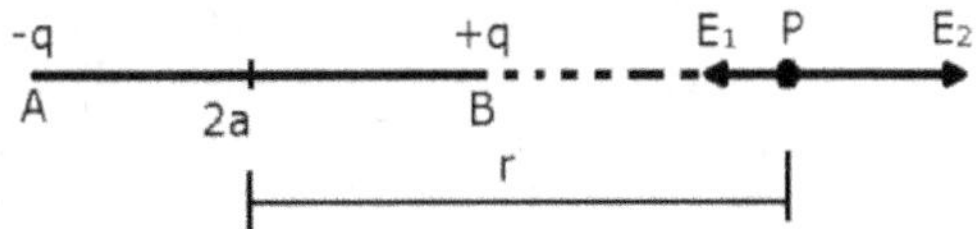

Electric field intensity at point P due to charge +q

$$E_2 = \frac{1}{4\pi\varepsilon_0}\frac{q}{BP^2} = \frac{1}{4\pi\varepsilon_0}\frac{q}{(r-a)^2}$$

It is along BP. **(½ Mark)**

Hence, the resultant field $E = E_2 - E_1$

$$= \frac{1}{4\pi\varepsilon_0}\frac{q}{(r-a)^2} - \frac{1}{4\pi\varepsilon_0}\frac{q}{(r+a)^2}$$

$$= \frac{q}{4\pi\varepsilon_0}\left[\frac{1}{(r-a)^2} - \frac{1}{(r+a)^2}\right]$$

$$= \frac{q}{4\pi\varepsilon_0}\left[\frac{4ar}{(r^2-a^2)}\right] \qquad \textbf{(½ Mark)}$$

$$E = \frac{q}{4\pi\varepsilon_0}\frac{2a \times 2r}{(r^2-a^2)^2}$$

Now, the dipole moment is $q \times 2a = p$

$$\therefore \quad E = \frac{p}{4\pi\varepsilon_0}\frac{2r}{(r^2-a^2)^2} \qquad \textbf{(1 Mark)}$$

(b) Graph of E versus r for r >> a

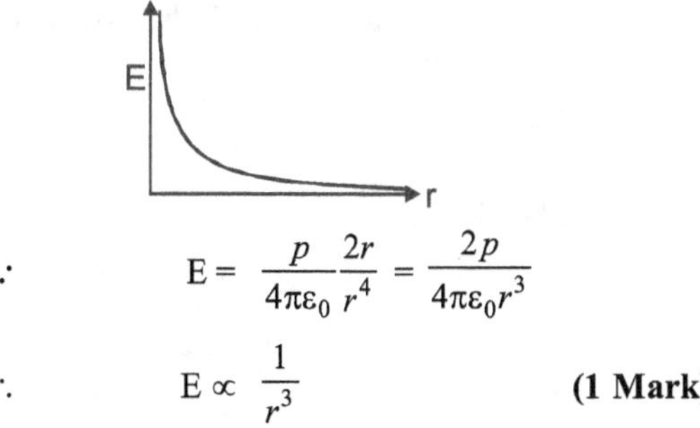

$$\therefore \quad E = \frac{p}{4\pi\varepsilon_0}\frac{2r}{r^4} = \frac{2p}{4\pi\varepsilon_0 r^3}$$

$$\therefore \quad E \propto \frac{1}{r^3} \qquad \textbf{(1 Mark)}$$

(c) Diagram representing the position of the dipole in stable equilibrium:

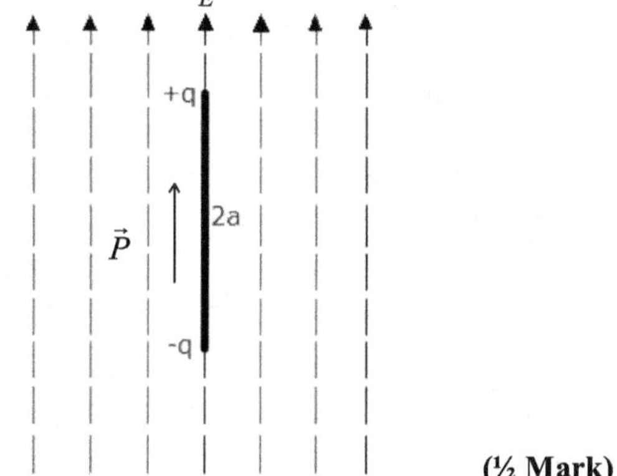

(½ Mark)

In this case, torque acting on the dipole,

$\tau = pE \sin\theta = pE \sin0$

Diagram representing the position of the dipole in unstable equilibrium:

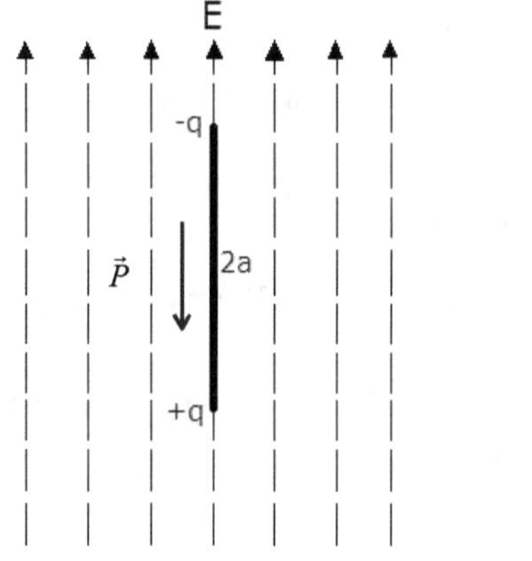

(½ Mark)

In this case, torque acting on the dipole,

$\tau = pE \sin\theta = pE \sin 180$ **(½ Mark)**

OR

(a) Consider a thin infinite plane uniformly charged sheet having a surface charge density σ.

To find electric field due to the plane sheet of charge at any point P distant r from it, choose a cylinder of area of cross-section A through the point P as the Gaussian surface.

The flux due to the electric field of the plane sheet of charge passes only through the two circular caps of the cylinder.

Let surface charge density = σ

According to Gauss's law

$$\oint \vec{E} \cdot \vec{dS} = q_{in} / \varepsilon_0 \qquad \textbf{(1 Mark)}$$

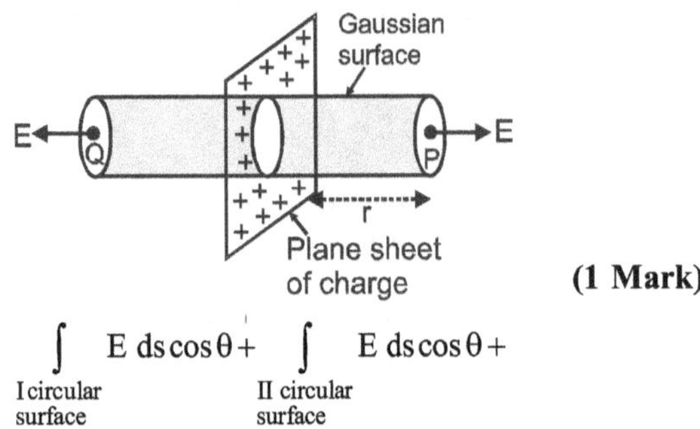

(1 Mark)

$$\int_{\substack{\text{I circular} \\ \text{surface}}} E\, ds\cos\theta + \int_{\substack{\text{II circular} \\ \text{surface}}} E\, ds\cos\theta +$$

$$\int_{\substack{\text{cylindrical} \\ \text{surface}}} E\, ds\cos\theta = \frac{\sigma A}{\varepsilon_0} \qquad \textbf{(1 Mark)}$$

$$\text{or,}\quad EA + EA + 0 = \frac{\sigma A}{2\varepsilon_0} \quad \text{or} \quad E = \frac{\sigma}{2\varepsilon_0} \quad \textbf{(1 Mark)}$$

(b) Let V_0 be the potential at the point in front of the large thin plane sheet. This point is at a distance r from its surface.

$$dV = E \cdot dr$$

$$\therefore\ V_0 - V = \frac{\sigma}{2\varepsilon_0} r = W \text{ (Work done)} \qquad \textbf{(1 Mark)}$$

25. (a) The device 'X' is a capacitor. **(1 Mark)**

(b) **Curve A:** Power consumed in the circuit

Curve B : Voltage

Curve C: Current

This is because current leads voltage in a capacitive circuit. **(1 Mark)**

(c) **Impedance:** $X_C = \dfrac{1}{2\pi f C}$

Therefore, impedance (X_C) is inversely proportional to frequency (f).

Graph of impedance (X_C) versus frequency (f)

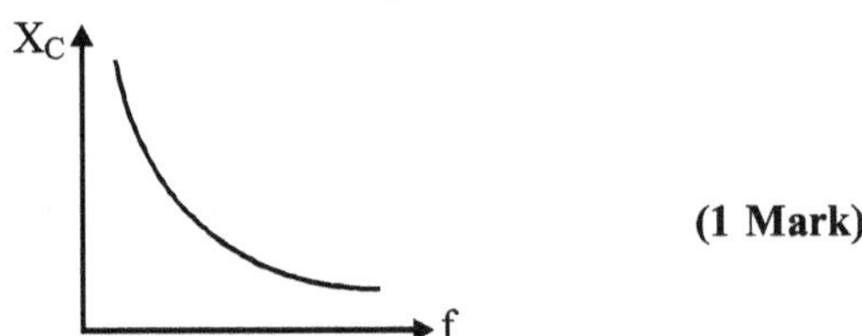

(1 Mark)

(d) Voltage applied to the circuit, $V = V_0 \sin \omega t$

Due to this voltage, a charge will be produced which will charge the plates of the capacitor with positive

and negative charges. If the potential difference across the plates of the capacitor is V, then

$$V = \frac{q}{C} \qquad\qquad \therefore\ q = CV$$

Therefore, the instantaneous value of the current in the circuit

$$i = \frac{dq}{dt} = \frac{d(cv)}{dt} = \frac{d}{dt}(CV_0 \sin \omega t)$$

$$\therefore\quad i = CV_0\, \omega \cos \omega t = \frac{V_0}{\dfrac{1}{\omega C}}\sin\left(\omega t + \frac{\pi}{2}\right) \quad \textbf{(1 Mark)}$$

Thus, the peak value of current $i_0 = \dfrac{V_0}{\dfrac{1}{\omega C}}$

$$\therefore\ i = i_0 \sin\left(\omega t + \frac{\pi}{2}\right)$$

Hence, current leads voltage by $\dfrac{\pi}{2}$ **(1 Mark)**

OR

(a) **AC Generator:** It is used to convert mechanical energy into electrical energy.

Principle : It works on the principle of electromagnetic induction.

Construction : The main components of ac generator are:

(i) Armature coil : It consist of large number of turns of insulated copper wire wound over iron core.

(ii) Magnet : Strong permanent magnet (for small generator) or an electromagnet (for large generator) with cylindrical poles in shape.

(iii) Slip rings : The two ends of the armature coil are connected to two brass rings R_1 and R_2. These rings rotate along with the armature coil.

(iv) Brushes : Two carbon brushes $(B_1$ and $B_2)$, are pressed against the slip rings. These brushes are connected to the load through which the output is obtained.

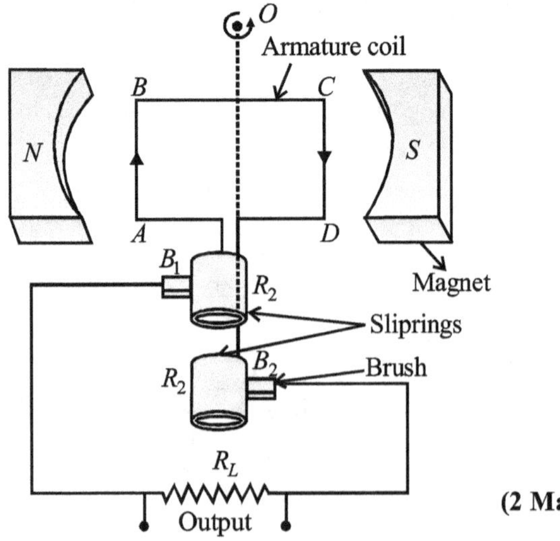

(2 Mark)

Expression for the emf induced:

When the coil is rotated with a constant angular speed ω, the angle θ between the magnetic field vector B and the area vector A of the coil at any instant t is

$\theta = \omega t$ (assuming $\theta = 0°$ at $t = 0$)

As a result, the effective area of the coil exposed to the magnetic field lines changes with time, and the flux at any time t is $\phi_B = BA \cos \theta = BA \cos \omega t$

From Faraday's law, the induced EMF for the rotating coil of N turns

$$\varepsilon = -N\frac{d\phi}{dt} = -NBA\frac{d}{dt}(\cos \omega t) \qquad \textbf{(1 Mark)}$$

Thus, the instantaneous value of the EMF $\varepsilon = NBA\omega \sin \omega t$ where $NBA\omega$ is the maximum value of the EMF

If we denote $NBA\omega$ as ε_0, then EMF, $\varepsilon = \varepsilon_0 \sin \omega t$

(1 Mark)

(b) Here, speed, $V = 5$ ms^{-1} length of conducting rod, $l = 10$ m and magnetic field, $B = 0.3 \times 10^{-4}$ wb/m^2

emf induced in the rod $\varepsilon = Blv$

$\therefore \varepsilon = 0.3 \times 10^{-4} \times 10 \times 5 = 1.5 \times 10^{-3}$ V $= 1.5$ mV

(1 Mark)

26. (a) **Wavefront:** A wavefront is defined as the surface of constant phase or the locus of all particles vibrating in the same phase. **(1 Mark)**

Verification of lwas of refraction by using Huygens principle

Let v_1 and v_2 be the speed of light in medium 1 and medium 2 $v_2 < v_1$ Suppose a plane wavefront AB is incident on $\overline{PP'}$ at an angle i.

Let t be the time taken by the wavefront to travel distance BC in medium 1. Thus, BC $= v_1 t$

In the same time the wavefront travels distance AE in medium 2. Thus, AE $= v_2 t$ and CE would represent the refracted wavefront.

In $\triangle ABC$, $\sin i = \dfrac{BC}{AC} = \dfrac{v_1 t}{AC}$;

In $\triangle AEC$, $\sin r = \dfrac{AE}{AC} = \dfrac{v_2 t}{AC}$

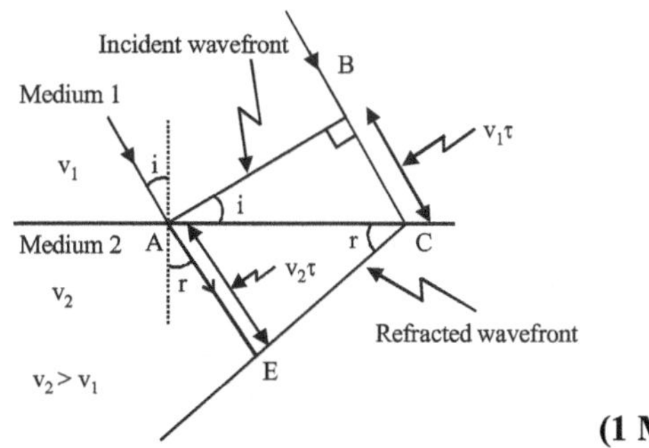

(1 Mark)

where i and r are the angle of incidence and of refraction respectively.

$\therefore \quad \dfrac{\sin i}{\sin r} = \dfrac{v_1}{v_2} \qquad \text{...(i)}$

Now, $n_1 = \dfrac{c}{v_1}$ and $n_2 = \dfrac{c}{v_2}$

$\therefore \quad \dfrac{n_2}{n_1} = \dfrac{v_1}{v_2}$ or $n_{21} = \dfrac{v_1}{v_2} \qquad \text{...(ii)}$

From eqs. (i) and (ii), $\dfrac{\sin i}{\sin r} = n_{21}$ **(1 Mark)**

This is the Snell's law of refraction.

Consider refraction of a plane wave at a rarer medium i.e., $v_2 > v_1$

As $\quad \sin i_c = \dfrac{n_2}{n_1}$

If $i = i_c$ then $\sin r = 1$ and $r = 90°$.

Therefore, for $i > i_c$ (critical angle), there cannot be any refracted wave. The wave will suffer total internal reflection.

(b) The unpolarised light coming from the sun encounter the air molecules of the earth's atmosphere. Under the influence of the electric field of the incident wave, the electrons in molecules are set in vibrations and emit the light waves in which electric field is perpendicular to the emitted light. An observer looking at 90° to the direction of sunlight will see the light polarised perpendicular to the plane, figure.

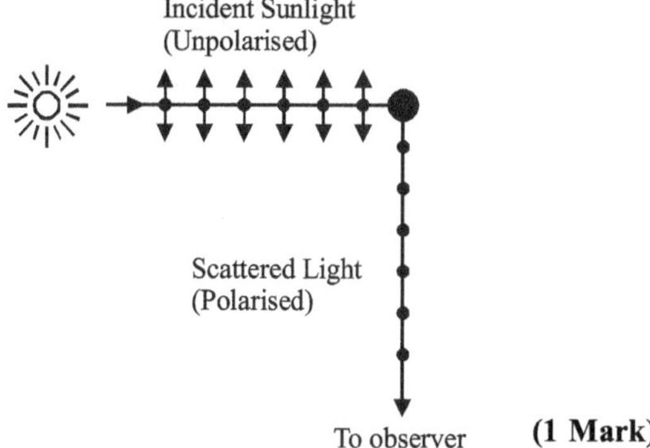

(1 Mark)

Brewster angle: It is related to refractive index as $\mu = \tan i_p$

$\therefore i_p = \tan^{-1} \mu = \tan^{-1} 1.5 = 56.3°$ **(1 Mark)**

OR

(a) Ray diagram to show the image formation by a combination of two thin convex lenses in contact:

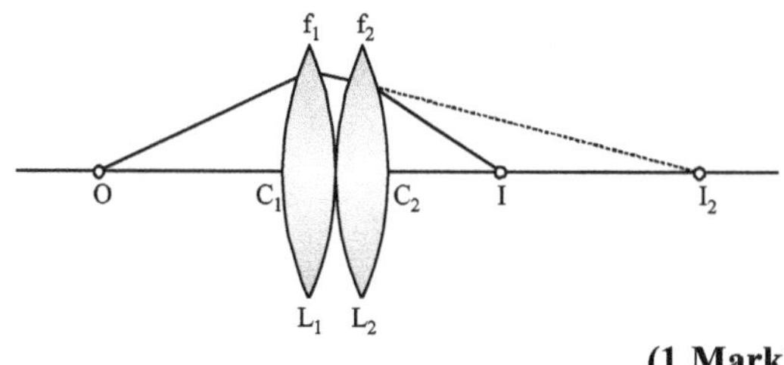

(1 Mark)

Let a point object O be placed on the common principal axis at a distance

$OC_1 = u$ (as lenses are thin)

Lens L_1 will form an image at I_2 $C_1I_2 = v_2$

Using lens formula, $\dfrac{1}{v} - \dfrac{1}{u} = \dfrac{1}{f}$

$$\dfrac{1}{v_2} - \dfrac{1}{u} = \dfrac{1}{f_1} \qquad \text{...(i) (½ Mark)}$$

Now, this image will act as an object for second lens L_2 and it will form an image at I with $C_2I = v$

As the lenses are thin, $u = C_2I_2 = C_1I = v_2$

$$\dfrac{1}{v} - \dfrac{1}{v_2} = \dfrac{1}{f_2} \qquad \text{...(ii) (½ Mark)}$$

Adding, eqns. (i) and (ii)

$$\dfrac{1}{v} - \dfrac{1}{u} = \dfrac{1}{f_1} + \dfrac{1}{f_2} = \dfrac{1}{f}$$

$$\therefore \qquad \dfrac{1}{f} = \dfrac{1}{f_1} + \dfrac{1}{f_2} \qquad \textbf{(1 Mark)}$$

Power (p) of the lens is the reciprocal of focal length(f).

$$\therefore \qquad P = \dfrac{1}{f_1} + \dfrac{1}{f_2}$$

If there is distance between the two lens, say 'd', then equivalent focal length is given as

$$\dfrac{1}{f} = \dfrac{1}{f_1} + \dfrac{1}{-f_2} - \dfrac{d}{f_1 f_2}$$

and equivalent power is given as

$$P = P_1 + P_2 - dP_1P_2$$

(b) According to the question, angle of prism A = 60°

(∵ Prism is an equilateral)

Here, $i = \dfrac{3}{4}A = 45°$

As the ray undergoes minimum deviation

∴ $i = e$

and $r_1 = r_2 = \dfrac{A}{2} = 30°$ $\qquad$ **(1 Mark)**

Using Snell's law

$$\mu = \dfrac{\sin i}{\sin r} = \dfrac{\sin 45°}{\sin 30°}$$

$$= \dfrac{\dfrac{1}{\sqrt{2}}}{\dfrac{1}{2}} - \dfrac{2}{\sqrt{2}} = \sqrt{2} = 1.414$$

∴ Speed of light in the prism

$$v = \dfrac{C}{\mu} = \dfrac{3 \times 10^8}{1.414} = 2.12 \times 10^8 \text{ m/s } \textbf{(1 Mark)}$$

CBSE Board Solved Paper

Time Allowed : 3 Hours   *Maximum Marks : 70*

General Instructions:
  (i)   There are **26** questions in all. All questions are compulsory.
  (ii) This question paper has **five** sections: Section **A**, Section **B**, Section **C**, Section **D** and Section **E.**
  (iii) Section **A** contains **five** questions of **one** mark each, Section **B** contains **five** questions of **two** marks each, Section **C** contains **twelve** questions of **three** marks each, Section **D** contains **one** value based question of **four** marks and Section **E** contains **three** questions of **five** marks each.
  (iv) There is no overall choice. However, an internal choice has been provided in **one** question of **two** marks, **one** question of **three** marks and all the **three** questions of **five** marks weightage. You have to attempt only **one** of the choices in such questions
  (v)   You may use the following values of physical constants wherever necessary:
  $c = 3 \times 10^8$ m/s
  $h = 6.63 \times 10^{-34}$ Js
  $e = 1.6 \ 10^{-19}$ C
  $\mu_0 = 4\pi \times 10^{-7}$ Tm A^{-1}
  $\varepsilon_0 = 8.854 \times 10^{-12}$ C^2 N^{-1} m^{-2}

  $$\frac{1}{4\pi\varepsilon_0} = 9 \times 10^9 \text{N m}^2 \text{ C}^{-2}$$

  Mass of electron $(m_e) = 9.1 \times 10^{-31}$ kg

  Mass of neutron $= 1.675 \times 10^{-27}$ kg

  Mass of proton $= 1.673 \times 10^{-27}$ kg

  Avogadro's number $= 6.023 \times 10^{23}$ per gram mole

  Boltzmann constant $= 1.38 \times 10^{-23}$ JK^{-1}

SECTION - A

1. Does the charge given to a metallic sphere depend on whether it is hollow or solid? Give reason for your answer.
2. A long straight current carrying wire passes normally through the centre of circular loop. If the current through the wire increases, will there be an induced emf in the loop? Justify.
3. At a place, the horizontal component of earth's magnetic field is B and angle of dip is 60°. What is the value of horizontal component of the earth's magnetic field at equator?
4. Name the junction diode whose I-V characteristics are drawn below :

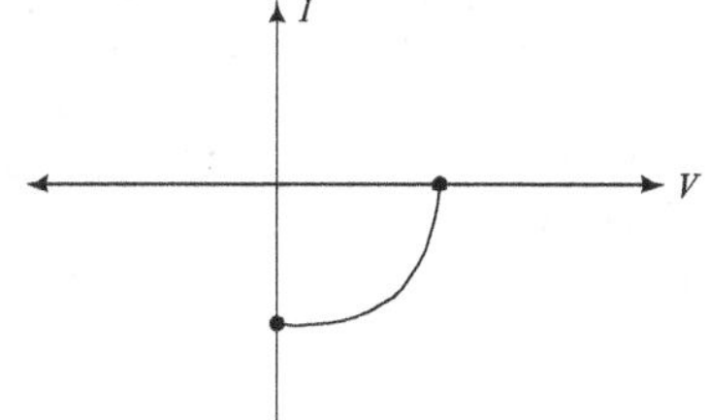

5. How is the speed of em-waves in vacuum determined by the electric and magnetic fields?

SECTION - B

6. How does Ampere-Maxwell law explain the flow of current through a capacitor when it is being charged by a battery ? Write the expression for displacement current in terms of the rate of change of electric flux.
7. Define the distance of closest approach. An α-particle of kinetic energy 'K' is bombarded on a thin gold foil. The distance of the closest approach is 'r' What will be the distance of closest approach for an α-particle of double the kinetic energy?

OR

Write two important limitations of Rutherford nuclear model of the atom.
8. Find out the wavelength of the electron orbiting in the ground state of hydrogen atom.
9. Define the magnifying power of a compound microscope when the final image is formed at infinity. Why must both

the objective and the eyepiece of a compound microscope has short focal lengths ? Explain.

10. Which basic mode of communication is used in satellite communication ? What type of wave propagation is used in this mode ? Write, giving reason, the frequency range used in this mode of propagation.

SECTION - C

11. (i) Find the value of the phase difference between current and the voltage in the series LCR circuit shown below. Which one leads in phase : current or voltage?

    (ii) Without making any other change, find the value of the additional capacitor C_1, to be connected in parallel with the capacitor C, in order to make the power factor of the circuit unity.

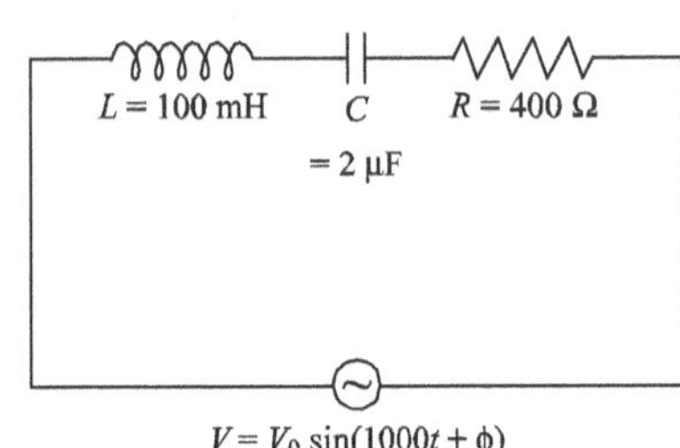

$$V = V_0 \sin(1000t + \phi)$$

12. Write the two processes that take place in the formation of a p-n junction. Explain with the help of a diagram, the formation of depletion region and barrier potential in a p-n junction.

13. (i) Obtain the expression for the cyclotron frequency.

    (ii) A deutron and a proton are accelerated by the cyclotron. Can both be accelerated with the same oscillator frequency ? Give reason to justify your answer.

14. (i) How does one explain the emission of electrons from a photosentive surface with the help of Einstein's photoelectric equation?

    (ii) The work function of the following metals is given: Na = 2.75 eV, K = 2.3 eV, Mo = 4.17 eV and Ni = 5.15 eV. Which of these metals will not cause photoelectric emission for radiation of wavelength 3300 Å from a laser source placed 1 m away from these metals ? What happens if the laser source is brought nearer and placed 50 cm away?

15. A resistance of R draws current from a potentiometer. The potentiometer wire, AB, has total resistance of R_0. A voltage V is supplied to the potentiometer. Derive an expression for the voltage across R when the sliding contact is in the middle of potentiometer wire.

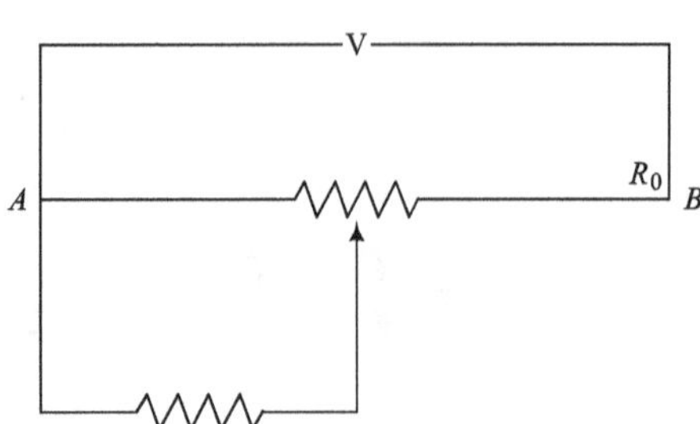

16. Define term amplitude modulation. Explain any two factors which justify the need for modulating a low frequency base-band signal.

17. (i) Find equivalent capacitance between A and B in the combination given below. Each capacitor is of 2 µF capacitance.

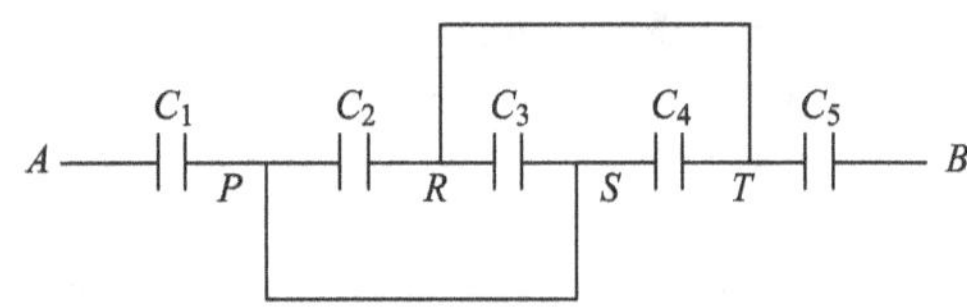

    (ii) If a dc source of 7 V is connected across AB, how much charge is drawn from the source and what is the energy stored in the network?

18. (i) Derive the expression for electric field at a point on the equatorial line of an electric dipole.

    (ii) Depict the orientation of the dipole in (i) stable, (ii) unstable equilibrium in a uniform electric field.

19. (i) A radioactive nucleus 'A' undergoes a series of decays as given below :

    $$A \xrightarrow{\alpha} A_1 \xrightarrow{\beta} A_2 \xrightarrow{\alpha} A_3 \xrightarrow{\gamma} A_4$$

    The mass number and atomic number of A_2 are 176 and 71 respectively. Determine the mass and atomic numbers of A_4 and A.

    (ii) Write the basic nuclear processes underlying β^+ and β^- decays.

20. (i) A ray of light incident on face AB of an equilateral glass prism, shows minimum deviation of 30°. Calculate the speed of light through the prism.

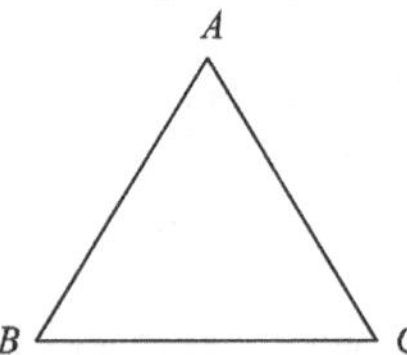

    (ii) Find the angle of incidence at face AB so that the emergent ray grazes along the face AC.

21. For a CE transistor amplifier, the audio signal voltage across the collector resistance of 2 kΩ is 2V. Given the current amplification factor of the transistor is 100, find the input signal voltage and base current, if the base resistance is 1 kΩ.

22. Describe the working principle of a moving coil galvanometer. Why is it necessary to use (i) a radial magnetic field and (ii) a cylindrical soft iron core in a galvanometer? Write the expression for current sensitivity of the galvanometer.

Can a galvanometer as such be used for measuring the current? Explain.

OR

(a) Define the term 'self-inductance' and write its S.I. unit.

(b) Obtain the expression for mutual inductance of two long co-axial solenoids S_1 and S_2 wound over the other, each of length L and radii r_1 and r_2 and n_1 and n_2 number of turns per unit length, when a current I is set up in the outer solenoid S_2.

SECTION - D

23. Mrs. Rashmi Singh broke her reading glasses. When she went to shopkeeper to order new spects, he suggested that she should get spectacles with plastic lenses instead of glass lenses. On getting the new spectacles, she found that the new ones were thicker than the earlier ones. She asked this question to the shopkeeper but he could not offer satisfactory explanation for this. At home, Mrs. Singh raised the same question to her daughter Anuja who explained why plastic lenses were thicker.

(a) Write two qualities displayed each by Anuja and her mother.

(b) How do you explain this fact using len's maker's formula?

SECTION - E

24. (a) Draw a labelled diagram of AC generator. Derive the expression for the instantaneous value of the emf induced in the coil.

(b) A circular coil of cross-sectional area 200 cm^2 and 20 turns is rotated about the vertical diameter with angular speed of 50 rad s^{-1} in a uniform magnetic field of magnitude 3.0×10^{-2} T. Calculate the maximum value of the current in the coil.

OR

(a) Draw a labelled diagram of a step-up transformer. Obtain the ratio of secondary to primary voltage in terms of number of turns and currents in the two coils.

(b) A power transmitted line feeds input power at 2200 V to a step-down transformer with its primary windings having 3000 turns. Find the number of turns in the secondary to get the power output at 220 V.

25. (a) Distinguish between unpolarized light and linearly polarized light. How does one get linearly polarised light with the help of a polariod ?

(b) A narrow beam of unpolarised light of intensity I_0 is incident on a polaroid P_1. The light transmitted by it is then incident on a second polaroid P_2 with its pass axis making angle of 60° relative to the pass axis of P_1. Find the intensity of the light transmitted by P_2.

OR

(a) Explain two features to distinguish between the interference pattern in Young's double slit experiment with the diffraction pattern obtained due to a single slit.

(b) A monochromatic light of wavelength 500 nm is incident normally on a single slit of width 0.2 mm to produce a diffraction pattern. Find the angular width of the central maximum obtained on the screen.

Estimate the number of fringes obtained in Young's double slit experiment with fringe width 0.5 mm, which can be accommodate within the region of total angular spread of the central maximum due to single slit.

26. (i) Derive an expression for drift velocity of electrons in a conductor. Hence deduce Ohm's law.

(ii) A wire whose cross-sectional area is increasing linearly from its one end to the other end, is connected across a battery of V volts. Which of the following quantities remain constant in the wire ?

(a) drift speed

(b) current density

(c) electric current

(d) electric field Justify your answer.

OR

(i) State the two Kirchoff's laws. Explain briefly how these rules are justified.

(ii) The current is drawn from a cell of emf E and internal resistance r connected to the network of resistors each of resistance r as shown in the figure. Obtain the expression for (i) the current drawn from the cell and (ii) the power consumed in the network.

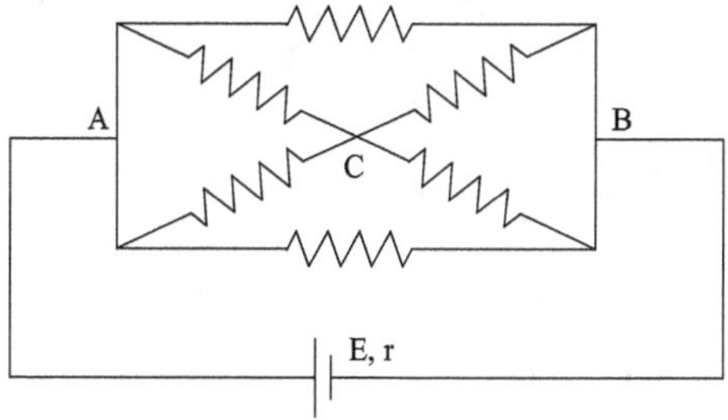

Solutions

SECTION - A

1. No, the charge given to a metallic sphere does not depend on whether it is hollow or solid because whatever charge is given to metallic sphere it will reside on its surface.

(½ + ½ = 1 Mark)

> **Note**
>
> *In static situation, whatever the charge given to conductor, they distribute themselves on the surface such that electrostatic field is zero inside a conductor. If there is any cavity inside conductor it remains shielded from outside electric influence. This is known as electrostatic shielding.*

2. No,

(½ Mark)

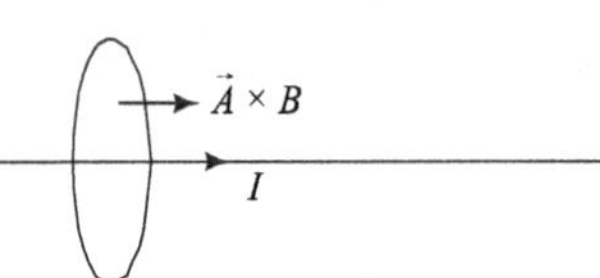

Induced emf is given as $\varepsilon = \dfrac{-d\phi_B}{dt}$

where ϕ_B = magnetic flux.

$$\phi_B = \vec{B} \cdot \vec{A}$$

Since $\vec{B}$ is the plane of the circular loop, angle between $\vec{A}$ and $\vec{B}$ is 90°

$$\therefore \qquad \phi_B = BA \cos 90°$$
$$= 0$$

$\therefore$ Induced emf will be zero when current through the wire increases as it will have no effect on magnetic flux.

(½ Mark)

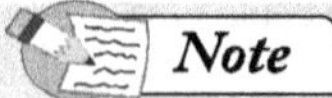

> **Note**
>
> *Self-induced emf is also known as back emf as it opposes any change in current in coil. Therefore self-inductance plays the role of inertia and is the electromagnetic analogue of mass in mechanics.*

3. Horizontal component of earth's magnetic field

$$B_H = B_E \cos \delta \qquad \text{(½ Mark)}$$

where B_E is earth's magnetic field

δ = angle of dip

Given $B_H = B$ and $\delta = 60°$

$$\therefore \qquad B = B_E \cos 60°$$

$$B_E = 2B \qquad \left(\because \cos 60° = \dfrac{1}{2}\right)$$

At equator, $\delta = 60°$

$$\therefore \qquad B_H = B_E \cos 0°$$
$$= 2B \times 1$$

B_H at equator $= 2B$

(½ Mark)

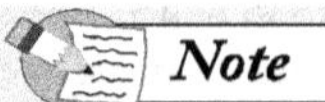

> **Note**
>
> *Magnetic dip is given as*
>
> $$\tan \delta = \dfrac{B_V}{B_H}$$
>
> *where B_V = vertical component of earth's magnetic field.*
>
> $$B_V = B_E \sin \delta$$

4. The I-V characteristics given in question is of solar cell.

(1 Mark)

5. Let E_0 = amplitude of electric field

B_0 = amplitude of magnetic field.

Then speed of em-waves,

$$C = \dfrac{E_0}{B_0} \qquad \text{(1 Mark)}$$

> **Note**
>
> *Speed of light C in vaccum is also given as*
>
> $$C = \dfrac{1}{\sqrt{\mu_0 \varepsilon_0}}$$
>
> *But if the light is travelling through medium of permittivity ε and magnetic permeability μ, then*
>
> *speed of light in that medium is,* $v = \dfrac{1}{\sqrt{\mu\varepsilon}}$

SECTION - B

6. Ampere-Maxwell law is given as

$$\oint \vec{B} \cdot d\vec{l} = \mu_0 (i_c + i_d)$$

where i_c = conductor current

$$i_c = \dfrac{dQ}{dt}$$

i_d = displacement current

$$i_d = \varepsilon_0 \dfrac{d\phi_E}{dt} \; ; \; \phi_E = \text{electric flux.} \qquad \text{(1 Mark)}$$

During charging, outside the capacitor there is conduction current i_c and current between the plates of capacitor is due to electric field on plates i.e. displacement current.

$\therefore$ Current through capacitor is displacement current, when it is being charged by battery.

(1 Mark)

Another way to ask this question.
Q. What modifications were made by maxwell to overcome the inconsistency in ampere's circuital law?

7. Distance of approach is defined as the distance where entire intial kinetic energy of the α-particle gets converted into electrostatic potential energy. **(1 Mark)**

   If 'K' is the kinetic energy of α-particle, then distance of approach 'r' is

   $$r = \frac{2Ze^2}{4\pi\varepsilon_0 K}$$

   if $K \to 2K$, then

   $$r \to \frac{2Ze^2}{4\pi\varepsilon_0(2K)} = \frac{Ze2}{4\pi\varepsilon_0 K} = \frac{r}{2}$$

   $$\therefore K \to 2K, \text{ then } r \to \frac{r}{2} \qquad \textbf{(1 Mark)}$$

   OR

   Two important limitations of Rutherford nuclear model of the atom are:-

   (i) An electron revolving around the nucleus is under continuous acceleration towards the centre. So, according to electromagnetic theory, it should continously lose energy and move in orbits of gradually decreasing radii. Thus the Rutherford' model cannot explain the stability of an atom.

   (ii) In Rutherford' model, an electron can revolve in orbits of all possible radii. So it should emit a continous spectrum.
   (1 × 2 = 2 Marks)

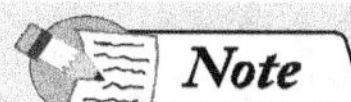

Rutherford's nuclear model:- Rutherford's model suggested that most of the mass of the atom and its positive charge are concentrated in a tiny nucleus and electrons revolve around it.

8. According to Bohr model
   $$2\pi r_n = n\lambda \qquad \textbf{(1 Mark)}$$
   where r_n = radius of nth orbit of hydrogen atom
   For ground state $n = 1$.
   $$2\pi r_1 = \lambda$$
   $$r_1 = \text{Bohr's radius} = 0.53 \text{ Å}$$
   $$= 0.53 \times 10^{-10} \text{ m}$$
   $$\therefore \quad \lambda = 2 \times 3.14 \times 0.53 \times 10^{-10} \text{ m}$$
   $$\lambda = 3.32 \times 10^{-10} \text{ m}$$
   $$\lambda = 3.32 \text{ Å}. \qquad \textbf{(1 Mark)}$$

9. Magnifying power of a compound microscope when final image is formed at infinity, is
   $$m = m_0 m_e$$
   $$= \frac{L}{f_0} \times \frac{D}{fe} \qquad \textbf{(1 Mark)}$$
   where　f_0 = focal length of objective

f_e = focal length of eyepiece

L = tube length of microscope

D = distance of distinct vision.

As from the expression of magnifying power we see that it is inversely proportional to both f_e and f_o. So to increase magnifying power both objective and eyepiece should have short focal lengths. **(1 Mark)**

Magnifying power of compound microscope when final image is at least distance of distinct vision,

$$m = \frac{L}{fo}\left(1 + \frac{D}{fe}\right)$$

10. Both broadcast and point to point mode of communication is used in satellite communication. **(1 Mark)**

    Space wave propagation is used in this mode. The frequency range of space wave propagation is above 40 MHz because frequencies above 40 MHz are not reflected back by ionosphere. **(1 Mark)**

SECTION - C

11. (i) $V = V_0 \sin(1000\, t + \phi)$
    $$\therefore \quad \omega = 1000$$
    $$C = 2 \text{ μF}$$
    $$L = 1000 \text{ mH}$$
    $$R = 400 \text{ Ω}$$

    $$X_C = \frac{1}{C\omega} = \frac{1}{2 \times 10^{-6} \times 1000} = 500 \text{ Ω}$$

    $$X_L = L\omega = 1000 \times 10^{-3} \times 100 = 100 \text{ Ω } \textbf{(1 Mark)}$$
    Phase angle ϕ is

    $$\tan\phi = \frac{X_l - X_c}{R} = \frac{100 - 500}{400} = -1$$

    $$\tan\phi = \tan\frac{\pi}{4} \quad \Rightarrow \quad \phi = -\frac{\pi}{4}$$
    Since phase angle is negative, current leads the voltage.
    (1 Mark)

    (ii) When additional capacitor C_1 is connected in parallel with C, then equivalent capacitor will be,
    $$C^1 = C + C_1 \text{ and } X_C \to X_{C^1}$$
    For power factor to be unity
    $$X_{C^1} = X_L$$

    $$\frac{1}{w(C + C_1)} = 100$$

    $$C + C_1 = 10 \times 10^{-6}$$
    $$C + C_1 = 10 \text{ μF}$$
    $$C_1 = (10 - C) = 10 - 2 = 8 \text{ μF}. \textbf{(1 Mark)}$$

12. The two processes that take place in the formation of a *p-n* junction are:-
(i)　Diffusion
(ii)　Drift　　**(½ Mark)**

When a *p-n* junction is formed, the p-side of the junction has a higher concentration of electrons while the *n*-side has a higher concentration of electron. Therefore, holes begin to diffuse from *p*-side to *n*-side and election begin to diffuse from *n*-side to *p*-side. This creates a positive charge on *n*-side and a region of negative charge on *p*-side, near the junction. This is called depletion region.　　**(1 Mark)**

Barrier Potential : The accumulation of negative charge in *p*-region and positive charges in the *n*-region sets up a potential difference across the junction. This acts as a barrier and is called barrier potential VB which opposes the further diffusion of electron and holes across junction.　**(1 Mark)**

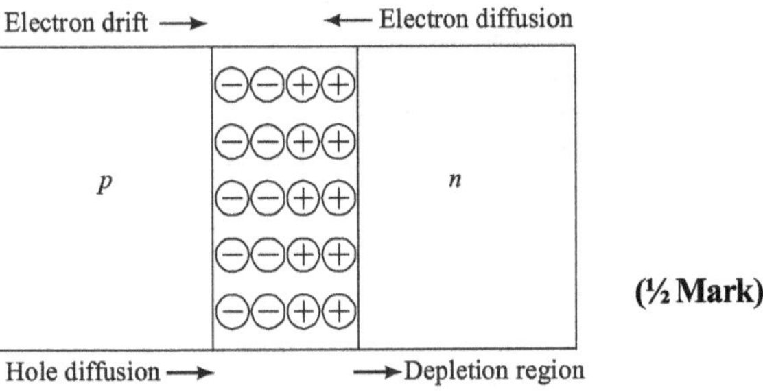

(½ Mark)

13. (i)　Let a charged particle of charge q, enters the region of magnetic field $\vec{B}$ that is normal to its velocity $\vec{u}$. Due to magnetic field, the particle will follow a circular path. The necessary centripetal force is provided by magnetic force.

So magnetic force = centripetal force.

$$\left[\vec{U}\times\vec{B}\right] = \frac{mv^2}{r}$$

$$q\,VB\sin 90° = \frac{mv^2}{r}$$

$$q\,VB = \frac{mv^2}{r} \quad\Rightarrow\quad r = \frac{mv}{qB} \quad \textbf{(1 Mark)}$$

Period of revolution T

$$T = \frac{2\pi r}{u} = \frac{2\pi}{u}\times\frac{mu}{qB}$$

$$T = \frac{2\pi m}{qB}$$

Now the frequency of revolution is

$$f = \frac{1}{T}$$

$$f = \frac{qB}{2\pi m} \quad \text{Cylctron frequency.} \quad \textbf{(1 Mark)}$$

(ii)　Cylctron frequency f is inversely proportional to mass of charged particle.

$$f\,\alpha\,\frac{1}{m}$$

Mass of deutron > mass of proton.

Therefore, their frequency of revolution will be different and hence they cannot be accelerated by same amount.　　**(1 Mark)**

Note

Deutron is nucleus of deuterium atom. Deutron consist of 1 proton and 1 neutron. Hence mass of deutron is more than mass of proton. But charge of both deutron and proten is equal.

14. (i)　Einstein's photoelectric equation is,

$$h\nu = \phi_0 + K.E_{max}$$

where $h\nu$ = energy of incident photon

ϕ_0 = work function of metal

$K.E_{max}$ = maximum kinetic energy of electrons ejected.

When a photon of energy '$h\nu$' is incident on metal surface, it provides energy to electron to ejectout from metal surface. Some part of photon's energy is utilized by electron to overcome the work function and the remaining part appears as the kinetic energy of ejected electron.　　**(1 Mark)**

(ii)　Wavelength of incident radiation
$\lambda = 3300\,\text{Å}$
$= 3.3\times10^{-7}\,\text{m}$
Energy of incident photon $E = h\nu$

$$E = \frac{hC}{\lambda}\ [\because \nu\lambda = C]$$

$$\therefore\quad E = \frac{6.63\times10^{-34}\times3\times10^{8}}{3.3\times10^{-7}\times1.6\times10^{-19}}eV$$

$$E = 3.77\,eV \quad\quad \textbf{(1 Mark)}$$

The work function of *Mo* and *Ni* is more than energy of incident radiation ($= 3.77\ eV$) so, photoelectric emission will not take place in *Mo* and *Ni* metal.

Kinetic energy of photoelectrons does not depend on the distance between source of radiation and metal surface. So, kinetic energy of photoelectron will not change but intensity of photoelectric current will change.　　**(1 Mark)**

15.

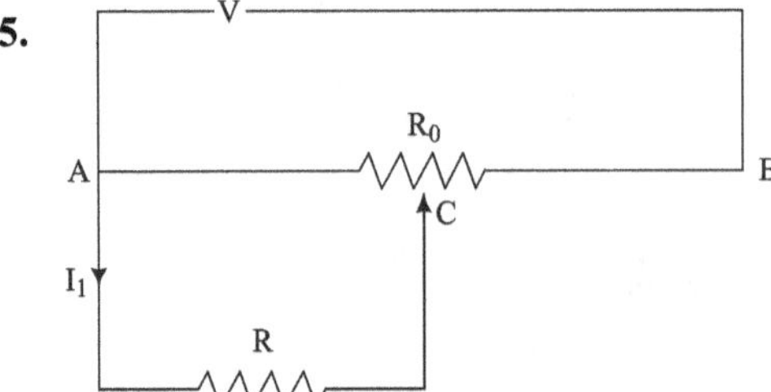

When the slide is in the middle of potentiometer, the effective resistance between AC will be $R_0/2$.

$\therefore$ Total resistance between A and C, R_1

$$\frac{1}{R_1} = \frac{1}{R} + \frac{1}{R_{0/2}}$$

$$R_1 = \frac{R_0 R}{R_0 + 2R}$$ **(1 Mark)**

The total resistance between A and B will be,

$$R_{AB} = R_1 + \frac{R_0}{2}$$

$$R_{AB} = \frac{R_0 R}{R_0 + 2R} + \frac{R_0}{2}$$

$\therefore$ Current flowing through potentiometer will be

$$I = \frac{V}{R_{AB}}$$

$$I = \frac{V}{R_1 + \dfrac{R_0}{2}} = \frac{2U}{2R_1 + R_0}$$ **(1 Mark)**

Voltage across R and R_1 will be same as they are in parallel.

So $V_1 = IR_1$

$$= \frac{2V}{2R_1 + R_0} \times R_1$$

$$= \frac{2V}{2\left[\dfrac{R_0 R}{R_0 + 2R}\right] + R_0} \times \left[\dfrac{R_0 R}{R_0 + 2R}\right]$$

$$V_1 = \frac{2VR}{2R + R_0 + 2R}$$

$$V_1 = \frac{2VR}{R_0 + 4R}$$ **(1 Mark)**

16. In amplitude modulation, a low frequency message signal is suprimposed over a high frequency carrier signal such that the amplitude of carrier wave is varied according to message signal.   **(1 Mark)**

The two factors justified for modulating a low frequency are:-

(i) *Size of antenna:-* For transmitting a signal we require an antenna whose size should have a size comparable to the wavelength of the signal ($\sim \lambda/4$). Therefore, for large wavelengths signal, the size of antenna is very large and not achieveable.

(ii) *Effective power radiated by antenna:-* It is inversely proportional to λ^2 *i.e.* $P \propto \ell/\lambda^2$. so for large wavelength (or low frequency) power radiated by antenna will be very less.   **(2 × 1 = 2 Marks)**

17. (i) The circuit can be re-drawn as

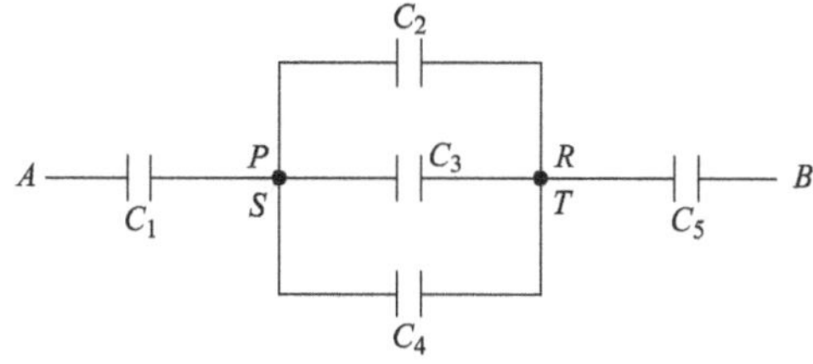

$\therefore$ Capacitor C_2, C_3 and C_4 are connected in parallel. Their equivalent capacitance will be,

$$C^1 = C_2 + C_3 + C_4$$

$$= 2 + 2 + 2$$

$$C^1 = 6 \,\mu F$$ **(½ Mark)**

Capacitance C_1, C^1 and C_5 are connected in sereis. Their equivalent capacitance will be,

$$\frac{1}{C} = \frac{1}{C_1} + \frac{1}{C^1} + \frac{1}{C_5}$$

$$\frac{1}{C} = \frac{1}{2} + \frac{1}{6} + \frac{1}{2}$$

$$\frac{1}{C} = \frac{3+1+3+}{6} = \frac{7}{6}$$

$\therefore$ Equivalent capacitance between AB is $\dfrac{6}{7}\,\mu F$.

                    (½ Mark)

(ii) Charge drawn from circuit

$$Q = CV$$

$$= \frac{6}{7} \times 7 \times 10^{-6} = 6 \times 10^{-6}\,C$$ **(1 Mark)**

$Q = 6\,\mu C$ and energy stored $E = \dfrac{Q^2}{2C}$

$$E = \frac{6 \times 6 \times 10^{-12}}{2 \times \dfrac{6}{7} \times 10^{-6}} J$$

$$E = 2_1 \times 10^{-6}\,J = 2_1\,\mu J$$ **(1 Mark)**

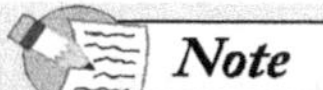

Note

While solving equivalent circuit consisting capacitance or resistance, first keep the points of same potential at one point and then solve the further circuit. For example, in the given circuit, point p and S are at same potential as they are connected by a simple wire. Similarly R and T are at same potential.

18. (i)   **(½ Mark)**

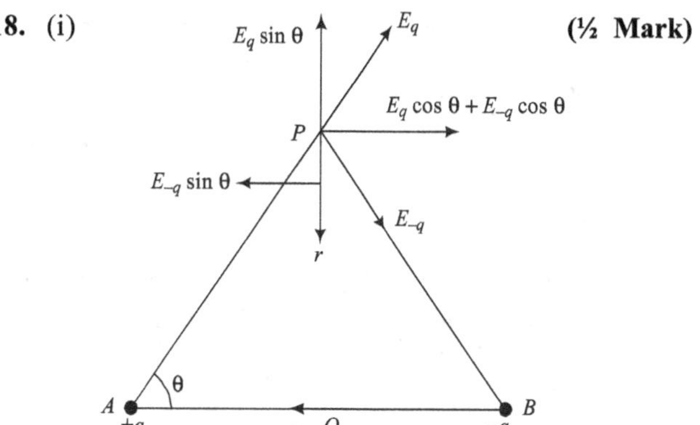

Let 'P' be equitorial point where electric field has to be calculated.

$$E_q = \frac{q}{4\pi\varepsilon_0 AP^2}$$

$$E_{-q} = \frac{q}{4\pi\varepsilon_0 PB^2}$$

From ΔPAO and ΔPBO

$$AP^2 = r^2 + a^2$$

and $\qquad BP^2 = r^2 + a^2$

$$\therefore \quad E_q = E_{-q} = \frac{q}{4\pi\varepsilon_0(r^2 + a^2)} \qquad \textbf{(1 Mark)}$$

From the figure, we see that at P the vertical component of E_q and E_{-q} are equal and opposite, hence cancel each other. Where as horizontal component are in same direction, therefore they add up.

So, net electric field due to dipole at point P is,

$$\vec{E} = -[E_q \cos\theta + E_{-q}\cos\theta]\hat{P}$$

Negative sign show that electric field is in opposite direction of $\vec{P}$ (dipole moment)

$$\cos\theta = \frac{a}{\sqrt{r^2 + a^2}}$$

$$\vec{E} = \frac{-2q}{4\pi\varepsilon_0(r^2 + a^2)} \times \frac{a}{\sqrt{r^2 + a^2}}\hat{P}$$

$$\vec{E} = \frac{-2qd}{4\pi\varepsilon_0(r^2 + a^2)3/2}\hat{P}$$

Since $|\vec{P}| = q \times 2a$

$$\therefore \quad \vec{E} = \frac{P}{4\pi\varepsilon_0(r^2 + a^2)3/2}\hat{P} \qquad \textbf{(½ Mark)}$$

(ii) For stable equilibrium, angle between dipole moment $\vec{P}$ and electric field $\vec{E}$ is $0°$ and for unstable equilibrium, it is $180°$.

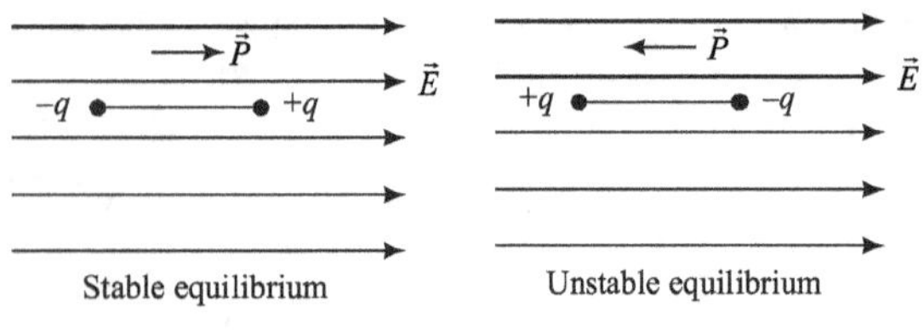

(1 Mark)

 **Note**

When torque $\vec{\tau} = \vec{P} \times \vec{E}$, on dipole due to uniform electric field is zero, the dipole is said to be in equilibrium position.
For stable equilibrium $\tau = PE \sin 0° = 0$
For unstable equilibrium $\tau = PE \sin 180° = 0$.

19. (i) $\quad {}^{176}_{71}(A_2) \xrightarrow{\alpha} {}^{172}_{69}A_3 + \alpha$

$$ {}^{172}_{69}A_3 \xrightarrow{y} {}^{172}_{69}A_4 + y$$

$${}^{176}_{70}(A_1) \xrightarrow{\beta^-} {}^{176}_{71}(A_2) + \beta^- + \overline{\nu}$$

$${}^{180}_{72}(A) \xrightarrow{\alpha} {}^{176}_{70}(A_1) + \alpha$$

$$\therefore \quad {}^{180}_{72}(A) \xrightarrow{\alpha} {}^{176}_{70}A_1 \xrightarrow{\beta^-} {}^{176}_{71}$$

$$A_2 \xrightarrow{\alpha} {}^{172}_{69}A_3 \xrightarrow{y} {}^{172}_{69}A_y$$

For $A_4 \rightarrow$ Mass number $= 172$

Atomic number $= 69$ $\qquad$ **(1 Mark)**

For $A \rightarrow$ Mass number $= 180$

Atomic number $= 72$ $\qquad$ **(1 Mark)**

 **Note**

Since it is not given in the question β^+ decay or β^- decay, you can choose either of them. If you choose β^+ decay, then values of A_4 will be same but for A, mass number will be 180 and atomic number will be 74.

(ii) Nuclear process for B^+ decay

$$P \rightarrow n + e^+ + \nu \qquad \textbf{(½ Mark)}$$

Nuclear process for B^- decay

$$n \rightarrow p + e^- + \overline{\nu} \qquad \textbf{(½ Mark)}$$

20. (i) Refractive index of prism μ is

$$\mu = \frac{\sin\left(\dfrac{A + D_m}{2}\right)}{\sin\dfrac{A}{2}}$$

where $A =$ Angle of prism $= 60°$ for equilateral prism

$D_m = 30°$ (given)

$$\therefore \quad \mu = \frac{\sin\left(\dfrac{60° + 30°}{2}\right)}{\sin\left(\dfrac{60°}{2}\right)}$$

$$= \frac{\sin 45°}{\sin 30°} = \frac{1}{\sqrt{2}} \times 2 = \sqrt{2} \qquad \textbf{(1 Mark)}$$

Also $\mu = \dfrac{\text{speed of light in vacuum}}{\text{speed of light in medium}}$

$$\therefore \quad \mu = \frac{c}{v}$$

$$\Rightarrow \quad \sqrt{2} = \frac{3 \times 10^8}{v}$$

$$\Rightarrow \quad v = 2.122 \times 10^8 \text{ m/s.} \qquad \textbf{(½ Mark)}$$

(ii)

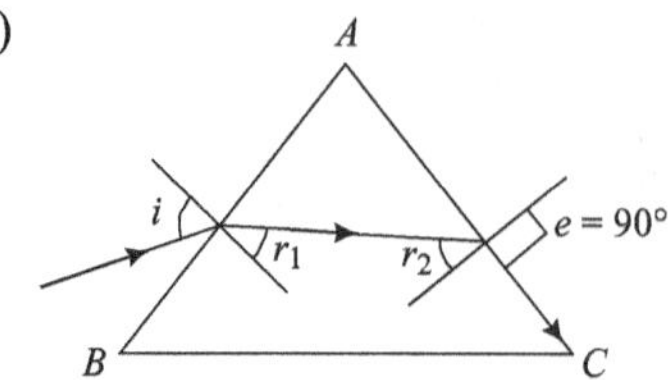

At face AC, angle of refraction $e = 90°$ and angle of incidence is r_2.

$\therefore$ *Applying snell's law at face AC*

$$\frac{\sin r_2}{\sin 90°} = \mu ap$$

where μap = refractive index of air wrt to prism

$\therefore \quad \dfrac{\sin r_2}{\sin 90°} = \dfrac{1}{\sqrt{2}} \qquad \left[\because \mu_p = \sqrt{2}\right]$

$$\frac{\sin r_2}{1} = \frac{1}{\sqrt{2}}$$

$$r_2 = \sin^{-1}\left[\frac{1}{\sqrt{2}}\right] = 45° \qquad \textbf{(½ Mark)}$$

Now, angle of prism $A = r_1 + r_2$

$\therefore \qquad 60° = r_1 + 45°$

$\qquad \qquad r_1 = 15°$

Applying snell's law at face AB $\dfrac{\sin i}{\sin r_1} = \mu pa$

where μpa = refractive index of prism wrt air

$$\frac{\sin i}{\sin 15°} = \sqrt{2}$$

$\qquad \sin i = \sqrt{2} \times 0.65 \ (\because \sin 15° = 0.65)$

$\qquad \sin i = 0.92$

$\qquad \quad i = \sin^{-1}(0.92)$

$\qquad \quad i = 66.9° \qquad \qquad \textbf{(1 Mark)}$

21. Given $R_C = 2 \ k\Omega = 2 \times 10^3 \ \Omega$

$\qquad \qquad R_B = 1 \ k\Omega = 1 \times 10^3 \ \Omega$

$\qquad \qquad V_{CE} = 2 \ V$

$\qquad \qquad \beta = 100$

Now, $\quad V_{CE} = I_C R_C$

$\therefore \qquad I_C = \dfrac{V_{CE}}{R_C} = \dfrac{2}{2 \times 10^3}$

$\qquad \qquad I_C = 1 \ mA \qquad \qquad \textbf{(1 Mark)}$

Current amplification $\beta = \dfrac{I_C}{I_B}$

$\therefore \qquad 100 = \dfrac{1 \ mA}{I_B}$

$\qquad \qquad I_B = 10^{-5} \ A \qquad \qquad \textbf{(1 Mark)}$

Input voltage $\quad Vi = I_B R_B$

$\qquad \qquad \qquad = 10^{-5} \times 10^3$

$\qquad \qquad \quad Vi = 10^{-2} \ V. \qquad \textbf{(1 Mark)}$

22. *Working principle of galvanometer:-* A current carrying coil placed in a magnetic field experiences a current dependent torque, which tends to rotate the coil and produces angular deflection. **(1 Mark)**

(i) *Radial magnetic field:* Radial magnetic field makes the arm of couple fixed and hence torque on the coil is always same in all position of the coil in the magnetic field. This provides a linear current scale, i.e. to have deflection proportional to current.

(ii) *A cylindrical soft iron core:* Due ot high permeability of soft iron, the magnetic lines of force crowd through the soft iron core. This increases the magnetic field and hence sensitivity of the galvanometer. **(½ × 2 = 1 Mark)**

No, a galvanometer only detects current. It cannot measure current. However by applying a low resistance in parallel with galvanometer, it can be converted into ammeter to measure current. **(1 Mark)**

OR

22. (a) Self-inductance of a coil may be defined as the induced emf set up in the coil due to a unit rate of change of current through it. **(½ Mark)**

Self-inductance, $L = \dfrac{\varepsilon}{dI/dt}$

where ε = induced emf

$\qquad \dfrac{dI}{dt}$ = rate of change of current.

S.I. unit = henry (H). **(½ Mark)**

(b) Consider two solenoid each of length L, S_1 and S_2 where S_2 is wound over S_1.

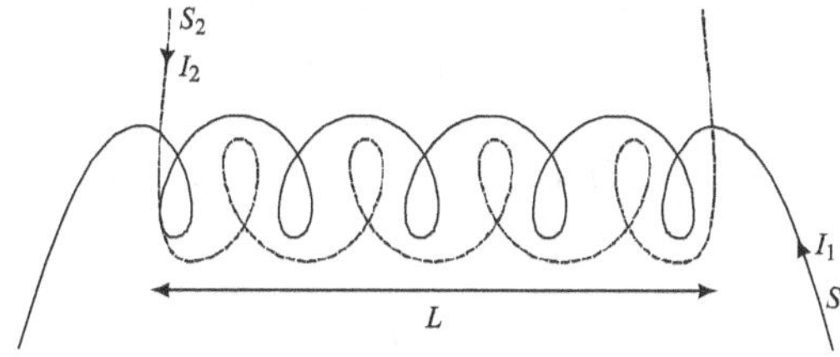

r_1, r_2 = radius of solenoid S_1 and S_2 respectively.

N_1, N_2 = no. of turns in S_1 and S_2

n_1, n_2 = no. of turns per unit length in S_1 and S_2

Let a current I_2 flow through S_2. This sets up a magnetic flux ϕ_1 through each turn of the coil S_1.

Flux linked with S_1

$N_1\phi_1 = M_{12} I_2$ ...(1) **(½ Mark)**

where m_{12} = mutual indutance between two solenoid.

The magnetic field set up inside S_2 due to I_2 is

$\qquad B_2 = \mu_0 \, n_2 I_2$ **(½ Mark)**

So, flux linked with S_1

$N_1\phi_1 = B_2 A N_1 \qquad \left(\because \phi_B = \vec{B} \cdot \vec{A}\right)$

$\qquad \quad = \mu_0 \, n_2 I_2 \cdot A N_1 \qquad \text{...(2)}$

Here $\qquad A = \pi r_1^2$

Equating equation (1) and (2)

$$M_{12} I_2 = \mu_0 \, n_2 I_2 \cdot \left(\pi r_1^2\right) N_1$$

$$M_{12} = \mu_0 \, n_2 \left(\pi r_1^2\right) (n_1 L) \quad \{\because N_1 = n_1 L\}$$

So, $\qquad M_{12} = \mu_0 \, n_1 n_2 \, \pi r_1^2 L.$ **(1 Mark)**

SECTION - D

23. (a) *Qualities displayed by Anuja:-* Knowledgeable, Scientific temperament. **(1 Mark)**

Qualities displayed by her mother:- Inquistive, Keen to learn. **(1 Mark)**

(b) Lens maker formula is

$$\frac{1}{f} = (\mu_{21} - 1)\left[\frac{1}{R_1} - \frac{1}{R_2}\right]$$

Now as refractive index of plastic material is less then that of glass, therefore to keep focal length same, radius of curvature 'R' has to be increased, making lens thicker. **(2 Marks)**

SECTION - E

24. (a) When a coil having N turns is rotated with a constant angular speed w, the angle θ between the magnetic field $\vec{B}$ and area vector $\vec{A}$ of coil at any instant t is $\theta = \omega t$

Magnetic flux $\phi_B = \vec{B} \cdot \vec{A}$

$$\phi_B = BA \cos \theta$$
$$= BA \cos wt \qquad \textbf{(½ Mark)}$$

From Faraday's law of electromagnetic induction, induced emf is

$$\varepsilon = -\frac{Nd\phi_B}{dt} \qquad \textbf{(½ Mark)}$$

$$\varepsilon = -N\frac{d}{dt}[BA \cos wt]$$

$$\varepsilon = -NBA\,(-\sin wt)\,\frac{d}{dt}\,(wt) \qquad \textbf{(½ Mark)}$$

$$\varepsilon = +NBAw \sin wt$$

$$\varepsilon = \varepsilon_0 \sin wt$$

where $\varepsilon_0 = NBA\omega$. **(1 Mark)**

(b) Given

$$N = 20$$
$$\omega = 50 \text{ rad } s^{-1}$$
$$A = 200 \text{ cm}^2 = 200 \times 10^{-4} \text{ m}^2$$
$$B = 3.0 \times 10^{-2} \text{ T}$$

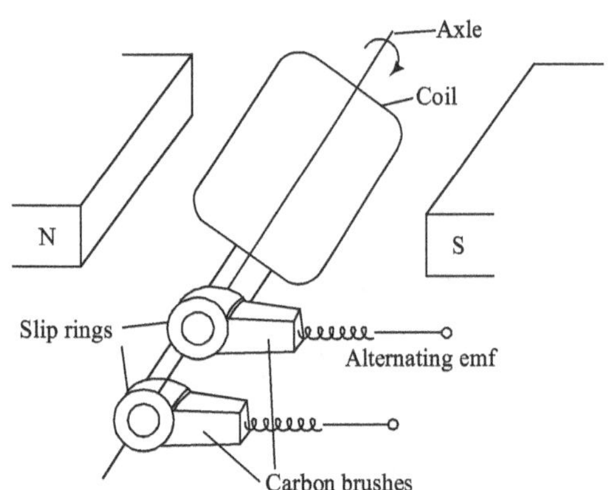

Maximum value of current $i_0 = \dfrac{\varepsilon_0}{R}$ **(½ Mark)**

where $\varepsilon_0 = NBAw$

$R =$ resistance of coil [not given]

$$i_0 = \frac{NBAW}{R} \qquad \textbf{(1 Mark)}$$

$$i_0 = \frac{20 \times 3 \times 10^{-2} \times 200 \times 10^{-4} \times 50}{R}$$

$$i_0 = \frac{600 \times 10^{-3} V}{R}$$

$$i_0 = \frac{600}{R} \text{ mA.} \qquad \textbf{(1 Mark)}$$

OR

24. (a)

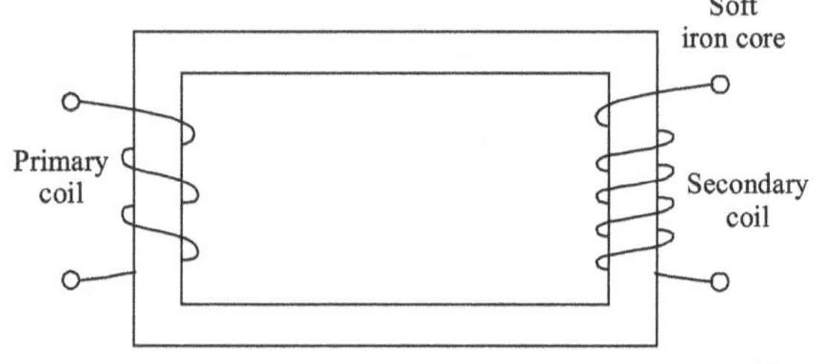

(1 Mark)

Consider the situation, input emf is ε_p (emf in primary). This incuced emf is]

$$\varepsilon_p = -NP\frac{d\phi}{dt} \qquad \textbf{(½ Mark)}$$

where $\phi =$ magnetic flux linked with each turn of the primary or secondary coil.

emf induced in secondary coil, ε_s is

$$\varepsilon_s = -N_S\frac{d\phi}{dt} \qquad \textbf{(½ Mark)}$$

Here N_S and $N_P =$ no. of turns in secondary and primary coil respectively.

$$\therefore \quad \frac{\varepsilon_S}{\varepsilon_p} = \frac{N_S}{N_p} \qquad \text{...(1) } \textbf{(1 Mark)}$$

Assuming transformer to be ideal one so that there is no energy losses, then

Input power = Output power

$$\varepsilon_P I_P = \varepsilon_S I_S$$

$$\frac{\varepsilon_S}{\varepsilon_p} = \frac{I_p}{I_S} \qquad \text{...(2) } \textbf{(1 Mark)}$$

(b) Input voltage $\varepsilon_P = 2200 \text{ V}$

Output voltage $\varepsilon_S = 220 \text{ V}$

$$NP = 3000$$

So $\quad \dfrac{N_S}{N_p} = \dfrac{\varepsilon_S}{\varepsilon_p}$

$$\Rightarrow \quad \frac{N_S}{3000} = \frac{220}{2200}$$

$$\therefore \quad N_S = 300 \qquad \textbf{(1 Mark)}$$

25. (a) *Unpolarized light:-* A light which has vibrations in all directions in a plane perpendicular to the direction of propagation is said to be unpolarised light. **(1 Mark)**

Polarized light:- If the electric field vector of a light wave vibrates just in one direction perpendicular to the direction of wave propagation, then it is said to be linearly polarised. **(1 Mark)**

An unpolarised light can easily be polarised using a polariod. A polariod contains long chain molecules aligned in a particular direction. The electric vectors of unpolarised light along the direction of aligned molecule get absorbed. Therefore, the light wave will get polarised linearly with the electric vector oscillating along a direction perpendicular to the aligned molecules.

(1 Mark)

(b) Intensity of light (unpolarised) after passing through

P_1 will reduced to half *i.e.* $\dfrac{I_0}{2}$.

According to Malus' law
$$I = I_0 \cos^2\theta \qquad \textbf{(1 Mark)}$$
where θ angle between pass axis of P_1 and P_2.

So, $\quad I = \dfrac{I_0}{2} \cos^2 60°$

$$I = \frac{I_0}{2} \times \frac{1}{4} = \frac{I_0}{8}$$

$\therefore$ The intensity of transmitted light through P_1 is $\dfrac{I_0}{8}$.

(1 Mark)

OR

(a)

Interference	Diffraction
(i) All bright and dark fringes are of equal width	(i) The width of central maxima is twice the width of secondary maxima.
(ii) All bright fringes are of equal intensity	(ii) Intensity of maxima decrease as we go away from central maxima.

(b) Angular width of central maxima is **(1 × 2 = 2 Marks)**

$$\theta = \frac{2\lambda}{a}$$

$$\lambda = 500\ nm = 500 \times 10^{-9}\ m$$

$$a = 0.2\ mm = 0.2 \times 10^{-3}\ m$$

$$\therefore \quad \theta = \frac{2 \times 500 \times 10^{-9}}{0.2 \times 10^{-3}}$$

$$\theta = 5 \times 10^{-3}\ rad \qquad \textbf{(1 Mark)}$$

Linear width of interference fringes, β

$$\beta = \frac{\lambda D}{d} \qquad \textbf{(½ Mark)}$$

where D = distance between screen and slit

d = distance between two slits.

Linear width of central maxima of diffraction pattern,

$$\beta^1 = \frac{2\lambda D}{a} \qquad \textbf{(½ Mark)}$$

where a = slit width.

$\therefore$ no. of fringes central maxima can accommodate are n

$$n = \frac{\beta^1}{\beta}$$

$$n = \frac{2\lambda D}{a} \times \frac{d}{\lambda D}$$

$$n = \frac{2d}{a} \qquad \textbf{(1 Mark)}$$

> **Note**
>
> *In interference and diffraction light energy is redistributed. Formation of dark fringe does not mean light energy has been lost, its been distributed to bright fringe. It is in accordance with conservation of energy.*

26. (i) The average velocity of free electrons in conductor is zero because their motion is random.

So, $\dfrac{1}{N} \sum \vec{v_i} = 0 = (Vi)\text{avg}$

where $\vec{v_i}$ = velocity of ith electron.

When electric field (E) is applied across conductor electrons will be accelerated towards positive end.

Acceleration $\vec{a} = \dfrac{-e\vec{E}}{m} \qquad \textbf{(1 Mark)}$

where $-e$ = charge of electron

m = mass of electron.

As electron move, they suffer collision with heavy fixed ions. The collisions of electron do not occur at regular interval but at random times. The average value of time between successive collisions is known as relaxation time τ.

The average velocity of N electron at any given time t is called drift velocity V_d.

$$\vec{V_d} = \left(\vec{V_i}\right)\text{avg} - \frac{e\vec{E}}{m}(t_i)\text{avg}$$

$$\vec{V_d} = 0 - \frac{e\vec{E}}{m}\tau$$

$$\vec{V_d} = \frac{-e\vec{E}}{m}\tau$$

Since $E = \dfrac{V}{l}$, where V = Potential difference and

l = length of conductor

$$\therefore \quad |\vec{V}d| = \dfrac{ev\tau}{ml} \qquad \textbf{(1 Mark)}$$

$$\left[\,|\vec{V}d| = \text{magnitude of } \vec{V}d\,\right]$$

If the cross-section of the conductor is A and n is no. of electron per unit volume, then current through conductor

$$I = enAvd$$

$$I = enA \times \dfrac{ev\tau}{ml}$$

$$I = \dfrac{e^2 nA\tau}{ml} V$$

$$V = \dfrac{ml}{e^2 nA\tau} I$$

$$\Rightarrow \boxed{V = RI} \to \text{Ohm's law.} \qquad \textbf{(1 Mark)}$$

where $R = \dfrac{ml}{e^2 nA\tau}$ = resistance of conductior.

(ii) Current $\qquad I = \dfrac{dQ}{dt}$

Drift velocity $\quad Vd = \dfrac{I}{enA}$

Current density $\quad J = \dfrac{I}{A}$

Electric field $\quad E = \dfrac{J}{\sigma} = \dfrac{I}{A\sigma}$

From the formula, we see that except current all other quantities depend on cross-sectional area A so, only current will remain constant. **(2 Marks)**

OR

(a) *Junction Rule:-* At any junction of circuit elements, the sum of currents entering the junction must be equal the sum of currents leaving it.

$$\Sigma I = 0$$

Justification:- This rule is justified on the basis of law of conservation of charge.

Loop Rule:- The algebraic sum of changes in potential around any closed loop must be zero.

$$\Sigma(\Delta V) = 0$$

Justification:- This rule is justified on the basis of law of conservation of energy. **(1 × 2 = 2 Marks)**

(b) The current can be redrawn as

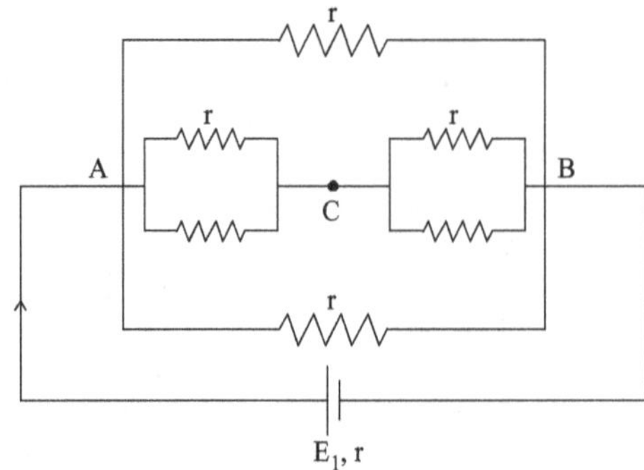

The equivalent resistance between A and C is r_{AC} =

$$r_{AC} = \dfrac{r \times r}{r + r} = \dfrac{r}{2}$$

Similarly $\quad r_{CB} = \dfrac{r \times r}{r + r} = \dfrac{r}{2}$

$\therefore$ Equivalent resistence in middle branch is

$$r_m = \dfrac{r}{2} + \dfrac{\mu}{2} = r$$

Equivalent resistance between A and B is

$$\dfrac{1}{R_{AB}} = \dfrac{1}{r} + \dfrac{1}{r} + \dfrac{1}{r} \qquad \Rightarrow R_{AB} = \dfrac{r}{3} \qquad \textbf{(1 Mark)}$$

(i) Current drawn from cell is

$$I = \dfrac{E}{R_{AB} + r} \qquad \Rightarrow \qquad I = \dfrac{E}{\dfrac{r}{3} + r}$$

or, $\quad I = \dfrac{3E}{r + 3r} = \dfrac{3E}{4r} \qquad \textbf{(1 Mark)}$

(ii) Power consumed is

$$P = I^2(R_{AB} + r)$$

$$P = \left(\dfrac{3E}{4r}\right)^2 \times \left(\dfrac{\mu}{3} + r\right)$$

$$P = \dfrac{9E^2}{16r^2} \times \dfrac{4r}{3}$$

$$P = \dfrac{3E^2}{4r} \qquad \textbf{(1 Mark)}$$

All India *2016*
CBSE Board Solved Paper

Time Allowed: 3 Hours   *Maximum Marks: 70*

General Instructions:

(i) There are **26** questions in all. All questions are compulsory.

(ii) This question paper has **five** sections: Section **A**, Section **B**, Section **C**, Section **D** and Section **E.**

(iii) Section **A** contains **five** questions of **one** mark each, Section **B** contains **five** questions of **two** marks each, Section **C** contains **twelve** questions of **three** marks each, Section **D** contains **one** value based question of **four** marks and Section **E** contains **three** questions of **five** marks each.

(iv) There is no overall choice. However, an internal choice has been provided in **one** question of **two** marks, **one** question of **three** marks and all the **three** questions of **five** marks weightage. You have to attempt only **one** of the choices in such questions

(v) You may use the following values of physical constants wherever necessary:

$c = 3 \times 10^8$ m/s

$h = 6.63 \times 10^{-34}$ Js

$e = 1.6 \, 10^{-19}$ C

$\mu_0 = 4\pi \times 10^{-7}$ Tm A^{-1}

$\varepsilon_0 = 8.854 \times 10^{-12}$ C^2 N^{-1} m^{-2}

$$\frac{1}{4\pi\varepsilon_0} = 9 \times 10^9 \text{N m}^2 \text{C}^{-2}$$

Mass of electron $(m_e) = 9.1 \times 10^{-31}$ kg

Mass of neutron $= 1.675 \times 10^{-27}$ kg

Mass of proton $= 1.673 \times 10^{-27}$ kg

Avogadro's number $= 6.023 \times 10^{23}$ per gram mole

Boltzmann constant $= 1.38 \times 10^{-23}$ JK^{-1}

SECTION - A

1. In what way is the behaviour of a diamagnetic material different from that of a paramagnetic, when kept in an external magnetic field.

2. The plot of the variation of potential difference across a combination of three identical cells in series, versus current is shown below. What is the emf and internal resistance of each cell ?

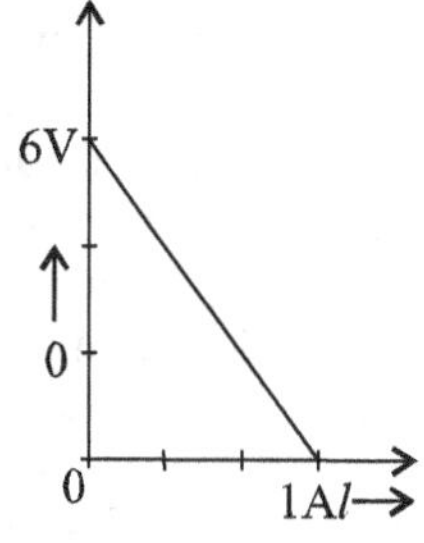

3. Why does sun appear red at sunrise and sunset?

4. A charge 'q' is moved from a point A above a dipole of dipole moment 'p' to a point B below the dipole in equatorial plane without acceleration. Find the work done in the process.

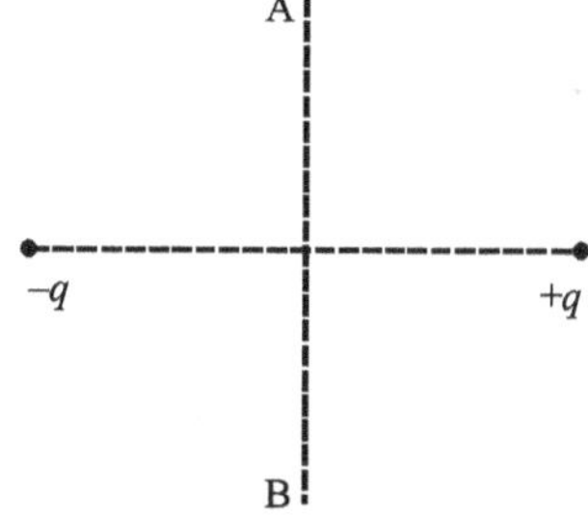

5. Name the essential components of a communication system.

SECTION - B

6. Calculate the de-Broglie wavelength of the electron orbitting in the $n = 2$ state of hydrogen atom.

7. A battery of emf 12 V and internal resistance 2 Ω is connected to a 4 Ω resistor as shown in the figure.

(a) Show that a voltmeter when placed across the cell and across the resistor, in turn, gives the same reading.

(b) To record the voltage and the current in the circuit, why is voltmeter placed in parallel and ammeter in series in the circuit?

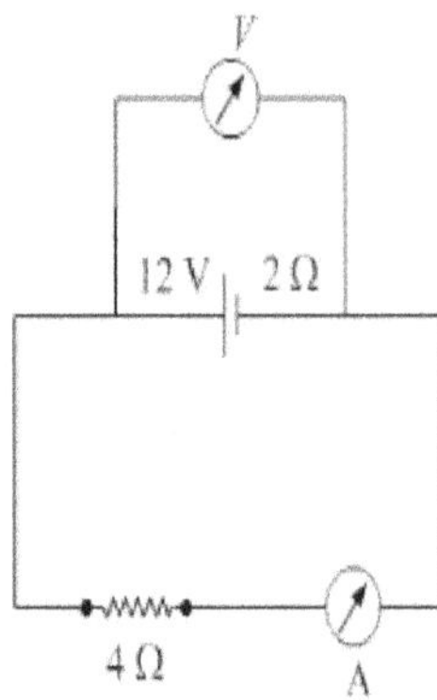

8. Define ionization energy.
How would the ionization energy change when electron in hydrogen atom is replaced by a particle of mass 200 times that of electron but having the same charge?

OR

Calculate the shortest wavelength of the spectral lines emitted in Balmer series.
[Given Rydberg constant, $R = 10^7 \, m^{-1}$]

9. Define modulation index. Why is it kept low? What is the role of a bandpass filter?

10. A ray PQ incident normally on the refracting face BA is refracted in the prism BAC made of material of refractive index 1.5. Complete the path of ray through the prism. From which face will the ray emerge? Justify your answer.

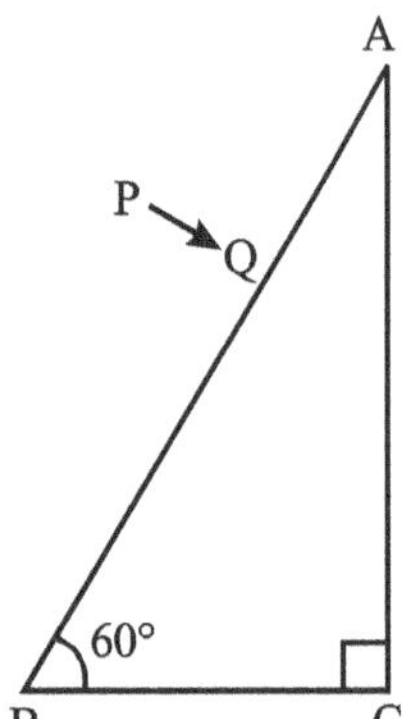

SECTION - C

11. (i) Derive an expression for drift velocity of free electrons.

(ii) How does drift velocity of electrons in a metallic conductor vary with increase in temperature?

12. (a) Write the basic nuclear process involved in the emission of β^+ in a symbolic form, by a radioactive nucleus.

(b) In the reactions given below :

(i) $^{11}_{6}C \rightarrow \, ^{z}_{y}B + x + v$

(ii) $^{12}_{6}C + \, ^{12}_{6}C \rightarrow \, ^{20}_{a}Ne + \, ^{c}_{b}He$

Find the values of x, y and z and a, b and c.

13. Sketch the graphs showing variation of stopping potential with frequency of incident radiations for two photosensitive materials A and B having threshold frequencies $v_A > v_B$.

(i) In which case is the stopping potential more and why?

(ii) Does the slope of the graph depend on the nature of the material used? Explain.

14. (i) State law of Malus.

(ii) Draw a graph showing the variation of intensity (I) of polarised light transmitted by an analyser with angle (θ) between polariser and analyser.

(iii) What is the value of refractive index of a medium of polarising angle 60°?

15. Define an equipotential surface. Draw equipotential surfaces :

(i) in the case of a single point charge and

(ii) in a constant electric field in Z-direction.
Why the equipotential surfaces about a single charge are not equidistant ?

(iii) Can electric field exist tangential to an equipotential surface ? Give reason.

16. Use Biot-Savart law to derive the expression for the magnetic field on the axis of a current carrying circular loop of radius R.

Draw the magnetic field lines due to a circular wire carrying current I.

17. Define the term wavefront. State Huygen's principle.

Consider a plane wavefront incident on a thin convex lens. Draw a proper diagram to show how the incident wavefront traverses through the lens and after refraction focusses on the focal point of the lens, giving the shape of the emergent wavefront.

OR

Explain the following, giving reasons :

(i) When monochromatic light is incident on a surface separating two media, the reflected and refracted light both have the same frequency as the incident frequency.

(ii) When light travels from a rarer to a denser medium, the speed decreases, Does this decrease in speed imply a reduction in the energy carried by the wave ?

(iii) In the wave picture of light, intensity of light is determined by the square of the amplitude of the wave. What determines the intensity in the photon picture of light?

18. For a CE-transistor amplifier, the audio signal voltage across the collector resistance of 2kΩ is 2V. Suppose the current amplification factor of the transistor is 100, find the input signal voltage and base current, if the base resistance is 1 kΩ.

19. (i) Identify the part of the electromagnetic specturm which is :

    (a) suitable for radar system used in aircraft navigation.

    (b) produced by bombarding a metal target by high speed electrons.

  (ii) Why does a galvanometer show a momentary deflection at the time of charging or discharging a capacitor ? Write the necessary expression to explain this observation.

20. (i) Which mode of propagation is used by shortwave broadcast services having frequency range from a few MHz upto 30 MHz? Explain diagrammatically how long distance communication can be achieved by this mode.

  (ii) Why is there an upper limit to frequency of waves used in this mode ?

21. (i) Explain with the help of a diagram the formation of depletion region and barrier potential in a pn Junction.

  (ii) Draw the circuit diagram of a half wave rectifier and explain its working.

22. (i) When an AC source is connected to an ideal inductor show that the average power supplied by the source over a complete cycle is zero.

  (ii) A lamp is connected in series with an inductor and an AC source. What happens to the brightness of the lamp when the key is plugged in and an iron rod is inserted inside the inductor? Explain.

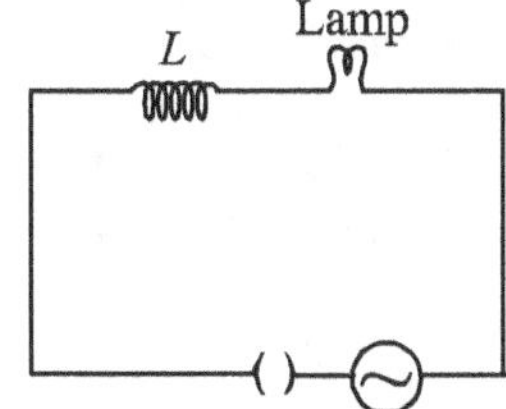

SECTION - D

23. Ram is a student of class X in a village school. His uncle gifted him a bicycle with a dynamo fitted in it. He was very excited to get it. While cycling during night, he could light the bulb and see the objects on the road. He, however, did not know how this device works. He asked this question to his teacher. The teacher considered it an opportunity to explain the working to the whole class.

Answer the following question :

  (a) State the principle and working of a dynamo.

  (b) Write two values each displayed by Ram and his school teacher.

SECTION - E

24. (i) Derive the mathematical relation between refractive indices n_1 and n_2 of two radii and radius of curvature R for refraction at a convex spherical surface. Consider the object to be a point since lying on the principal axis in rarer medium of refractive index n_1

and a real image formed in the denser medium of refractive index n_2. Hence, derive lens maker's formula.

  (ii) Light from a point source in air falls on a convex spherical glass surface of refractive index 1.5 and radius of curvature 20 cm. The distance of light source from the glass surface is 100 cm. At what position is the image formed?

OR

  (a) Draw a labelled ray diagram to obtain the real image formed by an astronomical telescope in normal adjustment position. Define its magnifying power.

  (b) You are given three lenses of power 0.5 D, 4 D and 10 D to design a telescope.

    (i) Which lenses should be used as objective and eyepiece? Justify your answer.

    (ii) Why is the aperture of the objective preferred to be large ?

25. (i) Use Gauss's law to find the electric field due to a uniformly charged infinite plane sheet. What is the direction of field for positive and negative charge densities ?

  (ii) Find the ratio of the potential differences that must be applied across the parallel and series combination of two capacitors C_1 and C_2 with their capacitances in the ratio 1 : 2 so that the energy stored in the two cases becomes the same.

OR

(i) If two similar large plates, each of area A having surface charge densities $+\sigma$ and $-\sigma$ are separated by a distance d in air, find the expressions for

  (a) field at points between the two plates and on outer side of the plates. Specify the direction of the field in each case.

  (b) the potential difference between the plates.

  (c) the capacitance of the capacitor so formed.

(ii) Two metallic spheres of Radii R and 2R are charged so that both of these have same surface charge density σ. If they are connected to each other with a conducting wire, in which direction will the charge flow and why?

26. (i) Draw a labelled diagram of a step-down transformer. State the principle of its working.

  (ii) Express the turn ratio in terms of voltages.

  (iii) Find the ratio of primary and secondary currents in terms of turn ratio in an ideal transformer.

  (iv) How much current is drawn by the primary of a transformer connected to 220 V supply when it delivers power to a 110V – 550 W refrigerator?

OR

  (a) Explain the meaning of the term mutual inductance. Consider two concentric circular coils, one of radius r_1 and the other of radius r_2 $(r_1 < r_2)$ placed coaxially with centres coinciding with each other. Obtain the expression for the mutual inductance of the arrangement.

  (b) A rectangular coil of area A, having number of turns N is rotated at 'f' revolutions per second in a uniform magnetic field B, the field being perpendicular to the coil. Prove that the maximum emf induced in the coil is $2\pi f$NBA.

Solutions

SECTION - A

1. When a diamagnetic material is placed in an external magnetic field, the field lines are repelled or expelled and the field inside the material is reduced.

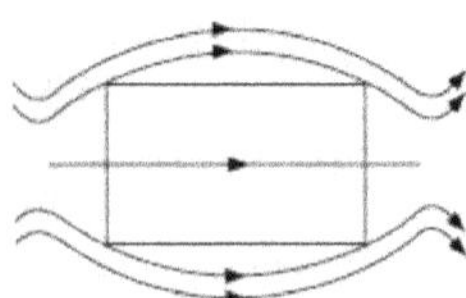

Diamagnetic material in external magnetic field.

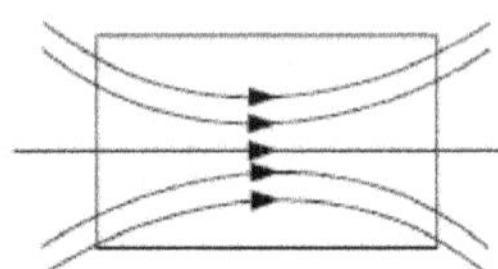

Paramagnetic material in external magneitc field.

Whereas when a paramagnetic material is placed in an external magnetic field, the field lines are attracted towards it. Thus the field lines get concentrated inside the material and the field inside is enhanced. **(1 Mark)**

> **Note**
>
> *In terms of susceptibility, diamagnetic material have negative susceptibility and paramagnetic materials have positive and small susceptibility.*

2. Let E and r be the EMF and internal resistance of all cells respectively and internal resistance of each cell respectively as cells are identical. As we know, according to the definition of the terminal potential difference,

$$V = E - Ir \qquad \ldots(i)$$

E is the EMF and r is the total internal resistance of the circuit.

From eqn (i) when

$$I = 0 \implies V = E$$

From the graph we can see, E = 6 V

As there are three cells

$$\therefore \quad E = 3 \times e = 6\,v \implies e = 2\,V \qquad \textbf{(½ Mark)}$$

And, when, V = 0, I = 1A from graph

$$E = Ir \implies r = \frac{E}{I} = \frac{6}{1} = 6\,\Omega$$

As the cells are connected in series, so internal resistance of each cell.

$$= \frac{r}{3} = \frac{6}{3} = 2\,\Omega \qquad \textbf{(½ Mark)}$$

3. At the time of sunset or sunrise, the Sun and its surroundings appear red because of the scattering of light.

$$\text{Scattering} \propto \frac{1}{\lambda^4}$$

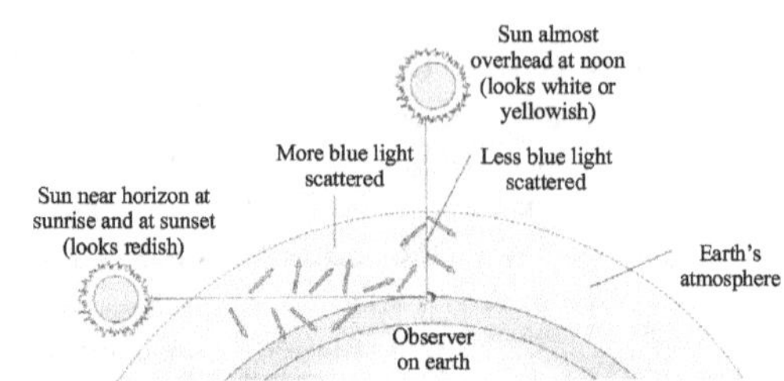

At noon, the light of sun travels relatively shorter distance through earth's atmosphere thus appears white as only a little of blue and violet colours are scattered. During sunrise or sunset, sun is near the horizon. So sunlight has to travel a relatively larger distance through earth atmosphere due to which low wavelength light waves like blue and violet get scattered out and sky appears red. **(1 Mark)**

> **Note**
>
> *Due to scattering, atmosphere appears blue as blue light have shorter wavelength and is scattered the most. And since red light is least scattered, therefore it is used in traffic light.*

4. The net force on the charge is directed parallel to the dipole and hence perpendicular to its motion along AB.

$$\therefore \quad \text{Work done} = 0 \qquad \textbf{(1 Mark)}$$

5. Communication is the act of transmission of information. Communication system has three essential components-transmitter, medium/channel and receiver. **(1 Mark)**

SECTION - B

6. As we know, according to Bohr's theory angular momentum

$$mvr = \frac{nh}{2\pi} \qquad \therefore \quad mvr_2 = \frac{nh}{2\pi}$$

The de-Broglie wavelength is given as,

$$\lambda = \frac{h}{p} = \frac{h}{mv} = \frac{h}{nh} \times (2\pi r_2) = \pi r_2$$

As $r_2 = 0.529 \times n^2 \times 10^{-10}\,m$ **(1 Mark)**

Therefore, wavelength

$$\lambda = \pi \times 0.529 \times 10^{-10} \times n^2$$
$$= 3.14 \times 0.529 \times 10^{-10} \times 2^2;$$
$$6.64 \times 10^{-10}\,m \qquad \textbf{(1 Mark)}$$

> **Note**
>
> *Radius of nth orbit for electron is*
>
> $$r_n = \left(\frac{n^2}{m}\right)\left(\frac{n}{2\pi}\right)^2 \frac{4\pi\varepsilon_0}{e^2}$$
>
> *or* $\quad r_n = 0.529 \times 10^{-10} \times n^2.$

7. (i) Given $\varepsilon = 12\,V, r = 2\pi, R = 4\,\Omega$

Total current in circuit I,

$$I = \frac{\varepsilon}{R + r}$$

$$I = \frac{12}{4+2} = 2\,A$$

$$\therefore \quad V = \varepsilon - I_r = 12 - 2 \times 2 = 8\,V$$

Voltage across 4Ω resistor,

$$V' = IR = 2 \times 4 = 8\,V$$

$\therefore$ Voltmeter when placed across cell and resistor show the same reading $V = 8V$. **(1 Mark)**

(ii) We connect voltmeter in parallel as we know that current chooses only the low resistance path. Voltmeter has very high resistance and ensure that its connection does not alter the flow of current in the circuit. Hence, it is connected in parallel to the load across which potential difference is to be measured. Ammeter measures value of current flowing through the circuit so it should be connected in the series. Ammeter has very low resistance to ensure that all the current flows through it. Thus, it gives a correct reading of the current when connected in series. **(1 Mark)**

8. The minimum amount of energy required to remove an electron from the outermost orbit of a neutral atom in its ground state is known as the **ionization energy** of that atom. **(1 Mark)**

The ionization energy of Hydrogen atom is directly proportional to mass of electron

$$E_H \propto m_e \qquad\qquad \text{...(i)}$$

When mass of electron is replaced by a particle having mass $= 200\,m_e$, then

$$E_H' \propto 200 m_e \qquad\qquad \text{...(ii)}$$

From eqs. (i) and (ii), we have

$$E_H' = 200\,E_H = 200 \times (-13.6) = -2720\,eV \ (\because E_H = -13.6\,eV)$$
(1 Mark)

OR

For shortest wavelength, of the spectral lines emitted in balmer series, $n = \infty$

As we know, $\quad \dfrac{1}{\lambda} = R\left(\dfrac{1}{2^2} - \dfrac{1}{n^2}\right)$ **(1 Mark)**

$$\therefore \qquad \frac{1}{\lambda} = R\left(\frac{1}{2^2} - 0\right) = \frac{R}{4}$$

$$\therefore \qquad \lambda = \frac{4}{R} = \frac{4}{10^7} = 4 \times 10^{-7}\,m \qquad \text{(1 Mark)}$$

9. Modulation index : It is defined as the ratio of the amplitude of the message signal to the amplitude of the carrier wave.

Modulation index, $\mu = \dfrac{A_m}{A_c}$ **(1 Mark)**

For effective amplitude modulation, μ is kept low to avoid distortion in the signal.

As the low-frequency modulating signal is mixed with a high-frequency carrier wave, the distortion is restricted due to the high-frequency carrier wave for modulation index lying between 0 and 1. If the amplitude of modulating wave is greater than the carrier wave then the carrier wave gets over-modulated. This over modulation results in distorted waveform envelope which will result in a distorted output signal. Hence modulation index is kept low.

Bandpass filter are those filter which allows a certain range of frequency to pass through it. **(1 Mark)**

10. Here, refractive index of the material of prism, $\mu = 1.5$

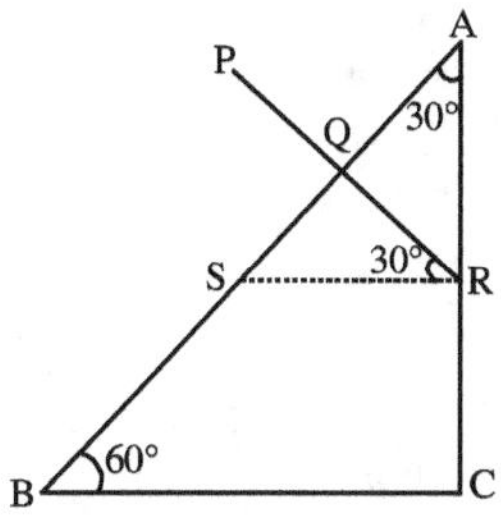

$\angle Q = 90°$

and $\angle S = 60°$ (as BC $\parallel$ SR)

$\therefore \ \angle R = 180° - 90° - 60° = 30°$.

As we know, $\quad \mu = \dfrac{1}{\sin i_c}$

$$\Rightarrow \quad \sin i_c = \frac{1}{\mu} = \frac{1}{1.5} = 0.66$$

And we know, $\sin 30° = 0.5$

i.e., $i_c > 30°$

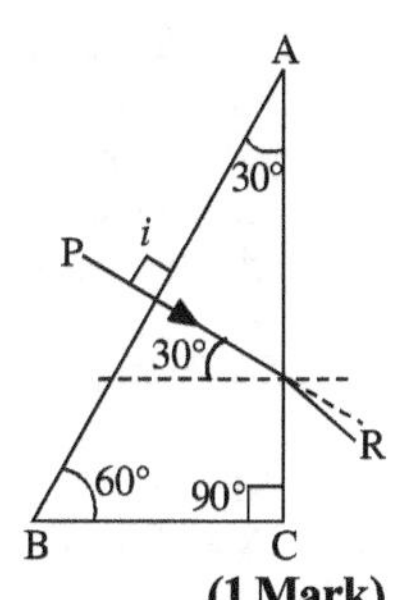

(1 Mark)

Thus, here light will emerge out from face AC. **(1 Mark)**

In $\triangle QRS$,

11. (i) Free electrons are in continuous random motion, They undergo change in direction at each collision and the thermal velocities are randomly distributed in all directions.

$\therefore$ Average thermal velocity,

$$u = \frac{u_1 + u_2 + ... + u_n}{n} = 0$$

Free electrons in a conductor move with the same speed but in random directions. Thus, the average velocity of all N electrons will be zero.

$$\frac{1}{N}\sum_{i=1}^{N} \vec{v_i} = 0$$

When an electric field (E) is applied across the conductor electrons will be accelerated towards the positive end.

$$\vec{a} = \frac{-eE}{m} \qquad\qquad \text{(1 Mark)}$$

Where $-e$ is the charge and m is the mass of an electron. As electrons move, they suffer collision with the heavy fixed ions. The collisions of the electrons do not occur at regular intervals but at random times. The average value of time between successive collisions is known as relaxation time (τ).

The average velocity of N electrons at any given time t is called the drift velocity (V_d).

$$\vec{V}_d = (\vec{V}_i)_{\text{average}} - \frac{e\vec{E}}{m}(t_i)_{\text{average}}$$

$$= 0 - \frac{e\vec{E}}{m}\tau$$

or, $\quad \vec{V}_d = -\frac{e\vec{E}}{m}\tau$ **(1 Mark)**

Hence average drift velocity, $\vec{V}_d = \dfrac{e\vec{E}}{m}\tau$

(ii) Drift velocity of electrons in a metallic conductor decreases with increase in temperature.

As we know,
with increase the temperature of the metallic conductor the collision between the electrons and ions increases, which results in the decrease in the relaxation time.

So, from the equation $\quad \vec{v}_d = \dfrac{e\vec{E}}{m}\tau$

$v_d \propto \tau$

Hence, the drift velocity decreased. **(1 Mark)**

Note

When electric field is applied across the conductor, it is almost instantly established causing at every point a local electron drift. Therefore, establishment of current does not have to wait for electrons from one end to travel to other end of conductor.

12. (a) The basic nuclear process involved in the emission of β^+ in a symbolic form, by a radioactive nucleus

$$p \to n + \beta^+ + \nu \quad \textbf{(1 Mark)}$$

For a beta-plus decay, a proton transforms into a neutron within the nucleus, according to the above reaction.

(b) (i) $\quad {}^{11}_{6}C \to {}^{z}_{y}B + x + \nu$

$\Rightarrow \quad {}^{11}_{6}C \to {}^{11}_{5}B + {}^{1}_{0}\beta + \nu$

The corresponding y and z are 5 and 11, respectively, the x is the positron. **(1 Mark)**

(ii) $\quad {}^{12}_{6}C + {}^{12}_{6}C \to {}^{20}_{a}Ne + {}^{c}_{b}He$

$\Rightarrow \quad {}^{12}_{6}C + {}^{12}_{6}C \to {}^{20}_{10}Ne + {}^{4}_{2}He$

The corresponding values of a, b and c are 10, 2 and 4, respectively. **(1 Mark)**

13. The variation of stopping potential with frequency of incident radiation for two photosensitive materials A and B having threshold frequencies $\nu_A > \nu_B$ is shown below.

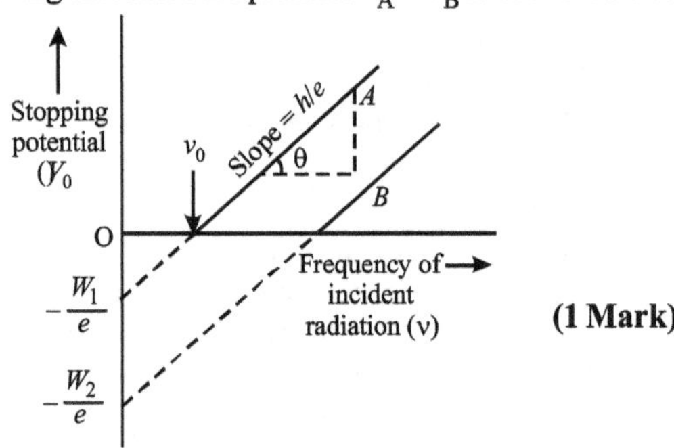

(1 Mark)

From the graph, it is very clear that
(i) the stopping potential is proportional to the threshold frequency, hence the stopping potential is higher for metal B.

(ii) the slope of the graph does not depend on the nature of the material used
As we know, from Einsteins photoelectric equation,
$$K_{\max} = h\nu - \phi_0 = eV_0$$
Dividing the whole equation by e, we get
$$\frac{h\nu}{e} - \frac{\phi_0}{e} = V_0$$
From the above equation, the slope of the graph is $\dfrac{h}{e}$ (on comparing with the straight line equation).
Thus, we see that the slope is independent of the nature of the photoelectric material. **(1 Mark)**

Note

The fact the stopping potential is independent of intensity of incident radiation and depend on frequency of incident radiation is crucial discriminator between the wave- picture and photon picture of photoelective effect.

14. (i) **Law of Malus :** It states that when a completely plane polarised light beam is incident on an analyser, the intensity of the emergent light varies as the square of the *cosine* of the angle between the plane of transmission of the analyser and the polariser.
i.e., $I = I_0 \cos^2 \phi$ **(1 Mark)**

(ii) 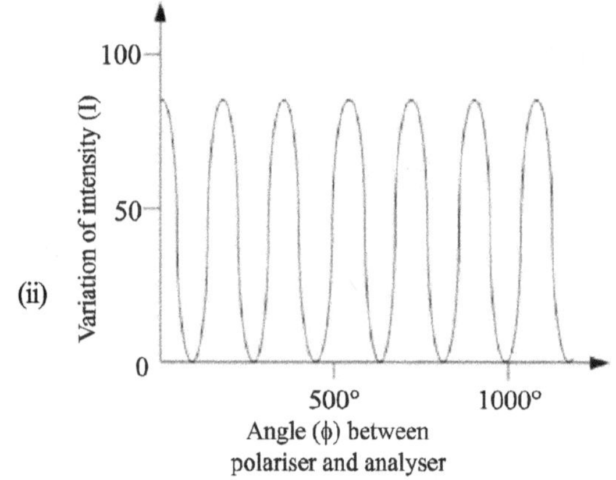

(1 Mark)

(iii) According to the Brewster law
Refractive index $\mu = \tan i_p$ where i_p is the polarising angle
$$\mu = \tan 60° = \sqrt{3}$$
The refractive index of the material is 1.73. **(1 Mark)**

15. An equipotential surface is that surface at every point of which, the electric potential is the same. **(½ Mark)**
(i) Equipotential surface in case of single point charge.

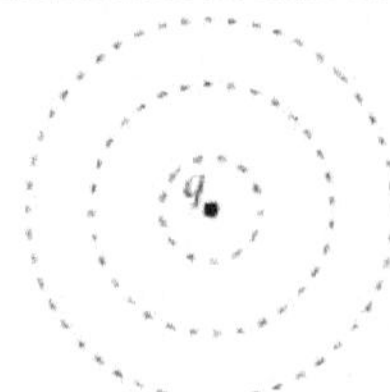

(½ Mark)

(ii) Equipotential surface in a constant electric field in z-direction.

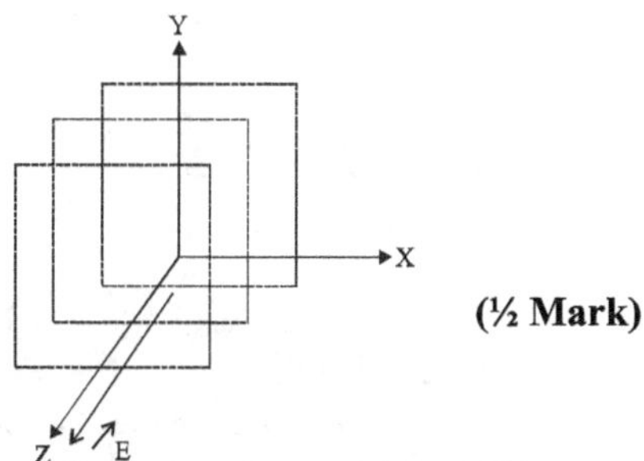

(½ Mark)

As electric field due to a single change is not constant so equipotential surfaces about a single charge are not equidistant. **(½Mark)**

(iii) No, if the electric field exists along tangential to an equipotential surface, a charged particle will experience a force along the tangential line and can move along it. As a charged particle can move only due to the potential difference (along the direction of change of potential), this contradicts the concept of an equipotential surface. **(1 Mark)**

16. Let these be a current carrying loop of radius R. Current flowing through the loop is I_0.

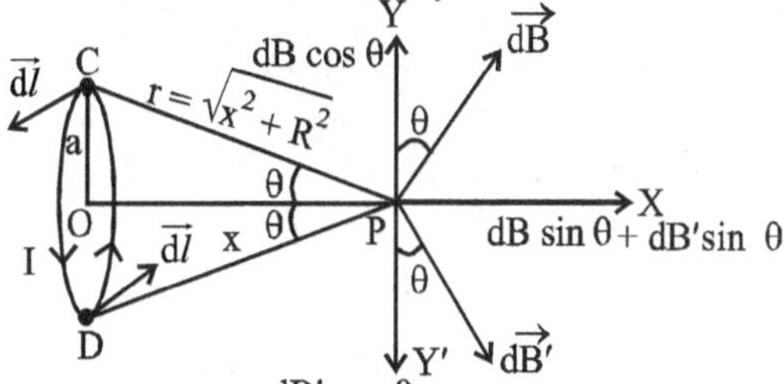

Consider two small elements of coil of length dl each, at C and D diametrically opposite to each other.

$PC = PD = r$

$$= \sqrt{R^2 + x^2} \text{ and } \angle CPO = \angle DPO = \theta$$

Magnetic field at P due to current element dl at C

$$dB = \frac{\mu_0}{4\pi} \cdot \frac{Idl\sin 90°}{r^2} [\theta = 90°]$$

$$dB = \frac{\mu_0}{4\pi} \cdot \frac{Idl}{r^2} = \frac{\mu_0}{4\pi} \cdot \frac{Idl}{(R^2 + x^2)}$$ **(½ Mark)**

Direction of dB is along PE perpendicular to CP.

Magnetic field at P due to current element dl at

$$D = dB' = \frac{\mu_0}{4\pi} \cdot \frac{Idl\sin 90°}{r^2} = \frac{\mu_0}{4\pi} \cdot \frac{Idl}{(R^2 + x^2)}$$

acting along PF $\perp$ DP.

$$\therefore \quad dB = dB' = \frac{\mu_0}{4\pi} \cdot \frac{Idl}{(R^2 + x^2)}$$ **(½Mark)**

Resolving dB and dB' in rectangular components,

(i) $dB\cos\theta$ along PY and $dB\sin\theta$ along PX

(ii) $dB'\cos\theta$ along PY' and $dB'\sin\theta$ along PX

Cosine components being equal and opposite will cancel each other.

Total magnetic field at P due to current through the whole circular coil.

$$B = \int dB\sin\theta = \int \frac{\mu_0\, Idl\sin\theta}{4\pi(R^2 + x^2)}$$ **(½Mark)**

$$= \frac{\mu_0 I\sin\theta}{4\pi(R^2 + x^2)} \int dl \left[\because \sin\theta = \frac{R}{\sqrt{R^2 + x^2}}\right.$$

$$\left. \text{and } \int dl = 2\pi a\right]$$

$$B = \frac{\mu_0 I}{4\pi(R^2 + x^2)} \cdot \frac{R}{(R^2 + x^2)^{1/2}} \cdot 2\pi a$$

$$= \frac{\mu_0 IR^2}{2(R^2 + x^2)^{3/2}} \text{ along PX}$$ **(1 Mark)**

If there are n number of turns of the coil,

$$B = \frac{\mu_0 nIR^2}{2(R^2 + x^2)^{3/2}} = \frac{\mu_0}{4\pi} \cdot \frac{2nIA}{x^3} = \frac{\mu_0}{4\pi} \cdot \frac{2M}{x^3}$$ **(½Mark)**

[Here A = πR^2 = area of the coil and x >> R

Figure showing magnetic field lines due to a circular wire carrying current I.

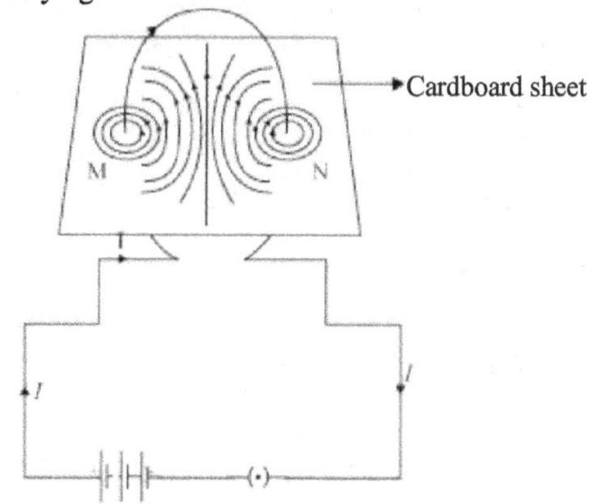

17. A **wavefront** is defined as the continuous locus of all the particles of a medium which are vibrating in the same phase. **(1 Mark)**

Huygens's Principle is based on the following assumptions:

(i) Each point on the primary wavefront acts as a source of secondary wavelets, sending out disturbances in all directions in a similar manner as the original source of light does.

(ii) The new position of the wavefront at any instant (called secondary wave front) is the envelope of the secondary wavelets at that instant. **(1 Mark)**

Diagram showing how the incident wavefront traverses through the lens.

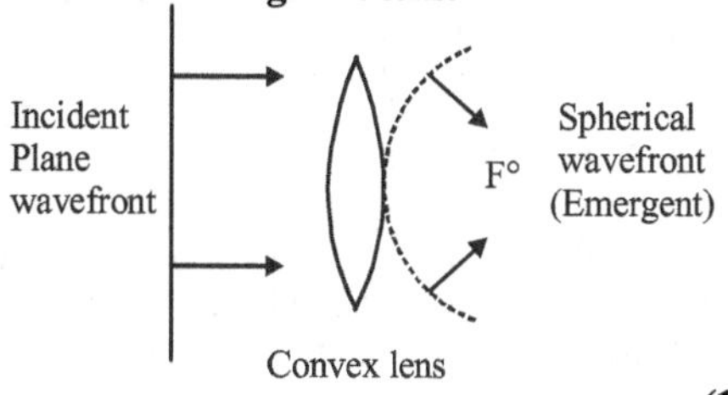

(1 Mark)

OR

(i) Frequency (ν) and wavelength (λ) of light are related as

$$\nu = \frac{v}{\lambda}$$

where v is the velocity of light. As the wave travels from one medium to another, the wavelength of light changes changing the speed of light with it. The frequency remains constant. **(1 Mark)**

(ii) No, as the energy of wave depends only on its frequency. Since the frequency does not change as wave travels from one medium to another, therefore, the energy of the wave remains same and does not decrease. **(1 Mark)**

(iii) In photon picture of light, the intensity of light is determined by the number of photons. **(1 Mark)**

Note

When light is incident on matter, the interaction between light with atoms of matter give rise to reflection and refraction. Thus, atoms may be viewed as oscillators, which take up the frequency of incident light causing forced oscillations. The frequency of light emitted by atomic oscillator equals its frequency of oscillation. Thus frequency of reflected and refracted light remains same.

18. Given: Output voltage, $V_O = 2\,V$, output resistance, $R_O = 2\,k\Omega$, base resistance, $R_i = 1\,k\Omega$
Current amplification factor, $\beta = 100$
Then input signal voltage is calculated as :

$$\frac{V_o}{V_i} = \frac{R_o}{R_i} \times \beta \Rightarrow \frac{2}{V_i} = \frac{2}{1} \times 100 \quad \Rightarrow V_i = 10\,mV \text{ (1 Mark)}$$

Now, collector current $I_C = \dfrac{V_o}{R_o} = \dfrac{2}{2} = 1\,mA$ **(1 Mark)**

Therefore, base current $I_B = \dfrac{I_C}{\beta} = \dfrac{1mA}{100} = 10\mu A$

(1 Mark)

19. (i) (a) Microwaves (b) X-rays **(1 Mark)**
(ii) As the capacitor is connected to the battery, the electrons start moving towards the plate connected to the negative terminal of the battery and electrons leave from the plate connected to the positive terminal of the battery. This happens until the potential of the capacitor becomes equal to that of the battery. As this happens very quickly, the charging current produces a deflection. The reverse process is repeated for discharging that is the charge is lost. As the galvanometer can be considered as a resistance, the circuit behaves like a R-C circuit having time constant equal to RC. Hence the expression governing this observation is

$$q = q_0\left(1 - e^{-\frac{t}{RC}}\right) \qquad \textbf{(2 Marks)}$$

20. (i) Sky wave: The sky waves reach the reciever after reflection from the ionosphere. The oscillating electric field of electromagnetic wave changes the velocity of the electrons in the ionosphere which changes the

effective dielectric constant and hence refractive index. **(1½ Marks)**

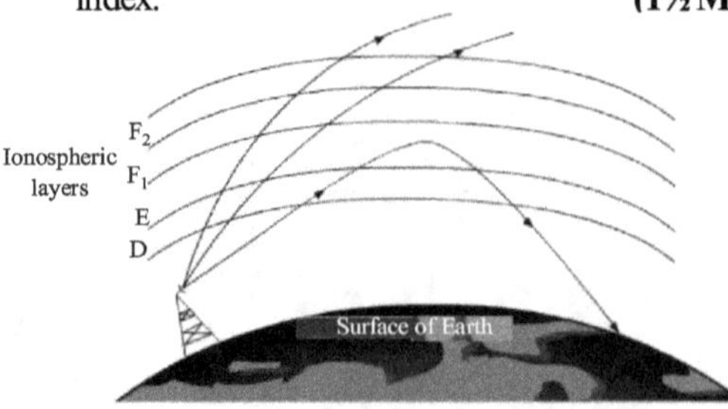

In a single reflection from the ionosphere, the radio-waves cover a distance of not less than 4000 km. In this way, a very long distance communication is possible with the help of sky waves.

(ii) The ionosphere acts as a reflector for a certain range of frequencies (1710 kHz to 40 MHz). Waves above 40 MHz get refracted through ionosphere and escape. This is why there is an upper limit to the frequency used in this mode. **(1½ Marks)**

21. (i) When a P-type semiconductor is suitably joined to an N-type semiconductor, then resulting arrangement is called P-N junction or P-N junction diode.

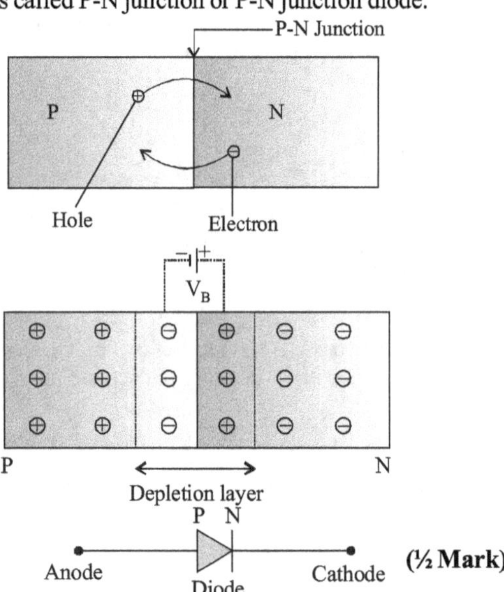

(½ Mark)

Depletion region : On account of difference in concentration of charge carriers in the two sections of P-N junction, the electrons from N-region diffuse through the junction into P-region and the hole from P region diffuse into N-region.

Due to diffusion, neutrality of both N and P-type semiconductor is disturbed. *A layer of negative charged ions appear near the junction in the P-crystal and a layer of positive ions appears near the junction in N-crystal. This layer is called depletion region or layer.* **(½ Mark)**

Potential barrier : *The potential difference created across the P-N junction due to the diffusion of electrons and holes is called potential barrier.*
For Ge $V_B = 0.3$ V and for silicon $V_B = 0.7\,V$
On an average the potential barrier in P-N junction is ~ 0.5 V and the width of depletion region $\sim 10^{-6}$m. **(½ Mark)**

(ii) The circuit diagram for a half wave rectifier is shown below:

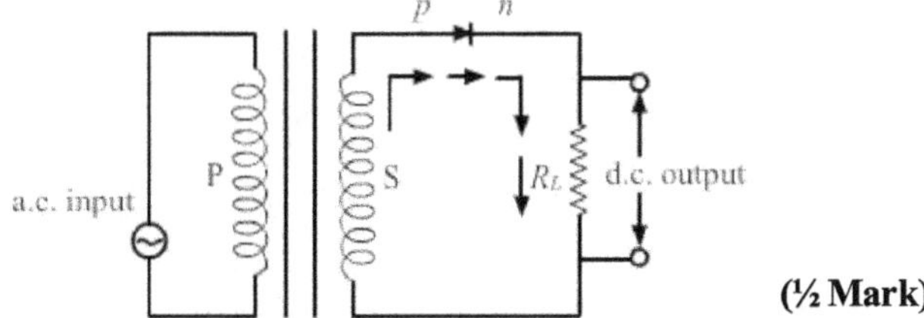

(½ Mark)

Working : During the positive half cycle of the input a.c., the p-n junction is forward biased i.e., the forward current flows from p to n and the diode offers a low resistance path to the current. Thus, we get output across-load **i.e.,** a.c input will be obtained as d.c output.

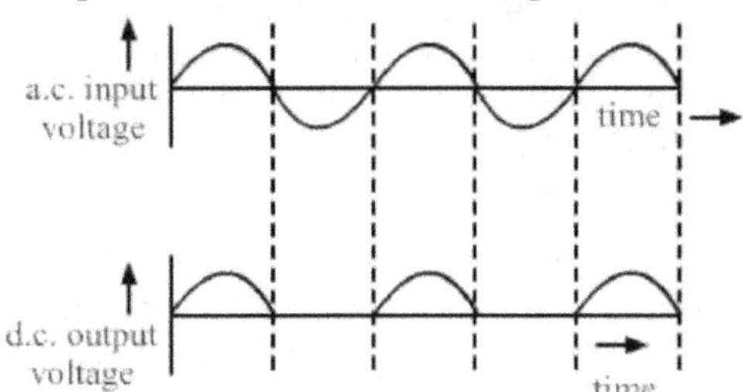

(½ Mark)

During the negative half cycle of the input a.c., the p-n junction is reversed biased *i.e.,* the reverse current flows from n to p, the diode offers a high resistance path to the current. Thus, we get no output across-load. **(½ Mark)**

> **Note**
>
> (i) *The thickness of depletion layer is 1 micron = $10^{-6}m$.*
>
> (ii) *Width of depletion layer $\propto \dfrac{1}{\text{Dopping}}$*
>
> (iii) *Depletion is directly proportional to temperature.*
>
> (iv) *The P-N junction diode is equivalent to capacitor in which the depletion layer acts as a dielectric.*

22. The average power supplied by the source over a complete cycle is given as
$P = VI \cos \phi$
where, $\cos \phi$ is the power factor. **(1 Mark)**
For pure inductive circuit, the phase difference between current and voltage is $\dfrac{\pi}{2}$ $\therefore \cos\phi = \cos\dfrac{\pi}{2} = 0$
Therefore, the average power supplied by the source over a complete cycle is zero. **(1 Mark)**

(ii) If an iron rod is inserted in the inductor, then the value of inductance L increases. So, voltage drop across inductor increases which results in decrease in voltage across bulb. Due to which, the current through the bulb will decrease, thus, decreasing the brightness of the bulb. **(1 Mark)**

SECTION - D

23. (a) **Principle of a dynamo:** A dynamo or generator is a device which converts mechanical energy into electrical energy. It is based on the principle of electromagnetic induction. **(1 Mark)**

Working: A dynamo includes a coil attached to a small turbine fitted with a plastic cap. The coil is placed in a magnetic field. When the plastic cap comes in contact with moving tyres of the bicycle, the coil placed between the poles of a magnet rotates, thus the flux through the coil changes continuously. This induces a current in the coil which is connected to a bulb which lights up. As long as the bicycle is moving, the coil keeps on rotating, and hence, the flux keeps on changing. At a steady rate, we get a steady current and hence a light of steady intensity. **(2 Marks)**

(b) The qualities shown by Ram are inquisitive and observing. The qualities shown by the teacher are: responsible as a teacher, and knowledgeable. **(1 Mark)**

SECTION - E

24. (i) Consider a spherical surface of radius R. The refractive indexes at left and right of the surface are μ_1 and μ_2 respectively.

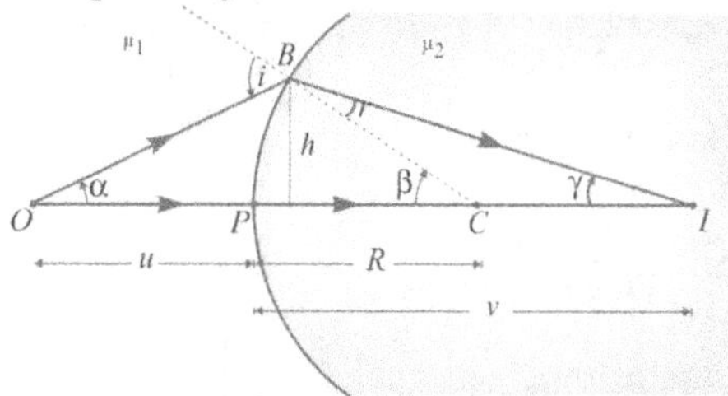

Let an object O be placed at a distance u from pole P of the surface in a medium of refractive index μ_1. Ray OP, incident normally, passes into the second medium without deviation. Ray OB, making an angle α with the principal axis, is incident at an angle i with the normal and is refracted at an angle r. These rays intersect at I at a distance v to the right of pole P. Thus I is the real image of the object O. **(1 Mark)**

From the triangles OBC and IBC, we have
$i = \alpha + \beta$
and $\beta = r + \gamma$ or $r = \beta - \gamma$
From Snell's law

$$\dfrac{\mu_2}{\mu_1} = \dfrac{\sin i}{\sin r} \text{ or } \mu_1 \sin i = \mu_2 \sin r$$

For small angle of incidence i, we can write
$\sin i \simeq i$ and $\sin r \simeq r$
Thus $\mu_1 i = \mu_2 r$
or $\mu_1 (\alpha + \beta) = \mu_2 (\beta - r)$ ...(i)
As i is small, and so α, β and γ are also small. Thus
$(\alpha + \beta) = \tan\alpha + \tan\beta$

$$= \dfrac{h}{-u} + \dfrac{h}{+R} \text{ and } (\beta - \gamma) = \dfrac{h}{R} - \dfrac{h}{v}$$

On substituting these values in equation (i), we have

$$\mu_1 \left[\dfrac{h}{-u} + \dfrac{h}{+R} \right] = \mu_2 \left[\dfrac{h}{R} - \dfrac{h}{v} \right]$$

After simplifying, we get

$$\dfrac{\mu_2}{v} - \dfrac{\mu_1}{u} = \dfrac{\mu_2 - \mu_1}{R}$$ **(1 Mark)**

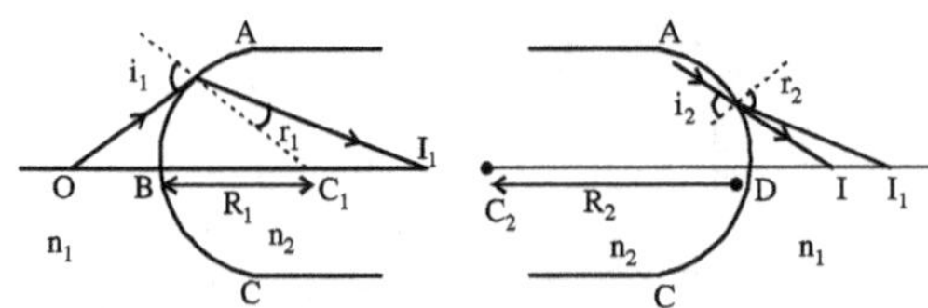

Applying relation, $\dfrac{\mu_2}{v} - \dfrac{\mu_1}{v} = \dfrac{\mu_2 - \mu_1}{R}$ on face ADC we get

$$\dfrac{-\mu_2}{DI_1} + \dfrac{\mu_1}{DI} = \dfrac{\mu_2 - \mu_1}{DC_2} \qquad \text{......(1)}$$

Applying same relation, on face ABC we get

$$\dfrac{\mu_1}{OB} + \dfrac{\mu_2}{BI_1} = \dfrac{\mu_2 - \mu_1}{BC_1} \qquad \text{......(2)}$$

Adding (1) and (2) and $BI_1 = DI_1$

$$\dfrac{\mu_1}{OB} + \dfrac{\mu_2}{DI} = (\mu_2 - \mu_1)\left[\dfrac{1}{BC_1} + \dfrac{1}{DC_2}\right] \qquad \textbf{(1 Mark)}$$

Here $OB \to \infty$

$DI \to f$

$BC_1 = +R_1$

$DC_2 = -R_2$

$$\therefore \quad \dfrac{\mu_1}{f} = (\mu_2 - \mu_1)\left[\dfrac{1}{R_1} - \dfrac{1}{R_2}\right]$$

$$\dfrac{1}{f} = (\mu_{21} - 1)\left[\dfrac{1}{R_1} - \dfrac{1}{R_2}\right] \Rightarrow \text{lens maker formula.}$$

(1 Mark)

(ii) Using the relation, $\dfrac{n_2}{v} - \dfrac{n_1}{u} = \dfrac{n_2 - n_1}{R}$

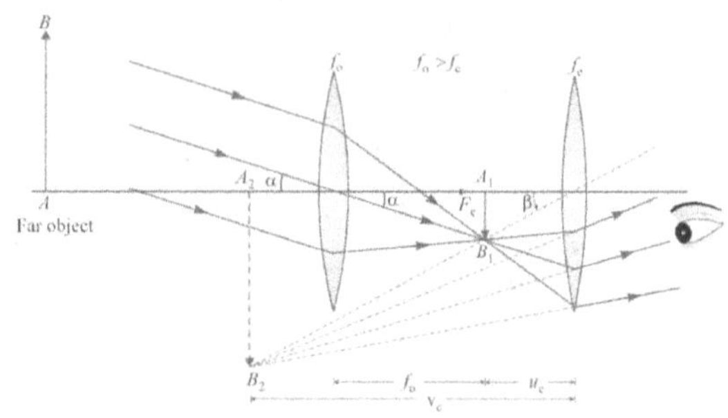

$$\Rightarrow \quad \dfrac{1.5}{V} - \dfrac{1}{(-100)} = \dfrac{1.5-1}{20} = \dfrac{1}{40}$$

$$\Rightarrow \quad \dfrac{1.5}{V} - \dfrac{1}{40} - \dfrac{1}{100} = \dfrac{5-2}{200} = \dfrac{3}{200}$$

$$\Rightarrow \quad v = \dfrac{1.5 \times 200}{3} = 100\,\text{cm}$$

Hence, the image is formed at 100 cm in the denser medium.

(1 Mark)

OR

(a) A ray diagram to obtain the real image formed by an astronomical telescope in normal adjustment position. Consider a distant object AB. Its real inverted image A_1B_1 is formed at focal point of the objective. This image becomes object for eyepiece, which finally forms virtual image A_2B_2. **(2 Marks)**

(2 Marks)

Magnifying power or angular magnification of an astronomical telescopoe is defined as the ratio of the angle subtended at the eye by the final image to the angle subtended at the eye, by the object directly, when the final image and the object, both are at infinity.

Angular magnification,

$$M = \dfrac{\text{angle subtended by image }(\beta)}{\text{angle subtended by object at eye }(\alpha)}$$

For distant object, the angle forms by object at objective lens is nearly same as that at eye, and so

$$M = \dfrac{\beta}{\alpha}$$

From the figure, $\dfrac{\beta}{\alpha} = \dfrac{-A_1B_1/(-u_e)}{-A_1B_1/f_o} = -\dfrac{f_o}{u_e}$

$$\therefore \quad M = -\dfrac{f_o}{u_e} \qquad \text{...(i)}$$

For eye piece; $u = -u_e,\ v = v_e,\ f = +f_e.$

By lens formula, $\dfrac{1}{v} - \dfrac{1}{u} = \dfrac{1}{f}$, we have

$$\dfrac{1}{-v_e} - \dfrac{1}{-u_e} = \dfrac{1}{f_e} \quad \text{or} \quad \dfrac{1}{u_e} = \dfrac{1}{f_e} + \dfrac{1}{v_e} = \dfrac{1}{f_e}\left(1 + \dfrac{f_e}{v_e}\right)$$

From equation (i), we have $M = -\dfrac{f_o}{f_e}\left(1 + \dfrac{f_e}{v_e}\right)$ ...(ii)

(1 Mark)

(b) (i) Lens with smallest power or largest focal length should be used as the objective i.e. lens with power 0.5 D.

Lens with largest power or smallest focal length should be used as the eye-piece i.e. lens with power 10 D. **(1 Mark)**

(ii) The aperture is preferred to be large so that the telescope can collect as much light coming from the distant object as possible. **(1 Mark)**

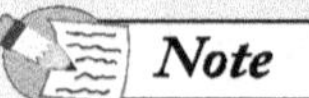 **Note**

Magnifying power of telescope $M = \dfrac{-f_0}{f_e}\left(1 + \dfrac{f_e}{v_e}\right)$

If final image is formed at infinity then $v_e = \infty$

$$M = \dfrac{-f_0}{f_e}\left(1 + \dfrac{f_e}{\infty}\right) = \dfrac{-f_0}{f_e}$$

25. Electric fields due to a uniformly charged infinite plane sheet: Suppose a thin non-conducting infinite sheet of uniform surface, charge density σ. **(1 Mark)**

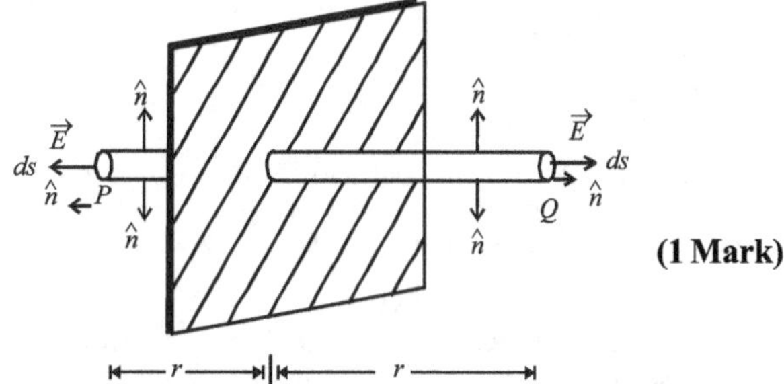

(1 Mark)

Electric field intensity $\vec{E}$ on either side of the sheet must be perpendicular to the plane of sheet having same magnitude at all points from sheets.

Let P be any point at a distance r from the sheet. Let the small area element $\vec{ds} = ds\,\hat{n}$.

$\vec{E}$ and $\hat{n}$ are parallel on the two cylinderical edges P and Q, which contributes electric flux.

∴ Electric flux over the edges P and Q of the cylinder is 2ϕ

$$\Rightarrow \quad 2\oint \vec{E}\cdot \vec{ds} = \frac{q}{\epsilon_0} \quad \Rightarrow \quad 2E\pi\,r^2 = \frac{q}{\epsilon_0}$$

$$E = \frac{q}{2\pi\,\epsilon_0\,r^2} \qquad \textbf{(1 Mark)}$$

Charge density, $\sigma = \dfrac{q}{s} \Rightarrow q = \pi\,r^2\,\sigma$

[Where S – area of circle]

$$E = \frac{\pi r^2 \sigma}{2\pi\,\epsilon_0\,r^2}$$

$$E = \frac{\sigma}{2\,\epsilon_0}, \text{ Vectorically } \vec{E} = \frac{\sigma}{2\,\epsilon_0}\,\hat{n}$$

where $\hat{n}$ is a unit vector normal to the plane and going away from it.

When σ > 0, E is directed away from both sides. Hence electric field intensity is independent of r.

The direction of an electric field for positive charge density is in outward direction and perpendicular to the plane infinite sheet. And for the negative charge density the direction of the field is in inward direction and perpendicular to the sheet. **(1 Mark)**

(ii) According to question, $C_2 = 2C_1$
When the capacitor are connected in parallel the total capactitance will be
$$C_P = C_1 + C_2 = 3C_1$$

Energy stored in the capacitor : $E = \dfrac{1}{2}C_P V_P^2 = \dfrac{3C_1 V_P^2}{2}$

(½ Mark)

When the capacitor are connected in series the total capacitance will be
$$\frac{1}{C_s} = \frac{1}{C_1} + \frac{1}{C_2} \Rightarrow C_s = \frac{2C_1}{3}$$

Energy stored in the capacitor : $E = \dfrac{1}{2}C_s V_s^2 = \dfrac{C_1 V_s^2}{3}$

(1 Mark)

According to the question
$$\frac{3C_1 V_P^2}{2} = \frac{C_1 V_s^2}{3}$$

$$\therefore \quad \frac{V_P}{V_s} = \frac{\sqrt{2}}{3} \qquad \textbf{(1 Mark)}$$

OR

(a) We are given two similar large plates separated by a small distance (d) and having area (A).

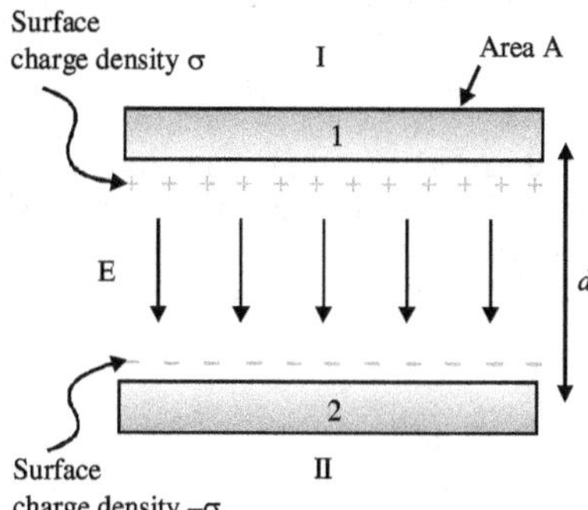

(½ Mark)

Let charge on each plate be Q
Surface charge density of plate 1, σ = Q/A, and that of plate 2 is –σ.
Electric field in different regions :
Outer region I,

$$E = \frac{\sigma}{2\varepsilon_0} - \frac{\sigma}{2\varepsilon_0} = 0 \qquad \textbf{(½ Mark)}$$

Outer region II,

$$E = \frac{\sigma}{2\varepsilon_0} - \frac{\sigma}{2\varepsilon_0} = 0 \qquad \textbf{(½ Mark)}$$

In the inner region between plates 1 and 2, the electric fields due to the two charged plates add up. So,

$$E = \frac{\sigma}{2\varepsilon_0} + \frac{\sigma}{2\varepsilon_0} = \frac{\sigma}{\varepsilon_0} = \frac{Q}{\varepsilon_0 A}$$

The direction of electric field is form the positive to the negative plate. **(½ Mark)**

(b) For uniform electric field, potential difference is simply the electric field multiplied by the distance between the plates,

$$i.e., \quad V = Ed = \frac{1}{\varepsilon_0}\frac{Qd}{A} \qquad \textbf{(½ Mark)}$$

(c) Capacitance C of the parallel plate capacitor,

$$C = \frac{Q}{V} = \frac{Q}{\dfrac{Qd}{\varepsilon_0 A}} = \frac{\varepsilon_0 A}{d} \qquad \textbf{(½ Mark)}$$

(ii) We know that the potential of the metallic sphere is given by,

$$V = \frac{Q}{4\pi\varepsilon_0 r} \text{ whee “}r\text{” is the radius of the sphere.}$$

Now, the potential of the metallic sphere of radius R is given by,

$$V_R = \frac{Q}{4\pi\varepsilon_0 R} = \frac{\sigma(4\pi R^2)}{4\pi\varepsilon_0 R}$$

$$V_R = \frac{\sigma R}{\varepsilon_0} \qquad ...(i) \qquad \textbf{(1 Mark)}$$

Similarly, the potential of the metallic sphere of radius 2R is given by,

$$V_{2R} = \frac{Q}{4\pi\varepsilon_0 2R} \Rightarrow V_{2R} = \frac{\sigma(4\pi(2R)^2)}{4\pi\varepsilon_0 2R}$$

$$V_{2R} = \frac{\sigma 2R}{\varepsilon_0} \qquad ...(ii)$$

From the relation (i) and (ii) it is very clear that $V_{2R} > V_R$ so, when both the spheres are connected the charge flow from the sphere of radius 2R to R. **(1 Mark)**

26. A labelled diagram of a Step-down transformer

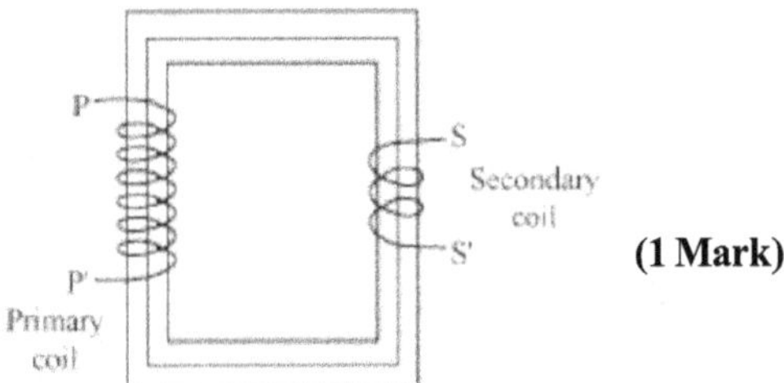

(1 Mark)

Principle : A transformer is based on the principle of electromagnetic mutual induction, *i.e.*, whenever the amount of magnetic flux linked with a coil changes, an e.m.f. is induced in the neighbouring coil. **(1 Mark)**
Working : Alternating emf is supplied to the primary coil PP', the resulting current induces a current in secondary coil. Magnetic flux linked with primary is also linked with the secondary. The induced emf in each turn of the secondary is equal to that induced in each turn of the primary.
Let, E_p - alternating emf applied to primary and n_p - number of turns in the primary

$\dfrac{d\phi}{dt}$ - Rate of change of flux through each turn of primary coil

$$\therefore \quad E_p = n_p \frac{d\phi}{dt} \qquad ...(i)$$

E_s - alternating emf of secondary and n_s - number of turns in secondary

$$\therefore \quad E_s = n_s \frac{d\phi}{dt} \qquad ...(ii)$$

Dividing equation (ii) by (i),

$$\frac{E_s}{E_p} = \frac{n_s}{n_p} = k \text{ (transformation ratio)} \qquad \textbf{(½ Mark)}$$

For step-up transformer, $K > 1 \therefore E_s > E_p$
For step-down transformer, $K < 1 \therefore E_s < E_p$ **(½ Mark)**

(ii) Turn ratio, $n = \dfrac{N_s}{N_p} = \dfrac{E_s}{E_p}$ **(½ Mark)**

(iii) In an ideal transformer
Input electrical power = Output electrical power

$$E_p I_p = E_s I_s \therefore \frac{E_s}{E_p} = \frac{I_p}{I_s}$$

$$\frac{I_p}{I_s} = \frac{E_s}{E_p} = \frac{N_s}{N_p} \Rightarrow \frac{I_p}{I_s} = n \qquad \textbf{(½ Mark)}$$

(iv) Given, $V_s = 110V, P = 550\,W, V_p = 220\,V, I_p = ?$
Power, $P = V_p I_p$

$$\therefore \quad I_p = \frac{P}{V_P} = \frac{550}{220} = 2.5A \qquad \textbf{(1 Mark)}$$

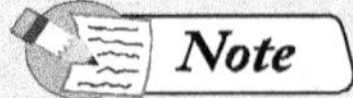 **Note**

A transformer does not violate the law of conservation of energy. If transformer changes a low-voltage into a high voltage then current is reduced by the same proportion.

OR

(a) **Mutual Inductance:** Consider two coils (Primary and secondary) placed very near to each other. Let N_1 and N_2 be the number of turns in the coils and i_1 be the current flowing in the first coil.
Let, due to this current, the magnetic flux linked with each turn of the secondary coil be ϕ_2. If N_2 be the number of turns in the secondary coil, then the number of flux-linkages in the coil will be $N_2\phi_2$. This number is proportional to the current i_1 flowing in the primary coil, *i.e.*,
$N_2\phi_2 \propto i_1$ or $N_2\phi_2 = Mi_1$, **(1 Mark)**
where M is a constant called the **'coefficient of mutual induction'** or **'mutual inductance'** between the two coils.
Mutual Inductance of two concentric coils, one of radius R_1 and the other of radius R_2 $(R_1 < R_2)$ placed coaxially with centres coinciding with each other:

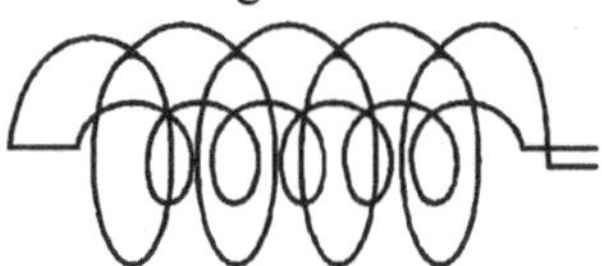

Let the number of turns in the primary and secondary coils be N_1 and N_2 respectively and the current in the primary be i_1 ampere. The magnetic field at the centre of primary coil is

$$B = \frac{\mu_0 N_1 i_1}{2R_1} \qquad \textbf{(1 Mark)}$$

where R_1 is the radius of the primary coil. Considering this magnetic field uniform over the entire surface area of the secondary coil, the magnetic-flux passing through the secondary coil is $\phi_2 = BA$

where $A = \pi R_2^2$ is the area of the secondary coil. Substituting for B in this equation, we get

$$\phi_2 = \frac{\mu_0 N_1 i_1}{2R_1} \times \pi R_2^2 \qquad \textbf{(1 Mark)}$$

Now, according to definition, the mutual inductance between the coils is

$$M = \frac{N_2\phi_2}{i_1} \quad \therefore \quad M = \frac{\mu_0 N_1 N_2 \pi R_2^2}{2R_1} \qquad \textbf{(1 Mark)}$$

(b) We know that flux $\phi = N\,B\,A\cos\theta$
And induced emf

$$e = -\frac{d\phi}{dt} = \left(-NBA(-\sin\theta)\frac{d\theta}{dt}\right)\left\{\frac{d\theta}{dt} = \omega = 2\pi f\right\}$$

$$= NBA\sin\theta\,(2\pi f)$$

For maximum induced emf
$\sin\theta = 1$

$$\therefore \quad e_{max} = NBA \times 1 \times (2\pi f) = NBA\,(2\pi f) \ \textbf{(1 Mark)}$$

Delhi *2016*

CBSE Board Solved Paper

Time Allowed : 3 Hours   *Maximum Marks : 70*

General Instructions:

(i)   There are **26** questions in all. All questions are compulsory.

(ii) This question paper has **five** sections: Section **A**, Section **B**, Section **C**, Section **D** and Section **E.**

(iii) Section **A** contains **five** questions of **one** mark each, Section **B** contains **five** questions of **two** marks each, Section **C** contains **twelve** questions of **three** marks each, Section **D** contains **one** value based question of **four** marks and Section **E** contains **three** questions of **five** marks each.

(iv) There is no overall choice. However, an internal choice has been provided in **one** question of **two** marks, **one** question of **three** marks and all the **three** questions of **five** marks weightage. You have to attempt only **one** of the choices in such questions

(v)   You may use the following values of physical constants wherever necessary:

$c = 3 \times 10^8$ m/s

$h = 6.63 \times 10^{-34}$ Js

$e = 1.6 \, 10^{-19}$ C

$\mu_0 = 4\pi \times 10^{-7}$ Tm A^{-1}

$\varepsilon_0 = 8.854 \times 10^{-12}$ C^2 N^{-1} m^{-2}

$$\frac{1}{4\pi\varepsilon_0} = 9 \times 10^9 \text{N m}^2 \text{C}^{-2}$$

Mass of electron $(m_e) = 9.1 \times 10^{-31}$ kg

Mass of neutron $= 1.675 \times 10^{-27}$ kg

Mass of proton $= 1.673 \times 10^{-27}$ kg

Avogadro's number $= 6.023 \times 10^{23}$ per gram mole

Boltzmann constant $= 1.38 \times 10^{-23}$ JK^{-1}

SECTION - A

1.   A point charge $+Q$ is placed at point O as shown in the figure. Is the potential difference $V_A - V_B$ positive, negative or zero?

$+Q$
$\overset{\bullet}{O} \text{-----------------------} \overset{\bullet}{A} \text{------------} \overset{\bullet}{B}$

2.   How does the electric flux due to a point charge enclosed by a spherical gaussian surface get affected when its radius is increased ?

3.   Write the underlying principle of a moving coil galvanometer.

4.   Why are microwaves considered suitable for radar systems used in aircraft navigation?

5.   Define 'quality factor' of resonance in series LCR circuit. What is its SI units?

SECTION - B

6.   Explain the terms (i) Attentuation and (ii) Demodulation used in communication.

7.   Plot a graph showing variation of de-Broglie wavelength λ versus $\dfrac{1}{\sqrt{V}}$, where V is accelerating potential for two particles A and B carrying same charge but of masses m_1, m_2 $(m_1 > m_2)$. Which one of the two represents a particle of smaller mass and why?

8.   A nucleus with mass number $A = 240$ and $B.E/A = 7.6$ MeV breaks into two fragments each of $A = 120$ with $B.E/A = 8.5$ MeV. Calculate the energy released.

OR

Calculate the energy in fusion reaction:

$$^2_1\text{H} + {}^2_1\text{H} \longrightarrow {}^3_2\text{He} + n,\ \text{where } B.E.\ \text{of } {}^2_1\text{H} = 2.23 \text{ MeV}$$

and of $^3_2\text{He} = 7.73$ MeV.

9. Two cells of emfs 1.5 V and 2.0 V having internal resistance 0.2 Ω and 0.3 Ω respectively are connected in parallel. Calculate the emf and internal resistance of the equivalent cells.

10. State Brewster's law.

   The value of Brewster angle for a transparent medium is different for light of different colours. Give reason.

11. A charge is distributed uniformly over a ring of radius 'a'. Obtain an expression for electric intensity E at a point on the axis of ring. Hence show that for points at large distances from ring, it behaves like a point charge.

12. Write three characteristic features in a photoelectric effect which cannot be explained on the basis of wave theory of light, but can be explained only using Einstein's equation.

13. (i) Write the expression for the magnetic force acting on a charged particle moving with velocity in the presence of magnetic field B.

   (ii) A neutron, an electron and an alpha particle moving with equal velocities, enter a uniform magnetic field going into the plane of paper as shown. Trace their paths in the field and justify your answer.

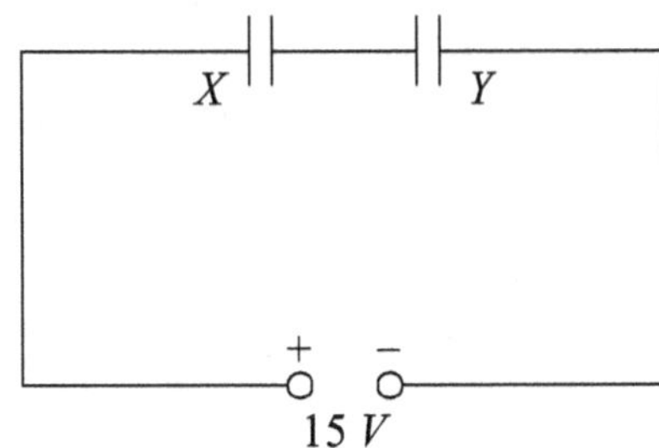

14. (i) Define Mutual Inductance.

   (ii) A pair of adjacent coils has a mutual inductance of 1.5 H. If the current in one coil changes from 0 to 20 A in 0.5 s, what is the change of flux linkage with the other coil?

15. Two parallel plate capacitor X and Y have the same area of plates and same separation between them. X has air between the plates while Y contains a dielectric medium $\varepsilon_r = 4$.

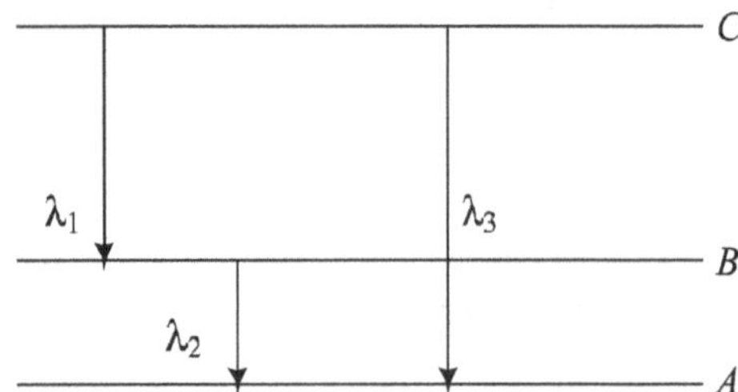

   (i) Calculate the capacitance of each capacitor if equivalent capacitance of the combination is 4 µF.

   (ii) Calculate the potential difference between the plates of X and Y.

   (iii) Estimate the ratio of electrostatic energy stored in X and Y.

16. Two long straight parallel conductors carry steady current I_1 and I_2 separated by a distance d. If the currents are flowing in the same direction, show how the magnetic field set up in one produces an attractive force on the other. Obtain the expression for this force. Hence define one ampere.

17. How are em waves produced by oscillating charges? Draw a sketch of linearly polarized em waves propagating in z-direction. Indicate the directions of the oscillating electric and magnetic fields.

OR

Write Maxwell's generalization of Ampere's Circuital law. Show that in the process of charging a capacitor, the current produced within plates of the capacitor is

$$i = \varepsilon_0 \frac{d\varphi_E}{dt}$$

where φ_E is the electric flux produced during charging of the capacitor plates.

18. (a) Explain any two factors which justify the need of modulating a low frequency signal.

   (b) Write two advantages of frequency modulation over amplitude modulation.

19. (i) Write the function of three segments of a transistor.

   (ii) Draw the circuit diagram for studying the input and output characteristics of n-p-n transistor in common emitter configuration. Using the circuit, explain how input, output characteristics are obtained.

20. (a) Calculate the distance of an object of height 'h' from a concave mirror of radius of curvature 20 cm, so as to obtain a real image of magnification 2. Find the location of image also.

   (b) Using a mirror formula, explain why does a convex mirror always produce a virtual image.

21. (i) State Bohr's quantization condition for defining stationary orbits. How does de-Broglie hypothesis explain the stationary orbits?

   (ii) Find the relation between the three wavelengths of λ_1, λ_2 and λ_3 from energy level diagram shown below.

22. Draw a schematic ray diagram of reflecting telescope showing how rays coming from a distant object are received at the eye-piece. Write its two important advantages over a refracting telescope.

SECTION - D

23. Meeta's father was driving her to school. At the traffic signal she noticed that each traffic light was made of many tiny lights instead of a single bulb. When Meeta asked this question to her father, he explained the reason for this.

Answer the following questions based on above information:

(i) What were the values displayed by Meeta and her father?

(ii) What answer did Meeta's father give?

(iii) What are the tiny lights in traffic signals called and how do these operate?

SECTION - E

24. (i) An a.c. source of voltage $V = V_0 \sin \omega t$ is connected to a series combination of LCR. Use the phasor diagram to obtain expressions for impedance of the circuit and phase angle between voltage and current. Find the condition when current will be in phase with the voltage. What is the circuit in this condition called?

(ii) In a series LR circuit $X_L = R$ and power factor of the circuit is P_1. When capacitor with capacitance C such that $X_L = X_C$ is put in series, the power factor becomes P_2. Calculate P_1/P_2.

OR

(i) Write the function of transformer. State its principle of working with the help of a diagram. Mention various energy losses in this device.

(ii) The primary coil of an ideal step up transformer has 100 turns and transformation ratio is also 100. The input voltage and power are respectively 220 V and 1100 W. Calculate

(a) number of turns in secondary coil

(b) current in primary

(c) voltage across secondary

(d) current in secondary

(e) power in secondary

25. (i) In Young's double slit experiment, deduce the condition for (a) constructive and (b) destructive interfence at a point on the screen. Draw a graph showing variation of intensity in the interference pattern against position 'x' on the screen.

(ii) Compare the interference pattern observed in Young's double slit experiment with single slit diffraction pattern, pointing out three distinguishing features.

OR

(i) Plot the graph to show the variation of angle of deviation as a function of angle of incidence for light passing through prism. Derive an expression for refractive index of the prism in terms of angle of minimum deviation and angle of prism.

(ii) What is the dispersion of light? What is its cause?

(iii) A ray of light incident normally on one face of right isosceles prism is totally reflected as shown in fig. What must be the minimum value of refractive index of glass? Give relevant calculations.

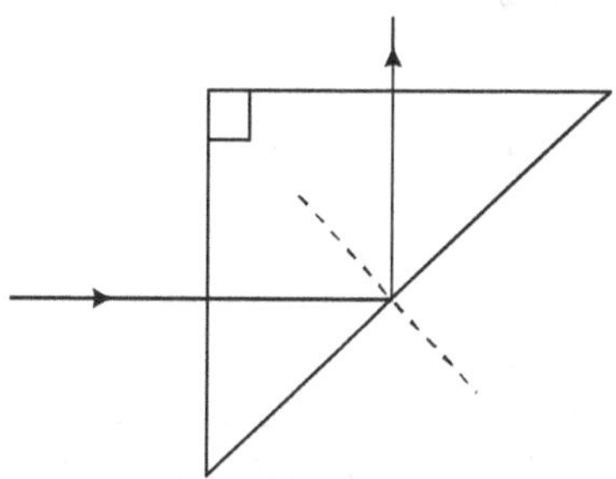

26. (i) Define the term drift velocity.

(ii) On the basis of electron drift, derive an expression for resistivity of a conductor in terms of number density of free electron and relaxation time. On what factors does resistivity of a conductor depend?

(iii) Why alloys like constantan and manganin are used for making standard resistors?

OR

(i) State the working principle of a potentiometer.

(ii) In the following potentiometer circuit AB is a uniform wire of length 1 m and resistance 10 Ω. Calculate the potential gradient along the wire and balance length $AO\,(=l)$.

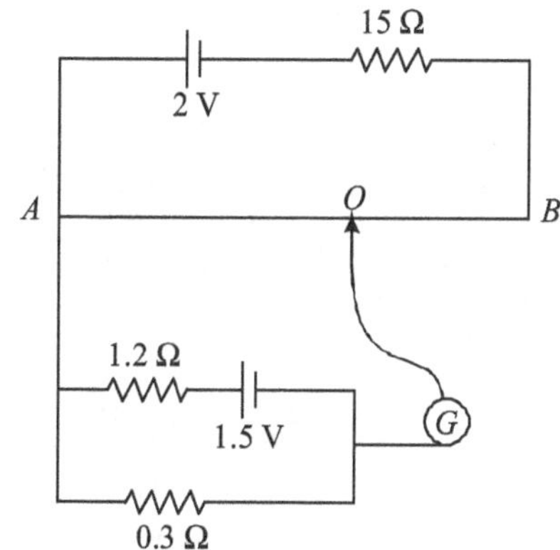

Solutions

1. Potential difference between two points in an electrostatic field is the amount of work in moving a unit +ve charge from one point to another against field.

Here, $V_A > V_B$ as we are moving charge (unit + ve charge) in the direction of field.

So $V_A - V_B = $ positive. **(1 Mark)**

Note

If instead of +Q charge, there was –Q charge at point O, then $V_B > V_A$ and hence

$$V_A - V_B = negative.$$

2. According to Gauss's law, electric flux through a gaussian surface is

$$\phi = \frac{q_{nc}}{\varepsilon_0} \qquad ...(i)$$

where q = charge enclosed by gaussian surface.

As we see from, eqn (i) the flux is independent of radius of spherical gaussian surface. So, electric flux would remain unchanged, when the radius of spherical gaussian surface is increased. **(1 Mark)**

3. *Principle of moving coil galvanometer: A* current carrying coil placed in a magnetic field experiences a current dependent torque, which tends to rotate the coil and produces angular deflection. **(1 Mark)**

4. Due to their short wavelength, microwaves are not diffracted or bent by objects of normal dimensions. So, microwaves are considered suitable for radar system used in aircraft navigation. **(1 Mark)**

5. The quality factor Q defined by

$$Q = \frac{\omega_o L}{R} = \frac{1}{\omega_o CR} \qquad \textbf{(½ Mark)}$$

is an indicator of the sharpness of resonance, the higher value of Q indicating sharper peak in the current.

Quality factor Q is unitless. **(½ Mark)**

Note

The resonance phenomenon occur when $X_L = X_C$ in a RLC circuit. For resonance to occur, the presence of both L and C elements in circuit is a must. With only one of these (L or C) elements, there is no possibility of voltage cancellation and hence no resonance is possible.

6. *Attentuation:* The loss of strength of a signal while propagating through a medium is known as attentuation.

Demodulation: The process of retrieval of information from the carrier wave at the receiver is termed as demodulation. This the reverse process of modulation.**(1 + 1 = 2 Marks)**

7. De-Broglie wavelength of a charged particle accelerating in potential V is

$$\lambda = \frac{h}{\sqrt{2mqV}} \qquad ...(i)$$

where q = charge of particle
m = mass of particle
From eqn (i), we can write,

$$\frac{\lambda}{\left(1/\sqrt{V}\right)} = \frac{h}{\sqrt{2mq}}$$

$$\Rightarrow \quad \frac{\lambda}{\left(1/\sqrt{V}\right)} \propto \frac{1}{\sqrt{m}} \qquad \textbf{(½ Mark)}$$

The graph between λ and $\dfrac{1}{\sqrt{V}}$ will be a straight line with

$$\text{Slope} = \frac{h}{\sqrt{2mq}}.$$

Since charge of particles is same,

$$\therefore \qquad \text{Slope} \propto \frac{1}{\sqrt{m}}$$

Given that $m_1 > m_2$, particle with mass m_2 will have greater slope. **(1 Mark)**

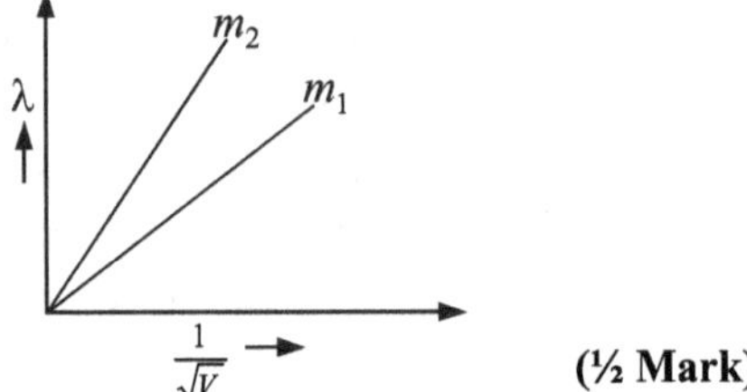

(½ Mark)

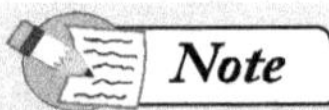

Note

When an electron is accelerated from rest through a potential V, the kinetic energy of an electron is equal to work done on electron by electric field.

$$\Rightarrow \qquad \frac{1}{2} mv^2 = eV$$

$$since \qquad p = mv$$

$$\therefore \qquad \frac{1}{2} m \left(\frac{p^2}{m^2}\right) = eV$$

$$p = \sqrt{2meV}$$

de-Broglie wavelength $\quad \lambda = \dfrac{h}{p}$

$$\therefore \qquad \lambda = \frac{h}{\sqrt{2meV}}.$$

8. Energy released = *B.E.* of daughter nuclei − *B.E.* of nuclei parent

B.E. | *A* for nucleus of *A* = 240 = 7.6 MeV

∴ *B.E.* for nucleus of *A* = 240 = 7.6 × 240

$\qquad$ = 1824 MeV $\qquad$ **(½ Mark)**

B.E. | *A* for nucleus of *A* = 120 = 8.5 MeV

∴ *B.E.* for nucleus of *A* = 120 = 8.5 × 120

$\qquad$ = 1020 MeV $\qquad$ **(½ Mark)**

Energy released = 2 × 1020 − 1824

$\qquad$ = 216 MeV. $\qquad$ **(1 Mark)**

 *Note*

The binding energy (per nucleon) curve show that exothermic nuclear reactions are possible, when two light nuclei fuse into nuclei with intermediate mass. However, for fusion, the light nuclei must have sufficient initial energy to overcome the coulomb potential barrier. That is why fusion requires very high temperatures.

OR

Total *B.E.* of reactants = 2 × 2.23

$\qquad$ = 4.46 MeV $\qquad$ **(½ Mark)**

Total *B.E.* of product = 7.73 MeV. $\qquad$ **(½ Mark)**

Energy released or fusion energy = *B.E.* of product − *B.E.* of reactants

$\qquad$ = 7.73 − 4.46

$\qquad$ = 3.27 MeV. $\qquad$ **(1 Mark)**

9. Given,

$$\varepsilon_1 = 1.5 V \quad r_1 = 0.2\,\Omega$$
$$\varepsilon_2 = 2.0 V \quad r_2 = 0.3\,\Omega$$

equivalent emf of cells connected in parallel is

$$\varepsilon_{eq} = \frac{\varepsilon_1 r_2 + \varepsilon_2 r_1}{r_1 + r_2}$$

$$= \frac{1.5 \times 0.3 + 2.0 \times 0.2}{0.2 + 0.3}$$

$$\varepsilon_{eq} = \frac{0.45 + 0.40}{0.5}$$

$$\varepsilon_{eq} = 1.7 V \qquad \textbf{(1 Mark)}$$

Equivalent internal resistance when cells are connected in parallel is

$$r_{eq} = \frac{r_1 r_2}{r_1 + r_2} = \frac{0.2 \times 0.3}{0.2 + 0.3}$$

$$r_{eq} = \frac{0.06}{0.5}$$

$$r_{eq} = 0.12\,\Omega \qquad \textbf{(1 Mark)}$$

10. The angle of incidence at which a beam of unpolarised light falling on a transparent surface is reflected as a beam of completely plane polarised light is called Brewster angle. It is denoted by i_p.

The Brewster's law states that the tangent of the polarising angle or Brewster angle i_p, of a transparent medium is equal to its refractive index.

$$\mu = \tan i_p \qquad \textbf{(1 Mark)}$$

Since refractive index (μ) of a transparent medium is different for different colours, hence Brewster angle is different for different colours. $\qquad$ **(1 Mark)**

SECTION - C

11.

Suppose that the ring is placed with its plane perpendicular to the *x*-axis as shown in figure.

Electric field $d\vec{E}$ due to charge element dq at point p, r distance from ring is

$$d\vec{E} = \frac{1}{4\pi\varepsilon_0} \frac{dq}{r^2}$$

Let λ = linear charge density

∴ $\qquad \lambda = \dfrac{dq}{dl}$

where dl = line element on ring

so $\qquad d\vec{E} = \dfrac{1}{4\pi\varepsilon_0} \dfrac{\lambda dl}{r^2} \qquad$ **(1 Mark)**

As show in figure, the field $d\vec{E}$ has two components, the axial component $dE\cos\theta$ and the perpendicular component $dE\sin\theta$.

Since perpendicular components of any two diametrically opposite element are equal and opposite, they will cancel out in pairs. Only the axial components will add up to produce the resultant field $\vec{E}$ at point *P*, which is given by,

$$E = \int_0^{2\pi a} dE\cos\theta$$

$$E = \int_0^{2\pi a} \frac{1}{4\pi\varepsilon_0} \frac{\lambda dl}{r^2} \times \frac{x}{r} \quad (\because \cos\theta = \frac{x}{r})$$

$$E = \frac{1}{4\pi\varepsilon_0} \frac{\lambda x}{r^3} \int_0^{2\pi a} dl$$

$$E = \frac{1}{4\pi\varepsilon_0} \frac{\lambda x}{r^3} [l]_0^{2\pi a}$$

$$E = \frac{1}{4\pi\varepsilon_0} \frac{\lambda x}{r^3} (2\pi a)$$

Now $\qquad \lambda = \dfrac{\text{Total charge } Q}{\text{Perimeter of ring} = 2\pi a}$

Also $\qquad r^2 = x^2 + a^2$ (from pythagorous thm.)

∴ $\qquad r^3 = (x^2 + a^2)^{3/2}$

∴ $\qquad E = \dfrac{1}{4\pi\varepsilon_0} \dfrac{Qx}{(x^2 + a^2)^{3/2}} \times \dfrac{(2\pi a)}{2\pi a}$

$$E = \frac{1}{4\pi\varepsilon_0} \frac{Qx}{(x^2 + a^2)^{3/2}} \qquad \textbf{(1 Mark)}$$

At large distance $x \gg a$,

$\therefore \qquad\qquad x^2 + a^2 \approx x^2$

So, E will become

$$E = \frac{1}{4\pi\varepsilon_0} \frac{Qx}{(x^2)^{3/2}}$$

$$E = \frac{1}{4\pi\varepsilon_0} \frac{Q}{x^2} \qquad \textbf{(1 Mark)}$$

which is electric field due to a point charge.

12. The three basic features in photoelectric effect which cannot be explained by wave theory but by using Einsteins equation are:-

(i) The photoelectric emission is an instantaneous process

(ii) There exists a threshold frequency for every metal below which emission does not take place.

(iii) The maximum kinetic energy of photoelectrons is independent of the intensity of incident radiation.

$$\textbf{(1 × 3 = 3 Marks)}$$

13. (i) The magnetic force acting on a charged particle 'q' moving with velocity 'v' in the presence of magnetic field $\vec{B}$ is,

$$\vec{F} = q\,(\vec{v} \times \vec{B})$$

$$\vec{F} = q\,v\,B \sin\theta$$

where θ = angle between $\vec{v}$ and $\vec{B}$. $\qquad$ **(1 Mark)**

(ii)

Since neutron is uncharged particle, it will have no effect due to $\vec{B}$ and will go in straight line undeflected.

The direction of α-particle (+ve charge) is given by either Fleming's left hand rule or right hand thumb rule. The direction of electron (–ve charge) will be opposite to that of α-particle (+ve charge). $\qquad$ **(1 Mark)**

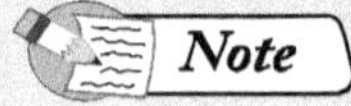

Magnetic force $\vec{F} = (\vec{V} \times \vec{B})q$, is perpendicular to the velocity of the charged particle. A force on a particle does work if the force has a component along the direction of motion of the particle. Therefore, magnetic force does no work on charge particle as magnetic force produces displacement perpendicular to the force.

14. (i) A changing current in one coil (coil 1) can induce an emf in a nearby coil (coil 2). This relation is given by,

$$\varepsilon_2 = -M_{21} \frac{dI_1}{dt}$$

The quantity M_{21} is called mutual inductance of coil 2 with respect ot coil 1.

S.I. unit of mutual inductance is Henry H. $\qquad$ **(1 Mark)**

(ii) Given

$$M = 1.5\,\text{H}$$
$$dI_1 = 0 \text{ to } 20\,\text{A}$$
$$dt = 0.5 \text{ seconds.}$$

Induced emf in other coil is

$$\varepsilon_2 = -M \frac{dI_1}{dt} \qquad \text{...(i)} \ (\textbf{½ Mark})$$

From Faraday's law of electromagnetic induction

$$\varepsilon = \frac{-d\phi}{dt} \qquad \text{...(ii)} \ (\textbf{½ Mark})$$

where $d\phi$ = change in flux.

From eqn (i) and (ii)

$$\frac{-d\phi_2}{dt} = -M \frac{dI_1}{dt}$$

$$d\phi_2 = M\,dI_1$$

$$= 1.5\,(20 - 0)$$

$$d\phi_2 = 30 \text{ weber} \qquad \textbf{(1 Mark)}$$

15. (i) Given $\qquad C_{eq} = 4\mu\text{F}$

Dielectric constant of medium between plates of $y = 4$.

$\therefore$ capacitance of y will by $C_y = 4C \qquad \{\because C = KC_0\}$

and capacitance of $x \Rightarrow C_x = C$

equivalent capacitance in series is

$$\frac{1}{C_{eq}} = \frac{1}{C_x} + \frac{1}{C_y}$$

$$\frac{1}{4} = \frac{1}{C} + \frac{1}{4C}$$

$$\frac{1}{4} = \frac{4+1}{4C} = \frac{5}{4C}$$

$$C = 5\,\mu\text{F}$$

$\therefore \qquad C_x = 5\,\mu\text{F}$

$\qquad\qquad C_y = 4 \times 5 = 20\,\mu\text{F} \qquad \textbf{(1 Mark)}$

(ii) In series total charge on capacitor plates is same for all the capacitors in series.

$\therefore \qquad$ Total charge $Q = C_{eq}\,\text{V}$

$\qquad\qquad\qquad V = 15\,\text{V (given)}$

$\Rightarrow \qquad\qquad Q = 4\,\mu\text{F} \times 15\,\text{V}$

$\qquad\qquad\qquad Q = 60\,\mu\text{C}$

Potential difference across capacitor x

$$V_x = \frac{Q}{C_x} = \frac{60}{5} = 12\text{V}$$

Potential difference across a capacitor C_y

$$V_y = \frac{Q}{C_y} = \frac{60}{20} = 3\text{V} \qquad \textbf{(1 Mark)}$$

(ii) Electrostatic energy stored in capacitor is

$$E = \frac{Q^2}{2C}$$

$$\therefore \qquad E_x = \frac{Q^2}{2C_x} \text{ and } E_y = \frac{Q^2}{2C_y}$$

$$\frac{E_x}{E_y} = \frac{Q^2/2C_x}{Q^2/2C_y} = \frac{C_y}{C_x}$$

$$\frac{E_x}{E_y} = \frac{20}{5}$$

so $\qquad E_x : E_y = 4 : 1.$ **(1 Mark)**

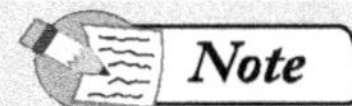

Note

From the question, we see that the potential difference between the plates of capacitor is very small (3 V or 12 V). This is because the capacitor is configured in such a way that it confines the electric field lines within a small region of space. Thus, even though electric field may have considerable strength, the potential difference between the two plates (or conductor) is very small.

16. d = distance between conductor 1 and 2
F_{21} = Force on conductor 1 due to B_1.

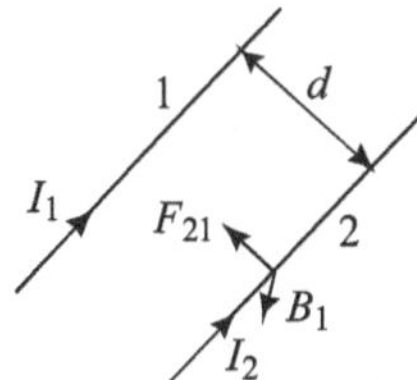

Consider two long parallel conductors 1 and 2 separated by distance d and carrying current I_1 and I_2, respectively. The conductor '1' produces same magnetic field B_1 at all points along the conductor '2'. The right hand thumb rule (or screw rule) tell us that the direction of this field is dawnward.

The magnetic field, due to current in conductor 1 I_1, enclosed in amperian loop $2\pi d$ is

$$B_1 = \frac{\mu_0 I_1}{2\pi d} \text{ (From Ampere's law)}$$

(½ Mark)

The conductor 2 carrying current I_2 will experience *a* force due to B_1 which will be

$$\vec{F}_{21} = I_2 \left[\vec{L} \times \vec{B}_1 \right] \qquad \textbf{(½ Mark)}$$

where $\qquad L$ = length of conductor.

From screw rule or right hand rule for vector or cross product, the direction of F_{21} is side ways such that conductor 1 attracts conductor 2. Hence force F_{21} is attractive.

From fig, angle between L and B is 90°.

$$\therefore \qquad F_{21} = I_2 L B_1 \sin 90°$$
$$F_{21} = I_2 L B_1$$

or $\qquad F_{21} = I_2 L \left[\frac{\mu_0 I_1}{2\pi d} \right]$

$$F_{21} = \frac{\mu_0 I_1 I_2 L}{2\pi d} \qquad \textbf{(1 Mark)}$$

Defination of one Ampere:- The ampere is the value of that steady current which, when maintained in each of two very long, straight, parallel conductors of negligible cross-section, and placed one metre apart in vacuum, would produce on each of these conductors a force eual to 2×10^{-7} newtons per meter of length. **(1 Mark)**

17. When a charge oscillates with some frequency, it produces an oscillating electric field in space, which produces an oscillating magnetic field, which in turn, produces oscillating electric field and so on. Thus, the oscillating electric and magnetic field regenerate each other as the wave propagates through the space. This is how em waves are produced.

(1½ Mark)

The direction of oscillating electric field $\vec{E}$ and magnetic field $\vec{B}$ are perpendicular to each other and also perpendicular to the direction of propagation of em waves.

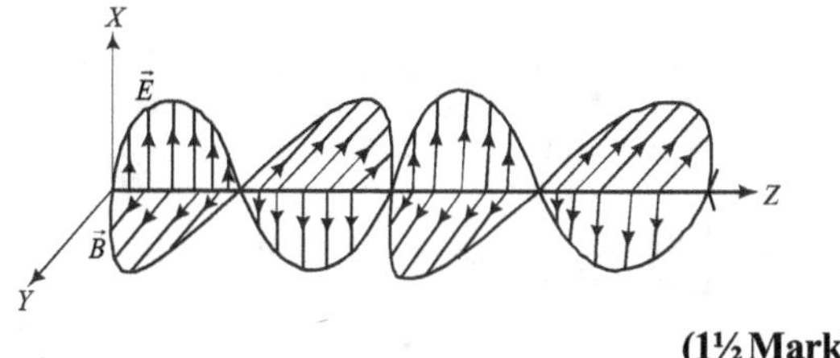

(1½ Mark)

OR

Maxwell's generalisation of Ampere's circuital law is that the total current passing through any surface of which the closed loop is the perimeter is the sum of the conduction current and the displacement current.

$$\oint \vec{B} \cdot \vec{dl} = \mu_0 i_c + \mu_0 \varepsilon_0 \frac{d\phi_E}{dt} \qquad \textbf{(1 Mark)}$$

where $\qquad i_C$ = conduction current

$$\frac{\varepsilon_0 d\phi_E}{dt} = i_D = \text{displacement current.}$$

We know that during the charging of capacitor, there develops an electric field $\vec{E}$ which is

$$E = \frac{Q}{\varepsilon_0 A} \qquad \textbf{(½ Mark)}$$

between the plates having area A and charge Q. Therefore electric flux between plates of capacitor,

$$\phi_E = \vec{E} \cdot \Delta \vec{S}$$
$$= E A$$

$$\phi_E = \frac{Q}{\varepsilon_0 A} \times A \qquad \textbf{(½ Mark)}$$

Since during charging the charge on plates is changing with time, there is a current $i = \dfrac{dQ}{dt}$.

$$\frac{d\phi_E}{dt} = \frac{1}{\varepsilon_0} \frac{dQ}{dt} = \frac{1}{\varepsilon_0} i$$

$$\therefore \qquad i = \varepsilon_0 \frac{d\phi_E}{dt} \qquad \textbf{(1 Mark)}$$

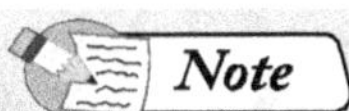

Another way to ask this question.

Q. Considering the case of a parallel plate capacitor being charged, show how one is required to generalize the ampere's circuital law to include the term displacement current.

18. (a) A low frequency signal modulation is needed for following reasons:

(i) For effective communication, the minimum height of antenna should be $\dfrac{\lambda}{4}$. So, for low frequency signal, wavelength will be large and hence the height of antenna will be impractically large. So there is a need of translating the information contained in our low frequency signal into high frequency.

(ii) Power radiated by antenna is proportional to $\left(\dfrac{l}{\lambda}\right)^2$. So for low frequency (high wavelength) power radiated would be less. So, the power radiated increases with decreasing λ i.e. increasing frequency.

$$(1 \times 2 = 2 \text{ Marks})$$

(b) The advantages of frequency modulation over amplitude modulation are:

(i) High efficiency can be acheived by frequency modulation

(ii) Frequency modulation produces less noise.

$$(\frac{1}{2} \times 2 = 1 \text{ Mark})$$

Frequency modulation:- To generate a frequency modulated signal, the frequency of carrier wave (radio wave) is changed in accordance with the message signal.

19. (i) (i) *Emitter:* Emitter is of moderate size and heavily doped segment of transistor. Its function is to supply a large number of majority carriers for the current flow through the transistor.

(ii) *Base:* Base is very thin and lightly doped segment of transistor which is in centre of transistor. It controls the movement of charge carries coming from emitter region.

(iii) *Collector:* Collector is moderately doped and large in size. It collects a major portion of the majority carriers supplied by the emitter. $\quad$ $(\frac{1}{2} \times 3 = 1\frac{1}{2}$ **Marks**$)$

(ii)

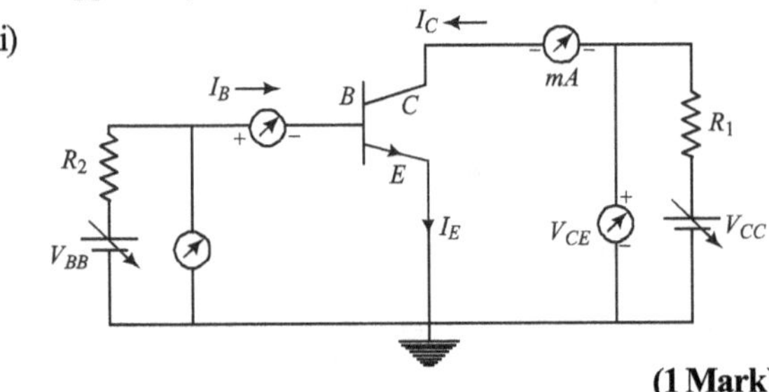

$$(1 \text{ Mark})$$

Input characteristics:- Graph between base current I_B and V_{BE} at constant V_{CE}.

Output characteristics:- Graph between collector current I_C and V_{CE} at constant I_B. $\quad$ $(\frac{1}{2}$ **Mark**$)$

20. (a) Radius of curvature of concave mirror $R = -20$ cm

$$\therefore \text{ Focal length } f = \frac{R}{2} = \frac{-20}{2} = -10 \text{ cm.}$$

Magnification, $m = -2$ $\qquad$ ($\because$ real image)

$$m = \frac{-v}{u} = -2$$

$$\therefore \qquad v = 2u.$$ $\qquad$ **(1 Mark)**

Mirror formula

$$\frac{1}{v} + \frac{1}{u} = \frac{1}{f}$$

where $\qquad v =$ image distance

$\qquad\qquad u =$ object distance

$$\frac{1}{2u} + \frac{1}{u} = \frac{1}{-10}$$

$$\frac{3}{2u} = \frac{1}{-10}$$

$$\therefore \qquad u = -15 \text{ cm}$$

So, $\qquad v = 2u = 2 \times (-15) = -30 \text{ cm.}$

$$(1 \text{ Mark})$$

(b) Mirror formula,

$$\frac{1}{f} = \frac{1}{v} + \frac{1}{u}$$

for a convex mirror f is always $+ve$ and u is always $-ve$.

$$f = +f \quad u = -u$$

$$\therefore \qquad \frac{1}{v} = \frac{1}{f} - \frac{1}{(-u)}$$

$$\frac{1}{v} = \frac{1}{f} + \frac{1}{u}$$

$\therefore$ v will be always $+ve$, hence image is always virtual.

$$(1 \text{ Mark})$$

For mirrors, the magnification is given as

$$m = \frac{-v}{u}.$$

For real and inverted image, m = −ve

For virtual and errect image, m = +ve

21. (i) Bohr's postulate states that the electron revolves around the nucleus only in those orbits for which the angular momentum is some integral multiple of $h/2\pi$ where $h =$ planck's constant. Thus the angular momentum L of the orbiting electron is quantised.

$$L = \frac{nh}{2\pi} \qquad ...(i) \text{ (1 Mark)}$$

de-Broglie wavelength of electron in n^{th} orbit is

$$\lambda = \frac{h}{P}$$

where P is momentum of electron.

For circular orbit angular momentum L

$L = r_n \times P = r_n P \qquad \{\because \theta = 90° \text{ and } \sin 90° = 1\}$

or $\qquad L = \dfrac{r_n h}{\pi} \qquad \qquad ...(ii)$

From *eqn* (i) and (ii)

$$\dfrac{r_n h}{T} = \dfrac{nh}{2\pi}$$

$\Rightarrow \qquad 2\pi r_n = n\lambda \qquad \qquad \textbf{(1 Mark)}$

$\therefore$ Perimeter of permitted stationary orbits are integral multiples of the wavelength λ.

(ii) From Bohr's third postulate, the energy of emitted photon, when electron makes transistion from one orbit to another orbit is given as

$$h\nu = E_i - E_f$$

where ν = frequency of emitted photon.

Also $\nu\lambda = C$ = speed of light.

$\therefore \qquad E_i - E_f = \dfrac{hC}{\lambda}$

From figure,

$E_C - E_B = \dfrac{hC}{\lambda_1} \qquad \qquad ...(i)$

$E_B - E_A = \dfrac{hC}{\lambda_2} \qquad \qquad (ii)$

$E_C - E_A = \dfrac{hC}{\lambda_3} \qquad \qquad ...(iii)$

Add eqn (i) and (ii)

$$E_C - E_B + E_B - E_A = \dfrac{hC}{\lambda_1} + \dfrac{hC}{\lambda_2}$$

$E_C - E_A = \dfrac{hC}{\lambda_1} + \dfrac{hC}{\lambda_2} \qquad ...(iv)$

Equating *eqn* (iv) and (iii), we get

$$\dfrac{hC}{\lambda_3} = \dfrac{hC}{\lambda_1} + \dfrac{hC}{\lambda_2}$$

$\therefore \qquad \dfrac{1}{\lambda_3} = \dfrac{1}{\lambda_1} + \dfrac{1}{\lambda_2} \qquad \textbf{(1 Mark)}$

22.

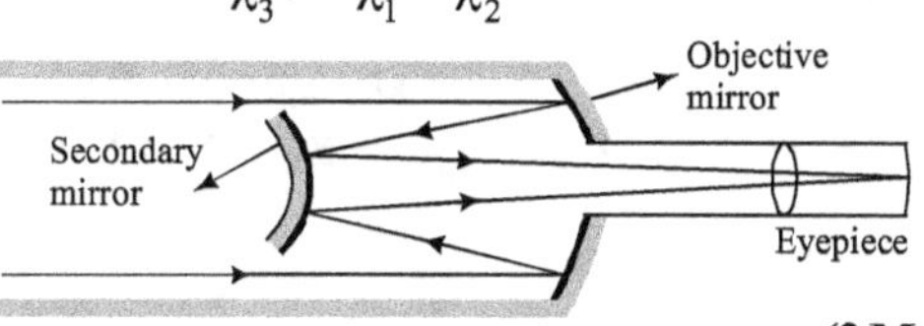

(2 Marks)

Two advantages of reflecting telescope over refractive telescope are:

(i) Reflecting telescope offer large magnifying power than refracting telescope.

(ii) There is no chromatic or spherical aberration in reflecting telescope. **(1 Mark)**

23. (i) *Meeta's values:*- Keen observer, inquistive *Father's values:*- Supporative, encouraging. **(1 Mark)**

(ii) Meeta's father answered that tiny bulbs in traffic lights are a semiconductor device called light emitting diodes (LED). **(1 Mark)**

(iii) Tiny bulbs in traffic bulb are light emitting diode (LED).

LED are diode that operate under forward bias. When the diode is forward biased, electrons are sent from $n \to p$ and holes are sent from $p \to n$. At the junction boundary on either side of junction, excess of minority carriers are there which recombine with majority carriers near junction. On recombination, the energy is released in form of photons of light. **(2 Marks)**

24. (i)

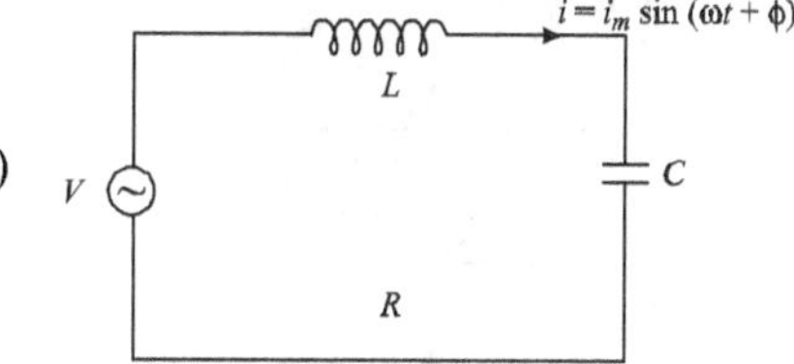

A.C. source of voltage is

$$V = V_0 \sin \omega t$$

Let I be the phasor representing current. Further, let V_L, V_R, V_C and V represent the voltage across the inductor, resistor, capacitor and source. We know, V_R is parallel to I, V_C is $\pi/2$ behind I and V_L is $\pi/2$ ahead of I. So, phase diagram of V_R, V_L, V_C and I is

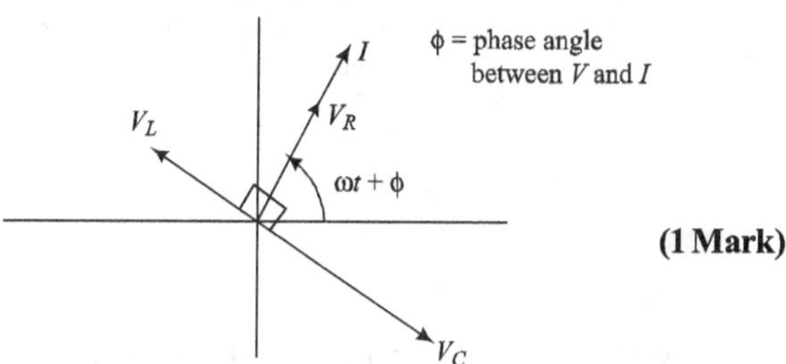

(1 Mark)

Since V_C and V_L are always along same line and in opposite direction, they combine into a single phase $(V_C + V_L)$.

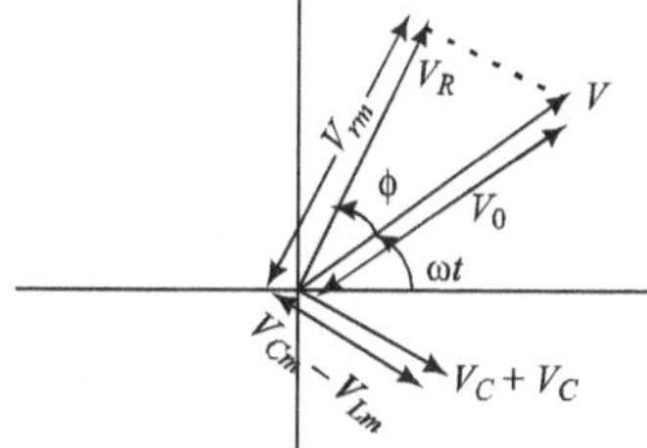

Length of phasors V_R, V_L and V_C is

$$V_R \Rightarrow V_{rm} = i_m R$$
$$V_C \Rightarrow V_{cm} = i_m X_C$$
$$V_L \Rightarrow V_{Lm} = i_m X_L$$

In second phasor diagram, V represents hypotenuse of a right-triangle whose base is V_R and perpendicular is $V_C + V_L$. Therefore, from pythagorean theorem,

$$V_0^2 = V_{rm}^2 + (V_{cm} - V_{Lm})^2$$
$$V_0^2 = i_m^2 R^2 + (i_m X_c - i_m X_L)^2$$
$$V_0^2 = i_m^2 \left[R^2 + (X_c - X_L)^2 \right]$$

$$i_m^2 = \frac{V_0^2}{R^2 + (X_c - X_L)^2}$$

$$i_m = \frac{V_0}{\sqrt{R^2 + (X_c - X_L)^2}}$$

By analogy to ohm's law $I = \dfrac{V}{R}$

Impedance $Z = \sqrt{R^2 + (X_C - X_L)^2}$ **(1 Mark)**

From second phasor diagram, we can write

$$\tan\phi = \frac{V_{cm} - V_{Lm}}{V_{rm}}$$

$$\tan\phi = \frac{i_m X_c - i_m X_L}{i_m R}$$

$$\tan\phi = \frac{X_C - X_L}{R}$$

$$\phi = \tan^{-1}\left(\frac{X_C - X_L}{R}\right)$$

For current and voltage to be in phase

$$X_C = X_L$$
then $\phi = 0$.

This is the condition of resonance when current in the circuit is maximum. **(1 Mark)**

(ii) Power factor is $\cos\phi$, where ϕ is the phase angle between V and I.

$\cos\phi$ can be calculated from phasor diagram.

$$\cos\phi = \frac{Vrm}{V_0}$$

$$\cos\phi = \frac{i_m R}{i_m Z}$$

$$\therefore \quad \cos\phi = \frac{R}{Z}$$

when L and R are connected in series, then

$$Z = \sqrt{X_L^2 + R^2}$$
$$= \sqrt{R^2 + R^2} \qquad [\because X_L = R \text{ given}]$$
$$Z = R\sqrt{2}$$

so power factor $P_1 = \dfrac{R}{R\sqrt{2}} = \dfrac{1}{\sqrt{2}}$ **(½ Mark)**

When $L_1 C$ and R are connected in series, then

$$Z = \sqrt{R^2 + (X_C - X_L)^2}$$
$$Z = R \qquad [\because X_C = X_L \text{ given}]$$

Power factor $P_2 = \dfrac{R}{R} = 1$ **(½ Mark)**

$$\therefore \quad \frac{P_1}{P_2} = \frac{\frac{1}{\sqrt{2}}}{1} = \frac{1}{\sqrt{2}}$$

$$P_1 : P_2 = 1 : \sqrt{2} \qquad \textbf{(1 Mark)}$$

OR

(i) Function of a transformer is to step up voltage change a.c. of low voltage to high voltage or to step down voltage - change a.c of high voltage to low voltage.

(½ Mark)

Working principle of transformer:- It works on the principle of mutual inductance *i.e.* when a changing current is passed through one of the two inductively coupled coils, an induced emf is set up in the other coil. **(1 Mark)**

Energy losses in transformer:-
(1) *Eddy currents:-* The alternating magnetic flux induces eddy current and causes heating in the iron core.
(2) *Flux leakage:-* There is always some flux leakage which means not all of flux due to primary passes through secondary coil. **(1 Mark)**

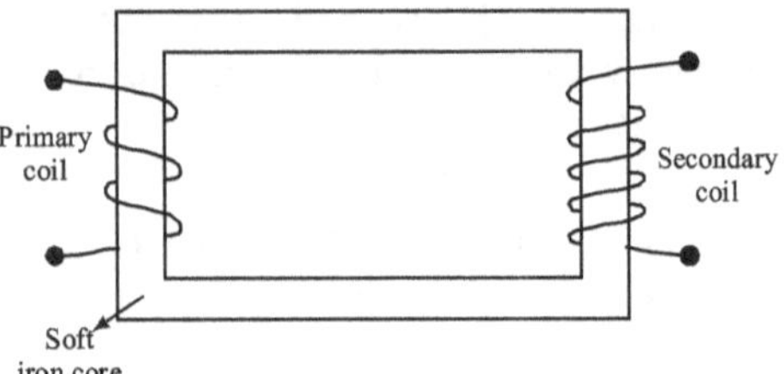

(ii) Given

Number of turns in primary coil $N_p = 100$

Transformation ratio $\dfrac{N_S}{N_P} = 100$

Input voltage/voltage across primary $= 220$ V
Input power/power in primary $= 1100$ w

(a) Number turns in secondary coil N_S,
$$N_S = 100 \times N_p$$
$$= 100 \times 100$$
$$N_S = 10{,}000 \qquad \textbf{(½ Mark)}$$

(b) Power in primary $=$ Voltage across primary $\times$ current in primary
$$\therefore \quad 1100 = 220 \times I_P$$
$$I_P = 5\text{ A} \qquad \textbf{(½ Mark)}$$

(c) Step up transformer *eqn* is
$$\frac{V_S}{V_P} = \frac{N_S}{N_P}$$
$$V_S = \frac{N_S}{N_P} \times V_P$$
$$= 100 \times 220 = 22000 \text{ V}$$
$\therefore$ Voltage accross secondary $V_S = 2.2 \times 10^4$ V
(½ Mark)

(d) Current in secondary
$$\frac{I_P}{I_S} = \frac{N_S}{N_P}$$
$$\frac{5}{I_S} = \frac{N_S}{N_P} = 100$$
$$\therefore \quad I_S = 0.05\text{ A} \qquad \textbf{(½ Mark)}$$

(e) Power in secondary $=$ Power in primary
$$= 1100 \text{ W.} \qquad \textbf{(½ Mark)}$$

 **Note**

A transformer does not violate the law of conservation of energy. If transformer changes a low-voltage into a high voltage then current is reduced by the same proportion.

25. (i)

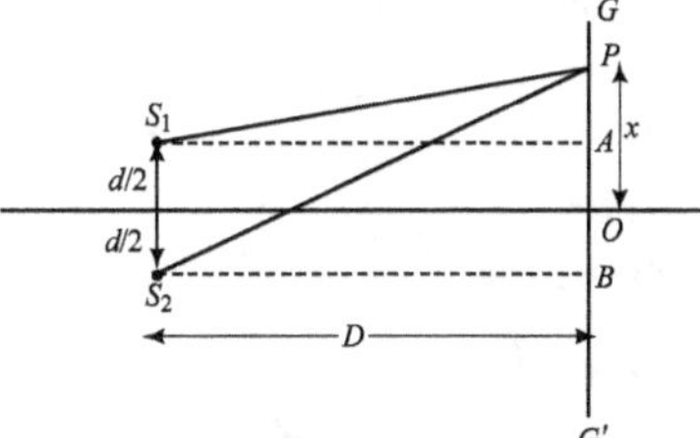

Consider two narrow slit at S_1 and S_2 which act as two coherent sources separated by distanced. Interferences pattern due to waves emanating from S_1 and S_2 are formed at screen GG', D distance away from slit.

Consider a point P on screen which is at x distance from O.

Path difference at $\quad P = S_2P - S_1P$.

From ΔS_2BP, using pythagorean thm.

$$S_2P^2 = S_2B^2 + PB^2 = D^2 + \left(x + \frac{d}{2}\right)^2 \qquad ...(i)$$

and from $\Delta S_1 AP$,

$$S_1P^2 = S_1A^2 + PA^2 = D^2 + \left(x - \frac{d}{2}\right)^2 \qquad ...(ii)$$

So, $S_2P^2 - S_1P^2 = \left[D^2 + \left(x + \dfrac{d}{2}\right)^2\right] - \left[D^2 + \left(x - \dfrac{d}{2}\right)^2\right]$

$$= xd + xd = 2xd \qquad \textbf{(1 Mark)}$$

$$(S_2P + S_1P)(S_2P - S_1P) = 2xd$$

$$(\because (a^2 - b^2) = (a+b)(a-b))$$

In practice the point P lies very close to O, so

$$S_2P \approx S_1P \approx D$$

$\therefore \qquad S_2P + S_1P = 2D$

so $\qquad S_2P - S_1P = \dfrac{2xd}{S_2P + S_1P} = \dfrac{2xd}{2D}$

So path difference $S_2P - S_1P = \dfrac{xd}{D} \qquad \textbf{(1 Mark)}$

For constructive interference,

$$S_2P - S_1P = n\lambda \qquad \text{where } n = 0, 1, 2$$

$\therefore \qquad \dfrac{xd}{D} = n\lambda \qquad \textbf{(½ Mark)}$

$$x_n = \dfrac{n\lambda D}{d} \rightarrow \text{position of bright}$$

fringes on screen.

For destructive interference,

$$S_2P - S_1P = (2n+1)\,\dfrac{\lambda}{2} \quad \text{where } n = 0, 1, 2$$

$\therefore \qquad \dfrac{xd}{D} = (2n+1)\,\dfrac{\lambda}{2}$

$$x_n = (2n+1)\,\dfrac{\lambda D}{2d} \rightarrow \text{position of dark fringes on screen.}$$

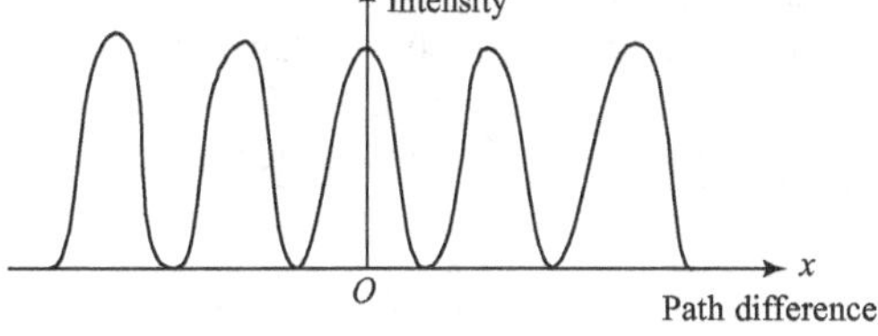

$$\textbf{(½ Mark)}$$

Interference	Diffraction
(i) All bright and dark fringes are of equal width	(i) The width of central maxima is twice the of secondary maxima width
(ii) All bright fringes are of equal intensity.	(ii) Intensity of maxima decreases as we move away from central maxima.
(iii) Bright fringes occur at $\dfrac{\lambda}{a}$, where a is slit width.	(iii) Dark fringe or minima occur at same $\dfrac{\lambda}{a}$ angle.

$$\textbf{(2 Marks)}$$

OR

(i)

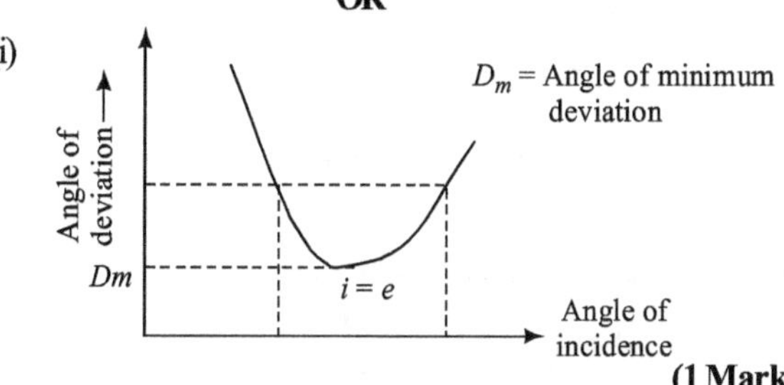

$$\textbf{(1 Mark)}$$

Angle of deviation for a triangular prism, is

$$\delta = i + e - A$$

where i = angle of incidence

$\qquad e$ = angle of emergence

$\qquad A$ = angle of prism $= r_1 + r_2$

From graph we see that,

at $\qquad \delta = Dm \quad i = e$

and $\qquad r_1 = r_2 \Rightarrow A = 2r$

$\therefore \qquad Dm = 2i - A$

or $\qquad i = \dfrac{Dm + A}{2}$

and $\qquad A = r_1 + r_2 = 2r$

where r_1 and r_2 are angle of refractions.

$\therefore \qquad r = \dfrac{A}{2}$

From Snell's law,

refractive index of prism $\mu = \dfrac{\sin i}{\sin r}$

$\therefore \qquad \mu = \dfrac{\sin\left[\dfrac{A + Dm}{2}\right]}{\sin \dfrac{A}{2}} \qquad \textbf{(1 Mark)}$

(ii) Dispersion of light is the phenomenon of splitting of light (white light) into its constituent colour.

We know that refractive index of material depends upon the wavelength (colour) of light. So when white light having 7 different colours or wavelength, they get deviated by different angle of deviation. This is because angle of deviation of prism is dependent on refractive index of material of prism by eqn. **(1 Mark)**

$$\mu = \frac{\sin\left[\dfrac{A + Dm}{2}\right]}{\sin\dfrac{A}{2}}.$$

(iii) As seen from figure, light is incident normally on prism. So its angle of incidence at second refracting surface is 45°. For total internal reflection,

$$i \geq i_C$$

Here $\quad i = 45°$

$\therefore \quad 45° \geq i_C$

or $\quad i_C \leq 45°$

$$\sin i_C \leq \sin 45° \qquad \textbf{(1 Mark)}$$

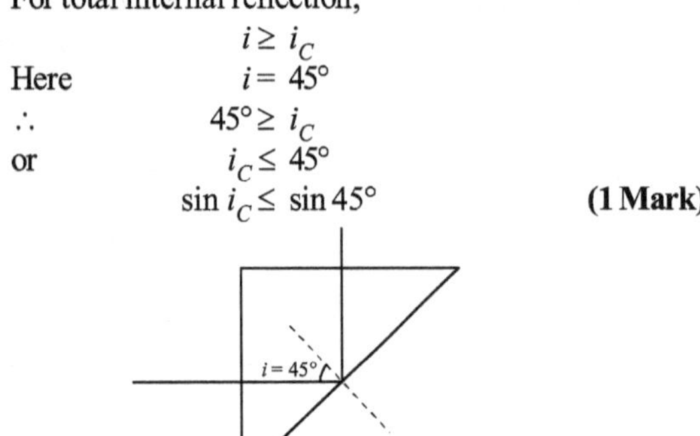

$\therefore \quad \sin i_C \leq \dfrac{1}{\sqrt{2}}$

For total internal reflection,

$$\sin i_C = \frac{1}{\mu}$$

where μ =refractive index of medium

So, $\quad \dfrac{1}{\mu} \leq \dfrac{1}{\sqrt{2}}$

$\Rightarrow \quad \mu \geq \sqrt{2} \qquad \textbf{(1 Mark)}$

$\therefore$ The minimum value of refractive index is $\sqrt{2}$.

26. (i) Drift velocity is defined as average velocity gained by the free electrons of a conductor in the opposite direction of the externally applied electric field.

$$V_d = \frac{-eE\tau}{m} \qquad \textbf{(1 Mark)}$$

where τ = relaxation time

E = applied electric field

(ii) Drift velocity V_d is

$$V_d = \frac{eE\tau}{m}$$

Also, $E = \dfrac{V}{l}$, where V is potential difference applied across a conductor of length 'l'

$\therefore \qquad V_d = \dfrac{eV\tau}{ml} \qquad \text{...(i)}$

If the area of cross-section of the conductor is A and n = number of electrons per unit volume, then current through conductor

$$I = enA\,Vd \qquad \textbf{(1 Mark)}$$

$$I = enA\,\frac{eV\tau}{ml} \qquad \text{(from eq. (i))}$$

$$I = \frac{e^2 nA\tau}{ml}\cdot V$$

$$\frac{V}{I} = \frac{ml}{e^2 nA\tau}$$

From ohm's law, we know

$$\frac{V}{I} = R \text{ (Resistance)}$$

$\therefore \qquad R = \dfrac{ml}{e^2 nA\tau}$

Also, resistance R is

$$R = \rho\,\frac{l}{A}$$

where ρ = resistivity of conductor

$\therefore \qquad \dfrac{ml}{ne^2 A\tau} = \rho\,\dfrac{l}{A}$

$\Rightarrow \qquad \rho = \dfrac{m}{ne^2 \tau} \qquad \textbf{(1 Mark)}$

Resistivity of a conductor depends on

(i) n = number of free electron per unit volume or electron density

(ii) τ = relaxation time, the average time between two successive collisions of an electron. **(1 Mark)**

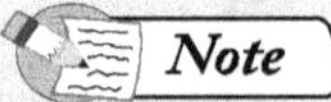

Note

Another way to ask this question is:
Using the concept of drift velocity, deduce ohm's law. Also write the expression for resistivity in terms of number density of free electrons and relaxation time.

(iii) Alloys like constantan or maganin are used for making standard resistances because they have small temperature coefficient. So their resistance does not change appreciably even for several degrees rise of temperature. **(1 Mark)**

OR

(i) *Working principle of potentiometer:* The basic principle of a potentiometer is that when a constant current flows through a wire of uniform cross-section area and composition, the potential drop across any length of the wire is directly proportional to that length. **(2 Marks)**

(ii) Total resistance of potentiometer circuit $= 15 + 10 = 25\,\Omega$

$\therefore$ Current in wire $AB = \dfrac{2}{25} = 0.08\,\text{A}$

So, potential difference across the wire AB, V_{AB}

$V_{AB} = $ current × resistance of wire AB

$\qquad = 0.08 \times 10 = 0.8\,\text{V}.$

Potential gradient $K = \dfrac{V_{AB}}{\text{length of wire}AB}$ **(1½ Marks)**

$$K = \frac{0.8V}{1.0m} = 0.8\,\text{V/m}$$

Now, total resistance of circuit containing cell

$$= 1.2 + 0.3 = 1.5\,\Omega$$

Current in circuit containing cell, $= \dfrac{1.5V}{1.5\Omega} = 1\,\text{A}$

Now potential difference between A and O is equal to potential difference across 0.3 Ω resistor.

$\therefore$ Potential difference between A and O

$$= 1\,A \times 0.3\,\Omega = 0.3\,\text{V}$$

So length of $AO = \dfrac{\text{Potential difference}}{\text{Potential gradient}}$

$$= \frac{0.3}{0.8} = 0.375\,\text{m} = 37.5\,\text{cm}$$

(1½ Marks)

All India *2015*
CBSE Board Solved Paper

Time Allowed : 3 Hours · *Maximum Marks : 100*

General Instructions:

(i) There are **26** questions in all. All questions are compulsory.

(ii) This question paper has **five** sections: Section **A**, Section **B**, Section **C**, Section **D** and Section **E.**

(iii) Section **A** contains **five** questions of **one** mark each, Section **B** contains **five** questions of **two** marks each, Section **C** contains **twelve** questions of **three** marks each, Section **D** contains **one** value based question of **four** marks and Section **E** contains **three** questions of **five** marks each.

(iv) There is no overall choice. However, an internal choice has been provided in **one** question of **two** marks, **one** question of **three** marks and all the **three** questions of **five** marks weightage. You have to attempt only **one** of the choices in such questions

(v) You may use the following values of physical constants wherever necessary:

$c = 3 \times 10^8$ m/s

$h = 6.63 \times 10^{-34}$ Js

$e = 1.6\ 10^{-19}$ C

$\mu_0 = 4\pi \times 10^{-7}$ Tm A^{-1}

$\varepsilon_0 = 8.854 \times 10^{-12}$ C^2 N^{-1} m^{-2}

$\dfrac{1}{4\pi\varepsilon_0} = 9 \times 10^9$ N m^2 C^{-2}

Mass of electron $(m_e) = 9.1 \times 10^{-31}$ kg

Mass of neutron $= 1.675 \times 10^{-27}$ kg

Mass of proton $= 1.673 \times 10^{-27}$ kg

Avogadro's number $= 6.023 \times 10^{23}$ per gram mole

Boltzmann constant $= 1.38 \times 10^{-23}$ JK^{-1}

SECTION - A

1. Draw a graph to show variation of capacitative-reactance with frequency in an a.c. circuit.

2. What is the function of a 'Repeater' used in communication system?

3. The line AB in the ray diagram represents a lens. State whether the lens is convex or concave.

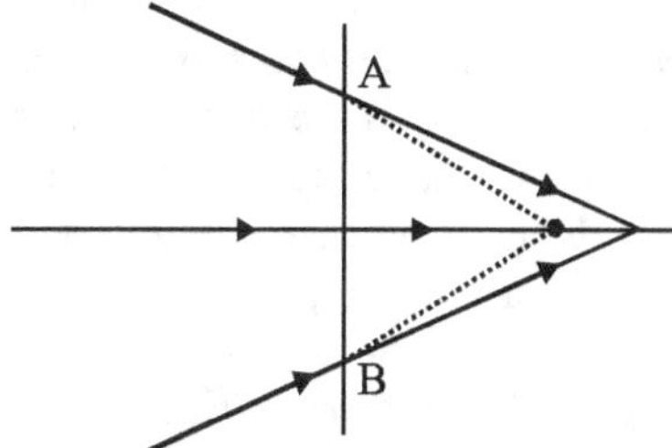

4. The field lines of a negative point charge are as shown in the figure. Does the kinetic energy of a small negative charge increase or decrease in going from B to A?

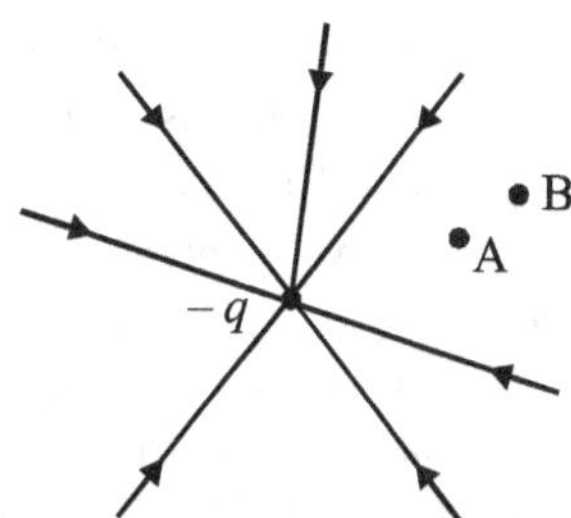

5. Distinguish between emf and terminal voltage of a cell.

SECTION - B

6. How does one explain, using de Broglie hypothesis, Bohr's second postulate of quantization of orbital angular momentum?

7. In a meter bridge shown in the figure, the balance point is found to be 40 cm from end A. If a resistance of 10 Ω is connected in series with *R*, balance point is obtained 60 cm from A. Calculate the values of *R* and *S*.

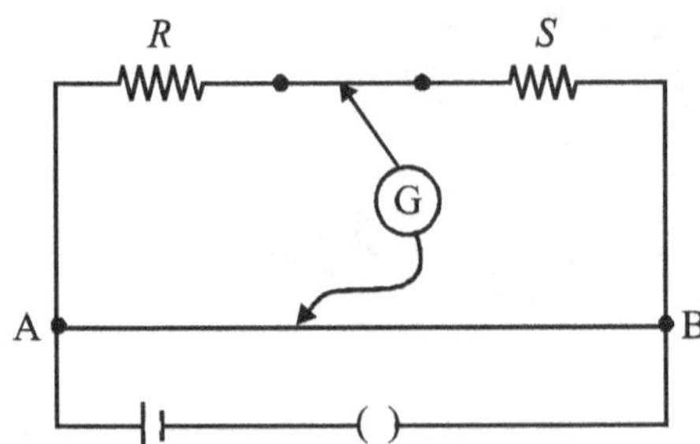

8. What is ground wave communication? Explain why this mode cannot be used for long distance communication using high frequencies.

9. The equivalent wavelength of a moving electron has the same value as that of a photon of energy 6×10^{-17} J. Calculate the momentum of the electron.

10. A ray of light passes through an equilateral glass prism such that the angle of incidence is equal to the angle of emergence and each of these angles is equal to 3/4 of angle of prism. Find the angle of deviation.

OR

Calculate the speed of light in a medium whose critical angle is 45°. Does critical angle for a given pair of media depend on the wavelength of incident light? Give reason.

SECTION - C

11. Write two important considerations used while fabricating a Zener diode. Explain, with the help of a circuit diagram, the principle and working of a Zener diode as voltage regulator.

12. Draw the necessary energy band diagrams to distinguish between conductors, semiconductors and insulators. How does the change in temperature affect the behaviour of these materials ? Explain briefly.

13. (a) What are the three basic units in communication systems?
Write briefly the function of each of these,

   (b) Write any three applications of the Internet used in communication systems.

14. (a) Write the necessary conditions to obtain sustained interference fringes.

   (b) In Young's double slit experiment, plot a graph showing the variation of fringe width versus the distance of the screen from the plane of the slits keeping other parameters same. What information can one obtain from the slope of the curve?

   (c) What is the effect on the fringe width if the distance between the slits is reduced keeping other parameters same?

15. A series LCR circuit is connected across an a.c. source of variable angular frequency 'ω'. Plot a graph showing variation of current 'i' as a function of 'ω' for two resistances R_1 and R_2 $(R_1 > R_2)$.

Answer the following questions using this graph.

   (a) In which case is the resonance sharper and why?

   (b) In which case is the power dissipation more and why?

16. (a) Give two reasons to explain why reflecting telescopes are preferred over refracting type.

   (b) Use mirror equation to show that convex mirror always produces a virtual image independent of the location of the object.

17. State Lenz's law. Illustrate, by giving an example, how this law helps in predicting the direction of the current in a loop in the presence of a changing magnetic flux.

In a given coil of self-inductance of 5 mH, current changes from 4 A to 1 A in 30 ms. Calculate the emf induced in the coil.

OR

In what way is Gauss's law in magnetism different from that used in electrostatics? Explain briefly.

The Earth's magnetic field at the equator is approximately 0.4 G. Estimate the Earth's magnetic dipole moment. Given : Radius of the Earth = 6400 km.

18. How are electromagnetic waves produced? What is the source of energy of these waves?

Draw a schematic sketch of the electromagnetic waves propagating along the $+ x$–axis. Indicate the directions of the electric and magnetic fields. Write the relation between the velocity of propagation of wave and the magnitudes of electric and magnetic fields.

19. Obtain the relation between the decay constant and half life of a radioactive sample.

The half life of a certain radioactive material against α-decay is 100 days. After how much time, will the undecayed fraction of the material be 6.25%?

20. Find the equivalent capacitance of the network shown in the figure, when each capacitor is of 1 μF. When the ends X and Y are connected to a 6 V battery, find out (i) the charge and (ii) the energy stored in the network.

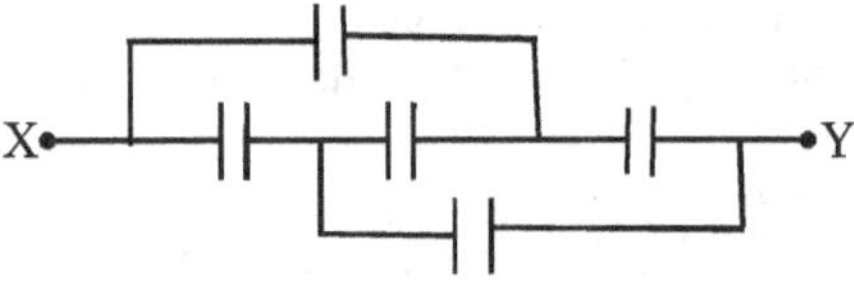

21. State the underlying principle of a potentiometer. Write two factors by which current sensitivity of a potentiometer can be increased. Why is a potentiometer preferred over a voltmeter for measurirg the emf of a cell?

22. (a) Define the term 'intensity of radiation' in terms of photon picture of light.

   (b) Two monochromatic beams, one red and the other blue, have the same intensity. In which case (i) the number of photons per unit area per second is larger, (ii) the maximum kinetic energy of the photoelectrons is more? Justify your answer.

SECTION - D

23. During a thunderstorm the 'live' wire of the transmission line fell down on the ground from the poles in the street. A group of boys, who passed through, noticed it and some of them wanted to place the wire by the side. As they were approaching the wire and trying to lift the cable, Anuj noticed it and immediately pushed them away, thus preventing them from touching the live wire. During pushing some of them got hurt. Anuj took them to a doctor to get them medical aid.

Based on the above paragraph, answer the following questions :

(a) Write the two values which Anuj displayed during the incident.

(b) Why is it that a bird can sit on a suspended live wire without any harm whereas touching it on the ground can give a fatal shock ?

(c) The electric power from a power plant is set up to a very high voltage before transmitting it to distant consumers. Explain, why.

SECTION - E

24 (a) State Kirchhoff's rules and explain on what basis they are justified.

(b) Two cells of emfs E_1 and E_2 and internal resistances r_1 and r_2 are connected in parallel. Derive the expression for the (i) emf and (ii) internal resistance of a single equivalent cell which can replace this combination.

OR

(a) "The outward electric flux due to charge + Q is independent of the shape and size of the surface which encloses it." Give two reasons to justify this statement.

(b) Two identical circular loops '1' and '2' of radius R each have linear charge densities $-\lambda$ and $+\lambda$ C/m respectively. The loops are placed coaxially with their centres $R\sqrt{3}$ distance apart. Find the magnitude and direction of the net electric field at the centre of loop '1'.

25. (a) Use Huygens' principle to show the propagation of a plane wavefront from a denser medium to a rarer medium. Hence find the ratio of the speeds of wavefronts in the two media.

(b) (i) Why does an unpolarised light incident on a polaroid get linearly polarised ?

(ii) Derive the expression of Brewster's law when unpolarised light passing from a rarer to a denser medium gets polarised on reflection at the inteface.

OR

A biconvex lens with its two faces of equal radius of cuivature R is made of a transparent medium of refractive index μ_1. It is kept in contact with a medium of refractive index μ_2 as shown in the figure.

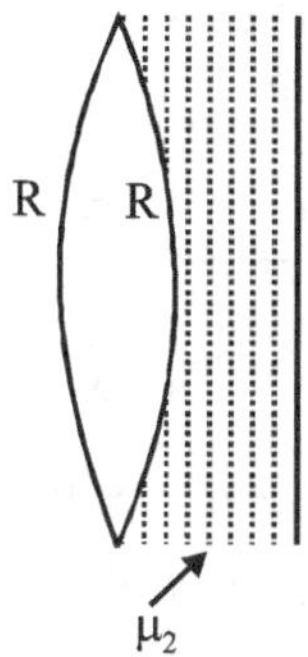

(a) Find the equivalent focal length of the combination.

(b) Obtain the condition when this combination acts as a diverging lens.

(c) Draw the ray diagram for the case $\mu_1 > (\mu_2 + 1)/2$, when the object is kept far away from the lens. Point out the nature of the image formed by the system.

26. Two infinitely long straight parallel wires, '1' and '2', carrying steady currents I_1 and I_2 in the same direction are separated by a distance d. Obtain the expression for the magnetic field $\vec{B}$ due to the wire '1' acting on wire '2'. Hence find out, with the help of a suitable diagram, the magnitude and direction of this force per unit length on wire '2' due to wire '1'. How does the nature of this force changes if the currents are in opposite direction? Use this expression to define the S.I. unit of current.

OR

Draw a necessary arrangement for winding of primary and secondary coils in a step-up transformer. State its underlying principle and derive the relation between the primary and secondary voltages in terms of number of primary and secondary turns. Mention the two basic assumptions used in obtaining the above relation.

State any two causes of energy loss in actual transformers.

Solutions

SECTION - A

1. As capacitative reactance

$$X_C = \frac{1}{\omega C} = \frac{1}{2\pi f C}$$

Hence, it is inversely proportional to frequency f.

Graph: X_C versus f

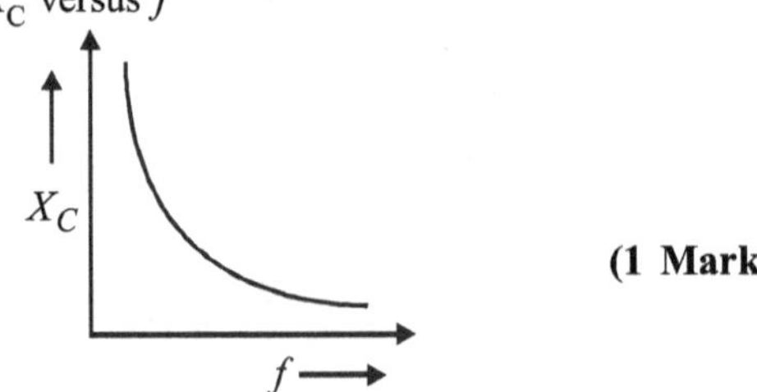

(1 Mark)

2. A Repeater is an amplifying device used to increase the range of the transmission in communication systems with the help of a set of receiver and transmitter. **(1 Mark)**

3. As the rays diverging from lens so, the lens is concave in nature. **(1 Mark)**

4. Since we know that a negative charge always experiences a force in the direction opposite to that of the electric field present, the negative charge will experience the force away from the centre. This will cause its motion to retard while moving from B to A. Hence, its kinetic energy will decrease in going from B to A. **(1 Mark)**

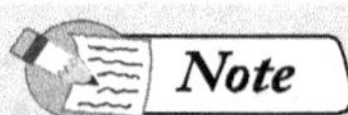 **Note**

Alternate solution.

Due to force of repulsion between two negative charge, the kinectic energy will decrease as the small negative charge tries to move towards the charge –q.

5.

EMF	Terminal voltage
It is the maximum potential difference that can be delivered by a cell when no current flows through the circuit.	It is the potential difference across the terminals of the load when current flows through the circuit.
It is represented by E and remains constant for a cell.	It is represented by V and depends on the internal resistance of the cell.

(1 Mark)

 **Note**

Relation between emf and terminal voltage of cell is

$$V = \varepsilon - Ir$$

where r = internal resistance of cell.

SECTION - B

6. According to de-Broglie hypothesis, a stationary orbit is the one that contains an integral number of de-Broglie waves associated with the revolving electron. **(1 Mark)**

For the permissible orbit, we have

$$2\pi r_n = n\lambda,$$

where λ is the wavelength, r_n - radius of orbit

According to de-Broglie, wavelength of matter waves

$$\lambda = \frac{h}{mv_n}$$

where $\quad v_n$ = speed of electron in n^{th} orbit

$$\therefore \quad 2\pi r_n = \frac{nh}{mv_n}$$

$$\Rightarrow \quad mv_n r_n = \frac{nh}{2\pi} \qquad \textbf{(1 Mark)}$$

This is Bohr's second postulate of quantisation of orbital angular momentum.

 **Note**

Bohr's second postulate states that the electron revolves around the nucleas only in those orbits for which angular momentum is integral multiple of $\dfrac{h}{2\pi}$.

$$Thus \quad L = mvr = n\frac{h}{2\pi}$$

7. When balance point is at 40 cm, we have

$$\frac{R}{S} = \frac{40}{100-40} = \frac{40}{60}$$

$$\Rightarrow \quad \frac{R}{S} = \frac{2}{3}$$

$$\Rightarrow \quad 3R = 2S \qquad \dots \text{(i)} \; \textbf{(½ Mark)}$$

When a resistance of 10 Ω is added in series with R,

Then, equivalent resistance of $R' = R + 10$

Now, balance point is obtained at 60 cm.

$$\therefore \quad \frac{R+10}{S} = \frac{60}{100-60} = \frac{60}{40}$$

$$\Rightarrow \quad \frac{R+10}{S} = \frac{3}{2}$$

$$\Rightarrow \quad 2R + 20 = 3S \qquad \dots \text{(ii)} \quad \textbf{(1 Mark)}$$

Solving eqs (i) and (ii), we get

$$S = 12 \; \Omega \text{ and } R = 8 \; \Omega \quad \textbf{(½ Mark)}$$

8. Ground waves are the radio waves that travel along the surface of the Earth. The propagation of the wave is guided along the Earth's surface and follows the curvature of the Earth. **(1 Mark)**

The propagation of high frequency wave is not possible through ground waves for long distance communication because while progressing, ground waves induce current in the ground and bend round the corner of the objects on the Earth due to which the energy of the ground waves of high frequency is almost absorbed by the surface of the Earth after travelling a small distance. Thus, ground wave communication is not suited for high frequency.

(1 Mark)

9. According to the de Broglie hypothesis, the momentum (p) of an electron is given by

$$p = \frac{h}{\lambda} \qquad \text{... (i)} \; \textbf{(1 Mark)}$$

Energy of photon, $E = \dfrac{hc}{\lambda} = 6 \times 10^{-17} J$ (Given)

$$\Rightarrow \quad \lambda = \frac{(6.625 \times 10^{-34})(3 \times 10^8)}{(6 \times 10^{-17})}$$

$$\Rightarrow \quad \lambda = 3.31 \times 10^{-9} \text{ m}$$

From eq^n (i), we have

$$p = \frac{6.626 \times 10^{-34}}{3.31 \times 10^{-9}} = 2 \times 10^{-25} \text{ kg m s}^{-1}$$

(1 Mark)

10. The angle of deviation δ for a ray of light in a prism is given by

$\delta = i + e - A$

where i = angle of incidence of ray

e = angle of emergence and

A = angle of prism

$$\Rightarrow \quad \delta = 2i - A \quad (\because e = i) \qquad \textbf{(½ Mark)}$$

Given : $i = e = \dfrac{3}{4}A$

$$\therefore \quad \delta = 2 \times \frac{3}{4}A - A = \frac{1}{2} A \qquad \textbf{(½ Mark)}$$

As the prism is equilateral, $\angle A = 60°$

$$\therefore \quad \delta = \frac{1}{2} \times 60° = 30° \qquad \textbf{(1 Mark)}$$

OR

According to Snell's Law, we know

$$\mu = \frac{1}{\sin i_c} \; ; \text{ where } i_c = \text{critical angle}$$

$$\therefore \quad \frac{c}{v} = \frac{1}{\sin i_c} \qquad \left(\because \mu = \frac{c}{V} \right)$$

$$\Rightarrow \quad v = \sin i_c \times c$$

$$\Rightarrow \quad v = \sin 45° \times 3 \times 10^8$$

$$\Rightarrow \quad v = 2.12 \times 10^8$$

Therefore, speed of light in the medium is 2.12×10^8 ms⁻¹.

(1 Mark)

We know that the critical angle of the medium depends on its refractive index and the refractive index μ of a medium is inversely proportional to the wavelength of incident light. So, the critical angle of the medium also depends upon the wavelength of incident light. **(1 Mark)**

When angle of incidence is equal to angle of emergence, then angle of deviation is minimum and known as angle of minimum deviation Dm.

SECTION - C

11. Two important considerations while fabricating a Zener diode are as follows:
    (i) The Zener diode should be fabricated by heavily doping both p and n junctions.
    (ii) Proper wafer-handling devices must be used to avoid contamination, which may affect the quality and stability of the diode. **(1 Mark)**

Principle

Zener diode when reverse biased shows a sudden increase in current to a high value at a certain voltage known as the breakdown voltage or the Zener voltage.

Working : Zener diode as voltage regulator:-

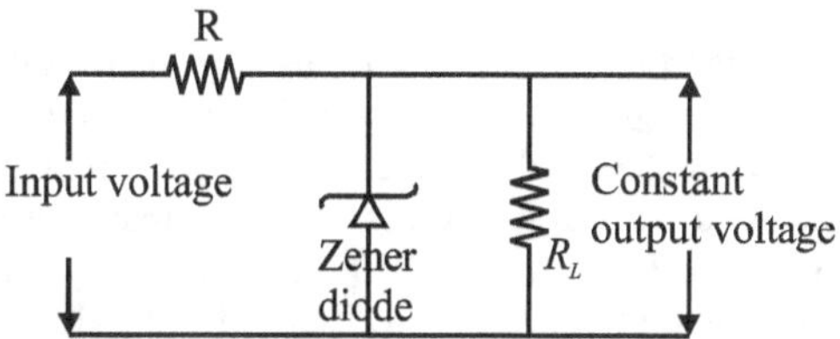

The fluctuating input dc voltage is connected to the zener diode through a series resistance R. If the input voltage increases, current through R and zener also increases. This increase voltage drop across R without any change voltage across zener diode. This is because in break down region, voltage across zener diode is independent of current change and remains constant.

Similarly, if imput voltage decreases, currrent through zener and resistance R decreases. And voltage drop across R decrease without changing the voltage across zener. Therefore, any change in input voltage does not effect the voltage across zener diode making it suitable for voltage regulation. **(2 Marks)**

12. In **conductors**, the conduction and the valence band overlap each other.

As the temperature increases, the conductivity of the conductors decrease due to increase in the thermal motion of the free electrons.

Energy band diagram for a conductor

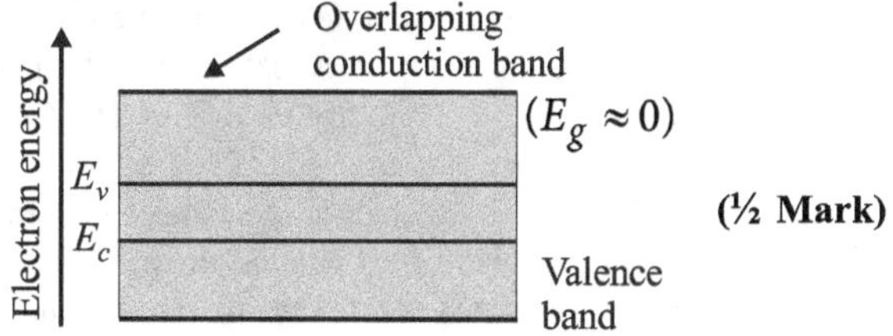

Energy band diagram for an insulator

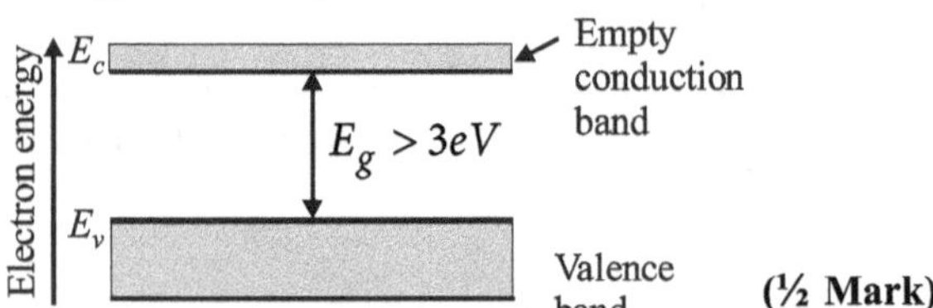

(½ Mark)

Here, the valence band is completely filled and the conduction band is empty. The energy band gap of the insulator is quite large. So, on increasing the temperature, the electrons of the valence band are not able to reach the conduction band. Therefore, electrical conduction in these materials is almost impossible.

Energy band diagram for a semiconductor

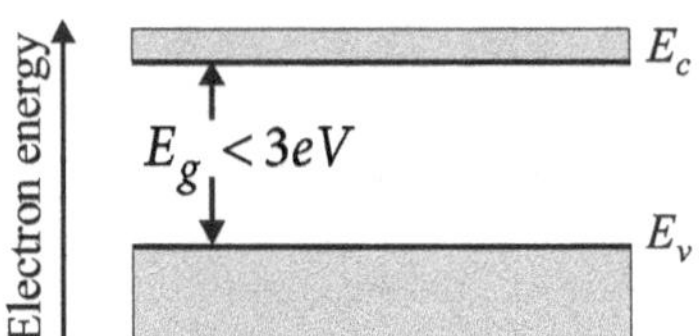

(½ Mark)

In **semiconductors,** the valence band is totally filled and the conduction band is empty but the energy gap between conduction band and valence band is quite small. At 0 K, electrons are not able to cross even this small energy gap and, hence, the conduction band remains totally empty. At room temperature, some electrons in the valence band acquire thermal energy greater than energy band gap, which is less than 3 eV and jump over to the conduction band where they are free to move under the influence of even a small change in the temperature. As the temperature increases more and more electrons crosses the band gap and hence conductivity increases. **(1½ Marks)**

13. (a) A communication system consists of three basic units:

(i) Transmitter: This unit is used for transmitting the information after modifying it to a suitable form. It basically consists of a transducer that converts signal in any physical form to electrical signal for transmission. After that, the signal is modulated to transmit over long distances.

(ii) Communication channel: This unit carries the modulated signal from the transmitter to the receiver. E.g free space, transmission lines acts as a communication channel.

(iii) Receiver: This receives the signal, followed by a demodulator, an amplifier and a transducer. The demodulator demodulates the modulated signal, the amplifier boosts up its intensity and the transducer converts it back again electrical form to the needed physical form. **(½ × 3 = 1½ Marks)**

(b) The list of uses of Internet is given below.

(i) **E-banking:** It is an electronic payment system that enables customers of a financial institution (usualy a bank) to proceed for financial transactions on a website operated by that institution. To bank online with an institution, it is required that the customer is a member of that institution and has the access of Internet.

(ii) **Internet surfing:** Navigation over World Wide Web (www) from one webpage/website to another is called Internet surfing. It is an interesting way of searching and viewing information on any topic of interest.

(iii) **E-shopping (E-commerce):** It is a form of electronic commerce, by which the consumers can buy the products or the services over Internet.

Apart from the above internet is used for sending e-mail, e-ticketing, etc. **(½ × 3 = 1½ Marks)**

14. (a) The necessary conditions to obtain sustained interference fringes are:

(i) The two sources of light must be coherent.

(ii) The two sources should preferably be monochromatic.

(iii) The coherent sources must be very close to each other. **(1 Mark)**

(b) The fringe width in Young's double slit experiment is given by

$$\beta = \frac{\lambda D}{d}$$

where λ = wavelength of source
D = distance between the slits and screen
d = distance between the slits

$$\Rightarrow \beta \propto D$$

The variation of fringe width with distance of screen from the slits is given by the graph shown below:

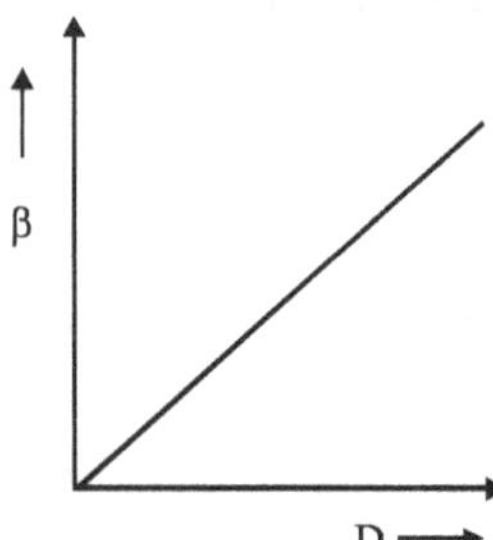

It is a linear graph with slope equal to λ/d, So. for the fringe width to vary linearly with distance of screen from the slits, the ratio of wavelength to distance between the slits should remain constant. Therefore, it is advised to take wavelengths of incident light nearly equal to the width of the slit. **(1 Mark)**

(c) Fringe width is given by $\beta = \frac{\lambda D}{d}$

Hence, if the distance between the slits is reduced then the width of the fringes increases. **(1 Mark)**

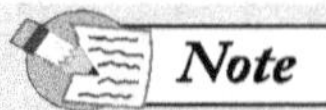

Note

In interference (or diffraction) light energy is redistributed. Formation of dark fringes does not mean light energy has been lost, its been distributed to other region producing bright fringe. Both interference and diffraction are consistent with conservation of energy.

15. The variation of current with angular frequency for the two resistances R_1 and R_2 shown in the graph below.

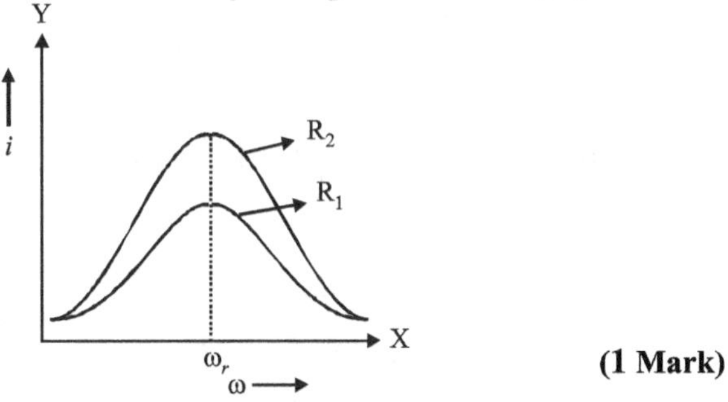

(1 Mark)

Here, ω_r = Resonance frequency

(a) From the graph, we can see that resonance for the resistance R_2 is sharper than for R_1 because resistance R_2 is less than resistance R_1. Therefore, at resonance, the value of peak current will rise more abruptly for a lower value of resistance. **(1 Mark)**

(b) Power associated with the resistance is given by

$$P = E_v I_v$$

From the graph, we can say that the current in case of R_2 is more than the current in case of R_1. Hence, the power dissipation in case of the circuit with R_2 is more than that with R_1. **(1 Mark)**

> ### Note
>
> *Quality factor, Q is also a measure of resonance.*
>
> $$Q = \frac{\omega_0 L}{R} \qquad \qquad ...(1)$$
>
> *Larger the value of Q, sharper is the resonance.*
>
> *From eqn (1), we see that $Q \propto \dfrac{1}{R}$. So, for R_2 will be sharper.*

16. (a) The reflecting telescopes are preferred over refracting type because of the following reasons:

(i) There is no chromatic aberration in case of reflecting telescopes as the objective is a mirror.

(ii) Spherical aberration is reduced in case of reflecting telescopes by using mirror objective in the form of a paraboloid. **(1 Mark)**

(b) For convex mirror, $f = +ve$

object distance, u = –ve or u < 0.

Using the mirror formula we have,

$$\frac{1}{f} = \frac{1}{v} + \frac{1}{u} \quad \Rightarrow \quad \frac{1}{v} = \frac{1}{f} - \frac{1}{u} \qquad \textbf{(1 Mark)}$$

Since $f > 0$ and $u < 0$, then from the above equations, we get that

$$\frac{1}{v} > 0 \quad \Rightarrow \quad v < 0$$

Hence, a image is always formed at the backside of the mirror. Therefore, the image formed by the convex mirror is always virtual in nature. **(1 Mark)**

17. According to Lenz's law, the polarity of emf induced in the coil always opposes the change in the magnetic flux responsible for production of induced emf. **(1 Mark)**

E.g., When a north pole of a bar magnet is brought closer to a coil, as shown in figure, the amount of magnetic flux linked with the coil increases. So, the emf induced in the coil is directed such that it opposes this change in magnetic flux responsible for production of induced emf, which is possible only when the current induced in the coil is in anticlockwise direction.

Similarly, the direction of induced current can be found when north pole of bar magnet is moved away from the coil. As the magnetic flux in this case decreases, the induced current is in the clockwise direction. **(1 Mark)**

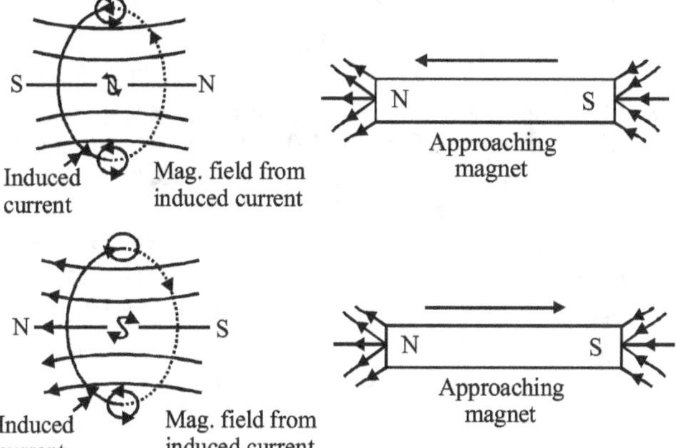

Given: Self inductance, $L = 5$ mH $= 5 \times 10^{-3}$ H

Change in current, $dI = (1 - 4) = -3$ A

Change in time, $dt = 30$ ms $= 30 \times 10^{-3}$ s

The emf induced in the coil is given by

$$e = -L\frac{dI}{dt}$$

$$\Rightarrow \quad e = \frac{(-5\times10^{-3})\times(-3)}{30\times10^{-3}}$$

$$\Rightarrow \quad e = 0.5 \text{ V} \qquad \textbf{(1 Mark)}$$

OR

Gauss's law for magnetism states that net magnetic flux ϕ_B through any closed surface is zero.

$$\phi_B = \oint \overline{B}.\overline{ds} = 0$$

On the other hand, Gauss's law for electrostatics states that electric flux through a closed surface S is given by

$$\phi_E = \oint \overline{E}.\overline{ds} = \frac{\sum q_{en}}{\varepsilon_0}$$

So, if an electric dipole is enclosed by surface, electric flux will be zero. But in magnetism there is no counterpart of isolated charge as in electricity. So, we can say that isolated magnetic poles or monopoles do not exist.

(1½ Marks)

As we know $\qquad B = \dfrac{\mu_0 M}{4\pi d^3} \qquad$ **(½ Mark)**

Here $\quad d = R =$ Radius of the Earth

Given: $\qquad B = 0.4G = 0.4 \times 10^{-4}$ T

$$\frac{\mu_0}{4\pi} = 10^{-7} \text{ Wb A}^{-1}\text{ m}^{-1}$$

$$d = 6400 \text{ km} = 6.4 \times 10^6 \text{ m}$$

$$\therefore \quad M = \frac{4\pi B d^3}{\mu_0}$$

$$\Rightarrow \quad M = \frac{(0.4\times10^{-4})(6.4\times10^6)^3}{10^{-7}}$$

$$\Rightarrow \quad M = 1.05 \times 10^{23} \text{ Am}^2 \qquad \textbf{(1 Mark)}$$

Note

The negative sign in the expression for faraday's law of electromagnetic induction indicates Lenz's law.

$$\varepsilon = \frac{-d\phi}{dt}.$$

18. Electromagnetic waves are produced by a moving charge with non-zero acceleration. When the charge moves with acceleration, both the magnetic and electric fields change continuously. This change produces electromagnetic waves. An accelerated charge is the source of energy of these waves. **(1½ Marks)**

Schematic sketch of the electromagnetic waves:

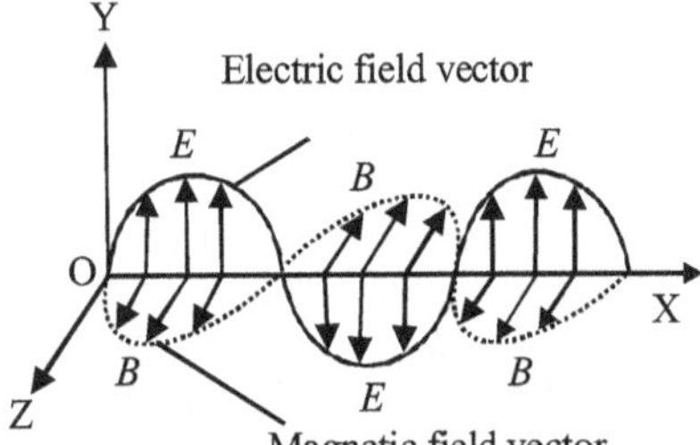

The relation between the velocity of propagation and the magnitudes of electric and magnetic fields is $E = cB_0$ where c = speed of em waves. **(1½ Mark)**

19. Relation between decay constant and half life of a radioactive substance:

The number of atoms at any instant in a radioactive sample is given by

$$N = N_0\, e^{-\lambda t} \qquad \textbf{(½ Mark)}$$

N = total number of atoms at any instant
N_0 = number of atoms in radioactive substance at $t = 0$

When $t = T$ (Where T is the half life of the sample)

$$N = \frac{N_0}{2}$$

$$\Rightarrow \quad \frac{N_0}{2} = N_0 e^{-\lambda T}$$

$$\Rightarrow \quad e^{\lambda T} = 2 \qquad \textbf{(½ Mark)}$$

Taking log on both the sides, we get

$$\lambda T = \log_e 2 = 2.303\ \log_{10} 2$$

$$\Rightarrow \quad T = \frac{2.303\log_{10} 2}{\lambda}$$

$$\Rightarrow \quad T = \frac{0.693}{\lambda} \qquad \textbf{(½ Mark)}$$

Let t be the required time after which the undecayed fraction of the material will be 6.25%.

$$\therefore \quad \frac{6.25}{100} = \frac{1}{16}$$

$$\therefore \quad N = \frac{N_0}{16}$$

But $\quad N = N_0\left(\dfrac{1}{2}\right)^n$ where $n = \dfrac{t}{T}$ **(½ Mark)**

$$\Rightarrow \quad \frac{N_0}{16} = N_0\left(\frac{1}{2}\right)^n$$

$$\Rightarrow \quad n = 4$$

$$\therefore \quad \text{Time'} \quad t = n \times T$$

$$\Rightarrow \quad t = 4 \times 100$$

$$t = 400 \text{ days} \qquad \textbf{(1 Mark)}$$

20. This is a wheatstone bridge configuration, So

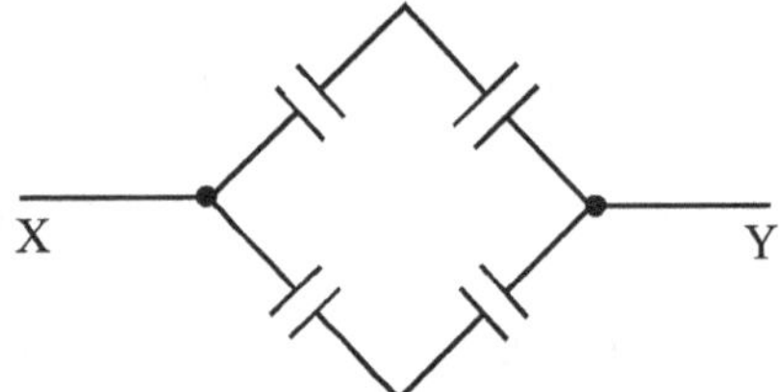

Capacictor in upper branch is in series.

$$C_{eq} = \frac{1\times1}{1+1} = \frac{1}{2}\mu F$$

Similarly, equivalent capacitor of lower branch

$$C_{eq} = \frac{1\times1}{1+1} = \frac{1}{2}\mu F$$

Now, two $\frac{1}{2}\mu F$ capacitor are in parallel. So equivalent capacitance across XY will be

$$C = \frac{1}{2}+\frac{1}{2} = 1\mu F \qquad \textbf{(1 Mark)}$$

(i) Charge on capacitor

$$q = CV$$
$$= 1 \times 10^{-6}$$
$$= 6 \times 10^{-6}\text{C}$$
$$= 6\mu C \qquad \textbf{(1 Mark)}$$

(ii) Energy stored in capacitor

$$E = \frac{1}{2}CV^2$$
$$= \frac{1}{2}\times1\times10^{-6}\times6\times6$$
$$E = 18 \times 10^{-6} \text{ J} \qquad \textbf{(1 Mark)}$$

21. (a) **Principle of potentiometer:** When a steady current flows through the potentiometer wire then, the potential difference across the uniform wire is directly proportional to the length of the part across which the potential is measured. **(1 Mark)**

(b) Current sensitivity can be increased by
(i)   increasing the length of the wire
(ii) decreasing the current in the wire using a rheostat
(1 Mark)

(c) Potentiometer is preferred over voltmeter because it measures accurate emf of the cell. It uses null method, so no current is drawn by the galvanometer from the cell in balanced condition of potentiometer and a voltmeter measures the voltage across the terminals of a cell when the cell is in closed circuit. This voltage is called terminal voltage of a cell not emf. **(1 Mark)**

22. (a) Intensity of radiation is defined as the number of photons falling per unit area in unit time. **(1 Mark)**

(b) (i)   Number of photons per unit per second in both the beams is same as they have the same intensity.

(ii) The maximum kinetic energy of photoelectrons is given by
$$E = hc/\lambda - \phi$$ **(1 Mark)**

We know that the wavelength of blue beam is less than that of red beam. So, we can say that the maximum kinetic energy of the photoelectrons of the blue beam will be more. **(1 Mark)**

SECTION - D

23 (a) During this incident, Anuj reflected the following values:
(i)   He was concerned about the lives of the individuals.
(ii) He was well aware about what would be the after effect of touching a live wire with naked hands and he immediately acted upon this situation and saved lives of the boys. **(2 Marks)**

(b) When the bird perches on a live wire, its body becomes charged for the moment and has same voltage as the live wire; however, no current flows into its body. Body is a poor conductor of electricity as compared to the copper wire, so there is no reason for electrons to take a detour through the bird's body. Therefore, no current flows from the body of the bird.

On the other hand, if the bird touches the ground while being in contact with the high voltage live wire, then the electric circuit gets complete and high current flows through the body of the bird, giving it a fatal shock. **(1 Mark)**

(c) The electric power from a power plant is set up at a very high voltage before transmitting it to distant consumers to reduce the loss of power during transmission.

The power loss during the transmission = $I^2 R$. So the power loss can be minimised by reducing the value of the current. Thus, to reduce the value of current, value of the voltage of the electric power should be kept high before transmitting. **(1 Mark)**

Power = voltage × Current

From the above equation, we can see that the current can be reduced by increasing the voltage of the electric power.

SECTION - E

24. (a) Kirchhoff's first rule (Junction rule): The algebraic sum of the currents meeting at a point in an electrical circuit is always zero.
$$\Sigma I = 0$$
This law is justified on the basis of law of conservation of charge. **(1 Mark)**

Kirchhoff's second law (Loop rule): In a closed loop, the algebraic sum of the emfs is equal to the algebraic sum of the products of the resistances and the current flowing through them.
$$\Sigma\varepsilon + \Sigma IR = 0$$
This law is justified on the basis of law of conservation of energy. **(1 Mark)**

(b)

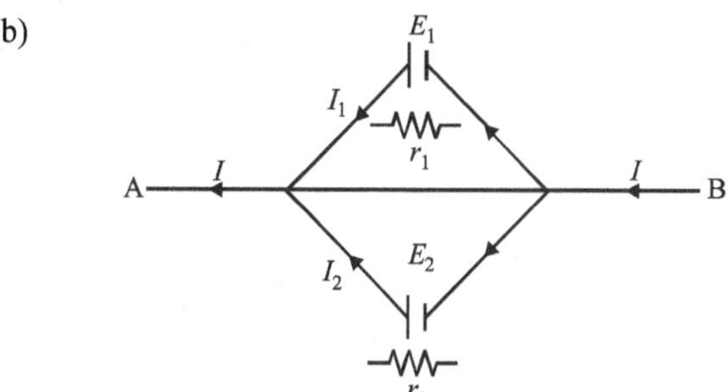

Terminal potential difference across the first cell is
$$V = E_1 - I_1 r_1$$
$$\Rightarrow \qquad I_1 = \frac{E_1 - V}{r_1} \qquad \text{(½ Mark)}$$

For the second cell, terminal potential difference will be equal to that across the first cell. So, V
$$= E_2 - I_2 r_2$$
$$\Rightarrow \qquad I_2 = \frac{E_2 - V}{r_2} \qquad \text{(½ Mark)}$$

Let E be effective emf and r is effective internal resistance. Let I be the current flowing through the cell.
$$I = I_1 + I_2$$
$$\Rightarrow \qquad I = \frac{E_1 - V}{r_1} + \frac{E_2 - V}{r_2}$$
$$\Rightarrow \qquad I = \frac{r_2(E_1 - V) + r_1(E_2 - V)}{r_1 r_2}$$
$$\Rightarrow \qquad I r_1 r_2 = E_1 r_2 + E_2 r_1 - (r_1 + r_2)V$$
$$\Rightarrow \qquad V = \frac{E_1 r_2 + E_2 r_1}{r_1 + r_2} - \frac{I r_1 r_2}{r_1 + r_2} \qquad \textbf{(1 Mark)}$$

Comparing the equation with
$$V = E - Ir, \text{ we get}$$
Emf,
$$E = \frac{E_1 r_2 + E_2 r_1}{r_1 + r_2} \qquad \text{(½ Mark)}$$

Internal resistance,
$$r = \frac{r_1 r_2}{r_1 + r_2} \qquad \text{(½ Mark)}$$

OR

(a) The outward electric flux due to charge $+Q$ is independent of the shape and size of the surface, which encloses it because:

(i) Number of electric field lines coming out from a closed surface enclosing the charge depends on the charge enclosed by the surface.

(ii) Number of electric field lines coming out from a closed surface enclosing the charge is independent of the position of the charge inside the closed surface. **(2 Marks)**

(b) Magnitude of electric field at any point on the axis of a uniformly charged loop is given by,

$$E = \frac{\lambda}{2\,\epsilon_0} \frac{rR}{(r^2 + R^2)^{\frac{3}{2}}} \quad ...(i) \text{ (1 Mark)}$$

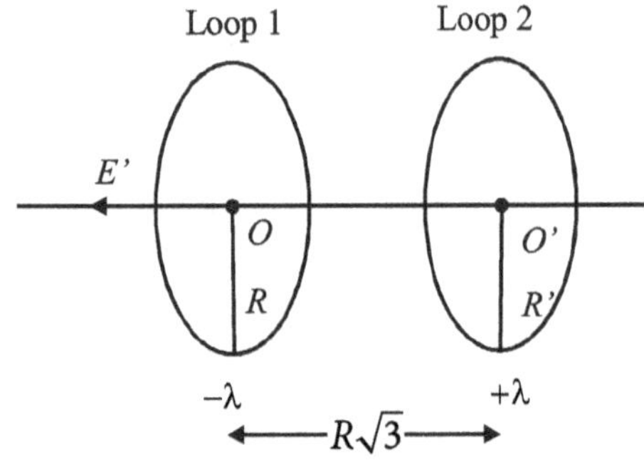

Electric field at the centre of loop 1 due to charge present on it is zero. [From (i), when $r = 0$]

Hence, electric field at the centre of the loop 1 due to charge present on the loop 2 is,

$$E = \frac{+\lambda}{2\,\epsilon_0} \frac{(R\sqrt{3})R}{[(R\sqrt{3})^2 + R^2]^{3/2}}$$

$$= \frac{\lambda}{2\varepsilon_0} \frac{R^2\sqrt{3}}{8R^3}$$

$$\Rightarrow \qquad E = \frac{\sqrt{3}}{16\,\epsilon_0} \frac{\lambda}{R} \qquad \text{(1½ Marks)}$$

The direction of this net field is from loop 2 to loop 1 as shown. **(½ Mark)**

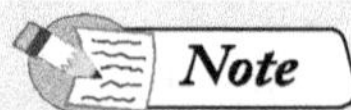 *Note*

Kirchhoff's junction rule is valid even for bending or reorientation of wire. This rule is based on conservation of charge. It is not affected by the shape of wire.

25. (a) Let XY be the surface separating the denser medium and the rarer medium. Let:

v_1 = Speed of light wave in the denser medium

v_2 = Speed of light wave in the rarer medium

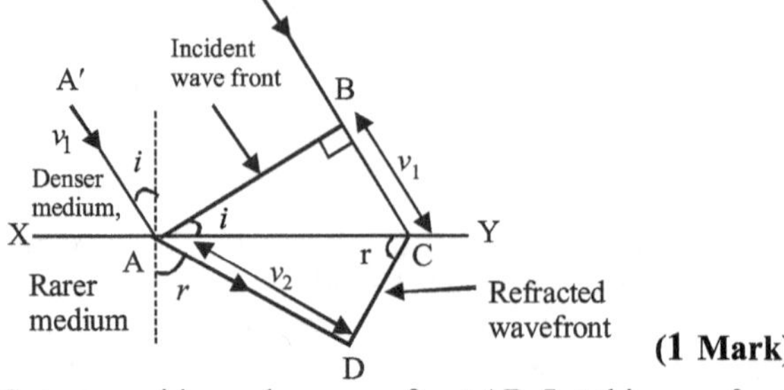

(1 Mark)

Let us consider a plane wavefront AB. Let this wavefront incident on the interface at an angle of incidence i.

Let t be the time taken by the wavefront to travel the distance BC in denser medium.

$$\Rightarrow \qquad BC = v_1 t$$

To determine the shape of refracted wavefront, we will draw a sphere of radius v_2t from point A in the rarer medium. Let CD represent a tangent plane drawn from point C onto the sphere.

Now, $\qquad AD = v_2 t$

Here, CD would represent the refracted wavefront. Considering the triangles ABC and ADC, we get

$$\sin i = \frac{BC}{AC} = \frac{v_1 t}{AC}$$

$$\sin r = \frac{AD}{AC} = \frac{v_2 t}{AC}$$

$$\Rightarrow \qquad \frac{\sin r}{\sin i} = \frac{v_2}{v_1} \qquad ....(1)$$

Since $r > i$, the speed of light in the rarer medium (v_2) will be greater than the speed of light in the denser medium (v_1).

Now, $\qquad \mu_1 = \dfrac{c}{v_1}; \ \mu_2 = \dfrac{c}{v_2}$

where

μ_1 = Refractive index of denser medium

μ_2 = Refractive index of rarer medium

Further, (1) can be written as $\mu_1 \sin i = \mu_2 \sin r$ **(1 Mark)**

This is the Snell's law of refraction.

(b) (i) When unpolarised light is passed through a polaroid, only those vibrations of light pass through the crystal that are parallel to the axis of the crystal. All other vibrations will be absorbed by the crystal. In this way, the unpolarised light gets linearly polarised. **(1 Mark)**

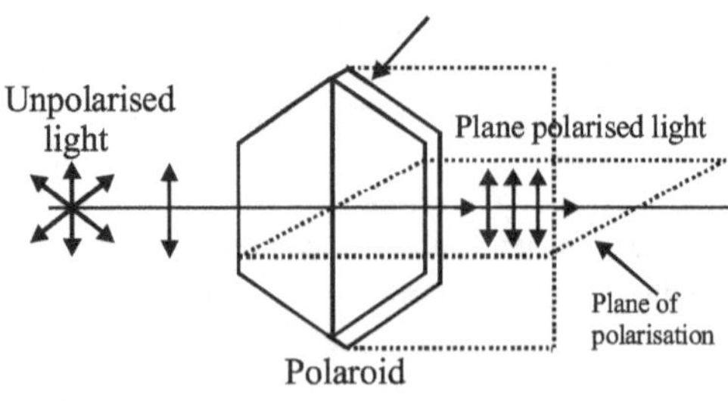

(ii) Let us consider that an unpolarised light is incident along XO at an angle i_p (angle of polarisation) on the interface AB, separating air, a rarer medium, from a denser medium of refractive index μ.

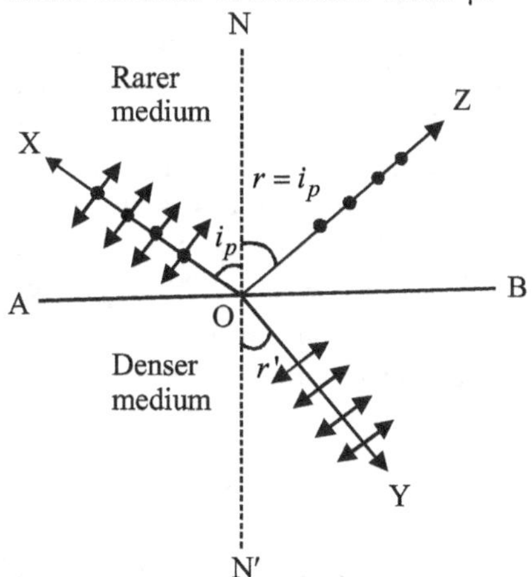

It has been experimentally observed that when unpolarised light is incident at polarising angle, the reflected components along OZ and OY are mutually perpendicular to each other. So, we have

$$\angle ZOB + \angle BOY = 90°$$

$$\Rightarrow \quad (90° - i_p) + (90° - r') = 90°$$

$$\Rightarrow \quad 90° - i_p = r' \qquad \textbf{(1 Mark)}$$

By Snell's law, $\quad \mu = \dfrac{\sin i_p}{\sin r'}$

$$\therefore \qquad \mu = \dfrac{\sin i_p}{\sin(90° - i_p)} = \tan i_p \qquad \textbf{(1 Mark)}$$

This gives us the required expression for Brewster's law.

OR

From the lens maker formula, we have

$$\dfrac{1}{f} = (\mu - 1)\left(\dfrac{1}{R_1} - \dfrac{1}{R_2}\right) \qquad \textbf{(1 Mark)}$$

Let f_1 anf f_2 be the focal lengths of the two mediums. Then,

$$\dfrac{1}{f_1} = (\mu_1 - 1)\left[\dfrac{1}{R} - \left(-\dfrac{1}{R}\right)\right]$$

$$\Rightarrow \quad \dfrac{1}{f_1} = (\mu_1 - 1)\left(\dfrac{2}{R}\right)$$

$$\dfrac{1}{f_2} = (\mu_2 - 1)\left[\left(-\dfrac{1}{R}\right) - \dfrac{1}{\infty}\right]$$

$$\Rightarrow \quad \dfrac{1}{f_2} = (\mu_2 - 1)\left(-\dfrac{1}{R}\right) \qquad \textbf{(1 Mark)}$$

(a) If f_{eq} is the equivalent focal length of the combination, then

$$\dfrac{1}{f_{eq}} = \dfrac{1}{f_1} + \dfrac{1}{f_2}$$

$$\Rightarrow \quad \dfrac{1}{f_{eq}} = \dfrac{2(\mu_1 - 1)}{R} - \dfrac{(\mu_2 - 1)}{R}$$

$$\Rightarrow \quad \dfrac{1}{f_{eq}} = \dfrac{2\mu_1 - \mu_2 - 1}{R}$$

$$\Rightarrow \quad f_{eq} = \dfrac{R}{2\mu_1 - \mu_2 - 1} \qquad \textbf{(1 Mark)}$$

(b) For the combination to behave as a diverging lens, $f_{eq} < 0$

$$\Rightarrow \quad \dfrac{R}{2\mu_1 - \mu_2 - 1} < 0$$

$$\Rightarrow \quad 2\mu_1 - \mu_2 - 1 < 0$$

$$\Rightarrow \quad m_1 < \dfrac{(\mu_2 + 1)}{2}$$

which is the required condition   **(1 Mark)**

(c) For $\mu_1 > (\mu_2 + 1)/2$. the combination will behave as the converging lens. So, an object placed far away from the lens will form image at the focus of the lens.

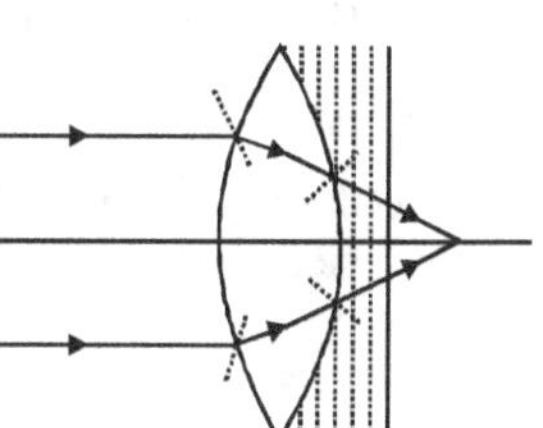

The image so formed will be real and diminished in nature.   **(1 Mark)**

Note

Huygens principle tells us that each point on a weavefront is a source of secondary waves, which add up to give the wavefront at a later time.

26. Consider a straight conductor XY lying in the plane of paper. Consider a point P at a perpendicular distance 'a' from straight conductor.

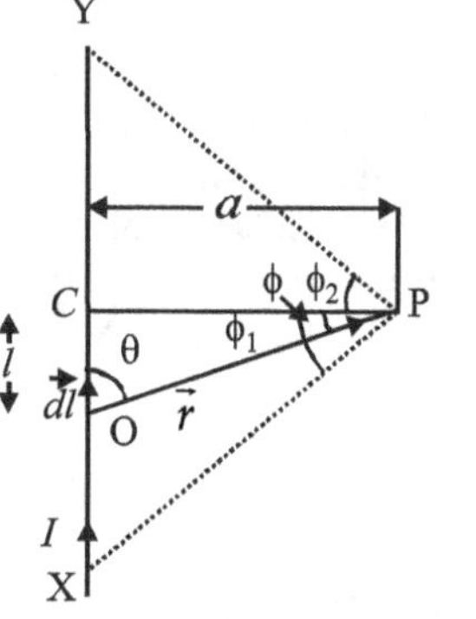

   (1 Mark)

Now Magnetic field induction at a point P due to current I passing through conductor XY is given by

$$B = \dfrac{\mu_0 I}{4\pi a}\left[\sin \phi_1 + \sin \phi_2\right]$$

At the centre of the infinite long wire,

$$\phi_1 = \phi_2 = 90°$$

$$\therefore \qquad B = \dfrac{\mu_0 I}{4\pi a}\left[\sin 90° + \sin 90°\right]$$

$$\Rightarrow \qquad B = \dfrac{\mu_0}{4\pi}\dfrac{2I}{a} \qquad ....(1) \textbf{ (1 Mark)}$$

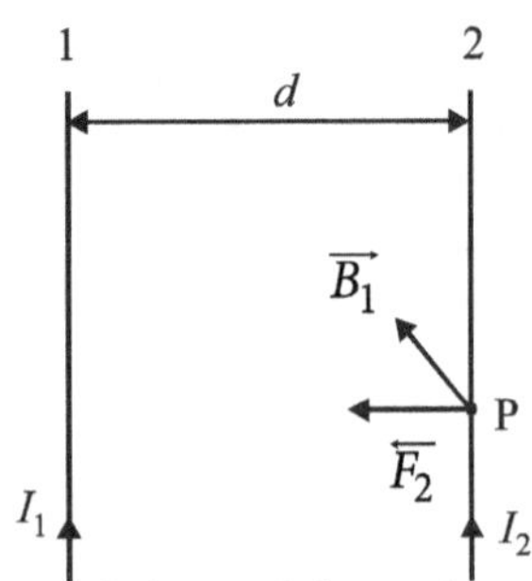

Consider two infinite straight conductors 1 and 2. Let I_1 and I_2 current flowing through the conductor 1 and 2 and they are d distance apart from each other.

The magnetic field induction (B) at a point P on conductor 2 due to current I_1 passing through conductor 1 is given by $B_1 = \dfrac{\mu_0 2I_1}{4\pi d}$

According to right hand rule, the direction of this magnetic field is perpendicular to the plane of the paper inward.

Now force experienced (F_2) by unit length of conductor 2 will be $F_2 = B_1 I_2 \times 1 = B_1 \, I_2$

$$\therefore \qquad F_2 = \dfrac{\mu_0}{4\pi} \dfrac{2I_1 I_2}{d} \qquad \textbf{(2 Marks)}$$

Conductor 1 also experiences the same amount of force, directed towards the conductor 2. Hence, conductor 1 and conductor 2 attract each other. Thus, two linear parallel conductors carrying currents in the same direction attract and repel each other when the current flows in the opposite direction.

Let $\qquad I_1 = I_1 = 1A; \; r = 1 \; m$

Then, $\qquad F_1 = F_2 = F = 10^{-7} \dfrac{2 \times 1 \times 1}{1}$

$\Rightarrow \qquad\quad F = 2 \times 10^{-7} \; \text{N/m}$

Definition of one ampere : One ampere is that value of constant current which when flowing through each of the two parallel uniform long linear conductors placed in free space at a distance of 1 m from each other will attract or repel each other with a force of 2×10^{-7} N per metre of their length. **(1 Mark)**

OR

Transformer

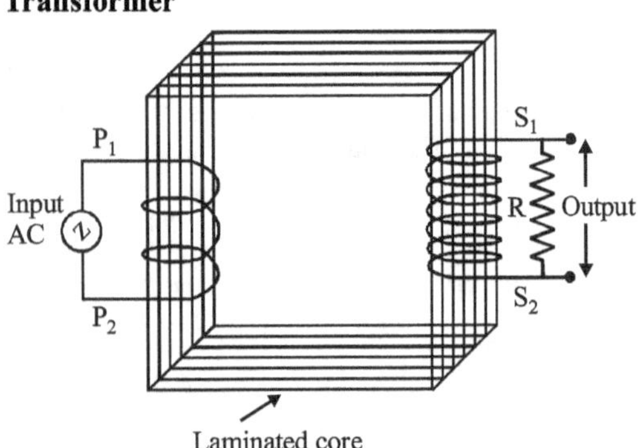

Laminated core

(1 Mark)

Principle: It works on the principle of mutual induction. Whenever magnetic flux linked with coil changes, an emf is induced in the neighbouring coil. **(1 Mark)**

Working: When an alternating emf is supplied to the primary coil then magnetic flux linked with the secondary coil changes. As a result, an emf is induced in the secondary coil. Voltage at the primary and the secondary coils depends on the number of turns. Magnetic flux that is linked with the primary coil is also linked with the secondary coil. The induced emf in each turn (E_{turn}) of the secondary coil is equal to that of the primary coil.

Let E_p be the alternating emf applied to primaiy coil and n_p be the number of turns in it. If ϕ be the electric flux associated with it, then

$$E_p = -n_p \dfrac{d\phi}{dt} \qquad ....(1)$$

Let E_s be the emf across the secondary coil and n_s be the no of turns in it. Then,

$$E_s = -n_s \dfrac{d\phi}{dt} \qquad ....(2)$$

Dividing (2) by (1),

$$\dfrac{E_s}{E_p} = \dfrac{n_s}{n_p} = k \qquad \textbf{(1 Mark)}$$

For step up transformer, $k > 1$

$$\therefore \qquad E_S > E_P$$

For step down transformer, $k < 1$

$$\therefore \qquad E_S < E_P$$

For ideal transformer, we assume that

1. The resistance of the primary and secondary windings are negligible.

2. The energy loss due to magnetic hysterisis in the iron core is negligible. **(1 Mark)**

Following are the two causes of energy loss:

(1) Iron loss: Loss in the bulk of iron core due to the induced eddy currents. It is minimised by using thin laminated core.

(2) Hysteresis loss: Alternately magnetising and demagnetising, the iron core causes loss of energy. It is minimised using a special alloy of iron core with silicon. **(1 Mark)**

Note

A transformer does not violate the law of conservation of energy. If transformer changes a low-voltage into a high voltage then current is reduced by the same proportion.

Delhi *2015*

CBSE Board Solved Paper

Time Allowed : 3 Hours —— *Maximum Marks : 70*

General Instructions:
(i) There are **26** questions in all. All questions are compulsory.
(ii) This question paper has **five** sections: Section **A**, Section **B**, Section **C**, Section **D** and Section **E**.
(iii) Section **A** contains **five** questions of **one** mark each, Section **B** contains **five** questions of **two** marks each, Section **C** contains **twelve** questions of **three** marks each, Section **D** contains **one** value based question of **four** marks and Section **E** contains **three** questions of **five** marks each.
(iv) There is no overall choice. However, an internal choice has been provided in **one** question of **two** marks, **one** question of **three** marks and all the **three** questions of **five** marks weightage. You have to attempt only **one** of the choices in such questions
(v) You may use the following values of physical constants wherever necessary:

$c = 3 \times 10^8$ m/s

$h = 6.63 \times 10^{-34}$ Js

$e = 1.6 \, 10^{-19}$ C

$\mu_0 = 4\pi \times 10^{-7}$ Tm A^{-1}

$\varepsilon_0 = 8.854 \times 10^{-12}$ C^2 N^{-1} m^{-2}

$\dfrac{1}{4\pi\varepsilon_0} = 9 \times 10^9$ N m^2 C^{-2}

Mass of electron $(m_e) = 9.1 \times 10^{-31}$ kg

Mass of neutron $= 1.675 \times 10^{-27}$ kg

Mass of proton $= 1.673 \times 10^{-27}$ kg

Avogadro's number $= 6.023 \times 10^{23}$ per gram mole

Boltzmann constant $= 1.38 \times 10^{-23}$ JK^{-1}

SECTION - A

1. Define capacitative reactance. Write its S.I. unit.
2. What is the electric flux through a cube of side 1 cm which encloses an electric dipole?
3. A concave lens of refractive index 1.5 is immersed in a medium of refractive index 1.65. What is the nature of the lens?
4. How side bands are produced?
5. Graph showing the variation of current versus voltage for material GaAs is shown in the figure. Identify the region of
   (i) negative resistance
   (ii) where ohm's law is obeyed.

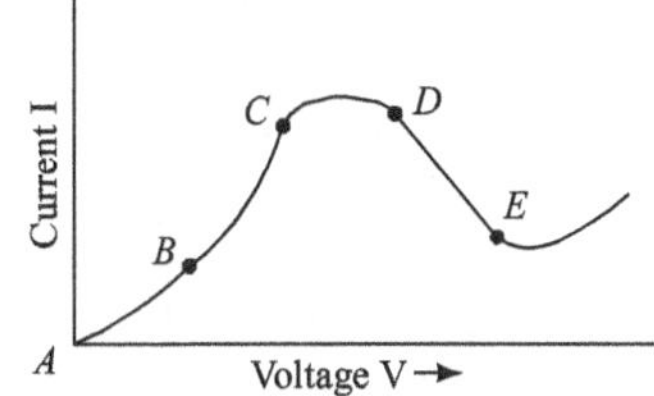

SECTION - B

6. A proton and an α-particle have same de-Broglie wavelength determine the ratio of (i) their accelerating potentials and (ii) their speeds.

7. Show that the radius of the orbit in hydrogen atom varies as n^2, where n is the principle quantum number of the atom.

8. Distinguish between 'intrinsic' and 'extrinsic' semiconductor.

9. Use the mirror equation to show that an object placed between f and $2f$ of a concave mirror produces a real image beyond $2f$.

OR

Find an expression for intensity of transmitted light when a polariod sheet is rotated between two crossed polariod. In which position of the polariod sheet will the transmitted intensity be maximum?

10. Use kirchhoff's law to obtain conditions for the balanced condition in a wheatstone bridge.

SECTION - C

11. Name the part of the electromagnetic spectrum which is
(a) suitable for radar system used in aircraft navigation
(b) used to treat muscular strain
(c) used as a diagnostic tool in medicine
Write in brief, how these waves are produced.

12. (i) A giant refracting telescope has an objective lens of focal length 15 m. If an eye piece of focal length 1.0 cm is used, what is the angular magnification of the telescope.
(ii) If this telescope is used to view moon, what is the diameter of the image of the moon formed by the objective lens? The diameter of the moon is 3.48×10^6 m and radius of lunar orbit is 3.8×10^8 m.

13. Write Einstein's photoelectric equation and mention which important features in photoelectric effect can be explained with the help of this equation.

The maximum kinetic energy of the photoelectrons gets doubled when the wavelength of light incident on the surfaces changes from λ_1 to λ_2. Derive the expressions for the threshold wavelength λ_0 and work function for the metal surface.

14. In the study of Geiger-Marsdon experiment on scattering of α-particles by a thin foil of gold, draw the trajectory of α-particles in the coulomb field of target nucleus. Explain briefly how one gets the information on the size of the nucleus from this study.

From relation $R = R_0 A^{1/3}$, where R_0 is constant and A is the mass number of the nucleus, show the nuclear density is independent of A.

OR

Distinguish between nuclear fission and fusion. Show now in both these processes energy is released.

Calculate the energy release in MeV in deuterium-tritium fusion reaction.

$$\, _1^2\text{H} + \, _1^3\text{H} \longrightarrow \, _2^4\text{He} + \, _0^1\text{n}$$

using data.

$$m\left(\, _1^2\text{H}\right) = 2.014102 \ u$$

$$m\left(\, _1^3\text{H}\right) = 3.016049 \ u$$

$$m\left(\, _2^4\text{He}\right) = 4.002603 \ u$$

$$m_n = 1.008665 \ u$$

$$1 \ u = 931.5 \ \text{MeV/c}^2$$

15. Draw a block diagram of a detector for AM signal and show, using necessary processes and the waveform how the original message signal is detected from the input AM wave.

16. A cell of emf 'E' and internal resistance 'r' is connected across a variable load resistor R. Draw the plots of the terminal voltage V versus (i) R and (ii) the current.

It is found that when $R = 4 \ \Omega$, the current is 1 A and when R is increased to 9 Ω, the current reduces to 0.5 A. Find the values of the emf E and internal resistance r.

17. Two capacitor of unknown capacitances C_1 and C_2 are connected first in series and then in parallel across a battery of 100 V. If the energy stored in the two combinations is 0.045 J and 0.25 J respectively, determine the value of C_1 and C_2. Also calculate the charge on each capacitor in parallel combination.

18. State the working principle of galvanometer.

A galvanometer of resistance G is converted into a voltmeter to measure upto V volts by connecting a resistance R_1 in series with the coil. If a resistance R_2 is connected in series with it, then it can measure upto V/2 volts. Find the resistance, in terms of R_1 and R_2, required to be connected to convert it into a voltmeter that can read upto 2V. Also find the resistance G of the galvanometer in terms of R_1 and R_2.

19. With what considerations in view, a photodiode is fabricated? State its working with the help of a suitable diagram.

Even though the current in the forward bias is known to be more than in the reverse bias, yet the diode works in reverse bias. What is the reason?

20. Draw a circuit diagram of a transistor amplifier in CE configuration.

Define terms: (i) input resistance and (ii) current amplification factor. How are these determined using typical input and output characteristics?

21. Answer the following questions:
(i) In a double slit experiment using light of wavelength 600 nm, the angular width of the fringe formed on a distant screen is 0.1°. Find the spacing between the two slits.
(ii) Light of wavelength 5000 Å. Propagating in air gets partly reflected from the surface of water. How will the wavelength and frequencies of the reflected and refracted light be affected?

22. An inductor L of inductance X_L is connected in series with a bulb B and an ac source. How would brightness of the bulb change when (i) number of turns in the inductor is reduced, (ii) an iron rod is inserted in the inductor and (iii) a capacitor of reactance $X_C = X_L$ is inserted in series in the circuit. Justify your answer in each case.

SECTION - D

23. A group of students while coming from the school noticed a box marked "Danger H.T. 2200 V" at a substation in the main street. They did not understand the utility of such a high voltage, while they argued, the supply was only 220 V. They asked their teacher this question the next day. The teacher thought it to be an important question and therefore explained to the whole class.

Answer the following question:

(i) What device is used to bring the high voltage down to low voltage of a.c. current and what is the principle of its working?

(ii) Is it possible to use this device for bringing down high d.c. voltage to the low voltage? Explain.

(iii) Write the values displaced by the students and the teacher.

SECTION - E

24. (a) State Ampere's circuital law. Use this law to obtain the expression for magnetic field inside an air cored toroid of average radius 'r' having 'n' turns per unit length and carrying a steady current I.

(b) An observer to the left of a solenoid of N turns each of cross-section area 'A' observes that a steady current I in it flows in the clockwise direction. Depict the magnetic field lines due to the solenoid specifying its polarity and show that it act as a bar magnet of magnetic moment $m = NIA$.

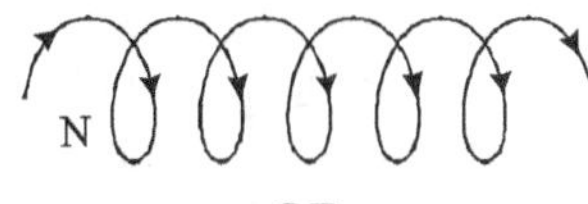

OR

(a) Define mutual inductance and write S.I. unit.

(b) Derive the expression for the mutual inductance of two long co-axial solenoids of same length wound over one another.

(c) In an experiment, two coils C_1 and C_2 are placed closed to each other. Find out the expression for the emf induced in the coil C_1 due to a change in current through the coil C_2.

25. (a) Using Huygen's principle of construction of secondary wavelets explain how a diffraction pattern is obtained on a screen due to a narrow slit on which a monochromatic beam of light is incident normally.

(b) Show that the angular width of the Ist diffraction fringe is half that of the central fringe.

(c) Explain why the maxima at $\theta = \left(n + \dfrac{1}{2} \right) \dfrac{\lambda}{a}$ become weaker with increasing n.

OR

(a) A point object 'O' is kept in a medium of refractive index n_1 in front of a convex spherical surface of radius of curvature R which separates the second medium of refractive index n_2 from the first one, as shown in figure.

Draw the ray diagram showing the image formation and deduce the relationship between object distance and image distance in terms of n_1, n_2 and R.

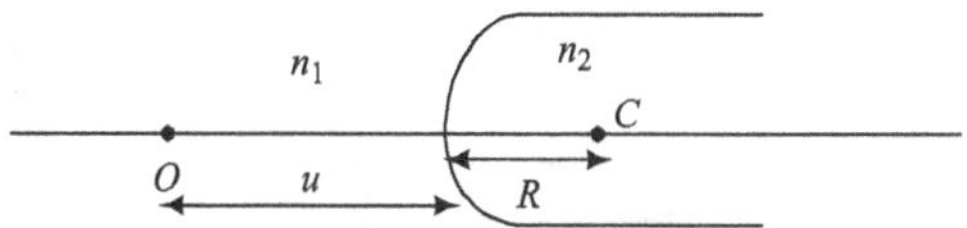

(b) When the image formed above act as a virtual object for concave spherical, surface separating the medium n_2 from n_1 ($n_2 > n_1$), draw this ray diagram and write the similar (similar to (a)) relation. Hence obtain the expression for lens maker's formula.

26. (a) An electric dipole of dipole moment $\vec{p}$ consists of point charges $+q$ and $-q$ separated by a distance $2a$ apart. Deduce the expression for the electric field $\vec{E}$ due to the dipole at a distance x from the centre of the dipole on its axis line in terms of the dipole moment $\vec{p}$. Hence show that in the limit $x \gg a$, $\vec{E} \to 2\vec{p}/(4\pi\varepsilon_0 x^3)$.

(b) Given the electric field in the region $\vec{E} = 2x\hat{i}$, find the net electric flux through the cube and the charge enclosed by it.

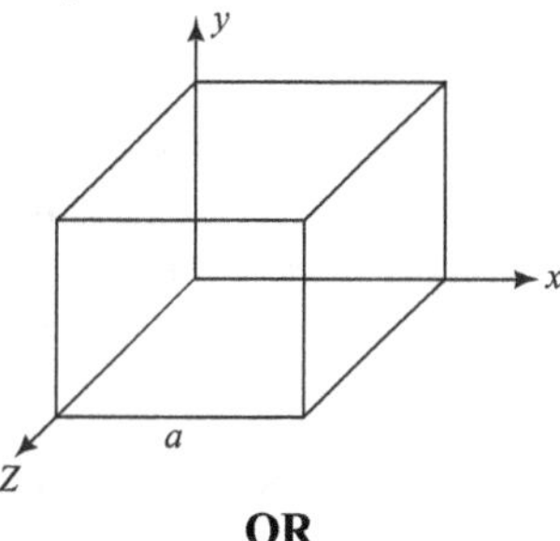

OR

(a) Explain, using suitable diagrams, the difference in the behaviour of a (i) conductor and (ii) dielectric in the presence of an external electric field. Define the terms polarization of a dielectric and write its relation with susceptibility.

(b) A thin metallic spherical shell of radius R carries a charge Q on its surface. A point charge $\dfrac{Q}{2}$ is placed at its centre C and an other charge $+2Q$ is placed outside the shell at a distance x from the centre as shown in figure. Find (i) the force on the charge at the centre of shell and at the point A and (ii) the electric flux through the shell.

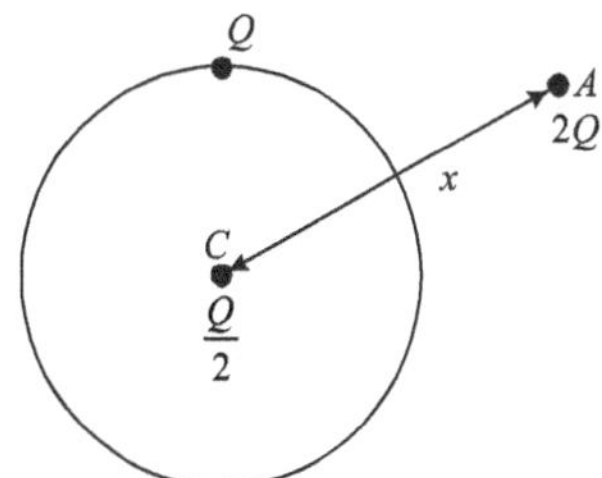

Solutions

SECTION - A

1. Capacitative reactance, $X_C = \dfrac{1}{\omega C}$, is the effective resistance or opposition offered by the capacitor to the flow of a.c. through it.   **(½ Mark)**

Its S.I. unit - ohm (Ω).   **(½ Mark)**

2. From gauss's law, electric flux

$$\phi = \frac{q}{\varepsilon_0} \qquad \textbf{(½ Mark)}$$

where q = total charge enclosed in gaussian surface.

Here, total charge is zero (as electric dipole consists of two equal and opposite charge) within the cube. So, since $q = 0$, flux ϕ through cube is also zero.   **(½ Mark)**

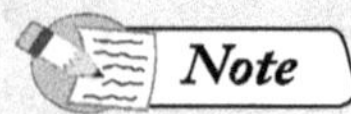

Note

In Gauss law, which states that $\phi = \dfrac{q}{\varepsilon_0}$

Electric flux, ϕ is due to all charges, outside or inside gaussian surface. But the term q, on the right side of Gauss's law, however represents only the charge inside gaussian surface.

3. The lens will behave as converging lens because the refractive index of lens (rarer medium), $\mu_L = 1.5$ is less than the refractive index of surrounding medium, $\mu_m = 1.6$ (denser medium). So, when the ray of light emerges out of the lens, it bends towards the normal as it is moving from a rarer to denser medium.   **(1 Mark)**

Note

If the concave lens given in question was immersed in a medium of refractive index less than refractive index of lens, then concave lens would behave as diverging lens.

4. Side bands are produced due to superposition of carrier waves of frequency ω_c over modulating/audio signal of frequency ω_m.

$\omega_c + \omega_m \rightarrow$ upper side band frequency   **(½ Mark)**

$\omega_c - \omega_m \rightarrow$ lower side band frequency.   **(½ Mark)**

Note

While choose carrier wave for amplitude modulation, care should be taken that broadcast frequencies (carrier wave) are sufficiently spaced out so that sidebands do not overlap and different stations can operate without interfering with each other.

5. (i) Negative resistance – DE **(½ Mark)**

    (ii) Where Ohm's law is obeyed – AB **(½ Mark)**

Note

Remember slope of a I–V graph $= \dfrac{1}{\text{resistance }(R)}$ slope of a V–I graph $=$ resistance (R)

In the given question, I–V graph is given. For both the graphs, if curve is a straight line through origin then ohm's law is obeyed.

+ve slope – +ve resistance

–ve slope – –ve resistance.

SECTION - B

6. (i) De-Broglie wavelength of a particle accelerating at a potential V is   **(½ Mark)**

$$\lambda = \frac{h}{\sqrt{2mqV}}$$

where m = mass of the particle

         q = charge of the particle

         h = planck's constant

For proton, let

$$m = m_p, \, q = q_p, \, \lambda = \lambda_p, \, V = V_p$$

For α–particle

$$m = m_\alpha = 4m_p, \, q = q_\alpha = 2q_p$$
$$\lambda = \lambda_\alpha, \, V = V_\alpha$$

Given, $\lambda_\alpha = \lambda_p$

$$\therefore \lambda_p = \lambda_\alpha = \frac{h}{\sqrt{2m_\alpha q_\alpha v_\alpha}} = \frac{h}{\sqrt{2m_p q_p v_p}}$$

$$\Rightarrow \sqrt{2m_\alpha q_\alpha V_\alpha} = \sqrt{2m_p q_p V_p}$$

Squaring both sides

$$2\,m_\alpha\,q_\alpha\,V_\alpha = 2\,m_p\,q_p\,V_p$$

$$\Rightarrow (4m_p)(2q_p)\,V_\alpha = m_p\,q_p\,V_p$$

$$\Rightarrow \frac{V_p}{V_\alpha} = \frac{4m_p \times 2q_p}{m_p q_p} = \frac{8}{1}$$

$$\therefore \qquad V_p : V_\alpha = 8 : 1 \qquad \textbf{(½ Mark)}$$

  (ii) De-Broglie wavelength of particle moving with speed v is   **(½ Mark)**

$$\lambda = \frac{h}{mv}$$

For proton $\lambda_p = \dfrac{h}{m_p v_p}$

For α-particle $\lambda_\alpha = \dfrac{h}{m_\alpha v_\alpha}$

as $\lambda_\alpha = \lambda_p$

$$\therefore \quad \frac{h}{m_p v_p} = \frac{h}{m_\alpha v_\alpha}$$

$$\Rightarrow \quad \frac{v_p}{v_\alpha} = \frac{m_\alpha}{m_p} = \frac{4m_p}{m_p} = 4 \qquad (\because m_\alpha = 4\,m_p)$$

$$\therefore \quad v_p : v_\alpha = 4 : 1 \qquad \textbf{(½ Mark)}$$

7. Consider a electron of charge '$-e$' revolving around nucleus with a positive charge '$+e$', in a circular orbit of hydrogen atom.

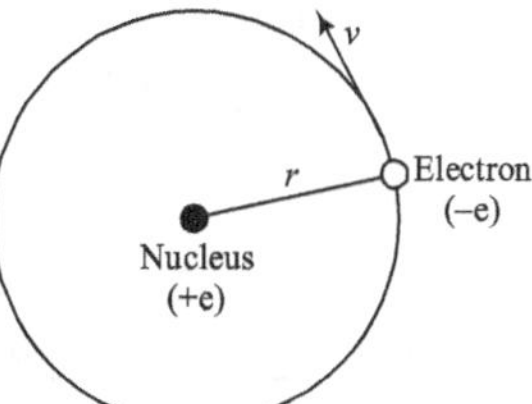

Let the radius of circular orbit = r.

The electrostatic attraction force between nucleus and electron is

$$F = \frac{ke^2}{r^2} \qquad ...(i) \qquad \textbf{(½ Mark)}$$

To keep the electron in its orbit, the centripetal force on the electron must be equal to electrostatic attraction. Therefore,

$$\frac{mv^2}{r} = \frac{ke^2}{r^2}$$
$$\Rightarrow \quad mv^2r = ke^2 \qquad ...(ii) \text{ (½ Mark)}$$

where m = mass of electron

$$k = \frac{1}{4\pi\varepsilon_0}$$

v = speed of electron in orbit.

Bohr's quantisation condition for angular momentum is

$$mvr = \frac{nh}{2\pi}$$
$$\text{or} \quad m^2v^2r^2 = \frac{n^2h^2}{4\pi^2} \qquad ...(iii) \quad \textbf{(½ Mark)}$$

Divide (iii) by (ii)

$$mr = \frac{n^2h^2}{4\pi^2} \times \frac{1}{ke^2}$$
$$\therefore \quad r = n^2 \times \frac{h^2}{4\pi^2e^2km} \quad \boxed{r \propto n^2} \qquad \textbf{(½ Mark)}$$

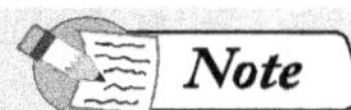

Note

While deriving the radius of orbit of hydrogen atom, an assumption has been made that orbits are circular. But orbits under inverse-square force (Here, coloumb force) are in general elliptical. However, it was shown by Arnold Sommerfeld that, when the restriction of circular orbit was removed, these equations continue to hold even for elliptical orbit.

8.

Intrinsic semiconductor	Extrinsic Semiconductor
(i) The presence of charge carrier (e and h) is an 'intrinsic' property of the material.	(i) The presence of charge carrier (e and h) is an 'extrinsic' as well as 'intrinsic' property.
(ii) Charge carrier are obtained by thermal excitation	(ii) Charge carriers are obtained by doping of a suitable impurity.
(iii) $n_e = n_h$	(iii) $n_e \neq n_h$

9. Mirror equation is

$$\frac{1}{v} + \frac{1}{u} = \frac{1}{f} \qquad \textbf{(½ Mark)}$$

where v = image distance

u = object distance

f = focal length of mirror.

For concave mirror,

$$f < 0, u < 0 \qquad \textbf{(½ Mark)}$$

Let us suppose, first $u = -f$.

Then using mirror equation, we get

$$\frac{1}{v} - \frac{1}{f} = \frac{1}{-f}$$
$$\therefore \quad v = \infty \qquad ...(i)$$

Now suppose $u = -2f$. **(½ Mark)**

Then using mirror equation, we get

$$\frac{1}{v} - \frac{1}{2f} = \frac{1}{-f}$$
$$\Rightarrow \quad \frac{1}{v} = \frac{-1}{f} + \frac{1}{2f} = \frac{-1}{2f}$$
$$\therefore \quad v = -2f \qquad ...(ii)$$

Our object lies between f and $2f$. So, from equation (i) and (ii), for $2f < u < f$, $v \geq -2f$ i.e., image will lie beyond $2f$.

(½ Mark)

OR

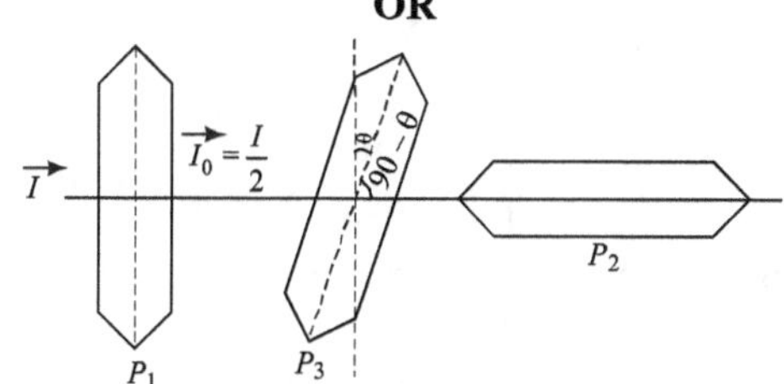

Let P_1 polariod and P_2 polariod be in crossed positions i.e., angle between their pass axis is 90°. A polariod P_3 is rotated between them. Let, at any instant, the angle between P_1 and P_3 is θ and angle between P_3 and P_2 is (90 – θ). Intensity of transmitted light coming out of P_3, according to Malus' law, is

$$I' = I_0 \cos^2 \theta \qquad \textbf{(½ Mark)}$$

Intensity of transmitted light coming out of P_2,

$$I'' = I' \cos^2 (90 - \theta)$$
$$I'' = (I_0 \cos^2\theta) [\cos^2 (90 - \theta)] \qquad \textbf{(½ Mark)}$$

Now, using trignometeric identities,

$$\cos (90 - \theta) = \sin \theta$$
$$\sin 2\theta = 2 \sin \theta \cos \theta$$
$$I'' = I_0 (\cos \theta \sin \theta)^2$$
$$= I_0 \frac{\sin^2 2\theta}{4}$$
$$I'' = \frac{I_0}{4} \sin^2 2\theta \qquad \textbf{(½ Mark)}$$

The value of 'sine' function is maximum when 'theta' is 90°. So, for I'' to be maximum, $\theta = 45° = \dfrac{\pi}{4}$. **(½ Mark)**

Note

According to Malus' law, the intensity of transmitted polarized light, when two polariod are kept such that they make angle θ between their pass axis, is given as, $I = I_0\cos^2 \theta$ where I_0 = max. intensity of polarised light after passing through Ist polariod.

10. For a balanced bridge, the current through galvanometer G is zero. So, $I_g = 0$.

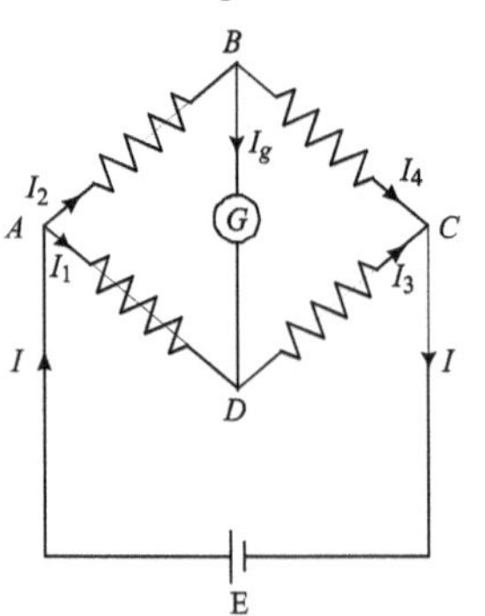

(½ Mark)

For $I_g = 0$, $I_2 = I_4$ and $I_1 = I_3$.

Applying Kirchhoff's loop rule in *ADBA*,

$-I_1 R_1 + 0 + I_2 R_2 = 0$ (½ Mark)

$\Rightarrow \quad I_1 R_1 = I_2 R_2$ ...(i)

Applying Kirchhoff's loop rule in *CBDC*,

$I_4 R_4 + 0 - I_3 R_3 = 0$

$\Rightarrow \quad I_4 R_4 = I_3 R_3$ ...(ii)

From equation (i)

$$\frac{I_1}{I_2} = \frac{R_2}{R_1}$$ ...(iii) (½ Mark)

From equation (ii)

$$\frac{I_3}{I_4} = \frac{I_1}{I_2} = \frac{R_4}{R_3}$$ ...(iv)

From equation (iii) and (iv)

$$\frac{R_2}{R_1} = \frac{R_4}{R_3}$$ (½ Mark)

This is the balanced condition of Wheatstone bridge.

SECTION - C

11. (a) Micro waves.

   Production:- They are produced using Gunn diodes or oscillating currents in vaccum tubes like klystrons.

   (b) Infrared waves.

   Production:- They are produced by hot bodies or molecules. When atoms or molecules move due to high temperature, they emit infrared radiations.

   (c) X-Rays.

   Production:- X-Rays are produced due to sudden deceleration of fast moving electron upon collision with the metal target.   **(3 × 1 = 3 Marks)**

12. (i) Angular magnification of telescope is

$$m = \frac{f_o}{f_e}$$ (½ Mark)

   where f_o = focal length of objective

   f_e = focal length of eyepiece.

   Given, $f_o = 15$ m

   $f_e = 1$ cm $= 10^{-2}$ m

   $\therefore \quad m = \dfrac{15}{10^{-2}} = 1500$ (½ Mark)

(ii) Diameter of moon 'd' $= 3.48 \times 10^6$ m

Radius of lunar orbit 'r' $= 3.8 \times 10^8$ m

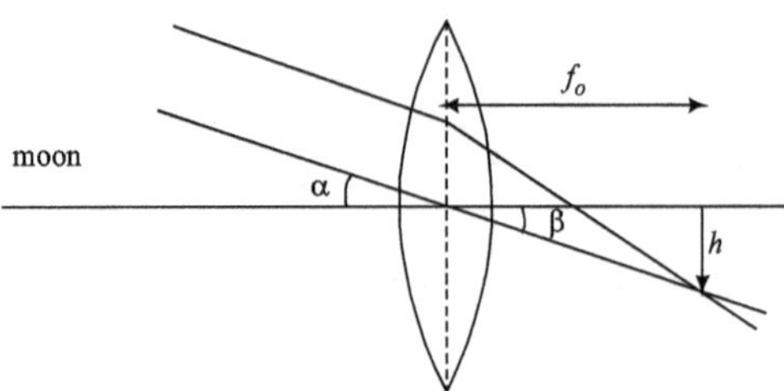

Objective lens

From the figure, we see that angle subtended by moon at objective lens is equal to angle subtended by image of moon formed by the objective.

Angle subtended by moon at objective lens,

$$\alpha = \frac{\text{Diameter of moon}}{\text{radius of lunar orbit}}$$

$$\alpha = \frac{3.48 \times 10^6}{3.8 \times 10^8}$$ ...(i) (½ Mark)

Angle subtended by image of moon at objective,

$$\beta = \frac{\text{diameter of image of moon}}{f_o}$$

$$\beta = \frac{\text{diameter of image of moon}}{15}$$ ...(ii) (½ Mark)

Since $\alpha = \beta$, from equation (i) and (ii)

$$\frac{3.48 \times 10^6}{3.8 \times 10^8} = \frac{\text{diameter of image of moon}}{15}$$

(½ Mark)

$\Rightarrow$ Diameter of image of moon

$$= \frac{3.48 \times 10^6}{3.8 \times 10^8} \times 15$$ (½ Mark)

$$= 13.73 \text{ cm}$$

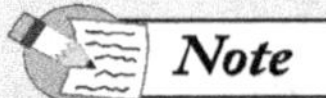 **Note**

Angular magnification, 'm', of telescope when final image is formed at (D = 25 cm) least distance of distinct vision is given as

$$m = \left(\frac{f_o}{f_e}\right)\left(1 + \frac{f_o}{D}\right)$$

13. Einstein's photoelectric equation is:-

$$K_{max} = h\nu - \phi_0$$ ...(i) (½ Mark)

where

K_{max} = max. kinetic energy of emitted electron

$h\nu$ = energy of incident photon

ϕ_0 = work function of metal.

Important feature of photoelectric equation:-

(i) According to equation K_{max} depends linearly on ν, frequency of incident radiation and is independent of intensity of radiation.   (½ Mark)

(ii) Equation tells that emission cannot take place if $h\nu <$ ϕ_0, since K_{max} cannot be negative. This gives the existence of threshold frequency.   **(½ Mark)**
Given, max. kinetic energy of photoelectrons gets doubled when wavelength of light incident changes from λ_1 to λ_2.
We know that $\nu\lambda = c$
Where c = speed of light.

Work function $\phi_0 = h\nu_0 = \dfrac{hc}{\lambda_0}$

where ν_0 = threshold frequency.
So, for wavelength λ_1,
$$h\nu_1 = \phi_0 + K_{max}$$
$$\Rightarrow \frac{hc}{\lambda_1} = \frac{hc}{\lambda_0} + K_{max} \qquad \text{...(ii)}$$
For wavelength λ_2
$$h\nu_2 = \phi_0 + 2 K_{max}$$
$$\Rightarrow \frac{hc}{\lambda_2} = \frac{hc}{\lambda_0} + 2 K_{max} \qquad \text{...(iii)}$$
From equation (ii) and (iii)
$$\frac{hc}{\lambda_2} = \frac{hc}{\lambda_0} + 2\left[\frac{hc}{\lambda_1} - \frac{hc}{\lambda_0}\right] \qquad \textbf{(½ Mark)}$$
$$\Rightarrow \frac{hc}{\lambda_2} = \frac{hc}{\lambda_0} + \frac{2hc}{\lambda_1} - \frac{2hc}{\lambda_0}$$
$$\Rightarrow \frac{2hc}{\lambda_1} - \frac{hc}{\lambda_2} = \frac{hc}{\lambda_0}$$
$$\Rightarrow \boxed{\frac{1}{\lambda_0} = \frac{2}{\lambda_1} - \frac{1}{\lambda_2}}$$
$$\Rightarrow \lambda_0 = \frac{\lambda_1\lambda_2}{2\lambda_2 - \lambda_1} \qquad \textbf{(½ Mark)}$$
so work function
$$\phi_0 = \frac{hc}{\lambda_0} = \frac{hc(2\lambda_2 - \lambda_1)}{\lambda_1\lambda_2} \qquad \textbf{(½ Mark)}$$

14.   **(1 Mark)**

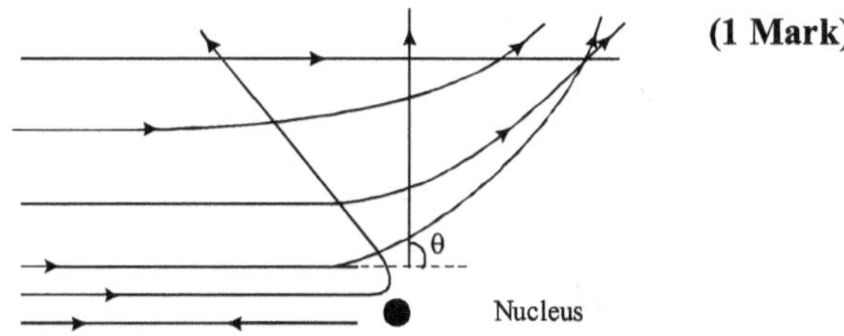

It is seen that an α-particle close to the nucleus suffers large scattering. The fact that only a small fraction of the number of incident particles rebound back indicates that the number of α-particles undergoing head on collision is small. This implies that the mass of the atom is concentrated in a small volume. So, this scattering gives the information on the size of the nucleus.   **(1 Mark)**
Radius of Nucleus is
$$R = R_0 A^{1/3} \qquad \textbf{(½ Mark)}$$

where A = mass number
             R_0 = constant.
$$\text{Density of Nucleus} = \frac{\text{Mass of Nucleus}}{\text{Volume of Nucleus}}$$
Assuming that nucleus is spherical in shape, volume of nucleus V will be,
$$V = \frac{4}{3}\pi R^3$$
$$= \frac{4}{3}\pi (R_0 A^{1/3})^3$$
$$V = \frac{4}{3}\pi R_0^3 A$$
The mass of nucleus = mass number A.
$$\therefore \text{Density of Nucleus} = \frac{A}{\frac{4}{3}\pi R_0^3 A}$$
$$= \frac{3}{4\pi R_0^3} \qquad \textbf{(½ Mark)}$$
which is independent of A.

> **Note**
>
> *Another way to ask this question.*
> *Q – Draw the trajectory of α-particles scattered by a thin foil of gold and briefly describe how the large angle scattering explains the existence of nucleus inside the atom.*

OR

Nuclear fission:- When a heavy nucleus ($A > 170$) decays into two or more daughter nuclei, some energy is released and this process is called nuclear fission.   **(1 Mark)**
Nuclear fusion:- When a light nucleus ($A < 30$) fuse with another light nucleus, to form a heavy stable nucleus, it is called nuclear fusion.   **(1 Mark)**

Given $${}_1^2 H + {}_1^3 H \rightarrow {}_2^4 He + {}_0^1 n$$
Energy Released
$$= \left[m\left({}_1^2 H\right) + m\left({}_1^3 H\right) - m\left({}_2^4 He\right) - m(n) \right]c^2 \qquad \textbf{(½ Mark)}$$
$$= [2.014102 + 3.016049 - 4.002603 - 1.008665]uc^2$$
$$= 0.018883\ uc^2$$
$$= 0.018883 \times 931.5\ \frac{\text{MeV}}{c^2}c^2$$
$$= 17.59\ \text{MeV.} \qquad \textbf{(½ Mark)}$$

15.
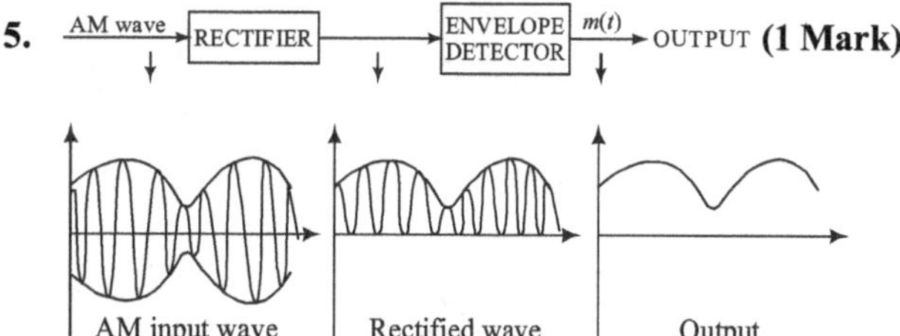

(1 Mark)

(2 Marks)

16.

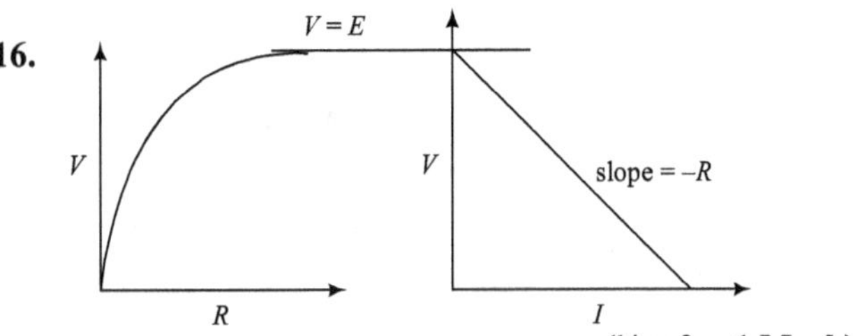

(½ × 2 = 1 Mark)

Terminal voltage $V = \varepsilon - Ir$

where $\varepsilon = emf$ of cell

       $I =$ current

       $r =$ internal resistance

Also, $V = IR$

$\therefore$ $IR = \varepsilon - Ir$

$\Rightarrow$ $\varepsilon = I(R + r)$

When $R = 4\Omega$, then $I = 1A$ **(½ Mark)**

        $\varepsilon = (4 + r)$ ...(i) **(½ Mark)**

When $R = 9\,\Omega$, then $I = 0.5\,A$

        $\varepsilon = 0.5\,(9 + r)$ **(½ Mark)**

        $\varepsilon = 4.5 + 0.5\,r$ ...(ii)

Solving equation (i) and (ii) we get

        $\varepsilon = 5\,V$ and $r = 1\,\Omega$ **(½ Mark)**

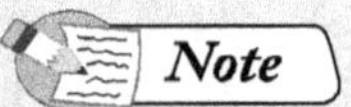 **Note**

Terminal voltage $V = \varepsilon - I_r$

or $V = (-r)\,I + \varepsilon$ ...(i)

Comparing equation (i) with equation of straight line

$y = mx + C$, we get

Slope of V–I graph $= -r$

$y =$ intercept $C = \varepsilon$

17. Given,

Energy stored in series combination, $E_S = 0.045\,J$

Energy stored in parallel combination, $E_P = 0.25\,J$

Energy stored in capacitor is

$$E = \frac{1}{2}CV^2$$

Capacitance in series

$$\frac{1}{C_S} = \frac{1}{C_1} + \frac{1}{C_2}$$

$$C_S = \frac{C_1 C_2}{C_1 + C_2} \qquad \textbf{(½ Mark)}$$

$\therefore$

$$E_S = \frac{1}{2}C_S V^2$$

$$0.045 = \frac{1}{2}\frac{C_1 C_2}{C_1 + C_2}(100)^2 \quad ..(i)\ \textbf{(½ Mark)}$$

Capacitance in parallel

$$C_P = C_1 + C_2$$

$\therefore$

$$E_P = \frac{1}{2}C_P V^2$$

$$0.25 = \frac{1}{2}(C_1 + C_2)(100)^2$$

$$C_1 + C_2 = 0.5 \times 10^{-4} \qquad \text{...(ii) }\textbf{(½ Mark)}$$

Putting the value $(C_1 + C_2)$ in equation (i), we get

$$0.045 = \frac{1}{2}\frac{C_1 C_2}{(0.5 \times 10^{-4})} \times (100)^2$$

$\Rightarrow$ $C_1 C_2 = 0.045 \times 10^{-8}$ ...(iii) **(½ Mark)**

Using the alegrabic identity,

$$(C_1 - C_2)^2 = (C_1 + C_2)^2 - 4C_1 C_2$$

$$(C_1 - C_2)^2 = (0.5 \times 10^{-4})^2 - 0.045 \times 4 \times 10^{-8}$$

(From eqn (ii) and (iii))

$$(C_1 - C_2)^2 = 0.25 \times 10^{-8} - 0.180 \times 10^{-8}$$

$$= 0.07 \times 10^{-8}$$

$$(C_1 - C_2) = 2.6 \times 10^{-5} = 0.26 \times 10^{-4} \quad \text{...(iv)}$$

Solving equation (ii) and (iv), we get

$$C_1 = 0.38 \times 10^{-4}\,F$$

$$C_2 = 0.12 \times 10^{-4}\,F \qquad \textbf{(½ Mark)}$$

Charges on capacitor C_1 and C_2 in parallel combination

$$Q_1 = C_1 V$$

$$= 0.38 \times 10^{-4} \times 100$$

$$Q_1 = 0.38 \times 10^{-2}\,C$$

$$Q_2 = C_2 V$$

$$= (0.12 \times 10^{-4})\,100$$

$$Q_2 = 0.12 \times 10^{-2}\,C. \qquad \textbf{(½ Mark)}$$

18. *Working principle of galvanometer:-* A current carrying coil placed in a magnetic field experiences a current dependent torque, which tends to rotate the coil and produces angular deflection.   **(1 Mark)**

Voltage when resistance R_1 is connected in series with galvanometer G,

$$V = I(G + R_1) \qquad \text{...(i)}$$

Voltage when resistance R_2 is connected in series with galvanometer G,

$$\frac{V}{2} = I(G + R_2) \qquad \text{...(ii) }\textbf{(½ Mark)}$$

From equation (i) and (ii)

$$2 = \frac{I(G + R_1)}{I(G + R_2)}$$

$\Rightarrow$ $2(G + R_2) = G + R_1$

        $2G + 2R_2 = G + R_1$

         $G = R_1 - 2R_2$ **(½ Mark)**

Let R_3 be the resistance required for conversion into voltmeter of range $2V$.

$\therefore$ $2V = I(G + R_3)$ ...(iii)

From equation (i) and (iii)

$$2 = \frac{G + R_3}{G + R_1} \qquad \textbf{(½ Mark)}$$

$\Rightarrow$ $R_3 = G + 2R_1$

Putting the value of G in above equation

$$R_3 = R_1 - 2R_2 + 2R_1$$
$$R_3 = 3R_1 - 2R_2 \qquad \text{(½ Mark)}$$

19. Photodiode is fabricated with a transparent window to allow light to fall on diode. **(½ Mark)**

Working of photodiode:-

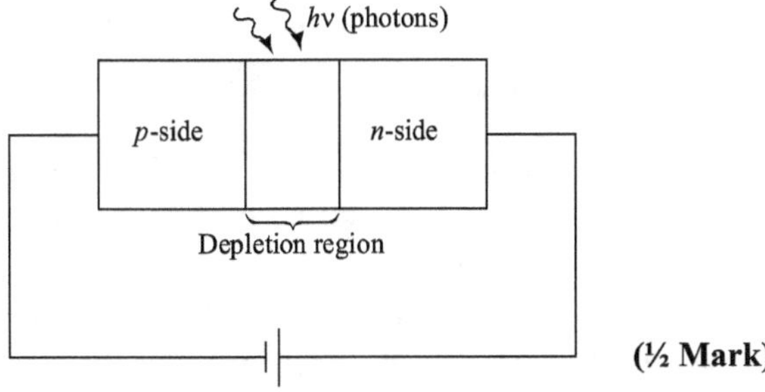

(½ Mark)

When photodiode is illuminated with light photons of energy hν greater than the energy gap E_g of the semiconductor, additional e-h pair are generated near depletion region. They get separated due to junction electric field and hence produce an emf. Electrons get collected on *n*-side and holes on *p*-side. **(1 Mark)**

Reason of reverse biasing of photodiode:-

The whole purpose of a photodiode is to detect light, and it does this by measuring the effect the light has on the current. When photodiode is illuminated with light, the fractional increase in majority carriers is much less than the fractional increase in minority carriers. Consequently, the increase in reverse bias current is more readily measurable than increase in forward bias current.

(1 Mark)

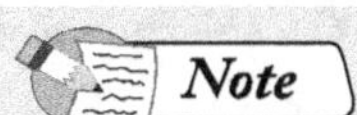

> ***Note***
>
> *Both solar cell and photodiode work on same principle that an emf is generated when radiation falls on p-n junction. But the difference between them is for solar cell there is no external bias (photodiode is reversed bias) and the junction area is kept much larger for solar radiation.*

20. *Input resistance:-* This is defined as the ratio of change in base - emitter voltage (ΔV_{BE}) to the change in base current (ΔI_B) at constant collector - emitter voltage (V_{CE}).

$$r_i = \left(\frac{\Delta V_{BE}}{\Delta I_B}\right)_{V_{CE}}$$

The value of input resistance is determined from the slope of I_B verses V_{BE} plot at constant V_{CE}. **(1 Mark)**

Current amplification:- This is defined as the ratio of the change in collector current to the change in base current at constant collector - emitter voltage (V_{CE}).

$$\beta_{ac} = \left(\frac{\Delta I_C}{\Delta I_B}\right)_{V_{CE}}$$

It is obtained from slope of collector I_C versus V_{CE} plot using different values of I_B. **(1 Mark)**

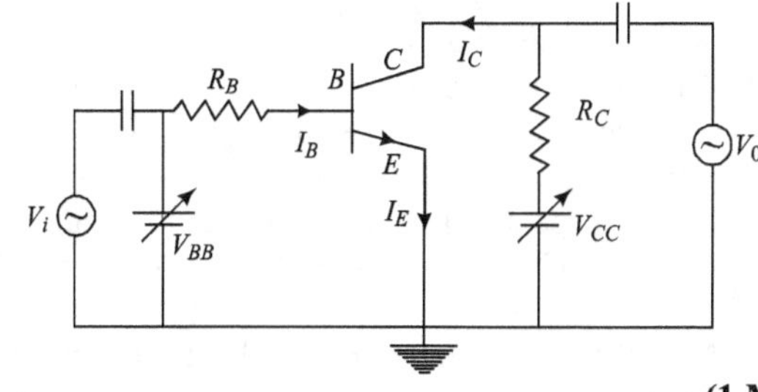

(1 Mark)

21. (i) In a double slit experiment, angular width of fringes is **(½ Mark)**

$$\theta = \frac{\lambda}{d}$$

where d = separation between slits.

Given, $\lambda = 600$ nm $= 600 \times 10^{-9}$ m

$$\theta = 0.1° = 0.1 \times \frac{\pi}{180} \text{ radian}$$

So, $0.1 \times \dfrac{\pi}{180} = \dfrac{600 \times 10^{-9}}{d}$

$\Rightarrow \qquad d = \dfrac{600 \times 10^{-9} \times 180}{0.1 \times \pi}$

$\Rightarrow \qquad d = 3.43 \times 10^{-4}$ m

$\qquad\qquad = 0.34$ cm **(½ Mark)**

(ii) Given

Wavelength of incident light $= 5000$ Å

For reflected wave:-

Reflected wave will have same frequency and wavelength as the incident wave. **(1 Mark)**

For refracted wave:-

Refracted wave will have same frequency as frequency depends on source. But its wavelength will be decreased because velocity of wave in water will be less than in air. **(½ Mark)**

22. (i) Brightness of bulb will increase when no. of turns in inductor is reduced.

When no. of turns in inductor is reduced, then, the inductance is $(L = \mu_0 n^2 Al)$ also reduced because $L \propto n^2$ (no. of turns per unit length).

Therefore, inductive reactance $X_L = \omega L$ will also get reduced. This will increase the brightness as current through it will increase. **(1 Mark)**

(ii) Brightness of lamp will decrease when an iron rod is inserted in inductor.

Inductance L when an iron rod is inserted is

$L = \mu_r \mu_0 n^2 Al$

where μ_r = relative permeability of iron.

Therefore, L will increase. So, $X_L = \omega_L$ will also increase due to which current in lamp gets decreased. **(1 Mark)**

(iii) Brightness of lamp will increase when capacitor of $X_C = X_L$ is connected in series with inductor. When $X_C = X_L$, we get maximum current in the circuit due to resonance which will increase the brightness of lamp. **(1 Mark)**

SECTION - D

23. (i) The device is transformer. **(1 Mark)**

Working principle of transformer:- It works on the principle of mutual induction, i.e. when a changing current is passed through one of the two inductively coupled coils, an induced emf is set up in the other coil. **(1 Mark)**

(ii) No, high d.c. voltage cannot be lowered using transformer because for d.c. voltages there is no induced emf. **(1 Mark)**

(iii) *Values of students:-* Inquistive nature, Scientific temperament.

Values of teacher:- Concern for students, Professional honesty. **(1 Mark)**

SECTION - E

24. (a) Ampere's circuital law states that the line integral of the magnetic field $\vec{B}$ around any closed circuit is equal to μ_0 times the total current I passing through this closed circuit.

$$\oint \vec{B} \cdot \vec{dl} = \mu_0 I \qquad \textbf{(1 Mark)}$$

Magnetic field due to toriod:-

Let I be the current flowing through each turn of toriod. From the sectional view of toroid, the direction of magnetic field $\vec{B}$ is clock-wise. Consider 3 Amperian loop 1, 2 and 3.

Let the magnetic field along loop 1 be B, and radius be r_1. But this loop encloses no current *i.e.*, $I = 0$. Thus

$$B_1 L = I_e \mu_0 = (0)\,\mu_0 = 0$$
$$\Rightarrow \qquad B_1 = 0 \qquad \textbf{(½ Mark)}$$

Similarly, let the magnetic field along loop 3 be B_3 and radius of loop be r_3. However, the current coming out of the plane of the paper is cancelled exactly by the current going into it. Thus $I = 0$ giving $B_3 = 0$.

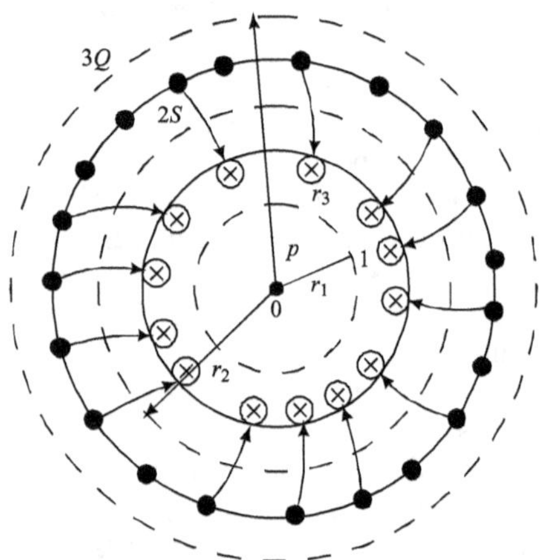

● – Current out of the plane of paper

⊗ – Current into the plane of paper **(½ Mark)**

The magnetic field along loop 2 be B_2. Radius of loop 2 is r. So, applying ampere circuital law for loop 2,

$$\oint \vec{B} \cdot \vec{dl} = \mu_0 I_e$$

$$\oint B_2 dl \cos 0° = \mu_0 I_e$$
$$B_2 (2\pi r) = \mu_0 I_e$$
$$\oint dl = \text{circumference of loop 2} = 2\pi r$$
$$\cos 0° = 1$$

Total current I_e due to N no. of turns will be
$$I_e = NI$$
$$\therefore \qquad B_2 (2\pi r) = \mu_0 NI$$
$$B_2 = \frac{\mu_0 NI}{2\pi r} \qquad \textbf{(½ Mark)}$$

Now, we can write

$N = 2\pi r n$ = perimeter of toroid × number of turns per unit length.

Thus, magnetic field due to toroid $= B = \mu_0 nI$ **(½ Mark)**

(b) 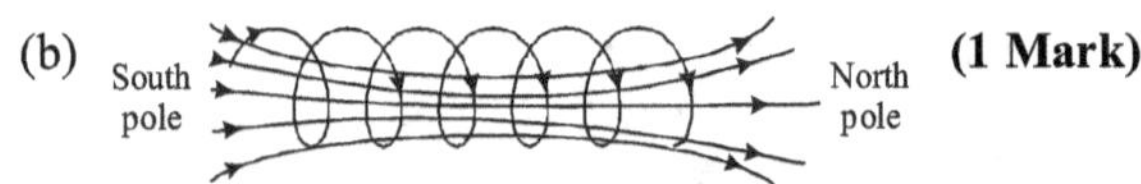

(1 Mark)

The solenoid contains N loops, each carrying a current I. Therefore each loop acts as a dipole.

Magnetic moment of loop of area A is
$$m = IA.$$

The magnetic moment of all loops are aligned along the same direction. Hence the magnetic moment equals to NIA. **(1 Mark)**

> **Note**
>
> *Ampere's circuital law holds for steady currents which do not fluctuate with time. Also, ampere's law is to Biot-Savart law, what Gauss's law is to Coulomb's law. Both ampere and Biot-Savart law relate magnetic field and the current.*

OR

(a) Mutual inductance is the phenomenon of production of induced emf in one coil due to a change of current in the neighbouring coil. **(½ Mark)**

S.I. units – Henry. **(½ Mark)**

(b) Consider two solenoid, each of length l_1 and where S_2 is wound over S_1.

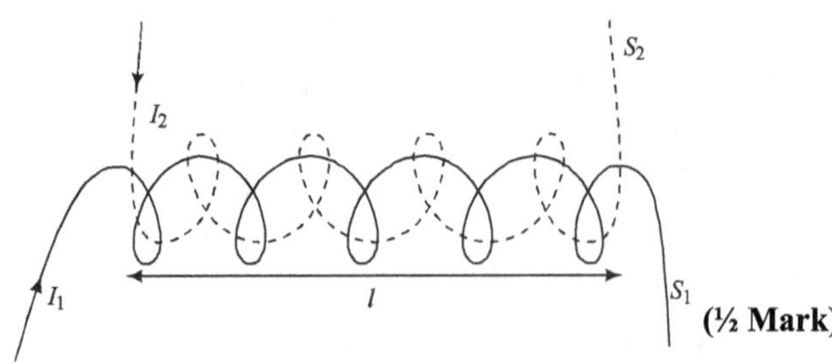

(½ Mark)

r_1, r_2 = radius of solenoid S_1 and S_2 respectively.

N_1, N_2 = number of turns in the two solenoid.

Let a current I_2 flow through S_2. This sets up a magnetic flux ϕ_1 through each turn of the coil S_1.

Flux linked with S_1

$$N_1\phi_1 = M_{12} I_2 \qquad \text{...(i)} \textbf{ (½ Mark)}$$

where M_{12} = mutual inductance between two solenoid.

The magnetic field set up inside S_2 due to I_2 is

$$B_2 = \mu_0 n_2 I_2 \qquad \textbf{(½ Mark)}$$

So, flux linked with S_1

$$N_1\phi_1 = B_2 A N_1$$
$$= \mu_0 n_2 I_2 \cdot A N_1 \qquad \text{...(ii)} \textbf{ (½ Mark)}$$

where A = area of cross-section of $S_1 = \pi r_1^2$

Equating (i) and (ii)

$$M_{12} I_2 = \mu_0 n_2 I_2 A N_1 \qquad \textbf{(½ Mark)}$$
$$M_{12} = \mu_0 n_2 \left(\pi r_1^2\right) N_1$$
$$M_{12} = \mu_0 n_1 n_2 \left(\pi r_1^2\right) l \qquad [\because N_1 = n_1 l]$$

$\therefore$ Mutual inductance = $\mu_0 n_1 n_2 \pi r_1^2 l$ **(½ Mark)**

(c) Let the current in $C_2 = I_2$

Magnetic flux linked with $C_1 = \phi_1$

From the concept of mutual inductance, we know magnetic flux ϕ_1 linked with coil C_1 is directly proportional to current I_2 in C_2

$$\therefore \quad \phi_1 \propto I_2$$
$$\Rightarrow \quad \phi_1 = M I_2$$
$$M = \text{mutual inductance}$$
$$\phi_1 = M I_2$$
$$\therefore \quad \frac{d\phi_1}{dt} = M \frac{dI_2}{dt} \qquad \text{...(i)} \textbf{ (½ Mark)}$$

Faraday's law of electromagnetic induction, states the magnitude of induced emf is equal to the rate of change of magnetic flux.

$$\varepsilon = \frac{-d\phi}{dt}$$

Therefore, equation (i) becomes

$$\varepsilon = -M \frac{dI_2}{dt}. \qquad \textbf{(½ Mark)}$$

Note

(b) *If we introduce a medium within solenoids of relative permeability* μ_r, *then mutual inductance would be*

$$M = \mu_r \mu_0 n_1 n_2 \pi r_1^2 l.$$

25. (a) Consider a slit LN of width 'a'. A parallel beam of light falls normally on it and the diffracted light goes to meet a screen.

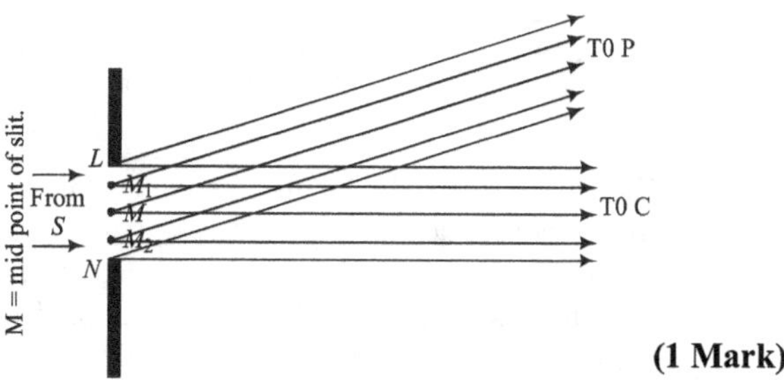

                                (1 Mark)

MC is a straight line perpendicular to the slit plane. The basic idea is to divide the slit into much smaller parts, and add their contribution at any point on screen with proper phase differences. We are treating different parts of the wavefront at the slit as secondary source.

For central point C, all the secondary wavelet are going straight across the slit. All the path differences are zero and we get maximum intensity at C. This is central maxima.

Consider a point P. Let at P we have a minima. To understand how a minima is formed at P, divide the slit into two halves, LM and NM. For every point in LM there is corresponding point in NM for which the path difference is $\dfrac{\lambda}{2}$. Therefore, wavelets from LM and NM are out of phase and cancel each other giving minima at P.

For a maxima, divide the slit into three values. The path difference between the wavelet arise from first two have will be $180°$ and hence they will cancel out each other. However, the remaining one-third of the slit contributes to the intensity and we get a secondary maxima but of much weaker intensity.   **(1 Mark)**

(b) The position of first minima on screen is

$$\theta = \frac{\lambda}{a} \qquad \textbf{(1 Mark)}$$

where λ = wavelength of incident light

a = slit width.

From figure, we can see that angular width of central maxima is $2\theta = \dfrac{2\lambda}{a}$.   **(½ Mark)**

Also, from figure, angular width of Ist diffraction fringe is $\theta = \dfrac{\lambda}{a}$.

$\therefore$ Angular width of central fringe is twice the angular width of first fringe.   **(½ Mark)**

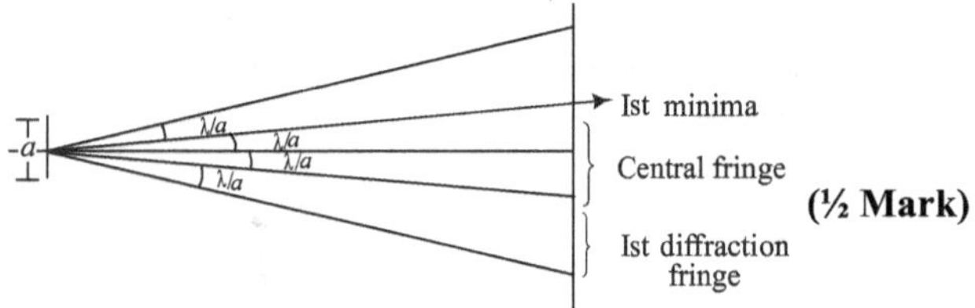

(½ **Mark**)

(c) The reason is that the intensity of central maxima is due to contribution of all part of the slit. Whereas for secondary maxima, only one-third part contributes to intensity of secondary maxima. This goes on decreasing as we increase 'n'. And hence, the intensity of secondary maxima becomes much weaker with increasing n.   (**1 Mark**)

OR

(a) Figure show the image I of an object O formed by refraction through spherical surface separating two media n_1 and n_2. The rays are incident from a medium of refractive index n_1 to another of refractive index n_2.

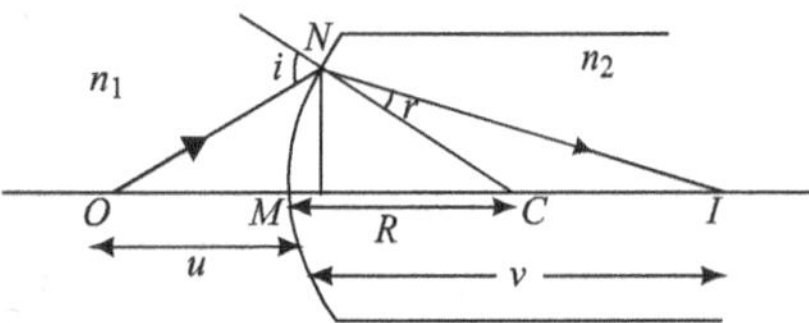

If we take the aperture of the surface to be small, the NM will be nearly equal to the length of the perpendicular from the point N on the principle axis.

In ΔNOM,

$$\tan \angle NOM = \frac{MN}{OM}$$ (½ **Mark**)

In ΔNCM,

$$\tan \angle NCM = \frac{MN}{MC}$$ (½ **Mark**)

In ΔNIM,

$$\tan \angle NIM = \frac{MN}{MI}$$ (½ **Mark**)

For small angles,

$\tan \angle NOM \approx \angle NOM$, $\tan \angle NCM \approx \angle NCM$

$\tan \angle NIM \approx \angle NIM$

For, ΔNOC, i is the exterior angle

$\therefore$ $i = \angle NOM + \angle NCM$

$$\Rightarrow i = \frac{MN}{OM} + \frac{MN}{MC}$$ (½ **Mark**)

Similarly, for ΔNIC,

$\angle NCM$ is exterior.

$\therefore$ $\angle NCM = r + \angle NIM$

or $r = \angle NCM - \angle NIM$

$$= \frac{MN}{MC} - \frac{MN}{MI}$$

Snell's law states

$$n_i \sin i = n_2 \sin r$$

for small angles, $\sin \theta \approx \theta$

$\therefore$ $n_1 i = n_2 r$

$$\Rightarrow n_1\left[\frac{MN}{OM} + \frac{MN}{MC}\right] = n_2\left[\frac{MN}{MC} - \frac{MN}{MI}\right]$$ (½ **Mark**)

or $\dfrac{n_1}{OM} + \dfrac{n_2}{MI} = \dfrac{n_2 - n_1}{MC}$

Applying the sign convention,

$$OM = -u,\ MI = +v,\ MC = +R$$

$\therefore$ $\dfrac{n_1}{-u} + \dfrac{n_2}{v} = \dfrac{n_2 - n_1}{R}$ ...(i) (½ **Mark**)

(b) 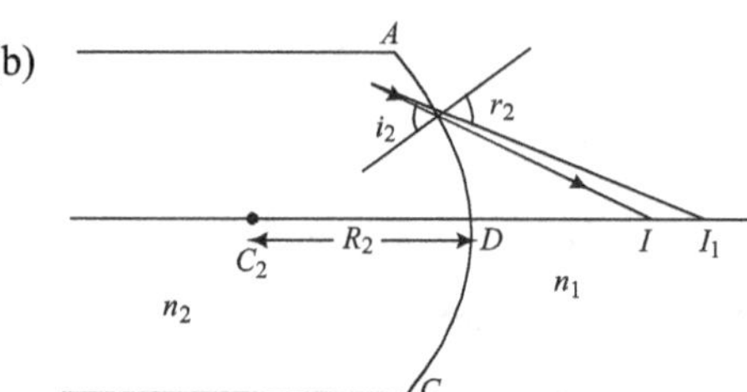

Applying the relation (i) to the interface ADC, we get

$$\frac{-n_2}{DI_1} + \frac{n_1}{DI} = \frac{n_2 - n_1}{DC_2}$$ ...(ii) (½ **Mark**)

For lens maker formula,

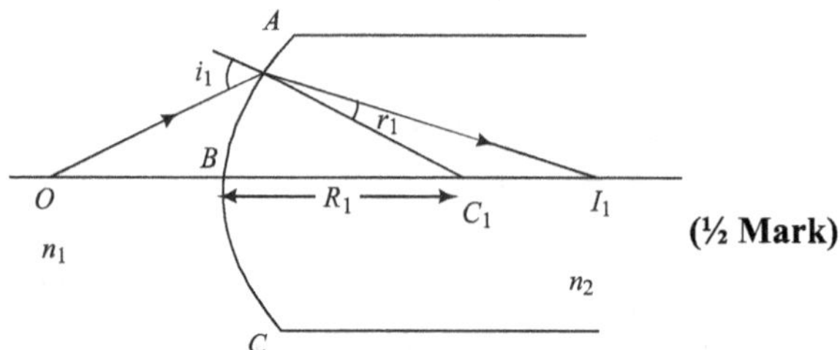

                                           (½ **Mark**)

Applying the relation (i) to the interface ABC, we get,

$$\frac{n_1}{OB} + \frac{n_2}{BI_1} = \frac{n_2 - n_1}{BC_1}$$ ...(iii)

For a thin lens $BI_1 = DI_1$. So adding equation (ii) and (iii).

$$\frac{n_1}{OB} + \frac{n_1}{DI} = (n_2 - n_1)\left[\frac{1}{BC_1} + \frac{1}{DC_2}\right]$$ (½ **Mark**)

Here OB = object distance. If we suppose object to be at infinity then $OB \to \infty$.

   $DI = f$

   $B\,C_1 = +R_1$

   $DC_2 = -R_2$

$$\therefore \frac{n_1}{f} = (n_2 - n_1)\left[\frac{1}{R_1} - \frac{1}{R_2}\right]$$

$$\frac{1}{f} = (n_{21} - 1)\left[\frac{1}{R_1} - \frac{1}{R_2}\right]\left\{\because n_{21} = \frac{n_2}{n_1}\right\}. \quad \textbf{(½ Mark)}$$

Note

This question can be asked in another way as

(a) Derive the relations between the distance of object, distance of image and radius of curvature of a convex spherical surface, when refraction takes place.

(b) Using the relation obtained in part (a), derive lens-maker formula.

26. (a) Let P be the point where electric field due to dipole has to be evaluated.

Here, $\vec{P}$ = dipole moment = $q \times 2a$ **(½ Mark)**
$2a$ = distance between two charges of dipole
x = distance from the centre of dipole to point p.
Electric field due to $+q$ at p is

$$\vec{E}_{+q} = \frac{1}{4\pi\varepsilon_0}\frac{q}{(x-a)^2} - (\hat{p}) \quad \textbf{(½ Mark)}$$

Electric field due to $-q$ at p is

$$\vec{E}_{-q} = \frac{1}{4\pi\varepsilon_0}\frac{q}{(x+a)^2}(-\hat{p}) \quad \textbf{(½ Mark)}$$

Total electric field at point p, E will be

$$\vec{E} = \vec{E}_q + \vec{E}_{-q}$$

$$\vec{E} = \frac{1}{4\pi\varepsilon_0}\left[\frac{1}{(x-a)^2} - \frac{1}{(x+a)^2}\right]\hat{p}$$

$$= \frac{q}{4\pi\varepsilon_0}\left[\frac{(x+a)^2 - (x-a)^2}{(x^2-a^2)^2}\right]\hat{p}$$

$$\vec{E} = \frac{q}{4\pi\varepsilon_0}\times\frac{4ax}{(x^2-a^2)^2}\hat{p} \quad \textbf{(½ Mark)}$$

$$\vec{E} = \frac{2\times 2aq\times x}{4\pi\varepsilon_0(x^2-a^2)^2}\hat{p}$$

$$\vec{E} = \frac{2px}{4\pi\varepsilon_0(x^2-a^2)^2}\hat{p} \quad \textbf{(½ Mark)}$$

For $x \gg a$
$$x^2 - a^2 \approx x^2$$

$$\therefore \quad \vec{E} = \frac{1}{4\pi\varepsilon_0}\frac{2px}{(x^2)^2}\hat{P}$$

$$\vec{E} = \frac{1}{4\pi\varepsilon_0}\frac{2p}{x^3}\hat{p}N/C^{-1} \quad \textbf{(½ Mark)}$$

(b) Electric flux ϕ is

$$\phi = \oint \vec{E}\cdot d\vec{s}$$

where $\vec{E}$ is electric field
$d\vec{s}$ is area element.

Given, Electric field $\vec{E} = 2x\,\hat{i}$

The faces perpendicular to $\vec{E}$ will not contribute in total flux as angle between $\vec{E}$ and $d\vec{s}$ will be 90°.
(½ Mark)

The faces parallel to $\vec{E}$ will contribute to the flux.
$$\phi = \phi_I + \phi_{II}$$
$$\vec{E}_I = 2\times 0\times\hat{i} = 0$$
$$\vec{E}_{II} = 2\times a\times\hat{i} = 2a\,\hat{i}$$

$$\therefore \quad \phi = \oint\vec{E}_I\cdot d\vec{s} + \oint\vec{E}_{II}\cdot d\vec{s}$$

$$= 0 + 2a\hat{i}.a^2\hat{i}$$

$$\phi = 2a^3\ Nm^2C^{-1} \quad \textbf{(½ Mark)}$$

The net charge enclosed by cube can be found out by Gauss law, which is

$$\phi = \frac{q}{\varepsilon_0} \quad \textbf{(½ Mark)}$$

$$\therefore \quad q = \phi\varepsilon_0 \quad \textbf{(½ Mark)}$$

$$q = 2a^3\varepsilon_0\ C \quad \textbf{(½ Mark)}$$

OR

(a) When a conductor is placed in an external electric field $\vec{E}_{ext}$, its free electrons begin to move in the opposite direction of $\vec{E}_{ext}$. Negative charges are induced on the left end and positive charges on right end of conductor. The process continues untill electric field due to induced charges becomes equal to external electric field. Therefore, net electric field inside the conductor becomes zero.

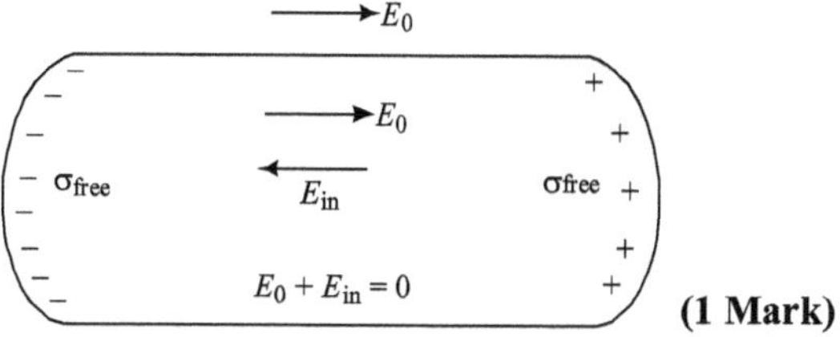

(1 Mark)

In dielectric, the external electric field induces dipole moment by stretching or re-orienting the moleules of dielectric. The induced dipole moment sets up an electric field which opposes $\vec{E}_{ex}$ but does not cancel this field. It only reduces it.

$$E_0 + E_{in} \neq 0$$

(1 Mark)

Polarization:- The polarization $\vec{P}$ is defined as the dipole moment per unit volume. For linear isotropic dielectrics having a susceptibility χ_e, we have

$$P = \chi_e E.$$

(1 Mark)

(b) Electric field inside the conductor (here shell) is always zero.

$\therefore$ Force on charge $\dfrac{Q}{2}$ at the centre is zero.

Force on charge $2Q$ at A due to charges $\dfrac{Q}{2}$ and Q will be

$$F = \frac{1}{4\pi\varepsilon_0} \frac{\left(Q + \dfrac{Q}{2}\right) \times 2Q}{x^2}$$

$$F = \frac{1}{4\pi\varepsilon_0 x^2} \times \frac{3Q}{2} \times 2Q$$

$\therefore$
$$F = \frac{3Q^2}{4\pi\varepsilon_0 x^2}$$

(1 Mark)

Electric flux through the shell can be calculated using Gauss law which is

$$\phi = \frac{q}{\varepsilon_0}$$

where q = total charge enclosed by shell.

Total charge enclosed by shell is $\dfrac{Q}{2}$

$\therefore$
$$\phi = \frac{Q/2}{\varepsilon_0} = \frac{Q}{2\varepsilon_0}.$$

(1 Mark)

All India *2014*
CBSE Board Solved Paper

Time Allowed: 3 Hours   *Maximum Marks: 70*

General Instructions:
(i)   All questions are compulsory.
(ii) There are 30 questions in total. Question No. **1** to **8** are very short answer type questions and carry **one** mark each.
(iii) Question No. **9** to **18** carry **two** marks each. Question Nos. **19** to **27** carry **three** marks each and question nos. **28** to **30** carry **five** marks each
(iv) One of the questions carrying **three** marks weightage is value based question
(v)   There is no overall choice. However, an internal choice has been provided in **one** question of **two** marks, **one** question of **three** marks and all **three** questions of **five** marks each weightage. You have to attempt only **one** of the choices in such questions.
(vi) Use of calculators is not permitted. However, you may use log tables if necessary.
(vii) You may use the following values of physical constants wherever necessary:

$c = 3 \times 10^8$ m/s

$h = 6.63 \times 10^{-34}$ Js

$e = 1.6 \times 10^{-19}$ C

$\mu_0 = 4\pi \times 10^{-7}$ T m A^{-1}

$\varepsilon_0 = 8.854 \times 10^{-12}$ C^2 N^{-1} m^{-2}

$\dfrac{1}{4\pi\varepsilon_0} = 9 \times 10^9$ N m^2 C^{-2}

Mass of electron $(m_e) = 9.1 \times 10^{-31}$ kg

Mass of neutron $= 1.675 \times 10^{-27}$ kg

Mass of proton $= 1.673 \times 10^{-27}$ kg

Avogadro's number $= 6.023 \times 10^{23}$ per gram mole

Boltzmann constant $= 1.38 \times 10^{-23}$ JK^{-1}

SECTION - A

1. Using the concept of force between two infinitely long parallel current carrying conductors, define one ampere of current.

2. To which part of the electromagnetic spectrum does a wave of frequency 5×10^{19} Hz belong?

3. Two equal balls with equal positive charge 'q' coulombs are suspended by two insulating strings of equal length. What would be the effect on the force when a plastic sheet is inserted between the two?

4. Define intensity of radiation on the basis of photon picture of light. Write its S.I. unit.

5. The electric current flowing in a wire in the direction from B to A is decreasing. Find out the direction of the induced current in the metallic loop kept above the wire as shown.

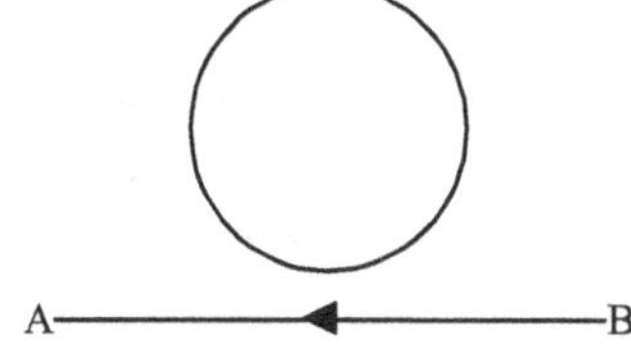

6. Why is it found experimentally difficult to detect neutrinos in nuclear -decay?

7. Why is the use of A.C. voltage preferred over D.C. voltage? Give two reasons.

8. A biconvex lens made of a transparent material of refractive index 1.25 is immersed in water of refractive index 1.33. Will the lens behave as a converging or a diverging lens? Give reason.

SECTION - B

9. Using Rutherford model of the atom, derive the expression for the total energy of the electron in hydrogen atom. What is the significance of total negative energy possessed by the electron?

OR

Using Bohr's postulates of the atomic model, derive the expression for radius of nth electron orbit. Hence obtain the expression for Bohr's radius.

10. A parallel plate capacitor of capacitance C is charged to a potential V. It is then connected to another uncharged capacitor having the same capacitance. Find out the ratio of the energy stored in the combined system to that stored initially in the single capacitor.

11. Considering the case of a parallel plate capacitor being charged, show how one is required to generalize Ampere's circuital law to include the term due to displacement current.

12. A cell of emf 'E' and internal resistance 'r' is connected across a variable resistor 'R'. Plot a graph showing variation of terminal voltage 'V' of the cell versus the current 'I'. Using the plot, show how the emf of the cell and its internal resistance can be determined.

13. Explain, with the help of a circuit diagram, the working of a *p-n* junction diode as a half-wave rectifier.

14. Estimate the average drift speed of conduction electrons in a copper wire of cross-sectional area 1.0×10^{-7} m^2 carrying a current of 1.5 A. Assume the density of conduction electrons to be 9×10^{28} m^{-3}.

15. Two monochromatic rays of light are incident normally on the face AB of an isosceles right-angled prism ABC. The refractive indices of the glass prism for the two rays '1' and '2' are respectively 1.35 and 1.45. Trace the path of these rays after entering the prism.

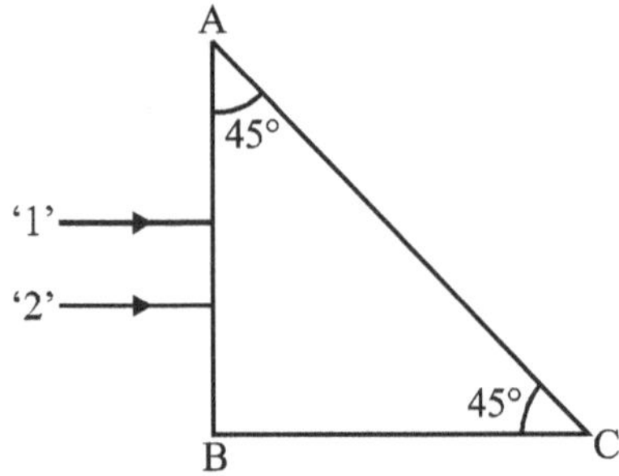

16. Write the functions of the following in communication systems:

(i) Transducer

(ii) Repeater

17. Show diagrammatically the behaviour of magnetic field lines in the presence of (i) paramagnetic and (ii) diamagnetic substances. How does one explain this distinguishing feature?

18. Draw a circuit diagram of n-p-n transistor amplifier in CE configuration. Under what condition does the transistor act as an amplifier?

SECTION - C

19. (a) Using the phenomenon of polarisation, show how the transverse nature of light can be demonstrated.

(b) Two polaroids P_1 and P_2 are placed with their pass axes perpendicular to each other. An unpolarised light of intensity I_0 is incident on P_1. A third polaroid P_3 is kept in between P_1 and P_2 such that its pass axis makes an angle of 30° with that of P_1. Determine the intensity of light transmitted through P_1, P_2 and P_3.

20. Define the term 'mutual inductance' between the two coils.

Obtain the expression for mutual inductance of a pair of long coaxial solenoids each of length l and radii r_1 and r_2 ($r_2 \gg r_1$). Total number of turns in the two solenoids are N_1 and N_2, respectively.

21. Answer the following:

(a) Why are the connections between the resistors in a meter bridge made of thick copper strips?

(b) Why is it generally preferred to obtain the balance point in the middle of the meter bridge wire?

(c) Which material is used for the meter bridge wire and why?

OR

A resistance of R Ω draws current from a potentiometer, as shown in the figure. The potentiometer has a total resistance R_o Ω. A voltage V is supplied to the potentiometer. Derive an expression for the voltage across R when the sliding contact is in the middle of the potentiometer.

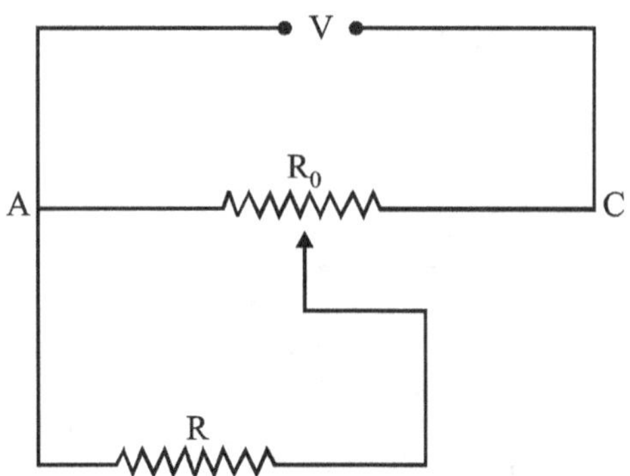

22. A convex lens of focal length 20 cm is placed coaxially with a convex mirror of radius of curvature 20 cm. The two are kept at 15 cm apart. A point object lies 60 cm in front of the convex lens. Draw a ray diagram to show the formation of the image by the combination. Determine the nature and position of the image formed.

23. A voltage $V = V_0 \sin \omega t$ is applied to a series LCR circuit. Derive the expression for the average power dissipated over a cycle.

Under what condition (i) no power is dissipated even though the current flows through the circuit, (ii) maximum power is dissipated in the circuit?

24. Write any two distinguishing features between conductors, semiconductors and insulators on the basis of energy band diagrams.

25. For the past some time, Aarti had been observing some erratic body movement, unsteadiness and lack of coordination in the activities of her sister Radha, who also used to complain of severe headache occasionally. Aarti suggested to her parents to get a medical check-up of Radha. The doctor thoroughly examined Radha and diagnosed that she has a brain tumour.

   (a) What, according to you, are the values displayed by Aarti?

   (b) How can radioisotopes help a doctor to diagnose brain tumour?

26. Write two basic modes of communication. Explain the process of amplitude modulation. Draw a schematic sketch showing how amplitude modulated signal is obtained by superposing a modulating signal over a sinusoidal carrier wave.

27. An electron microscope uses electrons accelerated by a voltage of 50 kV. Determine the de-Broglie wavelength associated with the electrons. Taking other factors, such as numerical aperture etc. to be same, how does the resolving power of an electron microscope compare with that of an optical microscope which used yellow light?

SECTION - D

28. Draw a labelled diagram of Van de Graaff generator. State its working principle to show how by introducing a small charged sphere into a larger sphere, a large amount of charge can be transferred to the outer sphere. State the use of this machine and also point out its limitations.

OR

   (a) Deduce the expression for the torque acting on a dipole of dipole moment $\vec{p}$ in the presence of a uniform electric field $\vec{E}$.

   (b) Consider two hollow concentric spheres, S_1 and S_2, enclosing charges 2Q and 4Q respectively as shown in the figure. (i) Find out the ratio of the electric flux through them. (ii) How will the electric flux through the sphere S_1 change if a medium of dielectric constant 'ε_r' is introduced in the space inside S_1 in place of air? Deduce the necessary expression.

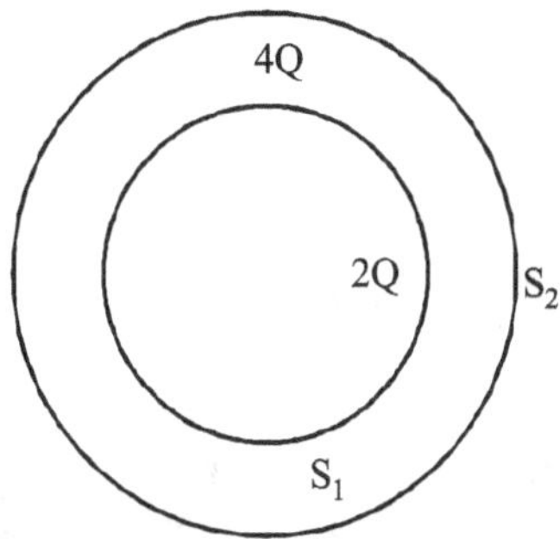

29. (a) In Young's double slit experiment, describe briefly how bright and dark fringes are obtained on the screen kept in front of a double slit. Hence obtain the expression for the fringe width.

   (b) The ratio of the intensities at minima to the maxima in the Young's double slit experiment is 9 : 25. Find the ratio of the widths of the two slits.

OR

   (a) Describe briefly how a diffraction pattern is obtained on a screen due to a single narrow slit illuminated by a monochromatic source of light. Hence obtain the conditions for the angular width of secondary maxima and secondary minima.

   (b) Two wavelengths of sodium light of 590 nm and 596 nm are used in turn to study the diffraction taking place at a single slit of aperture 2×10^{-6} m. The distance between the slit and the screen is 1·5 m. Calculate the separation between the positions of first maxima of the diffraction pattern obtained in the two cases.

30. (a) Deduce an expression for the frequency of revolution of a charged particle in a magnetic field and show that it is independent of velocity or energy of the particle.

   (b) Draw a schematic sketch of a cyclotron. Explain, giving the essential details of its construction, how it is used to accelerate the charged particles.

OR

   (a) Draw a labelled diagram of a moving coil galvanometer. Describe briefly its principle and working.

   (b) Answer the following:
   (i) Why is it necessary to introduce a cylindrical soft iron core inside the coil of a galvanometer?
   (ii) Increasing the current sensitivity of a galvanometer may not necessarily increase its voltage sensitivity. Explain, giving reason.

Solutions

SECTION - A

1. The amount of current which when flowing (in same direction) through two infinitely long parallel wires separated by one metre produces an attractive force of 2×10^{-7} N/m is called one ampere. The wires must have negligible cross-section and they must be placed in vacuum.

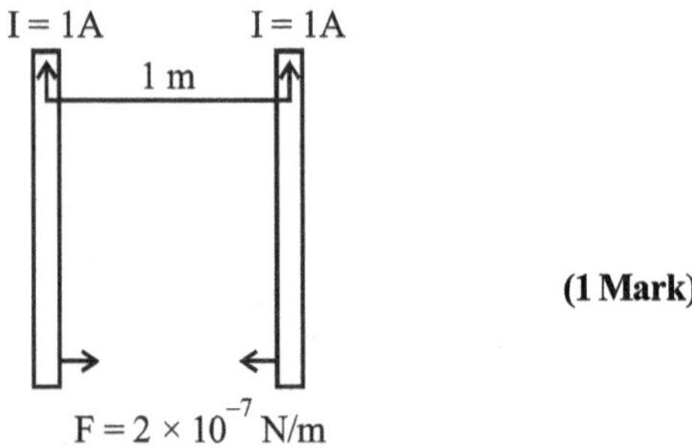

(1 Mark)

2. Gamma rays typically have frequency range 10^{19}–10^{24} Hz. Thus, the frequency 5×10^{19} Hz belongs to the gamma region of the electromagnetic spectrum. **(1 Mark)**

3. Electric field lines due to any of the charge will not be able to pass through plastic because it is an insulation of electricity. And in the absence of an external electric field both the charges will not experience any force due to each other. **(1 Mark)**

4. Intensity means strength or power. Therefore the intensity of radiation is defined as the number of photons per unit surface area per unit time. Its S.I unit is joule/meter^2 second. **(½ + ½ Mark)**

5. The current induced in the loop is in clockwise direction (using the right-hand thumb rule) because the decreasing magnetic field in the loop due to the decreasing current in wire AB is into the plane of the paper (perpendicular to the plane). So, the direction of the induced current in the loop will be such that it produces an inward magnetic field (perpendicular to the plane). **(1 Mark)**

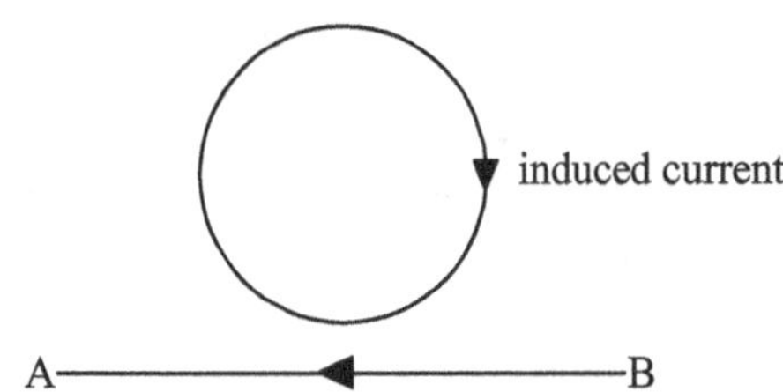

6. Neutrinos are uncharged particles with almost no mass and they interact very weakly with matter, so they are very difficult to detect. **(1 Mark)**

7. The reasons of using A.C. voltage over D.C. voltage are,

   (i) By using a transformer A.C. voltage can be stepped up and stepped down as per the requirement

   (ii) A.C. voltage can be transmitted over long distances without loss of energy as compared to D.C. voltage.

   (½ + ½ Mark)

8. The biconvex lens will behave as a converging lens, because refractive index of water (1.33) is more than the refractive index of the material of the lens (1.25).

   (½ + ½ Mark)

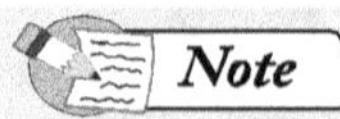 **Note**

It acts as a diverging lens in air because the refractive index of air is less than that of the material of the lens.

SECTION - B

9. If, F_c – centripetal force required to keep a revolving electron in orbit

   F_e – electrostatic force of attraction between the revolving electron and the nucleus then, for a dynamically stable orbit in a hydrogen atom, where Z = 1,

   $$F_c = F_e$$

   $$\frac{mv^2}{r} = \frac{(e)(e)}{4\pi\varepsilon_0 r^2} \qquad ...(i)$$

   $$r = \frac{e^2}{4\pi\varepsilon_0 mv^2} \qquad ...(ii)$$

   K.E. of electron in the orbit,

   $$K = \frac{1}{2}mv^2$$

   From equation (i),

   $$K = \frac{e^2}{8\pi\varepsilon_0 r}$$

   Potential energy of electron in orbit,

   $$U = \frac{(e)(-e)}{4\pi\varepsilon_0 r} = \frac{-e^2}{4\pi\varepsilon_0 r}$$

   Negative sign indicates that revolving electron is bound to the positive nucleus.

   ∴ Total energy of electron in hydrogen atom

   $$E = k + U = \frac{e^2}{8\pi\varepsilon_0 r} - \frac{e^2}{4\pi\varepsilon_0 r}$$

   $$\boxed{E = -\frac{e^2}{8\pi\varepsilon_0 r}} \qquad \textbf{(1½ Marks)}$$

   Therefore, total energy of electrons in orbit of hydrogen atom is negative. Hence, the electron bound to the nucleus *i.e.*, the electron is not free to leave the orbit around the nucleus. **(½ Marks)**

OR

According to the postulates of Bohr's atomic model, the electrons revolve around the nucleus only in those orbits for which the angular momentum is the integral multiple of $h/2\pi$. Where h is plank's constant.

$\therefore$ $L = nh/2\pi$

Angular momentum is given by

$L = mvr$

According to Bohr's postulate,

$$L_n = mv_n r_n = \frac{nh}{2\pi} \qquad \ldots(i)$$

Where,

$n \rightarrow$ Principle quantum number

$v_n \rightarrow$ Speed of moving electron in the nth orbit

$r_n \rightarrow$ Radius of nth orbit

$$v_n = \frac{nh}{2\pi m r_n}$$

From, Bohr's postulate of atomic model

$$\frac{mv_n^2}{r_n} = \frac{Kze^2}{r_n^2}$$

$$r_n = \frac{Kze^2}{mv_n^2}$$

Putting the value of vn and z = 1 (for hydrogen atom).

$$r_n = \frac{n^2 h^2}{4\pi^2 mKe^2} \qquad \textbf{(1 Mark)}$$

For Bohr's radius, n = 1

$$\therefore \quad r_1 = \frac{h_2}{4\pi^2 mke^2}$$

$$k = \frac{1}{4\pi\varepsilon_0}$$

$$\Rightarrow \quad r_1 = \frac{h^2 4\pi\varepsilon_0}{4\pi^2 me^2} = \frac{h^2 \varepsilon_0}{\pi e^2 m} = 5.29 \times 10^{-11} m \qquad \textbf{(1 Mark)}$$

This is the expression for Bohr's radius. This shows $r \propto n^2$.

10. Let 'q' be the charge on the charged capacitor. Energy stored in it is

$$U = q^2/2C$$

When another similar uncharged capacitor is connected, the net capacitance of the system is C' = 2C

The charge on the system is constant. So, the energy stored in the system now is

$$U' = q^2/2(C') \Leftrightarrow U' = q^2/2(2C) \Rightarrow U' = q^2/4C$$

Thus, the required ratio is

$$\frac{U'}{U} = \frac{q^2/4c}{q^2/2c} = \frac{1}{2} \qquad \textbf{(2 Marks)}$$

11. According to Gauss' law, the electric flux Φ_E of a parallel plate capacitor having an area A, and a total charge Q is given by,

$$\phi_E = \frac{Q}{\epsilon_0}$$

As the charge Q on the capacitor plates changes with time, so current is given by

$$i = dQ/dt$$

Also, $\dfrac{d\phi_E}{dt} = \dfrac{d}{dt}\left(\dfrac{Q}{\epsilon_0}\right) = \dfrac{1}{\epsilon_0}\dfrac{dQ}{dt}$

$$\Rightarrow \epsilon_0 \frac{d\phi_E}{dt} = \frac{dQ}{dt} = i$$

This is the missing term in Ampere's circuital law.

So the total current through the conductor is

$i = $ Conduction current (i_c) + Displacement current (i_d)

$$\therefore \quad i = i_c + i_d = i_c + \epsilon_0 \frac{d\phi_E}{dt} \qquad \textbf{(1 Mark)}$$

As Ampere's circuital law is given by

$$\therefore \quad \oint \vec{B}.\vec{dl} = \mu_0 I$$

After modification we have Ampere—Maxwell law is given as

$$\oint B.dl = \mu_0 i_c + \mu_0 \epsilon_0 \frac{d\phi_E}{dt} \qquad \textbf{(1 Mark)}$$

The total current passing through any surface, of which the closed loop is the perimeter, is the sum of the conduction current and displacement current.

Note

Another way to ask this question:-
What modification was made by maxwell to overcome the inconsistency in Ampere's circuital law?

12. If E is the emf of the cell, r is the internal resistance of the cell and I is the current through the circuit. Then Terminal voltage 'V' of the cell is $V = E - Ir$

So, $V = -Ir + E$

Comparing with the equation of a straight line

$y = mx + c$, we get:

$y = V; x = I; m = -r; c = E$

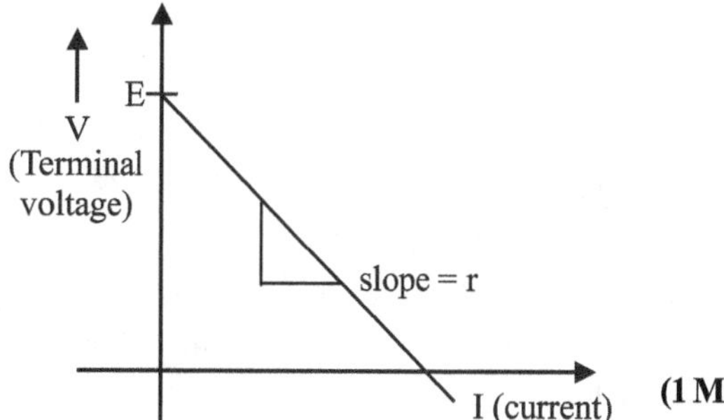

(1 Mark)

Graph showing variation of terminal voltage 'V' of the cell versus the current 'I'

Where,

Emf of the cell = Intercept on V axis   **(1 Mark)**

Internal resistance = slope of line.

13. For half wave rectification we have to use only one p-n juction. The arrangement is shown in fig.

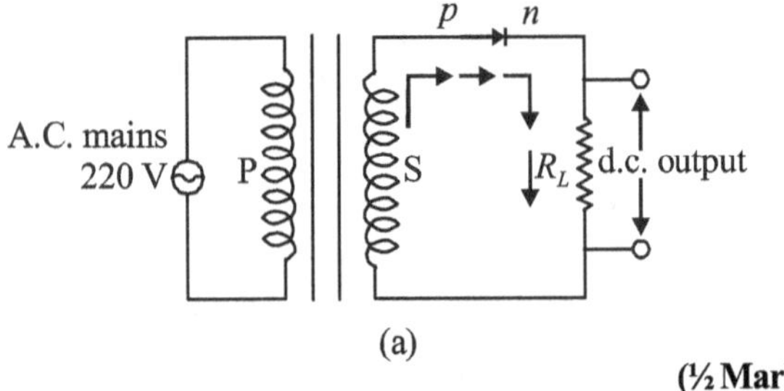

(a)   **(½ Mark)**

Working: During the positive half cycle of the input a.c. The p-n junction is forward biased i.e the forward current flows from p to n, the diode offers a low resistance path to the current. Thus we get output across load.

During the negative half cycle of the input a.c., the p-n junction is reversed biased i.e the reverse current flows from n to p, the diode offers a high resistance path to the current. Thus we get no output across load. **(1 + ½ Mark)**

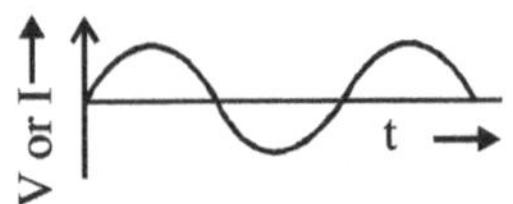

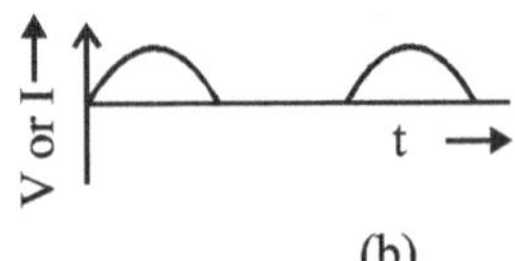

(b)

Thus, corresponding to an alternating input signal, we get undirectional pulsating output.

14. Drift velocity,

$$V_d = \frac{I}{neA}$$ **(1 Mark)**

where, I is the current, n is charge density, e is charge of electron and A is cross-section area.

$$V_d = \frac{1.5}{9 \times 10^{28} \times 1.6 \times 10^{-19} \times 1.0 \times 10^{-7}}$$

$$V_d = \frac{1.5}{14.4 \times 10^2}$$

$$V_d = 10.4 \times 10^{-4} \text{ m/s.}$$ **(1 Mark)**

15. Critical angle of ray 1:

$\sin(c_1) = 1/\mu_1 = 1/1.35 \Rightarrow c_1 = \sin^{-1}(1/1.35) = 47.73°$

Similarly, critical angle of ray 2:

$\sin(c_2) = 1/\mu_2 = 1/1.45 \Rightarrow c_2 = \sin^{-1}(1/1.45) = 43.6°$

Both the rays will fall on the side AC with angle of incidence (i) equal to 45°.

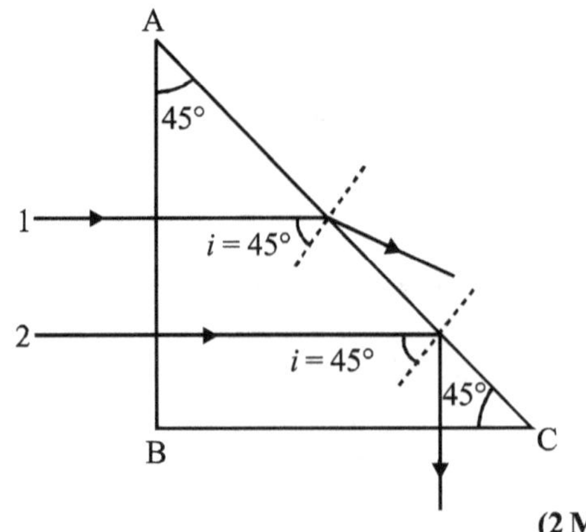

(2 Marks)

Critical angle of ray 1 is greater than that of i. Hence, it will emerge from the prism, as shown in the figure. Critical angle of ray 2 is less than that of i. Hence, it will be internally reflected.

 **Note**

If light is incident normally on one surface of a right angled prism, then angle of incidence on other surface of prism will always be 45°.

16. (i) Transducer : A transducer is a device that converts a non-electrical signal into electrical signal. Microphone, photo detector and Pizoelectric sensors are types of transducers. **(1 Mark)**

(ii) Repeater : A repeater is a combination of receiver and a transmitter. It picks up the signal from a transmitter, amplifies it and retransmits it to the receiver. A communications satellite is basically a repeater station in space. **(1 Mark)**

17. The behaviour of magnetic field lines in the presence of a diamagnetic substances (fig. a) and paramagnetic substances (fig. b) are shown below:

(i) Diamagnetic

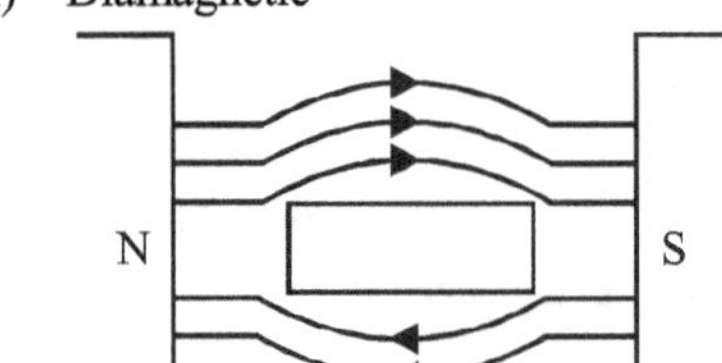

(½ Mark)

(a)

(ii) Paramagnetic

(½ Mark)

(b)

The distinguishing feature of magnetic substances is the difference in their relative permeabilities. The relative permeability of the diamagnetic substance is less than 1; so, the magnetic lines of force do not prefer passing through the substance. The relative permeability of a paramagnetic substance is greater than 1; so, the magnetic lines of force prefer passing through the substance. **(1 Mark)**

18. The circuit diagram of an n-p-n transistor amplifier in CE configuration is given below:

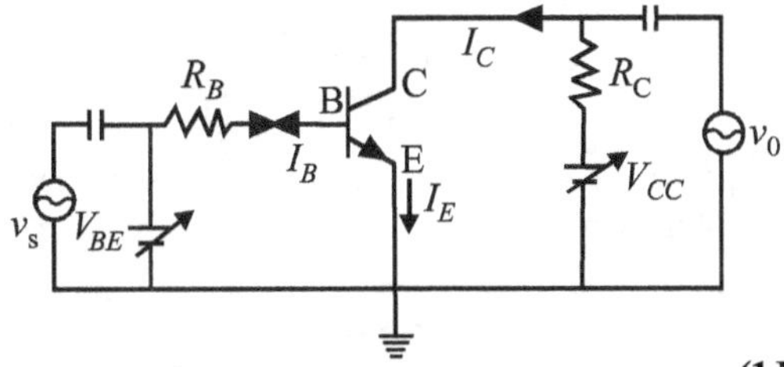

(1 Mark)

The transistor acts as an amplifier when the input circuit (emitter–base) is forward biased with low voltage V_{BE} and the output circuit (collector-base) is reverse biased with high voltage V_{CC}. **(1 Mark)**

SECTION - C

19. (a) When an ordinary light is incident normally on a pair of crystals C_1 and C_2. It gets plane polarised after passing crystal C_1, in the direction perpendicular to the length of crystal.

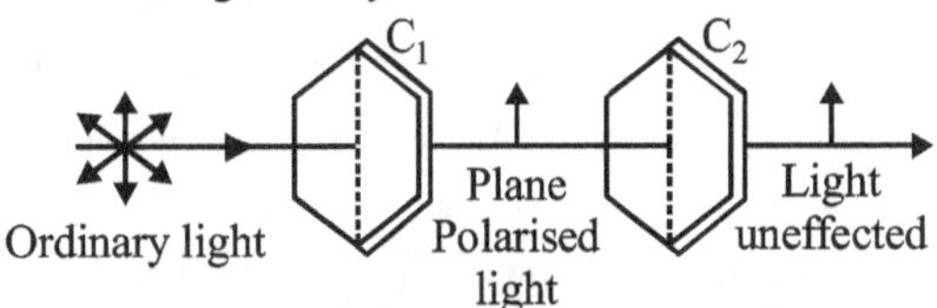

Now, we observe that when the axes of two crystals are parallel, the intensity of the emerging light will be maximum.

When the second crystal is placed perpendicular w.r.t the first crystal, the intensity of light observed is zero.

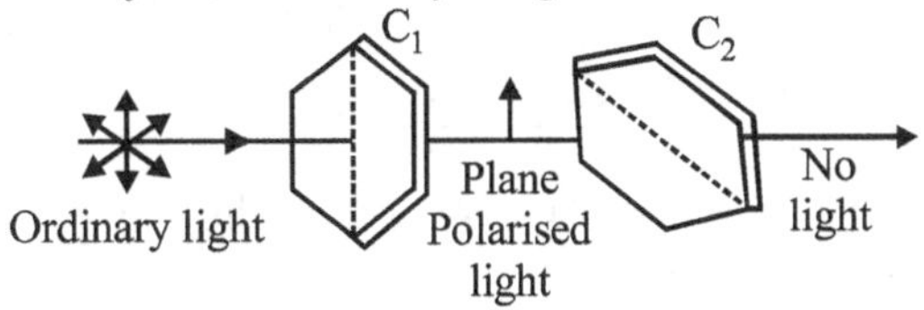

(1½ Marks)

This is because the electric field of the plane polarised light obtained from C_1 can vibrate only in one direction. Hence, when the axis of the crystal is perpendicular to its direction of vibration of electric field, it gets blocked. This depicts the transverse nature of light.

(b) According to the question P1, P2 and P3 are placed as shown in the diagram.

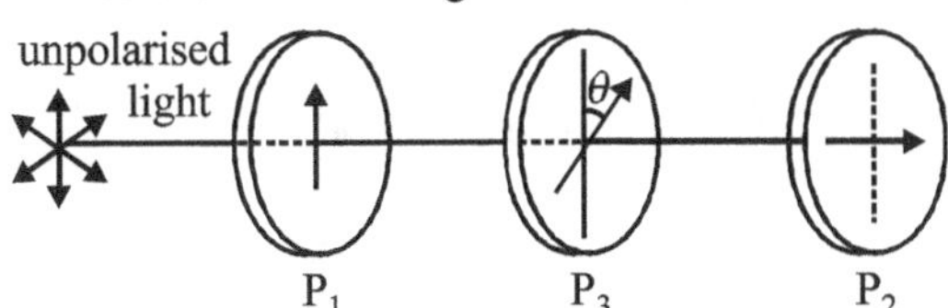

Intensity of light after falling on P_1, $I' = \dfrac{I_0}{2}$

Intensity of light after falling on P_3, $I'' = I' \cos^2\theta$

(½ + ½ + ½ Mark)

$$I'' = \frac{I_0}{2}\cos^2(30)$$

$$I'' = \frac{I_0}{2}\left(\frac{\sqrt{3}}{2}\right)^2$$

$$I'' = \frac{3I_0}{8}$$

Therefore, a light of intensity $3I_0/8$ will pass through P_3, and the angle between P_3 and P_2 will be 60° because of the condition given in the question.

Intensity of light after falling on P_2, $I''' = I''\cos^2(\theta)$

$$= \frac{3I_0}{8}\cos^2(60°) = \frac{3I_0}{32}$$

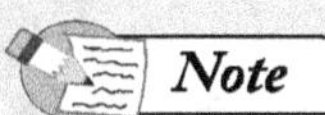 **Note**

Remember intensity coming out of a single polariod is half of the incident intensity. By putting second polariod, the intensity can furthur be controlled from 50% to zero of the incident intensity.

20. Production of induced e.m.f. in a coil due to the change of current in a neighbouring coil, is called mutual induction. **(1 Mark)**

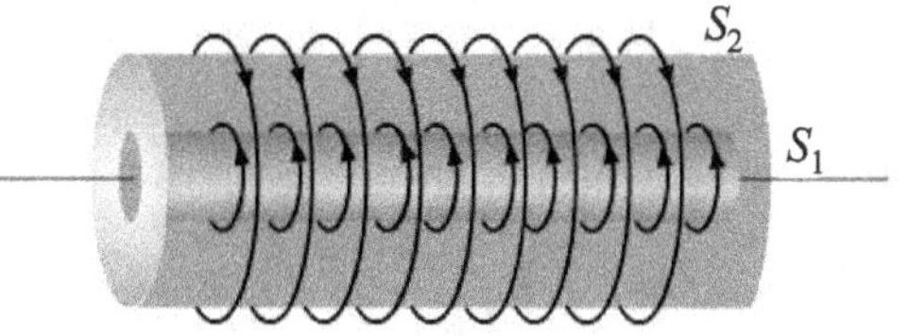

Suppose a current i is passed through the inner solenoid S_1. A magnetic field $B = \mu_0 n_1 i$ is produced inside S_1, whereas the field outside it is zero.

The flux through each turn S_2 is

$$B\pi r_1^2 = \mu_0 n_1 i\pi r_1^2$$

The total flux through all the turns in a length l of S_2 is

$$\phi = (\mu_0 n_1 i\pi r_1^2)n_2 l = (\mu_0 n_1 n_2 \pi r_1^2 l)i \qquad \textbf{(2 Marks)}$$

$$\Rightarrow M = \mu_0 n_1 n_2 \pi r_1^2 l$$

 **Note**

Between the two solenoid if a medium of relative permeability μ_r has been present, the mutual inductance would be

$$M = \mu_r v_0 n_1 n_1 \pi r_1^2 l \,.$$

Mutual inductance of a pair of coils, solenoids etc, depends on their separation as well as relative orientation.

21. (a) The resistivity of a copper wire of very low, and the connections are thick, so that the area is quite large and hence the resistance of the wires is almost negligible. $\left[\because R = \dfrac{\rho l}{A}, R \propto \dfrac{1}{A}\right]$ **(1 Mark)**

(b) To improves the sensitivity of the meter bridge, the balance point in the middle of the meter bridge. **(1 Mark)**

(c) Constantan is used for meter bridge wire because the temperature coefficient of constantan is almost negligible due to which the resistance of the wire does not change with increase in temperature of the wire due to flow of current. **(1 Mark)**

OR

Total resistance between A and B

$$R_{AB} = \dfrac{\dfrac{R_0}{2} \times R}{R + \dfrac{R_0}{2}} = \dfrac{RR_0}{2R + R_0}$$

Total resistance between A and C

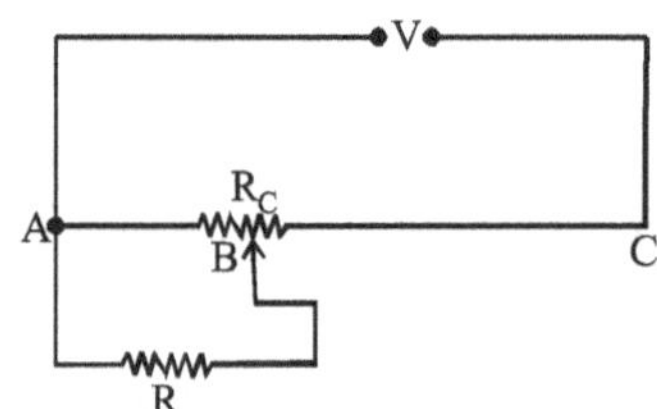

$$R_{AC} = R_{AB} + \dfrac{R_0}{2} = \left[\dfrac{RR_0}{2R + R_0} + \dfrac{R_0}{2}\right]$$

(1 Mark)

The current through the potentiometer wire

$$I = \dfrac{V}{R_{AC}}$$

The potential difference between A and B

$$V_{AB} = I\,R_{AB} = \dfrac{V}{R_{AC}} \times R_{AB}$$

$$= \dfrac{V}{\dfrac{RR_0}{R + R_0} + \dfrac{R_0}{2}} \times \dfrac{RR_0}{(2R + R_0)}$$

$$= \dfrac{V}{\dfrac{2RR_0 + R_0(2R + R_0)}{2(2R + R_0)}} \times \dfrac{RR_0}{(2R + R_0)}$$

$$= \dfrac{2V\,RR_0}{R_0[2R + 2R + R_0]}$$

$$V_{AB} = \dfrac{2\,VR}{R_0 + 4R}$$ **(2 Marks)**

22. For the position of image of the point object S formed by the convex lens,

$$u = -60 \text{ cm}$$
and $$f = 20 \text{ cm}$$

From the lens formula, we have

$$1/v - 1/u = 1/f \quad \Rightarrow \quad 1/v = 1/f + 1/u$$
$$\Rightarrow \quad 1/v = 1/20 + 1/(-60)$$
$$\Rightarrow \quad 1/v = \dfrac{1}{20} - \dfrac{1}{60} = \dfrac{3-1}{60} = \dfrac{2}{60}$$
$$= 2/60 \Rightarrow v = 30 \text{ cm}$$

The positive sign shows that the image is formed to the right of the lens.

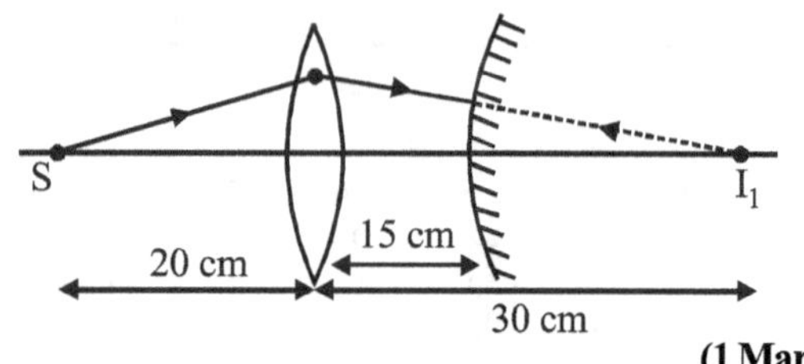

(1 Mark)

The image I_1 is formed behind the mirror and acts as a virtual source for the mirror. The convex mirror forms the image I_2, whose distance from the mirror can be calculated as:

$$1/v + 1/u = 1/f \quad \text{Here: } u = 15 \text{ cm}$$
And, $$f = R/2 = 10 \text{ cm} \Rightarrow 1/v = 1/f - 1/u$$
$$\Rightarrow \quad 1/v = 1/10 - 1/15 \Rightarrow 1/v = (3-2)/30 = 1/30$$
$$\Rightarrow \quad v = 30 \text{ cm}$$ **(1 Mark)**

Hence, the final virtual image is formed at a distance of 30 cm from the convex mirror, as shown in the figure below.

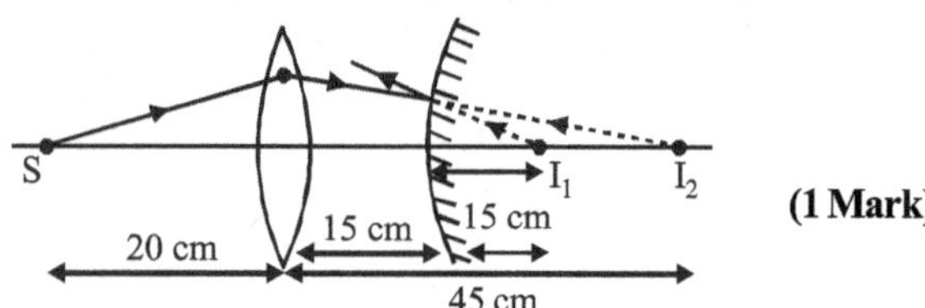

(1 Mark)

23. The power is defined as the rate of at which work is being done in the circuit.

When $V = V_0 \sin\omega t$ is applied to a series LCR circuit.

Current is $I = I_0 \sin(\omega t + \phi)$

$$I_0 = \dfrac{V_0}{Z} \quad \text{and} \quad \phi = \tan^{-1}\left(\dfrac{X_C - X_L}{R}\right)$$

Instantaneous power supplied by the source is

$$P = VI = (V_0 \sin\omega t) \times (I_0 \sin(\omega t + \phi))$$
$$P = V_0 I_0 \sin\omega t \sin(\omega t + \phi)$$
$$P = \dfrac{V_0 I_0}{2}\left[\cos\phi - \cos(2\omega t + \phi)\right]$$
$$P_{av} = \dfrac{V_0 I_0}{2}\left[\cos\phi - 0\right] \qquad \{\because\ <\cos(2\omega t) = 0\}$$

The average power $P_{av} = V_{rms} I_{rms} \cos\phi$

$$= \frac{V_0}{\sqrt{2}} \cdot \frac{I_0}{\sqrt{2}} \cdot \cos\phi \qquad \textbf{(1 Mark)}$$

In this expression $\cos\phi$ is known as the power factor.

Case I : For pure inductive circuit or pure capacitive circuit, the phase difference between current and voltage is $\frac{\pi}{2}$.

$$\therefore \qquad \phi = \frac{\pi}{2}, \cos\phi = 0$$

Therefore, $P_{av} = 0$. Thus no power is dissipated in the circuit. This current is sometimes referred to as wattless current and such a circuit is called wattless circuit.

(1 Mark)

Case II : For power dissipated at resonance in an LCR circuit,

$$X_C - X_L = 0, \ \phi = 0$$

$$\therefore \qquad \cos\phi = 1$$

So, maximum power is dissipated in the circuit. **(1 Mark)**

24. **Conductors:** (i) In conductors, the valence band is completely filled and the conduction band is—either partially filled with an extremely small energy gap between the valence and conduction bands or empty, with the two bands overlapping each other.

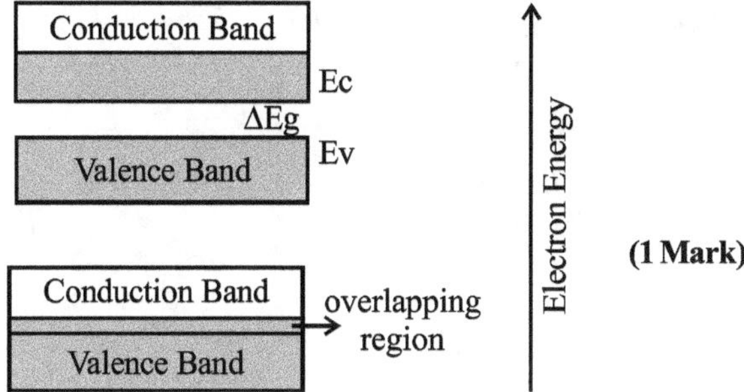

(1 Mark)

(ii) On applying an even small electric field, conductors can conduct electricity.

Semiconductors: (i) In semiconductors the energy band structure is similar to that of insulators, but in this case, the size of forbidden energy gap is much smaller than that of the insulators, as shown.

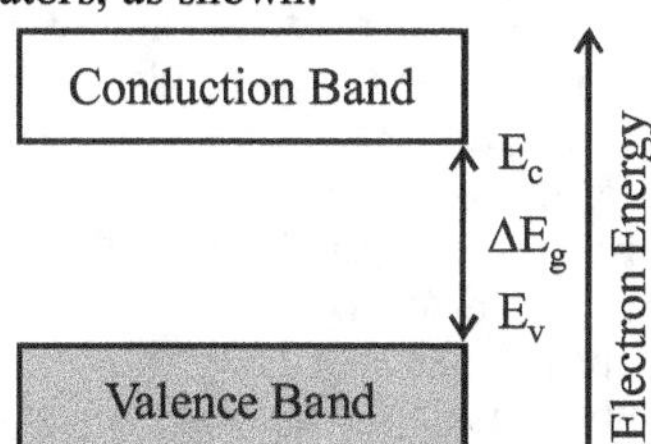

(ii) When an electric field is applied to a semiconductor, the electrons in the valence band find it comparatively easier to shift to the conduction band. So, the conductivity of semiconductors lies between the conductivity of conductors and insulators. **(1 Mark)**

Insulators: (i) In insulators, the energy gap between the conduction and valence band is very large. Also, the conduction band is practically empty.

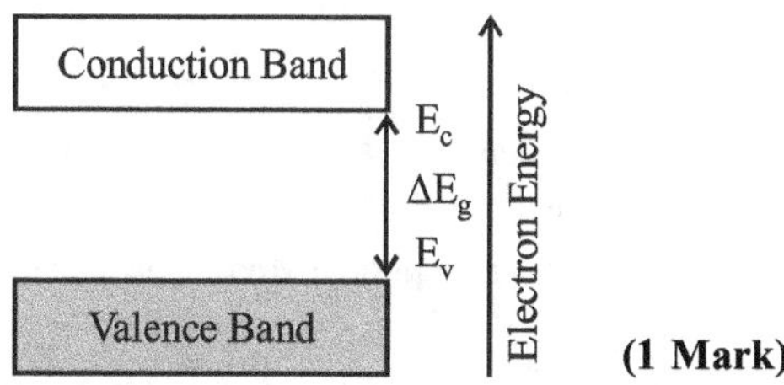

(1 Mark)

(ii) When an electric field is applied across such a solid, the electrons find it difficult to acquire such a large amount of energy to reach the conduction band. Thus, the conduction band continues to be empty. That is why no current flows through insulators.

25. (a) Aarti has displayed awareness, concern and caring towards the health of her sister. **(1 Mark)**

(b) During the intake of different elements and compounds, the biological organisms absorb them differently. Also, the exact distribution of the elements and their function in the various parts of organisms cannot be known clearly. For this, a radioisotope is made to enter the organism along with the elements and compounds, whose absorption, functioning and distribution to the brain has to be studied. The radioisotope acts as a tag of label for the element or compound under study. **(2 Marks)**

> **Note**
>
> *Radioisotopes are the unstable form of an element that emit radiation to transform into a stable form. Radiation is easily traceable and can cause changes in substances it falls upon. These special attributes make radioisotopes useful in medicine industry.*

26. The two basic modes of communication are:

(1) point-to-point communication

(2) broadcast communication **(½ Mark)**

Amplitude Modulation (AM): Amplitude modulation is the process in which one modulating wave of low frequency is superposed with carrier wave of high frequency such that the amplitude of carrier wave change in accordance with the amplitude of modulating wave.

Let the carrier wave be $c(t) = A_c \sin\omega_c t$

and the modulating signal be $m(t) = A_m \sin \omega_m t$, where $\omega_m = 2\pi f_m$ is the angular frequency of the message signal.

Modulated signal $c_m(t)$ is

$$c_m(t) = (A_c + A_m \sin \omega_m t) \sin \omega_c t$$

$$= A_c \left(1 + \frac{A_m}{A_c} \sin \omega_m t \right) \sin \omega_c t$$

$$\therefore \quad c_m(t) = A_c \sin \omega_c t + \mu A_c \sin \omega_m t \sin \omega_c t$$

where $\mu = A_m / A_c$ is the modulation index.

using trigonometeric identify

$$\sin A \sin B = \frac{1}{2}\left[\cos(A-B) - \cos(A+B)\right]$$

$$c_m(t) = A_c \sin\omega_c t + \frac{\mu A_c}{2}\cos$$

$$(\omega_c - \omega_m)t - \frac{\mu A_c}{2}\cos(\omega_c + \omega_m)t \qquad \textbf{(1½ Marks)}$$

$\omega_c - \omega_m$ and $\omega_c + \omega_m$ and are the lower side and upper side frequencies, respectively.

Production of Amplitude Modulated Wave

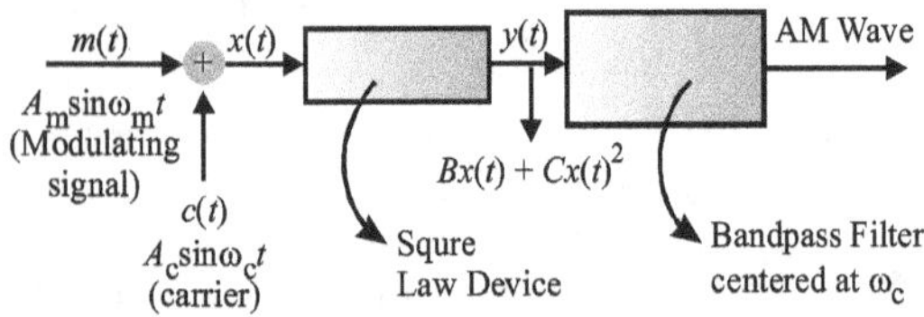

Amplitude modulated signal is obtained by superposing a modulating signal over a sinusoidal carrier wave is shown in the figure given below

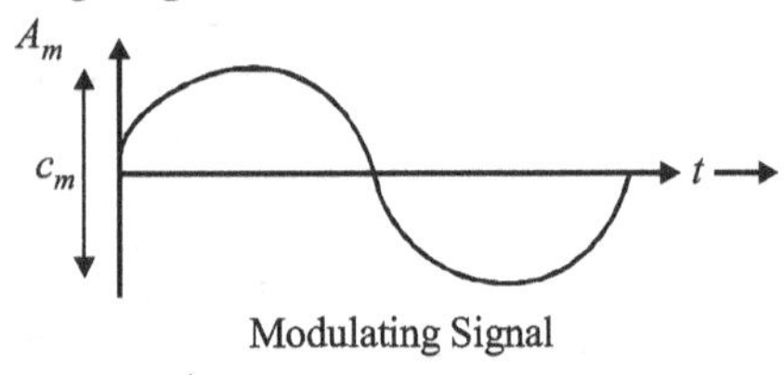
Modulating Signal

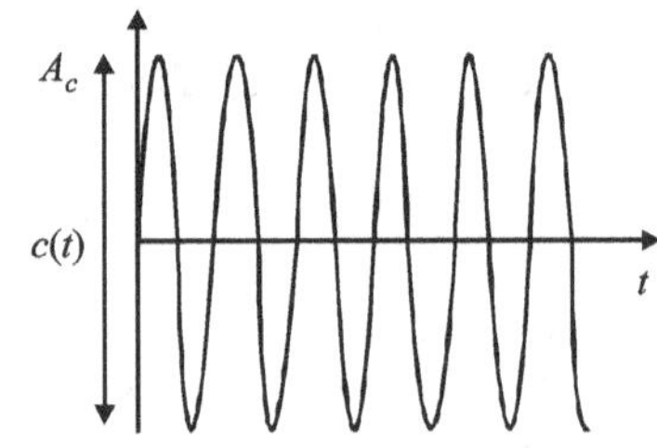
Carrier Wave

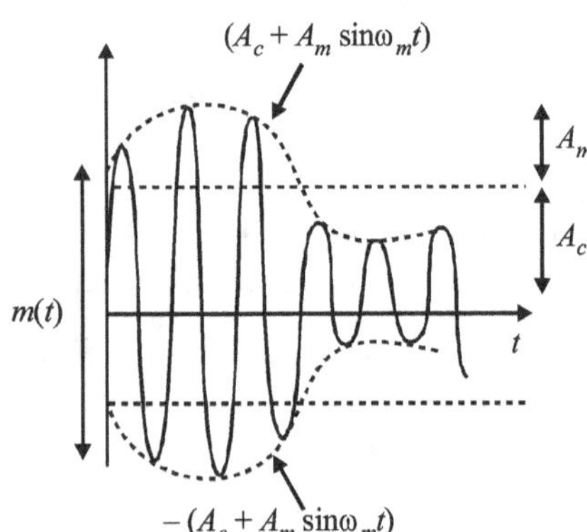

Amplitude Modulated Wave   **(1 Mark)**

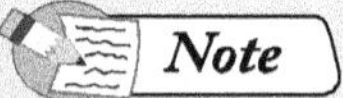 **Note**

Modulation Index $\mu = \dfrac{A_m}{A_c}$ *is always equal to or less than unity.*

When m exceeds unity, the carrier wave is overmodulated. The negative cycle (half) of the modulating signal is clipped and distortion will occur during reception.

27. The de-Broglie wavelength of the electrons is given by:

$$\lambda = \frac{h}{\sqrt{2meV}}$$

Here:

$m =$ mass of the electron $= 9.1 \times 10^{-31}$ kg
$e =$ charge on the electron $= 1.6 \times 10^{-19}$ C
$V =$ accelerating potential $= 50$ kV
$h =$ Planck's constant $= 6.626 \times 10^{-34}$ Js

$$\Rightarrow \quad \lambda = \frac{6.626 \times 10^{-34}}{\sqrt{2\,(9.1 \times 10^{-31})\,(1.6 \times 10^{-19})\,(50 \times 10^3)}}$$

$$\Rightarrow \quad \lambda = 0.0549\,\text{Å} \qquad \textbf{(1 Mark)}$$

Resolving power of a microscope, $R = 2\mu\sin\theta/\lambda$

For an electron microscope, the electrons are accelerated through a 60,000 V potential difference. Thus the wavelength of electrons is found to be,

$$\lambda = \frac{12.27}{\sqrt{V}} = \frac{12.27}{\sqrt{60000}} = 0.05\,\text{Å}$$

As, λ is very small (approximately 10^{-5} times smaller) for electron microscope than an optical microscope which uses yellow light of wavelength (5700 Å to 5900 Å). Hence, the resolving power of an electron microscope is much greater than that of optical microscope.   **(2 Marks)**

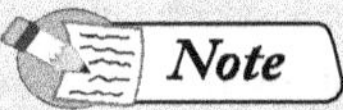 **Note**

Consider an electron accelerated from rest through a potential V. Kinetic energy = work done on electron by electric field.

$$\frac{1}{2}mv^2 = eV$$

Since $\qquad P = mv$

$$\therefore \quad \frac{1}{2}m\left(\frac{P^2}{m^2}\right) = eV$$

$$P = \sqrt{2meV}$$

De-Broglie wavelength $\lambda = \dfrac{h}{P}$

$$\therefore \lambda = \frac{h}{\sqrt{2meV}}.$$

28. Van de Graaff designed an electric generator capable of producing very high potential of the order of 10 MV.
Principle: It is based on the following two phenomena
(i) The electric charge always resides on the outer surface of a hollow cylinder.
(ii) The electric discharge in air or a gas takes place very fast through the pointed ends of the conductors. It is called corona discharge.
Construction: It consists of a large hollow metal sphere S mounted on two insulating columns A and B and an endless belt of rubber or silk is made to run on two pulleys, P_1 and P_2 by means of an eletric motor comb C_1 called spray comb and the upper comb C_2 called collecting comb. C_1 is connected to positive terminal of a very high voltage soource ($\approx 10^4$ volts) and upper comb C_2 is connected to the inner surface of the metal sphere S.

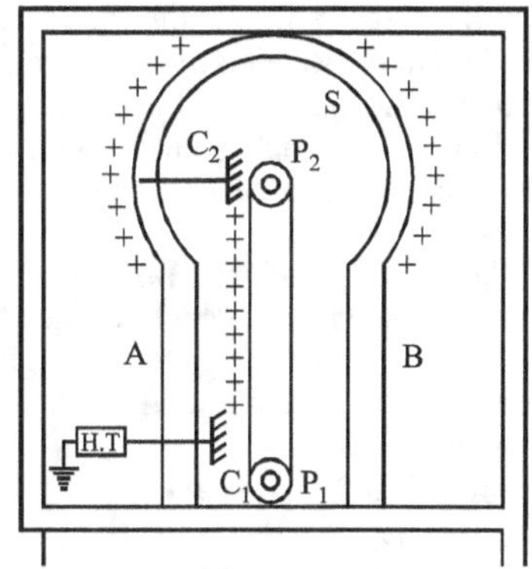

(1 Mark)

Working: When C_1 is connected to a very high potential, it produces ions near it, due to action of sharp points. The positive ions, so produced, get sprayed on the belt due to repulsion between positive ions and comb C_1. Positive ions are then carried upward by the moving belt. The comb C_2 collects positive charge from the belt and immediately shifts it to the outer surface of sphere S. Due to continuous motion of the belt, positive charges are continuously collected on S and the potential rises to a very high value. **(2 Marks)**

Use : Van de Graaff generator generates high potential differences that are used to accelerate charged particles such as electrons, protons, ions, etc. used for nuclear disintegration. **(1 Mark)**

Limitations : (1) It's a series combination that allows only one route for the movement of charge.

(2) It can accelerate only the charged particles not the uncharged particles. **(1 Mark)**

OR

(a) Dipole in a Uniform External Field

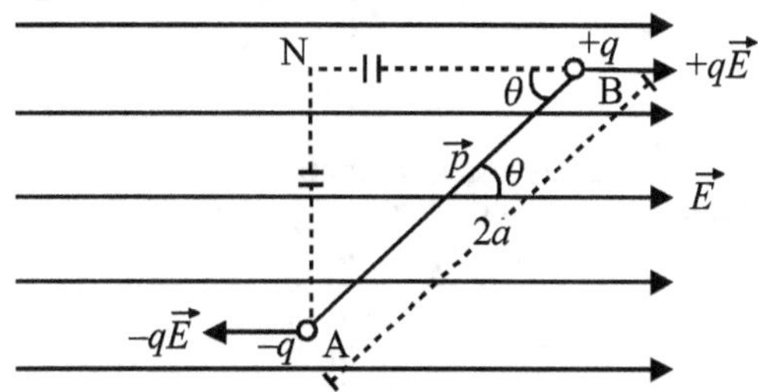

Consider an electric dipole consisting of charges $-q$ and $+q$ and of length $2a$ placed in a uniform electric field $\vec{E}$ making an angle θ with electric field.

Force on charge $-q$ at $A = q\vec{E}$ (opposite to $\vec{E}$)

Force on charge $+q$ at $B = q\vec{E}$ (along $\vec{E}$)

When electric dipole is placed under the action of two equal and opposite parallel forces, it gives rise a torque on the dipole.

$$\tau = \text{Force} \times \text{Perpendicular}$$
$$\text{distance between the two forces}$$
$$\tau = qE\,(AN) = qE\,(2a\sin\theta)$$
$$\tau = q(2a)\,E\sin\theta$$
$$\tau = pE\sin\theta \quad \{\because p = q\,(2a)\} \qquad \textbf{(2 Marks)}$$

$$\therefore \qquad \vec{\tau} = \vec{p} \times \vec{E}$$

(b) (i) Charge enclosed by sphere
$$S_1 = 2Q$$

By Gauss law, electric flux through sphere S_1 is $\phi_1 = 2Q/\varepsilon_0$

Charge enclosed by sphere
$$S_2 = 2Q + 4Q = 6Q$$
$$\therefore \qquad \phi_2 = 6Q/\varepsilon_0 \qquad \textbf{(1½ Marks)}$$

The ratio of the electric flux is
$$\phi_1/\phi_2 = 2Q/\in_0 \big/ 6Q/\in_0 = 2/6 = 1/3$$

(ii) For sphere S_1, the electric flux is
$$\phi' = 2Q/\varepsilon_r$$
$$\therefore \qquad \phi'/\phi_1 = \varepsilon_0/\varepsilon_r \Rightarrow \phi' = \phi_1.\varepsilon_0/\varepsilon_r$$
$$\because \qquad \varepsilon_r > \varepsilon_0$$
$$\therefore \qquad \phi' < \phi_1$$

Therefore, the electric flux through the sphere S_1 decreases with the introduction of the dielectric inside it. **(1½ Marks)**

 **Note**

$$\tau = \vec{P} \times \vec{E}$$
$$\tau = PE\sin\theta$$
at $\theta = 0°$ and $180°$, torque on dipole will be zero.
$\therefore$ At $\theta = 0°$, dipole is in stable equilibrium.
At $\theta = 180°$, dipole is in unstable equilibrium.

29. (a) Young performed the experiment by taking two coherent sources of light. The rays of light from two coherent sources S1 and S2 superpose each other on the screen and this leads to formation of alternate dark and bright fringes due to constructive and destructive interference, respectively.

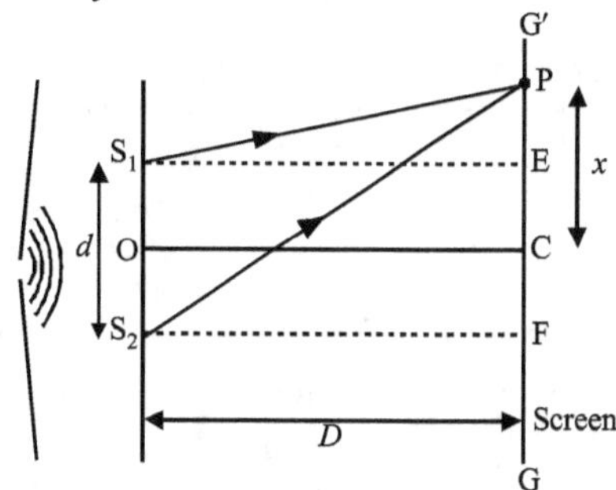

Let S_1 and S_2 be two slits separated by a distance d. GG' is the screen at a distance D from the slits S_1 and S_2. Point C is equidistant from both the slits. The intensity of light will be maximum at this point because the path difference of the waves reaching this point will be zero. **(2 Marks)**

At point P, the path difference between the rays coming from the slits S_1 and S_2 is $S_2P - S_1P$.

Now, $S_1 S_2 = d$, $EF = d$, and $S_2F = D$

$\therefore$ In $\triangle S_2PF$, from figure

$$S_2P = \left[S_2F^2 + PF^2\right]^{\frac{1}{2}}$$

$$S_2P = \left[D^2 + \left(x + \frac{d}{2}\right)^2\right]^{\frac{1}{2}}$$

$$= D\left[1 + \frac{\left(x + \frac{d}{2}\right)^2}{D^2}\right]^{\frac{1}{2}} \approx D\left[1 + \frac{1}{2}\frac{\left(x + \frac{d}{2}\right)^2}{D^2}\right]$$

Similarly, in ΔS_1PE, from figure
$$S_1P =$$

$$D\left[1+\frac{\left(x-\dfrac{d}{2}\right)^2}{D^2}\right]^{\frac{1}{2}} \approx D\left[1+\frac{1}{2}\frac{\left(x-\dfrac{d}{2}\right)^2}{D^2}\right]$$

($\because$ By Binomial expansion)

$$\therefore\ S_2P - S_1P = D\left[1+\frac{1}{2}\frac{\left(x+\dfrac{d}{2}\right)^2}{D^2}\right] - D\left[1+\frac{1}{2}\frac{\left(x-\dfrac{d}{2}\right)^2}{D^2}\right]$$

$$S_2P - S_1P = \frac{1}{2D}\left[4x\frac{d}{2}\right] = \frac{xd}{D}$$

For bright fringes (constructive interference), the path difference is an integral multiple of wavelengths, i.e. path difference is $n\lambda$.

$$\therefore\qquad n\lambda = \frac{xd}{D}$$

$$x = \frac{n\lambda D}{d}, \text{ where } n = 0, 1, 2, 3, 4, \ldots$$

Fringe width (β) $\rightarrow$ Separation between the centres of two consecutive bright fringes is called the width of a dark fringe.

$$\boxed{\therefore \beta_1 = x_n - x_{n-1} = \frac{\lambda D}{d}}\qquad \textbf{(2 Marks)}$$

Similarly, for dark fringes,

$$x_n = (2n-1)\frac{\lambda D}{2\,d}$$

The separation between the centres of two consecutive dark interference fringes is the width of a bright fringe.

$$\boxed{\therefore \beta_2 = x_n - x_{n-1} = \frac{\lambda D}{d}}$$

$$\therefore\qquad \beta_1 = \beta_2$$

All the bright and dark fringes are of equal width as $\beta_1 = \beta_2$

(b) Let the slit width is w, amplitude is a and intensity I. Then
$$I_{min}/I_{max} = (a_1 - a_2)^2/(a_1 + a_2)^2 = 9/25$$
$$(a_1 - a_2)/(a_1 + a_2) = 3/5 \text{ Or } a_1/a_2 = 4/1$$
and $\qquad w_1/w_2 = (a_1)^2/(a_2)^2 = 16/1$ $\qquad$ **(1 Mark)**

OR

(a) Consider a parallel beam of light from a lens falling on a slit AB. As diffraction occurs, the pattern is focused on the screen XY with the help of lens L2. We will obtain a diffraction pattern that is a central maximum at the centre O flanked by a number of dark and bright fringes called secondary maxima and minima.

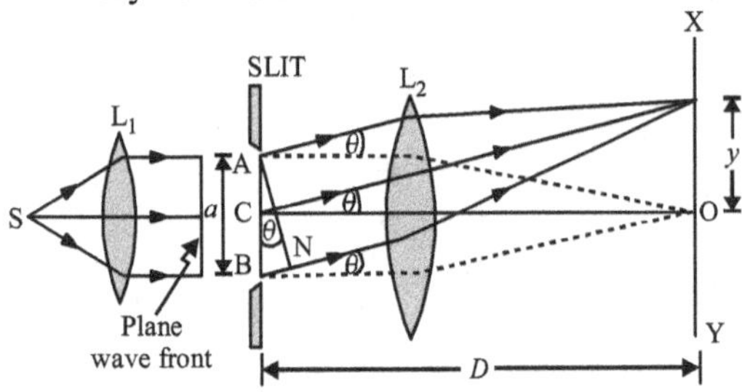

Central Maxima : Each point on the plane wave front AB sends out secondary wavelets in all directions. The waves from points equidistant from the centre C lying on the upper and lower half reach point O with zero path difference and hence, reinforce each other, producing maximum intensity at point O.

Positions and Widths of Secondary Maxima and Minima

Consider a point P on the screen at which wavelets travelling in a direction making angle θ with CO are brought to focus by the lens. The wavelets from points A and B will have a path difference equal to BN.

From the right-angled ΔANB, we have:
$$BN = AB \sin\theta$$
$$BN = a \sin\theta \qquad \ldots(i)$$
Suppose $\qquad BN = \lambda \quad$ and $\quad \theta = \theta_1$
Then, the above equation gives
$$\lambda = a \sin\theta_1$$

$$\boxed{\sin\theta_1 = \frac{\lambda}{a}}\qquad \ldots(ii)$$

This will be the position of first secondary minimum.
If $\qquad BN = 2\lambda$ and $\theta = \theta_2$, then
$$2\lambda = a \sin\theta_2$$
$$\sin\theta_2 = \frac{2\lambda}{a} \qquad \ldots(iii)$$
This will be the position of second secondary minimum.
In general, for n^{th} minimum at point P,
$$\sin\theta_n = \frac{n\lambda}{a} \qquad \ldots(iv)$$
If y_n is the distance of the nth minimum from the centre of the screen, from right-angled ΔCOP, we have:
$$\tan\theta_n = \frac{OP}{CO}$$
$$\tan\theta_n = \frac{y_n}{D} \qquad \ldots(v)$$
In case θ_n is small, $\sin\theta_n \approx \tan\theta_n$
$\therefore$ Equations (iv) and (v) give
$$\frac{y_n}{D} = \frac{n\lambda}{a}$$
$$y_n = \frac{nD\lambda}{a}$$
Width of the secondary maximum,
$$\beta = y_n - y_{n-1} = \frac{nD\lambda}{a} - \frac{(n-1)D\lambda}{a}$$
$$\beta = \frac{D\lambda}{a} \qquad \ldots(vi)$$
$\therefore$ β is independent of n, all the secondary maxima are of the same width β.

If $BN = \dfrac{3\lambda}{2}$ and $\theta = \theta_1'$, from equation (i), we have:

$$\sin\theta_1' = \frac{3\lambda}{2a} \qquad \textbf{(1½ Marks)}$$

This will be the position of the first secondary maximum.
Corresponding to path difference,

$$BN = \frac{5\lambda}{2} \text{ and } \theta = \theta_2', \text{ the second secondary maximum is produced}$$

In general, for the nth maximum at point P,

$$\sin\theta'_n = \frac{(2n+1)\lambda}{2a} \qquad \text{... (vii)}$$

If y'_n is the distance of nth maximum from the centre of the screen, then the angular position of the nth maximum is given by

$$\tan\theta'_n = \frac{y'_n}{D} \qquad \text{...(viii)}$$

When θ'_n is small,

$$\sin\theta'_n \approx \tan\theta'_n$$

$$\therefore \qquad y'_n = \frac{(2n+1)D\lambda}{a}$$

Width of the secondary minimum,

$$\beta' = y'_n - y'_{n-1} = nD\lambda/a - (n-1)D\lambda/a$$

$$\boxed{\beta' = \frac{D\lambda}{a}} \qquad \text{... (xi)}$$

(1½ Marks)

Since β' is independent of n, all the secondary minima are of the same width β'.

(b) For first maxima of the diffraction pattern we know $\sin\theta = 3\lambda/2a$ where a is aperture of slit.

For small values of θ, $\sin\theta \approx \tan\theta = y/D$

Where y is the distance of first minima from central line and D is the distance between the slit and the screen.

So, $$y = \frac{3\lambda}{2a}D$$

For 590 nm,

$$y_1 = \frac{3 \times 590 \times 10^{-9}}{2 \times 2 \times 10^{-6}} \times 1.5 = 0.66375\,\text{m}$$

For 596 nm,

$$y_2 = \frac{3 \times 596 \times 10^{-9}}{2 \times 2 \times 10^{-6}} \times 1.5 = 0.6105\,\text{m}$$

Separation between the positions of first maxima $= y_2 - y_1$
$= 0.00675\,\text{m}$ **(2 Marks)**

30. (a) When a charged particle with charge q moves inside a magnetic field $\vec{B}$ with velocity v, it experiences a force, which is given by:

$$\vec{F} = q(\vec{v} \times \vec{B})$$

Here, $\vec{v}$ is perpendicular to $\vec{B}$ and $\vec{F}$ is the force on the charged particle which acts as the centripetal force and makes it move along a circular path.

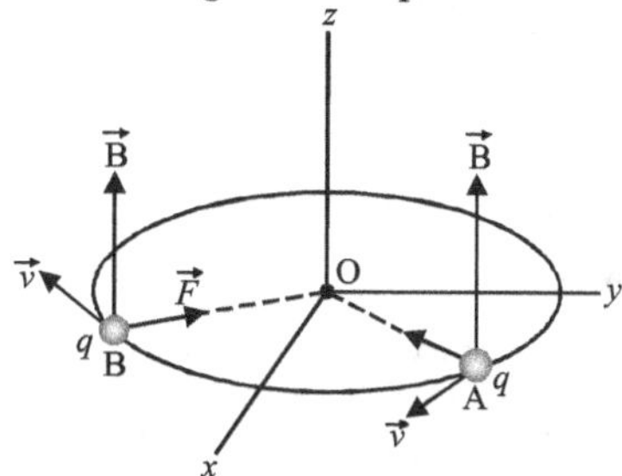

Let m be the mass of the charged particle and r be the radius of the circular path.

$$q(\vec{v} \times \vec{B}) = \frac{mv^2}{r}$$

Since, v and B are perpendicular to each other.

$$\therefore \qquad qvB = \frac{mv^2}{r}$$

$$\boxed{r = \frac{mv}{Bq}}$$

Time period of circular motion of the charged particle can be calculated as shown below:

$$T = \frac{2\pi r}{v} = \frac{2\pi}{v}\frac{mv}{Bq}$$

$$T = \frac{2\pi m}{Bq}$$

$\therefore$ Angular frequency is

$$\omega = \frac{2\pi}{T}$$

$$\boxed{\therefore \omega = \frac{Bq}{m}} \qquad \qquad \textbf{(2 Marks)}$$

Therefore, the frequency of the revolution of the charged particle is independent of the velocity or the energy of the particle.

(b) Cyclotron :

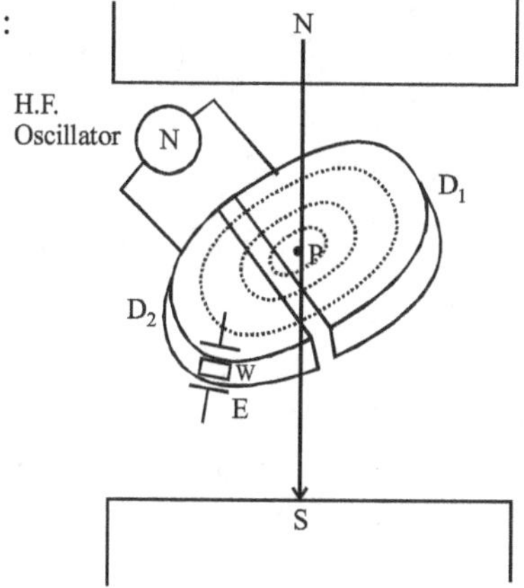

(½ Mark)

Principle: A positively charged particle is subjected to two perpendicular electric and magnetic fields. It is accelerated and hence gains energy due to the oscillating electric field by crossing the field again and again, whereas due to the magnetic field it travels in a circular path. **(½ Mark)**

Construction:

(i) D_1 and D_2 are two hollow, 'D' shaped, evacuated, metal chambers called Dees.

(ii) H.F. oscillator produces a high potential difference of the order of 10^4 volt between D_1 and D_2.

(iii) N, S are pole pieces of a strong electromagnet which produces a strong magnetic field perpendicular to the plane of the dees. **(½ Mark)**

(iv) P is a source of positively charged particle.

(v) W is a window through which accelerated charged particle will come out.

(vi) E is a pair of deflecting plates which produces electric field to take out accelerated charged particle.

Working:

Let initially D_1 is at a negative potential and D_2 is at positive potential. Therefore, positive ions from P will be accelerated towards D_1 and in D_1, there will be a field free space so the particles will move with a constant speed v. But due to perpendicular magnetic field of strength B, it will describe a circular path of radius r in D_1.

$\therefore$ $Bqv = \dfrac{mv^2}{r}$ (centripetal force is provided by the magnetic Lorentz force)

$\therefore$ $r = \dfrac{mv}{Bq}$

Time to travel the semicircular path

$= t = \dfrac{\pi r}{v} = \dfrac{\pi m}{Bq} = $ constant.

If this time is equal to half the time of cycle of electric oscillator, so as the particle will reach at the end of D_1, the polarities of D_1 and D_2 will change and the ion will be accelerated in D_2. In D_2 it will move with a constant speed and will travel another semicircular path of slightly greater radius. In this way, each time the particle will travel in a circular path of slightly greater radius and will acquire more energy. Finally it is taken out through the window (w) by applying an electric field across the deflecting plates E.

Maximum K.E. of the particle

$= \dfrac{1}{2}mv^2 = \dfrac{1}{2}m\left(\dfrac{Bqr}{m}\right)^2$ $\left[\because \dfrac{mv^2}{r} = Bqv \Rightarrow v = \dfrac{Bqr}{m}\right]$

$(K.E.)_{Max} = \dfrac{B^2q^2r^2}{2m}$ **(1½ Marks)**

Time period of the oscillating electric field

$= T = 2t = \dfrac{2\pi m}{Bq}$

Cyclotron frequency $= \nu = \dfrac{1}{T} = \dfrac{Bq}{2\pi m}$

OR

(a) **Principle:** When a current carrying coil is placed in a magnetic field, it experience a torque.

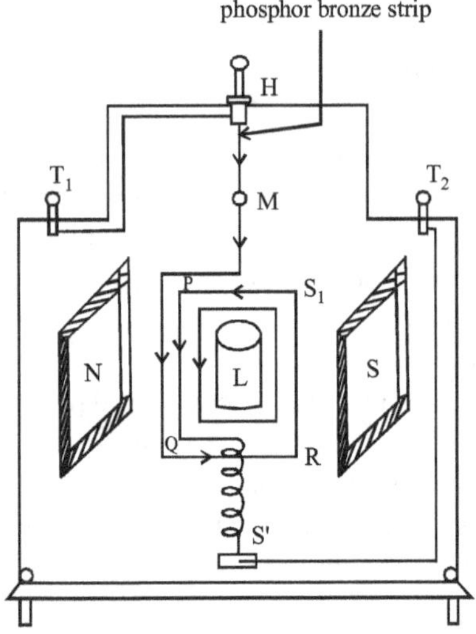

Construction:

(i) PQRS, is a coil with large number of turns of insulated copper wire which is wound over a nonmagnetic frame.
(ii) H is a Torsion head from which the coil is suspended by means of a phosphor bronze fibre within the uniform magnetic field of two cylindrical magnetic pole pieces N and S.
(iii) S' is a hair spring made by quartz or phosphor bronze.
(iv) L is a soft iron core to make the magnetic field radial.
(v) M is a concave mirror used to note the deflection of the coil by a lamp and scale arrangement.
(vi) T_1, T_2 are terminals through which the galvanometer is connected in the circuit.

Theory & Working : Let, ℓ = length of the coil, b = breadth of the coil, n = number of turns of the coil

$\ell \times b = A$ = Area of the coil, B = magnetic field strength, I = current through the coil

α = angle between the normal to the plane of the coil and $\vec{B}$.

$\therefore$ Torque on the coil $= \tau = nIBA \sin \alpha$

For radial magnetic field *i.e.*, when plane of the coil is parallel to the magnetic field, then $\sin \alpha = 1$ *i.e.*, $\alpha = 90°$

$\therefore$ $\tau = nIBA$

Due to this torque the coil rotates and the phosphor bronze strip gets twisted. So a restoring torque comes into play within the strip which tries to bring the coil back to its original position. In equilibrium, deflecting torque = Restoring torque

$nIBA = k\theta$ [k = Restoring torque/unit twist of the strip]

(½ + ½ + 2 Marks)

$\therefore$ $I = \dfrac{k}{nBA}\theta = G\theta$ [θ = twist]

where G = Galvanometer constant $= \dfrac{k}{nBA}$

$\therefore$ $I \propto \theta$

(b) (i) When cylindrical soft iron core, is placed inside the coil of a galvanometer, it makes the magnetic field stronger and radial in the space between it and pole pieces, such that whatever the position of the rotation of the coil is, the magnetic field is always parallel to its plane. Thus it is necessary to introduce a cylindrical soft iron core inside the coil of a galvanometer. **(1 Mark)**

(ii) Current sensitivity is

$\dfrac{\phi}{I} = \dfrac{NAB}{k}$ ...(i)

Voltage sensitivity is

$\dfrac{\phi}{V} = \left(\dfrac{NAB}{k}\right)\dfrac{1}{R}$ ...(ii)

Let's increase current sensitivity by doubling no. of turns $N \to 2N$.

Then from equation (i),

$\dfrac{\phi}{I} \to 2\dfrac{\phi}{I}$

i.e current sensitivity also gets doubled. **(1 Mark)**

But for $N \to 2N$, $R \to 2R$ as resistance is proportional to length of wire.

$\therefore$ from equation 2, $\dfrac{\phi}{V} \to \dfrac{2NAB}{k} \times \dfrac{1}{2R}$

$\dfrac{\phi}{V} \to \dfrac{\phi}{V}$

i.e., voltage sensitivity remains unchanged.

Delhi *2014*

CBSE Board Solved Paper

Time Allowed : 3 Hours   *Maximum Marks : 70*

General Instructions:

(i)   All questions are compulsory.

(ii) There are 30 questions in total. Question Nos. **1** to **8** are very short answer type questions and carry **one** mark each.

(iii) Question Nos. **9** to **18** carry **two** marks each. Question Nos. **19** to **27** carry **three** marks each and question nos. **28** to **30** carry **five** marks each

(iv) One of the questions carrying **three** marks weightage is value based question

(v)   There is no overall choice. However, an internal choice has been provided in **one** question of **two** marks, **one** question of **three** marks and all **three** questions of **five** marks each weightage. You have to attempt only **one** of the choices in such questions.

(vi) Use of calculators is not permitted. However, you may use log tables if necessary.

(vii) You may use the following values of physical constants wherever necessary:

$c = 3 \times 10^8$ m/s

$h = 6.63 \times 10^{-34}$ Js

$e = 1.6 \times 10^{-19}$ C

$\mu_0 = 4\pi \times 10^{-7}$ T m A^{-1}

$\varepsilon_0 = 8.854 \times 10^{-12}$ C^2 N^{-1} m^{-2}

$\dfrac{1}{4\pi\varepsilon_0} = 9 \times 10^9$ N m^2 C^{-2}

Mass of electron $(m_e) = 9.1 \times 10^{-31}$ kg

Mass of neutron $= 1.675 \times 10^{-27}$ kg

Mass of proton $= 1.673 \times 10^{-27}$ kg

Avogadro's number $= 6.023 \times 10^{23}$ per gram mole

Boltzmann constant $= 1.38 \times 10^{-23}$ JK^{-1}

---

1. Define the term 'mobility' of charge carriers in a conductor. Write its S.I. unit

2. The carrier wave is given by

$$C(t) = 2\sin(8\pi t) \text{ volt.}$$

The modulating signal is a square wave as shown. Find modulation index.

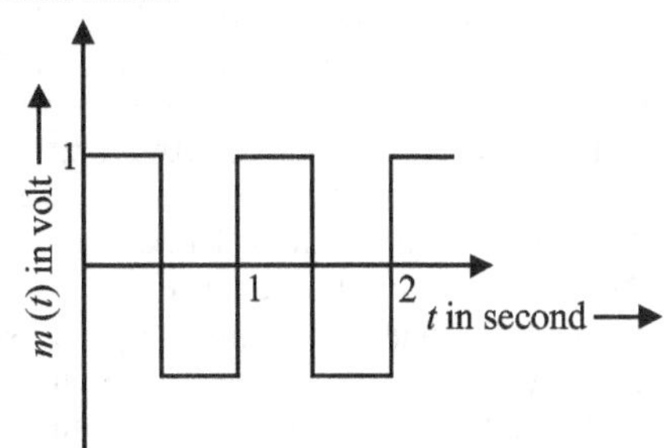

3. "For any charge configuration, equipotential surface through a point is normal to the electric field." Justify.

4. Two spherical bobs, one metallic and the other of glass, of the same size are allowed to fall freely from the same height above the ground. Which of the two would reach earlier and why?

5. Show variation of resistivity of copper as a function of temperature in a graph.

6. A convex lens is placed in contact with a plane mirror. A point object at a distance of 20 cm on the axis of this combination has its image coinciding with itself. What is the focal length of the lens?

7. Write the expression, in a vector form, for the Lorentz magnetic force due to a charge moving with velocity in a magnetic field. What is the direction of the magnetic force?

8. The figure given below shows the block diagram of a generalized communication system. Identify the element labelled 'X' and write its function.

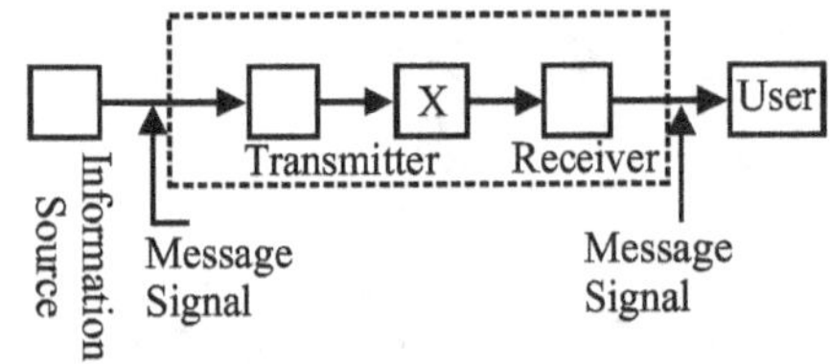

9. Out of the two magnetic materials, 'A' has relative permeability slightly greater than unity while 'B' has less than unity. Identify the nature of the materials 'A' and 'B'. Will their susceptibilities be positive or negative?

10. Given a uniform electric field $\vec{E} = 2 \times 10^3\, \hat{i}$ N/C, find the flux of this field through a square of side 20 cm, whose plane is parallel to the y–z plane. What would be the flux through the same square, if the plane makes an angle of 30° with the x-axis ?

11. For a single slit of width "a", the first minimum of the diffraction pattern of a monochromatic light of wavelength λ occurs at an angle of λ/a. At the same angle of λ/a, we get a maximum for two narrow slits separated by a distance "a". Explain.

12. Write the truth table for the combination of the gates shown. Name the gates used.

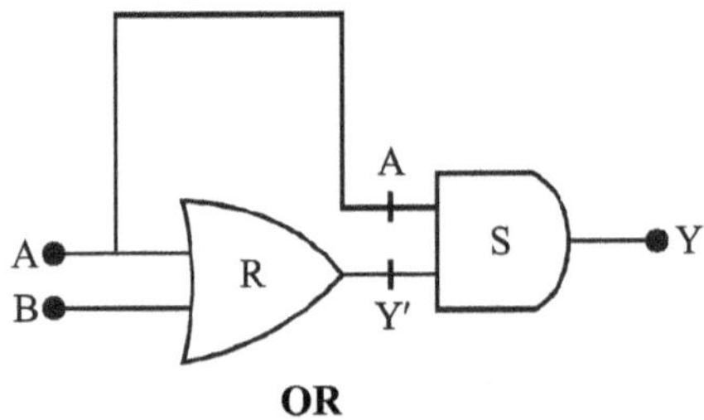

OR

Identify the logic gates marked 'P' and 'Q' in the given circuit. Write the truth table for the combination.

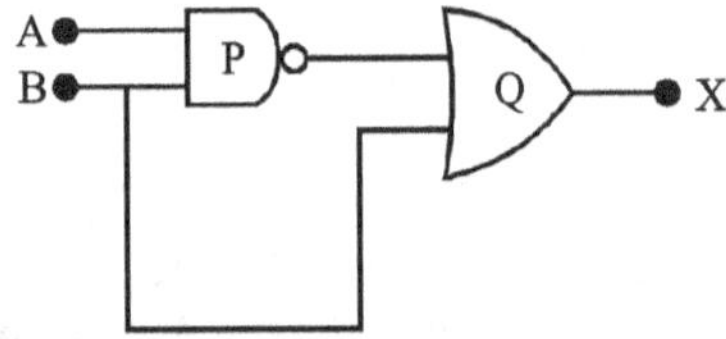

13. State Kirchhoff's rules. Explain briefly how these rules are justified.

14. A capacitor 'C', a variable resistor 'R' and a bulb 'B' are connected in series to the ac mains in circuit as shown. The bulb glows with some brightness. How will the glow of the bulb change if (i) a dielectric slab is introduced between the plates of the capacitor, keeping resistance R to be the same; (ii) the resistance R is increased keeping the same capacitance?

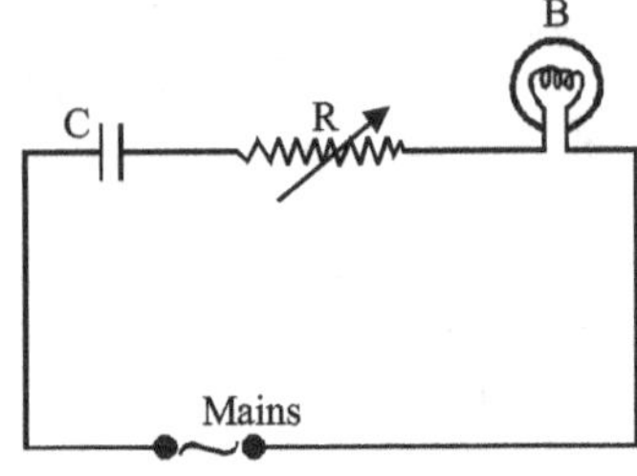

15. State the underlying principle of a cyclotron. Write briefly how this machine is used to accelerate charged particles to high energies.

16. An electric dipole of length 4 cm, when placed with its axis making an angle of 60° with a uniform electric field, experiences a torque of $4\sqrt{3}$ Nm. Calculate the potential energy of the dipole, if it has charge ±8 nC.

17. A proton and a deuteron are accelerated through the same accelerating potential. Which one of the two has
(a) greater value of de-Broglie wavelength associated with it, and
(b) less momentum?
Give reasons to justify your answer.

18. (i) Monochromatic light of frequency 6.0×10^{14} Hz is produced by a laser. The power emitted is 2.0×10^{-3} W. Estimate the number of photons emitted per second on an average by the source.
(ii) Draw a plot showing the variation of photoelectric current versus the intensity of incident radiation on a given photosensitive surface.

19. A 12.5 eV electron beam is used to bombard gaseous hydrogen at room temperature. Upto which energy level the hydrogen atoms would be excited?
Calculate the wavelengths of the first member of Lyman and first member of Balmer series.

20. When Sunita, a class XII student, came to know that her parents are planning to rent out the top floor of their house to a mobile company she protested. She tried hard to convince her parents that this move would be a health hazard.
Ultimately her parents agreed :
(1) In what way can the setting up of transmission tower by a mobile company in a residential colony prove to be injurious to health?
(2) By objecting to this move of her parents, what value did Sunita display?
(3) Estimate the range of e.m. waves which can be transmitted by an antenna of height 20 m. (Given radius of the earth = 6400 km)

21. A potentiometer wire of length 1 m has a resistance of 10 Ω. It is connected to a 6 V battery in series with a resistance of 5 Ω. Determine the emf of the primary cell which gives a balance point at 40 cm.

22. (a) Draw a labelled ray diagram showing the formation of a final image by a compound microscope at least distance of distinct vision.
(b) The total magnification produced by a compound microscope is 20. The magnification produced by the eye piece is 5. The microscope is focussed on a certain object. The distance between the objective and eyepiece is observed to be 14 cm. If least distance of distinct vision is 20 cm, calculate the focal length of the objective and the eye piece.

23. (a) A mobile phone lies along the principal axis of a concave mirror. Show, with the help of a suitable diagram, the formation of its image. Explain why magnification is not uniform.
(b) Suppose the lower half of the concave mirror's reflecting surface is covered with an opaque material.

What effect this will have on the image of the object? Explain.

24. (a) Obtain the expression for the energy stored per unit volume in a charged parallel plate capacitor.

(b) The electric field inside a parallel plate capacitor is E. Find the amount of work done in moving a charge q over a closed loop a b c d a.

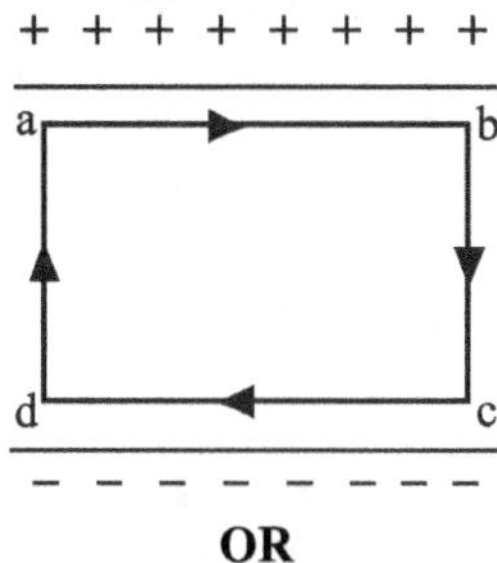

OR

(a) Derive the expression for the capacitance of a parallel plate capacitor having plate area A and plate separation d.

(b) Two charged spherical conductors of radii R_1 and R_2 when connected by a conducting wire acquire charges q_1 and q_2 respectively. Find the ratio of their surface charge densities in terms of their radii.

25. (a) State Ampere's circuital law, expressing it in the integral form.

(b) Two long coaxial insulated solenoids, S_1 and S_2 of equal lengths are wound one over the other as shown in the figure. A steady current "I" flow thought the inner solenoid S_1 to the other end B, which is connected to the outer solenoid S_2 through which the same current "I" flows in the opposite direction so as to come out at end A. If n_1 and n_2 are the number of turns per unit length, find the magnitude and direction of the net magnetic field at a point (i) inside on the axis and (ii) outside the combined system.

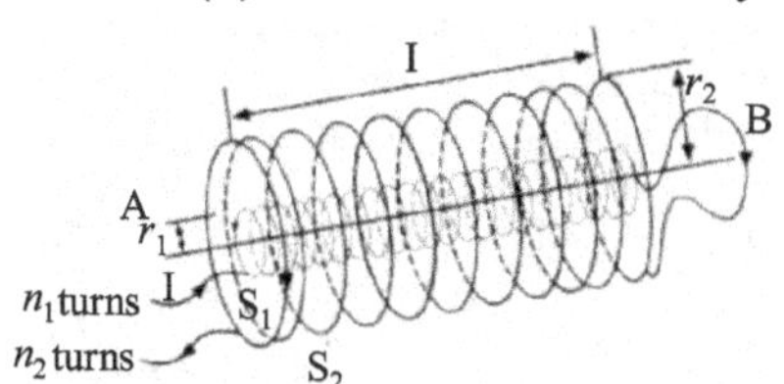

26. Answer the following:
(a) Name the em waves which are suitable for radar systems used in aircraft navigation. Write the range of frequency of these waves.

(b) If the earth did not have atmosphere, would its average surface temperature be higher or lower than what it is now? Explain.

(c) An em wave exerts pressure on the surface on which it is incident. Justify.

27. (a) Deduce the expression, $N = N_0 e^{-\lambda t}$, for the law of radioactive decay.

(b) (i) Write symbolically the process expressing the β^+ decay of $^{22}_{11}\text{Na}$. Also write the basic nuclear process underlying this decay.

(ii) Is the nucleus formed in the decay of the nucleus $^{22}_{11}\text{Na}$, an isotope or isobar?

28. (a) (i) 'Two independent monochromatic sources of light cannot produce a sustained interference pattern'. Give reason.

(ii) Light waves each of amplitude "a" and frequency "ω", emanating from two coherent light sources superpose at a point. If the displacements due to these waves is given by $y_1 = a \cos \omega t$ and $y_2 = a \cos(\omega t + \phi)$ where ϕ is the phase difference between the two, obtain the expression for the resultant intensity at the point.

(b) In Young's double slit experiment, using monochromatic light of wavelength λ, the intensity of light at a point on the screen where path difference is λ, is K units. Find out the intensity of light at a point where path difference is λ/3.

OR

(a) How does one demonstrate, using a suitable diagram, that unpolarised light when passed through a Polaroid gets polarised?

(b) A beam of unpolarised light is incident on a glass-air interface. Show, using a suitable ray diagram, that light reflected from the interface is totally polarised, when $\mu = \tan i_B$, where μ is the refractive index of glass with respect to air and i_B is the Brewster's angle.

29. (a) Describe a simple experiment (or activity) to show that the polarity of emf induced in a coil is always such that it tends to produce a current which opposes the change of magnetic flux that produces it.

(b) The current flowing through an inductor of self inductance L is continuously increasing. Plot a graph showing the variation of
(i) Magnetic flux versus the current
(ii) Induced emf versus dI/dt
(iii) Magnetic potential energy stored versus the current.

OR

(a) Draw a schematic sketch of an ac generator describing its basic elements. State briefly its working principle. Show a plot of variation of
(i) Magnetic flux and time
(ii) Alternating emf versus time generated by a loop of wire rotating in a magnetic field.

(b) Why is choke coil needed in the use of fluorescent tubes with ac mains?

30. (a) State briefly the processes involved in the formation of *p-n* junction explaining clearly how the depletion region is formed.

(b) Using the necessary circuit diagrams, show how the V-I characteristics of a *p-n* junction are obtained in
(i) Forward biasing
(ii) Reverse biasing

How are these characteristics made use of in rectification?

OR

(a) Differentiate between three segments of a transistor on the basis of their size and level of doping.

(b) How is a transistor biased to be in active state?

(c) With the help of necessary circuit diagram, describe briefly how *n-p-n* transistor in CE configuration amplifies a small sinusoidal input voltage. Write the expression for the ac current gain.

Solutions

1. Drift velocity per unit electric field is called Mobility. It is denoted by μ.

$$\mu = \frac{V_d}{E} \qquad (½ + ½ = \textbf{1 Mark})$$

S.I. unit of mobility is $m^2 v^{-1} s^{-1}$

2. The generalised equation of a carrier wave is given as, $C(t) = A_c \sin\omega_c t \dots$ (i)

Modulation index (μ) is the ratio of the amplitude of modulating signal to the amplitude of the carrier wave.

$$\mu = \frac{A_m}{A_c} \qquad (\textbf{½ Mark})$$

On comparing equations with the given equation of carrier wave, we get:

Amplitude of carrier wave, $A_c = 2V$

From given amplitude madulated wave form Amplitude of modulating signal, $A_m = 1V$

$$\Rightarrow \mu = \frac{1}{2} = 0.5 \qquad (\textbf{½ Mark})$$

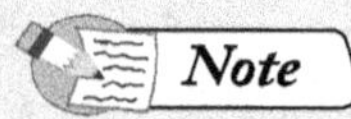 **Note**

Modulation index m is always equal to or below 1, to avoid distortion. While solving question care should be taken that m £ 1.

3. An equipotential surface is that at every point of which electric potential is same. Consider two points A and B on the equipotential surface.

By definition, potential difference between two points A and B = work done in carrying a unit positive charge from A to B.

$$\Rightarrow V_A - V_B = W_{AB} = \vec{E}.d\vec{\ell} \qquad (\textbf{1 Mark})$$

But $V_A = V_B$ $\qquad \therefore \vec{E}.d\vec{\ell} = 0$

$\Rightarrow E dl \cos\theta = 0 \qquad \Rightarrow \cos\theta = 0$

$\Rightarrow \theta = 90° \qquad \therefore \vec{E} \perp d\vec{\ell}$

$\therefore$ Electric field ($\vec{E}$) is directed perpendicular to the equipotential surface.

 **Note**

So, the work done (W) in moving a test charge along an equipotential surface is zero. An equipotential surface is a surface with a constant value of potential at all the points on the surface.

4. Glass bob is non-conducting in nature. Due to the non-conducting nature of the glass bob, it will only experience the Earth's gravitational pull. So, the glass bob will reach the ground earlier.

While a metallic bob is conducting in nature. So, Eddy current is induced in the metallic bob as it falls through the magnetic field of the Earth. By Lenz's law, the current induced is such that it opposes the motion of the metallic bob. So, the metallic bob will experience a force in the upward direction. This will slow down the metallic bob by some extent.

Hence, it will reach the Earth after the glass bob.

$$(½ + ½ = \textbf{1 Mark})$$

5. 
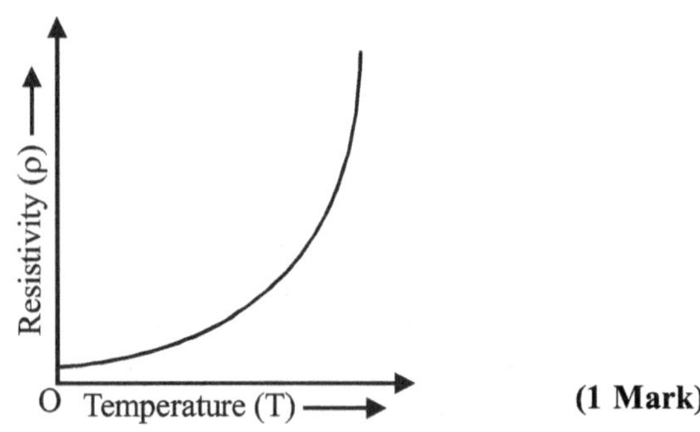

$(\textbf{1 Mark})$

 **Note**

The value of temperature coefficient (α) is positive for metals, like copper, because resistance of metal increases with rise in temperature. Thus the variation of resistivity of copper with temperature is parabolic in nature. This is shown in the following graph:

6. The convex lens is in contact with a plane mirror. The image distance is equal to the object distance. Thus, it is clear that the point object is placed at the centre of the curvature of the lens.

From relations $f = \dfrac{R}{2}$ $\qquad (\textbf{1 Mark})$

We use the relation, where R is the distance between the centre of the curvature

and the pole and f = focal length.

Here, R = 20 cm

$\therefore$ Focal length of the lens = 20/2 = 10 cm

7. The force acting on a particle having a charge q and moving with velocity $\vec{v}$ in an uniform magnetic field $\vec{B}$ is given

by, $\vec{F} = q(\vec{v} \times \vec{B})$ $\qquad (½ + ½ = \textbf{1 Mark})$

The direction of the magnetic force is perpendicular to the plane containing the velocity vector and the magnetic field vector.

8. The element labelled 'X' is called 'channel'. Channel in the medium through which message travels from the transmitter to the receiver. A channel may either be wireless or in the form of wires connecting the transmitter and the receiver. $\qquad (½ + ½ = \textbf{1 Mark})$

9. Relation between relative permeability (μ_r) and susceptibility (χ) of a magnetic material is,

$$\mu_r = 1 + \chi$$

For a paramagnetic material, the relative permeability lies between $1 < \mu_r < 1$ and its susceptibility lies between $0 < \chi < E$.

Hence, 'A' is a paramagnetic material and its susceptibility is positive.

For a diamagnetic material, the relative permeability lies between $0 \leq \mu_r < 1$ and its susceptibility lies between $-1 < \chi < 0$. **(1 + 1 = 2 Marks)**

Hence, 'B' is a diamagnetic material and its susceptibility is negative.

10. When the plane is parallel to the y-z plane:

$$\phi = \vec{E} \cdot \vec{A} \qquad \textbf{(1 + 1 = 2 Marks)}$$

Here: $\vec{E} = 2 \times 10^3\, \hat{i}$ N/C

$$\vec{A} = (20\ \text{cm})^2\, \hat{i} = 4 \times 10^{-2}\, \hat{i}\ \text{m}^2$$

$\therefore \qquad \phi = (2 \times 10^3\, \hat{i}) \cdot (4 \times 10^{-2}\, \hat{i})$

$\Rightarrow \qquad \phi = 80$ weber

When the plane makes a $30°$ angle with the x-axis, the area vector makes a $60°$ angle with the x-axis.

$$\phi = \vec{E} \cdot \vec{A}$$
$\Rightarrow \qquad \phi = EA \cos\theta$
$\Rightarrow \qquad \phi = (2 \times 10^3)\,(4 \times 10^{-2})\cos 60°$
$\Rightarrow \qquad \phi = 80/2$
$\Rightarrow \qquad \phi = 40$ weber

11. In single slit diffraction, the path difference between two secondary wavelets is

path difference $= a\sin\theta$

if path difference in 'n λ', the we get a minima

$\therefore \qquad a\sin\theta = n\lambda$
for $\qquad n = 1$
$\qquad a\sin\theta = \lambda$

$$\sin\theta = \frac{\lambda}{a} \qquad \ldots(1)$$

In double slit interference, the path difference between waves from two coherent sources is

path difference $= \dfrac{xd}{D}$

For bright fringes,

$$\frac{xd}{D} = n\lambda$$
For $\qquad n = 1$

$$\frac{x}{D} = \frac{\lambda}{d}$$

if d-distance between slit $= a$ - width of single slit

then, $\qquad \dfrac{x}{D} = \dfrac{\lambda}{a}$

Here $\qquad \dfrac{x}{D} = \sin\theta$

$$\therefore \qquad \sin\theta = \frac{\lambda}{a} \qquad \ldots(2)$$

From (1) and (2), it is clear that for same angle λ/a we get a minima in diffraction pattern and maxima in interference pattern. **(2 Marks)**

12. In the given combination of gates,

R – OR GATE **(1 + 1 = 2 Marks)**

S – AND GATE

Truth table–

A	B	Y' = A+B	Y = Y'.A
0	0	0	0
0	1	1	0
1	0	1	1
1	1	1	1

OR

In the given combination of gates,

P – NAND GATE **(1 + 1 = 2 Marks)**

Q – OR GATE

Truth table–

A	B		X
0	0	1	1
0	1	1	1
1	0	1	1
1	1	0	1

13. Kirchhoff's 1st rule or Junction rule The algebraic sum of electric currents at any junction of electric circuit is equal to zero *i.e.*,

$$\Sigma I = O \qquad \textbf{(1 + 1 = 2 Marks)}$$

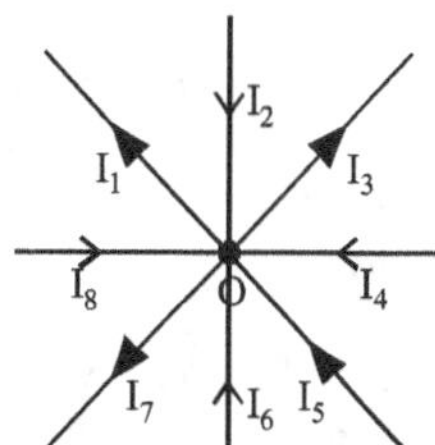

I_1, I_2, I_3, I_4, I_5 I_6, I_7 and I_8 are the currents flowing through the respective wires.

Convention: The current flowing towards the junction is taken as positive.

The current flowing away from the junction is taken as negative.

$$I_2 + I_4 + I_5 + I_6 + I_8 + (-I_1) + (-I_3) + (-I_7) = 0$$

This law is based on the law of conservation of charge.

Kirchhoff's IInd rule or voltage law In any closed mesh of electric circuit, the algebraic sum of emfs of cells and the product of currents and resistances is always equal to zero.

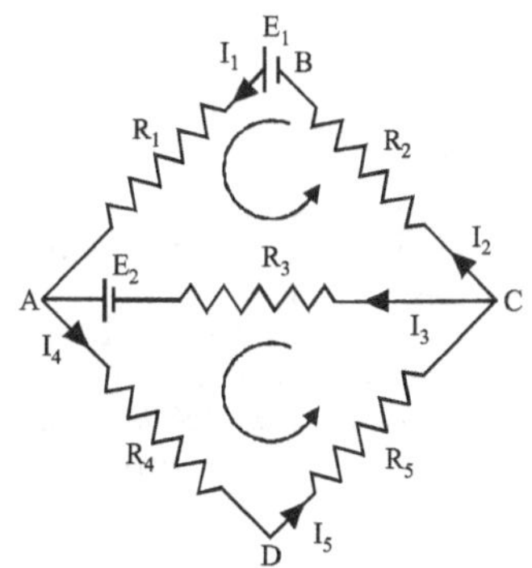

i.e., $\Sigma E + \Sigma IR = 0$

For the closed loop BACB:

$E_1 - E_2 = I_1 R_1 + I_2 R_2 - I_3 R_3$

For the closed loop CADC:

$E_2 = I_3 R_3 + I_4 R_4 + I_5 R_5$

This law is based on the law of conservation of energy.

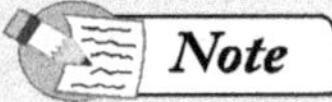 **Note**

In a 100p if current enters positive terminal of battery, then voltage of that battery is taken as negative and if it leaves the positive terminal, then voltage is taken as positive.

14. (i) When the dielectric slab is introduced between the plates of the capacitor, its capacitance will increase. Hence, the potential drop across the capacitor will decrease (since both are connected in series) ($V = Q/c$), as a result, the potential drop across the bulb will increase. So, its brightness will increase.

   (ii) As the resistance (R) is increased, the potential drop across the resistor will increase (since both are connected in series) as a result, the potential drop across the bulb will decrease. So, its brightness will decrease. **(1 + 1 = 2 Marks)**

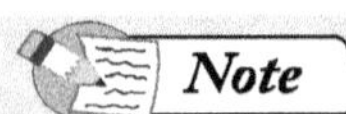 **Note**

When a dielectric slab of dielectric constant k is introduced between capcitor plates, then the capacitance becomes $C = kC_o$. Thus, capacitance increases.

15. **Principle of cyclotron :** A positive ion can acquire sufficiently large energy with a comparatively smaller alternating potential difference by making them to cross the same electric field again and again by making use of a strong magnetic field. **(1 + 1 = 2 Marks)**

In case of the cyclotron, the particle moves in a circular path, the centripetal force required is provided by magnetic force,

$$\therefore \quad qvB = \frac{mv^2}{r}$$

$$r = \frac{mv}{qB} \Rightarrow v = \frac{qBr}{m}$$

$$\therefore \quad KE = \frac{1}{2}mv^2 = \frac{1}{2}\left(\frac{qBr}{m}\right)^2$$

$$= \frac{q^2 B^2 r^2}{2m}$$

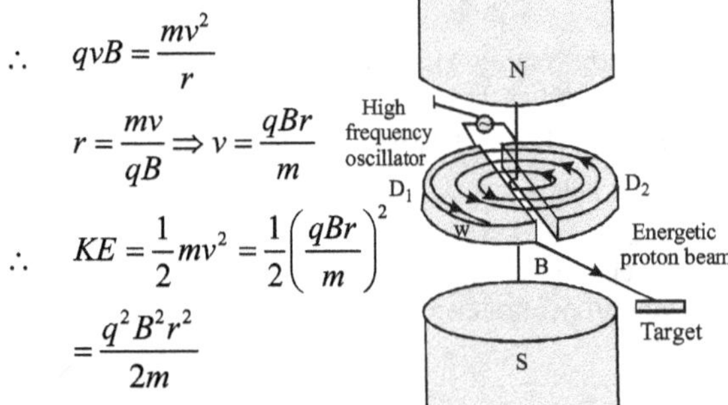

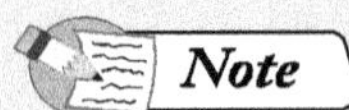 **Note**

A cyclotron involves the use of an electric field to accelerate charge particles across the gap between the two D-shaped magnetic field regions. The magnetic field is perpendicular to the paths of the charged particles that makes them follow in circular paths within the two Ds. An alternating voltage accelerates the charged particles each time they cross the Ds. The radius of each particle's path increases with its speed. So, the accelerated particles spiral toward the outer wall of the cyclotron.

The accelerating electric field reverses just at the time the charge particle finishes its half circle so that it gets accelerated across the gap between the Ds.

The particle gets accelerated again and again, and its velocity increases. Therefore, it attains high kinetic energy, which is given by

$$KE = q^2 B^2 r^2 / 2m$$

16. Torque on a dipole which is placed in an uniform electric field (E) is given by,

$$\tau = PE \sin\theta = (ql) E \sin\theta \qquad ...(1) \qquad \textbf{(½ Mark)}$$

Here, l is the length of the dipole, Q is the charge and E is the electric field.

Potential energy,

$$U = -PE \cos\theta = -(ql) E \cos\theta \qquad ...(2)$$

Dividing (2) by (1), $\dfrac{\tau}{U} = \dfrac{ql E \sin\theta}{-ql E \cos\theta} = -\tan\theta$

$$\Rightarrow \quad U = \frac{-\tau}{\tan\theta} \quad \Rightarrow \quad U = \frac{-\tau}{\tan 60°}$$

$$\Rightarrow \quad U = \frac{-4\sqrt{3}}{\sqrt{3}} \quad \Rightarrow \quad U = -4J \qquad \textbf{(1½ Marks)}$$

17. (a) de-Broglie wavelength of a charged particle is given by, $\lambda = \dfrac{h}{\sqrt{2mqV}}$ **(1 + 1 = 2 Marks)**

If m_p and e are mass and charge of a proton respectively,

and, m_D and e are mass and charge of a deutron respectively, then

$$\frac{\lambda_p}{\lambda_o} = \sqrt{\frac{m_D q_D}{m_p q_p}} = \sqrt{\frac{(2m_p)(e)}{(m_p)(e)}} = \sqrt{2} \quad (\because V \text{ is same})$$

$$\lambda_p = \sqrt{2}\lambda_D$$

Thus, de-broglie wavelength associated with proton is $\sqrt{2}$ times of the de-broglie wavelength of deutron and hence it is more.

(b) Momentum, is given by, $P = \dfrac{h}{\lambda}$ or, $p \propto \dfrac{1}{\lambda}$

where, h = plank's constant

Since the wavelength of a proton is more than that of deutron thus, the momentum of a proton is lesser than that of deutron. Hence, the momentum of proton is less.

 **Note**

When an electron is accelerated from rest through a potential V, then kinetic energy of electron is equal to work done on electron by electric field

$$\Rightarrow \frac{1}{2}mv^2 = eV$$

Since P = mv

$$\frac{1}{2}m\left(\frac{P^2}{m^2}\right) = eV$$

$$P = \sqrt{2meV}$$

de-Broglie wavelength $\lambda = \dfrac{h}{P}$

$$\therefore \ \lambda = \dfrac{h}{\sqrt{2meV}}$$

18. (i) Energy of a photon is given by, v **(1 Mark)**

   $E = h\nu$

   Number of photons emitted per second,

   $n = \dfrac{P}{E}$ where, P = power emitted

   On putting the values, we get,

   $$n = \dfrac{2 \times 10^{-3}}{6 \times 10^{14} \times 6.63 \times 10^{-34}}$$
   $$= 5.03 \times 10^{15}$$

   (ii) The photoelectric current is known to be directly proportional to the intensity of incident light with fixed frequency. So, the plot will be a straight line shown as, **(1 Mark)**

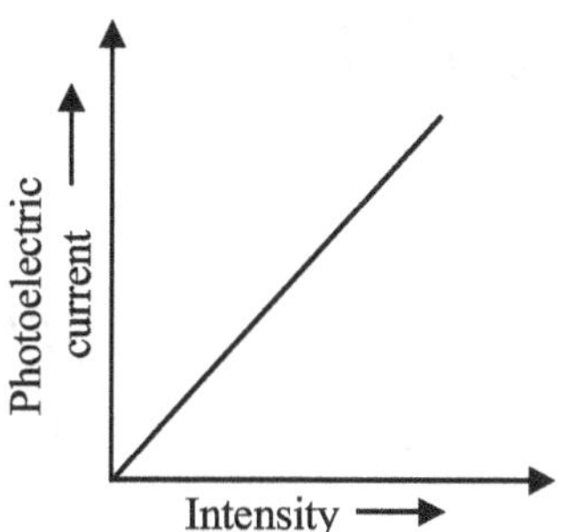

19. Energy of the electron in the nth state of an atom is given as,

$$E_n = \dfrac{-13.6Z^2}{n^2}\,eV$$

Here, z is the atomic number of the atom.
For hydrogen atom, $z = 1$
Energy required to excite an atom from the initial state

(n_i) to the final state (n_f) $= \dfrac{-13.6}{n_f^2} + \dfrac{13.6}{n_i^2}\,eV$

This energy must be equal to or less than the energy of the incident electron beam.

$$\therefore \ \dfrac{-13.6}{n_f^2} + \dfrac{13.6}{n_i^2} = 12.5$$

Energy of the electron in the ground state

$$\dfrac{-13.6}{1^2}eV = -13.6\ eV$$

$$\therefore \ \dfrac{-13.6}{n_f^2} + 13.6 = 12.5$$

$$\Rightarrow \ -13.6 + 12.5 = \dfrac{-13.6}{n_f^2}$$

$$\therefore \qquad n_f = 3.5$$

State cannot be a fraction number.

$\therefore \ n_f = 3$ **(2 Marks)**

Hence, hydrogen atom would be excited up to 3rd energy level.

Rydberg formula for the spectrum of the hydrogen atom is given below:

$$\dfrac{1}{\lambda} = R\left[\dfrac{1}{n_1^2} - \dfrac{1}{n_2^2}\right] \qquad (\frac{1}{2} + \frac{1}{2} = \textbf{1 Marks})$$

Here, λ is the wavelength and R is the Rydberg constant.

$$R = 1.097 \times 10^7 \ m^{-1}$$

For the first member of the Lyman series: $n_1 = 1$ and $n_2 = 2$

$$\dfrac{1}{\lambda} = 1.097 \times 10^7 \left[\dfrac{1}{1^2} - \dfrac{1}{2^2}\right]$$
$$\lambda = 1215 \ \text{Å}$$

For the first member of Balmer series: $n_1 = 2$ and $n_2 = 3$

$$\dfrac{1}{\lambda} = 1.097 \times 10^7 \left[\dfrac{1}{2^2} - \dfrac{1}{3^2}\right]$$
$$\Rightarrow \qquad \lambda = 6563 \ \text{Å}$$

20. (1) The setting up of transmission tower by a mobile company in a residential colony prove to be injurious to health because it makes use of electromagnetic waves such as microwaves, exposure to which can cause severe health hazards like tumour and cancer. Also, the transmitting antenna operates on a very high power, so the risk of someone getting severely burnt in a residential area increases. **(1½ Marks)**

   (2) Sunita has displayed awareness towards the health and environment of her society. **(½ Mark)**

   (3) Range of the transmitting antenna is given as,

   $$d = \sqrt{2hR}$$

   Here, h is the height of the transmitting antenna and R is the radius of the Earth.

   $$R = 6400 \ km = 64 \times 10^5 \ m$$
   $$d = \sqrt{2 \times 20 \times 64 \times 10^5} = 16{,}000 \ m$$

21. Total resistance of the circuit,

   $$R = (R_{PQ} + 5) \ \Omega = 15 \ \Omega \qquad \textbf{(3 Marks)}$$

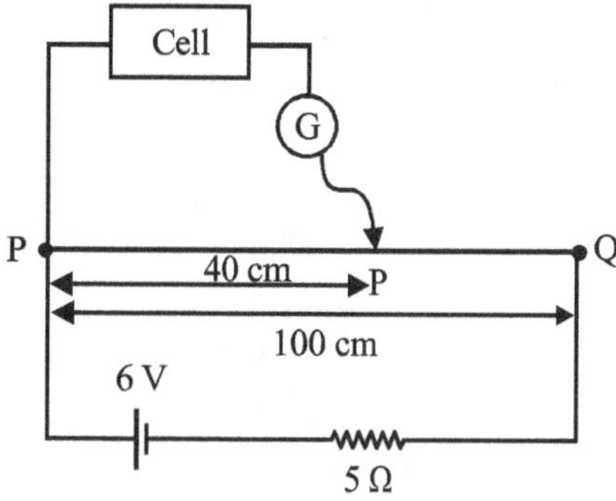

Current in the circuit, $\quad i = \dfrac{V}{R} = \dfrac{6}{15}\,A$

$\therefore$ Voltage across PQ, $V_{PQ} = i.R_{PQ} = 4$ V

emf of the cell, $e = \dfrac{l}{L} V_0$

Here: balance point is at,

$$l = 40 \text{ cm}$$

Total length of wine $PQ = L = 1 \text{ m} = 100 \text{ cm}$

$\therefore$ $e = \dfrac{40}{100}(4) = 1.6V$

22. (a) Ray diagram of compound microscope   **(1 Mark)**

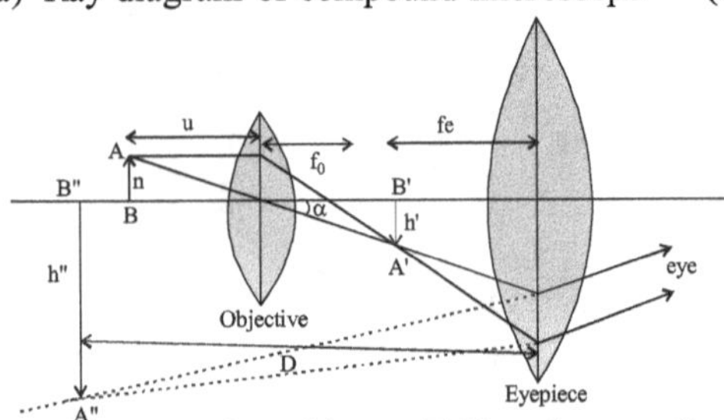

where, PQ = object, $P'Q'$ = image formed by objective and $P''Q''$ = image formed by eyepiece

$\quad f_o$ = focal length of objective,

$\quad u_o$ = object distance from objective

$\quad v_o$ = image distance from objective

$\quad d$ = distance of least distinct vision

$\quad D$ = length of the microscope

(b) For the least distance of clear vision, the total magnification is given by: **(1 + 1 = 2 Marks)**

$$m = \dfrac{-D}{f_0}\left(1 + \dfrac{d}{f_e}\right) = m_o m_e \qquad ...(i)$$

where, D is the separation between the eyepiece and the objective

f_o is the focal length of the objective

f_e is the focal length of the eyepiece

d is the least distance for clear vision

Also, the given magnification for the eyepiece:

$$m_e = 5 = 5 = 1 + \dfrac{d}{f_e}$$

$$\Rightarrow \qquad 5 = 1 = 1 + \dfrac{20}{f_e}$$

$$\Rightarrow \qquad f_e = 5 \text{ cm}$$

Substituting the value of m and m_e in equation (1), we get; $m_o = \dfrac{20}{5} = 5$

Now, we have;

$$m = \dfrac{D}{|f_0|} \Rightarrow f_0 = \dfrac{14}{4} = 3.5 \text{ cm}$$

23. (a)

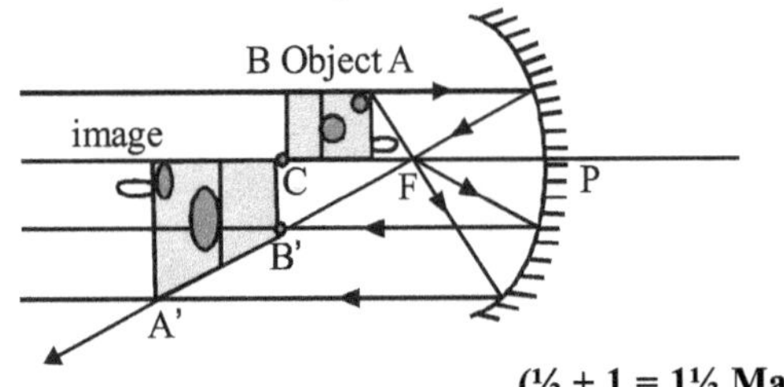

(½ + 1 = 1½ Marks)

The part of the mobile phone that is at C will form an image of the same size only at C.

B'C = BC. But, the part of the mobile phone that lies between C and F will form enlarged image beyond C as shown in the figure. It can be observed that the magnification of each part of the mobile phone cannot be uniform on account of different locations. That is why the image formed is not uniform.

(b) The laws of reflection are true for all points of the mirror. So, the height of the whole image will be produced. However, as the area of the reflecting surface has been reduced, the image intensity will be reduced. In other words, the image produced will be less bright.   **(½ + 1 = 1½ Marks)**

24. (a) Energy stored in capacitor.

Consider a parallel plate capacitor, of capacitance C which is given as :

$$C = \dfrac{\varepsilon_0 A}{d} \qquad \textbf{(2 Marks)}$$

where A = area of each plate

$\qquad$ d = distance between the plates.

If σ is the surface charge density on plates, the electaic field between plates

$$E = \dfrac{\sigma}{\varepsilon_0}$$

or $\sigma = \varepsilon_0 E$

charge on plate $Q = \sigma A = \varepsilon_0 EA$

Energy stared in capacitor $E_c = \dfrac{Q_2}{2C}$

$$E_c = \dfrac{(\varepsilon_0 EA)^2}{2 \times \dfrac{\varepsilon_0 A}{d}} = \dfrac{1}{2}\varepsilon_0 AdE^2$$

Energy stored per unit volume $= \dfrac{E_c}{\text{Volume}}$

$$u = \dfrac{E_c}{Ad}$$

$$u = \dfrac{\dfrac{1}{2}\varepsilon_0 AdE^2}{Ad}$$

$$u = \dfrac{1}{2}\varepsilon_0 E^2.$$

Suppose the plates of the capacitor are almost touching each other and a charge Q is given to the capacitor. One of the plates, say a, is kept fixed and other say b, is slowly pulled away from plate a to increase the separation from zero to d. The attractive force on the plate b at any instant due to first plate is given by, $F = \dfrac{Q^2}{2A\varepsilon_0}$

The person pulling the plate b must apply an equal and opposite force (F) in the opposite direction if the plate is moved slowly.

Work done by the person during the displacement of the second plate;

$$W = F.d = \frac{Q^2 d}{2A\varepsilon_0} = \frac{Q^2}{2C}$$

Here, $C = \dfrac{A\varepsilon_0}{d}$ which is the capacitance of the capacitor in the final position.

The work done by the person must be equal to the increase in the energy of the system.

Thus, the capacitor has a stored energy,

$$U = \frac{Q^2}{2C}$$

Now, if we pull the plates of the capacitor apart, we have to do work against the electrostatic attraction between the plates. When we increase the separation between the plates from d_1 to d_2, an amount $\dfrac{Q^2}{2A\varepsilon_0}(d_2 - d_1)$ of work is performed by us and this much energy goes into the capacitor. On the other hand, new electric field is created in a volume $A(d_2 - d_1)$.

The energy stored per unit volume is thus given by,

$$u = \frac{Q^2(d_2 - d_1)}{2A\varepsilon_0}$$

$$A(d_2 - d_1) = \frac{Q^2}{2A^2\varepsilon_0}$$

$$= \frac{1}{2}\varepsilon_0\left(\frac{Q}{A\varepsilon_0}\right)^2 = \frac{1}{2}\varepsilon_0 E^2$$

Here, E is the intensity of the electric field.

(b) Work done is given as $W = F.d$

Here, F is the force exerted on the charge (q) due to electric field (E) and is given by, $F = qE$ **(1 Mark)**

Net displacement, $d = 0$

$\therefore W = 0$

OR

(a) A parallel plate capacitor consists of two large plane parallel conducting plates separated by a small distance. **(1½ Marks)**

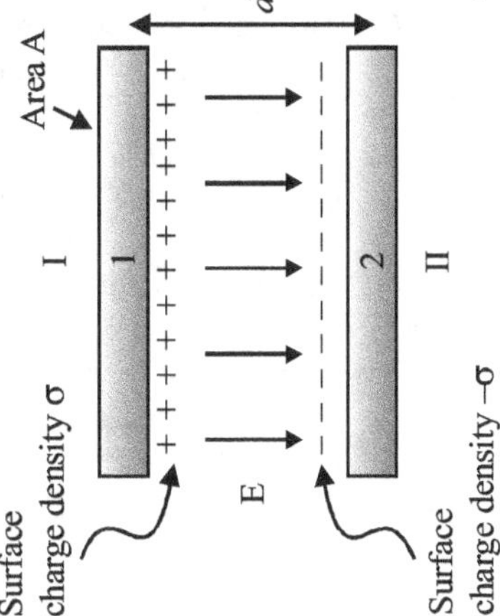

Let A be the area of each plate and d be the separation between them. The two plates have charges Q and –Q. Plate 1 has surface charge density, $\sigma = Q/A$, And plate 2 has a surface charge density $-\sigma$.

Electric field in, Outer region I,

$$E = \frac{\sigma}{2\varepsilon_0} - \frac{\sigma}{2\varepsilon_0} = 0$$

outer region II,

$$E = \frac{\sigma}{2\varepsilon_0} - \frac{\sigma}{2\varepsilon_0} = 0$$

In the inner region between plates 1 and 2, the electric fields due to the two charged plates add up.

$$E = \frac{\sigma}{2\varepsilon_0} + \frac{\sigma}{2\varepsilon_0} = \frac{\sigma}{\varepsilon_0} = \frac{Q}{\varepsilon_0} = \frac{Q}{\varepsilon_0 A}$$

The direction of electric field is from positive to the negative plate. For uniform electric field, potential difference is simply the electric field times the distance between the plates.

$$V = E\, d = \frac{1}{\varepsilon_0}\frac{Qd}{A}$$

Capacitance (C) of the parallel plate capacitor,

$$C = \frac{Q}{V} = \frac{\varepsilon_0 A}{d}$$

(b) The surface charge density for a spherical conductor is given by,

$$\sigma = \frac{Q}{4\pi r^2} \qquad \textbf{(1½ Marks)}$$

For spherical conductor R_1, the surface charge density is given by,

$$\sigma_1 = \frac{q_1}{4\pi R_1^2}$$

Similarly, for spherical conductor R_2, the surface charge density is given by,

$$\sigma_2 = \frac{q_2}{4\pi R_2^2}$$

$$\therefore \quad \frac{\sigma_1}{\sigma_2} = \left(\frac{q_1}{q_2}\right)\left(\frac{R_2^2}{R_1^2}\right)$$

Since the two conductors are connected, we have,

$$q_1 = q_2$$

$$\therefore \quad \frac{\sigma_1}{\sigma_2} = \frac{R_2^2}{R_1^2} = \left(\frac{R_2}{R_1}\right)^2$$

25. (a) The line integral of magnetic field $\vec{B}$ around any closed path in vacuum is μ_0 times the total current through the closed path. Mathematically, $\oint \vec{B}.d\vec{\ell} = \mu_0 I$.

(1 Mark)

(b) (i) The magnetic field due to a current carrying solenoid is given by, $B_0 = \mu_0 n_i$

where, **(1 + 1 = 2 Marks)**

n = number of turns per unit length

i = current through the solenoid

Now, the magnetic field due to solenoid S_1 will be in the upward direction and the magnetic field due to S_2 will be in the downward direction (by right-hand screw rule).

$$B_{net} = B_{s_1} - B_{s_2}$$
$$\Rightarrow \quad B_{net} = \mu_0 n_1 I - \mu_0 n_2 I$$
$$= \mu_0 I (n_1 - n_2)$$

In the upward direction

(ii) The magnetic field is zero outside a solenoid.

Note

Magnetic field at a point P at a distance r from the conductor = B

$$= \frac{\mu_0}{4\pi} \cdot \frac{2I}{r}$$

$\vec{B}$ is directed along the tangent to the circle at every point and is in same direction as $d\ell$ at the point.

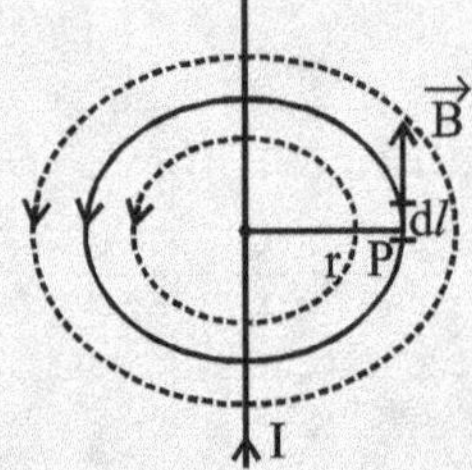

$$\therefore \quad \oint \vec{B} \cdot d\vec{\ell} = \oint B d\ell \cos 0° = \oint B d\ell = \oint \frac{\mu_0 I}{2\pi r} \cdot d\ell$$

$$\frac{\mu_0 I}{2\pi r} \cdot \oint d\ell = \frac{\mu_0 I}{2\pi r} \cdot 2\pi r = \mu_0 I$$

26. (a) Microwaves are suitable for radar systems used in aircraft navigation. The range of frequency for these waves is 10^9 Hz to 10^{12} Hz. **(1 + 1 + 1 = 3 Marks)**

(b) If the earth did not have atmosphere, there would be no greenhouse effect on the surface of the Earth. So, the temperature of the Earth would decrease rapidly, would be difficult for survival of living beings.

(c) The linear momentum carried by a portion of wave having energy U is given by, $P = \dfrac{U}{C}$

Thus, if the wave incident on a material surface is completely absorbed, it delivers energy U and momentum $P = \dfrac{U}{C}$ to the surface. If the wave is totally reflected, the momentum delivered $P = \dfrac{2U}{C}$ is because the momentum of the wave changes from p to $-p$. Therefore, it follows that an em waves incident on a surface exert a force and hence a pressure on the surface.

27. (a) **Radioactive decay law :** The rate of disintegration of radioactive sample at any instant is directly proportional to the number of undisintegrated nuclei present in the sample at that instant.

$$\because \quad \frac{dN}{dt} = -\lambda N \qquad \qquad \textbf{(1½ Marks)}$$

where λ = decay constant

N = number of undisintegrated nuclei in the sample of radioactive substance.

or $\quad \dfrac{dN}{N} = -\lambda dt$

Integrating both sides, we get,

$$\int \frac{dN}{N} = -\lambda \int dt$$
$$\ln N = -\lambda t + C$$

At t = 0, N = N_0 = number of undisintegrated nuclei present in the sample, initially

$$\Rightarrow \quad \ln N_0 = -\lambda \times 0 + C$$
$$\Rightarrow \quad C = \ln N_0$$
$$\Rightarrow \quad \ln N = -\lambda t + \ln N_0$$
$$\Rightarrow \quad \ln N - \ln N_0 = -\lambda t$$
$$\ln \frac{N}{N_0} = -\lambda t$$
$$\Rightarrow \quad \log_e \frac{N}{N_0} = -\lambda t$$
$$\Rightarrow \quad \frac{N}{N_0} = e^{\lambda t}$$
$$\text{or} \quad N = N_0 e^{-\lambda t}$$

(b) (i) The β^+ decay for $^{22}_{11}Na$ is given below:

$$^{22}_{11}Na \rightarrow {}^{22}_{10}Na + \beta^+ + v$$

If the unstable nucleus has excess protons than required for stability, a proton converts itself into a neutron. In the process, a positron e^+ (or a β^+) and a neutrino v are created and emitted from the nucleus. **(1 Mark)**

$$p \rightarrow n + \beta^+ + v$$

This process is called beta plus decay.

(ii) The nucleus so formed is an isobar of $^{22}_{11}Na$ because the mass number is same, but the atomic numbers are different. **(½ Mark)**

28. (a) (i) Two independent sources of light cannot be coherent and hence cannot produce interference pattern.

Two sources are monochromatic if they have the same frequency and wavelength. Since they are independent, i.e. they have different phases with irregular difference, they are not coherent sources. **(½ Mark)**

(ii) There is a narrow slit illuminated by a monochromatic source of light. Two fine slits A and B (about 0.5 mm apart) are placed equidistant from the source (S). A screen is placed at a suitable distance from the slits. **(2 Marks)**

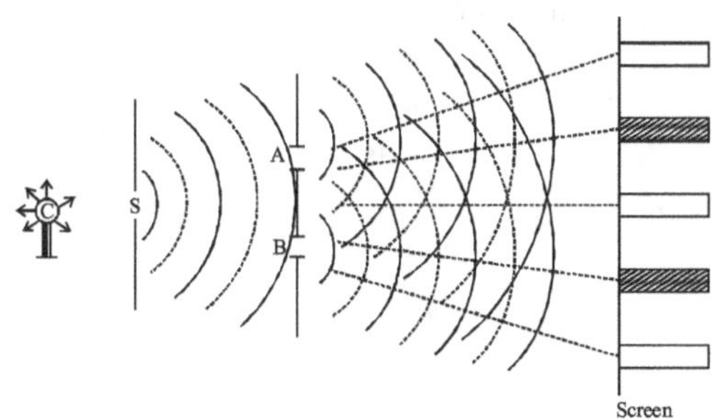

Supoose the phase difference between two waves arising from slits A and B is ϕ. Then,

$$y_1 = a\cos\omega t \text{ and}$$
$$y_2 = a\cos(\omega t + \phi).$$

Therefore the resultant displacent will be given by

$$y = y_1 + y_2$$
$$= a\cos\omega t + a\cos(\omega t + \phi)$$

using terigonometric identity

$$\cos A + \cos B = 2\cos\left(\frac{A+B}{2}\right)\cos\left(\frac{A-B}{2}\right)$$

$$y = 2a\cos\frac{\phi}{2}\cdot\cos(\omega t + \frac{\phi}{2})$$

The amplitude of the resultant displacent is given by

$$R = 2a\cos\left(\frac{\phi}{2}\right)$$

As, intensity $\propto$ (amplitude)^2
$I_0 \propto a^2$ and $I \propto R^2$

$\therefore$ Resultant intensity, $I = 4I_0\cos^2\left(\frac{\phi}{2}\right)$

(b) Phase difference $= \dfrac{2\pi}{\lambda} \times$ Path difference

$$\phi_1 = \frac{2\pi}{\lambda}\times\lambda = 2\pi$$

Where, ϕ_1 is the phase difference when the path difference is λ and the corresponding Intensity is $I_1 = K$

$$\phi_2 = \frac{2\pi}{\lambda}\times\frac{\lambda}{3} = \frac{2\pi}{3}$$

Where, ϕ_2 is the phase difference when the path difference is $\dfrac{\lambda}{3}$ and corresponding Intensity is I_2.

Using equation (iv), we get,

$$\frac{I_1}{I_2} = \frac{4a^2\cos^2\dfrac{\phi_1}{2}}{4a^2\cos^2\dfrac{\phi_2}{2}}$$

$$= \frac{\cos^2\left(\dfrac{2\pi}{2}\right)}{\cos^2\left(\dfrac{2\pi}{6}\right)} = \frac{\cos^2\pi}{\cos^2\left(\dfrac{\pi}{3}\right)} = 4$$

$$\Rightarrow \frac{K}{I_2} = 4 \qquad \Rightarrow I_2 = \frac{K}{4} \qquad \textbf{(2 Marks)}$$

OR

(a) Suppose an unpolarised light of intensity I_0 passes through a polaroid sheet P_1. Intensity of light beam that emerges from P_1 is reduced by half (i.e. becomes $\dfrac{I_0}{2}$). Thus, the light is plane polarised. The intensity of transmitted beam remains constant even if P_1 is being rotated.

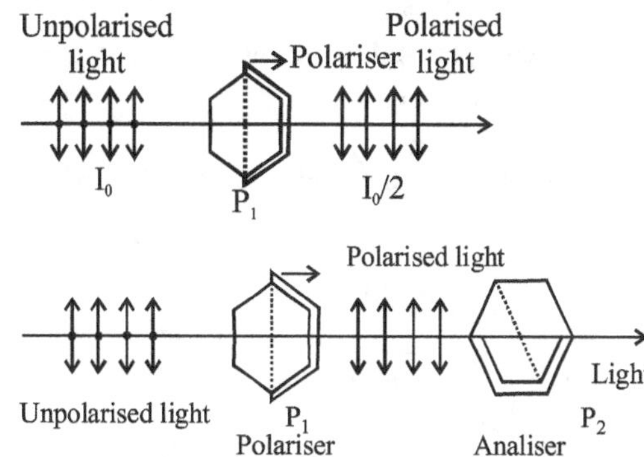

Now, an other polaroid P_2 is placed after P_1. In one position, when two polaroids are crossed, the intensity transmitted by P_2 is zero. Thus, by putting a second polariod, the intensity can be further reduced from 50% to zero of the incident intensity by adjusting the angle between the pass-axes of two polaroids.

The light coming from the blue portion of the sky is also polarised. The unpolarised light coming from the sun encounter the air molecules of the earth's atmosphere. Under the influence of the electric field of the incident wave, the electrons in molecules are set in vibrations and emit the light waves in which electric field is perpendicular to the emitted light. An observer looking at 90° to the direction of sunlight will see the light polarised perpendicular to the plane of figure.   **(1 + 2 = 3 Marks)**

(b)

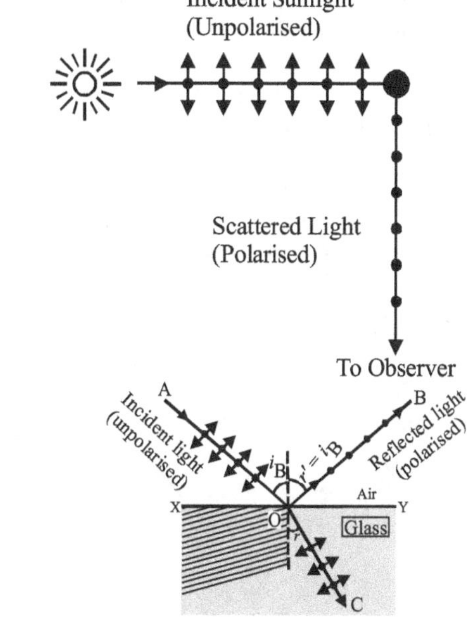

When unpolarised light is incident on the glass-air interface at Brewster angle i_B, then reflected light is totally polarised. This is called Brewster's Law.

When light is incident at Brewster angle, the reflected component OB and the refracted component OC are mutually perpendicular to each other.

From the figure, we have:

$$\angle BOY + \angle YOC = 90°$$
$$(90° - i_B) + (90° - r) = 90°$$

where, r is angle of refraction

$$90° - i_B = r$$

According to the Snell's law: $\mu = \dfrac{\sin i}{\sin r}$

(1 + 1 = 2 Marks)

$$i = i_B \text{ and } r = (90° - i_B)$$

$$\mu = \dfrac{\sin i_B}{\sin(90° - i_B)} = \dfrac{\sin i_B}{\cos i_B}$$

$$\mu = \tan i_B$$

29. (a) **Lenz's law and conservation of energy:** Lenz's law is according to law of conservation of energy because when N-pole of a magnet is moved towards the coil, the upper face of the coil acquires north polarity. So work has to be done against the force of repulsion in bringing the magnet closer to the coil. **(2 Marks)**

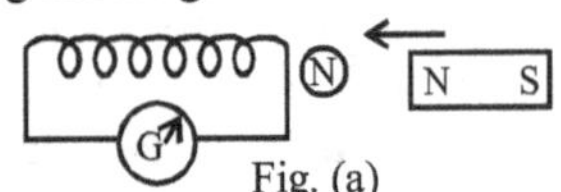

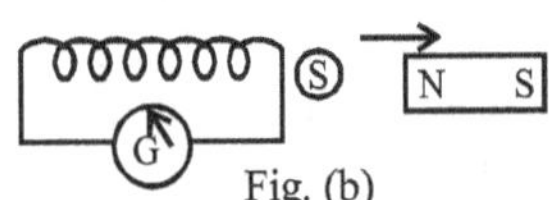

When the N-pole is moved away, south polarity is developed on the upper face of the coil. Therefore, work has to be done against the force of attraction in taking the magnet away from the coil.

∴ Mechanical work done is converted into electrical energy of the coil.

When the magnet does not move work done is zero, so no electrical energy is produced.

(b) (i) Since $\phi = LI$ **(1 + 1 + 1 = 3 Marks)**

where,

    I = Strength of current through the coil at any time

    ϕ = Amount of magnetic flux linked with all turns of the coil at that time

and,

    L = Constant of proportionality called coefficient of self induction

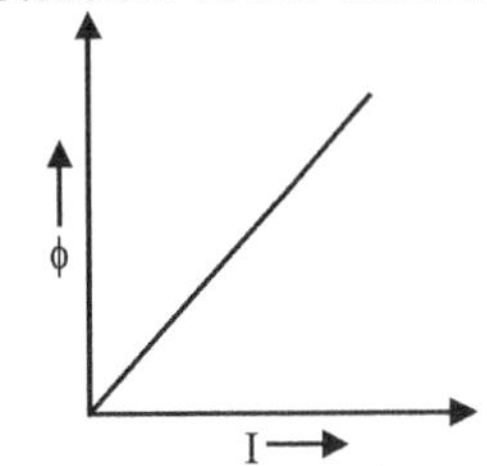

(ii) Induced emf,

$$e = \dfrac{-d\phi}{dt} = \dfrac{-d}{dt}(LI)$$

i.e., $e = -L\dfrac{dI}{dt}$

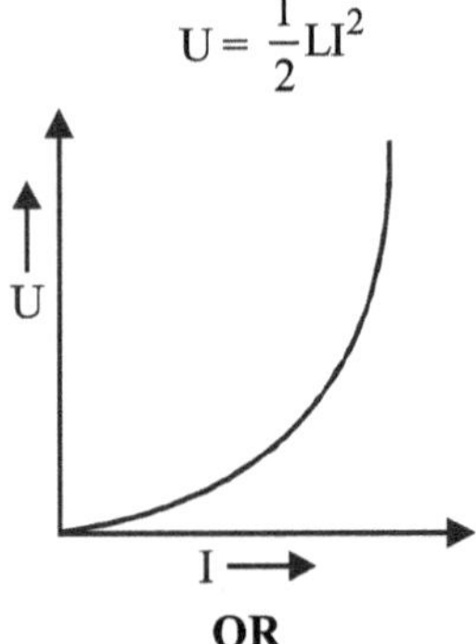

[The graph is drawn considering only magnitude of e]

(iii) Since magnetic potential energy is given by,

$$U = \dfrac{1}{2}LI^2$$

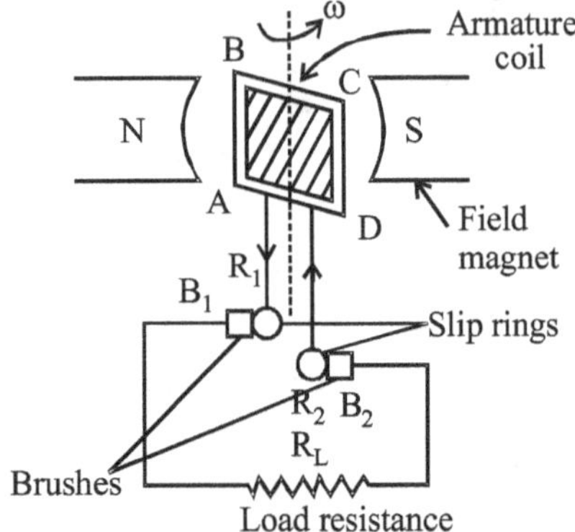

OR

(a) **Principle:** A dynamo or an ac generator is a device which converts mechanical energy into electrical energy. It is based on the principle of electromagnetic induction. **(1 Mark)**

Construction: It consists of four main parts-

(i) **Field magnet:** It produces the magnetic field. For a low power dynamo, the magnetic field in generated by a permanent magnet but for a large power dynamo, the magnetic field is produced by an electromagnet.

(ii) **Armature:** It consists of a large number of turns of insulated copper wire on a soft iron core. It can revolve round the axis between the two poles of the field magnet. The soft iron core provides support to the coils and increases the magnetic field through the coil.

(iii) **Slip rings:** The slip rings R_1 and R_2 are two metal rings to which the ends of the armature coil are connected. These rings are fixed to the shaft which rotates the armature coil so that the rings also rotate along with the armature.

(iv) **Brushes (B_1 and B_2):** These are flexible metal plates or carbon rods which are fixed and constantly touch the revolving rings. The output current in external load resistance R_1 is taken through these brushes.

Working: When the armature coil is rotated in the strong magnetic field, the magnetic flux linked the coil changes and the current is induced in the coil. The direction of current is given by Flemming's left hand rule. It remains same during the first half turn of the armature. During the second half revolution, the direction of current is reversed.

If N is the number in the coil, f is the frequency of rotation, A is the area of the coil and B is the magnetic field intensity then induced emf.

$$e = -\frac{d\phi}{dt} = \frac{d}{dt}(NBA \cos 2\pi ft)$$
$$= 2\pi NBAf \sin 2\pi ft$$

Therefore, the emf produced is alternating in nature and the current is also alternating. **(1 Mark)**
Current produced in a.c. generator can not be measured by moving coil galvanometer, because average value of a.c. over full cycle is zero.

(i) Graph between magnetic flux and time, is shown below:

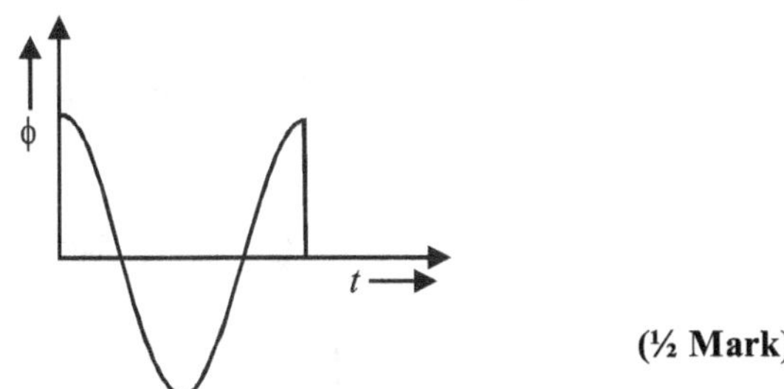

(½ Mark)

(ii) The graph between alternating emf versus time is shown below:

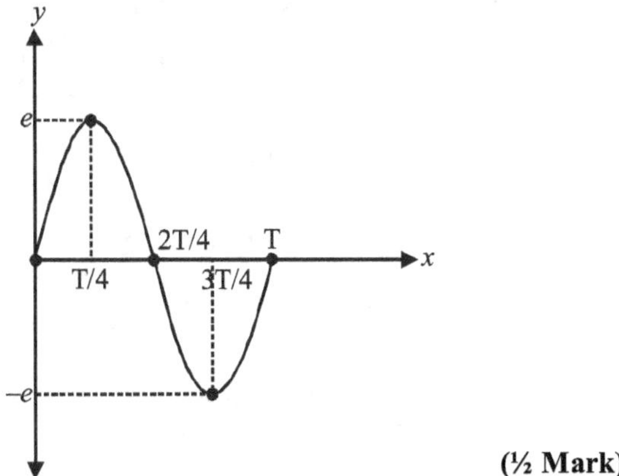

(½ Mark)

(b) A choke coil is an electrical appliance used for controlling current in an a.c. circuit. Therefore, if we use a resistance R for the same purpose, a lot of energy would be wasted in the form of heat etc. **(2 Marks)**

30. (a) When p– and n– type semiconductors are joined in thin wafer form they form a junction. In p– type semiconductor concentration of holes is more and on n – side electrons are in majority, hence due to this gradient both electrons and holes diffuse to the other side leaving behind ionised donor and acceptor atoms which are immobile. As charges diffuse a layer of negative charges (acceptor) is found on p–side and positive charges (donor) on n–side near the junction. This is depletion layer and creates an electric field due to which electrons on p– side move to n–side. This is called drift current. Thus space charge region of either side extends, forming p–n junction. **(2 Marks)**

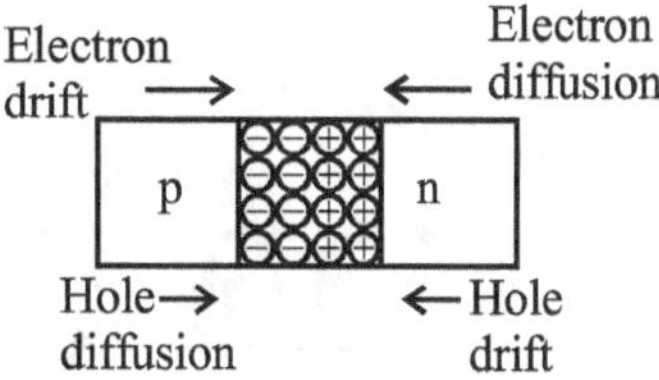

Hence, a space-charge region is formed on either side of the junction, which has immobile ions and is devoid of any charge carrier, called as depletion layer or depletion region.

(b) **V – I characteristics of a diode:** The circuit to study the variation of current as a function of applied voltage is shown. Battery is connected to potentiometer (or rheostat) to change applied voltage. In forward bias we use milliammeter and reverse bias we use microammeter. **(1 + 1 + 1 = 3 Marks)**

(i)

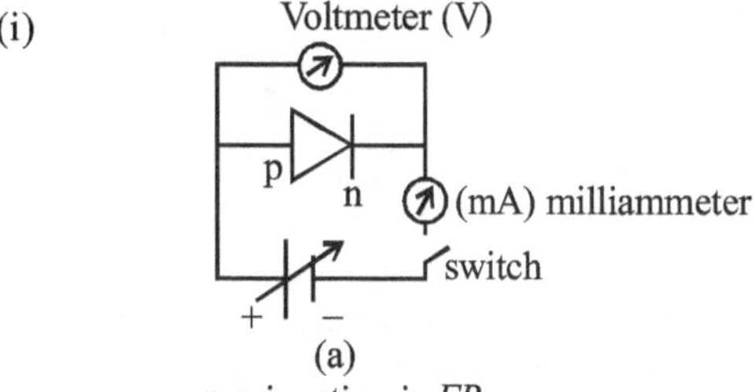

(ii)

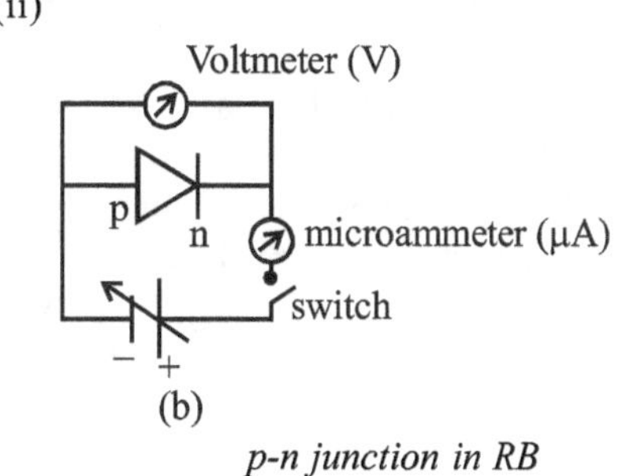

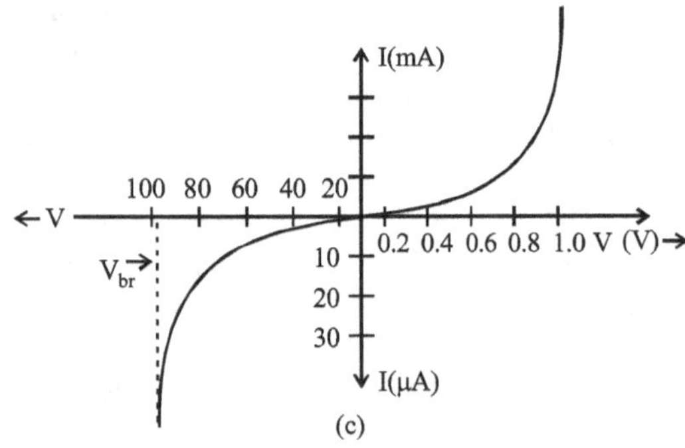

V - I. characteristics graph

p-n junction diode is used as a rectifier. Its working is based on the fact that the resistance of *p-n* junction becomes low when forward biased and becomes high when reverse biased. These characteristics of diode is used in rectification.

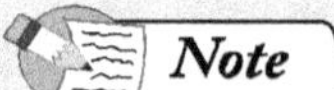

Note

p – n junction under forward bias: *When p –side is connected to positive terminal and n – side to negative terminal of external voltage, it is said to be **forward biased**. The applied voltage V is opposite to built in potential V_0, hence depletion layer width decreases and barrier height is reduced to $(V_0 - V)$. There is minority carrier injection, hence charges begin to flow. Current is in the order of mA.*

p – n junction under reverse bias: *The direction of applied voltage is same as direction of barrier potential, so barrier height increases to $(V_0 + V)$. This suppresses flow of electrons from n → p and holes from p → n. Diffusion current decreases but drift of electrons and holes under the electric field affect remains. This drift current is few μA. The current under reverse bias is independent of applied voltage upto a critical value known as breakdown voltage (V_{br}) when $V = V_{br}$, diode reverse current increases sharply. If the reverse current is not limited below this, the diode gets destroyed due to overheating.*

$$\text{Dynamic resistance} = \frac{\text{Small change in voltage}}{\text{Small change in current}}$$

$$\Rightarrow r_d = \frac{\Delta V}{\Delta I}$$

OR

Difference between three segments of a transistor on the basis of their size and level of dopping.

(a) Emitter (E) - It is the left hand side thick layer of the transistor, which is heavily doped.

Base (B) - It is the central thin layer of the transistor, which is lightly doped.

Collector (C) - It is the right hand side thick layer of the transistor, which is moderately doped.

Structure: (i) Emitter (E), (ii) Base (B), (iii) Collector (C)   **(1½ Marks)**

Emitter size > base

Collector size > emitter

$\therefore$ C > E > B (size wise)

Doping wise E > C > B.

Representation:

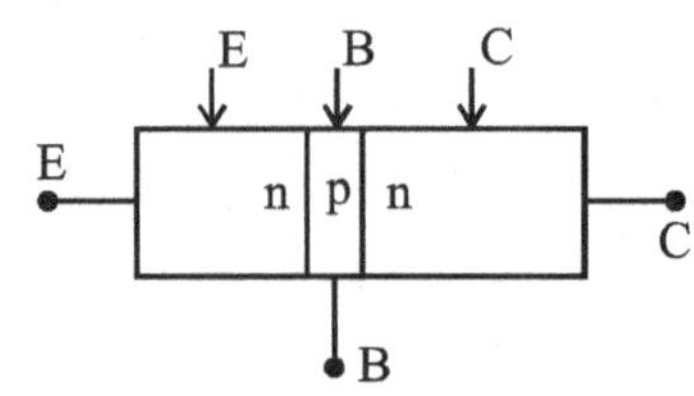

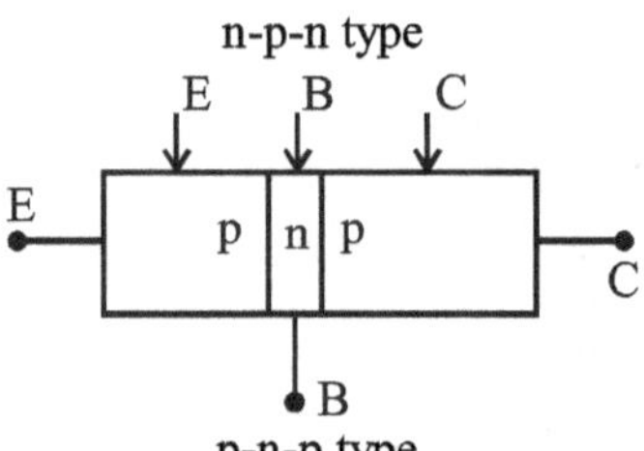

(b) There are two conditions for a transistor to be into an active region.

1. The input circuit should be forward biased by using a low voltage battery.   **(1 Mark)**
2. The output circuit should be reverse biased by using a high voltage battery.

(c) **Transistor as an amplifier (C E configuration):** Transistor works in active region.

Output, $V_0 = V_{CC} - I_C R_C$ ...(1)

If input voltage increases, output voltage decreases. V_i and V_0 are out of phase.

$$A_V = \text{small signal voltage gain} = \frac{\Delta V_0}{\Delta V_i} \quad ...(2)$$

(2 + ½ = 2½ Mark)

Since V_{CC} and R_C are constant,

$\Delta V_0 = 0 - R_C \, \Delta I_C$ (from (1), differentiate)

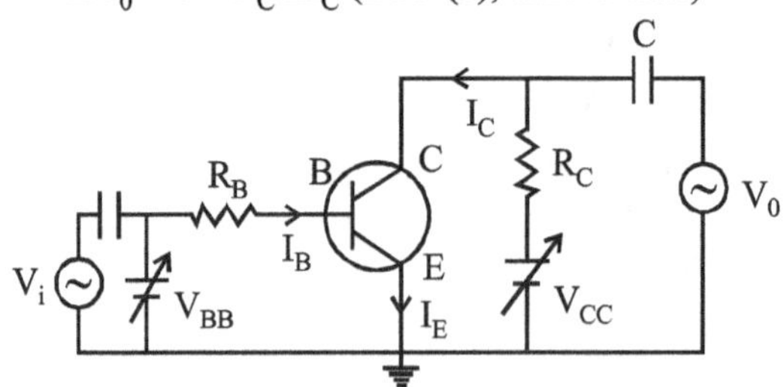

Input $V_i = I_B R_B + V_{BE}$

$\Rightarrow \Delta V_i = R_B \, \Delta I_B + \Delta V_{BE}$ ...(3)

Since $\Delta V_{BE} = $ small, neglect it, using (1), (3) in (2),

$$A_V = -\frac{R_C \Delta I_C}{R_B \Delta I_B} = -\beta_{ac}\left(\frac{R_C}{R_B}\right) \text{ where}$$

$$\beta_{ac} = \frac{\Delta I_C}{\Delta I_B} = \text{a.c. current gain}$$

All India *2013*
CBSE Board Solved Paper

Time Allowed: 3 Hours   *Maximum Marks: 70*

(i) All questions are compulsory.

(ii) There are **29** questions in total. Question Nos. **1** to **8** are very short answer type questions and carry **one** mark each.

(iii) Question Nos. **9** to **16** carry **two** marks each, Question Nos. **17** to **25** carry **three** marks each and Question Nos. **27** to **29** carry **five** marks each.

(iv) There is no overall choice. However, an internal choice has been provided in **one** question of **two** marks, **one** question of **three** marks and all **three** questions of **five** marks each. You have to attempt only one of the choices in such questions.

(v) Question No. 26 is value based question carries **four** marks.

(vi) Use of calculators is not permitted. However, you may use log tables if necessary.

(vii) You may use the following values of physical constants wherever necessary:

$c = 3 \times 10^8$ m/s

$h = 6.63 \times 10^{-34}$ Js

$e = 1.6 \: 10^{-19}$ C

$\mu_0 = 4\pi \times 10^{-7}$ Tm A^{-1}

$\varepsilon_0 = 8.854 \times 10^{-12}$ C^2 N^{-1} m^{-2}

$\dfrac{1}{4\pi\varepsilon_0} = 9 \times 10^9$ N m^2 C^{-2}

Mass of electron $(m_e) = 9.1 \times 10^{-31}$ kg

Mass of neutron $= 1.675 \times 10^{-27}$ kg

Mass of proton $= 1.673 \times 10^{-27}$ kg

Avogadro's number $= 6.023 \times 10^{23}$ per gram mole

Boltzmann constant $= 1.38 \times 10^{-23}$ JK^{-1}

---

1. Two charge of magnitudes $-2Q$ and $+Q$ are located at points $(a, 0)$ and $(4a, 0)$ respectively. What is the electric flux due to these charges through a sphere of radius '3a' with its centre at the origin?

2. How does the mutual inductance of a pair of coils change when :
   (i) distance between the coils is increased and
   (ii) number of turns in the coils is increased?

3. The graph shown in the figure represents a plot of current versus voltage for a given semiconductor. Identify the region, if any, over which the semiconductor has a negative resistance.

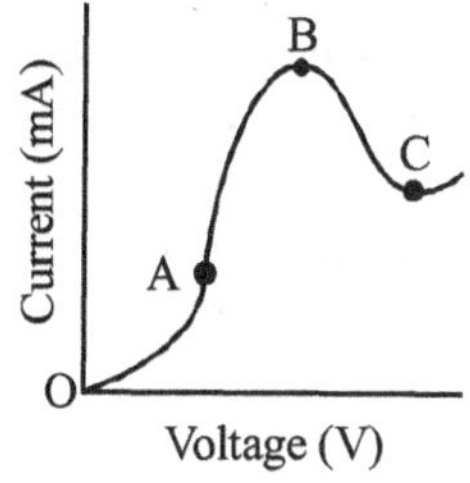

4. Two identical cells, each of emf E, having negligible internal resistance, are connected in parallel with each other across an external resistance R. What is the current through this resistance?

5. The motion of copper plate is damped when it is allowed to oscillate between the two poles of a magnet. What is the cause of this damping?

6. Define the activity of a given radioactive substance. Write its S.I. unit.

7. Welders wear special goggles or face masks with glass windows to protect their eyes from electromagnetic radiations. Name the radiations and write the range of their frequency.

8. Write the expression for the de Broglie wavelength associated with a charged particle having charge 'q' and mass 'm', when it is accelerated by a potential V.

9. Draw typical output characteristics of an n-p-n transistor in CE configuration. Show how these characteristics can be used to determine output resistance.

10. A parallel beam of light of 500 nm falls on a narrow slit and the resulting diffraction pattern is observed on a screen 1 m away. It is obsreved that the first minimum is at a distance of 2.5 nm from the centre of the screen. Calculate the width of the slit.

11. A slab of material of dielectric constant K has the same area as that of the plates of a parallel plate capacitor but has the thickness d/2, where d is the separation between the plates. Find out the expression for its capacitance when the slab is inserted between the plates of the capacitor.

12. A capacitor, made of two parallel plates each of plate area A and separation d, is being charged by an external ac source. Show that the displacement current inside the capacitor is the same as the current charging the capacitor.

13. Explain the term 'drift velocity' of electrons in a conductor. Hence obtain the expression for the current through a conductor in terms of 'drift velocity'.

OR

Describe briefly, with the help of a circuit diagram, how a potentiometer is used to determine the internal resistance of a cell?

14. A convex lens of focal length f_1 is kept on contact with a concave lens of focal length f_2. Find the focal length of the combination.

15. In the block diagram of a simple modulator for obtaining an AM signal, shown in the figure, identify the boxes A and B. Write their functions.

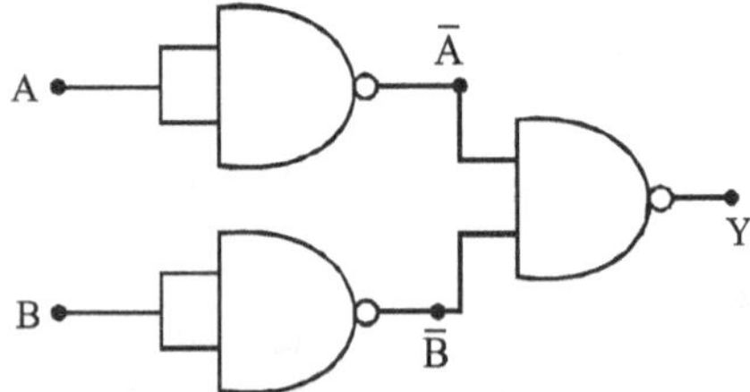

16. In the circuit shown in the figure, identify the equivalent gate of the circuit and make its truth table.

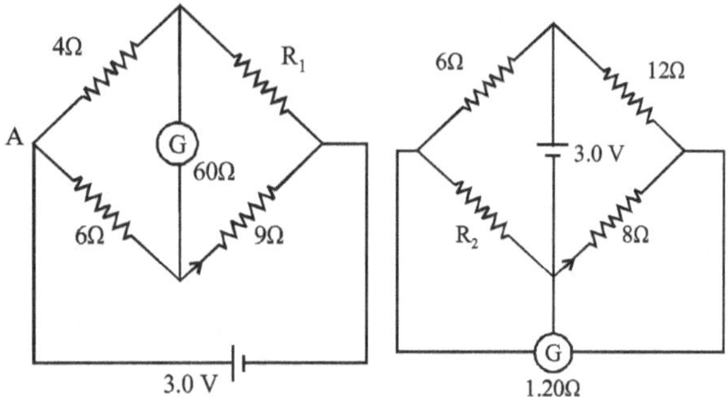

17. (a) For a given ac, $i = i_m \sin \omega t$, show that the average power dissipated in a resistor R over a complete cycle is $\dfrac{1}{2} i_m^2 R$.

   (b) A light bulb is rated at 100 W for a 220 V ac supply. Calculate the resistance of the bulb.

18. A rectangular conductor LMNO is placed in a uniform magentic field at 0.5 T. The field is directed perpendicular to the plane of the conductor. When the arm MN of length of 20 cm is moved towards left with a velocity of 10 ms⁻¹, calculate the emf inducted in the arm. Given the resistance of the arm to be 5Ω (assuming that other arms are of negligible resistance) find the value of the current in the arm.

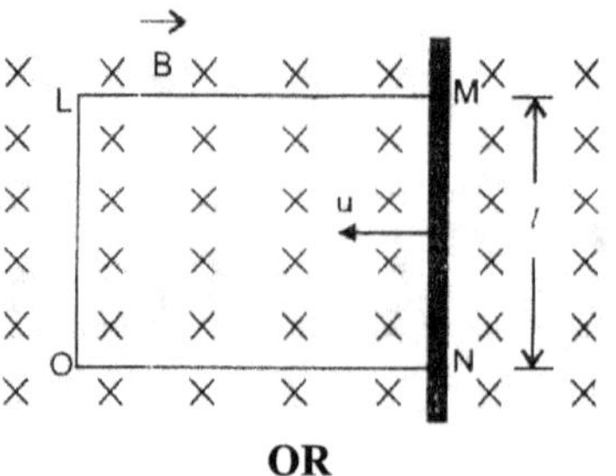

OR

A wheel with 8 metallic spokes each 50 cm long is rotated with a speed of 120 rev/min. in a plane normal to the horizontal component of the Earth's magnetic field. The earth's magnetic field at the place is 0.4 G and the angle of dip is 60°. Calculate the emf induced between the axle and the rim of the wheel. How will the value of emf be affected if the number of spokes were increased?

19. Define the current sensitivity of a galvanometer. Write its S.I. unit

Figure shows two circuits each having a galvanometer and a battery of 3V.

When the galvanometer in each arrangement do not show any deflection, obtain the ratio R_1/R_2.

20. A wire AB is carrying a steady current of 12A and is lying on the table. Another wire CD carrying 5A is held directly above AB at a height of 1 mm. Find the mass per unit length of the wire CD so that it remains suspended at its position when left free. Give the direction of the current flowing in CD with respect to that in AB. [Take the value of g = 10 ms⁻²]

21. Draw V-I characteristics of a *p-n* junction diode. Answer the following questions, giving reasons :

   (i) Why is the current under reverse bias almost independent of the applied potential upto a critical voltage?

   (ii) Why does the reverse current show a sudden increase at the critical voltage?

   Name any semiconductor device which operates under the reverse bias in the breakdown region.

22. Draw a labelled ray diagram of a refracting telescope. Define its magnifying power and write the expression for it.

Write two important limitations of a refracting telescope over a reflecting type telescope.

23. Write Einstein's photoelectric equation and point out any two characteristics properties of photons on which this equation is based.

    Briefly explain the three observed features which can be explained by this equation.

24. Name the type of waves which are used for line of sight (LOS) communication. What is the range of their frequencies?

    A transmitting antenna at the top of a tower has a height of 20 m and the height of the receiving antenna is 45 m. Calculate the maximum distance between them for satisfactory communication in LOS mode.
    (Radius of the Earth = 6.4×10^6 m)

25. (a) What is linearly polarised light? Describe briefly using a diagram how sunlight is polarised.

    (b) Unpolarised light is incident on a polaroid. How would the intensity of transmitted light change when the polaroid is rotated?

26. One day Chetan's mother developed a severe stomach ache all of a sudden. She was rushed to the doctor who suggested for an immediate endoscopy test and gave an estimate of expenditure for the same. Chetan immediately contacted his class teacher and shared the information with her. The class teacher arranged for the money and rushed to the hospital. On realising that Chetan belonged to a below average income group family, even the doctor offered concession for the test fee. The test was conducted successfully.

    Answer the following questions based on the above information:

    (a) Which principle in optics is made use of in endoscopy?

    (b) Briefly explain the values reflected in the action taken by the teacher.

    (c) In what way do you appreciate the response of the doctor on the given situation?

27. (a) Using Biot-Savart's law, derive the expression for the magnetic field in the vector form at a point on the axis of a circular current loop.

    (b) What does a toroid consist of? Find out the expression for the magnetic field inside a toroid for N turns of the coil having the average radius r and carrying a current I. Show that the magnetic field in the open space inside and exterior to the toroid is zero.

OR

(a) Draw a schematic sketch of a cyclotron. Explain clearly the role of crossed electric and magnetic field in accelerating the charge. Hence derive the expression for the kinetic energy acquired by the particles.

(b) An α-particle and a proton are released from the centre of the cyclotron and made to accelerate.

    (i) Can both be accelerated at the same cyclotron frequency? Give reason to justify your answer.

    (ii) When they are accelerated in turn, which of the two will have higher velocity at the exit slit of the dees?

28. (a) Define electric dipole moment. Is it a scalar or a vector? Derive the expression for the electric field of a dipole at a point on the equatorial plane of the dipole.

    (b) Draw the equipotential surfaces due to an electric dipole. Locate the points where the potential due to the dipole is zero.

OR

Using Gauss' law deduce the expression for the electric field due to a uniformly charged spherical conducting shell of radius R at a point (i) outside and (ii) inside the shell. Plot a graph showing variation of electric field as a function of $r > R$ and $r < R$. (r being the distance from the centre of the shell).

29. Using Bohr's postulates, derive the expression for the frequency of radiation emitted when electron in hydrogen atom undergoes transition from higher energy state (quantum number n_i) to the lower state, (n_f).

    When electron in hydrogen atom jumps from energy state $n_i = 4$ to $n_f = 3, 2, 1$. Identify the spectral series to which the emission lines belong.

OR

(a) Draw the plot of binding energy per nucleon (BE/A) as a function of mass number A. Write two important conclusions that can be drawn regarding the nature of nuclear force.

(b) Use this graph to explain the release of energy in both the processes of nuclear fusion and fission.

(c) Write the basic nuclear process of neutron undergoing β-decay. Why is the detection of neutrinos found very difficult?

Solutions

1. When a sphere of radius 3a is drawn with origin O at the centre, the charge $+Q$ will be outside the sphere. So charge $-2Q$ will contribute to flux.

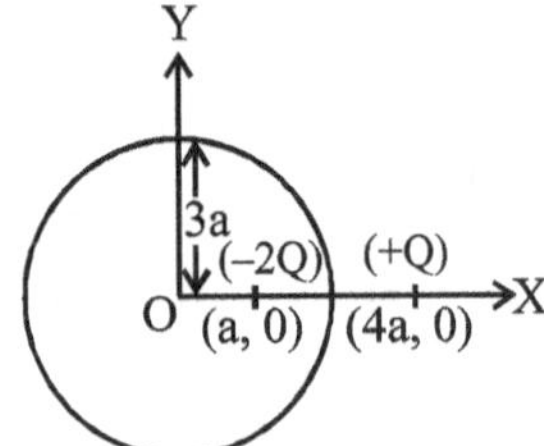

∴ Flux through the sphere,

$$\Phi = \frac{Q}{\epsilon_0} = \frac{-2Q}{\epsilon_0} \qquad \textbf{(1 Mark)}$$

Note

Only the changes inside the gaussian surface contributes to electric flux through that surface. Do not include the charge outside the gaussian surface.

2. Mututal inductance $M = \dfrac{\mu_0 N_1 N_2 A}{l}$. Hence the mutual inductance will

(i) decrease with the increase in distance and

(ii) increase with increase of number of turns in the coils.

$$\textbf{(½ + ½ = 1 Mark)}$$

3. In region BC of the graph semiconductor has a negative resistance. **(1 Mark)**

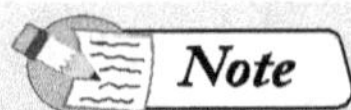

Note

In I-V graph or V-I graph, the slope of graph represents resistence. if slope is negative, then negative resistance if slope is positive, then positive resistance.

4. The net emf of cells, each of emf value E in parallel combination is E **(1 Mark)**

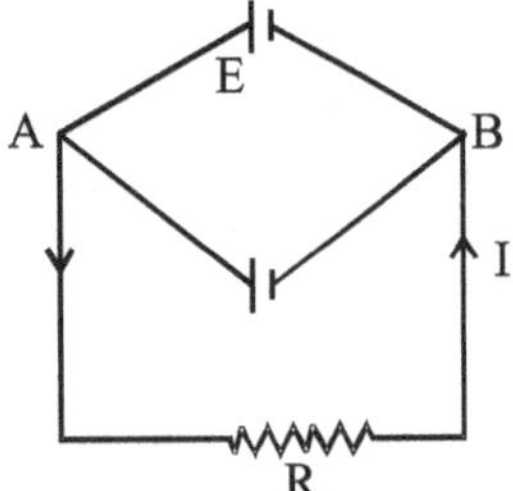

Therefore, by Ohm's law, current in the resistor R is

$$I = \frac{E}{R}$$

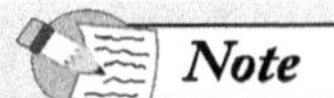

Note

If 'm' cells each of emf ε and internal resistance 'r' be connected in parallel, then equivalent resistance R'

$$R' = \frac{r}{m}$$

and, total emf of parallel combination = emf due to single cell = ε.

5. The cause of damping is the inducted emf (e) produced in the copper plate due to change in magnetic flux ($d\phi$), which produces eddy current. **(1 Mark)**

6. Activity is defined as the decay rate of the radioactive sample. Its S.I. unit is becquerel. (Bq) **(½ + ½ Mark)**

7. Ultraviolet radiations; Frequency range is 10^{14} to 10^{17} Hz. **(½ + ½ = 1 Mark)**

8. de Broglie wavelength,

$$\lambda = \frac{h}{p} = \frac{h}{\sqrt{2mqV}} \qquad \textbf{(1 Mark)}$$

9. Output characteristics of an n-p-n transistor in CE configuration : **(1 + 1 = 2 Marks)**

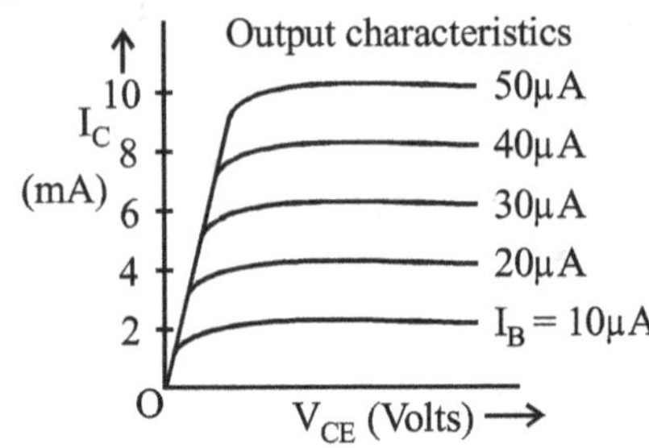

Now, output resistance r_0 is given by

$$r_0 = \frac{\Delta V_{CE}}{\Delta I_C} \text{ for constant } I_B$$

Thus for small values of V_{CE}, I_C almost increases linearly. And after small increase of V_{CE}, the current changes very little. Hence, output resistance is very high.

10. Given $\lambda = 500$ nm $= 500 \times 10^{-9}$ m

$D = 1$ m, d = ?

Distance of the first minima $= 2.5 \times 10^{-3}$ m = x

We know that the distance of the first minima on the screen is given by

$$d \sin \theta = \lambda \qquad \textbf{(1 Mark)}$$

$$d\frac{x}{D} = \lambda \quad \Rightarrow \quad d = \frac{\lambda D}{x}$$

$$d = \frac{500 \times 10^{-9} \times 1}{2.5 \times 10^{-3}} = 2 \times 10^{-4} \text{m} \qquad \textbf{(1 Mark)}$$

11. Let V be the potential difference between the plates and E_0 the electric field

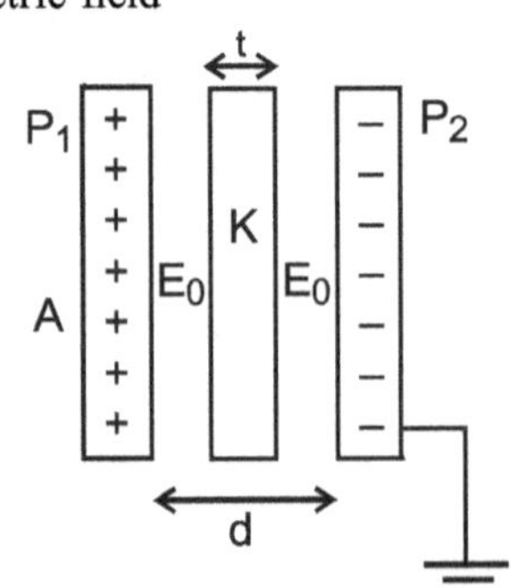

Capacitance of capacitor with dielectric slab of thickness t is

$$C = \frac{\varepsilon_0 A}{d - t + \dfrac{t}{k}} \qquad \text{Here} \quad t = \frac{d}{2} \qquad \textbf{(1 Mark)}$$

$$\therefore \qquad C = \frac{\varepsilon_0 A}{d - \dfrac{d}{2} + \dfrac{d}{2k}} = \frac{\varepsilon_0 A}{d\left[1 - \dfrac{1}{2} + \dfrac{1}{2k}\right]} = \frac{2k\varepsilon_0 A}{d(k+1)}$$

Therefore capacitance,

$$C = \frac{Q}{V} = \frac{2A\,\epsilon_0}{d\left(1 + \dfrac{1}{K}\right)} \qquad \textbf{(1 Mark)}$$

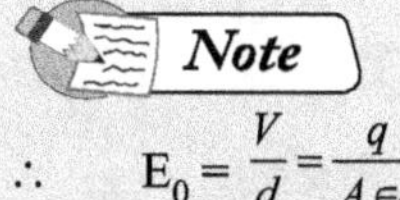 **Note**

$$\therefore \qquad E_0 = \frac{V}{d} = \frac{q}{A\,\epsilon_0}$$

where q is he charge and A is the area of the plates.

When a slab of thickness $t = \dfrac{d}{2}$ is introduced between the plates, then potential

$$V = E_0\left(d - \frac{d}{2}\right) + E \cdot \frac{d}{2} \qquad ...(i)$$

where E is the elctric field inside the dielectric of dielectric constant K

$$E = \frac{E_0}{K}$$

Putting this value of E in eq. (i)

$$V = E_0 \frac{d}{2} + \frac{E_0}{K}\frac{d}{2}$$

$$V = \frac{E_0 d}{2}\left(1 + \frac{1}{K}\right)$$

$$V = \frac{q}{A\,\epsilon_0} \cdot \frac{d}{2}\left(1 + \frac{1}{K}\right)$$

12. Current I through the capacitor is given by

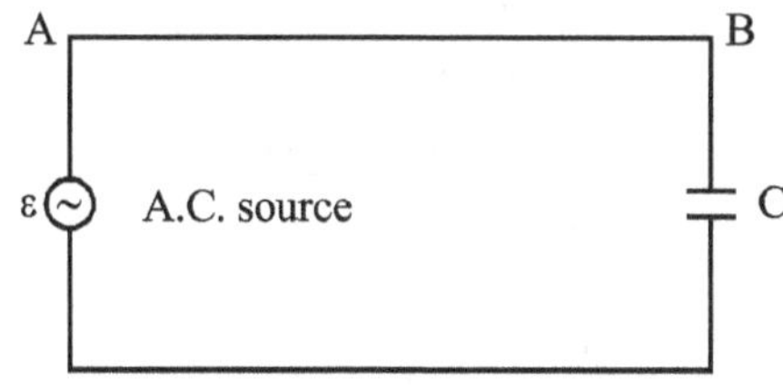

$$I = I_0 \sin\left(\omega t + \frac{\pi}{2}\right)$$

$$V = V_0 \sin \omega t$$

As we know, the displacement current

$$I_d = \epsilon_0 \frac{d}{dt}(\phi_E) = \epsilon_0 \frac{d}{dt}(AE) \qquad \textbf{(1 Mark)}$$

where A is area and E be the instantaneous electric intensity between the plates of the capacitor.

$$I_d = A\,\epsilon_0 \frac{d}{dt}\left(\frac{V}{d}\right) \qquad \left[\because E = \frac{V}{d}\right]$$

$$= \left(\frac{A\,\epsilon_0}{d}\right)\frac{d}{dt}(V_0 \sin \omega t)$$

$$= \frac{A\,\epsilon_0}{d} V_0 \cos \omega t \cdot \omega = CV_0 \omega \sin\left(\omega t + \frac{\pi}{2}\right)$$

$$\text{where } C = \frac{A\,\epsilon_0}{d} = \frac{V}{\dfrac{1}{C\omega}}\sin\left(\omega t + \frac{\pi}{2}\right) \qquad \left[\because I_0 = \frac{V}{X_C}\right]$$

$$I_d = I_0 \sin\left(\omega t + \frac{\pi}{2}\right) = I \text{ (Instantaneous current)}$$

(1 Mark)

13. When potential difference V is applied across the conductor, an electric field is produced and the electrons are accelerated from one end to the other. On the way, they suffer collisions, come to rest and are again accelerated. Thus, they drift from one end to the other with a very small velocity called the drift velocity and is denoted by v_d.   **(1 + 1 = 2 Marks)**

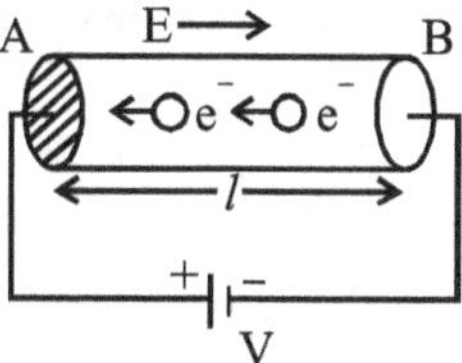

Let n = no. of electrons *i.e.*, charge carriers per unit volume

     a = area of cross-section

     I = current through the conductor

t = time taken by the electrons to drift from one end to other end of the conductor.

Clearly, in time t, whole charge Q will move from one end to the other.

Now,   Q = Ne,

where N is the total number of electrons

$$= a \times l \times ne$$

or $Q = nale$

$$\therefore \qquad \text{Current } i = \frac{Q}{t} = \frac{nale}{t}$$

or $i = n\,a\,e\,v_d \qquad \left[\because V_d = \frac{l}{t}\right]$

OR

A potentiometer is an arrangement of a long wire of uniform cross-section and composition.

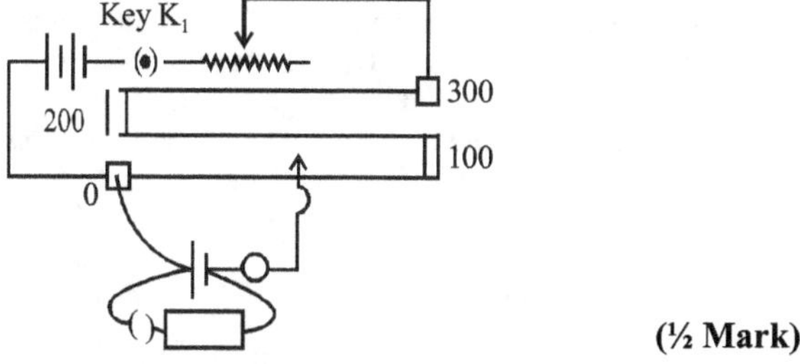

(½ Mark)

According to the principle of potentiometer $V \propto 1$

Internal resistance of the cell

$$r = \left(\frac{\varepsilon}{V} - 1\right)R = \left(\frac{\ell_1 - \ell_2}{\ell_2}\right)R$$

First, the key K_1 is inserted and key K_2 is not inserted. In this state, no current is drawn from the cell. The jockey is moved on the wire to fnd the balance point. Let the balancing length be ℓ_1. This length balanced the emf ε of the cell.

Therefore, by potentiometer principle,

$$\varepsilon \propto \ell_1 \qquad ...(i)$$

Now, key K_2 is also closed. A suitable resistance R is introduced in the circuit with the help of the resistance box (R.B.). In this state, current is drawn from the cell. The jockey is moved on the wire to find the balance point. Let the balancing length is ℓ_2. This length balances the terminal potential difference (V) of the cell.

Therefore, by potentiometer principle, we have

$$V \propto \ell_2 \qquad ...(ii)$$

From eq. (i) and (ii), we have

$$\frac{\varepsilon}{V} = \frac{\ell_1}{\ell_2} \qquad ...(iii)$$

Therefore, the internal resistance of the cell is given by the expression

$$r = \left(\frac{\varepsilon}{V} - 1\right)R = \left(\frac{\ell_1 - \ell_2}{\ell_2}\right)R \qquad \text{(1½ Marks)}$$

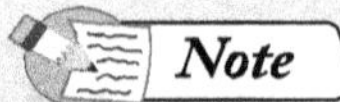

Note

Drift velocity $\hat{v}_d$ is also given as, $\hat{v}_d = \dfrac{-e\vec{E}}{m}\tau$

where $\vec{E}$ = *electric field*
    m = *mass of electron*
    τ = *relaxation time*
    e = *chanrge of electron.*

14. Let us consider an object O lying at a distance u from a combination of two lenses of focal length f_1 and f_2. The image of O is formed at I due to two lenses at a distance v from the combination.

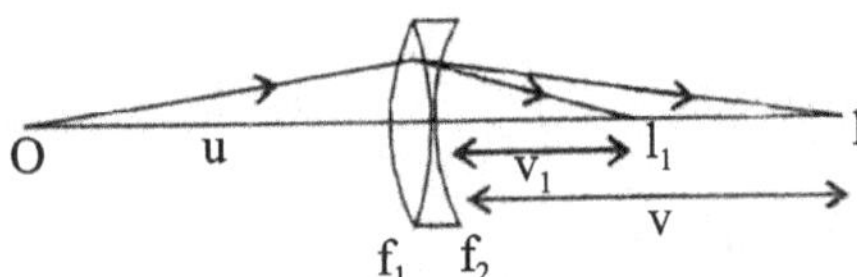

The image may be thought of as being formed in two stages. The convex lens forms the image of O at I_1 at a distance v_1 from the lens. The image I_1, then serves as a virtual object for the concave lens and its image is formed at I.

For refraction at the first lens, which is a convex lens,

$$\frac{1}{f_1} = \frac{1}{v_1} - \frac{1}{u} \qquad ...(i) \qquad \text{(½ Mark)}$$

For refraction at the second lens which is a concave lens

$$-\frac{1}{f_2} = \frac{1}{v} - \frac{1}{v_1} \qquad ...(ii) \qquad \text{(½ Mark)}$$

$(u = v_1, v = v)$

Adding eq. (i) and (ii)

$$\frac{1}{f_1} - \frac{1}{f_2} = \frac{1}{v} - \frac{1}{u} \qquad ...(iii)$$

If F is the focal length of the combination, then

$$\frac{1}{F} = \frac{1}{v} - \frac{1}{u} \qquad ...(iv)$$

From eq. (iii) and (iv)

$$\frac{1}{F} = \frac{1}{f_1} - \frac{1}{f_2}$$

or $\quad F = \dfrac{f_1 f_2}{f_2 - f_1} \qquad$ **(1 Mark)**

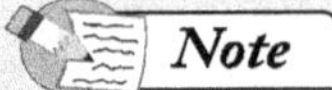

Note

Focal length of convex lens $= +f_1$
Focal length of concave lens $= -f_2$
The equivalent focal length f is given as

$$\frac{1}{f} = \frac{1}{f_1} + \frac{1}{(-f_2)} \Rightarrow \frac{1}{f} = \frac{f_2 - f_1}{f_1 f_2} \quad f = \frac{f_1 f_2}{f_2 - f_1}$$

15. Box A square law device and box B is a band pass filter.

(½ + ½ = 1 Mark)

Functions : A works as a detector and B allows a band of frequencies to pass through it. **(½ + ½ = 1 Mark)**

16. The given circuit is a combination of three NAND gates. The first two gates for the inputs A and B are NOT gates and third gates serves as a NAND gate for the inputes $\bar{A}$ and $\bar{B}$.

$$\therefore \quad Y = \overline{\bar{A} \cdot \bar{B}} = \bar{\bar{A}} + \bar{\bar{B}} = A + B$$

Hence, the three gates together form 'OR' gate.

(1 + 1 = 2 Marks)

The truth table of the 'OR' gate is :

A	B	Y = A + B
0	0	0
0	1	1
1	0	1
1	1	1

17. (a) Average power

$$P_a = \frac{1}{T}\int_0^T P_i\,dt = \frac{1}{T}\int_0^T i^2 R\,dt$$

$$= \frac{1}{T}\int_0^T i_m^2 \sin^2 \omega t\, R\,dt$$

$$= \frac{1}{T} i_m^2 R \int_0^T \frac{(1 - \cos 2\omega t)}{2}\,dt$$

$$= \frac{1}{T}\frac{I_m^2}{2} R\left[T - \frac{\sin 2\omega t}{2\omega}\right]_0^T \qquad \text{(2 Marks)}$$

$$= \frac{1}{T}\frac{I_m^2}{2} R\,[T - 0] = \frac{1}{2}I_m^2 R\,[\because \sin 2\omega T = 0]$$

(b)　Given, P = 100 W, V = 220 V

As we know power,

$$P = \frac{V^2}{R}, \text{ R is the resistance}$$

$$\therefore\quad R = \frac{V^2}{P} = \frac{220 \times 220}{100} = 484\ \Omega \qquad \textbf{(1 Mark)}$$

Note

The average value of a function F(t) over a period T is given by

$$<f(t)> = \frac{1}{T}\int_0^T F(t)dt.$$

Average value of cos 2ωt and sin 2ωt is always zero. So, instead of evaluating the complete integral, directly use
$<cos 2\omega t> = <sin 2\omega t> = 0$
Also

$$<cos^2 \omega t> = <cos^2 \omega t> = \frac{1}{2}.$$

18.　Given, $B = 0.5\ T, l = 20\ cm = 0.2\ m, v = 10\ ms^{-1}$

$$\textbf{(1½ + 1½ = 3 Marks)}$$

Induced emf e = BlV

$$\Rightarrow\quad 0.5 \times 0.2 \times 10 \text{ Volt}$$

or　e = 1.0 V

Current through this conductor

$$i = \frac{e}{R} = \frac{1V}{5\Omega} = 0.2\ A$$

OR

Given : Length of each spoke = 50 cm = 0.5 m

$$\omega = \frac{120}{60} = 2 \text{ rps}$$

$$= 2 \times 2\pi = 4\pi\,\text{radian s}^{-1}$$

$$B = 0.4\,G$$

$$\delta = 60°$$

Horizontal component of Earth's magnetic field

$$B_H = \quad B\cos\delta = 0.4 \times \cos 60° = 0.2\ G$$

Now,　$e = \dfrac{1}{2}B_H \omega l^2 = \dfrac{1}{2} \times 0.2 \times 4\pi \times 0.5 \times 0.5$ V

$$= 0.314\ V \qquad \textbf{(2 Marks)}$$

The emf will be uneffected by the increase in the number of spokes because they are in parallel. **(1 Mark)**

19.　(i)　Current sensitivity of a galvanometer is defined as the deflection produced in the galvanometer per unit current.

i.e.　$I_S = \dfrac{\theta}{i}$, its S.I. unit is division/ A

$$\textbf{(1 + 1 = 2 Marks)}$$

Larger the deflection produced more sensitive is the galvanometer.

(ii)　In both the arrangements, since the galvanometer shows no deflection, therefore, the bridge is balanced.

The battery and the galvanometer can be interchanged in a balanced Wheatstone bridge without effecting the balance point.

In the first arrangement, $\dfrac{P}{Q} = \dfrac{R}{S}$

$$\Rightarrow\quad \frac{4}{R_1} = \frac{6}{9} \quad \text{or,} \quad R_1 = \frac{9 \times 4}{6} = 6\Omega$$

and in the second arrangement

$$\frac{6}{12} = \frac{R_2}{8} \quad \Rightarrow \quad R_2 = \frac{8 \times 6}{12} = 4\Omega$$

$$\therefore\quad \frac{R_1}{R_2} = \frac{6}{4} = 1.5 \qquad \textbf{(1 Mark)}$$

20.　**Given :** $r = 1\ mm = 1 \times 10^{-3}\ m, i_1 = 12A, i_2 = 5A$

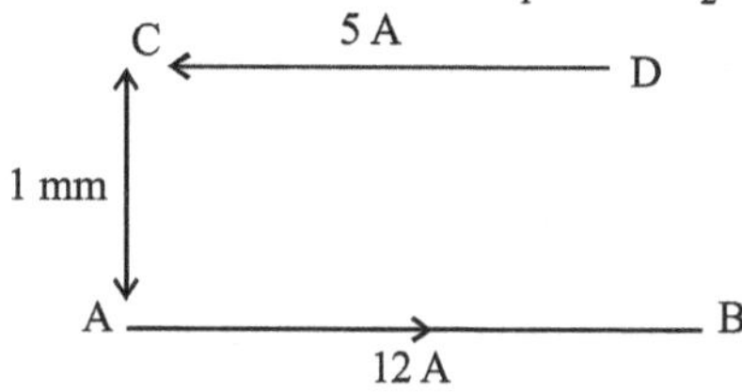

Since the wire CD is supported in air, the force of repulsion between the wire should be just equal to the weight of the wire.

Force of repulsion per unit length between the two wires **(1 Mark)**

$$\frac{dF}{dl} = \frac{\mu_0}{4\pi} \cdot \frac{2i_1 i_2}{r}\,\text{Nm}^{-1}$$

Let m kg be the mass per unit length of the wire CD
Downward force on a unit length

$$= mg = m \times 10\ \text{Nm}^{-1}$$

$$m \times 10\quad = \frac{dF}{dl} = \frac{\mu_0}{4\pi} \cdot \frac{2i_1 i_2}{r}$$

or,　$m \times 10\quad = \dfrac{10^{-7} \times 2 \times 5 \times 12}{10^{-3}}$ **(1 Mark)**

$$\therefore\qquad m = 12 \times 10^{-4}\,\text{kg/m} \qquad \textbf{(1 Mark)}$$

The current in the wire CD is in a direction opposite to that of AB.

Note

Force on another wire CD due to wire AB has to be replusive so that it remains suspended when left free. As gravity attracts the wire, force between both wire has to be equal and replasive. Therefore, current in wire CD will flow in opposite direction to AB wire, as anti-parallel currents repel each other.

21.　V— I characteristics of a p-n junction diode. **(½ Mark)**

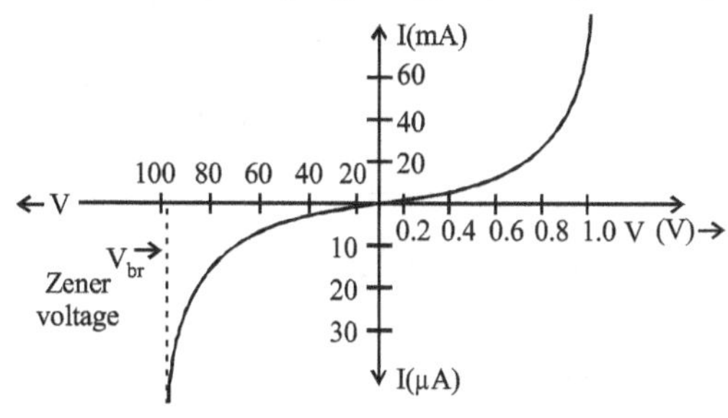

(i) In the reverse bias of the *p-n* junction, the electrons in the *p*-type crystal are repelled towards the junction and so are the holes in the *n*-region. The depletion layer width increases. The minority charge carriers however are pushed through the junction causing a little current through the *p-n* junction diode. This current is very small and is almost independent of applied voltage in the reverse bias. **(1 Mark)**

(ii) The reverse current shows a sudden increase in the current when the reverse bias increases. Reverse current is due to the flow of minority carriers *i.e.*, electrons from *p* to *n* and holes from *n* to *p*. As the reverse bias is increased the electric field at the junction becomes strong enough to pull the electrons from the *p* side which are accelerated to *n* side. These electrons account for the high current observed at the breakdown voltage. **(1 Mark)**

Zener diode operates under the reverse bias in the breakdown region. **(½ Mark)**

22. Ray diagram of a refracting type telescope.

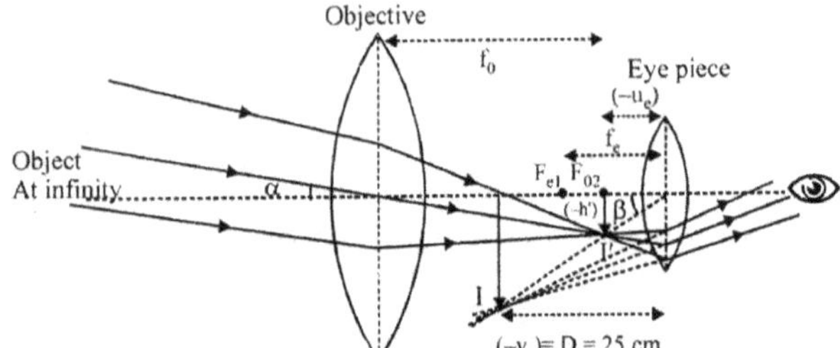

(½ Mark)

Magnifying power (M) of a telescope is defined as the ratio of angle subtended by the image at the eye when formed at the near point to the angle subtended at the unaided eye by the object at infinity.

Expression for magnifying power of a telescope. **(1 Mark)**

$$M = \frac{f_0}{f_e}\left(1+\frac{f_e}{D}\right), \text{ where}$$

f_0 = focal length of the objective
f_e = focal length of the eye piece
D = distance of distinct version

If the final image is formed at infinity *i.e.*, D = ∞, then

$$M = \frac{f_0}{f_e}$$ **(½ Mark)**

Limitations :

1. The image formed by a refracting telescope is not as bright as in the case of reflecting type telescope.

2. The image formed by a refraction type telescope suffers both spherical aberration and chromatic aberration which is not in case of reflecting type telescope. **(1 Mark)**

23. Einstein's photoelectric equation

$$h\nu = h\nu_0 + \frac{1}{2}mv^2$$

or, $\quad h\nu = h\nu_0 + eV_s,$

where v is the velocity of the ejected electrons and V_s is the stopping potential **(½ Mark)**

This equation is based on the following **properties of photons :**

(i) A photon is a packet of energy. It has an energy equal to hν wher *v* is its frequency and *h* plank's constant.

(ii) When a photon is incident on a photoelectric material, it is completely absorbed by the electron. The energy of the photon is used in ejecting electron and the balance if any is used up in imparting kinetic energy to the electron. **(½ + ½ = 1 Mark)**

Three **observed features** which can be explained by this equation :

(i) The photoelectric emission takes place only if the incident light has a frequency greater than the threshold frequency ν_0. If $\nu < \nu_0$, then $\frac{1}{2}mv^2$ will be –ve, which is not possible. Hence, electron will not be emited. **(1½ Marks)**

(ii) When the frequency of the incident light increases, then $\frac{1}{2}mv^2$ *i.e.*, kinetic energy of electron increases because work function = $h\nu_0$ is fixed. With increase in frequency more and more energy is available to the electron ejected and hence stopping potential also increases.

(iii) When we increase the intensity of the incident light, keeping its frequency constant the number of photons increases. Since each photon ejects one electron, the number of electrons ejected per sec also increases and hence the photoelectric current also increases.

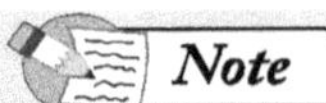

> ***Note***
>
> *The graph between intensity of light and photoelectric current is a straight line as shown.*

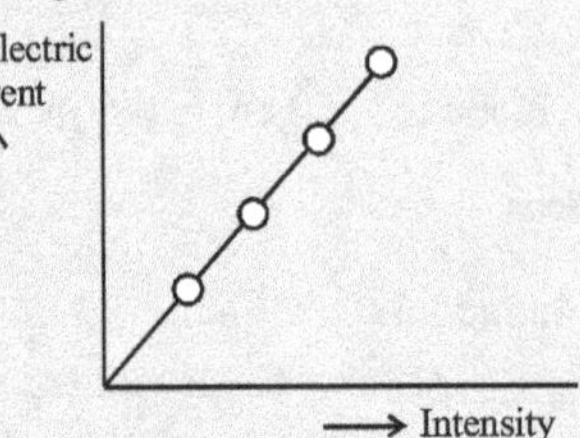

24. Space waves are used for line of sight commu-nication (LOS). Television broadcast microwave links and satellite communication are some examples that use space wave mode of propagation.

The range of frequencies used in space wave communication is 10^4 Hz to 10^{11} Hz.

Maximum LOS distance between two antenna's is given by **(1 + 1 + 1 = 3 Marks)**

$$d_m = d_T + d_R = \sqrt{2h_T R} + \sqrt{2h_R R}$$

$$= \sqrt{2 \times 20 \times 6.4 \times 10^6} + \sqrt{2 \times 45 \times 6.4 \times 10^6}$$

$$= \sqrt{256 \times 10^6} + \sqrt{576 \times 10^6} = 16 \times 10^3 + 24 \times 10^3$$

$$= 40 \times 10^3 \text{ m} = 40 \text{ km}$$

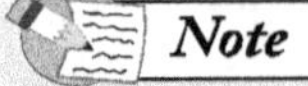

> ***Note***
>
> *A space wave travels in a straight line from transmitting antenna to the receiving anternna. Space wave are used for both line of sight communication as well as satellite communication.*

25. (a) If the electric field vector of light wave vibrates just in one direction perpendicular to direction of wave propagation, then it is said to be linearly palarised.

(½ Mark)

When a beam of sunlight is incident on small particles of dust or air molecules, it is scattered in all directions. The light scattered by the molecules in the perpendicular direction is found to be plane polarised. Ordinary light has components of the electric field vector both in the plane of paper represented by doubles arrow ($\updownarrow$) and perpendicular to the plane of the paper represented by dot ($\bullet$) in the fig. However, in the scattered light only components represented by dots are present i.e., scattered light is polarised perpendicular to the plane of the paper as shown below. **(1½ Marks)**

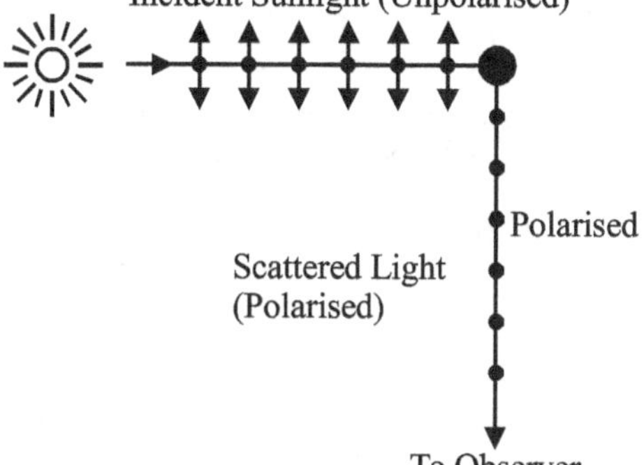

(b) When unpolarised light is incident on a polaroid, the transmitted light is polarised, its intensity is reduced to half and is unaffected by the rotation of polaroid.

(1 Mark)

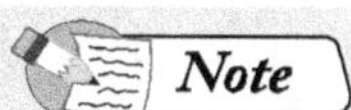
Note

Do not answer the question using malus law. Malus law is for intensity of transmitted light that has already passed through a polariod. Malus law in not for unpalarised light (incident light).

26. (a) Endoscopy is used to see inner organs. It uses optical fibres. It is based on the principle of total internal reflection. **(2 Marks)**

(b) Helpful, concern for the welfare of the students and their families. **(1 Mark)**

(c) Humanity and a sense of generosity. **(1 Mark)**

27. (a) Let there be a circular loop of wire of radius R and having N-turns located in the YZ plane and carrying a steady current I as shown in figure. **(2 Marks)**

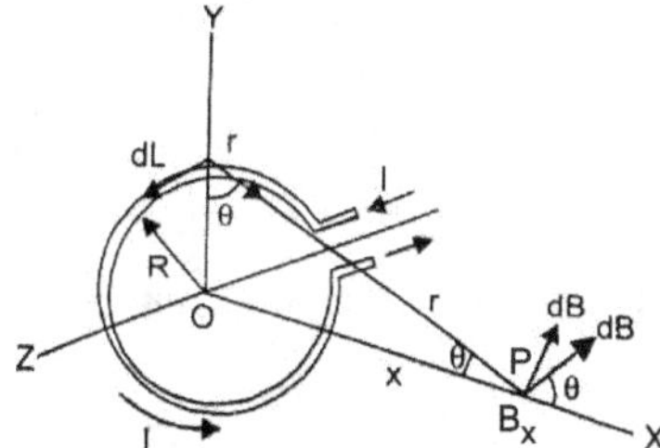

Let us calculate the magnetic field at an axial point P at a distance x from the centre of the loop.

From the figure, it is clear that any element dL is perpendicular to $\hat{r}$, furthermore all the elements around the loop are at the same distance r from P, where $r^2 = x^2 + R^2$.

By Biot-Savart's law, the magnetic field at point P due to the current element dL is given by

$$dB = \frac{\mu_0}{4\pi} \frac{I|\overrightarrow{dL} \times \hat{r}|}{r^2} = \frac{\mu_0}{4\pi} \frac{I\,d\,L}{(x^2 + R^2)} \quad ...(i)$$

The direction of the magnetic field dB due to the element dL is perpendicular to the plane formed by $\hat{r}$ and dL. The vector dB can be resolved into components dB_x along the X-axis and dB_y perpendicular to the X-axis. When the components perpendicular to the X-axis are added over the whole loop, the resultant is zero.

By integrating the components

$$dB_x = dB \cos\theta$$

We have $B = \oint dB \cos\theta = \dfrac{\mu_0 I}{4\pi} \oint \dfrac{dL \cos\theta}{x^2 + R^2} \quad ...(ii)$

The integral is to be taken over the entire loop since θ, x and R are constant for all elements of the loop and

$$\cos\theta = \frac{R}{\sqrt{x^2 + R^2}}$$

$$\therefore \quad B = \frac{\mu_0 IR}{4\pi\left(x^2 + R^2\right)^{3/2}} \oint dL = \frac{\mu_0\, IR^2}{2\left(x^2 + R^2\right)^{3/2}}$$

$$[\because \oint dL = 2\pi R]$$

If there are N number of turns, then

$$\vec{B} = \frac{\mu_0\, NIR^2}{2\left(x^2 + R^2\right)^{3/2}} \cdot \hat{i}$$

where $\hat{i}$ is unit vector in the direction of the x-axis

(b) A toroid consists of hollow circular ring on which a large number of turns of a wire are closely wound as shown in figure.

Let N be the number of turns and I be the current passed through the toroid. r be the average radius. If the coils are closely spaced, the field inside the toroidal coil is tangent to the dotted circular path and is same at all points. **(½ + 1½ + 1 = 3 Marks)**

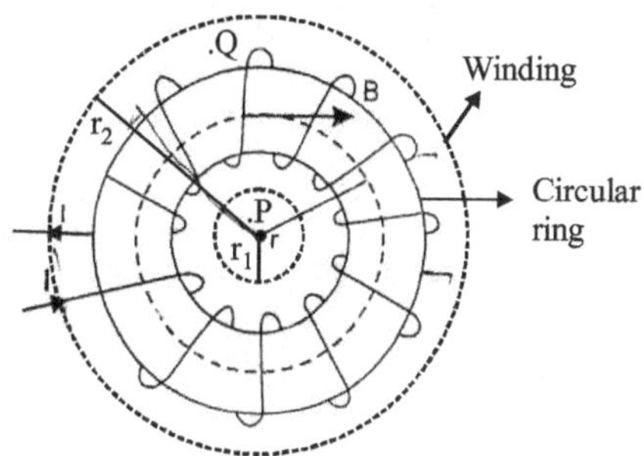

By Ampere's circuital law,

$$\oint \vec{B} \cdot \overline{dL} = B \oint dL = B(2\pi r) = \mu_0 NI$$

or $B = \dfrac{\mu_0 NI}{2\pi r} = \mu_0 nI$

$\because \quad n = \dfrac{N}{2\pi r}$ (number of turns per unit length)

This is the expression for magnetic field inside a toroidal solenoid.

(i) Inside the toroid at point P :

$$B_{(inside)}\,(2\pi r_1) = \mu_0\, I_e$$

As loop encloses no current.

So, $I_e = 0$

$\therefore \quad B_{(inside)} = 0$

(ii) Exterior to the toroid at point Q :

Magnetic field in the open space.

$$B_{(outside)}\,(2\pi r_2) = \mu_0\, I_e$$

Here current coming out of the plane of the paper is cancelled exactly by the current going into it

So, $I_e = 0$

$\therefore \quad B_{(outside)} = 0$

OR

(a) Schematic sketch of a cyclotron :

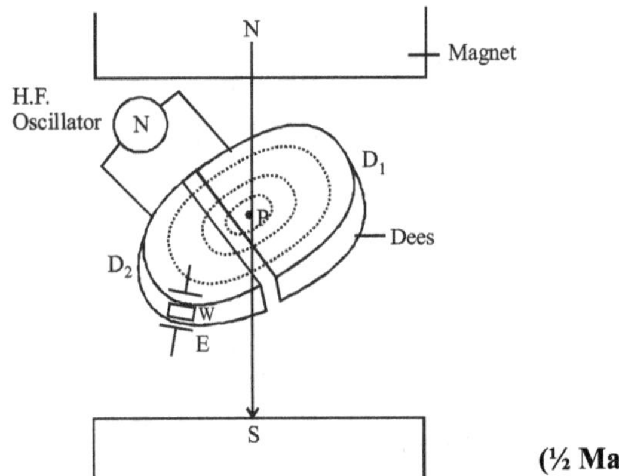

(½ Mark)

The role of crossed electric and magnetic fields is to increase the energy of charged particles. Cyclotron uses the fact that the frequency of revolution of the charged particle in a magnetic field is independent of its energy. **(1 Mark)**

The electric field imparts kinetic energy to the charged particle, the magnetic field makes the particle move in a circular path of increasing radius. If r is the maximum radius of the circular path before the charged particle comes out, then

$$v_{max} = \dfrac{BQ}{m}r$$

KE acquired by the charged particle

$$= \dfrac{1}{2} m.v_{max}^2$$

$$= \dfrac{1}{2} m \cdot \dfrac{B^2 Q^2}{m^2} \cdot r^2$$

$$= \dfrac{1}{2}\dfrac{B^2 Q^2 r^2}{m} \qquad \textbf{(1½ Marks)}$$

This is the required expression for the kinetic energy.

(b) (i) No, the time for which a charged particle remains inside a 'dee' for continuous acceleration is given by

$$t = \dfrac{2m\pi}{BQ},$$

For t be the same, the ratio of $\dfrac{m}{Q}$ must be the same.

For proton, $\dfrac{m}{Q} = \dfrac{m_p}{e}$

For α particle, $\dfrac{m}{Q} = \dfrac{4m_p}{2e} = \dfrac{2m_p}{e}$ **(1 Mark)**

$i.e.,\ \dfrac{m}{Q}$ is not same for both α-particle and proton, hence they cannot be accelerated by the same cyclotron frequency.

(ii) As, $v = \dfrac{BQ}{m}r$

$\therefore \quad v \propto \dfrac{Q}{m}$ **(1 Mark)**

and $\dfrac{Q}{m}$ is more for the proton, therefore, proton will have higher velocity at the exit slit of the dees.

28. (a) Electric dipole moment is defined as the product of either charge of the dipole and the distance between them.

$i.e.,\ \vec{p} = q \times \overrightarrow{2l}$, where $\overrightarrow{2l}$ is the vector distance from the –ve to +ve charge **(½ + ½ + 2 = 3 Marks)**

It is a vector quantity.

Expression for the electric field of a dipole at a point on the equatorial plane of the dipole :

Let there be a point P (on the equatorial plane of the dipole) at a distance r from the centre of a dipole formed by two charges –q and +q and having dipole moments $\vec{p} = 2\,\vec{ql}$. We have to find the electric field intensity at point P.

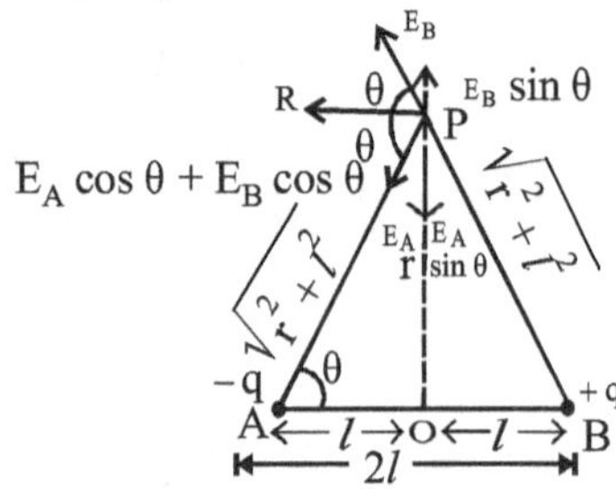

The electric field intensity at point P due to +q (at B)

$$E_A = \dfrac{1}{4\pi \in_0} \cdot \dfrac{q}{\left(r^2 + l^2\right)} \text{ along BP}$$

and electric field intensity at P due to –q charge (at A)

$$E_B = \frac{1}{4\pi \in_0} \cdot \frac{q}{\left(r^2 + l^2\right)} \text{ along PA}$$

Clearly, $E_A = E_B$ in magnitude.

E_A and E_B can be resolved into two rectangular components.

Components of E_A

(i) $E_A \cos\theta$ along PX

(ii) $E_A \sin\theta$ along PY

Components of E_B

(i) $E_B \cos\theta$ along PX

(ii) $E_B \sin\theta$ along YP

Vertical components being equal and opposite cancel each other.

Therefore, net electric field intensity along PX

$$E = E_A \cos\theta + E_A \cos\theta \qquad (\because E_A = E_B)$$
$$= 2E_A \cos\theta \text{ along PX}$$

$$= 2 \cdot \frac{1}{4\pi \in_0} \cdot \frac{q}{\left(r^2 + l^2\right)} \cdot \frac{1}{\sqrt{r^2 + l^2}}$$

or, $\quad E = \dfrac{1}{4\pi \in_0} \cdot \dfrac{p}{\left(r^2 + l^2\right)^{3/2}}$ along PX$(\because p = q \times 2l)$

If $l << r$ so that it can be neglected, then

$$E = \frac{1}{4\pi \in_0} \cdot \frac{p}{r^3} \text{ along PX}$$

$$\therefore \quad E \propto \frac{1}{r^3}$$

(b) Equipotential surfaces due to an electric dipole.

(1 + 1 = 2 Marks)

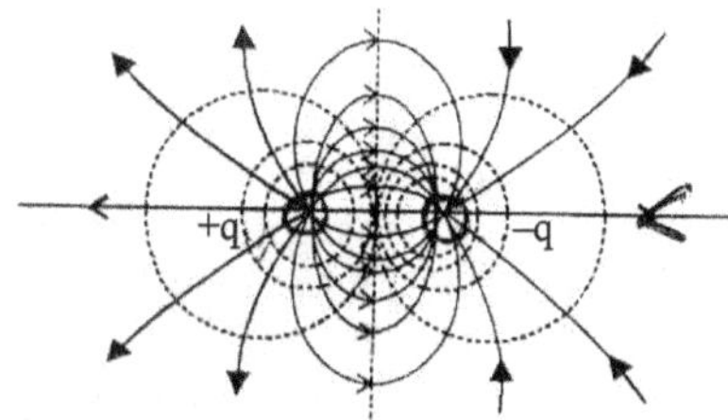

Potential due to the dipole is zero at the line bisecting the dipole length.

OR

Expression for the electric field due to a uniformly charged conducting shell :

Let there be a spherical conducting shell whose radius is R.

Let σ be the uniform surface charge density.

(i) We have to find electric field intensity at a point P *i.e.*, outside the shell. Imagine a sphere of radius r with its centre at O to serve as Gaussian surface.

Electric field intensity at P, $\vec{E}$ and area element $\overrightarrow{ds}$ are mutually perpendicular at every point on the Gaussian surface.

(2 Marks)

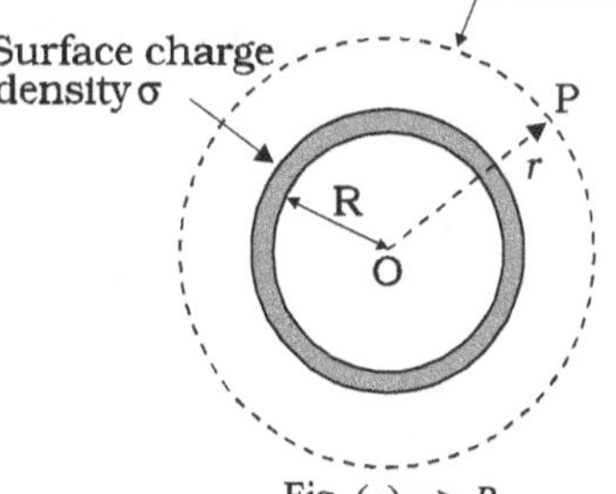

$$\therefore \quad \oint_S \vec{E} \cdot \overrightarrow{ds} = E \int_S ds = E \times S$$

or, $\quad \phi = E \times 4\pi r^2 \qquad \text{..... (i)}$

According to Gauss's theorem

$$\phi = \frac{Q}{\in_0}$$

$$\therefore \quad \vec{E} \cdot \overrightarrow{ds} = \frac{1}{\in_0} \cdot Q = \frac{1}{\in_0} \cdot \sigma \times 4\pi R^2 \quad \text{....(ii)}$$

$$\therefore \quad E \times 4\pi r^2 = \frac{\sigma}{\in_0} \cdot 4\pi R^2$$

or, $\quad E = \dfrac{q}{4\pi \in_0 r^2} \cdot R^2 \qquad$ (for $r > R$)

where q is the total charge on the shell.

(ii) When the point P lies inside the shell : In this case, the spherical Gaussian surface lies inside the cell. Since the charge lies outside the surfaces the Gaussian surface enclose no charge. **(2 Marks)**

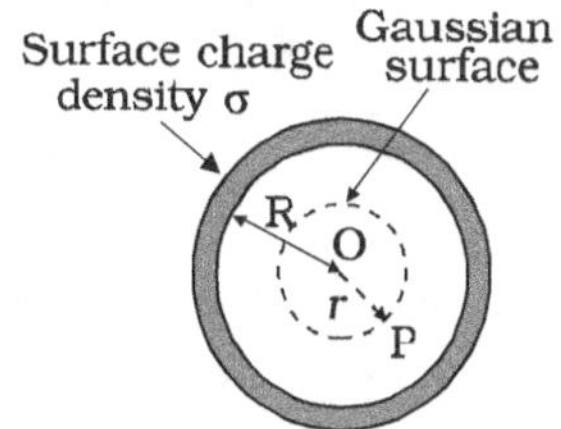

$$\therefore \quad \oint \vec{E} \cdot \overrightarrow{ds} = E \oint S = E \times 4\pi r^2 = \frac{q}{\in_0}$$

(from Gauss's law)

or, $\quad E \times 4\pi r^2 = 0 \qquad (\because q = 0)$

$\therefore \quad E = 0 \qquad$ (for $r < R$)

Graph showing variation of the electric field E with distance r from the centre : **(1 Mark)**

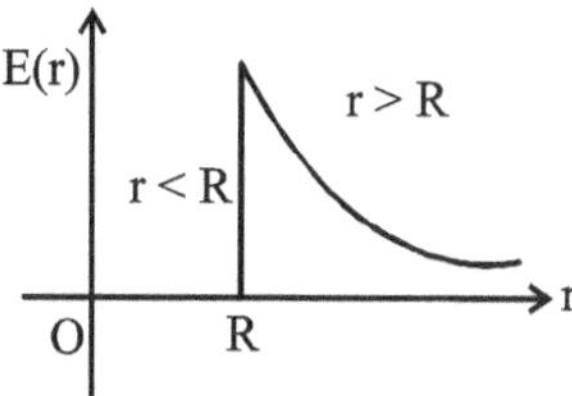

29. Let an electron of mass m, carrying a charge e revolving around the nucleus of hydrogen atom carrying a charge +e. Let r_n be the radius of the orbit and v_n is the speed of the electron in that orbit. The necessary centripetal force

to revolve the electron is provided by the electrostatic force between the electron and hydrogen nucleus

(3½ Marks)

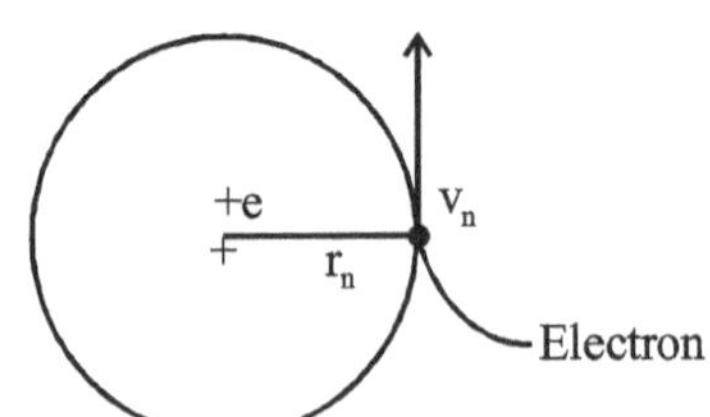

$$\therefore \quad k\frac{e^2}{r_n^2} = m\frac{v_n^2}{r_n}, \text{ where } k = \frac{1}{4\pi \in_0}$$

$$\therefore \quad r_n = \frac{ke^2}{mv_n^2} \qquad \qquad ...(i)$$

$$\text{or,} \quad mv_n^2 = \frac{ke^2}{r_n} \qquad \qquad ...(ii)$$

According to the angular momentum postulate

$$mv_n r_n = \frac{nh}{2\pi}$$

$$v_n = \frac{nh}{2\pi m r_n} \qquad \qquad ...(iii)$$

Putting the value of v_n from (iii) into (i), we have

$$r_n = \frac{ke^2}{m.n^2 h^2} 4\pi^2 m^2 r_n^2$$

$$\text{or} \quad r_n = \frac{n^2 h^2}{4\pi^2 ke^2 m} \qquad \qquad ....(iv)$$

KE of the electron

$$= \frac{1}{2}mv_n^2 = \frac{1}{2}\frac{ke^2}{r_n}$$

$$= \frac{1}{2}\frac{ke^2}{n^2 h^2}\cdot 4\pi^2 kme^2 = \frac{2\pi^2 k^2 me^4}{n^2 h^2} \qquad ....(v)$$

Potential energy of the electron

$$PE = -\frac{kq_1 q_2}{r} = -\frac{k.e.e}{r_n} = -\frac{ke^2}{r_n}$$

$$= \frac{-ke^2}{n^2 h^2} 4\pi^2 ke^2 m$$

$$PR = \frac{-4\pi^2 k^2 e^4 m}{n^2 h^2}$$

$\therefore$ Total energy of the electron

$$= \frac{2\pi^2 k^2 me^4}{n^2 h^2} - \frac{4\pi k^2 me^4}{n^2 h^2}$$

$$\text{or,} \quad E_n = \frac{-2\pi^2 k^2 me^4}{n^2 h^2}$$

If E_{ni} and E_{nf} are the energies of the electron for which n = n_i and n_f

$$\therefore \quad E_{ni} = \frac{-2\pi^2 k^2 me^4}{n_i^2 h^2} \text{ and } E_{nf} = \frac{-2\pi^2 k^2 me^4}{n_f^2 h^2}$$

If hv is the energy of the photon when the electron jumps from n = n_i to n = n_f, then

$$hv = \frac{2\pi^2 k^2 me^4}{h^2 n_f^2} + \frac{-2\pi^2 k^2 me^4}{h^2 n_i^2}$$

$$\Rightarrow \quad hv = \frac{2\pi^2 k^2 me^4}{h^2}\left[\frac{1}{n_f^2} - \frac{1}{n_i^2}\right]$$

$$\text{or,} \quad v = \frac{2\pi^2 k^2 me^4}{h^3}\left[\frac{1}{n_f^2} - \frac{1}{n_i^2}\right]$$

Spectral series when the transition of the electron takes place from **(1½ Marks)**

$n_i = 4$ to $n_f = 3 \rightarrow$ Paschen series

$n_i = 4$ to $n_f = 2 \rightarrow$ Balmer series

$n_i = 4$ to $n_f = 1 \rightarrow$ Lyman series

OR

(a) Plot of binding energy per nucleon (BE/A) as a function of mass number A :

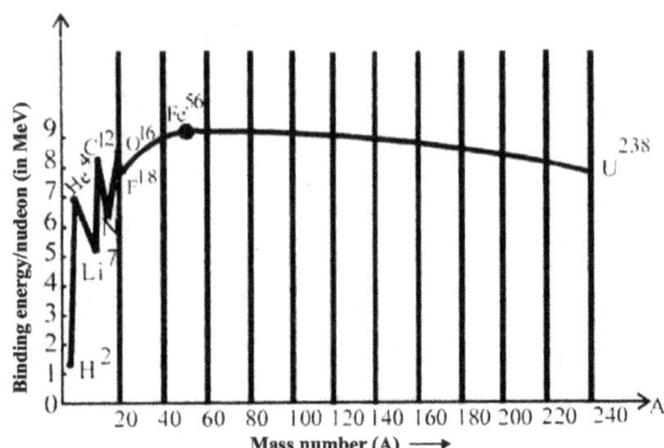

(1 Mark)

Two conclusions regarding the nature of nuclear force: **(½ + ½ = 1 Mark)**

(i) The nculear force is strong and attractive in nature.

(ii) The constantancy of binding energy for A > 30 and A < 170 shows the nuclear forces are short range forces.

(b) From the graph, it is clear that the binding energy both for lighter and heavy nuclei is small. The curve has a maxima of about 8.75 MeV for A = 56. A heavy nucleus say A = 200 has a lower binding energy. Thus, when a heavy nucleus breaks up into two nuclei, (i.e. nuclear fission) the two nuclei produced are more tightly bound. Thus, there is a larger mass defect. Hence, during fission energy will be released.

(1 + 1 Marks)

Similarly, when two lighter nuclei fuse to form a heavier nuclei, (*i.e.*, nuclear fusion), the binding energy increases *i.e.*, the nuclei become more tightly bound. Thus, there will be a large mass defect and energy will be released. Thus, during fusion also energy is released.

(c) The nuclear process of a neutron undergoing a β-decay is given as **(½ + ½ = 1 Mark)**

$$n \rightarrow p + e^- + \bar{v}$$

where $\bar{v}$ is a neutrino. The neutrinos are difficult to detect because they are chargeless and are of very small non-zero mass. It has very weak interaction with other particles.

CBSE Board Solved Paper

Time Allowed : 3 Hours *Maximum Marks : 100*

General Instructions:
(i) All questions are compulsory.
(ii) There are **29** questions in total. Question Nos. **1** to **8** are very short answer type questions and carry **one** mark each.
(iii) Question Nos. **9** to **16** carry **two** marks each, Question Nos. **17** to **25** carry **three** marks each and Question Nos. **27** to **29** carry **five** marks each.
(iv) There is no overall choice. However, an internal choice has been provided in **one** question of **two** marks, **one** question of **three** marks and all **three** questions of **five** marks each. You have to attempt only one of the choices in such questions.
(v) Question No. **26** is value based question carries **four** marks.
(vi) Use of calculators is not permitted. However, you may use log tables if necessary.
(vii) You may use the following values of physical constants wherever necessary:

$c = 3 \times 10^8$ m/s

$h = 6.63 \times 10^{-34}$ Js

$e = 1.6 \ 10^{-19}$ C

$\mu_0 = 4\pi \times 10^{-7}$ Tm A^{-1}

$\varepsilon_0 = 8.854 \times 10^{-12}$ C^2 N^{-1} m^{-2}

$\dfrac{1}{4\pi\varepsilon_0} = 9 \times 10^9$ N m^2 C^{-2}

Mass of electron $(m_e) = 9.1 \times 10^{-31}$ kg

Mass of neutron $= 1.675 \times 10^{-27}$ kg

Mass of proton $= 1.673 \times 10^{-27}$ kg

Avogadro's number $= 6.023 \times 10^{23}$ per gram mole

Boltzmann constant $= 1.38 \times 10^{-23}$ JK^{-1}

1. What are permanent magnets? Give one example.

2. What is the geometrical shape of equipotential surfaces due to single isolated charge?

3. Which of the following waves can be polarized (i) Heat waves; (ii) Sound waves? Give reason to support your answer.

4. A capacitor has been charged by a dc source. What are the magnitudes of conduction and displacement currents, when it is fully charged?

5. Write the relationship between angle of incidence 'i', angle of prism 'A' and angle of minimum deviation for a triangular prism.

6. The given graph shows the variation of photoelectric current (I) versus applied voltage (V) for two different photosensitive materials and for two different intensities of the incident radiation. Identify the pairs of curves that correspond to different materials but same intensity of incident radiation.

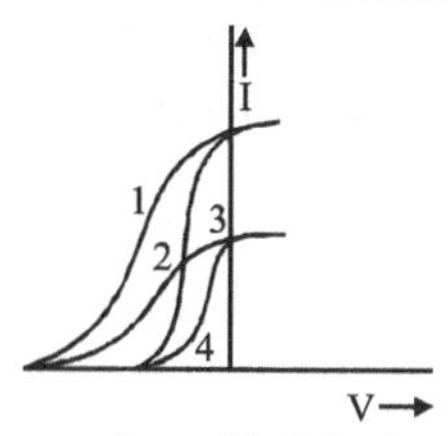

7. A 10 V battery of negligible internal resistance is connected across a 200 V battery and a resistance of 38 Ω as shown in the figure. Find the value of the current in the circuit.

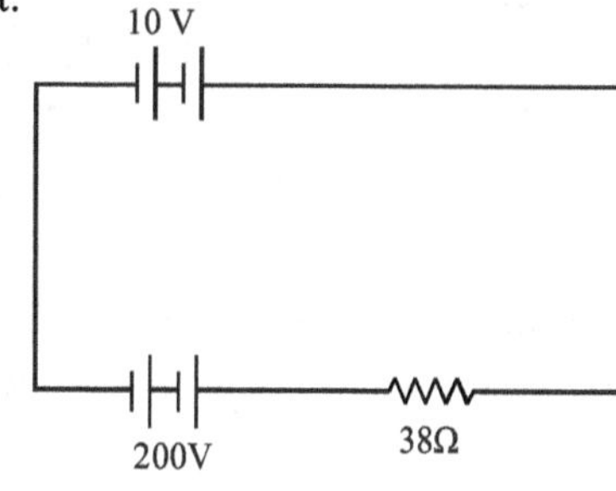

8. The emf of a cell is always greater than its terminal voltage. Why? Give reason.

9. (a) Write the necessary conditions for the phenomenon of total internal reflection to occur.

(b) Write the relation between the refractive index and critical angle for a given pair of optical media.

10. State Lenz's law.

A metallic rod held horizontally along east-west direction, is allowed to fall under gravity. Will there be an emf induced at its ends? Justify your answer.

11. A convex lens of focal length 25 cm is placed coaxially in contact with a concave lens of focal length 20 cm. Determine the power of the combination. Will the system be converging or diverging in nature?

12. An ammeter of resistance $0.80\ \Omega$ can measure current upto 1.0 A.

(i) What must be the value of shunt resistance to enable the ammeter to measure current upto 5.0 A?

(ii) What is the combined resistance of the ammeter and the shunt?

13. In the given circuit diagram, a voltmeter 'V' is connected across a lamp 'L'. How would (i) the brightness of the lamp and (ii) voltmeter reading 'V' be affected, if the value of resistance 'R' is decreased? Justify your answer.

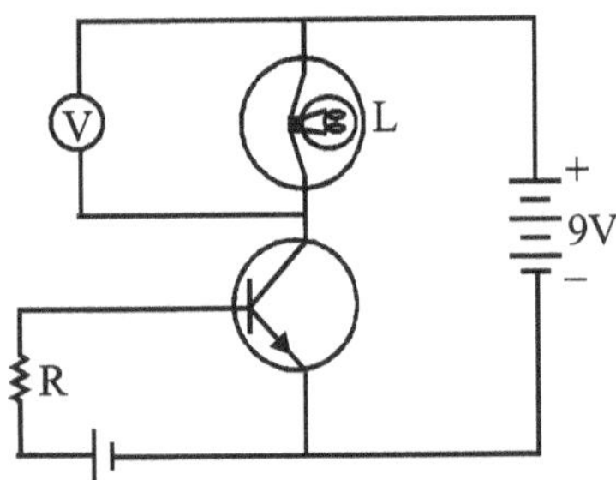

14. (a) An em wave is travelling in a medium with a velocity $\vec{v} = v\hat{i}$. Draw a sketch showing the propagation of the em wave, indicating the direction of the oscillating electric and magnetic fields.

(b) How are the magnitudes of the electric and magnetic fields related to the velocity of the em wave?

15. Block diagram of a receiver is shown in the figure :

(a) Identify 'X' and 'Y'

(b) Write their functions.

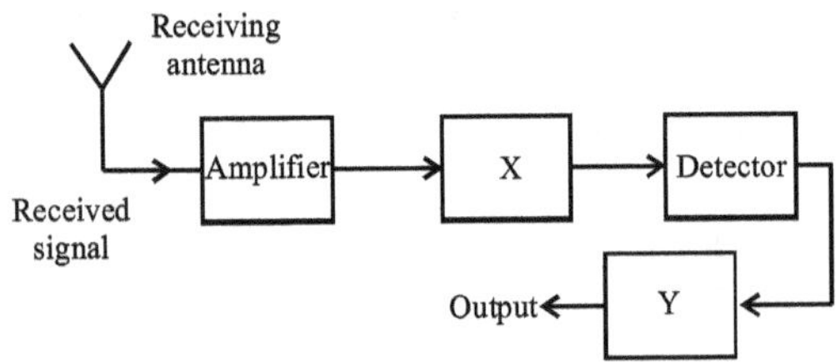

16. Explain, with the help of a circuit diagram, the working of a photo-diode. Write briefly how it is used to detect the optical signals.

OR

Mention the important considerations required while fabricating a p-n junction diode to be used as a Light Emitting Diode (LED). What should be the order of band gap of an LED if it is required to emit light in the visible range?

17. Write three important factors which justify the need of modulating a message signal. Show diagrammatically how an amplitude modulated wave is obtained when a modulating signal is superimposed on a carrier wave.

18. A capacitor of unknown capacitance is connected across a battery of V volts. The charge stored in it is 360 μC. When potential across the capacitor is reduced by 120 V, the charge stored in it becomes 120 μC.

Calculate :

(i) The potential V and the unknown capacitance C.

(ii) What will be the charge stored in the capacitor, if the voltage applied had increased by 120 V?

OR

A hollow cyindrical box of length 1 m and area of cross-section 25 cm^2 is placd in a three dimensional coordinate system as shown in the figure. The electric field in the region is given by $\vec{E} = 50\ x\hat{i}$, where E is in NC^{-1} and x is in metres.

Find :

(i) Net flux through the cylinder

(ii) Charge enclosed by the cylinder

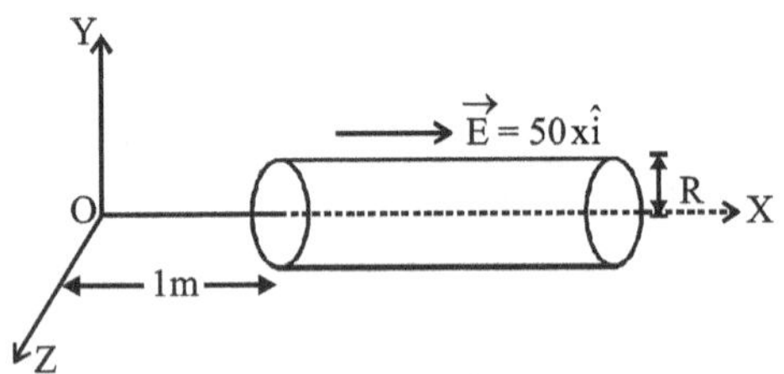

19. (a) In a typical nuclear reaction, e.g.

$$^2_1H + {}^2_1H \longrightarrow {}^3_2He + n + 3.27\ \text{MeV}$$

although number of nucleons is conserved, yet energy is released. How? Explain.

(b) Show that nuclear density in a given nucleus is independent of mass number A.

20. (a) Why photoelectric effect cannot be explain on the basis of wave nature of light? Give reasons.

(b) Write the basic features of photon picture of electromagnetic radiation on which Einstein's photoelectric equation is based.

21. A metallic rod length 'l' is rotated with a frequency ν with one end hinged at the centre and the other end at the circumference of a circular metallic ring of radius r, about an axis passing through the centre and perpendicular to the plane of the ring. A constant uniform magnetic field B parallel to the axis is present everywhere. Using Lorentz force, explain how emf is induced between the centre and the metallic ring and hence obtain the expression for it.

22. Output characteristics of an n-p-n transistor in CE configuration is shown in the figure. Determine :
- (i) dynamic output resistance
- (ii) dc current gain and
- (iii) ac current gain at an operating point $V_{CE} = 10V$, when $I_B = 30\,\mu A$

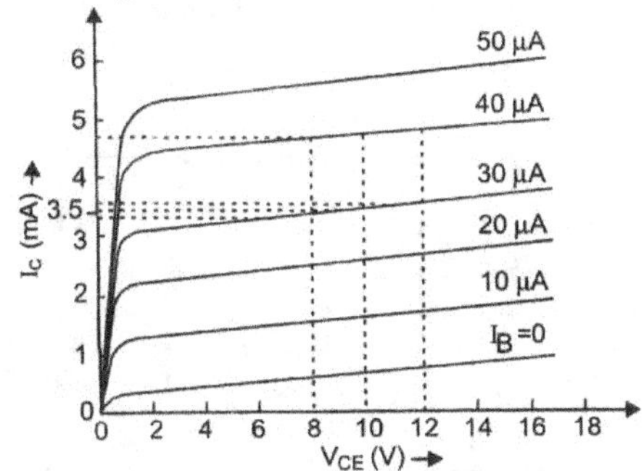

23. Using Bohr's postulates, obtain the expression for the total energy of the electron in the stationary states of the hydrogen atom. Hence, draw the energy level diagram showing how the line spectra corresponding to Balmer series occur due to transition between energy levels.

24. (a) In what way is diffraction from each slit related to the interference pattern in a double slit experiment?

(b) Two wavelengths of sodium light 590 nm and 596 nm are used, in turn, to study the diffraction taking place at a single slit of aperture 2×10^{-4} m. The distance between the slit and the screen is 1.5 m. Calculate the separation between the positions of the first maxima of the diffraction pattern obtained in the two cases.

25. In a series LCR circuit connected to an ac source of variable frequency and voltage $v = v_m \sin \omega t$, draw a plot showing the variation of current (I) with angular frequency (ω) for two different values of resistance R_1 and R_2 ($R_1 > R_2$). Write the condition under which the phenomenon of resonance occurs. For which value of the resistance out of the two curves, a sharper resonance is produced? Define Q-factor of the circuit and give its significance.

26. While travelling back to his residence in the car, Dr. Pathak was caught up in a thunderstorm. It became very dark. He stopped driving the car and waited for thunderstorm to stop. Suddenly he noticed a child walking alone on the road. He asked the boy to come inside the car till the thunderstorm stopped. Dr. Pathak dropped the boy at his residence. The boy insisted that Dr. Pathak should meet his parents. The parents expressed their gratitude to Dr. Pathak for his concern for safety of the child.

Answer the following questions based on the above information :
- (a) Why is it safer to sit inside a car during a thunderstorm?
- (b) Which two values are displayed by Dr. Pathak in his actions?
- (c) Which values are reflected in parents response to Dr. Pathak?
- (d) Give an example of a similar action on your part in the past from everyday life.

27. (a) Draw a ray diagram showing the image formation by a compound microscope. Hence obtain expression for total magnification when the image is formed at infinity?

(b) Distinguish between myopia and hypermetropia. Show diagrammatically how these defects can be corrected.

OR

(a) State Huygen's principle. Using this principle draw a diagram to show how a plane wave front incident at the interface of the two media gets refracted when it propagates from a rarer to a denser medium. Hence verify Snell's law of refraction.

(b) When monochromatic light travels form a rarer to a denser medium, explain the following, giving reasons :
- (i) Is the frequency of reflected and refracted light same as the frequency of incident light?
- (ii) Does the decrease in speed imply a reduction in the energy carried by light wave?

28. (a) State the working principle of a potentiometer. With the help of the circuit diagram, explain how a potentiometer is used to compare the emf's of two primary cells. Obtain the required expression used for comparing the emfs.

(b) Write two possible causes for one sided deflection in a potentiometer experiment.

OR

(a) State Kirchhoff's rules for an electric network. Using Kirchhoff's rules, obtain the balance condition in terms of the resistances of four arms of Wheatstone bridge.

(b) In the meterbridge experimental set up, shown in the figure, the null point 'D' is obtained at a distance of 40 cm from end A of the meterbridge wire. If a resistance of 10 Ω is connected in series with R_1, null point is obtained at AD = 60 cm. Calculate the values of R_1 and R_2.

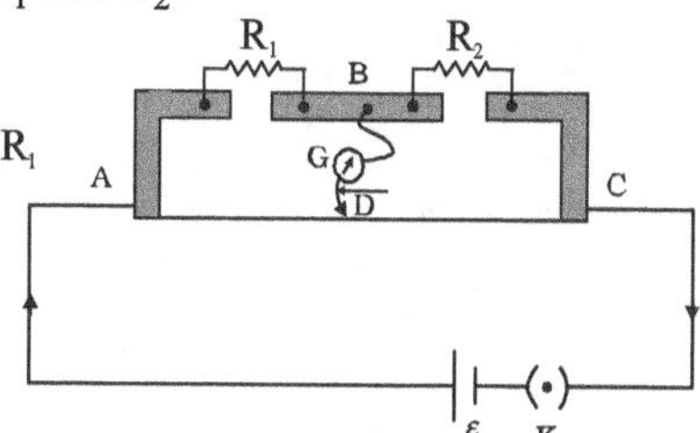

29. (a) Derive the expression for the torque on the rectangular current carrying loop suspended in a uniform magnetic field.

(b) A proton and a deuteron having equal momenta enter in a region of uniform magnetic field at right angle to the direction of the field. Depict their trajectories in the field.

OR

(a) A small compass needle of magnetic moment 'm' is free to turn about an axis perpendicular to the direction of uniform magnetic field 'B'. The moment of inertia of the needle about the axis is 'I'. The needle is slightly disturbed from its stable position and then released. Prove that it executes simple harmonic motion. Hence deduce the expression for its time period.

(b) A compass needle, free to turn in a vertical plane orients itself with its axis vertical at a certain place on the earth. Find out the values of (i) horizontal component of earth's magnetic field and (ii) angle of dip at the place.

Solutions

1. The magnets which have high retentivity and high coercivity are called permanent magnets. Example - steel.

(½ + ½ = 1 Mark)

2. Spherical. (1 Mark)

3. Heat waves can be polarized as they are electromagnetic and transverse in nature. (½ + ½ = 1 Mark)

4. The magnitudes of both conduction and displacement currents are zero. Displacement current flows only when the capacitor is being charged. A capacitor is a complete block for a dc source. **(1 Mark)**

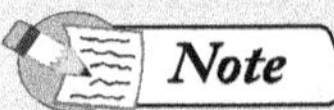

Conduction current $i_c = \dfrac{dQ}{dt}$

Displacement current $i_d = \varepsilon_0 \dfrac{d\phi_E}{dt}$

where Q = charge on the plates of capacitor

ϕ_e = *electric flux between the plates of capacitor.*

From Gauss law

$$\phi_E = \frac{Q}{\varepsilon_0}$$

$$\frac{d\phi_E}{dt} = \frac{1}{\varepsilon_0}\left(\frac{dQ}{dt}\right)$$

When capacitor is fully charged then,

$$\frac{dQ}{dt} = 0 \quad \Rightarrow \quad \frac{d\phi_E}{dt} = 0$$

$$\therefore \qquad i_c = 0 \text{ and } i_d = 0$$

5. The required relation is

$$i = \frac{A + D_{min}}{2}$$

where, D_{min} = angle of minimum deviation **(1 Mark)**

6. The pairs of curves (1 and 3) and (2 and 4) represent different materials because stopping potential is different for different materials. (½ + ½ = 1 Mark)

7. As the positive terminals are connected to opposite ends of the resistor, they send the current in opposite directions.

Hence, the net emf = 200 − 10 = 190 V (½ + ½ = 1 Mark)

$$\therefore \text{ Current in the circuit } I = \frac{V}{R} = \frac{190\,V}{38\,\Omega} = 5\,A$$

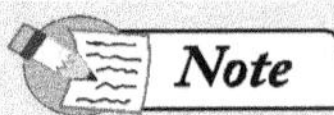

Applying Kirchhoff's law in 100p we get

10 + 38 i − 200 = 0

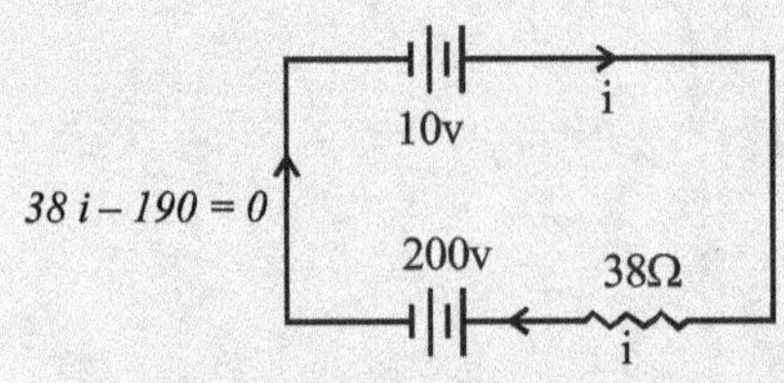

$$\therefore i = \frac{190v}{38\Omega} = 5A$$

8. Every cell has a characteristic emf E and some internal resistance. When the cell is in a closed circuit, a current flows through the cell. As a result some potential drop takes place inside the cell. The terminal voltage V = E − ir, clearly, V < E. **(1 Mark)**

9. (a) The necessary conditions for the phenomenon of total internal reflection to occur are :

   (i) The light rays must pass from the denser medium to rarer medium.

   (ii) The angle of incidence in the denser medium must be greater than the critical angle i_c.

(½ + ½ = 1 Mark)

   (b) If $^a\mu_b$ is the refractive index of the denser medium (b) w.r.t. the rarer medium (a) and i_c be the critical angle, then **(1 Mark)**

$$^a\mu_b = \frac{1}{\sin i_c}$$

10. (i) **Lenz's law :** Whenever the magnetic flux linked with a circuit changes, an induced emf is produced and the direction of the induced current is such that it opposes the cause which produces it. **(1 Mark)**

   (ii) Yes, emf will be induced in the metallic rod because there will be a change of magnetic flux. The metallic rod will cut the magnetic field lines of the earth's magnetic field. (½ + ½ = 1 Mark)

Faraday's law of electromagnetic induction is

$$\varepsilon = \frac{-d\phi_B}{dt}$$

ϕ_B = *magnetic flux*

ε = *induced emf.*

So, whenever flux changes through any conducting body an emf will be induced.

11. Given : focal length of convex lens

$$f_1 = 25 \text{ cm} = 25 \times 10^{-2}\text{m} \qquad \textbf{(½ Mark)}$$

focal length of concave lens

$$f_2 = -20 \text{ cm} = -20 \times 10^{-2}\text{m}$$

Let P_1 and P_2 be the powers of the two lenses, then

$$P_1 = \frac{100}{25} = 4D \text{ and } P_2 = \frac{-100}{20} = -5D$$

$$\left(\because P = \frac{1}{f\,(\text{in metre})}\right) \qquad \textbf{(½ Mark)}$$

$\therefore$ Power of the combination

$$P = P_1 + P_2 = 4D - 5D = -1D \qquad \textbf{(½ Mark)}$$

–ve sign shows that the combination is diverging in nature.

$$\textbf{(½ Mark)}$$

12. Given : $G = 0.80\,\Omega$, $I_g = 1.0\,A$

$I = 5.0\,A$, $S = ?$

From formula

(i) $\quad S = \dfrac{GI_g}{I - I_g} = \dfrac{0.8 \times 1}{5 - 1} = 0.2\,\Omega \qquad \textbf{(1 Mark)}$

(ii)   Combined resistance of the ammeter and shunt(R)

$$\frac{1}{R} = \frac{1}{G} + \frac{1}{S} \text{ or } R = \frac{G \times S}{G + S} \qquad \textbf{(1 Mark)}$$

$$= \frac{0.8 \times 0.2}{0.8 + 0.2} = 0.16\,\Omega$$

13. If the value of resistance R decreases, the input circuit will become more forward biased, decreasing the base current I_B, increasing emitter current I_E hence increases collector current I_C as

$$I_E = I_B + I_C \qquad \textbf{(1 Mark)}$$

(i)   as I_C increases which passes through the lamp so brightness of the lamp increases.

(ii)   the reading of voltmeter will also increase.

14. (a)   From $\vec{V} = V\hat{i}$, it is clear that the wave is propagating along the x-axis. The direction of electric field is along the y-axis and that of the magnetic field along the z-axis as shown below.

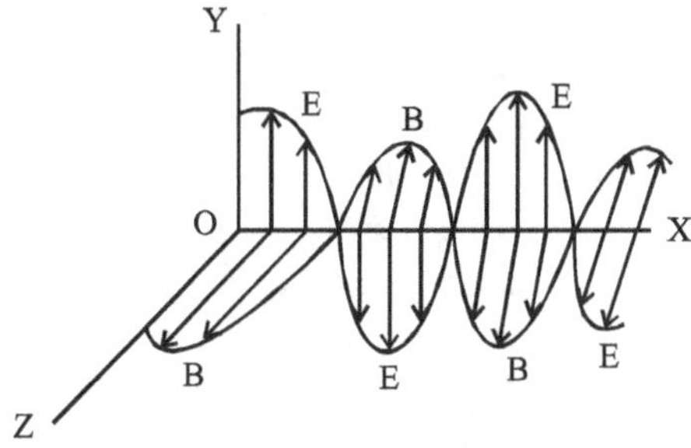

$$\textbf{(1 + ½ = 1½ Marks)}$$

(b)   The required relation between magnitude of electric field E_0 and magnitude of magnetic field B_0 is

$$\frac{E_0}{B_0} = C \qquad \textbf{(½ Mark)}$$

where c = speed of light (em wave)

15. (a)   X is an I.F. stage and Y is an amplifier. **(½ + ½ = 1 Mark)**

(b)   **Function of 'X' I.F. stage :** It is usually used to lower the frequency of the carrier waves to a lower frequency.
'Y' Amplifier : To amplify the detected signal before giving to the output device.   **(½ + ½ = 1 Mark)**

16. The circuit diagram of a photodiode is as shown in the fig.

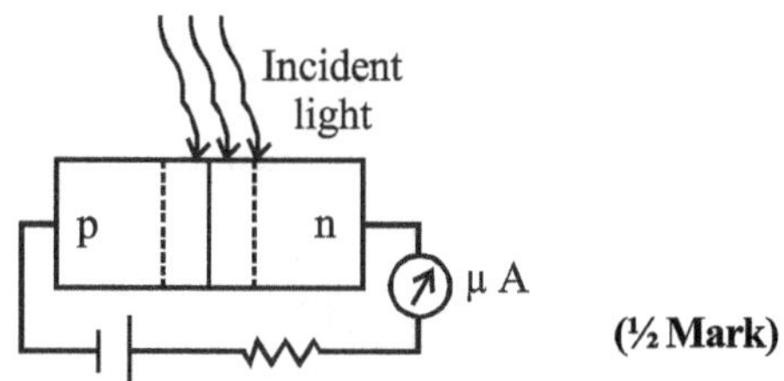

$$\textbf{(½ Mark)}$$

Working : A photodiode is always reverse biased. It conducts only when incident light photons having energy greater than the energy gap of a photodiode are incident on it.   **(1½ Mark)**

Reverse voltage is kept a little below the breakdown voltage. Now, light of frequency v is allowed to fall on the junction. If the energy of the incident photon is greater than the forbidden gap of the semiconductor, then electrons from the valence band start moving to the conduction band and current through the resistance increases.

The current depends upon the intensity of the incident light. The current in the photodiode is thus a measure of the intensity of the incident light.   **(½ Mark)**

OR

The **important considerations** for a p–n junction are :

(i)   Low power consumption.

(ii)   Light emitted should be visible and preferably monochromatic.   **(1 Mark)**

(iii)   Quick response.

(iv)   Low working voltage.

The order of band gap of an LED required to emit light in the visible range is 3eV to 1.8 ev.   **(1 Mark)**

17. The three important factors which justify the need of modulating a message signal are :

(i)   **Size of the antenna :** For transmitting a signal we require an antenna whose size should have a size comparable to the wavelength of the signal $\left(\sim \dfrac{\lambda}{4}\right)$.

Therefore, for large wavelengths signal, the size of antenna is very large.   **(½ + ½ + ½ = 1½ Marks)**

(ii) Effective power radiated by antenna : It is inversely proportional to λ^2. i.e. $p \propto \dfrac{l}{\lambda^2}$. So for large wavelength power radiated by antenna will be very less.

(iii) Mixing up of signals : If a number of transmitter transmit base band signal simultaneously then all these signal cover the same frequency range and will get mixed up. To avoid it, the transmission should be done at high frequency. This provides an adequate band width.

Amplitude Modulated Wave

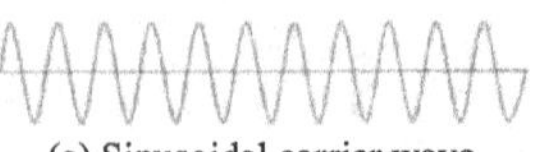

(a) Sinusoidal carrier wave

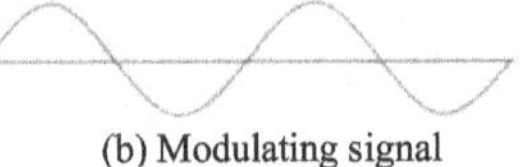

(b) Modulating signal

(c) Amplitude modulation   **(½ Mark)**

18. **(i)** Charge stored in the capacitor = CV

From question,

$Q = CV = 360 \times 10^{-6}$ ...(i)   **(½ Mark)**

$C(V - 120) = 120 \times 10^{-6}$ ...(ii)

Dividing eq. (i) by (ii)

$$\frac{V}{V-120} = 3$$

$\Rightarrow \quad V = 3V - 360$

$\Rightarrow \quad 2V = 360$

$\therefore \quad V = 180\,V$

Voltage V of the capacitor is 180 V   **(½ Mark)**

and unknown capacitance $C = \dfrac{Q}{V}$

$$= \frac{360 \times 10^{-6}}{180} = 2 \times 10^{-6}\,F$$ **(½ Mark)**

(ii) When the voltage across the capacitor increases by 120 V, the new voltage will be $180\,V + 120\,V = 300\,V$

Therefore, new charge stored in the capacitor

$Q' = CV' = 300 \times 2 \times 10^{-6} = 600\,\mu C$ **(1 Mark)**

OR

(i) From question, it is clear that the electric field $\vec{E} = 50\,x\hat{i}$

is directed along the x-axis. Hence, there is no electric flux through the curved surface.

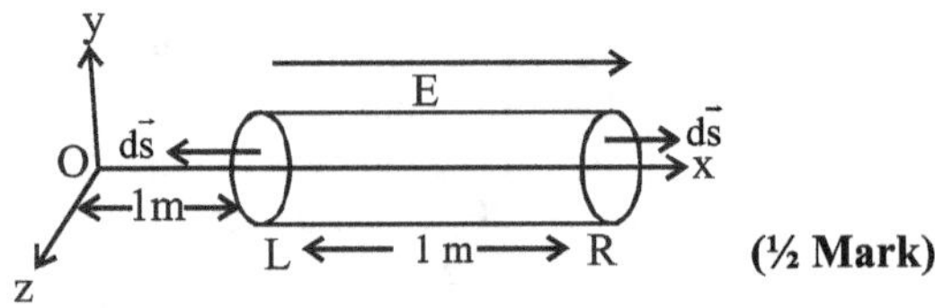

    (½ Mark)

Electric field on the left face of the cylinder,

$$E = 50\,\hat{i} \quad (\because x = 1\,m)$$

$\therefore$ Electric flux through this face

angle between E and ds is $180°$

So, $\phi_1 = \oint \vec{E}\cdot\overrightarrow{ds} = -E \times A$ $(\because \cos 180 = -1)$

$$= 50 \times 25 \times 10^{-4}\,m^2 \quad (\because A = 25\,cm^2)$$
$$= -0.125\,NC^{-1}\,m^2$$

Electric flux through the other face   **(½ Mark)**

angle between E and ds is $0°$.

So, $\phi_2 = E \times A \quad \left(\because E = 50\,\hat{i},\ x = 2\,m\right) \cos 0 = 1$

$$= 100 \times 25 \times 10^{-4}$$
$$= 0.25\,NC^{-1}\,m^2$$

Net flux through the cylinder $= \phi_1 + \phi_2$ **(1 Mark)**

$$= 0.25 - 0.125\,NC^{-1}m^2$$
$$= 0.125\,NC^{-1}\,m^2$$

(ii) Let q be the charge enclosed by the cylinder. According to Gauss's theorem

$$\phi = \frac{q}{\epsilon_0}$$

$\therefore \quad q = \phi\,\epsilon_0$

$$= 0.125 \times 8.854 \times 10^{-12}\,C$$ **(1 Mark)**
$$= 1.11 \times 10^{-12}\,C$$

19. **(a)** In the nuclear reaction, for example

$$_{1}^{2}H + _{1}^{2}H \longrightarrow _{2}^{3}He + _{0}n^{1} + 3.27\,MeV$$

Total number of nucleons is conserved.

i.e., number of neutrons + protons of the reactants is equal to the number of neutrons + protons of the products.

But the sum of the masses of the reactants and the sum of the masses of the products is not the same *i.e.*, there is some mass defect (Δm). Energy equivalent to the mass defect is released in the nuclear reaction.   **(1 Mark)**

According to Einstein's mass energy equivalence relation,

$$\Delta E = \Delta mc^2$$

(b) Let A be the mass number and R the radius of the nucleus.

Then mass of the nucleus = A amu

$$M = A \times 1.6 \times 10^{-27} \text{ kg}$$ 　　**(1 Mark)**

Now, 　$R = R_0 A^{1/3}$

where R_0 is a constant whose numerical value is (1.2×10^{-15})

∴ Volume of the nucleus which is considered spherical

$$= \frac{4}{3}\pi R^3 = \frac{4}{3}\pi R_0^3 A$$

∴ Density of the nucleus

$$= \frac{M}{V} = \frac{A \times 1.6 \times 10^{-27} \text{ kg} \times 3}{4 \times 3.14 \times \left(1.2 \times 10^{-15}\right)^3 \times A}$$ 　　**(1 Mark)**

$$= 2.2 \times 10^{17} \text{ kg m}^{-3}$$

which is independent of A.

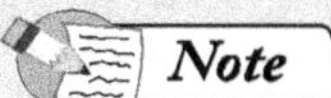 *Note*

If student does not remember the values of all the constant used in solution, then there is another way to approach the solution.

$$R = R_0 A^{1/3}$$

Density $\rho = \dfrac{\text{mass}}{\text{volume}}$

volume $v = \dfrac{4}{3}\pi R^3$

$$= \frac{4}{3}\pi \left[R_0 (A)^{1/3} \right]^3 = \frac{4}{3}\pi R_0^3 A$$

∴ 　$\rho = \dfrac{A}{\dfrac{4}{3}\pi R_0^3 A}$ 　$\rho = \dfrac{3}{4\pi R_0^3}$ *which is a constant.*

20. (a) When light wave is incident on photoelectric material, the photoelectrons should be emitted (after a long time) if work function is large. But no photoelectron is emitted by incident radiations if the frequency is less than the threshold frequency. The energy of the ejected electrons also has no relevance with the intensity of incident light, although according to the wave nature, it should be there. If the light is incident for a longer interval of light, the energy should also have increased. That is why photoelectric effect is not explained on the basis of wave nature of light. 　**(1½ Marks)**

(b) Basic features of photon picture :
　(i)　A photon of frequency ν is a packet of energy $E = h\nu$, where h is a planck's constant.
　(ii)　While interacting with matter photons behave as if they are all particles.

(iii)　All photons travel in vacuum with the same velocity. However, their velocity in different media is different. 　**(1½ Marks)**

(iv)　There is no charge on a photon. They are not deflected by electric and magnetic fields.

(v)　The energy of a photon does not depend upon the intensity of radiation.

(vi)　When it interacts with a photoelectric material, it is completely absorbed and loses its identity.

(vii)　Its collisions with the electron in the photoelectric material is elastic i.e., total energy and momentum are conserved during the collision.

 *Note*

Einstein's photoelectric equation is
　$h\nu = \phi_0 + K.E_{max}$
where $h\nu$ *= photon's energy*
　ϕ_0 *= work function of metal*
$K.E_{max}$ *= maximum K.E. of photoelectrons.*

21. Let there be a metallic rod of length l whose one end is hinged at the centre O of the metallic ring of radius r and other end at point A on the circumference of the ring.

　　　　　　　　　　　　　　　　(½ Mark)

When rod revolves (in anti-clock wise) direction, free electrons in the rod move towards the outer end due to Lorentz force and get distributed over the ring (Direction from fleming's right hand rule). This results in the production of an induced emf across the ends of the rod in the steady state when there is no further flow of electrons. Let us consider a small element at a distance x from the centre O. The small induced emf produced across this element.

　　　　　　　　　　　　　　　　(1 Mark)

$de = Bv\,dx$ where v is the velocity of the element at a distance x.
∴ The emf produced across the length of the conductor i.e., between centre O and circumference of the ring is

$$e = \int_0^r Bv\,dx$$

If ω is the angular frequency of the rod, then
$$v = x\,\omega$$

∴ 　　$$e = \int_0^r Bx\,\omega\,dx = B\omega \cdot \left[\frac{x^2}{2} \right]_0^r$$

or 　　$$e = \frac{1}{2} B\omega r^2$$

Also, 　$e = \dfrac{1}{2} B . 2\pi\nu\,r^2$ 　$(\because \omega = 2\pi\nu)$ 　**(1½ Marks)**
　　　　$= \pi B\nu r^2$

22. From the characteristics curve,

(i) dynamic output resistance

$$R_0 = \frac{\Delta V_{CE}}{\Delta I_C} = \frac{12-10}{(3.6-3.5)\times 10^{-3}} = \frac{2}{10^{-4}}$$

(1 + 1 + 1 = 3 Marks)

$$= 2 \times 10^4 = 20000\,\Omega = 20\,k\Omega$$

(ii) dc current gain $= \dfrac{I_C}{I_B} = \dfrac{3.5\times 10^{-3}}{30\times 10^{-6}}$

$$= \frac{3.5}{30}\times 10^3 = 1.17\times 10^2 = 117$$

(iii) ac current gain at ($V_{CE} = 10\,V$)

$$= \frac{\Delta I_C}{\Delta I_B} = \frac{(4.6-3.5)\times 10^{-3}}{(40-30)\times 10^{-6}}$$

$$= \frac{1.1}{10}\times 10^3 = 110$$

23. Let there be an electron of mass m carrying a charge e revolving around a nucleus of hydrogen atom carrying a charge +e. Let r_n be the radius of nth the orbit and v_n the speed of the electron. The electrostatic force supplies the centripetel force required to revolve the electron

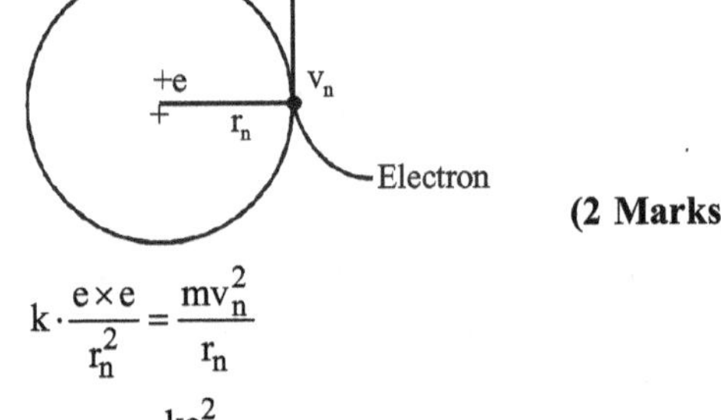

(2 Marks)

$$\therefore \quad k\cdot\frac{e\times e}{r_n^2} = \frac{mv_n^2}{r_n}$$

$$\therefore \quad r_n = \frac{ke^2}{mv_n^2} \qquad \dots(1)$$

Also $\quad mv_n^2 = \dfrac{ke^2}{r_n} \qquad \dots(2)$

According to Bohr's postulates only those orbits are allowed in which angular momentum is quantised, therefore,

$$mv_n r_n = n\frac{h}{2\pi}$$

$$\therefore \quad v_n = \frac{nh}{2\pi\, mr_n} \qquad \dots(3)$$

Putting this value of v_n in eq. (1), we have

$$r_n = \frac{ke^2 \times 4\pi^2 m^2 r_n^2}{mn^2 h^2}$$

$$\therefore \quad r_n = \frac{n^2 h^2}{4\pi^2 ke^2 m}$$

i.e., $\quad r_n \propto n^2$

Energy of the electron : The revolving electron possesses both kinetic and potential energy.

$\therefore \quad$ Total energy $= KE + PE$

$$= \frac{1}{2}mv_n^2 - k\frac{e^2}{r_n} = \frac{1}{2}\frac{ke^2}{r_n} - \frac{ke^2}{r_n}$$

$$\text{T.E.} = -\frac{ke^2}{2r_n} = -\frac{ke^2}{2n^2 h^2}\cdot 4\pi^2 ke^2 m$$

$$\text{TE} = -\frac{2\pi^2 k^2 e^4 m}{n^2 h^2}$$

By putting the values of the various constant, we get

$$\text{TE} = \frac{-13.6}{n^2}\,eV$$

Energy level diagram : The Balmer series is produced when transition take place from higher orbits to n = 2 as shown in the figure.

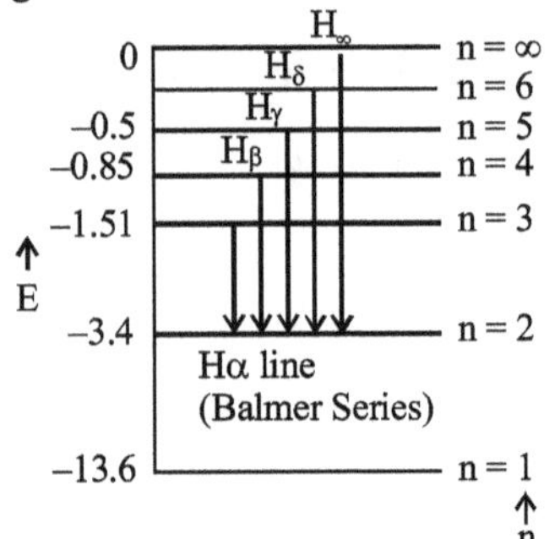

(1 Marks)

> **Note**
>
> *Bohr model is valid only for hydrogenic atom i.e., atoms consisting of a nucleus with positive charge +Ze and a single electron, example - hydrogen, singly ionised helium, doubly ionised lithium.*
> *Total energy when nucleus has a charge Ze would be*
> $$T.E. = -Z\frac{2\pi^2 k^2 e^4 m}{n^2 h^2}$$

24. (a) In double slit experiment an interference pattern is observed by waves from two slits but as each slit provide a diffraction pattern of its own, thus the intensity of interference pattern in Young's double slit experiment is modified by diffraction pattern of each slit. **(1 Mark)**

(b) Given : $a = 2\times 10^{-4}\,m$, $D = 1.5\,m$, $\lambda_1 = 590\,nm = 590\times 10^{-9}\,m$, $\lambda_2 = 596\,nm = 596\times 10^{-9}\,m$

Position of maxima is $\quad y = (2n+1)\dfrac{D\lambda}{Za}$

For $\quad n = 1$

$$y = \frac{3}{2}\frac{D\lambda}{a}$$

$\therefore \quad y_1 = \dfrac{3}{2}\dfrac{D}{a}\lambda_1$ and $y_2 = \dfrac{3}{2}\dfrac{D}{a}\lambda_2$ **(1 Mark)**

$\therefore \quad$ Separation between the positions of the first maxima

$$= y_2 - y_1 = \frac{3}{2}\frac{D}{a}(\lambda_2 - \lambda_1)$$

$$= \frac{3}{2}\times\frac{1.5}{2\times 10^{-4}}\times(596-590)\times 10^{-9}$$

$$= \frac{3}{2} \times \frac{1.5}{2 \times 10^{-4}} \times 6 \times 10^{-9}$$

$$= 6.75 \times 10^{-5} \text{ m} \qquad \textbf{(1 Mark)}$$

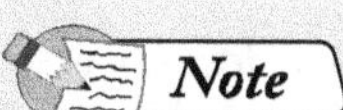

Note

To obtain first maxima, phase difference

$$a \sin \theta = (2n+1)\frac{\lambda}{2},$$

for $\qquad n = 1$

$$a \sin \theta = 3\frac{\lambda}{2}$$

or $\qquad a \cdot \frac{y}{D} = 3\frac{\lambda}{2}$

$$\Rightarrow \qquad y = \frac{3}{2}\lambda \frac{D}{a}$$

25. In a series LCR circuit, the impedance of the circuit is given

by $Z = \sqrt{\left(L\omega - \dfrac{1}{c\omega}\right)^2 + R^2}$, where ω is the angular

frequency. Clearly, as ω varies Z also varies and hence the current also varies. At a certain frequency (resonant frequency) $\omega = \omega_0$, Z becomes minimum and the current becomes maximum. This is the condition of resonance. Z is

minimum when $L\omega_0 = \dfrac{1}{C\omega_0}$. $\qquad$ **(1 Mark)**

$$Z_{min} = R$$

Plot showing variation of current with frequency:

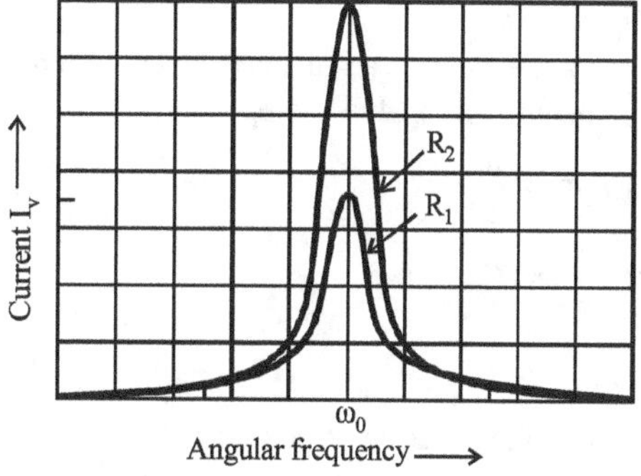

$\qquad\qquad\qquad\qquad\qquad\qquad$ **(1 Mark)**

Current at resonance

$$i_v = \frac{E_v}{Z} = \frac{E_v}{R} \quad \left(\text{as } L\omega_0 = \frac{1}{C\omega_0} \right)$$

Smaller the value of R, sharper the resonance curve. Q-factor of the circuit is defined as the ratio of inductive reactance at resonance to the resistance R in the circuit

$$i.e., \qquad Q = \frac{L\omega_0}{R} = \frac{1}{C\omega_0 R} \quad i.e., \ Q \propto \frac{1}{R}$$

Significance of Q-factor : The Q-factor of an LCR circuit is a measure of the sharpness of the resonance. Larger the value of Q-factor sharper is the resonance curve. **(1 Mark)**

26. (a) It is because the charge so electric field inside the conducting hollow car is zero. It is electrostatic shielding. $\qquad$ **(1 + 1 + 1 + 1 = 4 Marks)**

(b) (i) Concern about the safety of the child.

(ii) Knowledgeable, open mindedness and humanity

(c) Intellectual, obliged

(d) One day I saw a blind man was trying to cross the road. I stopped my bike took him on my bike and dropped him to his house.

27. (a) Diagram of compound microscope: $\qquad\qquad$ **(1 Mark)**

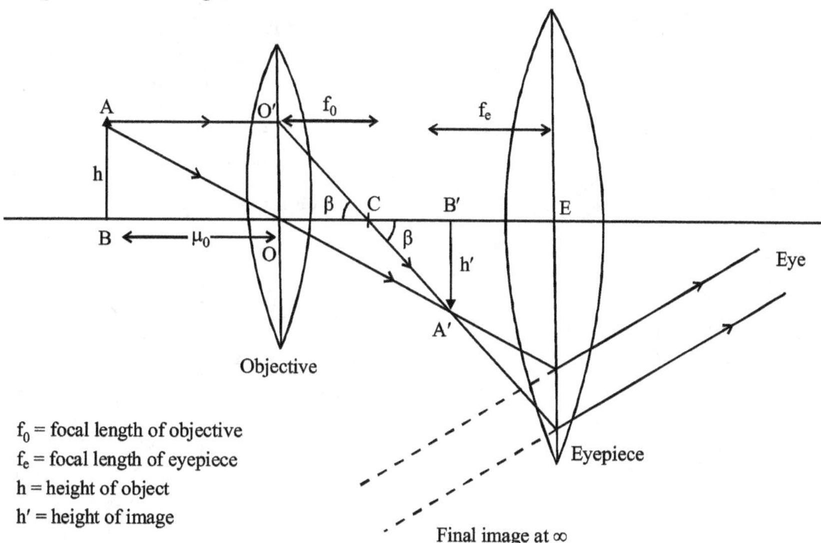

Expression of magnification when image is at infinity

Total magnification of compound microscope m is given as $\qquad\qquad$ **(2 Marks)**

$m = m_0 \times m_e$

where m_0 = magnification due to objective lens

m_e = magnification due to eyepiece.

Now, $m_0 = \dfrac{h'}{h}$.

From $\Delta OO'C$ $\quad \tan\beta = \dfrac{h}{f_0}$

From $\Delta CB'A'$ $\quad \tan\beta = \dfrac{h'}{L}$

where L = distance between f_0 and f_e

$\therefore \ \tan\beta = \dfrac{h}{f_0} = \dfrac{h'}{L} \ \Rightarrow \ \dfrac{h'}{h} = \dfrac{L}{f_0}$

So, $m_0 = \dfrac{h'}{h} = \dfrac{L}{f_0}$ $\qquad$ ...(i)

Since eyepiece act as simple microscope, angular magnification of eyepiece m_e is given as:-

$$m_e = \dfrac{D}{f_e} \qquad \text{...(ii)}$$

when final image is at infinity.

From (i) and (ii)

$$\boxed{m = \left(\dfrac{L}{f_0}\right)\left(\dfrac{D}{f_e}\right)}$$

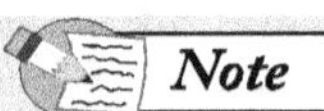

Note

When final image is at v = – D then,

$$m = \dfrac{L}{f_0}\left(1 + \dfrac{D}{f_e}\right)$$

The magnification is given by the expression.

$$M = \dfrac{\text{angle subtended by image } \beta}{\text{angle subtended by object } \alpha}$$

From triangles A'B'C' and A"C'Q as shown in figure, we have

$$\tan\alpha = \dfrac{QA''}{C'A''} = \dfrac{AB}{C'A''}$$

and $\qquad \tan\beta = \dfrac{A''B''}{C'A''}$

As angles are small

$\therefore \ \tan\alpha = \alpha \ \text{ and } \tan\beta = \beta$

$\therefore \ \alpha = \dfrac{AB}{C'A''} \text{ and } \beta = \dfrac{A''B''}{C'A''}$

Substituting values of α and β we get

$$M = \dfrac{\beta}{\alpha} = \dfrac{A''B''}{C'B''} \times \dfrac{C'B''}{AB} = \dfrac{A''B''}{A'B'} \times \dfrac{A'B'}{AB}$$

$$= m_0 \times m_e$$

where $m_e = \dfrac{A''B''}{A'B'}$ *and* $m_0 = \dfrac{A'B'}{AB}$

Now, we know that $m_e = 1 + \dfrac{D}{f_e}$, *and* $m_0 = \dfrac{v_0}{u_0}$

Therefore, the expression of magnification produced by compound microscope when the image is formed at infinity

(b) **Myopia :**

(i) A person suffering from this defect can see nearby objects clearly but cannot see the far away objects clearly.

(ii) Eyeball is longer than normal

(iii) The focal length of the lens decreases so, insufficient to produce a clearly formed image on the retina.

Myopia can be corrected with a diverging or concave lens as shown below :

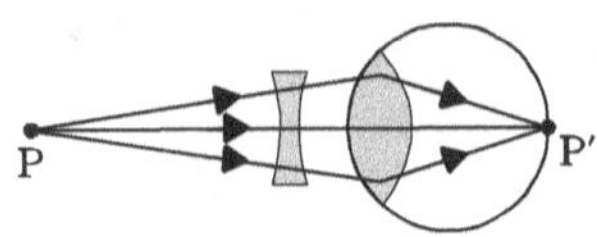

(1 + 1 = 2 Marks)

Hypermetropia :

(i) A person suffering from this defect can see distant objects clearly but cannot see nearby objects clearly.

(ii) Eyeball is too short

(iii) The ciliary muscle is unable to change the shape of the lens enough to properly focus the image i.e., the focal length of the lens increases.

Hypermetropia can be corrected with a converging or convex lens as shown below :

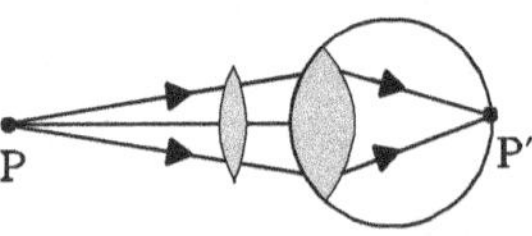

OR

(a) **Huygens Principle:-** Huygen's principle tells how a wavefront propagates through medium. According to the principle, each point on a wavefront is a source of secondary waves, which add up to give a wavefront at any later time.

Let surface PP' separating a rarer medium of refractive index n_1 from a denser medium of refractive index n_2. c_1 and c_2 be the values of velocity of light in the two media. A plane wavefront AB incident on PP' at an angle i. **(1 + 1 = 2 Marks)**

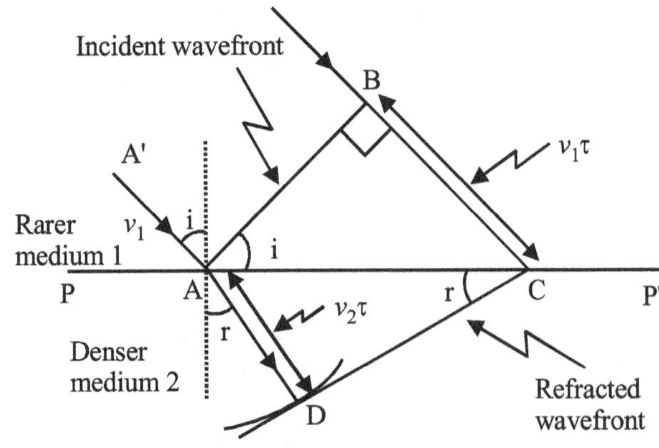

$v_2 < v_1$

According to Huygen's principle, point A meanwhile begins to act as secondary source of light and secondary wavelets from it will cover a distance c_2t in seconds medium in time t. Draw a circular arc with A as centre and c_2t as radius and draw a tangent CD from point C on this arc. Then CD is the refracted wave front. The refracted wave front subtends an angle r from surface PP'.

Now, from $\triangle ABC$

$$\sin i = \frac{BC}{AC} = \frac{c_1t}{AC}$$

and from $\triangle ADC$

$$\sin r = \frac{AD}{AC} = \frac{c_2t}{AC}$$

Therefore, $\dfrac{\sin i}{\sin r} = \dfrac{c_1t/AC}{c_2t/AC} = \dfrac{c_1}{c_2} = \dfrac{n_2}{n_1}$ **(1 Mark)**

This verify Snell's law of refraction.

(b) (i) Yes, when monochromatic light suffers reflection or refraction, there is no change in frequency although the velocity of light changes. The velocity of light decreases as light travels from rarer to denser medium.

(ii) No, because the energy of the wave do not depend on speed however it depends upon its frequency which remains the same. **(1 + 1 = 2 Marks)**

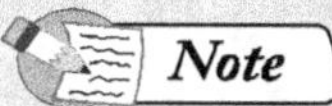

Note

Frequency of em waves depends only on the source producing the wave. Thus it does not change with medium.
However to keep the frequency constant, wavelength and velocity of light changes when light enters a certain medium.

$$v\lambda = \upsilon$$
$\upsilon\ = velocity\ of\ em\ waves$
$v\ = frequency$
$\lambda\ = wavelength$

28. (a) **Working principle of a potentiometer :** The basic principle of a potentiometer is that when a constant current flows through a wire of uniform cross-section, the potential drop across any length of the wire is directly proportional to that length. **(1 Mark)**

Circuit diagram for comparing the emfs of two cells :

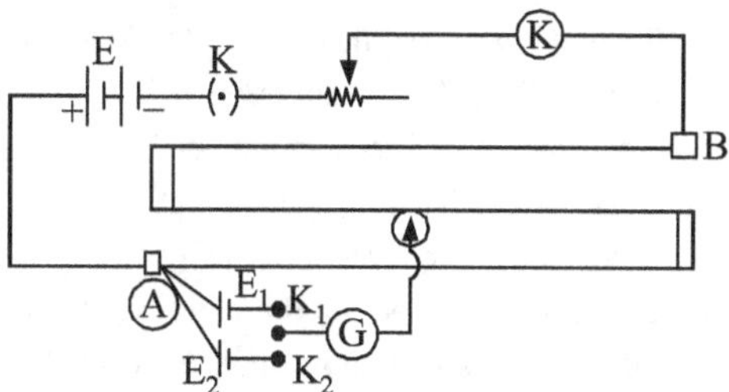

(1 Mark)

When the key K_1, is closed, the galvanometer is connected to the cell of emf E_1 in the circuit. The jockey is moved on the wire to obtain a balance point, *i.e.*, a point on the wire where the galvanometer gives zero deflection. Let the balancing length be L_1. Therefore, by the potentiometer principle,

$$E_1 \propto L_1 \qquad \text{...(i)}$$

Now, the key K_2 is closed. The galvanometer is connected to the cell of emf E_2 in the circuit. The jockey is again moved on the wire to obtain the balance point. Let the balancing length be L_2. Then by potentiometer principle,

$$E_2 \propto L_2 \qquad \text{...(ii)}$$

Dividing equation (i) by (ii),

$$\frac{E_1}{E_2} = \frac{L_1}{L_2} \qquad \text{...(iii)}$$

This is the required expression for comparing emf's **(1 Mark)**

Knowing the values of L_1 and L_2, the emf's of the cells can be compared.

(b) Two possible causes for one sided deflection in a potentiometer experiment.

(i) +ve ends of all the cells are not connected to the same end of the wire. **(1 + 1 = 2 Marks)**

(ii) The emf of the cell connected to the main is less than the emf's of cells whose emf's have to be compared.

OR

(a) **Kirchhoff's first rule or junction rule :** The algebraic sum of currents meeting at a junction in a closed circuit is zero.

i.e., $\qquad \Sigma I = 0 \qquad$ **(½ + ½ = 1 Mark)**

Kirchhoff' second rule or loop rule : The algebraic sum of changes in potential around any closed loop, including those with emf's and those of resistive elements is zero.

The circuit shown in figure is called **Wheatstone bridge.**

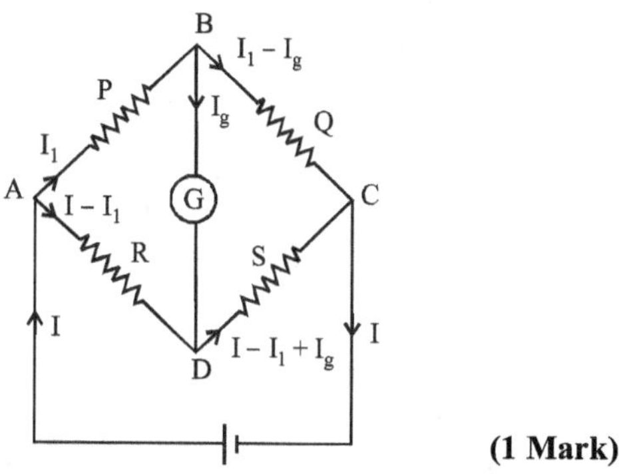

(1 Mark)

Now, applying Kirchhoff's loop rule to the closed loop ABDA, we have

$$-I_1P - I_gG + (I - I_1)R = 0 \qquad \text{...(i)}$$

Again, applying Kirchhoff's loop rule to closed loop BCDB, we have

$$-(I_1 - I_g)Q + (I - I_1 + I_g)S + I_gG = 0 \quad \text{...(ii)}$$

The value of P, Q, R and S are so adjusted that the galvanometer gives zero deflection. This means that both B and D will be at the same potential and hence no current will flow through the galvanometer *i.e.,*

$I_g = 0$. The Wheatstone bridge is said to be in balance condition. Putting $I_g = 0$ in equation (i) and (ii)

$$-I_1 P + (I - I_1) R = 0$$

or $I_1 P = (I - I_1) R$ ...(iii)

and $-I_1 Q + (I - I_1) S = 0$

or $I_1 Q = (I - I_1) S$ ...(iv)

Dividing equation (iii) by (iv) we have

$$\frac{P}{Q} = \frac{R}{S} \qquad ...(v)$$

This is the balanced condition in terms of resistance of four arms of a Wheatstone bridge.   **(1 Mark)**

(b) Meter bridge is based on Wheatstone bridge principle

i.e., $\dfrac{P}{Q} = \dfrac{R}{S}$

where $P = R_1$

$Q = R_2$

$R = l_1$

$S = 100 - l_1$

When null point D is at 40 cm from end A

$l_1 = 40 \text{ cm}$

and $l_2 = 100 - 40 = 60 \text{ cm}$

$\therefore \quad \dfrac{R_1}{R_2} = \dfrac{40}{60} = \dfrac{2}{3} \qquad ...(i)$

When a resistance of $10\,\Omega$, is connected in series with R_1,

$l_1 = 60 \text{ cm}$

$l_2 = 100 - 60 = 40 \text{ cm}$

$\therefore \quad \dfrac{R_1 + 10}{R_2} = \dfrac{60}{40} = \dfrac{3}{2} \qquad ...(ii)$

Dividing (ii) by (i)

$$\frac{R_1 + 10}{R_2} \times \frac{R_2}{R_1} = \frac{\frac{3}{2}}{\frac{2}{3}} = \frac{9}{4}$$

$\therefore \quad 4(R_1 + 10) = 9R_1$

or $40 = 5R_1$

$\therefore \qquad R_1 = 8\,\Omega$ **(1 + 1 = 2 Marks)**

and $R_2 = \dfrac{3}{2} R_1 = \dfrac{3}{2} \times 8 = 12\,\Omega$

29. (a) Let there be a rectangular current carrying loop ABCD placed in a uniform magnetic field B as shown in figure. The loop can be considered to be consisting of a series of a straight line segments. We will find that the total force acting on the loop is zero but there is net torque acting on it.

Let the forces acting on the various sides of the loop be $\vec{F_1}, \vec{F_2}, \vec{F_3}$ and $\vec{F_4}$ as shown.

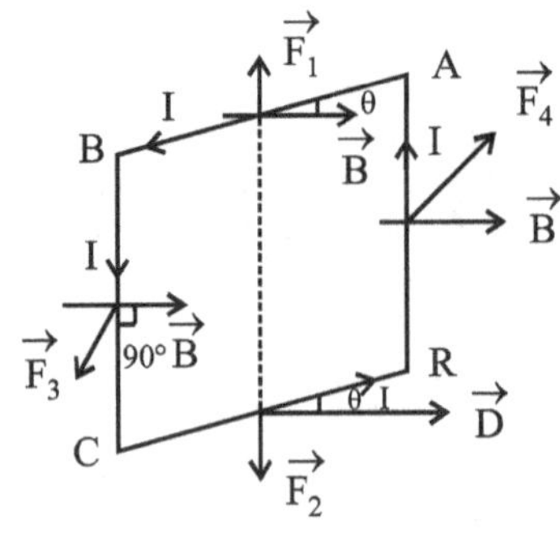

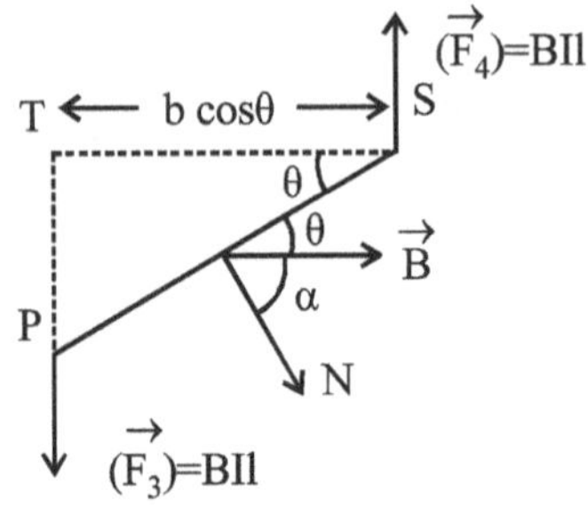

(1 Mark)

It follows from the expression for the force experienced by a conductor in a magnetic field that force on arm AB is

$$\vec{F_1} = I\,(\overrightarrow{AB} \times \vec{B}) \quad ...(i)$$

Here, $I\,(\overrightarrow{AB})$ is a vector in the direction of the current.

In accordance with Fleming's left hand rule, this force acts in the plane of the paper and is directed upwards as shown in figure.

The force on arm CD is

$$\vec{F_2} = I\,(\overrightarrow{CD} \times \vec{B}) \quad ...(ii)$$

Here, $I\,(\overrightarrow{CD})$ is a vector in the direction of the current.

In accordance with Fleming's left hand rule, this force acts in the plane of the paper and is directed downwards as shown.

The sides with length 'b' i.e., AB and CD make an angle $(90° - \theta)$ with the direction of the magnetic field. Therefore, the forces acting on these two sides given by equations (i) and (ii) are equal and opposite.

Since, these two forces are equal and opposite and have the same line of action therefore, they cancel out each others effect and their resultant effect on the coil is zero.

Now, the force on arm BC is

$$\vec{F_3} = I\,(\overrightarrow{BC} \times \vec{B}) \quad ...(iii)$$

Here, $I\,(\overrightarrow{BC})$ is a vector in the direction of the current.

In accordance with Fleming's left hand rule, this force

acts perpendicular to the plane of the paper and is directed downwards.

Finally, the force on arm DA is

$$\overrightarrow{F_4} = I(\overrightarrow{DA} \times \vec{B}) \quad ...(iv)$$

Here, I $(\overrightarrow{DA})$ is a vector in the direction of the current.

In accordance with Fleming's left hand rule, this force acts perpendicular to the plane of the paper and is directed inwards.

Forces F_3 and F_4 make an angle of 90° with the direction of magnetic field. Therefore, in magnitude these forces are given by

$$F_3 = F_4 = I\,l\,B \sin 90° = I\,l\,B \qquad ...(v)$$

The lines of action of both these forces are perpendicular to the plane of the paper.

The two forces F_3 and F_4 lie along, different lines and each gives rise to a torque about the X-axis. The two torques, produce a resultant torque in +X direction.

Arm of couple = b sin θ [From fig.] ...(vi)

By definition of torque

Torque = either force × arm of couple   **(2 Marks)**

Using equations (v) and (vi)

Torque = I B a × b sin θ

But ab = A, area of the coil, therefore, torque

$$\tau = I\,BA \sin θ$$

(b)   Proton $_1H^1$

Deuteron $_1H^2$

$$\therefore \quad Q_{proton} = Q_{deuteron}$$
$$P_{proton} = P_{deuteron} \qquad \text{(given)}$$

where, P = momentum and Q = charge

When a charged particle is subjected to a uniform magnetic field, then

$$\frac{mv^2}{r} = BQv \sin θ$$

As p and B are constant therefore

$$r \propto \frac{1}{Q}$$

Since their charges are equal, their trajectories in the field will be identical as shown below :

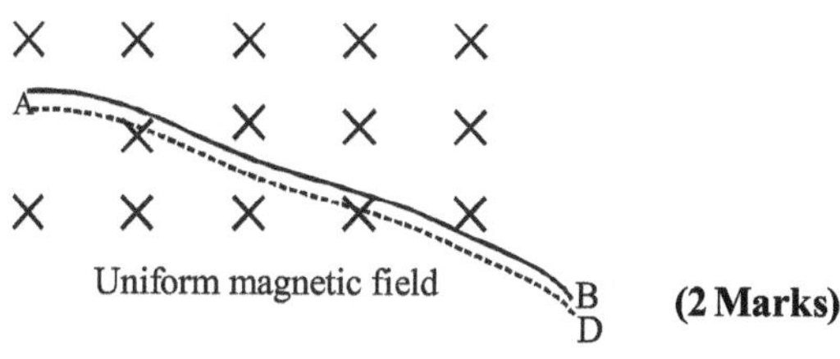

Uniform magnetic field   **(2 Marks)**

Deutron is nucleus of deuterium atom. Deutron consist of 1 proton and 1 neutron. Hence charge = +1

OR

(a)   **(1½ Marks)**

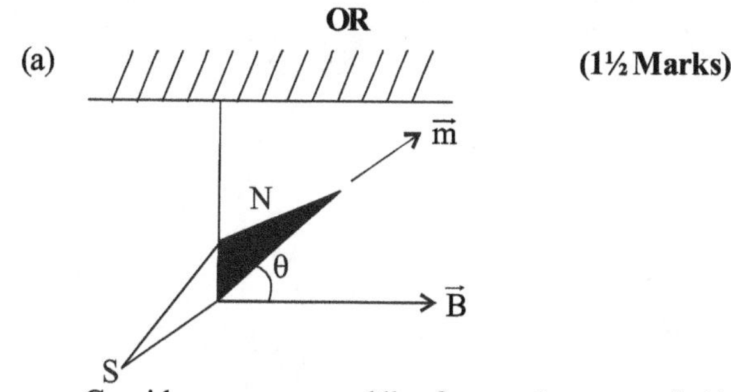

Consider a compass neddle of magnetic moment 'm' in magnetic field $\vec{B}$. In equilibrium position, the needle lies along $\vec{B}$. When it is slightly disturbed from its stable position and released, it begins to oscillate under restoring torque.

Now, torque on magnetic dipole in external magnetic field is given as

$$\vec{\tau} = \vec{m} \times \vec{B}$$

$\therefore$ Restoring torque $\vec{\tau} = -\vec{m} \times \vec{B} = -mB \sin θ$

The −ve sign incidates that the direction of torque τ is such as to decrease θ.

For small θ, sin θ ≈ θ

$$\therefore \quad \vec{\tau} = -mBθ \qquad ...(i)$$

Also torque is given as

$$\vec{\tau} = I\vec{\alpha} \qquad ...(ii)$$

where I = moment of inertia

$\vec{\alpha}$ = angular acceleration

In equilibrium condition,

$$I\vec{\alpha} = -mBθ$$

$$I\frac{d^2θ}{dt^2} = -mBθ \qquad \left[\because \; \alpha = \frac{d^2θ}{dt^2}\right]$$

$$\frac{d^2θ}{dt^2} = \frac{-mB}{I}θ$$

$$\frac{d^2θ}{dt^2} = -\omega^2θ \qquad \left[\omega^2 = \frac{mB}{I}\right]$$

This is simple harmonic motion.

Angular frequency ω,

$$\omega = \sqrt{\frac{mB}{I}}$$

Time period of oscillation is given as

$$T = \frac{2\pi}{\omega} = 2\pi\sqrt{\frac{I}{mB}} \qquad \text{**(1½ Marks)**}$$

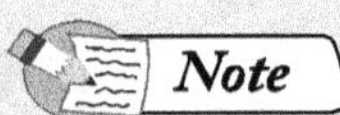

Note

Simple Harmonic Motion (SHM).

An object is undergoing simple harmonic motion if :-

(i) the acceleration of the object is directly proportional to its displacement

(ii) the acceleration is always directed towards the equilibrium position.

i.e., a $\alpha - x$

a = acceleration

x = displacement.

In question, it is

$$\frac{d^2\theta}{dt^2} \alpha - \theta$$

$\dfrac{d^2\theta}{dt^2}$ *= angular acceleration*

θ *= angular displacement.*

Let the needle is turned through an angle θ from the direction of the magnetic field, both north and south poles experience a magnetic force pB but their directions are opposite. These two forces form a couple

τ = either force × arm of the couple

= pB × NT

$\therefore \quad \dfrac{NT}{2l} = \sin\theta$ *or NT = 2l sin θ*

$\therefore \tau = pB\,2\,l \sin\theta = (p \times 2l)\,B \sin\theta$

As p × 2l = m

$\therefore \quad \tau = m\,B \sin\theta \qquad \qquad ... (i)$

This torque tries to align the magnet in the direction of the electric field. And due to inertia, it over shoots the mean position and begins to vibrate in SHM.

Also, $\tau = I\,\alpha$ $\qquad \qquad \qquad ... (ii)$

α *is the angular acceleration and I moment of inertia of the needle about the axis.,*

Therefore, from e.q. (i) and (ii), we have

$I\alpha = -mB \sin\theta$

(–ve sign shows it is a restoring torque)

$\qquad = -mB\theta$

or, $\qquad \alpha = \dfrac{-mB\theta}{I}$

$\therefore \qquad \alpha \propto -\theta$

Thus, motion is SHM

Time period T is given by

$$T = 2\pi\sqrt{\frac{\theta}{\alpha}} = 2\pi\sqrt{\frac{\theta}{\dfrac{mB\theta}{I}}}$$

or $\qquad T = 2\pi\sqrt{\dfrac{I}{mB}}$

This is the required expression for its time period.

(b) As the axis of the needle is vertical, the angle of dip δ at the place is 90°.

From formula

$$\tan\delta = \frac{B_V}{B_H}$$

$$\tan 90° = \frac{B_V}{B_H}$$

or $\quad B_H = \dfrac{B_V}{\infty} = 0 \qquad \left(\because \tan 90° = \infty\right)$

Hence,

(i) horizontal component of the earth's magnetic field is zero. **(1 + 1 = 2 Marks)**

(ii) Angle of dip at the place $\delta = 90°$